E. E. URBACH

THE SAGES — THEIR CONCEPTS AND BELIEFS

I

Publications of the Perry Foundation
in the Hebrew University of Jerusalem

EPHRAIM E. URBACH

THE SAGES

THEIR CONCEPTS AND BELIEFS

Translated from the Hebrew by
ISRAEL ABRAHAMS

AT THE MAGNES PRESS, THE HEBREW UNIVERSITY
JERUSALEM, 1979

First Edition 1975
Second Enlarged Edition 1979

ISBN 965–223–319–6
Printed in Israel
at Central Press, Jerusalem

To the memory of my son
AVRAHAM YEHUDA
who gave his life
in defence of the Land of Israel
18 Tevet 5728
19 January 1968

TRANSLATOR'S FOREWORD

In my rendering of Prof. Ephraim E. Urbach's work, *The Sages — Their Concepts and Beliefs*, I have endeavoured to keep as close to the Hebrew original as English usage would permit.

My reason for adopting this course was not only the desire for fidelity, although this was, needless to say, a major consideration, but the nature of Prof. Urbach's work and the qualities of his style. The author is essentially a scholar; he is not only eminently objective in his approach, but he writes with exemplary precision and economy of expression. Thus the basic structure and aims of the book made it vitally necessary for the translator to observe the greatest care in reflecting the exactitude and nuances of the Hebrew; any deviation from this standard would have distorted Prof. Urbach's presentation of his subject.

It must not, however, be supposed that the exigencies of scientific scholarship have voided *The Sages* of literary distinction. While remaining true to its genre, the work makes a notable contribution to modern Hebrew literature by its classical, idiomatic patina and by its streamlined, architectonic construction.

I must regretfully admit that, for a number of reasons, I could not reproduce these characteristics in my translation. But I did attempt to preserve one dominant feature of the work. On almost every page three — or at the very least two — literary strata are discernible: Biblical quotations, Rabbinic dicta, and the author's own comments, analysis, and general discussion. To reflect this threefold literary tapestry, I have employed Elizabethan English (I had recourse mainly, though not invariably, to The Jewish Publication Society version, *The Holy*

Scriptures) for the Biblical citations; the Rabbinic passages I translated myself in a slightly antiquated English (but without the use of 'thou', 'thee', or 'ye'); and for the writer's own discourse I used the modern English idiom. By this means I have sought to convey, in a modest — and admittedly imperfect — measure, the stylistic characteristics of the original.

Translators are often stigmatized — and not altogether without warrant — as traitors (*traduttori, traditori*). But curiously enough in the present instance the translation has one distinct advantage of which, I would hope, even Hebrew scholars will avail themselves. The spectrum of Prof. Urbach's quotations from Talmudic and Midrashic literature is unusually wide and inevitably includes a number of obscure passages. Whereas the Hebrew work cites these dicta in their original form, without necessarily adding elucidatory annotations, the translator has consistently been compelled, by his rendering, to interpret them, since every translation is also, by its very nature, a commentary. All my translations of Rabbinic dicta have, like the rest of the English version, the approval of the author.

Consideration for the needs of the English (and perhaps non-Jewish) reader has necessitated, at times, the addition of a few explanatory notes. To avoid overloading the book, these annotations have been kept to an absolute minimum. They will be found in square brackets. The round brackets, on the other hand, where these do not reproduce the writer's own parenthesis, indicate, as a rule, additions in the translation required to make sense in the English.

The renderings of extracts from Philo and Josephus follow the translation of the Loeb Classical Library, which was considered the most suitable for the purpose.

Generally the retention of Hebrew words has been avoided. But this could not be done in the case of personal (or place-) names, technical terms, and the titles of Hebrew books. For this purpose transcription was used wherever possible. However, in quoting variant readings and in exceptional instances where transliteration would not fully convey the Hebrew spelling, the Hebrew characters were retained.

The question of transcription presented a number of problems, which I endeavoured to solve with due regard to the convenience of the English reader. Biblical names are given the accepted spelling found in the majority of English versions. In the case of Rabbinic references, a compromise plan was adopted: the well-known names are spelt according to the most popular convention (e.g. Akiba, Joḥanan). But in the case of the less familiar names the transliteration is more (though not always completely) scientific. The transcription of technical terms and book titles accords with the rules given in the 'Key to the Transliteration'. The signs for the vowels are used for fully transliterated words, but are often omitted if the word is frequently repeated.

The titles of Hebrew works cited in the Text are generally translated (in square brackets) on their occurrence. But book names that are essentially of a poetic character and would, if translated, only serve to puzzle the English reader, are left in their original Hebrew form. Likewise Hebrew books referred to in the notes are not rendered into English; translation, in this case, would have made the annotations far too unwieldy.

The old Rabbinic teaching that 'All sacrifices will ultimately be abolished, except the thanksgiving offering' comes spontaneously to mind when I consider those who have helped in various ways to bring this work of translation to fruition.

First, I wish to recall, with abiding gratitude, that the late Mr. Silas S. Perry ז״ל made this publication possible not only by his financial generosity, but also by his life-long, loving interest in Jewish scholarship, which he fervently believed would ultimately spread the light and wisdom of Jewish knowledge among the broad masses of the Jewish (and non-Jewish) laity. His constant encouragement to me personally in my work for the Perry Foundation I can never forget.

My translation of *The Sages* could never have achieved its present form without the careful attention given to the translation in all its stages by Prof. Urbach. He has been a veritable tower of strength to me, and I record my appreciation of his friendship and inspiring erudition with deepfelt thanks.

Mrs. Yvonne Glickson (a daughter of Mr. Perry) has, with true filial piety, made a noteworthy contribution to the project by her valuable suggestions in matters of styling and presentation. Her association with the work will, I am sure, be a source of gratification to the entire Perry family.

I wish also to acknowledge, with appreciative thanks, my indebtedness to Mr. Ch. Toren, the director of the Magnes Press, for his unfailing interest in the progress of the translation and its publication; to the staff of the Central Printing Press, for the care and devotion with which they carried out their tasks.

Jerusalem

Nisan, 5733
April, 1973

ISRAEL ABRAHAMS

*
* *

An index of non-rabbinic sources and corrigenda are added to the second English edition. I am most grateful to Dr. Robert Brody for his help in preparing the index.

EPHRAIM E. URBACH

Jerusalem,
13 Tevet 5739
12 January 1979.

AUTHOR'S PREFACE TO THE ENGLISH EDITION

The English translation of this book is based on the second Hebrew edition without additions or changes. The printing started in spring of 1973. It was still in progress when to the great sorrow of his friends and all who knew him, Professor Israel Abrahams passed away after a brief illness on 26 October 1973. He managed to read most of the chapters in proof before he became ill.

The publication schedule had to be postponed because of his untimely death and also because of delays following the Yom Kippur War.

While working on the translation, Professor Abrahams used to pass to me drafts of each chapter; we would then meet to clarify any problems that had arisen. These hours we spent together discussing and studying the text, trying to achieve the most correct renderings of words, idioms and terminology, gave me great pleasure and will remain in my memory.

Mrs. Yvonne Glickson undertook an additional reading of the proofs; she suggested a few stylistic and linguistic alterations which I have accepted and which, I believe, would have been approved by the translator. The exacting task of proofreading was undertaken by Miss Susan Corb and Mrs. Janet Shvili. Dr. Yosef (Alan) Unterman prepared the indices and Mrs. E. Even Shoshan helped in compiling the bibliography. The publishers and staff of the Hebrew University's Magnes Press and the Central Press, Jerusalem, devoted a great deal of time and effort to complete the work in difficult conditions. To all of these I am most grateful.

Jerusalem, Hebrew University
10 Kislev, 5735
24 November, 1974

EPHRAIM E. URBACH

FROM THE PREFACE TO THE FIRST HEBREW EDITION

The aim of this work is to describe the concepts and beliefs of the Tannaim and Amoraim and to elucidate them against the background of their actual life and environment. Fidelity to the character of the sources dictated that the book should not present a monolithic whole, but should consist of chapters and segments of chapters that link up and form a single structure. Subjects that I treated in paragraphs, or combined into one paragraph, merited chapters to themselves; but I was concerned that the discussions might become unduly protracted and matters of primary importance might suffer.

Of the studies that I have published on the religious and social thought of the Sages since 1946, I have incorporated in this work only one ('On Providence'), and even in this essay I have introduced changes. Other articles served me only in part as material for the construction of a few paragraphs. My conclusions formed the basis of various chapters. The methods I adopted in this book I have briefly explained in the first chapter entitled 'The Study of the History of the Beliefs and Concepts of the Sages' and I shall not add to what I have stated there.

29 Av, 5729
13 August, 1969

FOREWORD TO THE SECOND HEBREW EDITION

It is less than two years ago since the first edition of this book was published, and there is now need of a second edition. Printing errors have been rectified and bibliographical references brought up to date. Some additions and amplifications have been introduced. These are based on further studies and on readers' comments which are acknowledged by name in each case.

1 Tammuz, 5771
24 June, 1971

KEY TO THE TRANSLITERATION OF THE HEBREW

(a) Consonants

א	= ’	ל	= l
בּ	= b	מ, ם	= m
ב	= v	נ, ן	= n
גּ	= g	ס	= s
ג	= gh	ע	= ‘
דּ	= d	פּ	= p
ד	= dh	פ, ף	= ph
ה	= h	צ, ץ	= ṣ
ו	= w	ק	= q
ז	= z	ר	= r
ח	= ḥ	שׂ	= ś
ט	= ṭ	שׁ	= š
י	= y	תּ	= t
כּ, ךּ	= k	ת	= th
כ, ך	= kh		

Note: (1) Unsounded ה at the end of a word is not represented in the transcription;

(2) the customary English spelling is retained for Biblical names and rabbinic works and authorities.

(b) Vowels

Long			*Short*		
ָ	(*Qāmeṣ gādhōl*)	= ā	ַ		= a
ִי, ִ	(*Ḥīreq gādhōl*)	= ī	ֶ		= e
ֵי, ֵ		= ē	ִ	(*Ḥīreq qāṭān*)	= i
וֹ, ֹ		= ō	ָ	(*Qāmeṣ qāṭān*)	= o
וּ		= ū	ֻ		= u

ְ	(*Šewā’*)	= ĕ
ֲ		= ă
ֳ		= ŏ
ֱ		= ĕ

CONTENTS

VOLUME I

Akiba — the order of creation and the dispute between the School of Shammai and the School of Hillel — creation in thought and the doctrine of Ideas — rejection of the theory of creation from *materia prima* — mythological dicta at the end of the Tannaitic period and the beginning of the Amoraic period — anti-Gnostic polemic — the Torah and the creation of the world — the problem of the influence of Philo's thought — the angels and the creation of the world — the creation of light — the sequence of times and worlds that preceded creation — the world was created by an utterance — the dogma that God created the world. pp. 184–213

Chapter X: Man

Man as the goal of creation — the body-*nefesh* relationship and the nature of the *nefesh* according to the Bible — the creation of man in the image of God — the three parts of man — the separation of body from *nefesh* and the doctrine of recompense — the creation of the body — the difference between Adam and his descendants — residual myths and legends, whose objectionable element has been removed, in the Amoraic homilies — Rav's teaching and the Iranian myth — the spirit of Adam — the formation of the child — man as a microcosm — the pre-existence of the *nefesh* — the treasure-house of souls — the problem of the integration of the *nefesh* with the body — is the embryo a living entity, or only 'its mother's thigh'? — the tractate of the creation of the child and the Platonic myth — the attitude to the body in the Hellenistic and Gnostic doctrines — the Tannaitic and Amoraic attitude and the parallelism in Zarathustra's conception — the dispute between the School of Hillel regarding the creation of man pp. 214–254

Chapter XI: On Providence

Josephus' testimony concerning the concepts of the sects regarding fate and free will — the Qumran Sect's doctrine of fate — the term 'Providence' and its meaning — R. Akiba's teaching — the opposition to the ancient doctrine of fate and Paul's teaching of grace — reward and punishment in relation to Providence — emphasis on the principle of freedom of choice — the integration of man's free will and the ways of Providence in the School of R. Ishmael — Ben Azzai's doctrine regarding the reward of the precepts — the restriction of reward to the world to come — the restriction of free will to the first decision — the influence of faith on astrology and its restriction — the view of the last of the Amoraim — a complementary approach. pp. 255–285

Chapter XII: The Written Law and the Oral Law

The term 'Torah' and its connotation — Torah and νόμος — the term 'Oral Law' and the unwritten law — the antithesis between letter and spirit — extreme allegorization and the anti-Paulinian polemic — the removal of the Torah from dependence on supernatural forces — Torah and prophecy — abolition of the difference between the Written Law and the Oral Law. pp. 286–314

Chapter XIII: The Commandments

Chapter XIV: Acceptance of the Yoke of the Kingdom of Heaven. Love and Reverence

Chapter XV: Man's Accounting and the World's Accounting

Chapter XVI: The People of Israel and its Sages

VOLUME II

CHAPTER I

THE STUDY OF THE BELIEFS AND CONCEPTS OF THE SAGES

The term 'Sages' is customarily used to denote the Sages of the Oral Law, who are mentioned in its literary sources: the Mishna, Tosefta, Halakhic Midrashim, Talmuds and Haggadic Midrashim. The earliest of the scholars lived in the era preceding the Maccabean revolt, and the last, when the Mediterranean countries were conquered by the Arabs — that is, their activities extended over a period of more than nine hundred years. This long interval was rich in events and acts that changed the face of the world. The beginning of this epoch witnessed the Hellenization of the lands of the East Mediterranean. After Alexander the Great had destroyed the Persian empire, the eastern countries, including Eretz-Israel, were opened to Greek culture, but at the same time the Orient — its beliefs and cultures — also began to influence Greek culture, and the synthesis, known as Hellenistic civilization, was formed. This civilization determined the physiognomy of Egypt, Syria, some of the lands of the Euphrates and Asia Minor even after their political conquest by the Romans. The Jewish people, whose country was conquered by Alexander the Great in 332 B.C.E., was also drawn into the process of Hellenization. After the wars of the Diadochi, it was subject for a century to the dominion of the Ptolemies, and only the victory of Antiochus III over the Ptolemies in 200–198 B.C.E. brought it under the rule of the Seleucids. Then for the first time there broke out an open clash between internal forces of the nation — between the Hellenistic party, who forsook the ancestral customs and found an ally in Antiochus IV, Epiphanes, and the Hasidim ('Pietists'), who were opposed to them.

The revolt, begun by the Hasidim, led to the establishment of the Maccabean state. The Greek cities were destroyed, and in the era of the Hasmoneans there arose within the nation movements that contended for leadership of the people. In this struggle religious, political and social elements were interlinked, and it continued after political independence had been lost and the Roman empire had spread the tentacles of its dominion over the whole country, until the destruction of the Temple. The Destruction did not end the struggle for political sovereignty, and the national centre remained in the Land for a long period, but the Jewish Diaspora and its centres acquired increased importance. The beginning of the Babylonian, and also of the Egyptian, dispersion dates back to the destruction of the First Temple, but the Diaspora was subsequently reinforced both by the cultural and commercial ties that grew between Eretz-Israel and the Hellenistic kingdoms, and by the stream of emigration from the Land in the wake of the internal disputes, rebellions, and wars, as well as by the conversion of many Gentiles who accepted Israel's Torah in some measure. One of the sectarian groups that sprang up in the last century before the destruction of the Temple, and also remained linked — at least in part — to the corporate nation for some time after the Destruction, penetrated primarily the Jewish communities in the Greek Diaspora, and as a result of proselytization, complete and partial, in which it widely engaged, it infiltrated also into the Gentile world. From being a persecuted and tolerated religion, Christianity became the dominant faith in the Roman empire. On the one hand it is clear that the events enumerated — and many others besides — left their mark on the thought and doctrines of their times; but on the other, the Sages, in each generation, introduced, by their beliefs and concepts, a ferment into the ranks of the nation, and by waging a constant struggle they achieved the crystallization and formulation of ideas and sentiments that were accepted as credal principles and were held in common by the scholars and the nation as a whole. These principles are few in number, but actually enter into many spheres of life and encompass them from various aspects, both large and small. Alongside the matters that formed common ground, there also remained subjects and issues on which the views of the Sages were not identical with the beliefs and views prevailing among the people, while on many matters even the scholars were divided among themselves.

These differences of opinion are explicable, apparently, in the light of the divergence of political, economic, and social background, when Sages living in different periods are spoken of. If the reference is to members of the same generation, the disagreements would be indicative of individual disparities between diverse religious types. But such differentiations are very difficult to determine, on account of the particular character of the sources with which we are dealing. Not only are there many dicta, the names of whose authors are unknown to us, but even in cases where they are attributed to Sages whom we know, there is no assurance whatsoever that these statements are the product of their thinking, for conceivably they were only transmitted by these scholars while their source is much older; thus they do not represent the individual opinion of this or that Rabbi but a generally accepted view. Attention must also be paid to the literary form of the source. The Talmuds and Midrashim contain sayings in which the Sages expressed religious and ethical ideas. These dicta are distinguished by their lapidary form, by their felicitous abstract formulation, by their pithiness, which is capable of condensing in a few words complete and complicated themes. With sayings and aphorisms of this kind there are bound up exegetical problems, but it cannot be doubted that they pertain to our subject. The position is different in respect of other literary forms: parables, homilies, narratives, and prayers; here we have to enquire how much weight should be given to the ideas that we tend to find in them, and what should be credited to the rhetorical-homiletic tendency and the artistic aspiration of the authors and editors.

We shall add one more source, which has been little used in relation to our subject, namely the Halakha. The Halakha does not openly concern itself with beliefs and concepts; it determines, in practice, the way in which one should *walk*, that which is permitted and forbidden, obligatory and exempted, clean and unclean. Nevertheless beliefs and concepts lie at the core of many Halakhot; only their detection requires exhaustive study of the history of the Halakha combined with care to avoid fanciful conjectures and unfounded explanations.

Common to all the sources is the fact that none of them provides systematic treatment of the subject of beliefs and conceptions, and there are almost no continuous discourses dealing with a single theme. In most instances we have to integrate and arrange the scattered material into one unit of thought. A great fund of terms and concepts was created in the era of the Sages, some of which are not known — at least in their present formulation — in the Bible, and some, although found in Scripture, have acquired a different meaning and content. It will suffice to mention the following concepts: 'this world' and 'the next world', 'good inclination' and 'evil inclination', 'penitence' and 'redemption', 'resurrection of the dead', 'reward' and 'punishment', *miṣwā* ('precept', 'good deed') and transgression, 'the kingdom of Heaven', 'the bestowal of lovingkindness', 'Gehinnom' ('Hell') and 'the Garden of Eden' ('Paradise'); likewise the new epithets and designations of God, such as: the Omnipresent (*Māqôm*, literally: 'Place'), 'Sovereign of the universe', 'the Holy One, blessed be He', 'the All-Merciful', 'the Almighty', 'Heaven'. The signification of these concepts is not defined or discussed in detail in the sources, and no attempt has been made to relate them or to reveal their common elements. Such attempts on our part are likely to show contradictions between the conclusions drawn from one set of ideas and those derived from another. It is just this lack of consistency and system that provided subsequent generations with a great measure of freedom in defining the principles of faith. The teachings of the Sages were accepted by them as a source of the highest authority, challenged by none, but the freedom allowed in the interpretation of its truths opened up multi-faceted possibilities. The philosophers of the Middle Ages, the Cabbalists, and the Hasidim all based themselves on Rabbinic dicta in expounding their systems.

Since their respective systems were of primary importance to these thinkers, the original meaning of the words of the Sages was dimmed and even set aside, especially as their modes of expression and literary form made them a tree of many boughs and branches, on which extraneous ideas could easily be appended. This method is prevalent also in our days in a particular category of books that is widely disseminated, especially in non-Hebrew languages, and whose theme is the presentation of 'Judaism'. They appear under the general title

'Judaism' or bear more piquant names. The authors largely make use of the sayings of the Rabbis — their parables and stories — but place upon them the interpretation given to them by Maimonides or Judah ha-Levi, by the Cabbalists and the Hasidic leaders, and even introduce into them modern concepts that are current in the philosophical and theological systems of our times. Needless to say, each writer quotes what seems to him to approximate to his own views, while disregarding other sources. Undoubtedly we may not completely deny the value of works of this nature as reading matter for those who are interested in them and in their authors' outlook — if, indeed, they have a view and outlook of their own — but they are of no value for our study, which is concerned with the history of *the beliefs and concepts of the Sages against the background of the reality of their times and environment.*

Modern Jewish scholarship ('Wissenschaft des Judentums') has paid but little attention to our subject. The scholars who were interested in philosophical thought and doctrine devoted their talents to medieval philosophy. They had an affinity with its rationalistic trends and succeeded in adapting to its study the accepted methods employed in the field of medieval philosophy, both Arabic and Christian scholastic. Here and there the introductions to general works on the Jewish philosophy of the Middle Ages incorporate brief surveys of Rabbinic thought. The best of them is that in Julius Guttmann's book, *Philosophies of Judaism,*[1] I, 3, 'The Religious Ideas of Talmudic Judaism'. But apart from several pertinent notes, this chapter contains only a summary survey that skims lightly over a number of problems. Research on the Talmud and Midrash was mainly concerned with literary and exegetical questions. It is true that a few monographs have been written, but this does not amount to a compendious account, unless we are prepared to regard as such the presentation of Isaac Hirsch Weiss in his *Dor Dor we-Doreshaw* ('Zur Geschichte der jüdischen Tradition'),[2] published in 1871.

Solomon Schechter's work, *Some Aspects of Rabbinic Theology,*[3] 1909, is certainly a fine book. But Schechter himself emphasized that the circumstances in which he began to write his work — the lack of preliminary monographic treatises — prevented him from writing the history of Jewish theology and its development, and consequently he confined himself to giving a general account of a few themes. He also admitted that in his treatment of the subject he had in mind principally the ideas that had become an integral part of the religious consciousness of the bulk of the Jewish people, or, as he terms it, of 'Catholic Israel'. Schechter did not, in truth, ignore the actual existence of differences of opinion, but he posited that views that failed to receive general approval — the particular time being irrelevant — were not of particular importance even in their own day. Hence he was also prepared to forgo the exposition of beliefs and concepts that show a special resemblance to those found in the Pseudepigrapha. He regarded them as chaff that somehow got mixed up with the wheat. But despite these prefatory remarks about his guiding principles and notwithstanding that sixty years have elapsed since the publication of the work, many of its sections have not lost their significance.

Kaufmann Kohler's *Jewish Theology Systematically and Historically Considered*, 1928, largely belongs to the class of general books on 'Judaism'. He himself defined his task thus: to provide 'a Jewish Theology by which the Jew can comprehend his own religious truths in the light of modern thought and at the same time defend them against the aggressive attitude of the ruling religious sects.'[4]

Studies in Christianity devoted special attention to the world of Jewish faith in the period close to the time of Jesus, at the outset in order to entrench and reinforce the polemic against the Pharisees found in the Gospels and in ancient Christian literature, and to stress the superiority of Christianity and its dogmas over Judaism. An outstanding example of this approach is found in Wilhelm Bousset's *Die Religion des Judentums in neutestamentlichen Zeitalter*, Berlin 1903. This title of the first edition is indicative of the trend to regard Judaism as merely the background of Christianity. In the second edition, revised by Hugo Gressmann, which appeared in 1926, the name of the book was changed to *Die Religion des Judentums im späthellenistischen Zeitalter*. The Jewish religion is described in this treatise primarily on the basis of external sources — the apocryphal literature and the Hellenistic literature — and relies only to a small extent on Rabbinic works, and even this was done without sufficient knowledge and with the help of secondary authorities, with the result that some gross errors have been perpetrated.

One of the sources used by Bousset, as by other Christian scholars — until the publication of the work by Strack and Billerbeck[5] — was Weber's book, *Jüdische Theologie auf Grund des Talmud und verwandten Schriften* (2 verb. Aufl. hrg. von F. Delitzsch und G. Schnederman, Leipzig 1897). Despite the reservation expressed by Bousset and Gressmann[6] about Weber's lack of historical discernment, they nevertheless preserved his aim, an aim that is reflected even in the order of the chapters, which seeks to underscore the legalistic character of Judaism. Felix Perles devoted an entire volume to a comprehensive critique of Bousset's work.[7] Bousset replied to this in a brochure entitled *Volksfrömmigkeit und Schriftgelehrtentum*, 1903. This polemic, which was waged sixty years ago, is itself a historic document. Perles was easily able to demonstrate Bousset's gross ignorance in dealing with Rabbinic sources as well as the tendentiousness of his book, which was partly conscious and partly the result of Christian education and the belief that Judaism was only a preparation for Christianity, combined, to put it mildly, with a lack of sympathy for existing Judaism. On the other hand, Perles's rejoinder is marked by a distinctly apologetic tone, which spoils the case. Actually Perles often adopts Bousset's method, only he uses it for his own purposes. The opinions and concepts of Christianity are also accepted by him as a criterion, only he finds them already in Judaism. His contention against Bousset that, whenever the latter finds in Christianity good and noble features and also objectionable and surprising elements, he regards the good things as the creation of Christianity, and the bad things as the heritage from Judaism, can almost be reversed in his own case. Perles wished to find in Judaism everything that appeared good and proper in the estimation of the humanitarian Christian liberalism of Germany at the beginning of the present century and to exclude, as alien to its spirit, whatever was not to his liking.

Perles's approach is characteristic of an entire generation of Jewish scholars. In the same year that Perles published his book against Bousset, another learned savant, Benno Jacob, wrote: 'Judaism must protest, if she is indiscriminately charged with responsibility for the pseudepigraphical literature.... Judaism can no more be portrayed by the *Book of Enoch*, or *Jubilees*, or *Ezra IV*, and similar writings, than Christianity can be depicted on the basis of the apocryphal gospels, spurious "acts", or Gnostic fantasies.' However, Jacob admits that it is difficult to find clear criteria in Judaism as to what is of its essence and what is not, for no dogmas were formulated in it as in Christianity; but on the pseudepigrapha — he declares — source-true Judaism has already passed judgment and rejected them; hence they are primarily a witness to Christianity, which preserved them. 'If a more fitting epithet cannot be found for what is contained in the pseudepigraphical works than the term "Jewish", then the study must avoid giving the impression that what is quoted from these writings is "Judaism". The latter can be depicted not only by means of the Haggada, but even better by having recourse to the Halakha, and to this end a beginning has not yet been made.'[8] It is a pity that Perles, Jacob, and other Jewish scholars like them did not write, in place of polemics, the history of the beliefs and opinions of the Sages. They would undoubtedly have arrived at a less uniform and monochromatic view of all the periods, at a different evaluation of the function of the trends that they term sub-currents, and of phenomena with which they have no sympathy, and which they find for some reason only in the marginal trends. Instead of showing that the pseudepigraphical works do not represent 'Judaism', they would have found them a great help in discovering the ideas and emotions that stirred Judaism from within, in uncovering the processes and struggles that preceded the formulation of the dicta and rulings of the Sages. But, unhappily, these Jewish scholars ally themselves with Christian scholars (whom they criticize in their writings) in positing that Judaism is fossilized, devoid of dynamism or vitality. Thus Benno Jacob writes that parallels to Christian teachings in Talmudic-Midrashic literature cannot be regarded as sources for Christianity, for they were composed later than the Christian writings, and should research prove the antiquity of a source, then, if the subject is not to be found in the Bible, the question arises whether the parallel passages do not have a common source. The premise is that spiritual life and religious thinking were extinguished among the Jewish people with the close of the Bible, and that outside Scripture and after it nothing was created, no emotions were felt, no thinking was done.

Bousset's tendentiousness and one-sidedness are manifest, and almost require no proof; but at the same time we must not wrong him, for he presented quite a number of problems in a form and mode acceptable to religious research. No less tendentious are most of the studies that treat Judaism as the background to Christianity or as the soil upon which it grew.

A change came about with the publication of the work of G. Foot Moore, *Judaism in the First Centuries of the Christian Era — The Age of the Tannaim* (vols. I–II, 1927; Notes, 1930). Moore does not portray Judaism merely as the background to the understanding of Christian origins, and his portrayal is based chiefly on Rabbinic literature and not on apocryphal and Hellenistic literature. The author's objectivity and his moderation and caution deserve commendation. He also made greater use than any of his predecessors of the researches of Jewish writers, and was not averse to learning from them. The influence of Schechter's work is discernible in many places. Christian scholars considered Pharisaic Judaism, as they are accustomed to call it, the Judaism of legalistic Halakha and the antithesis of prophetic Judaism, which became the heritage of apocalyptic Judaism. The consolidation of legalistic Judaism and its separation from other elements took place, according to some, with the rise of Christianity, and according to others, upon the destruction of the Temple. Some writers argue that in the Judaism preceding the Destruction there was evidence of universalistic elements and the desire to transcend the boundaries of people and country. But the Destruction, followed by rebellions among Diaspora Jewry in the reign of Trajan and the revolt of Bar Kokhba in Eretz-Israel in the time of Hadrian, led to the triumph of the nationalist elements, to the narrowing of horizons and to petrifaction; thereafter Christianity replaced Judaism as a missionary and universalistic religion. Another view[9] holds that the development took the opposite course. Judaism of the first century, with which Jesus, his apostles, and disciples dispute, was less spiritual. Only the destruction of the Temple and the consequences of the revolt brought about its spiritualization.

Against these and similar views, Foot Moore emphasizes the continuity of the teaching of 'normative Judaism', that is, of Judaism as it is reflected in the Tannaitic literature of the second century. In his opinion there is no antithesis between 'ethical-prophetic' and legalistic religion. The particular literary character of the apocalyptic literature and its kinship with prophetic literature does not yet make it the opponent of Halakhic literature; nor may we ignore the ethical instruction contained in Tannaitic literature. The restriction of proselytization, especially in the days of Hadrian, did not affect the essential character of the teaching of the Tannaim. The wars of 66–72 brought about changes in the social structure. The Sadducees and the priestly aristocracy left the stage of history. The Zealots perished in the course of the fighting, and the voice of the Essenes was also stilled immediately afterwards. The revival of Judaism after the Destruction was the work of the Pharisees. Judaism, which had been splintered into various sects, achieved, in the two generations after the Destruction, a homogeneity and authority that characterize it to this day. Although a ramified development in the details of the Halakha took place in the schools of the Tannaim in the second century, yet this unfoldment does not evince different principles or new features in relation to the earlier epochs, nor are such to be found in the fundamentals of the religion and ethic. The basic tenets and principles had been fixed long ago and it was necessary to emphasize them and to make each generation more fully conscious of them, but not to search for them and reveal them.

Caution and moderation, which rightly appeared to Moore essential after the fanciful expositions that he had encountered in the writings of his predecessors, caused him to confine himself to a presentation of normative Judaism (a parallel expression to Schechter's 'Catholic Judaism') in the epoch of the Tannaim. He admits that he bypassed the problems of 'the history of religion' (*religionsgeschichtliche Probleme*), that is to say, the question of the origin of beliefs and concepts found among Jews and known also to others, because he considered that these problems belong to the general history of religion and not specifically to the history of Judaism. But this is not the main defect. Moore did not always go deeply enough into the essence of the problems that he discussed. He failed to give an account of the origin of the beliefs and concepts, of their struggles and evolution, of their entire chequered course till their crystallization, of the immense dynamism and vitality of the spiritual life of the Second Temple period, of the tension in the relations between the parties and sects, and between the various sections of the Sages themselves. The character and status of the Rabbis are not elucidated.

The very concept of normative Judaism as finally crystallized is untenable from many aspects. There are Halakhot and concepts that were crystallized at an early period, and others that reached their accepted formulation only at the end of the era of the Sages, and not a few of them never attained even to that. The close of the Tannaitic epoch certainly cannot be regarded as a turning point or termination. The argument voiced by Moore against the scholars who set a boundary at the time of the destruction of the Temple, or against those who draw a distinction between ethical-prophetic and legalistic religion, applies equally to the line of demarcation that he set. A literary boundary is by no means of itself a demarcation or turning point in respect to the content of that literature. It is a well-known fact that Amoraic literature comprises topics and dicta for which there are parallels in the apocryphal literature and these prove to be much older than the age of the Tannaim, although their works contain no mention of them. The religious significance of the Halakha and its place among the spiritual treasures of Judaism did not receive adequate treatment and suitable exposition, despite Moore's recognition, in principle, of the importance of the phenomenon.[10]

These criticisms could already be levelled when Moore's book first appeared. But in the course of the decades that have elapsed since its publication, new sources have become available — it will suffice to mention the Qumran Scrolls — and the Rabbinic sources themselves have been equipped with critical commentaries based on a more reliable examination of the texts, while a long series of monographs has been added on specific subjects. These alone necessitate and justify renewed study of the history of the beliefs and concepts of the Sages. Such research is required no less by the recent studies in the Jewish history of the period and the new approaches that have come to light in them. The fresh data — archaeological, epigraphic and papyrological — have enriched our knowledge of the material and social life of the era, and also of the extent to which the Halakha controlled it. The more thorough use of external sources has changed considerably the picture of the relationship between the world of the Sages and that round about them — the Hellenistic-pagan and Christian worlds combined. This added information also brought in its train novel general insights.

Yitzhak Baer[11] presented a comprehensive, overall view of the course of Jewish history. The decisive era, to his mind, for laying the foundations of Judaism was the period between the conquest of the Orient by Alexander the Great and the Diadochi and the rise of the Hasmonean state. In this interval the special character of Judaism and of the Jewish people assumed the form it was destined to have for generations to come. At its commencement — in the Hellenistic, pre-Hasmonean period — there were created socio-religious ideals of an ascetic, spiritual, and martyrological nature, on the basis of which the society of the First Hasidim was built. This was followed by the epoch of the earlier Hasmoneans in which the attempt was made to establish a theocratic state according to these ideals, and which ended in a ruthless struggle between the Hasidim and the secular rulers. The circles of the Hasidim and the Sages were divested of their official influence in politics, but in practice they remained dominant in religious and social life. The attempt to restore a complete theocracy during the war against Rome failed, and the renewal of the regime of the spiritually-minded Sages came as a result of the recurrent collapse of the natural foundations of society. The spiritual-ascetic and eschatological trends continued also after the Destruction and even after the close of the Mishna, but in the closing of the Mishna there was implicit a conscious feeling of the continuous decline of creative power. The Jewish Hasid-Sage was born, according to Baer, by the meeting of the Hebrew prophetic tradition with Greek culture. Common elements in the ethical aims of the types of Sages and Pietists are to be found in Judea and in Greece: to live in accordance with the laws of nature and to maintain in the social order the ideals of natural life. Baer sets the contact between Judaism and Hellenism in the first generations of the spread of Hellenism, in the third century B.C.E., or at latest in the second. The Jewish Hasidim and Sages sought to realize ideals similar to the political ideals of Plato, only the concepts that appeared in an intellectual guise in the West, assumed among them a completely religious character, both in content and in form. These Sages and Hasidim were identical, according to Baer, with the Essenes as they are known to us from works of Philo and Josephus. They are even to be regarded as the prototype of the later Christian monks.

They were ascetics, inspired by the highest religious idealism, who, in the Hasmonean revolt, set an example of self-sacrifice for the sake of religion to all the monotheistic faiths. The Sages of the Mishna who lived after the destruction of the Temple were, in Baer's view, weak types in comparison with the Sages and the Hasidim who preceded the Hasmonean state. The latter, although they remained mostly anonymous, acted historically as creative forces far stronger than the later Sages, who wished merely to walk in the footsteps of their predecessors. The spiritual outlook that prevailed in the time of the Second Temple served as the starting point in the history of Christianity, and above all remained authoritative among the Jewish people for all generations. This outlook is marked by unity of ideas and teachings — a complete *Weltanschauung*, religious ideas that were generated and developed according to laws well known in the history of religion. They came into being through living contact with prophetic teaching, on the one hand, and also, on the other, as a result of the living encounter with the Western world.

There is a common aspect to Baer's approach and to Moore's. Baer also postulates continuity from the earliest period (of Judaism) to the close of the Mishna, but while Moore sets the epoch of creativity and crystallization at the end of this era, in the second century C.E., Baer places it specifically at the beginning, that is in the second century B.C.E. Another feature common to Moore and Baer is that both of them minimize the importance of the external tradition and of the problem of the sects; only in this regard, too, the motivating factors are different. Moore dates the crystallization of Judaism to the time when these factions had already passed away and ceased to exert any influence. Baer, on the contrary, states that the Halakha, in its basic aspects and with most of its details, was formed before the secession and schism of the sects. These sects were the result of external and internal decline and disintegration, and contrary to the express testimonies of Josephus and the Talmudic sources, this historian is inclined to transfer them from the days of the earlier Hasmoneans to the last period before the Destruction.[12]

The comprehensive, overall view of Baer, which represents the Sages and Hasidim as a creative factor on the stage of ancient history, is attractive and enticing. But it calls for a thorough and unbiased examination of the sources, and this, it would seem, leads to different results not only in details, but also in the general conception. One must admit, however, that Baer has restored a historic dimension to problems that require discussion and has raised questions that cannot be evaded.

Another attempt to give a general picture of the world of the Sages was made in our time by Louis Finkelstein in his English work *The Pharisees — The Sociological Background of their Faith.*[13]

Since Max Weber gave us his large tomes on the sociology of religion, no one doubts the importance of elucidating the relationship between socio-economic data and religious teachings, and undoubtedly there is need for an exposition of this kind in the sphere of the history of the Jewish religion regarding the centrality of the Halakha, which deals expressly with civil law, torts and the like. But, regrettably, the two volumes of Finkelstein do not advance our knowledge or understanding of the subject. The book is an ingenious amalgam of fanciful and far-fetched conjectures, of construction on unproven suppositions and premises, together with apologetical arguments. The apologetic orientation compels the author to explain away everything, or, more correctly, to 'sweeten' everything and make it plausible. This type of apologetic differs from that which was customary in 'Wissenschaft des Judentums' in Europe. The aim of the latter was to demonstrate that 'the teaching of Judaism' is in no way inferior to Christianity, and even transcends it. But it never claimed that the teaching of Judaism had been realized. As against this Finkelstein states that Pharisaism became the cornerstone of modern civilization. Judaism, Christianity, and Islam are the product of the Pharisaic party and its activity. 'Fully half of the world adheres to Pharisaic faiths.'[14] Christianity is only a facet of Pharisaism. Paul was a propagator of Pharisaism; the Gentile peoples that abandoned idolatry were won over by 'Pharisaism', which is common to both religions — to Judaism and to Christianity.[15] Finkelstein discovers a close resemblance between the Puritan movement of England and of New England and Pharisaism. Although Milton decried the Pharisees, his plea for intellectual freedom is the basis of Pharisaism. The persistent social conflict between Town and Country and the clear tendency towards urbanization with its problems can find a course of instruction, in his opinion, in the synthesis of urban and rural life that he discovers in Pharisaism. In the Foreword to the second edition Finkelstein seeks to allay somewhat the astonishment aroused by his presentation of Christianity as a part of Pharisaism by distinguishing between the Pharisaic Order and the acceptance of the principles of their teaching. He attributes to the Pharisees the desire to disseminate primarily their philosophic truth and to receive affirmation of their universal ethic. In the addenda to the third edition Finkelstein identifies the Pharisees with the Hasidim. The difference between the Pharisees and Sadducees was not primarily one of economic standing, the difference between rich and poor (a theory that he himself maintained in his book on R. Akiba). He also rejects Geiger's thesis that the Pharisees were innovators and reformers. The Pharisees, in Finkelstein's opinion, were burghers of Jerusalem, market people, traders and artisans, while the Sadducees were priests, owning great estates in the neighbourhood of Jericho and in Galilee. The Pharisees possessed ancient Jerusalem traditions, and the Sadducees provincial traditions. Many of the disputes between them had already originated in the time of the First Temple. Nowadays Finkelstein frequently uses such terms as 'Proto-Sadducees', 'Proto-Pharisees', and even 'Proto-Hillelites'. It was actually the Pharisees, or 'Proto-Pharisees', who guarded the written word of the Torah, whereas it was the Sadducees who deviated from the Scriptural text. On the other hand, the divergences of opinion among the Pharisees centred on the texts that could be interpreted in various ways. 'Difference of opinion ... was, at least in the early ages of Pharisaism, the glory of the whole movement.'[16] The Pharisees inherited their views from the Prophets, and the Sadducees from the tradition of the priests and the aristocracy, and many of their ideas have their origin in the last centuries of the First Temple period. Finkelstein seeks to prove all this by delving into the inner reasons of the Halakhot. But most of his interpretations and theories are not sufficiently grounded in the sources. Finkelstein wrote his book in the hope that it would help to shed light on our contemporary problems,[17] but we are not exempt from enquiring whether this hope serves to illumine the teaching of the Pharisees. The truth is that Pharisaic Judaism did not become a world religion, but remained a world on its own; and it is the image of this world that arouses our curiosity.

The desire to underscore the universal significance of Rabbinic teaching and to present it as a practical source of instruction for the solution of contemporary problems is understandable. 'The State of our Sages', writes Baer,[18] 'is part of the great historic world, which embraces and unites East and West. It is impossible to comprehend ancient history — including Christianity — unless we understand this determinant factor.... an organic chain links the different generations together. The epoch of the Second Temple is essentially and ultimately the period when the foundation of all facets of our Tradition was laid. In the measure that this structure is revealed to us as a true and actual reality of its time, in the same measure there are dispersed and forgotten, before the grandeur of the subject, all thoughts of concrete political or dogmatic religious connection with the present, and the structure remains standing before us as an ideal and as a testament for generations to come.' The words do honour to the author. But when we come to make generalizations of this nature, we must bear in mind the possibility that they may only be the result of inner conviction. It is just the person who holds that historical research is not intended to be merely an interesting pastime, but must fulfil a function, yet at the same time does not seek to pretend that it is possible to dispense with all evaluations, who may not overlook the difference between the researcher and the preacher. The historian is also permitted to be a mentor and preacher, but he must distinguish between these two functions for the benefit of both.

Our critical observations serve to outline our own approach. It is not our aim to portray Judaism of the Second Temple and of the centuries following the Destruction. We wish to describe the beliefs and concepts of the Sages, realizing that there were other trends, too, whose traces have been left not only in the pseudepigraphical literature and in the Qumran Scrolls, but also in the words of the Sages themselves, whether these ideas were rebutted in polemic or accepted by integration. Hence, in our discussions we have to take into account external and sectarian sources. Comparison of the external and internal sources shows that not every idea and teaching appearing in the writings of a sect represent an original concept belonging to it specifically. Sometimes they are only a part of older traditions that were adopted for tendentious reasons. In Rabbinic sources, too, there are to be found beliefs and concepts and even Halakhot that first germinated and became current in altogether different circles. Our method will be philological-historical. Main attention will be devoted to the elucidation of the sources on the basis of a reliable and clarified text against the historic background in which they originated and grew. Only if they yield sufficient evidence and proof, shall we permit ourselves to draw inferences relative to earlier periods. The primary basis of the Sages' teaching is the Bible. The work of the Sages is to be viewed as a protracted process aimed at the realization of the Torah and the ideals of the prophets in the reality and framework of their time. This reality influenced not only the Rabbis' manner of preaching and exposition, and determined to no small extent the formulation of their dicta and their underlying reasons, but also stamped their content. Just as we must clarify the nature and compass of the effect exerted by religious beliefs on social phenomena, so we must trace the influence of political and social forces on religious conceptions. Israel's contact with the world around them not only subjected them to various influences, but also gave rise to struggles and polemics. We shall rigorously eschew any trace of apologetics. We shall learn from the sources what is to be learnt from them by the methods developed by Talmudic research, which are simply the accepted philological techniques. This research has produced enduring results both in exegesis and in identifying and analysing the sources. The philological basis set bounds to conjectures and homiletical interpretations, for which the very type and nature of our sources provided ample opportunity. Careful attention must also be given both to the exegetical and homiletical methods used by the Sages in their Halakhot and Haggadot and to the artistic form that they gave to their own words.[19] Only the study of these aspects can teach us what weight to attach to a dictum, a homily, or a Halakhic discussion as expressing a substantive idea, and what must be put down to method, form, and formulation. Without philological examination and form—criticism of the sources it is impossible to give a historical account of religious ideas.[20]

The aim of our work is to give an epitome of the beliefs and concepts of the Sages as the history of a struggle to instil religious and ethical ideals into the every-day life of the community and the individual, while preserving at the same time the integrity and unity of the nation and directing its way in this world as a preparation for another world that is wholly perfect. In discussing the beliefs and concepts of the Sages, we shall not lose sight of the Sages themselves. Although their image and character were moulded by the Torah, which was their heritage, yet the world of the Sages was diversified and rich in varied types, who left the impress of their individuality upon their thinking and teaching. The author of the *Letter of Aristeas* writes (§§ 140–141): 'Hence the leading Egyptian priests... call us "men of God". This is a title which does not belong to the rest of mankind, but only to those who worship the true God. The rest are men (not of God), but of meats and drinks and clothing. For their whole disposition leads them to find solace in these things. Among our people such things are reckoned of no account, but throughout their whole life their main consideration is the sovereignty of God.' Certainly the words befit the majority of the Tannaim and Amoraim.

Their eyes and their hearts were turned Heavenward, yet one type was not to be found among them — not even among those who occupied themselves with the 'Work of the Chariot' and the 'Work of Creation' — namely the mystic who seeks to liberate himself from his ego, and in doing so is preoccupied with himself alone. They saw their mission in work here in the world below. There were Sages who inclined to extremism in their thoughts and deeds, and there were those who preached the way of compromise, which they did not, however, determine on the basis of convenience. Some were severe and exacting, while others demonstrated an extreme love of humanity and altruism. The vast majority of them recognized the complexities of life with its travail and joy, its happiness and tragedy, and this life served them also as a touchstone for their beliefs and concepts.

Without doubt our account will be found lacking in continuity, and at times the lacunae will preponderate, but we have preferred to acknowledge our ignorance and to reveal our doubts rather than take the way of facile and attractive generalizations.

CHAPTER II

THE BELIEF IN ONE GOD

The monotheistic concept of One God, beside whom there is no other, was at the beginning of our epoch the heritage of the whole Jewish people. It was not given a new formulation as a dogma, but the duty was introduced to read the verse Deuteronomy vi 1 ('Hear, O Israel', etc.) twice a day, and this very act implied the establishment of the belief in the Unity of God as the supreme creed. When was this practice made obligatory? We have no tradition on the subject. The Mishna assumes the existence of the custom as something well known, as though it were Scriptural, and asks 'From what time is the *Shĕma*ʿ ('Hear') to be read in the evening?' 'From what time is the *Shĕma*ʿ to be read in the morning?'[1] With regard to the details of the recital of the *Shĕma*ʿ, the Tannaim who lived about the time of the destruction of the Temple — namely the School of Shammai and the School of Hillel, and R. Eliezer and R. Joshua — hold different views. In the Mishna describing the order of service in connection with the daily sacrifice in the Temple it is stated 'They read the Decalogue, *Shĕma*ʿ, *wĕ-hāyā 'im shāmōa*ʿ ("And it shall come to pass, if ye shall hearken"), and *wa-yō'mer* ("And [the Lord] spoke").'[2] This combination of the Decalogue and the *Shĕma*ʿ is found in the Nash Papyrus, about whose exact date scholars are divided. Some date it as early as the second century B.C.E., and others as late as the first century C.E. The abolition of the recital of the Ten Commandments we shall discuss in another context. The precedence given to the recitation of the Decalogue, which obtained not only in the Temple but also outside Jerusalem, apparently points to the fact that it antedated the recital of the *Shĕma*ʿ. To the question 'Why are these two sections recited every day?' the Amora R. Levi already replied 'Because the Ten Commandments are comprised in them.'[3] The recitation of the content of the Sinaitic Revelation at the time when the sacrifice was being offered up constituted a renewal, as it were, of the covenant made by the Lord with His people. Now this section — unique in character and as a historic occurrence — is given prominence even in the Torah. When, however, was the section of the *Shĕma*ʿ added? We may possibly find a clue to the time, if we note what its first verse adds to the opening commandments of the Decalogue. In the Decalogue it is stated that God is the God of Israel, whom He brought forth from Egypt, and Israel is commanded 'Thou shalt have no other gods before Me', 'Thou shalt not make unto Thee a graven image, nor any likeness'. But they contain no express negation of the existence of other gods, such as find expression in the sharp polemic of the prophets, and emerges clearly from the proclamation 'The Lord is our God, the Lord is One.' In the Persian period the Jews encountered a religion (Hebrew, *dat*, which is, incidentally, of Persian origin) that was different in many respects from the religions that they had known hitherto, a religion that did not recognize idols.[4] Even if the Achaemenidian kings did not accept the teaching of Zarathustra, but held to the ancient Persian religion, or to the conception that Ahura-Mazda is the god of both day and night and transcends the antithesis of good and evil, yet he is still the father of the twins (*mainyū*),[5] between whom exists perpetual antagonism; it is clear, therefore, that to people from without the dualistic principle was more in evidence than the distinctions that present-day scholars point out. If in the eyes of Herodotus, the Greek, the Iranian gods, in contradistinction to the Greek deities, appeared far removed from human nature, to the Jews they were gods. The daily proclamation in the one Temple at Jerusalem, 'The Lord is our God, the Lord is One', expressed the great difference. The verse preceding 'Hear, O Israel' in the Bible is, 'Hear therefore, O Israel, and observe to do it; that it may be well with thee, and that ye may increase mightily, as the Lord, the God of thy fathers, hath promised unto thee — a land flowing with milk and honey.' But in the Septuagint we have the following addition: 'And these are the statutes and the ordinances that the Lord commanded the children of Israel in the wilderness, when they went forth from the land of Egypt.' This addition is found in the Nash Papyrus, and the probability is that it was interpolated into the Septuagint from the liturgy and not *vice versa*.[6] The recital of the verse amounted to a proclamation *vis-à-vis* the world, that the God of Israel is the God of the universe and there is none beside Him, which is the sense, in truth, that the Tannaim gave to the text: ' "The Lord is our God" — over us, "the Lord is One" — over all mankind.'[7]

The concept of Absolute Unity was deemed climactic in the understanding of God. To attain to the comprehension of this concept was not considered a simple matter in so far as 'all mankind' was concerned; the Sages regarded it as the outcome of a process of evolution, and found the various stages thereof in Scriptural verses. In a homiletical interpretation, which is not later than the second century, it is stated: ' "Now I know that the Lord is greater than all the gods": the Rabbis declared that Jethro did not omit to worship a single idol in the world, hence he said "than all the gods". Rahab said, "for the Lord your God, He is God in heaven above, and on earth beneath." Naaman acknowledged even more than they did, for it is stated: "Behold now, I know that there is no God in all the earth, but in Israel." '[8] Jethro attributed substance to idolatry, and acknowledged only the supremacy of the God of Israel over other divinities; Rahab set Him in heaven and on earth, but did not say that there was no other deity beside Him; Naaman went further and said, 'there is no God in all the earth, but in Israel'; but he did not say 'in heaven and on earth'. The concept of the Oneness and Uniqueness of God was expressed by Moses: 'that the Lord, He is God in heaven above and upon the earth beneath; there is none else'; in a still later Midrash the Sages interpreted this to mean: 'even throughout the expanse of the universe.'[9]

The belief in the One God finds expression in the complete negation of every other deity — in Rabbinic phraseology, of 'strange service' (i.e. idolatry) — that is to say, of any form of worship that is not unqualified 'service', which means service of the Lord. This thought was formulated in the dictum 'Whoever acknowledges idolatry disavows the whole Torah, and whoever disavows idolatry acknowledges the whole Torah.'[10] He who disavows idolatry does not deny its existence, but its reality;[11] he who acknowledges it acknowledges its reality. To whom is the dictum directed? It is addressed to those people who do not observe the whole of the Torah, but disavow idolatry, and also to another group who acknowledge the Torah but also idolatry. These circles were to be found among 'those who fear Heaven' — semi-proselytes — in the Jewish Exile. However, the prevailing view of the Sages in the third century was that the craving for idolatry had been uprooted and removed from Israel already at the beginning of the Second Temple period,[12] and there is parallel testimony for this in the Book of Judith: 'For there arose none in our age, neither is there any of us today, tribe, or kindred, or family, or city, which worship gods made with hands, as was done in the former days.'[13] This statement is corroborated by external evidence. Hecataeus of Abdera, a contemporary of Alexander the Great, deemed the essence of Judaism to lie in the fact that Moses introduced no image in the service of God on account of the dogma that God has no form.[14] He also noted the devotion with which the Jews of his day guarded their faith. The Jews of Babylonia refused to participate in the rebuilding, enjoined by Alexander the Great, of the ruined temple of Bel, and accepted severe afflictions and punishments in consequence; while the Jews of Eretz-Israel broke down the sanctuaries and altars erected by aliens who entered the country, without heeding the penalties imposed upon them.[15] Without doubt, in the period of Hellenization, which preceded the Hasmonean revolt, regression had set in in this sphere, too, a fact to which the account in Maccabees also bears witness:[16] 'Next day [after the battle with Gorgias], when the troops of Judas went — as it was high time they did — to pick up the corpses of the slain, in order to bring them home, to lie with their kinsfolk in their fathers' sepulchres, they discovered under the shirts of every one of the dead men amulets of the idols of Jamnia — a practice forbidden the Jews by law. All saw at once, that this was why they had perished.' The last part of the statement points to the activity of the earlier Maccabees in removing idolatry from the Land. Their conquests and mass proselytization were connected with the eradication of foreign cults and the destruction of their sanctuaries. But under the rule of the House of Herod and the Roman procurators these cities became Hellenistic cities again in all respects. Following upon the attempt of the Jews of Jabneh [Jamnia] to destroy a pagan altar, the Emperor issued an edict ordering them, according to Philo's account,[17] to set up a costly image and an altar in the Temple of Jerusalem. This incident serves to explain R. Joḥanan b. Zakkai's warning: 'Be not hasty to destroy the high places of the Gentiles lest you rebuild them with your own hand; lest you destroy structures of brick and they say to you, Make them of stone; of stone, and they say to you, Make them of wood!'[18] We may assume that it was in the time of the Maccabees that the Mishnaic benediction was composed: 'If one sees... a place from which idolatry has been rooted out, one should say: Blessed be He that rooted out idolatry from our land.'[19] In the Tosefta there is added the prayer: 'May it be Thy will, O Lord our God, that idolatry be rooted out from all Jewish places, and that Thou restore the hearts of their worshippers to worship Thee.'[20] Evidently this prayer belongs to a later period, when the Jews were no longer able to destroy Gentile idols, and it was even necessary to formulate a benediction for one who sees an idolatrous object — 'Blessed be He who is slow to anger'.[21] To a period of much proselytization — whether by compulsion or persuasion — or to a time when many of these 'dragged-in' converts reverted to paganism we must attribute the saying: 'Whoever acknowledges idolatry disavows the whole Torah, and whoever disavows idolatry acknowledges the whole Torah.'

The repudiation of idolatry became the common heritage of the Jewish people in the days of the Hasmoneans, and with the limitation of proselytization the feeling prevailed that idolatry presented no danger, since it had no substance; and this view was so deeply rooted that it even posited that actually even the Gentiles cannot believe in the reality of idolatry.[22] In truth there were many pagans in the second and third century, who regarded the images and idols not as having intrinsic worth, but as symbols. But the Sages, needless to say, looked even upon such a cult as a form of idolatry, and certainly did not accept the view that the idols were only the work of demons who are active through the medium of representations and images, a view that was widely current in Hellenistic literature and in the writings of the Church Fathers (in the Septuagint the word δαίμονες frequently occurs instead of idols). This notion is reported by Amoraim in the third century, but there is no evidence that they agreed with this explanation and did not look upon the Gentiles who credited it as fetishists. This also emerges explicitly from the source where this belief is mentioned: 'It has been stated: If an idol was broken of its own accord, R. Joḥanan said that (its broken parts) are prohibited, but Resh Laqish said that they are permitted. R. Joḥanan said that they are prohibited, because (the idolater) had not annulled it; and Resh Laqish said that they are permitted, because it may be assumed that (the idolater) certainly annulled it, saying to himself, It could not save itself, how then can it save me?... R. Joḥanan put an objection to Resh Laqish; (it is written:) "And the head of Dagon and both the palms of his hands lay cut off", and it is written: "Therefore the priests of Dagon do not tread... on the threshold of Dagon in Ashdod", etc. He answered him: Can proof be brought from there? In that instance, they abandoned Dagon and served the threshold, for they argued thus: Dagon's genius has left him and come to dwell upon the threshold' (*T.B. ʿAvoda Zara* 41b).

Resh Laqish merely reports the argument of the pagans.[23] But in later Midrashim this notion also took root.[24] The difference becomes evident when we compare two narratives, in which this motif is developed. Even the sceptics among the Gentiles were won over by the facts, namely the miracles — particularly, the healing of the sick — that were wrought in the temples, especially in those of Asklepios.[25] In a story from the period of the Tannaim it is recounted: 'Zonin said to R. Akiba, We both know in our hearts that an idol is only a sham, yet we see men go (to the temple) crippled and return cured. How do you explain this? He replied to him: I will tell you a parable. To what can the matter be compared? To a trustworthy man in a city, in whose keeping all the citizens used to deposit (their valuables) without witnesses. One man, however, used to come and place his deposits with him in the presence of witnesses. On one occasion he forgot and left (his valuables) in his custody without witnesses. Said his wife to him, Come, let us deny it! He answered her: Because this fool acted improperly, shall we lose our reputation for honesty? It is so with the afflictions (of illness), too. When they are sent upon a man, they are adjured to come upon him only on a given day, and to leave him only on a given day, and through the medium of such-

and-such a person and such-and-such a remedy. When their time came to depart, (the sick person) happened to go to his idolatrous shrine. Thereupon the afflictions said: Rightly we should not leave, but because this fool acted improperly shall we renounce our oath?' (*T.B.* *ʿAvoda Zara* 55a). This narrative, which is of interest from many aspects, is entirely rationalistic, and the answer it contains could have been given by any Stoic. Contrariwise we find in a later work of the tenth century: 'It once happened that a certain lame Jew heard that there was an idol in a given place, to which all the sick in the world used to come and be healed. So he went to be cured. He entered the shrine with the sick people at midnight; a man came holding in his hand a small cruse filled with oil, and he anointed all the sick and they were cured. When he came to the Jew, he said: Are you not a Jew? He replied, Yes! Then what are you doing here? He replied, (I came) to be healed. Thereupon (his interlocutor) said to him: Know you not that (the idol) itself is a demon who does these things in order to entice people to idolatry, so that he can destroy them from the world? Verily you are guilty; tomorrow, actually, your time had arrived to be cured, but because you have come here, you will not be healed.'[26] The narrator used R. Akiba's answer, but made it apply only to Jews; the Gentiles are misled by the demons who are active in the idols. Although the idea of the deception of the Gentiles is expressly mentioned in the homily of Rav on Deuteronomy iv 19: ' "which the Lord thy God *ḥālaq* [correctly: 'hath allotted'] unto all the peoples" — this teaches *she-heḥĕlîqān* ['He caused them to slip'] with words in order to drive them from the world' (*T.B.* *ʿAvoda Zara, ibid.*), yet his statement contains no reference to demons who are active in the idols. Possibly this conception, which influenced also the readings of the Talmud,[27] percolated into popular belief already at an early period, but it was given a literary version only in a late source. The view of the Sages is expressed in the story concerning R. Akiba, to wit, that the idol has no reality. This view produced important Halakhic consequences. It led to lenient decisions by most of the Rabbis in the period between the second and fourth centuries in all that related to the use of the art of imagery and its production. But the painting of pictures in Synagogues, the making of mosaic floors, and the ornamentation of sarcophagi did not sanctify or deify the subject of the painting or the mosaic. Despite the consideration the Sages gave to the various reasons and factors that induced them to mitigate the prohibition 'Thou shalt not make unto thee a graven image', the motivation 'for ye saw no manner of form on the day that the Lord spoke unto you in Horeb out of the midst of the fire' (Deuteronomy iv 15) remained in full force. No *Ars Sacra* came into being, and even those who interpreted the law most leniently expounded the verse: 'Ye shall not make with Me [אתי] a god of silver — ye shall not make Me [אותי].'[28]

The belief in One God is the principle creed, and whoever negates it is called כופר בעיקר *kōfēr bā-ʿIqqār* ['one who denies the primary principle of the faith']. *Kāfar* in the sense of 'to deny' is found only in the Rabbinic idiom. *ʿIqqār* is an Aramaic loan-word and means 'root'. God is *ʿIqqār*, that is to say, He is the Root of all things (see the Targum to Job xix 28). The disavowal of the Lord does not connote denial of the existence of God in general. Athens always knew unbelievers. Plato states in his *Laws*[29] that there are some people who think that there are no gods at all, and there are others who hold that the gods do indeed exist, but they pay no heed to man. The term *kōfēr bā-ʿIqqār* refers to both types. At the end of the first century C.E. R. Ṭarfon declared that if the books of the Minim — which were almost certainly the writings of the early Christians — fell into his hands, he would burn them, including the Divine Names that they contain, 'for even if a pursuer were pursuing me, I would enter an idolatrous shrine, but not one of their temples, because idolaters disavow Him (כופרין אותו; *var. lect.*, כופרין בו) out of ignorance, whereas these know Him and yet deny Him.'[30] The idolaters disavow Him; they believe in their own gods and do not acknowledge the God of Israel. The Minim know Him, that is to say, they are familiar with the Jewish conception of One God, but they introduce other elements into it. If the Minim are Gnostics, the reference is to dualism; and if the Christians are meant, the allusion is to Jesus, the Son.[31] Thus both — the idolaters and the Minim — disavow Him, that is, the Root.

The *kōfēr-bāʿIqqār* is seen as the most extreme example of a man's estrangement from the world of the Torah and commandments, but this self-alienation is intrinsic testimony to the denial of God, without its being linked to any speculative declaration whatsoever. This conception is widely current among the Tannaim in the middle of the second century, and particular importance attaches to the following evidence: 'Once R. Reuben spent the Sabbath in Tiberias and a certain philosopher found him, and said to him: "Who is hated in the world?" (The Rabbi) replied: "This is the one who denies Him who created him [הכופר במי שבראו]." Said he to the Rabbi: "How so?" (The Sage) answered him: "Honour thy father and thy mother; thou shalt not murder; thou shalt not commit adultery; thou shalt not steal; thou shalt not bear false witness against thy neighbour; and thou shalt not covet. Thus a man does not deny anything until he disavows the Root, and a man does not go to commit a transgression unless he first denies Him who enjoined us (not to do) it." '32 Here כופר בעיקר appears as a parallel expression to כופר במי שבראו. We do not know who the philosopher was, but R. Reuben stresses in his reply that the hated one is he who denies Him who created him — not just God in general, but the Creating God. This emphasis seeks to controvert the view that not the God of Israel, but the Demiurge, is the Creator of the World. The omission of the name of the Lord in the second part of the Decalogue teaches that no man commits a sin, unless he has first disavowed Him who enjoined us not to do it. 'He who denies the Root' is not therefore just one who denies God generally, but one who disavows God, the Creator of the universe, the God who gave the Torah and the commandments. It was necessary to stress this thought not only *vis-à-vis* a non-Jewish philosopher, but also, in the light of Tannaitic teaching in the second century, internally. Possibly this R. Reuben was none other than R. Reuben b. Strobilus of whom it is related that he went to make representations to have the imperial edict prohibiting the observance of the precepts revoked, the reference being to Hadrian's decrees (*T.B. Meʿila* 13a).

Of interest is the account of the religious position in Egypt ascribed to Hadrian himself. In a letter to the Consul Servianus, the Emperor writes: 'Hadrian Augustus sends greetings to Consul Servianus! Egypt, which you praised so highly to me, my dear Servianus, I have come to know as a frivolous land, which is quickly swayed to accept all nonsense. Here the worshippers of Serapis are Christians, and those who call themselves Christian bishops worship Serapis. Here you cannot find a head of a Jewish synagogue, a Samaritan, a Christian presbyter, who is not at the same time also an astrologer, a haruspex, and a magician all rolled in one... their One God is no God at all. He is worshipped by both Christians and Jews and all the other peoples.'[33]

In this situation of conceptual confusion and religious eclecticism it was necessary to emphasize that *kōfēr bāʿ-Iqqār* was one who does not believe in the Divine Creator of the universe and in Him who enjoined the observance of the Torah. He who transgresses precepts between man and man, he who deals falsely with his neighbour, and those who lend on interest,[34] are deemed to be 'deniers of the Root', because by their deeds they ignore the presence of God, who sees them.

The widespread use of the term *kōfēr bā-ʿIqqār* in a hyperbolical sense in the middle of the second century shows that the term was known long before, apparently with the meaning of denying the very existence of God.

A special expression was employed to describe an affront to God's glory. He who blasphemed or cursed the Lord was called פושט יד בעיקר *pōšēṭ yād bā-ʿIqqār* ['He who puts forth his hand against the Root'],[35] and the phrase also denotes an idolater.[36] On the other hand, with regard to the verse, Psalms xii 5 [4], 'Those who say, "With our tongue we will prevail, our lips are with us; who is our master?" ' it is stated: 'R. Joḥanan said in the name of R. Jose b. Zimra: If a man tells slanderous tales, it is as though he denied the Root.'[37] The *kōfēr bā-ʿIqqār* is the one who says 'who is our master?' He does not say, 'there is no master'; he does not deny the existence of God, but disregards Him. He denies that God's providence watches over the actions of His creatures. R. Akiba annotated the verse Psalms x 13, 'Why does the wicked man renounce God, and say in his heart, "Thou wilt not call to account?" ', as follows: '(The wicked man says:) There is neither judgment nor Judge — but there is judgment and there is a Judge' (*Gen. Rab.* xxvi 6, p. 252). His disciple, R. Me'ir, said with respect to the generation of the Flood: 'That generation declared, "The Lord does not judge; there is no Judge in the world, the Omnipotent has forsaken the world" ' (*'Avot de-R. Nathan*, Recension I, xxxii). In this spirit, the Targum renders the verse Psalms xiv 1, 'The fool says in his heart, "There is no God" ': 'The fool says in his heart,

"There is no dominion of God upon earth." ' Similarly, the Amoraim expounded the verse as referring to the wicked 'who say, "We plot in our heart", as though to say: the Holy One blessed be He does not know what is in our heart (*Midrash Tehillim*, xiv 1), and concerning them Isaiah says (xxix 15): "Woe to those who hide deep from the Lord their counsel, whose deeds are in the dark, and who say, "Who sees us? Who knows us?" ' The Amoraim viewed the disregard shown for the All-seeing Eye — that is, the conduct of the man who seeks to evade Providence and is inclined to delude himself into believing that he is concealing his deeds successfully — as a matter of daily occurrence; hence, when they preached, their words were directed not against those who denied the Root in theory, but against those who denied Him in practice. 'R. Levi said: To what can the matter be compared? To an architect who built a city and made therein secret places, hide-outs and chambers, and eventually he became the ruler. He then sought to seize the bandits in the city, and they fled and hid themselves in those hiding-places. Said he to them: "Fools! are you seeking to hide from me? I, after all, am the craftsman who built the city, and I, therefore, know all the secret places, and the entrances and exits of the hide-outs, better than you." Even so the Holy One, blessed be He, said to the wicked: "Fools! wherefore do you conceal the wickedness in your hearts? It is I who have built man, and I know all the chambers and secret recesses within him." '[38] Although the dicta that regard one who negates Divine Providence as a *kōfēr ba-ʿIqqār* belong to the second century, yet it can easily be shown that they merely formulate a view and concept current in previous generations. In the light of this premise we can understand why the name of the Greek philosopher Epicurus became a widespread epithet for a sectarian and a heretic. According to the philosophical system of Epicurus, the gods are indifferent to all that happens in the world. They are not active, but abide in absolute tranquility. The Sages were not acquainted with Greek philosophy, and not one of its great representatives is mentioned anywhere in Rabbinic literature, except Epicurus. In the *Mishna Sanhedrin* x, 1, the Epicurean is counted among those who have no share in the world to come, but it is not explained wherein lay the Epicurean's disqualification. This we can learn, however, from the teaching of R. Eleazar b. ʿArakh (*M. 'Avot* ii, 14): 'Be alert to learn Torah, and know what answer to give to the Epicurean. And know before whom you labour, and faithful [*ne'ĕmān*] is the Master of your work to give you the wages of your toil.'[39] The knowledge of 'before whom you labour', that is to say, the relationship existing between man's acts and his God, is linked with the answer to the Epicurean, for this knowledge clearly posits God's interest in His creatures. In a later Midrash, indeed — but the dictum is anonymous — we are given a homiletical exposition of Proverbs xv 7, ' "The lips of the wise spread knowledge" — these are the Israelites who proclaim the Holy One, blessed be He, King every day continually, and declare the unity of His name every day continually, morning and evening. "Not so the hearts of fools" — these are the sectarians [*mīnīm*] who say: The world is self-moving (αὐτόματος).'[40] The disciples of Epicurus did in truth teach, τὸν κόσμον αὐτόματον εἶναι. Even Josephus, the contemporary of R. Eleazar b. ʿArakh, wages a polemic against this Epicurean view: '... and learn from these facts how mistaken are the Epicureans, who exclude Providence from human life and refuse to believe that God governs its affairs or that the universe is directed by a blessed and immortal Being to the end that the whole of it may endure, but say that the world runs by its own movement without knowing a guide or another's care.'[41]

He who does not believe that God governs the world is an 'Epicurean' or *kōfēr bā-ʿIqqār*. The proclamation of the Almighty's unity, evening and morning, serves not only to testify to the existence of One God, but also to the fact that the world is not automatous, but that God created it and He rules it. From our portrayal of the character of the *kōfēr bā-ʿIqqār*, it follows that belief in the One God included also the belief in a God who created and administers it.

The recognition of the Creator of Abraham, the first believer, is depicted in R. Isaac's parable: 'It is like one who was travelling from place to place and saw a castle in flames. "Is it to be supposed (he asked) that the castle has no governor?" Thereupon the owner of the castle looked out and said to him "I am the owner of the castle." So, too, because our father Abraham said "Is it to be supposed that the world has no Governor?" the Holy One blessed be He looked out and said to him "I am the Governor, the Lord of the whole world" '

(*Gen. Rabba* xxxix, 1, p. 365). In this case also R. Isaac is only reporting an ancient tradition. Josephus said of Abraham: 'He was thus the first boldly to declare that God, the Creator of the universe, is one, and that, if any other being contributed aught to man's welfare, each did so by His command and not in virtue of its own inherent power.'[42]

The antithesis to heresy is faith. But just as we find that heresy is not the negation of God's existence, but the denial of His providence, so the belief in God is not merely the recognition of His existence, but trust in Him. Israel are 'believers, children of believers' (*T.B. Shabbat* 97a), says the Amora Resh Laqish (end of the third century), and he finds support in the verse 'And the people believed' (Exodus iv 31) with regard to Israel, and in the verse 'And he believed the Lord; and He reckoned it to him as righteousness' (Gen. xv 6) with respect to Abraham. These two verses were already cited as an example of faith in the first century B.C.E. by Shemaʻya and Avṭalyon, the teachers of Hillel and Shammai. 'Shemaʻya said: (The Lord declared) "The faith in Me evinced by their father Abraham merits that I should divide the sea for them", as it is said "And he believed the Lord; and He reckoned it to him as righteousness." Avṭalyon said: (The Lord declared) "The faith that they showed in Me merits that I should divide the sea for them"' (*Mekhilta de-R. Ishmael*, Massekhta de-Wa-yĕhî, iii, p. 99). The dispute between them concerns the question whether the merit of the fathers or their own merit was responsible for the miracle, but both ascribe the parting of the Sea of Reeds to faith, that is, to trust in God. The succeeding Tannaim elaborated their words and interpreted them; for instance: 'Others say: Israel did a great thing. The faith they showed in Me merits that I should divide the sea for them. For they said not to Moses "How shall we go forth to the wilderness, when we have no provisions for the way?" But they believed and followed Moses' (*ibid.*). In this spirit the verse was rendered with reference to Abraham in the Targum Pseudo-Jonathan: 'And he had faith in the word of the Lord, and He accounted it to him as a merit that he did not speak rebelliously to Him.' Here emphasis is given to the meaning of Israel's faith as the Psalmist in Psalms cvi 12 already understood it, when he paraphrased the Torah verses 'And they believed in the Lord and in Moses his servant. Then Moses and the children of Israel sang', in the form 'Then they believed

His words and sang His praise.' In the Septuagint, too, faith means trust in a promise, and the signification of ἐπίστευσεν τῷ θεῷ is the same as the Hebrew *wĕ-he'ĕmîn ba-A'dōnay* ['and he believed in the Lord'], but the Greek πίστις implies more of the intellectual element of faith, as we learn already from Philo.[43] To the question whether Abraham was deserving of praise for believing in God — 'When it is God who speaks and promises, who would not pay heed, even though he were the most unjust and impious of mankind?' — Philo answers: 'If you should be willing to search more deeply and not confine yourself to the mere surface, you will clearly understand that to trust in God alone and join no other with Him is no easy matter, by reason of our kinship with our yokefellow, mortality, which works upon us to keep our trust placed in riches and repute and office and friends and health and strength and many other things. To purge away each of these, to distrust created being... to trust in God, and in Him alone... this is a task for a great and celestial understanding which has ceased to be ensnared by aught of the things that surround us.'

In the Rabbinic expositions of the verses in Genesis xv relating to Abraham's faith and of the passage in Exodus xv concerning Israel's faith, a given situation in which man finds himself is envisaged, and his behaviour in these circumstances is deemed 'faith in the Lord'. This is the conception that had been accepted from time immemorial. This is shown by the words addressed by Mattathias to his sons (*I Maccabees* ii 52): 'Was not Abraham found faithful when tested?'; thereafter he refers to the conduct of Joseph, Phinehas, etc. In Philo's statement the term expresses not an individual act, but the general attitude of a man to God. Although in his aforementioned statement faith still has the meaning of trust, yet this trust is the result of speculative thought and bears an intellectual character. Philo's observations on faith in other passages have a still more marked overtone of mystical knowledge and cognition. 'Faith', he states, 'is the knowledge of piety (γνῶσις εὐσεβείας), the heritage of happiness, the exaltation of the soul...' (*De Abr.* 268). Those who are endowed with the gift of contemplation, who strive to perceive the immaterial and ideal, and do not use their senses, but only their intellect and understanding, attain to faith in God. The first believer was Abraham.[44] The lacking in faith are the multitude. The believers are those who love wisdom (*De Somniis*, I, 151). The concept of faith in Philo's writings thus goes beyond trust in the Lord's word. It denotes man's relationship to his God as one that not every person can achieve. We may posit that in Hellenistic Judaism the word πίστις came to mean belief in One God (*IV Maccabees* xvi 22, and even more so, xvii 2). 'Those who feared the Lord', φοβούμενοι τὸν θεόν,[45] even when they were not converted, accepted the belief in One God, and joined the Jewish community by declaration. Paul, who addressed his words to these congregations, certainly did not give the word a new meaning, only a new orientation. While the verse 'And he believed the Lord; and He reckoned it to him as righteousness' (Genesis xv 6) is translated in the Septuagint καὶ ἐπίστευσεν Αβραμ τῷ θεῷ and πιστεύειν always occurs there with the dative, in Christian writings this verb is used with εἰς or is followed by the genitive.[46] The missionary character of the new religion found expression in a combination of declaration and faith (I Tim. iv 1, 6). πίστις became identified with Christianity (Tit. i 4). In Judaeo-Christian writings this concept is strongly opposed. In the Epistle of James we read:[47]

> What doth it profit, my brethren, though a man saith he has faith but have not works? Can faith save him?... Yea, a man may say, 'Thou hast faith and I have works.' Shew me thy faith without thy works, and I will shew thee my faith by my works. Thou believest that there is one God; thou doest well: the devils also believe, and tremble. But wilt thou know, O vain man, that faith without works is dead? Was not Abraham our father justified by works, when he had offered Isaac his son upon the altar? Seest thou how faith was wrought with his works and by works was faith made perfect? And the scripture was fulfilled which saith, Abraham believed God, and it was imputed unto him for righteousness; and he was called the Friend of God. Ye see then how that by works a man is justified, and not by faith only. Likewise also was not Rahab the harlot justified by works, when she had received the messengers, and had sent them out another way? For as the body without the spirit is dead, so faith without works is dead also (James ii 14–26).

Contrariwise, Paul speaks of 'obedience to the faith', ὑπακοὴν πίστεώς (Romans i 5). Faith recognizes no other obedience. 'The righteousness which is of faith' annuls 'the righteousness which is of the Law which a man doeth' (*ibid.* x 5–6). Faith ῥῆμα τῆς πίστεως means: 'That if thou shalt confess with thy mouth the Lord Jesus, and shalt believe in thine heart that God hath raised him from the dead, thou shalt be saved. For with the heart man believeth unto righteousness; and with the mouth confession is made unto salvation' (*ibid.* vv. 9–10). 'Faith' assumes a dogmatic character, and there is a parallelism between *faith* and *confession.* Faith no longer means trust, piety. It is only grace — grace that is independent of works, 'But if it be of works, then is it no more grace: otherwise grace is no more grace' (*ibid.* xi 6). Faith is by grace (*ibid.* iv 16), and is, in practice, identical with grace: 'For I say, through the grace given unto me, to every man that is among you, not to think of himself more highly than he ought to think; but to think soberly, according as God hath dealt to every man the measure of faith.'[48] Paul also bases himself on Abraham, but the meaning of Abraham's faith remained on a different conceptual plane from that of his own, which is altogether new. Although attempts to find support for Paul's view[49] were not lacking, yet they met with no success. In *IV Esdras* xiii 23 it is stated: 'He who shall bring the peril in that time, He Himself shall keep them who have fallen into the peril, even such as have *works* and *faith* towards the Almighty'; and *ibid.* ix 7 (vii 7): 'And everyone that shall be saved, and shall be able to escape *by his works*, or *by faith*, whereby he hath believed.' The question is whether we may not infer too much from the word 'or'. *IV Esdras (IV Ezra)* has been preserved in Latin translation, made from the Greek; its original language was Hebrew. The translators were Christians, and it appears likely that they understood the connotation of 'faith' according to their own conception. The original signification of this faith we may deduce from the context: this is belief in wonders, mighty deeds, and perils that had been foretold. In other passages, too, the sense is not different from the accepted meaning, not even in the Apocalypse of Barukh.[50]

In the Bible faith is man's reaction to the promise of God, or to His manifestation or action. This is the case in Genesis xv 6 and Exodus iv 31, which served us as our starting point, and so it is also in Exodus xiv 31: 'And Israel saw the great work... and the people feared the Lord; and they believed in the Lord and in His servant Moses'; and in Habakkuk ii 4: 'But the righteous shall live by his faith', which the Septuagint renders ἐκ πίστεώς μου. Paul cites the verse without the personal pronoun, that is ἐκ πίστεώς only: 'But that no man is justified by the law in the sight of God, it is evident: for the just shall live by faith' (Galat. iii 11). Faith stands over against the Torah, and in antithesis to it.

The saying of the Tanna R. Nehemiah, which belongs to the middle of the second century, appears to be directed against these views: 'R. Nehemiah said: Whoever accepts one precept in faith (*var. lect.*, 'Whoever fulfils one precept...') is worthy that the Holy Spirit should rest upon him, for so we find in the case of our fathers, that, in reward for the faith that our ancestors had in the Lord, they merited that the Holy Spirit should rest upon them, and they sang a song, as it is said: "and they believed in the Lord, and in His servant Moses" ' (*Mekhilta de-R. Ishmael*, Massekhta de-Wa-yĕhî, vi, p. 114). The Holy Spirit as the reward of faith is found also in Philo, but, as we have seen, the nature of the faith is different (see above p. 32 ff).

In the whole of this passage from the *Mekhilta*, *'ămānā* [literally, 'trust'] is used for 'faith', and also in the preceding excerpt the text in the MSS. is: 'Great is faith [*'ămānā*] before Him who spoke and the world came into being.' It appears that it is actually intended to identify *'ĕmūna* ['faith'] with *'ămānā*. In Nehemiah x 1 the Septuagint (*II Esdras* 20 1) renders διατιθέμεθα πίστιν, that is to say, entering into a covenant [*'ămānā*] to keep the commandments constitutes faith. Whoever accepts a precept fulfils the *'ămānā*; he is the believer, who trusts in the Lord, who enjoins and gives the Torah. In the Rabbinic idiom, the word *'ĕmūnā* retained its original sense of 'trust'; in *M. Bava Batra* x, 8 it is stated, 'for he had lent him the money through his trust in him [*'ĕmûnātô*]', that is, through the 'assurance' of the guarantor of the loan. In this very same sense the Tanna uses the word *'ĕmūnā* with respect to God. 'R. Joḥanan said in the name of R. Eleazar b. R. Simeon: The Holy One, blessed be He, said to Israel, "My sons, borrow on My account and celebrate the holiness of the day, and trust in Me, and I shall pay (the debt)." '[51] The term has the same connotation in the dictum of R. Eliezer the Great:

'Whoever has bread in his basket, yet says, "What shall I eat to-morrow?", is evidently of those who have little faith.' On this dictum R. Isaac based his interpretation of the expression *'anshê 'ămānā* ['men of faith'] in the Mishna: 'These are people who believe in the Holy One, blessed be He.'[52] Faith in the Holy One, blessed be He — that is, that He fulfils His word[53] — accompanies the believer in all that he does.[54]

A single thread, clearly manifest, runs from the time of the earliest Hasmoneans to the last of the Amoraim. The concept of faith in the Lord does not find exhaustive expression in the recognition of God's existence or in a declaration proclaiming this recognition, but includes the conviction that there is a permanent relationship between the Deity and the world and its creatures. Faith is trust in the existence of Divine Providence. The manifestations of man's faith are the love and fear of the Lord. But before we consider the ways of Providence and the expressions of faith, we must examine the signification attributed by the Sages to the Biblical names of God and to the epithets coined in their own days, for they reflect their views regarding the entire pattern of relationship between man and his God.

CHAPTER III

THE *SHEKHINA* —
THE PRESENCE OF GOD IN THE WORLD

God's names bear testimony to His attributes and deeds and His relationship to man. A summary, as it were, of the connotations ascribed by the Sages to the Divine Names is found in the following statement of R. Abba bar Memel, who belonged to the first generation of the Palestinian Amoraim: 'The Holy One, blessed be He, said to Moses: "What dost thou seek to know? *I am called according to My acts*. Sometimes I am called *'Ēl Shadday* ['Almighty God'], or *Ṣĕvā'ôt* ['Hosts'], or *'Ĕlōhîm* ['God'], or *YHWH* ['Lord']. When I judge mankind I am called *'Ĕlohim*; when I make war against the wicked I am called *Ṣĕvā'ôt*; when I suspend man's sins I am called *'Ēl Shadday*, and when I have compassion on My world I am called *YHWH*," for the Tetragrammaton signifies none other than the quality of mercy, as it is said: "O *YHWH, YHWH*, God, merciful and gracious.' This is the meaning of the verse אהיה אשר אהיה, ['I am that I am'] — I am named according to my acts."[1] This interpretation of the Names, which implicitly nullifies all mythological exegesis, also holds good for the Names that were coined after the Biblical period.[2] From the Bible the Sages acquired their supramythological and supranatural conception of the Deity. He is spirit and not flesh. All possibility of representing God by means of any creature upon earth or the hosts of heaven is completely negated. 'To whom then will ye liken God? Or what likeness will ye compare unto Him?' (Isaiah xl 18). The war against the images was a war against the corporealization of the Godhead, against the belief that there is something divine in matter and its natural or magical-artistic forms. On the other hand, the idea of abstraction is wanting in the Bible.[3] God appears and reveals Himself to human vision in various likenesses — like a King sitting on His throne, or an Old Man full of compassion.[4] These literary images and other anthropomorphic expressions were able to convey the consciousness of God's nearness, but at the same time they could open the door to the infiltration of myth. On the other hand, complete and consistent abstraction of the concept of God was likely to lead to a deistic outlook, which removes God from the world and its affairs and leaves Him only a place as a passive observer. It has been rightly stated[5] that in the tension between the two aims — the insistence on the purity of the monotheistic idea on the one side, and on the vitality of faith on the other — is comprised the history of Israel's religion. The banishment of magic and myth demanded the creation of a gulf between God and man, but nevertheless the believer wishes to feel God's proximity, to recognize His character and to conceive to some extent His relationship to man and the world. This dualism is found in Scripture, where the two elements are found side by side. The Omnipotent God, the Creator of the universe, who governs it and cares for His creatures, is necessarily removed from the world, being above and beyond it; but in the same measure the concept of Providence incorporates God's nearness. The gulf is stressed in verses like 'It is He that sitteth above the circle of the earth, and the inhabitants thereof are as grasshoppers...' (Isaiah xl 22); 'For My thoughts are not your thoughts, neither are your ways My ways... For as the heavens are higher than the earth, so are My ways higher than your ways....' (*ibid.* lv 8–9). God is far from us; He is incomparable, and cannot be conceived; as Job puts it, 'Behold, God is great, and we know Him not' (xxxvi 26). Contrariwise, we find verses like 'Whither shall I go from Thy Spirit, Or whither shall I flee from Thy presence? If I ascend to heaven, Thou art there! If I make my bed in Sheol, Thou art there! If I take the wings of the morning and dwell in the uttermost parts of the sea, even there Thy hand shall lead me, and Thy right hand shall hold me' (Psalms cxxxix 7–10). His glory, therefore, fills the world, yet it is not, in consequence, a whit less sublime and wonderful. Thus the verses cited are preceded by 'Such knowledge is too wonderful for me, it is high I cannot attain it,' and they are followed (v. 14) by the words 'Wonderful are Thy works; and that my soul knoweth right well.'

The entire history of the patriarchs and the people is one multifaceted testimony to the immanence of God, or in the words of the Torah: 'Because the Lord thy God walketh in the midst of thy camp' (Deuteronomy xxiii 15 [14]). In many passages, God appears as a Father who compassionates His children, the work of His hands (Psalms ciii 13; Isaiah lxiv 7). And the same prophet that gave expression to the vast distance between the thoughts of God and the thoughts of man, adds to the Divine glorification an expression that remains true to His nearness: 'For thus says the high and lofty One who inhabits eternity, whose name is Holy: "I dwell in the high and holy place, and also with him who is of a contrite and humble spirit, to revive the spirit of the humble, and to revive the heart of the contrite" (Isaiah lvii 15). The psalmists have immortalized their trust in and their consciousness of God's nearness in verses like: 'I keep the Lord always before me', 'O taste and see that the Lord is good!' God is thus both near and far. Recognizing the enormous interval between the transcendental God — a consciousness that exists in every religion that has passed the mythical stage — and himself, the believer also yearns to attain to the realization of his nearness, without reverting to dangerous identification. A great part of the history of religions, including the religion of Israel, consists of the quest for the solution of the problem of bridging the abyss that cannot be closed. It is just the extreme exclusion of all similitudes and anthropomorphic qualities from the concept of the Deity that leads to the filling, by means of intermediate beings, of the vacuum thus created. This is the way of Hellenistic Judaism in its various manifestations. The Jewish Hellenists, like the neo-Pythagorians and the later disciples of Plato, posited the existence of intermediate powers, through the medium of which God works in the world of phenomena. These forces are not God. They are an expression and reflection of God, but not God Himself, nor separate personalities. Already in the *Letter of Aristeas* (132; 195) a distinction is drawn between the ruling power of God, which is omnipresent, and God Himself, the greatest of all entities and the Lord of everything, who is not in need of anything, and dwells in heaven. But the world is governed by Divine power. This intermediary power appears most clearly in *The Wisdom of Solomon* — the estimated date of whose composition is in the eighties B.C.E. — in the form of Wisdom, which penetrates to all parts of the world as the force of life operating perpetually. Undoubtedly, there is to be observed here the influence of the doctrine of the *pneuma* — the Stoic reason (ἔννουν τὸ πνεῦμα), only the Jewish author of the *Book of the Wisdom of Solomon* holds that the *pneuma* is not immanent in the world and linked to its physical conception, but is the breath of life, which the Creator breathed into Adam.[6]

Philo, to whom God is just 'Existence' (ὁ ὤν), declares that He cannot be conceived by the intellect beyond the fact that He *is*.[7] He bridges the gulf between God and matter by means of the Logos.

The problem before us is not openly discussed in the Rabbinic sources, but it emerges from the manner in which many names and epithets of God are used. One of these is the title *Shĕkhînā* ['Divine Presence']. At this stage we may already enquire how close is the relationship between the concept of Wisdom (*Sophia*) and that of the Shekhina. The designation Shekhina connotes the personification and hypostasis of God's presence in the world, that is, of God's immanence. Gershom Scholem[8] has rightly stressed the importance of elucidating this term in all its ramifications and metamorphoses in the history of Israel's religion. Shekhina does not mean the place where the Deity is to be found, that is, the Dwelling Place, but His manifest and hidden Presence. Reference is made to 'the glory of the Shekhina', to 'the wings of the Shekhina'[9], or to 'pressing the feet of the Shekhina' [i.e. acting haughtily towards the Shekhina]. The question before us is whether the concept of the Shekhina and its use in the Talmuds and Midrashim evidences a view that separates the Shekhina from God. The scholars of the Middle Ages already differed on this issue. The philosophers among them — like R. Saadia Gaon, Maimonides, and even R. Judah ha-Levi — held the view that the Shekhina, which they identified with the Divine Glory, 'is a form superior to the angels, mighty in its creation, radiant with majesty and light, and it is called "the glory of the Lord" ... and the Sages refer to it as Shekhina'[10]; it is the creation of God — the first of His works, having preceded the formation of matter, and, in the language of Maimonides, is 'the created light, which God caused to dwell in a given place in order to show the distinction of that place'.[11] This view appeared less dangerous than the acceptance of the hypostasis of an uncreated being, which implies a complete contradiction of the principle of excluding all corporeality from the conception of God. The view of Maimonides, who wished to find support for his theory in Onkelos's method of translation, was already rejected by Naḥmanides in his commentary on Genesis xlvi 1. He raised the serious objection: 'If one should say that it is a created glory, in accordance with the view of the Master [Maimonides] in regard to the verse "and the glory of the Lord filled the tabernacle" and others, how can we apply thereto *bārûkh* ['Blessed be'] and *ha-mĕvōrākh* ['the blessed'] ? Moreover, one who prays to a created glory is, as it were, an idolater! However, many statements by our Sages point to the fact that the name Shekhina stands for God, be He blessed.' With this opinion a scholar like Moore finds himself in agreement; he observes that the concept of the Shekhina is 'a verbal smoke to conceal the difficulty presented by the anthropomorphic language'.[12] On the other hand, J. Abelson,[13] who devoted a complete monograph to the Shekhina, is inclined to find in the sources a conception of the Shekhina as light or some other material object, as well as the use of this concept in a personal sense. But it is doubtful if his interpretation of the sources that he cites is always correct, and if his apologetic purpose, which is to demonstrate the doctrine of 'immanence' in Rabbinic literature, did not overstep the mark. He also quotes dicta that can be related to the subject discussed by him only by forced exegesis. We must examine the relevant sources ourselves.

The term Shekhina is added in Onkelos's rendering of verses in which the verb *shākhan* ['to dwell'] is used in relation to God, or where reference is made to 'causing His name to dwell' or to 'putting His name', for example: 'And He shall dwell in the tents of Shem' — Onkelos: 'And He will cause His Shekhina to dwell in the dwelling-place of Shem' (Genesis ix 27); 'And let them make Me a sanctuary, that I may dwell among them' — Onkelos: 'And they shall make before Me a sanctuary and I shall cause My Shekhina to dwell among them' (Exodus xxv 8); 'But unto the place which the Lord your God shall choose out of all your tribes to put His name there, even unto His habitation shall ye seek, and thither thou shalt come' — Onkelos: 'But unto the place which the Lord your God shall choose out of all your tribes to cause His Shekhina to dwell there, even to the House of His Shekhina shall ye seek and thither shall ye come' (Deuteronomy xii 5). But the addition of the word Shekhina is also found in passages of another kind, where its purpose is to avoid the use of anthropomorphic expressions, such as 'And the Lord passed by before him' — Onkelos: 'And the Lord caused His Shekhina to pass before him' (Exodus xxxiv 6);[14] 'For I will not go up in the midst of thee' — Onkelos: 'For I will not remove My Shekhina from among thee' (*ibid.* xxxiii 3); 'For I lift up My hand to heaven' — Onkelos: 'For I shall establish the House of My Shekhina in heaven' (Deuteronomy xxxii 40); 'For what good is there in heaven?' — Onkelos: 'For Thou art the God whose Shekhina is in heaven above' (*ibid.* iv, 39); 'And the shouting for the king is among them' — Onkelos: 'And the Shekhina of their king is among them' (Numbers xxiii 21). The translator did not deviate from the wording of the text on his own initiative, but translated as he did because his generation considered that certain verses could not be rendered literally, as the Tanna R. Judah observed: 'He who translates a verse literally is a liar.'[15] The translator chose to add the epithet 'Shekhina', because in his time it was already used to indicate the presence of God in His sanctuary and among His congregation. In these contexts the designation appears in Tannaitic literature. It is noteworthy that in the Mishna the term occurs only twice — both references being in effect one — and belongs to the era of Bar Kokhba. R. Ḥanania b. Ṭeradion said: 'If two sit together and occupy themselves with words of the Torah, the Shekhina abides in their midst.'[16] About two generations later R. Ḥalafta of the village of Ḥanania said: 'If ten men sit together and occupy themselves with words of the Torah, the Shekhina is in their midst, as it is said, "God standeth in the congregation of the godly." '[17]

The use of Shekhina is more prevalent in the Tosefta, and especially in the Halakhic Midrashim. The Tabernacle [*Mishkan*, 'Dwelling-place'] is the sphere of the Sanctuary, which is the 'Camp of the Shekhina' (*Tosefta Kelim*, Bava Qamma, i, 12). 'From the entrance of the Temple Court inward is the Camp of the Shekhina' (*Sifre*, Nāśō, § 1, p. 4); the House in which the Lord dwells is 'the House of the Shekhina' — 'The land of Canaan is fit to contain the House of the Shekhina, but Transjordan is not fit for the House of the Shekhina' (*Sifre Zuṭa*, Nāśō, v. 2, p. 228). Whenever the manifestation of the Lord, His descent, ascent, or going forth, is spoken of, the term Shekhina is used.[18] 'The Shekhina went before Israel and prepared a place for them to dwell in.'[19] Whereas at first this epithet was used to denote a theophany at a given place, after the destruction of the Temple this designation was specifically chosen when reference was made to the Divine Presence not at a definite place but in the midst of the people. 'Wherever Israel went into exile, the Shekhina, as it were, was exiled with them; they were exiled to Egypt, the Shekhina was with them... they were exiled to Babylon, the Shekhina was with them... they were exiled to Elam, the Shekhina was with them, as it is said, "And I will set My throne in Elam" (Jeremiah xlix 38).'[20] The verse from Jeremiah provides clear evidence of the sense of 'presence' inherent in the designation Shekhina. The use of the epithet Shekhina, however, expresses not only 'presence' but also 'nearness', and has made possible expressions of intimacy. At times God speaks of the Shekhina as though it were separate from Himself: 'The Omnipresent said to Israel... the fact that I have put My Shekhina in your midst...'; 'therefore the Omnipresent detained for her [Miriam's] sake the Shekhina, the Ark, the priests and the Levites....'[21] Similarly, it is possible to speak of acts — bloodshed, incest,[22] perversion of justice, and falsification of measures[23] — that cause the Shekhina to depart. 'For whoever is humble will ultimately cause the Shekhina to dwell with man upon earth... but whoever is haughty brings about the defilement of the earth and the departure of the Shekhina....'[24] R. Eliezer said: 'Now if on one who cleaves to uncleanness the spirit of uncleanness rests, then it follows that on one who cleaves to the Shekhina, the Shekhina rests upon him.'[25]

We may sum up as follows: In Tannaitic literature the term Shekhina is used when the manifestation of the Lord and His nearness to man are spoken of.[26] It is in this sense that R. Akiba uses the epithet Shekhina in the following homily: 'When man and wife are worthy the Shekhina abides in their midst; if they are unworthy fire consumes them' (*T.B. Soṭa* 17a). The same applies to Rabban Gamaliel's answer to the Gentile who asked 'Why did the Holy One blessed be He reveal Himself to Moses in a thorn-bush?', 'It teaches us that there is no place upon earth void of the Shekhina.'[27] The mention of this Divine designation in the dicta of these Tannaim and in those of their contemporaries is no indication of the date of their origin; nor is the explanation probable that the use of this epithet became prevalent, as it were, only after the destruction of the Temple, in order to stress that God's Presence among Israel did not cease with the destruction of the sanctuary.[28] It is inconceivable that a new and unknown designation would have been used to emphasize the Divine Presence at a time of crisis. It is more probable that to give emphasis to the Lord's Presence it was actually an epithet expressing this concept in Temple times that was chosen. Moreover we found, in Targum Onkelos and in the works of the Tannaim, that the term Shekhina was used in respect of Biblical passages that appeared to them as anthropomorphic. It is not to be assumed that they would have done this unless the epithet had been widely current and well known for a long time. It is a fact that the use of this designation in Tannaitic literature is the most prevalent and always serves to denote certain phenomena. Exceptions that seem to occur in printed editions are not to be found in the MSS. In almost every instance where we should have expected the designation Shekhina to appear and it does not, the epithet occurs in MSS; and *vice versa*, when it is found in an unsuitable place, it is wanting in the MSS. This consistent usage shows that we have indeed before us a systematic tradition that continued for generations.

Abelson wished to prove that the Shekhina is light, that is to say, tangible matter, and he bases himself on various sources that speak of 'the splendour of the Shekhina', or 'the light of the Shekhina'. With reference to the verse 'The Lord make His face to shine upon thee' (Numbers vi 25) R. Nathan said: 'This means the brightness of the Shekhina' (*Sifre*, Nāśō, No. 41, p. 44); but this contains no more than the Targum of Onkelos, 'May the Lord cause His Shekhina to shine', which is interpreted in *Num. Rabba* xi 6 to mean 'that He will look upon thee with kindly [literally, 'shining'] and not angry mien'.[29] In the light of what we learnt concerning the origin of the concept 'Shekhina', we see that 'the brightness of the Shekhina' simply means the light of the Lord, and refers to the manifestation of the Lord, Shekhina being substituted for the Tetragrammaton in order to avoid anthropomorphism. Ezekiel's statement (xliii 2) 'and behold, the glory of the God of Israel came from the way of the east; and His voice was like the sound of many waters; and the earth did shine with His glory' is explained in *'Avot de-Rabbi Nathan* (Recension I, ii) thus: ' "And the earth did shine with His glory" — that is, the face of the Shekhina'. There is nothing more here than in the Targum 'And the earth shone with the splendour of his glory'; nor is it stated that the Shekhina is a definite, separate, or material entity; only transcendence and sublimity are expressed here. A number of the sources cited by Abelson even prove the reverse of what he wished to demonstrate. With reference to the verse 'that Moses knew not that the skin of his face sent forth beams' (Exodus xxxiv 29) it is stated in the *Tanḥuma* (Kî Tiśśa', xxxiii): 'Whence did Moses acquire the beams of glory? The Sages declare: From the cave, as it is said "And it shall come to pass, while My glory passeth by, that I will put thee in a cleft of the rock" — the Holy One, blessed be He, placed His hand over him and thence he acquired the beams of glory... Others say that at the time when the Holy One, blessed be He, taught him [Moses] Torah, he received the beams of glory from the sparks that issued from the Shekhina.' Here the Shekhina is none other than the Holy One, blessed be He, and neither of them is light.

Nor is the concept that the Shekhina is separated light to be found in the following Midrash, which describes Moses' eminence as compared with that of Isaac, who claims: ' "I am greater than thou, for I stretched forth my neck on the altar and saw the face of the Shekhina." Moses answered him: "I rose to higher heights than thou. Thou didst behold the face of the Shekhina and thine eyes grew dim, as it is said: 'And it came to pass, that when Isaac was old, and his eyes were dim, from seeing'; what is meant by 'from seeing'? — from seeing the Shekhina. But I spoke with the Shekhina face to face, yet my eyes were not dimmed...." '[30] The use also of the figure 'the splendour [*zîv*] of the Shekhina' lends no support to Abelson's interpretation.[31] In the Mishna *zîv* is mentioned only in the phrases 'the splendour [*zîv*] of the priesthood' and 'the splendour of wisdom' (*M. Soṭa* ix, 15). In the *Tosefta* the word does not occur at all. 'The splendour of the Shekhina' is found a number of times in the Halakhic Midrashim, and principally in the sayings of the Amoraim, such as 'Until their homes were filled with the splendour of the Shekhina' (*Mekhilta*, Ba-ḥōdesh, Jethro, ii, p. 220); 'They enjoy the splendour of the Shekhina' (*T.B. Berakhot* 13a); 'The Holy One, blessed be He sates them with the splendour of the Shekhina' (*T.B. Bava Batra* 10a); 'The splendour of the Shekhina from on high was bestowed upon them' (*Ecclesiastes Rabba*, viii, 3). *Zîv*, like *ma'or* ['light', 'brightness'], links the concept of Shekhina with a corporeal act, and the usage serves to make the incident comprehensible, but actually there is no difference whatsoever between 'the splendour of the Shekhina' and 'the Shekhina'. In truth we find that an expositor will use both of them alternately in a single homily, for example: ' "The inside thereof being inlaid with love": R. Judan said, This means the merit of the Torah... R. Azariah in the name of R. Juda in the name of R. Simon said, This refers to the Shekhina. One verse states, "So that the priests could not stand to minister by reason of the cloud; for the glory of the Lord filled the house of the Lord (I Kings viii 11)"; and another verse states, "And the court was full of the brightness of the Lord's glory" (Ezekiel x 4). How are the two verses to be reconciled? R. Joshua of Sikhnin in the name of R. Levi (said): To what could the Tent be likened? To a cave situated next to the sea. The sea was turbulent and flooded the cave; the cave was filled (with water), yet the sea was in no way diminished. So, too, was the Tent filled with the splendour of the Shekhina, yet the world lacked not a whit of the Shekhina' (Canticles iii 8). The splendour of the Shekhina is the same as the Shekhina, just as the water that flooded the cave is identical with the water of the sea.

Sometimes the sources speak of the 'light' ['*ôr*] of God, without using the term Shekhina. The verse 'In the light of the king's countenance is light' (Proverbs xvi 15) the Sages expounded as referring to 'the light of the Holy One, blessed be He', and to the 'fire from on high';[32] and when they declared that 'the Holy One, blessed be He, is all light', or spoke of 'this people whose God is light'[33] they did not mean to say that He was a substance of light, but that the light was His own, and that He had no need of any other light.[34] On the verse in Daniel (ii 22) 'and the light dwelleth with Him' the Rabbis comment: 'Thou dost find that he who is in darkness can see what is in the light, whereas he who is in the light cannot see what is in darkness; but the Holy One, blessed be He, can see both what is in the darkness and what is in the light. Said Daniel "He revealeth the deep and secret things; He knoweth what is in the darkness, and the light dwelleth with Him." ' (*Tanḥuma* ii Tĕṣawwe, § 6). God is the Source of light; hence here, too, the light does not denote the essence of God. The light is the δόξα that is linked to the Deity.[35]

Even the metaphor 'the wings of the Shekhina' is not a material figure of speech; again the Shekhina is none other than God, for thus we read in the *Mekhilta*:[36] 'R. Joshua said that when Amalek came to harm Israel beneath the wings of their Father in heaven, Moses said before the Holy One, blessed be He: "Sovereign of the universe, this wicked man comes to destroy Thy children beneath Thy wings. Who now shall read the Book of the Torah that Thou hast given them?" ' A similar dictum occurs there in the name of R. Eleazar of Modiʿim. God, or the Shekhina, spreads His wings over Israel 'As an eagle that stirreth up her nest, hovereth over her young' (Deuteronomy xxxii 11). He who joins Israel — the proselyte — enters beneath the wings of the Shekhina (*'Avot de-R. Nathan*, Recension I, xii). 'For Abraham, our father, used to convert them and bring them beneath the wings of the Shekhina' (*Sifre*, Wā-'etḥannan, § 32, p. 54; *'Avot de-R. Nathan*, Recension I, xii). Jethro said: 'Behold, I shall go to my land, and I shall convert all the people of my country, and I shall lead them to the study of the Torah, and I shall bring them under the wings of the Shekhina' (*Mekhilta de-R. Ishmael*, Massekhta da-'Amalek, Jethro, ii, p. 2). Abelson's interpretation that it is precisely the image of 'the wings of the Shekhina' that expresses the omnipresence[37] of God is a good example of his forced explanations. This presence is expressed by the term Shekhina alone. To be beneath the wings of the Shekhina signifies to be under the Lord's protection, as the Bible phrases it (Ruth ii 12): 'And be thy reward complete from the Lord, the God of Israel, under whose wings thou art come to take refuge';[38] and alongside 'wings of the Shekhina' we find 'wings of Heaven'.[39]

The omnipresence of God-Shekhina is one of the primary postulates. The dicta that speak of the Shekhina do not attempt to describe her, but to explain and reconcile her with the manifestations and presence of God at fixed places and times, whilst avoiding the solution of positing the existence of powers that are separate and emanate from the Lord. A question was asked by Gentiles and not by them alone: 'The Emperor said to Rabban Gamaliel: "You say that wherever there is a company of ten (Jews) the Shekhina abides in their midst. How many Shekhinas are there then?" '[40] In reply Rabban Gamaliel takes the sun as an example: It shines upon each individual and, at the same time, upon the world as a whole. Now the sun is but one of the thousand myriad attendants of the Holy One, blessed be He, 'how much more so (can) the Shekhina of the Holy One, blessed be He (do this)!' Here the Shekhina is not a separate entity, nor is it light. The fear that the Shekhina's presence in the world detracts, as it were, from her transcendentalism is popularly and naively expressed in a dialogue between the Holy One, blessed be He, and the angels: ' "And it came to pass [*wa-yĕhî*] on the day that Moses had made an end of setting up the tabernacle" — woe [*way*] was it to the ministering angels on the day that Moses made an end. They said: "Now He will take His Shekhina away from our midst and cause His glory to abide with His children." The Holy One, blessed be He, answered them: "Pay no heed to this, for My Shekhina is ever with you on high", as it is said, "whose majesty is rehearsed above the heavens". But it was vain comfort that He gave them, so to speak. On the contrary, primarily His Shekhina is below, as it is said "His glory is upon the earth" — first, and only afterwards — "(upon) the heavens." '[41] The reference is to Psalms cxlviii 13, 'His glory is upon [E.V. 'above'] the earth and the heavens.' The anonymous expositor stresses, from the human standpoint, the superiority of immanence. What is stated in this dialogue concerning the Shekhina is expressed in another discussion relative to the Almighty Himself. A certain Cuthean asked R. Me'ir: ' "Is it possible that He of whom it is written 'Do not I fill heaven and earth?' spoke with Moses from between the two staves of the Ark?" He replied: "Bring me magnifying mirrors!"; he did so. (R. Me'ir then) said to him: "Look at your reflection!" He saw it magnified. (He thereupon said:) "Bring me diminishing mirrors!" He did so. "Look at your reflection there!" He saw it diminished. (Whereupon R. Me'ir) said to him: "If you, who are but flesh and blood can alter yourself in whatever way you wish, how much more so (can) He who spoke and the world came into being!... When He wishes — 'Do not I fill heaven and earth?'; and when He wishes — He speaks with Moses from between the staves of the Ark" ' (*Genesis Rabba* iv 4, pp. 27–28). An entirely different view is voiced by R. Me'ir's colleague — R. Jose — which is found in the following Baraita: 'It is taught, R. Jose said: The Shekhina never descended to earth, nor did Moses and Elijah ever ascend to Heaven, as it is said "The heavens are the heavens of the Lord, but the earth hath He given to the sons of men."'[42] R. Jose's words astonished the Amoraim, since they are emphatically contradicted by many Biblical verses, and the Sages reconciled them by a compromise. In truth the Shekhina did descend, but not below ten handbreadths, and Moses and Elijah ascended heavenward, but not above ten (handbreadths). Ten handbreadths constitute another domain.[43] Despite the great proximity a certain distance was preserved. But this was not the original purport of R. Jose's statement. The extreme form of its wording is in keeping with his other dictum 'The Holy One, blessed be He, is the Place of the world, but the world is not His place',[44] and seeks to negate the view that the revelation of God is connected with ascent and descent; they are only figurative expressions. It may be assumed that R. Jose, who disputed with sectarians, sought to obviate arguments of the kind put by the Cuthean to R. Me'ir, and to contradict dangerous answers given in reply. Actually the question of the Cuthean implies an answer like this: He of whom it is written 'Do not I fill heaven and earth?' is not the same as He that spoke with Moses from between the staves of the Ark. The Cuthean-Samaritan, whose question hints at this answer, is a Gnostic, who distinguished between the Supreme Deity and the demiurge, who created the world. The early fathers of the Christian Church also used this doctrine in order to reconcile the aforementioned contradiction, for it opened the way for them to introduce a Christological interpretation. It will suffice to cite the words of Justin Martyr, who was born in Shechem and was the contemporary of R. Me'ir and R. Jose. He said: 'Let it not be thought that the uncreated God ascends or descends, for the Father and Master does not go to any place, does not walk about, does not sleep and does not wake; He remains in His place....' (*Dialogue*, 56, 60). So far we hear the words of R. Jose,[45] but not so in another passage. There Justin writes: 'How is it possible that He should speak to anyone, or appear to anyone, or that He should manifest Himself in a finite place, since the people cannot see the glory of Him who sent it?... Hence, neither

Abraham, nor Isaac, nor Jacob, nor any other human being saw the Father, the Lord of all things, who is ineffable; they only saw him who was deified by the will of the Father, namely, His son, being similar to His angel, who ministers before Him' (*ibid.* 127). R. Jose's teaching did not close the door to interpretations of the type advanced by Justin; indeed, it remained an individual opinion. The Amoraim, who sensed the contradiction between belief in God, whose glory fills the universe, and His speaking to Moses from between the staves of the Ark, followed the exegetical method of R. Me'ir. The example of the reflection in the mirror lessened the force of the question. The emphasis laid on the absolute will and omnipotence of God did not remove the actual contradiction, but made it a component of the Divine capacity and might, which in no way conform to the standards of human reason.

It is reported in the name of R. Joḥanan that when Moses heard from the Almighty the words 'And let them make Me a sanctuary' (Exodus xxv 8), he retreated in consternation, saying 'Sovereign of the universe, lo, the heavens and the heavens of the heavens cannot contain Thee, yet Thou sayest "And let them make Me a sanctuary"!' In reply the Holy One, blessed be He, said to him: 'Moses, it is not as thou dost think, but twenty boards to the north and twenty boards to the south, eight in the west, and I shall descend and confine My Shekhina among you upon earth.'[46] The term 'confinement of the Shekhina', which appears in a few other passages,[47] signifies special concentration of the Divine Presence in a given place,[48] and the more limited the space is the greater is His might. When He confines His Shekhina among five elders, who entered to intercalate the year, the Ministering Angels laud Him, saying: 'This is the Mighty One, this is the Mighty One, this is God, this is God. He of whom it is written "A God feared in the great council of the holy ones" leaves the assembly on high and descends and confines His Shekhina among those below.'[49] The confinement of the Shekhina in one place does not imply withdrawal from another place. We have already quoted in a different context the analogy of the sea and the cave, which seeks to illustrate the truth that 'although it is written "and the glory of the Lord filled the tabernacle", neither the beings on high nor those below lacked anything of the splendour of His glory.'[50]

The general opinion is that nothing is too low or too humble for the Shekhina to be manifested thereon. 'A Gentile once put the following question to Rabban Gamaliel: "Why did the Holy One blessed be He reveal Himself to Moses in a thorn-bush?" He replied: "Had He revealed Himself to him on a carob tree or a fig tree, what wouldst thou have said then? It serves only to teach that no place on earth is void of the Shekhina." '[51] In the middle of the third century, the Amoraim debated the manner chosen by God to dwell with the humble and contrite: ' "With him also that is of a contrite and humble spirit" (Isaiah lvii 15) — Rav Huna and Rav Ḥisda (discuss the verse): one says (it means) "the contrite is with Me"; the other says "I am with the contrite." ' The Talmud concludes: 'It appears that the one who holds "I am with the contrite" is right. For the Holy One, blessed be He, left all the (other) mountains and hills and caused His Shekhina to dwell on Mount Sinai, but Sinai did not rise up....' From this it is deduced that pride encroaches upon the Shekhina: 'Whoever is imbued with an overweening spirit, the Holy One, blessed be He, declares "I and he cannot abide together in the world" ', and hence the moral that a man 'should learn from the mind of his Maker'.[52]

These views are opposed to the concept of the immanence of the Deity in the world, which was widely accepted by the Greeks, and according to which the Divine immanence in nature is an immutable law. 'To say that God turns His face away from sinners is exactly like saying that the sun withdraws its face from the blind.'[53] The Rabbinic view is that God's presence in the world and the modes of His theophanies are linked to man's conduct and deeds.[54] Regarding the fact that God caused the Shekhina to dwell in the Tabernacle, there is a difference of opinion between R. Simeon b. Yoḥai and Rabbi. According to Rabbi,[55] this event was 'a new phenomenon'; R. Simeon b. Yoḥai, on the other hand, declared: 'It had once existed and then had ceased for a long period, and finally it reverted to the former position.' His words were elucidated by the Amoraim. R. Abba bar Kahana[56] explained: 'Primarily the Shekhina dwelt among the inhabitants of the earth', but since Adam sinned, it departed to the first heaven and in the subsequent generations it withdrew on account of the wicked from heaven to heaven as far as the seventh heaven, until Abraham, our father, arose and brought it down to the sixth heaven; his descendants up to Amram then brought it down from heaven to heaven as far as the first heaven. Only Moses succeeded in bringing it back again to earth, and erected the Tabernacle. The basic thought underlying the dramatic account of how the Shekhina came to dwell on earth is explained in the following homily of R. Isaac:[57] 'It is written "The righteous shall inherit the land, and dwell therein for ever" (Psalms xxxvii 29). Wherein shall the wicked dwell? In the air? This is the meaning: The wicked caused the Shekhina to leave the earth, but the righteous caused the Shekhina to dwell upon the earth.' The connection between the Shekhina's dwelling among the denizens of the earth and human merit is to be inferred also from Rabbi's view that the Shekhina did not abide among the terrestrial inhabitants when the world was created, but only when the Tabernacle was erected. Obviously, Rabbi did not deny all the manifestations of the Shekhina to people upon earth, which are expressly mentioned in the Torah and preceded the erection of the Tabernacle, but referred to the Shekhina's dwelling below permanently — in one place. This must be credited to the merit and high status of the generation that accepted the Torah. R. Judah bar Il'ai already relates the following parable: 'It may be likened to the case of a king who had a daughter who was a minor. Until she grew up and came of age, he used to speak to her when he saw her in the street; he spoke to her in the alleyways. But when she grew up and came of age, he said: "It is not in keeping with my daughter's dignity that I should talk to her in public. Make her therefore a pavilion (παπυλιών), and I shall speak with her inside the pavilion." Thus at first it is written "When Israel was a child, then I loved him" (said God) — they saw Me in Egypt... they saw Me at the Red Sea... they saw Me at Sinai... But once they had accepted the Torah and become a complete nation unto Him, He said: "It is not in keeping with the dignity of My children that I should talk with them publicly, but let them make Me a Tabernacle and I shall speak (with them) from the midst of the Tabernacle." '[58] The first phase was deemed primitive, comparable to the age of childhood, when one does not insist on absolute propriety. But religious maturity cannot acquiesce in a state of anarchy.

The unique character of the Tabernacle, and subsequently of the

Temple, as the place of the Shekhina is related to the idea of election. The place 'where He shall choose to cause His name to dwell' (Deuteronomy xiv 23) is 'the Chosen House' [*Bêt ha-Bĕḥîrā*, i.e. the Temple].[59] The existence of the Shekhina in the Temple not only does not contradict its presence throughout the world, but, on the contrary, it is itself an essential condition of the maintenance of this presence, without which the latter would not be possible. Rabbi, who linked the descent of the Shekhina to the dwellers on earth with the erection of the Tabernacle, is also the author of the following homily: '...Thou dost say "and Mine eyes and My heart shall be there perpetually" (I Kings ix 3). Are they then there only? Behold, it has already been stated "the eyes of the Lord [that] run to and fro through the whole earth" (Zechariah iv 10) and it says "The eyes of the Lord are [in] every place, keeping watch upon the evil and the good" (Proverbs xv 3). What then is the significance of "and Mine eyes and My heart shall be there perpetually"? They are not, so to speak, only there, but since they are there, they are everywhere' (*Sifre Deuteronomy*, § 40). The perpetual, concentrated Presence in one place is essential to the recognition of the universality of the Divine Existence. When the Temple was built, the world was firmly established, as R. Samuel bar Naḥmani stated: 'Until the Temple was constructed the world stood on a throne of two legs; once the Temple was built the world was firmly established' (*Tanḥuma*, Tĕrūmā, § 9). The existence of the Deity in the world becomes firm, as it were, through His existence in one place.

It should be noted here that a distinction must be drawn between the existence of God, His presence and readiness to listen to those who pray unto Him, and the revelation of the Shekhina to individuals. This differentiation is required for the understanding of the following Tannaitic homily: '...It is to be inferred that the Shekhina does not reveal itself outside of Israel, for it is stated "But Jonah rose up to flee unto Tarshish from the presence of the Lord" (Jonah i 3). Was he then fleeing from the Lord's presence? Lo, it has already been said "Whither shall I go from Thy spirit?... If I ascend up into heaven, Thou art there..." (Psalms cxxxix 7–10), and it is written "the eyes of the Lord, that run to and fro through the whole earth" (Zechariah iv 10), and it is further written "The eyes of the Lord are in every place, keeping watch upon the evil and the good" (Proverbs xv 3)... The meaning is that Jonah said "I shall hie me beyond the borders of the Land of Israel, where the Shekhina does not reveal itself, for the Gentiles readily repent, lest (by comparison) I bring guilt upon Israel." '[60] Here the reference is to the manifestation of the Shekhina in the sense of Divine communication to the prophet, which takes place only in the Land; but the Shekhina's presence is, needless to say, throughout the world.[61]

The paradoxical concept that the specific presence of the Deity in a particular place not only does not contradict His presence throughout the world, but actually makes it possible, helped to solve a concrete, historical problem, namely the presence of God among His people and the singling out of this people as His dwelling place even after the destruction of the Temple and the nation's banishment from its land. Commenting on the verse '[in driving out] from before Thy people, whom Thou didst redeem to Thee out of Egypt, the nations and their gods?' (II Samuel vii 23; the *Mekhilta* reads 'nation', in the singular), R. Akiba stated: 'Were it not so written in Scripture, it would be impossible to voice such a thought. The Israelites said, as it were, to the Holy One, blessed be He: "Thou didst redeem Thyself." So, too, it is found that wherever Israel went into exile, the Shekhina, as it were, was exiled with them. When they were exiled to Egypt, the Shekhina was with them, as it is said "Did I reveal Myself unto the house of thy father, when they were in Egypt?" (I Samuel ii 27); when they were exiled to Babylon, the Shekhina was with them... and when they are destined to return, the Shekhina will return, so to speak, with them....'[62] However, there are dicta that speak of the departure of the Shekhina, when the Temple was destroyed. In a dramatic account, recalling that of the withdrawal of the Shekhina from the world after Adam had sinned, ten journeys[63] are mentioned, which preceded the departure of the Shekhina heavenward at the time of the destruction of the Temple. This account belongs to the Tannaitic period, for the early Amoraim base themselves upon it. 'R. Jonathan said[64]: Three and a half years the Shekhina abode on the Mountain of Olives and proclaimed thrice daily, saying "Return, ye backsliding children, I will heal your backslidings" (Jeremiah iii 22). Since they did not return, the Shekhina began to hover in the air, uttering the verse "I will go and return to My place, till they acknowledge their guilt and seek My face; in their trouble they will seek Me earnestly" (Hosea v 15).' According to another version, the Shekhina's station before returning to its place was the wilderness, and with reference to this 'R. Joḥanan[65] said: Six months the Shekhina waited for Israel in the wilderness, perchance they would return in penitence. Since they did not repent, the Shekhina said "Perish thy soul!"[66], as it is said "But the eyes of the wicked shall fail, and they shall have no way to flee, and their hope shall be the drooping [= perishing] of the soul" (Job xi 20).' This motif of the departure of the Shekhina, when the Temple was destroyed, recurs in the homilies of the Amoraim, for example: 'Zavdai b. Levi began his discourse thus: "God maketh the solitary to dwell in a house" (Psalms lxviii 7 [6]). You find that before the Israelites were redeemed from Egypt, they dwelt by themselves and the Shekhina by itself; but when they (the Israelites) were redeemed, they both (the Shekhina and Israel) formed an undivided whole (ὁμονοια). But when they were (again) exiled, the Shekhina once more dwelt by itself and the Israelites by themselves....'[67] Or, to take another example: 'When the Holy One, blessed be He, wished to destroy the Temple, He said: "So long as I am in it, the Gentile nations will not harm it. I shall, therefore, cease to regard it and I shall swear not to give it heed till the time of the End...." At that moment the enemy entered the Temple and burned it. When it was burnt, the Holy One, blessed be He, said "I no longer have a seat upon earth; I shall remove My Shekhina therefrom and ascend to My first habitation... At that moment the Holy One, blessed be He, wept and said: "Woe unto Me, what have I done! I caused My Shekhina to dwell below for Israel's sake, and now that they have sinned I have returned to My original place." '[68]

These homilies, expressing the shock and the sense of grief resulting from the destruction of the Temple, which disrupted the concord and created a division between the Shekhina and the people of Israel, conflict with the dicta of R. Akiba,[69] and of those who followed in his footsteps[70] which state that the Shekhina accompanied the people in exile. The difference between the two views is well reflected in two versions of Tannaitic homilies on the verses Deuteronomy xviii 11–12. In one Baraita it is reported: When R. Eliezer came to this verse, he used to say 'Alas for us! Now if on one who cleaves to uncleanness, the spirit of uncleanness rests, then it follows that on one who cleaves to the Shekhina, the Shekhina rests. And who caused it [i.e. that the Shekhina should not rest on us]? ' "But your iniquities have separated between you and your God." ' (Isaiah lix 2)[71] R. Eliezer attributes the withdrawal of the Shekhina from Israel to their sins. Just as repentance alone can bring, to his mind, redemption (see below, chapter XV), so only the removal of iniquities can restore the Shekhina to its place. On the other hand, it is reported in another Baraita: ' "Or that consulteth the dead" — this refers to one who starves himself and goes and spends the night in a cemetery, so that an unclean spirit may rest upon him. And when R. Akiba reached this verse, he wept, saying: 'If one who starves himself that the spirit of uncleanness should rest upon him (has his wish fulfilled), he who fasts that the spirit of purity should rest upon him how much more so! But what is one to do, seeing that his iniquities have brought this upon him, as it is said "But your iniquities have separated between you and your God"?'[72] Here the homily has changed and assumed an individual character: the spirit of purity — that is, of prophecy, the holy spirit — which does not rest upon a man who starves himself and is imbued with iniquity, is spoken of and not the Shekhina, which leaves Israel on account of their sins. R. Akiba's statement is connected with his Messianic outlook: 'All the time that Israel is in bondage, the Shekhina, so to speak, is in bondage with them.' The end of the homily explains its intent: 'And when they are destined to return, the Shekhina will return with them.' This is a homily of comfort, whereas the homily concerning the journeys of the Shekhina and its withdrawal is one of rebuke. The Shekhina is not with the people, but in heaven, and the conclusion of the homily, according to one of its versions, is: 'Behold, Israel seeks the Shekhina, but it will not return until the End comes.' But the continuation of the verse 'I will go and return to My place', which was expounded with reference to the departure of the Shekhina, is 'till they acknowledge their guilt, and seek My face; in their trouble they will seek Me earnestly'. Even when the Shekhina is in heaven, the possibility of offering supplications and prayers to heaven is not excluded, for God has not taken away His Providence from His people, in accordance with the words of R. Jannai: 'Although His Shekhina is in heaven, His eyes behold, His eyelids scrutinize, the children of men.'[73] However, at the end of the third century the Palestinian Amoraim still debated the question whether the Shekhina departed from the site of the Temple when the Temple was destroyed. While R. Samuel bar Naḥman held that 'Before the Temple was destroyed, the Shekhina rested in the Temple... but when the Temple was destroyed... He removed His Shekhina to heaven', his great contemporary, R. Eleazar b. Pedat, said 'Whether (the Temple) is destroyed or not, the Shekhina does not stir from its place.'[74] About a century later the Amora R. Aḥa gave the following exposition[75]: 'The Shekhina will never leave the Western Wall of the Temple, as it is said, "Behold, he standeth behind our wall" (Canticles ii 9)'; in an anonymous exposition of this verse a reason is added: 'Why? Because the Holy One, blessed be He, had sworn to it that it would never be destroyed.'[76] Since the Wall was not destroyed, there remains the part of the Sanctuary site from which the Shekhina has not departed. It is probable that this view underlies the testimony of R. Joshua: 'I have heard that sacrifices may be offered up although there is no Temple, and that the most holy offerings may be eaten although there are no curtains, the lesser holy offerings and the second tithe, although there is no wall, for the sanctity of the First Temple availed for its own time and for the future.'[77]

At all events, the view finds support in the Halakha relative to the orientation for praying, whose origin is old, but in whose various phases there is discernible the wrestling with the problem of the place of the Shekhina after the destruction of the Temple. It is true that prayer in the Bible[78] is not linked with any given site, and every place is deemed fit for prayer; nevertheless a certain uniqueness was attributed to the Temple even in respect of prayer. The worshipper is answered 'from His holy mountain' (Psalms iii 5 [4]), and Jonah's prayer from the bowels of the fish comes 'into Thy holy Temple' (Jonah ii 8).

In Solomon's prayer it is said of the captives in the land of the enemy: 'And they shall pray unto Thee toward their land, which Thou gavest unto their fathers, the city which Thou hast chosen, and the house which I have built for Thy name; then hear Thou this prayer

... in heaven Thy dwelling-place' (I Kings viii 48–49). Prayer from outside the Land of Israel reached His dwelling-place in heaven by way of the Land, the City and the Temple. Daniel prayed in his upper chamber, whose windows were open towards Jerusalem (Daniel vi 11). Accordingly, the Mishna teaches (*M. Berakhot* iv 5) that he who prays [i.e. recites the Eighteen Benedictions] must turn his face towards the Holy of Holies. A more detailed statement is found in a Baraita: 'Those who stand and pray [i.e. recite the Eighteen Benedictions] outside the Land of Israel should turn their faces towards the Land of Israel. What is the reason? (Because it is written:) "and they pray unto Thee toward [their land], which Thou gavest unto their fathers". Those who stand and pray in the Land of Israel should turn their faces towards Jerusalem. What is the reason? (Because it is written:) "and they pray unto the Land toward the city which Thou hast chosen". Those who stand up and pray in Jerusalem should turn their faces towards the Temple Mount, as it is said "and toward the house which I have built for Thy name". Those who stand and pray on the Temple Mount should turn their faces towards the Holy of Holies. What is the reason? (Because it is written:) "when they shall pray toward this place; yea, hear Thou in heaven Thy dwelling-place; and when Thou hearest, forgive". It is thus found that those who stand in the north face south, those who stand in the south face north, those who stand in the east face west, those in the west face east. In this way all Israel pray towards one place.'[79] The prayer-orientation, which is the same for the entire people, integrates them all around the place where God has chosen to cause His name to dwell. The turning of the face towards the Land, the City, and the Temple, is not merely an extraneous act but an expression of inner intent. Indeed, in the parallel sources to the text of the Baraita cited we find, instead of 'turn their faces', 'direct their hearts'[80], and this direction of the heart means two things: orientating the body and also one's thoughts. If one is so situated that he cannot orient his body, he can still direct his mind, his thoughts. Another significant variation, worthy of note, is this: while we are told in the Mishna that he who cannot determine the direction 'should turn his heart towards the Holy of Holies', it is stated in the Tosefta 'they direct their mind to the Omnipresent', and in the Baraita of the Palestinian

Talmud, 'they pray towards heaven'. These variant readings reflect the difference of opinion between the last Tannaitic Sages on the interpretation of the Mishna: 'To which Holy of Holies?' R. Ḥiyya Rabba said: Towards the heavenly Holy of Holies; R. Simeon b. Ḥalafta said: Towards the earthly Holy of Holies.' If it is not possible to orientate one's body to the earthly Holy of Holies, R. Ḥiyya holds that one's mind and thoughts should be directed straight to heaven. The Amora of Eretz-Israel, R. Phinehas bar Ḥama, reconciles the divergence of opinion by saying: 'They do not disagree: the earthly Holy of Holies faces the heavenly Holy of Holies.'[81] In orienting oneself towards the earthly Holy of Holies, one orients oneself at the same time to that in heaven. This ancient concept that the heavenly Temple faces the earthly one provides a special reason for directing the prayer of the Eighteen Benedictions towards the site of the Sanctuary even after the destruction of the Temple, that is, after the Shekhina had declared 'I will go and return to My place'. However, the orientation for the recitation of the prayer of the Eighteen Benedictions was not determined solely by the views concerning the place of the Shekhina.

The forms of cultic ritual and worship are not only decided by inner reasons of faith; frequently they are influenced by the rites of other religions either through adoption accompanied by the advancement of new reasons, or by negation and rejection. It happens at times that a new religion, or a nonconformist sect, by taking over a conventional religious custom and giving it a new interpretation, causes the custom to be changed or abandoned in its religious homeland, in whose soil it grew. The standing of the worshipper and his orientation were matters over which religions and sects were in conflict. Ezekiel (viii 16) sees in his vision an abomination perpetrated in the Temple: 'There were about five and twenty men, with their backs toward the Temple of the Lord, and their faces toward the east; and they worshipped the sun toward the east.' These people prostrated themselves to the sun and in this way linked sun-worship to the Temple. In the Mishnaic description of *simḥat bêt ha-Shô'ēvā* [the rejoicing in connection with the water-drawing ceremony on the second night of Succot],[82] it is related that when the procession of celebrants reached the gateway leading eastward, 'they turned their faces to the west and said: "Our ancestors who were in this place, their backs were toward the Temple of the Lord and their faces toward the east, and they prostrated themselves eastward to the sun; but as for us, our eyes are turned to the Lord"' (*M. Sukka* v, 4). Although the passage from Ezekiel is cited, it is not to be assumed that 'our ancestors who were in this place' refers to the men whom Ezekiel saw, and it is almost certain that the celebrants did not mean to say that their forefathers were sun-worshippers, but there is preserved here an allusion to a custom of praying towards the sun as an expression of reverence for the light. Josephus relates of the Essenes: 'Before the sun is up they utter no word on mundane matters, but offer to him certain prayers, which have been handed down from their forefathers, as though entreating him to rise' (*Wars* II, 8, 5). Philo reports a similar custom practised by the Therapeutae: 'Twice every day they pray, at dawn and at eventide; at sunrise they pray for a fine, bright day, fine and bright in the true sense of the heavenly daylight which they pray may fill their minds. At sunset they ask that the soul may be wholly relieved from the press of the senses and the objects of sense and, sitting where she is consistory and council chamber to herself, pursue the quest of truth.'[83] Even if we do not attribute mystical-philosophic thoughts of this kind to the ancestors of the participants in the Water-drawing Celebration, it is not impossible that the prostration to the sun contained an expression of reverence to the Creator of light. The worshipper came to the Sanctuary praying 'that I may walk before God in the light of the living' (Psalms lvi 14 [13]) and 'Many there are that say: "Oh that we could see some good!" Lord, lift Thou up the light of Thy countenance upon us' (*ibid.* iv 7 [6]). The joy at appearing in the Sanctuary of God, who is portrayed as 'The Lord is my light and my salvation' (Psalms xxvii 1),[84] found expression in the custom of prostration to the sun. It is not surprising that this custom aroused opposition on account of the part played by worship of the sun and the light both in the East — in the Persian religion — and in the Hellenistic-Roman world,[85] and also in view of our present knowledge concerning the dualistic *Weltanschauung* of the Qumran sectarians and the place that 'light' holds therein. 'The Sons of Light' — like the authors of *The Book of Jubilees*, The *Book of Enoch*, and *The Testaments of the Twelve*

Patriarchs — reckoned the annual calendar according to the course of the 'Great Luminary', the sun.[86] It appears that there has been preserved in the Mishna a tradition relating to a demonstration that caused an ancient custom to be abrogated in order to show the error of deviationists and sectarians. The worshipper faces only towards the west — 'as for us, our eyes are turned towards the Lord', and there is no need for him to face the sun in order to be vouchsafed 'the light of the Lord's countenance'. The light and the splendour are of the Shekhina.

However, the fixing of the praying-orientation towards Jerusalem also created a problem when Christianity came into being and was disseminated. The Church Father Epiphanius[87] relates that Elchasai, the founder and head of a Judeo-Christian sect,[88] who flourished *circa* 100 C.E., forbade his followers to turn in prayer towards the east, but enjoined them to face, from all the cardinal points, in the direction of Jerusalem: 'Those who live in the east — towards the west, facing Jerusalem; those who live in the west — towards the east, facing the same city; those who live in the north — towards the south; and those living in the south — towards the north. Thus from all directions they would turn towards Jerusalem.' The words of Elchasai seem exactly like a quotation from the Baraita on the prayer-orientation cited above. Other Judeo-Christian sects acted in the same way. Irenaeus relates[89] that the Ebionites revere Jerusalem as though it were the House of the Lord. It is obvious, however, that the reasons advanced for this attitude by these sectarians were not the same as those of the Sages. Epiphanius argues against Elchasai that on the one hand he negates the Temple services, and denies God's desire for sacrifices, and on the other he enjoins that one should pray towards Jerusalem. In truth, the Judeo-Christian traditions do not refer to praying towards the Sanctuary, but towards Jerusalem, and it may be presumed that their reason was not different from that found in the writings of the later Church Fathers,[90] who expounded the passages in Psalms cxxxii 7 'Let us go to His dwelling place; let us worship at His footstool!' and in Zechariah xiv 4 'On that day His feet shall stand on the Mount of Olives' as referring to the place where Jesus appeared. It appears that the tendency of a number of Sages to do away with a fixed prayer-orientation altogether, for the reason that 'the Shekhina is everywhere',[91] is a reaction to the arguments of the Judeo-Christians. This interpretation seems probable in so far as R. Ishmael is concerned, for he declared that 'The books of the sectarians create enmity, envy, and contention between Israel and their Father in Heaven... and should be burned together with their Divine names'.[92] Christianity in Egypt and in Western countries accepted in the second century a prayer-orientation to the east, taking into account the widespread practice in prayer among the Gentiles who had become Christians,[93] and in the third century it became universal in the Christian world even in Eastern countries. In the ordinances of the Syrian Church the rule was laid down that one had to face east in prayer, and, at the same time, a reason was given for it, namely that in time to come Jesus would appear from the east.[94] In the Land of Israel the Amoraim regarded the fixing of the orientation towards the Holy of Holies in the west as a barrier separating them completely from those who faced east. Particularly noteworthy is the dictum of R. Joshua b. Levi,[95] both from the viewpoint of style and of content. He said 'Come let us be grateful to our ancestors, who made known to us the place of prayer, as it is written "And the host of heaven worshippeth Thee". ' The words 'Let us be grateful to our ancestors' recall the words of the Mishna in the declaration made at the time of the Water-drawing Festival: 'Our ancestors who were in this place'. R. Joshua b. Levi invites us to be grateful to those ancestors who abrogated the practice of prostration towards the sun, and support for this action is to be found in the passage in Nehemiah (ix 6), which states that the host of heaven themselves, including the sun, prostrate themselves to the west. The view that 'the Shekhina is in the west'[96] is reflected in the Halakha that determined the form of the Synagogue structure: 'The entrances of the Synagogues are to be made only towards the east.'[97] Indeed, this ruling governed the construction of many synagogues that have been discovered in excavations both in Eretz-Israel and in the Diaspora, as, for example, in Dura-Europos.[98] In Babylonia there were Amoraim who continued to favour R. Ishmael's view that the Shekhina was everywhere. Rav Sheshet, who was blind, told his servant to position him for prayer facing whichever direction he pleased, but he excluded the east, 'because the sectarians teach this'. In the light of the observations that we have made above, there can be no doubt as to who the sectarians were that gave such instructions.[99]

The sources dealing with the orientation of prayer in relation to the place of the Shekhina corroborate that which we find also in other sources, namely that the epithet 'Shekhina' expresses the presence and proximity of God. But even in the epoch of the Tannaim it is not used to weaken the anthropomorphic character of Scriptural verses. On the contrary, we find that the designation Shekhina itself is accompanied by the expression *ki-vĕ-yākhôl* ['as it were', 'so to speak'][1] in passages that appear unduly daring.

A survey of all the passages referring to the Shekhina leaves no doubt that the Shekhina is no 'hypostasis' and has no separate existence alongside the Deity. This fact is stressed by Gershom Scholem,[2] even with respect to the literature of the *Hekhalot* ['Heavenly Halls'] and the surviving fragments of *Shiʿur Qoma* ['The Dimensions of God']. These do not regard the Shekhina as the embodiment of a separate entity. An exception to this rule, according to Scholem, is the dictum in *Midrash Proverbs*, xxii, 29: ' "Seest thou a man diligent in his business?" — When the Sanhedrin wished to count him [King Solomon] with the three kings and four commoners,[3] the Shekhina stood before the Holy One, blessed be He, and said unto Him: "Sovereign of the universe! Seest Thou a man diligent? — they wish to count him with 'mean men'." At that moment a Heavenly Voice went forth and said to them: "He shall stand before kings; he shall not stand before mean men." '[4] Scholem finds in this Midrash 'the beginning of a new development. For the first time a clear distinction is made between the Shekhina and the Holy One, blessed be He. They both appear in a dialogical relationship.' It seems that Scholem was influenced by the negative attitude of R. Moses b. R. Ḥasdai[5] to the aforementioned Midrash. The severe critic of both R. Saadia Gaon and Maimonides and the German Ḥasidim regarded the language of Midrash Proverbs as a source from which the philosophers could draw support for their conception of the Shekhina as 'a created form'.[6] R. Moses proceeded to deny them this source and declared: 'And now we need pay no heed to the reading in *Midrash Proverbs*, for our Talmud takes precedence.' But we are compelled to ask if we are permitted to ascribe a different intention to the expression 'the Shekhina stood before the Holy One, blessed be He' than to the phrase 'a Heavenly Voice went forth and said'. We have before us a Midrash that employs the well-known technique of interpreting a verse as a dialogue.[7] The verse (Proverbs xxii 29) is divided between two speakers. The first says: 'Seest thou a man diligent? — they wish to count him with mean men'; and the second answers: 'He shall stand before kings; he shall not stand before mean men.' There is no difference whatsoever between 'Shekhina' and 'Heavenly Voice'; they are both alternative expressions for 'the holy spirit' that speaks out of the language of Scripture. Indeed, we even find the holy spirit 'saying to the Holy One, blessed be He', and actually in an early Midrash[8] 'R. Aḥa said: This holy spirit is a counsel of defence — it defends both sides. It says to Israel: "Be not a witness against thy Friend without cause" (Proverbs xxiv 28); and it says to the Holy One, blessed be He: "Say not: 'I will do so to him as he hath done to Me.' " ' It will thus be seen that the concept of the Shekhina as a separate created being is not to be found in any Rabbinic source, not even in a late Midrash like *Pirqe de-R. Eliezer*. It is, in truth, stated there in chapter IV, with regard to the four companies of angels, 'The first company, of Michael, is on His right; the second company, of Gabriel, is on His left; the third company, of Uriel, is in front of Him; the fourth company, of Raphael, is behind Him; and the Shekhina of the Holy One, blessed be He, is in the middle; and He Himself sits on a throne, high and exalted.' But it seems that 'His Shekhina' and 'He' are one and the same. Even these Midrashim have not gone beyond what we found in the Halakhic Midrashim (above, p. 43). Only in the Midrash known as *Bẹreshit Rabbati*, which emanated from the circle of R. Moses ha-Darshan of Narbonne, in the eleventh century, which may have already been influenced by the philosophical exegesis of R. Saadia Gaon, is it stated: 'R. Akiba said: When the Holy One, blessed be He, scrutinized the action of the generation, and saw that they were corrupt and bad, *He withdrew Himself and His Shekhina from among them.*'[9] It is this very change in the conventional formula — 'the Holy One, blessed be He, withdrew His Shekhina'[10] — that points to a change of conception.

It is also necessary to emphasize that in the ideology of the Sages of the Talmud and the Midrash the term 'Shekhina' is not connected with 'Wisdom', and the two are not identified. In all the sayings and Haggadot in which reference is made to the Shekhina, figurative expressions like Princess, Matron (Lady), Queen or Bride, are absent. In brief, they contain no feminine element, an element that subsequently played a significant role in the Cabbala, under the influence of Gnostic doctrines,[11] and which, relative to Wisdom, is already found in Hellenistic literature. We must dwell on this for a moment in order to underline the difference, and thus we return to the starting point of this chapter. In *The Wisdom of Solomon*, Wisdom — whose gender is feminine in both Hebrew and Greek — is spoken of in one passage (viii 3) as the Bride and Spouse of God. The sublime source of Wisdom lies in its symbiosis with the Deity. The thought is even more clearly expressed by Philo. In his book *De Ebrietate*, 30, we read: 'Now "father and mother" is a phrase which can bear different meanings. For instance we should rightly say and without further questions that the Architect who made this universe was at the same time the father of what was thus born, whilst its mother was the knowledge (ἐπιστήμη) possessed by its Maker. With His knowledge God had union, not as men have it, and begat created being. And knowledge, having received the divine seed (τοῦ θεοῦ σπέρματα)... bore the only beloved son who is apprehended by the senses, the world which we see.' Such portrayals are found also in other passages of Philo. There is, of course, always a link between them and the verses that he expounds, as, for instance, in the example cited, the law of the stubborn and rebellious son (Deuteronomy xxi 20). But it is of consequence that in the Talmuds and the Midrashim such interpretations were never advanced, although the gender of Shekhina is feminine. We can observe here again the gulf between the way of thinking of the Talmudic and Midrashic Sages and speculative, philosophical thought. The concept of the Shekhina does not aim to solve the question of God's quiddity, but to give expression to His presence in the world and His nearness to man, without, at the same time, destroying the sense of distance.

CHAPTER IV

NEARNESS AND DISTANCE — OMNIPRESENT AND HEAVEN

The epithet 'Shekhina' expresses the presence of God, without any limitation whatsoever to this presence. There was no doubt in regard to the general meaning of the designation, and it could be used with a number of variations according to the degrees of proximity and distance in relation to God. It provides release from the tension of the polarity that marks the relationship between man and his God, and leaves the door wide open to a host of images that could not easily be linked to the classical Scriptural names of God, nor even to post-Biblical designations like 'Omnipresent' [*Māqôm*, literally: 'Place'] and 'Heaven', which we shall now discuss.

The use of the epithet 'Omnipresent' is very old. It occurs in a Baraita that tells of a Nazirite who came from the south to Simon the Just and told him the circumstances that had induced him to assume Naziriteship, and Simon the Just answered him 'My son, may those who do the Omnipresent's will like you multiply in Israel!' (*Tosefta Nezirut* iv, 7). There is no reason to doubt the authenticity of the expression, since it appears in all the parallel sources.[1] This epithet is employed even by the early Tannaim. Simon b. Sheṭaḥ sent word to Ḥoni ha-Meʿaggel [Ḥoni the Circle-Drawer]: 'But what can I do to you? You act like a spoilt child before the Omnipresent' (*M. Taʿanit* iii, 8). Akavya b. Mahalal'el said: 'Rather would I be called a fool all my life than become, for a moment, wicked before the Omnipresent' (*M. ʿEduyot* v, 6). The term is found in the ancient formula used by the Great Sanhedrin of Israel, when it judged the priests and investigated their genealogy. Of a priest in whom no disqualification was found, they said: 'Blessed be the Omnipresent that no disqualification was found in the seed of Aaron' (*M. Middot* v, 4). Concerning the early Hasidim it is reported: 'They used to wait an hour and then pray, so that they might direct their hearts to the Omnipresent' (*M. Berakhot* v, 1); 'R. Judah said: He vowed to become a Nazirite, for the Hasidim of old used to assume Naziriteship as a free-will offering, for the Omnipresent did not permit any inadvertent error to be made by them' (*Tosefta Nedarim* i, 5). It is related of R. Joḥanan b. Zakkai that all his days he taught 'that Job served the Omnipresent only out of fear'.[2] Also in the Tannaitic sources in our possession — in the Midrash, Tosefta and the Halakhic Midrashim — the use of the epithet 'Omnipresent' is extremely common.[3] Although 'the Holy One, blessed be He' occurs in many passages in our printed editions, comparison with MSS., or parallel sources, nearly always produces witnesses, or at least one testimony, to the reading 'the Omnipresent'.[4] On the other hand, the number of passages where 'the Omnipresent' occurs in our texts, but there is evidence that the reading should be 'the Holy One, blessed be He', is negligible. In the majority of places where 'the Omnipresent' occurs, the reading is supported by all the textual evidence. It should also be noted that in many passages we find the abbreviation הב״ה in the MSS., and in the first editions, and that this has been interpreted as *Ha-Qādôsh bārûkh Hû* ['the Holy One, blessed be He'], but it could also stand for *Ha-Māqôm bārûkh Hû* ['the Omnipresent, blessed be He'].[5] Furthermore, the possibility of contamination can only explain the change of 'Omnipresent' to 'the Holy One, blessed be He', not *vice versa*. The scribes and copyists were accustomed to uttering and writing the latter designation and not the former, for 'the Holy One, blessed be He' is the one commonly found in the Amoraic sources, and even ousted the epithet 'Omnipresent'. In the Babylonian Talmud the use of 'the Omnipresent' remained restricted primarily to aphorisms and benediction formulas — for example, 'because there is no elevation before the Omnipresent' (*T.B. Berakhot* 10b), 'May the Omnipresent make good your loss!' (*ibid.* 16b), 'the Omnipresent visit thee in peace!' (*T.B. Shabbat* 12b) — and to passages containing stories or traditions about Tannaim. In *Genesis Rabba*, where 'the Holy One, blessed be He' occurs hundreds of times, 'the Omnipresent' appears only in three instances, but in two of them the MSS. — the best among them — read 'the Holy One, blessed be He'.[6] 'There is thus left in this great Amoraic Midrash only one instance of the use of 'the Omnipresent', namely in the saying of R. Ammi, cited below, which discusses the meaning of the epithet. It seems that in the light of this discovery we cannot doubt that a change took place in the use of the designation 'the Omnipresent' in the period of the Amoraim. No surprise should be felt at the passages where 'the Holy One, blessed be He' occurs in Tannaitic sources, but at their paucity; they evidence the great fidelity with which the teaching of the Tannaim was transmitted through the generations.

The signification and source of the epithet 'the Omnipresent' were no longer known to the Amoraim at the end of the third century. This is shown by R. Ammi's question:[7] 'Why is the Holy One, blessed be He, given an epithet and called Omnipresent?' His answer 'Because He is the Place of His world' is derived from the teaching of R. Jose b. Ḥalafta: 'We do not know whether the Holy One, blessed be He, is the Place of His world, or His world is His place. Since it is written "Behold, there is a place by Me" (Exodus xxxiii 21), it is to be inferred that the Holy One, blessed be He, is the Place of His world, and His world is not His place.' We have already dealt with the connection between this dictum of R. Jose and his statement that the Shekhina did not descend to the earth and that Moses did not ascend to heaven, and with the intent of these observations to stress the gulf between God and the world and to remove any semblance of corporeality from the Divine manifestations and revelations. R. Jose's saying seeks to repudiate the view that 'His world is the place' of God, and the question is: Does R. Ammi's explanation of the epithet 'the Omnipresent', which is based on this dictum, also come to exclude another — original-signification of the designation? In its concrete sense the word *māqôm* [literally, 'Place', rendered: 'Omnipresent'] is related to the world, and there is no place outside it. *Māqôm*, in connection with the manifestation of the Lord in the Bible, always refers to a concrete place, be it on earth or in heaven, for example, 'For, behold, the Lord cometh forth out of His place to visit upon the inhabitants of the earth their iniquity' (Isaiah xxvi 21), or 'I will go and return to My place, till they acknowledge their guilt, and seek My face'

(Hosea v 15; in Targum Pseudo-Jonathan *ad loc.*: 'I shall remove My Shekhina, I shall return to My holy dwelling place, which is in heaven'). The fact that the epithet *ha-Māqôm* is not to be found in the Targumim, rendered in Aramaic as *'Atar* or *'Atrā*, does not fit the premise that this designation had an abstract, speculative connotation, but, on the contrary, can only be understood if we suppose that the word had a concrete, corporeal meaning, and that in consequence the translators refrained from using this title, which was undoubtedly known to them.

This view also finds corroboration in the parallelism between *māqôm* and *shāmayim* ('heaven'). In the Bible God utters His voice from heaven ('Out of heaven He made thee to hear His voice' [Deut. iv 36]); the heavens are His holy habitation ('Look forth from Thy holy habitation, from heaven' [Deut. xxvi 15]) and His dwelling place (I Kings viii 30). The phrase 'the God of heaven' occurs in Jonah i 9 — 'and I fear the Lord, the God of heaven' — and is frequently found in Ezra and Nehemiah. In his proclamation Cyrus declares '... the Lord, the God of heaven, hath given me' (Ezra i 2). Nehemiah prays to the God of heaven (Nehemiah i 4–5; ii 4, 20). In all the authentic and official Aramaic documents in Ezra we find 'the God of heaven'; so, too, in Daniel we read, 'God of heaven' alongside 'King of heaven', 'Lord of heaven', and once even 'heaven' by itself — 'after that thou shalt have known that the heavens do rule' (iv 23). We thus have here metonymy of place, which is common in Semitic languages, that is, the use of the name of a place in the sense of the people of the place, as, for example, 'And the whole earth was of one language' (Genesis xi 1) instead of 'the inhabitants of the earth'; 'and to the land wherein thou hast sojourned' (*ibid.* xxi 23) = 'to the inhabitants of the land'; 'and the cry of the city went up to heaven' (I Samuel v 12) = 'the cry of the inhabitants of the city'.[8] This usage is common in the Apocryphal literature, and especially in the *Books of the Maccabees*, as in the famous speech of Judas 'and with Heaven (τοῦ οὐρανοῦ) it is all one, to deliver with a great multitude, or a small company'.[9]

In the Tannaitic literature, we find the epithet 'Heaven' in the same tradition as that which is linked with the name of Simon the Just, in which we first found the designation 'Omnipresent'. In the story about the one who came from the south — his eyes were beautiful, his appearance was handsome, and his locks were curly — the Nazirite recounts his vow in the words 'I shall cut thee off (O my hair) in the name of Heaven', and with reference thereto Simon the Just said to him 'May those who do the Omnipresent's will like you multiply in Israel!'[10] There is no reason to question the authenticity of this tradition, for we find it confirmed at the beginning of the period of the Hasmoneans, in the Book of Daniel and in the words of Judas Maccabeus. Antigonos of Sokho, who received the tradition from Simon, likewise speaks of 'the fear of Heaven'. Whence is the expression derived? Some have thought to discern extraneous influence in the usage;[11] and, indeed, it is correct that the Iranian religions regarded heaven as the highest deity, who is omniscient. Mithra is considered the god of heaven — particularly of the night — and so, too, Ahura Mazda, in the theology of Zarathustra. Herodotus (I, 131) informs us that the Persians designate the whole vault of the heavens 'Zeus', that is to say, god.[12] 'The god of heaven', or 'heaven', was a comprehensible expression to the Persians, and is almost natural in Cyrus's utterances in all those official documents. The concept 'heaven' (οὐρανός), in the sense of cosmos, was current in Greece before Pythagoras coined the term κόσμος, and it was also used subsequently.[13] Various Syrian gods were presented to the Roman world in the guise of Jupiter, the god of heaven, and, *vice versa*, Antiochus introduced Zeus as the god of heaven. In the *Books of the Maccabees* (II, vi, 2) Zeus is called in the Syriac rendering 'Baal ['Lord'] of heaven', and some have conjectured that *shiqqûṣ shōmēm* ['the detestable thing that causeth appalment'] in Daniel (xii 11) is a dysphemistic epithet for *baʿal shāmayim* ['baal of heaven'].[14] These facts help to explain the widespread use by Jews, in the early days of the Second Temple, of the expression 'the God of heaven' in their contacts with the outer world, without any fear that those who use this designation might be considered sky-worshippers.[15] A self-identification like that of Jonah, 'I fear the Lord, the God of heaven', implied a declaration attesting his faith in the God who is the God of the universe and not a deity of a given country or temple. However, the metonym 'Heaven' stems naturally from the language of the Bible and its figures of speech.[16] The use of the word 'Heaven' in the sense of 'the God of heaven' expressed primarily the attitude of reverence and homage of man towards his God, and stressed the difference between God and human beings. This is evidenced by the phrases 'fear of Heaven' (*M. 'Avot* i, 3; iv, 12), 'kingdom of Heaven' (*Mekhilta de-R. Ishmael*, Ba-ḥōdesh, v, p. 219), 'the yoke of the kingdom of Heaven' (*M. Berakhot* ii, 2), 'the yoke of Heaven' (*Tosefta Soṭa* xiv, 4; *Sifra*, Bĕ-har, v, 109c), 'the things dedicated to Heaven' (Baraita, *T.B. Pesaḥim* 57a), and the antitheses: 'the honour of Heaven' as opposed to 'the honour of man' (*Tosefta Yoma* ii, 8), 'the laws of Heaven' in contrast to the 'laws of man' (*M. Bava Qamma* vi, 4), 'a thing devoted to Heaven' as against 'a thing devoted to the priests' (*M. Nedarim* ii 4), and 'the Father in Heaven' in contradistinction to 'a father of flesh and blood' (*M. Yoma* viii, 9, etc.) or 'his father upon earth' (*Sifre Deuteronomy* § 48, p. 113). In the course of time, however, the specific character of the epithet 'Heaven' was blurred and came to be used in various other phrases. Thus, instead of 'the name of the Lord' we find 'the name of Heaven'.[17] But the note of reverence and awe (*tremendum*) is preserved in its use in votive formulas, oaths, and dedications.[18] But it should be pointed out that in respect of dedicated things the use of the epithet 'Most High' [*Gāvôah*] tended to oust that of 'Heaven', especially when the reference was to the domain, property, and ownership of the Temple in antithesis to the domain, money, property, and ownership of a person. Actually 'Most High' is not an epithet of God but a synonym for *heqdēsh* ['dedicated'] things,[19] in which the tone of reverence instinct in the designation 'Heaven' is not felt.

Bousset understood the meaning of the epithet 'Heaven', but the deductions he drew therefrom are unfounded. In his view, the use of this designation led to the strangulation of the living faith in God. 'When it becomes customary to speak of God in the abstract, religion becomes anaemic. How different is the way the New Testament speaks of God — a way full of life and light — from that of Judaism!'[20] This last sentence not only reveals the tendentiousness of Bousset's remarks, but also his basic failure to understand the tension between the sense of reverence and exaltation that fills the soul of the believer and the feeling of God's nearness and of being drawn to Him in love. The multiplicity of names and titles is not an indication of the absence of a sense of the strong and living reality that marks God's relation to man, but actually expresses a variegated and multifaceted reality. The tension that we have mentioned found its resolution in the pair of epithets *Shāmayim* ['Heaven'] and *Māqôm* ['Omnipresent']. The primary meaning of *Māqôm* is not space, and is not to be construed as 'the most abstract of all terms'.[21] Just as 'Heaven' is a metonym for 'the God of heaven', so is also *Māqôm* [literally, 'Place'] used metonymically and refers to the God who reveals Himself in whatever place He wishes; this epithet thus expresses God's nearness. The youth who was suddenly seized by his evil inclination, says to it: 'Wicked one, I vow to cut thee off in the name of Heaven...', but when Simon the Just wishes to say that his action found favour with God, he declares: 'May those who do the Omnipresent's will like you multiply in Israel.'[22] This difference remains firmly entrenched in the Tannaitic sources. Israel does the will of the Omnipresent,[23] and the Omnipresent is pleased;[24] and if 'will' [*rāṣôn*] and 'Heaven' are associated, it is only through the medium of 'Father' [*'Av*], as, for example, 'the will of his Father in Heaven', '[the public sacrifices] appease [*mĕraṣṣîn*, from the same stem as *rāṣôn*] and atone for Israel before their Father in Heaven'.[25] Moreover, in all the accounts of the reciprocal relations between Israel and God[26] and in the dialogues between God and individuals or the people of Israel,[27] the dominant epithet is 'Omnipresent', even as 'Heaven' expresses God's farness and withdrawal from man.[28] The few exceptions prove the rule.[29] Of special interest are the passages in which 'Omnipresent' and 'Heaven' occur together and preserve the distinction alluded to above; we shall give two examples. One is from the *Sifra* (Nĕdāvā, iv, 8, 5d), ' "and it shall be accepted for him": this teaches us that the Omnipresent accepts him [i.e. forgives him]. But for what does "the Omnipresent" forgive him? Should you say for offences for which one is liable to execution by the court, or death at the hands of Heaven, or extinction [*kārēt*, premature death] by Heaven... then for what does the Omnipresent forgive him?...' The second is from the *Sifre* (Numbers § 95, p. 95): 'If one drew a ballot on which "elder" was inscribed, Moses said to him "the Omnipresent has already sanctified you." But if one drew a ballot on which "elder" was not inscribed, Moses said to him "It is from Heaven...." '

In the light of what has been stated above, it is clear already that the views that ascribe a foreign origin to the epithet 'the Omnipresent' are to be disregarded; but, as we shall see, there is no real basis for these conjectures, whether it is a Persian or Greek source that is suggested, and they have nothing to support them. The theory of Persian influence[30] is based on the testimony of Eudemos of Rhodes, the disciple of Aristotle, 'that the Magi and the entire Aryan tribe gave the Totality possessed of reason, which is not subject to analysis, the designation "Time" or "Place", from which were separated a good god and an evil daemon, and, according to others, darkness and light before them'.[31] This is the Zarvanite myth, according to which the two principles — light and darkness, Ormuzd and Ahriman — have their origin in the Infinite Time-Space, and is based on the worship of Infinite Time and Space in the Iranian liturgy. It is difficult to find any connection between these notions and the epithet 'Omnipresent' and its usages; and, needless to say, there is no significance for our subject in Iranian texts that postdate the Sassanian epoch, and in which is discernible the influence of Greek speculation on time and space.[32] At first blush, it would seem that the view postulating Greek influence is better founded. Philo in his book *On Dreams*[33] interprets Jacob's dream, and when he comes to the words 'And he alighted upon the place' (Genesis xxviii 11), he states that the word 'place' [Hebrew, *Māqôm*], τόπος, has three meanings; first, space in the physical sense; secondly, 'the word of God', θεῖος λόγος, which God has imbued with immaterial powers. He finds this signification in the verse 'and they saw the God of Israel; and there was under His feet the like of a paved work of sapphire stone' (Exodus xxiv 10), citing the verse in the form 'and they saw the place (τὸν τόπον) where the God of Israel stood', in accordance with the Septuagint. 'There is also', he declares, 'a third signification, in keeping with which God Himself is called a place, by reason of His containing things, and being contained by nothing whatever, and being a place for all to flee into, and because He is Himself the space which holds Him... I, mark you, am not a place, but in a place; and each thing likewise that exists; for that which is contained is different from that which contains it, and the Deity, being contained by nothing, is of necessity Itself Its own place — ἀναγκαίως ἐστὶν αὐτὸ τόπος ἑαυτοῦ. In proof, Philo quotes the verse 'And he went unto the place of which

God had told him... and Abraham lifted up his eyes, and saw the place afar off' (Genesis xxii 3–4). Philo uses the Greek expression ὁ ἐλθὼν in the sense of 'and he came to the place' and he asks: How is it possible that a man who comes to the place should see it afar off? The explanation is that 'place' has two meanings here. First it signifies the Logos, and secondly — the God above it. He who attains to the Logos sees that the Deity is far removed from the whole of creation, and that the possibility of perceiving Him is very remote. The resemblance between the words of Philo and the dictum of R. Jose bar Ḥalafta led to the fact that for a century almost[34] scholars keep reiterating the view that the designation *Māqôm* is only a translation of the Greek term τόπος. Latterly Yitzhak Baer has dealt with the subject.[35] The basis of the epithet *Māqôm* is, in his view, to be found in Plato's teaching, and denotes the place beyond the perception of the senses, including all the entities of the world on high. The physical place on earth has no independent existence, but is subsidiary to the transcendental 'place'. Although the distinction made by Philo between 'the place' as Logos and 'the Place' as the Deity above it is not expressly mentioned in the Midrash, he holds that the Midrashic tradition preferred 'not to speak too openly about the primary power that was created and appointed to stand at the side of God.' The epithet *Māqôm* came into being, according to Baer, when our ancient Sages first encountered Greek wisdom, and it is one of the earliest signs of the meeting of Israel's religious intuition with Western abstract thinking.[36] Baer's conclusions are far-reaching, but do not accord with the sources. The designation *Māqôm*, as it is used in the Rabbinic sources, has no abstract, transcendental character, but, on the contrary, expresses the nearness of man to God, and contains not the slightest allusion to *Māqôm* as the Divine Logos, which was created and appointed to stand at the side of God. On the other hand, Abraham Geiger[37] already noted that among the men of Alexandria *Māqôm* was not in constant use as an epithet. Philo only interprets Pentateuchal verses allegorically, and the word 'place' occurring in them symbolizes the Logos. It is probable that R. Jose b. Ḥalafta, who lived in the middle of the second century, used the formulation of Philo's concept 'that He is the Place of His world but not His world His place' and brought Scriptural evidence in support of it. From the wording of his statement 'We do not know whether....' we recognize its novelty, and only about a century later did the Amoraim R. Isaac and R. Ammi, on the basis of his statement, explain the epithet *Māqôm*, which by that time had gone out of use. So long as the epithet was employed, it denoted the immanence of God, His nearness to man and to the place where he was.[38] The Amoraic interpretation sought to give also to this epithet a transcendental signification, but even their words are devoid of Philo's speculative thought and certainly of his concept of the Logos.[39] Unlike Philo, the Sages (even the Amoraim) refrained from identifying the word *Māqôm* in the Scriptures — apart from the passage on which R. Jose b. Ḥalafta based himself — as a Divine epithet. Even the verse 'and he saw the place afar off' (Genesis xxii 4), which plays such an important role in Philo's exposition, is interpreted in Midrash *Genesis Rabba* (lvi, 2, p. 595) in a different manner: 'What did he see? He saw a cloud attached to them. (Thereupon) he said: It appears that this is the place where the Holy One, blessed be He, told me to offer up my son.' Only in a late Midrash,[40] in *Pirqe de-R. Eliezer* (xxxi), do we find a version that identifies *Ha-Māqôm* in the verse as the Shekhina: 'On the third day they came to Scopos, and having reached Scopos, he saw the glory of the Shekhina standing upon the mountain, as it is said: 'On the third day Abraham lifted up his eyes and saw the place afar off.' The change in the interpretation of the epithet *Māqôm* has the same background as its elimination from use.

As stated above, 'Heaven' is also used *vis-à-vis* the outer world, while *Māqôm*, which is not found either in the Apocryphal literature, in Aramaic, or in the New Testament, is an epithet that came into being in the world of the early Sages out of a desire to emphasize the immanence of God, namely that the world is His place. 'Heaven' and *Māqôm* complemented each other. To the outer world only 'Heaven' remained — possibly to avoid creating the impression of dualism. But when Gnostic sects, which professed the concept of dualism, made their appearance within the Jewish camp as well, they refrained from using *Māqôm*, which was also open to the suspicion of identifying God with the world, and chose instead the name 'the Holy One, blessed be He', which puts the designation beyond the question of immanence or transcendentalism. The use of 'Heaven', in the course of time, also began to decline, and remained in the Midrashim only in the phrase 'the name of Heaven'. The controversial sting in the disuse of the designation *Māqôm* is evident in R. Ammi's observation, 'the world is not His place'.

Echoes of the polemic against Gnostic views, in which the use of the epithets 'Heaven' and '*Māqôm*' played a role, are to be heard in our sources. 'R. Ishmael asked R. Akiba a question, when they were going on a journey. He said to him: "You who have studied for twenty-two years under Nahum of Gimzo, who interpreted every את *'et* [sign of the accusative] in the Torah, (tell me) how did he interpret את השמים ואת הארץ *'et ha-shāmayim wĕ-'et ha-'āreṣ* ['the heaven and the earth'] ?" He replied: "Had it said *shāmayim wā-'āreṣ*, I might have thought, *shāmayim wā-'āreṣ* are names of the Holy One, blessed be He;[41] but now that it says *'et ha-shāmayim wĕ-'et hā-'āreṣ, shāmayim* means the actual heavens, *'āreṣ* means the actual earth." '[42] Clearly, 'Heaven' stands for a Divine epithet, but 'Earth' is only a synonym for '*Māqôm*'; thus we have proof here that the two epithets provided the Gnostic sects with the opportunity of pointing to a Scriptural source in support of the doctrine of dualism. Possibly, for this reason the Sages discontinued using 'Heaven' except in phrases like 'the name of Heaven', 'desecration of the name of Heaven', 'sanctification of the name of Heaven'.

Evidence in support of this interpretation of the aforementioned debate is to be found in a statement of the Church Father Irenaeus, who was born *ca.* 130 in the neighbourhood of Izmir, and was a younger contemporary of R. Akiba. He writes in his work *Contra Haereses*[43] that the Gnostics assert that Moses alluded at the beginning of his book to 'the mother of all',[44] when he declared 'In the beginning God created the heaven and the earth.' In naming the four of them — אלהים *'Ĕlōhîm* ['God'], ראשית *Rē'shît* ['beginning'], *Shāmayim* ['heaven'], and *'Ereṣ* ['earth'] — he expresses their fourfold relationship'.[45] Arguments of this kind played a great part in restricting the use of the epithets 'Heaven' and *Māqôm*. Indeed, these epithets retained their place in the ancient traditions, only the designation *Māqôm*, which commonly occurs in them, acquired a totally new meaning, which gave it a transcendental connotation and approximated it to the epithet 'Heaven'. From the third century onward, the designation 'the Holy One, blessed be He' gained increasing currency.

In our examination of the epithet *Māqôm* we found[46] a patent difference between the Tannaitic and Amoraic sources. While in the former *Māqôm* is usual, and in most cases where 'the Holy One, blessed be He' occurs there are variant readings in the MSS. or parallel sources, in the latter the position is reversed: the primary epithet is 'the Holy One, blessed be He' and variant readings testify against the few deviations. This discovery shows clearly that the designation 'the Holy One, blessed be He' belongs to a later period. Nehemiah Brüll[47] was the first to note the existence of the title הקדש *Ha-Qōdesh* ['Holiness'] and posited that this was the ancient form in the light of the Aramaic קודשא בריך הוא *Qudshā bĕrîkh Hû* ['the Holy One (literally, 'Holiness'), blessed be He']. He was followed by other scholars and latterly by Saul Esh,[48] who collected the passages in which the reading 'the Holiness' remained and came to the conclusion that 'the Holiness' parallels *Māqôm* in Tannaitic literature and can only be understood on the basis of the same metonymy, namely that Zion, the holy place, is used as an epithet for Him who dwells in the Sanctuary.[49] But we still do not know why 'the Holiness' ousted *Māqôm*, seeing that there is no difference in their signification, nor do we understand why the noun-form 'the Holiness' was preferred to the adjective 'the Holy (One)' [הקדוש *Ha-Qādôsh*], which is common in the Bible. But the main objection to this view lies in the fact that it ignores the religious connotation of the epithet, and it is precisely this that makes it impossible to regard it as a metonym. Not only is *qādôsh* linked to the names of God in the Bible as an adjective, but the word is also found as a substantive. It parallels אלוה *'Elôah* ['God'] in Habakkuk iii 3, 'God cometh from Teman, and the Holy One from mount Paran', and in Isaiah lvii 15 it is stated, 'the High and Lofty One, that inhabiteth eternity, whose name is Holy'. God is the source of holiness; He sanctified the Tent of Meeting (Exodus xxix 44) and He dedicated the Temple to His name (I Kings ix 7), and whatever is designated 'holy' is holy to the Lord. It cannot, therefore, be supposed at all that the epithet 'the Holiness' is used instead of 'the Sanctuary'. The designation denotes precisely what the word connotes — the entire religious content that it enshrines. It comprises a synthesis of the meanings and nuances of 'Heaven' and *Māqôm*. The attributive 'Holy' expresses the exaltation and sublimity of transcendentalism and also nearness. God is 'the Holy One of Israel', and with His sanctity He sanctified His people, His land, His city, and His Temple. On the one hand the prophet says 'For great is the Holy One of Israel in the midst of thee' (Isaiah xii 6), and on the other 'Yea, thou hast lifted up thine eyes on high, even against the Holy One of Israel!' (*ibid.* xxxvii 23).

It appears that it was actually the Greek-speaking Jewish dispersion that first used the epithet 'the Holy One.' In the Apocryphal and pseudepigraphical works ὅ ἅγιος[50] often occurs, and it undoubtedly renders 'the Holy' [*ha-Qādôsh*] and not 'the Holiness' [*ha-Qōdesh*]. If we find in one or two places in the Hebrew Sirach the expression 'the Holiness',[51] we must bear in mind that even those who assign an early date to the Hebrew text of the Genizah MSS. do not go further back than the second half of the second century,[52] that is, the close of the Tannaitic period, when we find 'the Holiness' in use. On the other hand we often find in the Greek version of Sirach ὅ ἅγιος, while the Hebrew has in these passages אדני *'Ădōnay* ['Lord'], אל *'Ēl* ['God'], or עליון *'Ēlyôn* ['Most High'].[53] We may presume that Ben Sira's grandson employed ὅ ἅγιος, because its use was current in the Egyptian exile some three hundred years before the epithet 'the Holiness' came into use in Eretz-Israel.[54] Semantically, there is no difference between *ha-qōdesh* and *ha-qādôsh*, and in not a few passages they are interchanged. *Qōdesh* is used as an adjective in the saying of R. Akiba 'For all the Scriptures are holy [*qōdesh*], but the Song of Songs is most holy [*qōdesh qodāshîm*]'[55] (*M. Yadayim*, iii, 5) and the term כתבי הקדש *kitvê ha-qōdesh* does not mean 'the writings of God' or 'the writings of the Temple'[56] but 'holy writings' [Hagiographa]. The expression לשון הקדש *lĕshôn ha-qōdesh* and רוח הקדש *rûaḥ ha-qōdesh* can be interpreted respectively both as 'holy tongue' and as 'the tongue of God', as 'the holy spirit' and as 'the spirit of God'. Why then was the form *ha-qōdesh* chosen? The probable explanation is that *ha-qādôsh* was used at the close of the Tannaitic period also as an attributive in connection with men,[57] and consequently an abstract and less common form was chosen; but not content with that the Sages added to the epithet the benediction ברוך הוא *bārûkh Hû* ['blessed be He'], in order to obviate any misunderstanding. However, when this distinguishing addendum was made, the abbreviation of it הקב״ה *HQBH* was interpreted as הקדוש ברוך הוא *Ha-Qādôsh bārûkh Hû* ['the Holy One, blessed be He'] and only Aramaic retained the formula [with the abstract noun, 'Holiness'] קודשא בריך הוא *Qudshā bĕrîkh Hû*. The epithets *Qōdesh* and קב״ה *QBH* express — like the designation קדוש ישראל *Qĕdôsh Yiśrā'ēl* ['the Holy One of Israel'], which occurs frequently in the Book of Isaiah (in the first and second parts) — both the sense of exaltation, sublimity, and reverence towards God, and the concept inclining to the ethical and rational aspect.[58]

Among the appellations that have been ousted and changed is to be counted also עליון *'Elyôn* ['Most High']. The word occurs forty-four times in the Bible. In thirty-four of these it is an attributive of God (for example, 'God Most High') or serves as an epithet — 'the Most High' — in place of the Divine name. So, too, in Aramaic in the Book of Daniel: אלהא עליא *'Ĕlāhā 'Illā(y)'ā* ('God Most High' — iii 26, 32; v 18, 21) alongside *'Illā(y)'ā* ('the Most High' — iv 21, 29, 31). It has now also been established beyond doubt that the designation ὕψιστος, which occurs so frequently in the Greek Sirach, is only the translation of *'Elyôn* in the Hebrew original.[59] In the fragments discovered at Massada, *'Elyôn* appears even in passages where the Greek version renders κύριος. The widespread use of ὕψιστος in the pseudepigraphical literature, and in the Jewish diaspora, in papyri and in tombstone inscriptions, has already been noted by many scholars.[60] But no explanation has been given of the fact that *'Elyôn* does not occur either as an attributive of God, or as His by-name,[61] in the Midrash, or Tosefta,[62] or other Rabbinic sources. Incidentally, in the Dead Sea Scrolls,[63] too, the word is found only a few times, mostly in prayers, as in the Eighteen Benedictions or in rhetorical phrases borrowed from the Bible. The cause of this phenomenon lies, apparently, in the fact that *'elyôn* ['upper'] is very common in Rabbinic sources as an adjective applied to various objects and their parts in contrast to תחתון *taḥtôn* ['lower']. Whereas this usage is infrequent in the Bible, it is the rule in Rabbinic language and completely ousted the use of the word as a Divine epithet. In several sources *'elyôn* is replaced by מעלה *ma'ălā* ['on high'].[64] The occurrence of the Greek word ὕψιστος in the Midrash is rather doubtful.[65]

CHAPTER V

THE EPITHET *GĔVÛRĀ* AND THE MIGHT OF GOD

In our discussion thus far, one great fundamental was stressed — the omnipresence of God. With this Divine attribute is conjoined another, namely His 'omnipotence'. The idea of the power and ability of the Deity is deeply embedded in the foundation of every religion, beginning with the primitive cults. We know the Melanesian concept of *mana*, which expresses power, and the corresponding terms of other tribes including the names *'Ēl—'Ēlîm* [literally, 'power—powers'; rendered 'god—gods'].[1]

The power and might of God play an important role in many Rabbinic dicta, and it appears that the emphasis given to them had a practical significance in various periods. This significance is clearly evident in the homily of R. Abbahu in the name of R. Eleazar[2]: ' "Happy is he that hath the God of Jacob for his help..." What is written thereafter? — "who made heaven and earth..." But what is the connection between the one verse and the other? The answer is that if a human king has a patron, he rules over one province, but does not rule over any other; even if you take a cosmocrator, he rules over the land — does he also rule over the sea? But[3] the Holy One, blessed be He, rules over the sea and over the land, and He delivers on the sea from the water, and on land from fire; it was He who delivered Moses from the sword of Pharaoh, Jonah from the bowels of the fish, Hananiah, Mishael and Azariah from the fiery furnace, and Daniel from the pit of lions.' The images of the homily are borrowed from the *milieu* of the Roman Orient. The patron is the governor of a province, beneath whom are the *duces* and various kings. The cosmocrator is the Roman emperor, but above him is a Ruler of vaster and more embracing power and ability.

This omnipotence does not inspire dread, but, on the contrary, strengthens the feeling of nearness and man's trust in this proximity. The following story, which forms the sequel to the above exposition, expresses the thought with unique simplicity, showing how deeply the concept had penetrated the popular strata.

> R. Tanḥuma said: There is a story about a ship carrying Gentiles that was sailing from the Mediterranean [literally, 'the Great Sea'], and there was a Jewish youth [*tînôq*] on board. A great storm arose on the sea, and each passenger arose and began taking his god in his hand and calling (unto it), but to no avail. When they saw that (their prayers) did not avail, they said to the Jew: 'My son, arise, call unto thy God! For we have heard that He answers you when you cry unto him, and that He is mighty.' Forthwith, the youth arose and cried with all his heart, and the Holy One, blessed be He, accepted his prayer and the sea grew calm. When they reached land, they all disembarked to buy their requirements. Said they to the youth: 'Do you not want to sell anything?' Said he to them: 'What would you require from a poor stranger like me?' They replied: 'You are a poor stranger? It is they who are poor strangers! Some of them are here and their idols are in Babylon; others are here and their idols are in Rome; others again are here and their idols are with them, yet profit them nought. But you, wherever you go your God is with you', as it is written: 'as the Lord our God is whensoever we call upon him' (*T.P. Berakhot* ix, 1, p. 13b).

The narrative is noteworthy in that it puts these arguments in the mouth of non-Jews, and the representative of the absolute faith is a *tînôq* (literally, 'a child'; in Rabbinic literature and in the Middle Ages it denotes 'a young man'); and two truths are underlined here: first that God is mighty. The Deity must perforce have absolute power. The Gentiles on board ship mention Babylon and Rome. If their gods are active, they remain bound to a given place, whereas you, O Jew! — God is with you everywhere. The omnipotence of God — an omnipotence that brings into relief His greatness in the sense of sublimity, which in effect serves to underscore His farness — contains an assurance that this nearness is not a mere fantasy, lacking all value, and a figment of mythology. 'The Holy One, blessed be He, appears far away, yet is there none nearer than He', but 'the idol appears near, yet is actually far away' (*T.P. ibid.*, p. 13a). Here there is also an answer to the charges levelled by Gentiles against the Jewish faith, to wit, that they cannot accept a faith that is not represented by images and idols; such an abstract faith seemed to them a form of atheism, of denial of the Godhead. Hence came the reply: The Holy One, blessed be He, appears far away, yet none is nearer than He; and *vice versa* in the cases of the idol.

In order to elucidate the Rabbinic conception of God's all-embracing power and might, it is advisable to make a few preliminary observations about the problem inherent in this term and the manner of its solution in other religions. In the Greek religion, as it is reflected in the poems of Homer, the gods are clearly not omnipotent. There are bounds to the sphere of their dominion — not only to that of each invididual divinity, who is limited by another deity, but also to their collective power. The boundary is *death*. There is no god that can revive the dead. Even a goddess is unable to save her beloved from death, if the *Moira* — the decree of death — has decided it. We are familiar with the saying, found already in Herodotus, that the power of the gods cannot withstand fate and necessity. Fate is also intrinsically different from the gods. The latter help man, bestow good and light upon him. Fate is essentially negative. From it stems death, calamity, annihilation. The question, of course, arises: If calamities and misfortunes, and particularly death, are unalterable, what use or value is there in the help of the gods? Walter Otto answers[4] that, in truth, relative to a religion whose God transcends nature, the answer to such a question is necessarily negative. If the deity is outside Nature and is unable to obviate Fate, he is useless. But in the Greek religion, in which the divine is identical with the bliss of life, there is a gulf separating the divine from death. The gods differ from man only in knowing what the *Moira* determined. Now *Moira* is not a personality; it is the law that transcends everything and determines each one's fate,[5] that is, death and collapse. Death is outside the sphere of the dominion of the gods, which are a part of life. This conception implicitly raised the problem that was also formulated in the fifth century by Euripides, the author of the tragedies: If there exists something like Fate, the gods are superfluous; and if the gods are dominant, then Fate is of no consequence. In truth, the boundaries become blurred, and when the godhead, or a god, is spoken of in general terms, the reference is to Destiny or Fate — in effect to 'the course of events in the world', and the term 'god' is only 'an abstraction devoid of personality'.[6]

The religion of Israel included, *ab initio*, also death in the capacity and power of God. It thus excluded from its teaching any dualistic belief or magical concept, which necessarily posits the existence of forces that can affect the Deity and detract from His omnipotence. The God of the Bible contains all powers: He is the 'Almighty God' — He is the 'Lord of Hosts'. His might is expressed in His absolute dominion over nature, both in the normal course of its phenomena and in catastrophic occurrences. Of both categories the poet sang in Psalms civ 9, 'Thou didst set a bound which they should not pass, so that they might not again cover the earth' and also 'Who looketh on the earth, and it trembleth; He toucheth the mountains, and they smoke' (*ibid.* v. 32), and He is the God, who 'slayeth, and maketh alive; He bringeth down to the grave, and bringeth up' (I Samuel ii 6).

His might is manifested with special emphasis in the sphere of the history of the individual person and the nations. Of this the poet sang in Psalms cvi 2, 'Who can express the mighty acts of the Lord, or make all His praise to be heard?' He delivered Israel from Egypt 'that He might make His mighty power to be known'. His might also assures redemption, for God 'will punish the host of the high heaven on high, and the kings of the earth upon the earth' (Isaiah xxiv 21). This might is cited by the prophet of consolation as a reason, when he proceeds to describe the end of days and the universal goal of history. In Nebuchadnezzar's dream, according to Daniel's interpretation, God is the source of the kingdom, the power and the might, and He causes kingdoms to pass away and kings to rule (Daniel ii 31 ff). These two aspects of the Lord's might — His absolute dominion over nature and over history — are also emphasized in the teachings of the Sages, but their doctrine also has other aspects. They coined the epithet *Gĕvûrā* ['might'], which serves to stress the power and the omnipotence of God. In the Septuagint, *Ṣĕvā'ôt* ['Hosts'] is rendered παντοκράτωρ — the 'Omnipotent Ruler', and *YHWH Ṣeva'ôt* is Κύριος παντοκράτωρ. The pseudepigraphical literature also uses this expression, but does not call God *Gĕvûrā* ['Might'].[7]

In order to understand the specific character of this epithet, with all the ideas and intentions implicit in its use, we must carefully examine the passages in which it occurs. We find this designation as part of the phrase *mi-pî ha-Gĕvûrā* ['from the mouth of the Almighty'], but also apart from it already in the time of R. Eliezer and R. Joshua: ' "With the edge of the sword" ... R. Eliezer said ...from this we learn that this battle was fought specifically at the command of the Almighty [*'al pî ha-Gĕvûrā'*]' (*Mekhilta de-R. Ishmael*, Massekhta da-'Amalek, Bĕ-shallaḥ, i, p. 181); 'R. Joshua said: Before they turned (to look towards the wilderness) the Almighty [*Ha-Gĕvûrā*] had revealed Himself' (*ibid.*, Massekhta de-Wa-yissa', ii, pp. 162–163). ' "And Moses led": R. Joshua said: On this journey (the Israelites) went only at the bidding of Moses, but on all the other journeys they went at the injunction of the Almighty [*'al pî ha-Gĕvûrā*]... R. Eliezer said: They journeyed at the injunction of the Almighty...' (*ibid.*, Wa-yissa', i, p. 152; in the *Mekhilta de-R. Simeon b. Yoḥai*, p. 101: 'R. Eleazar of Modi'im'). ' "And the people murmured against Moses" ... R. Eleazar of Modi'im said: The Israelites were accustomed to complain against Moses, and not against Moses only did they speak, but (even) against the Almighty [*Ha-Gĕvûrā*]' (*Mekhilta de-R. Ishmael, op. cit.*, p. 155; *Mekhilta de-R. Simeon b. Yoḥai*, p. 103). ' "I will give thee counsel, and God be with thee" — go and consult the Almighty [*Gĕvûrā*]' (*Mekhilta de-R. Ishmael*, Massekhta da-'Amalek, Jethro, ii, p. 197; *Mekhilta de-R. Simeon b. Yoḥai*, p. 133). The Tannaim, beginning with R. Ishmael, and likewise the Amoraim, use the epithet *Gĕvûrā* particularly in connection with the giving of the Torah and the revelation of God. On the verse 'Because he hath despised the word of the Lord, and hath broken His commandment' (Numbers xv 31) it is stated: 'Rabbi Ishmael said: Scripture speaks here of idolatry, for it is said, "Because he hath despised the word of the Lord" — he was contemptuous of the First Commandment uttered to Moses by the mouth of the *Gĕvûrā* "I am the Lord thy God... Thou shalt have no other gods before Me"' (*Sifre Numbers*, § 112, p. 121); and in the name of the same R. Ishmael it is reported: ' "I am" and "Thou shalt not have" we heard from the mouth of the *Gĕvûrā*' (*T.B. Horayot* 8a). In a Baraita it is further stated: 'The Rabbis have taught: What was the procedure of instruction in the Oral Law? Moses learnt from the mouth of the *Gĕvûrā*, then Aaron entered and Moses taught him his lesson...' (*T.B. ʿEruvin* 54b). In another Baraita that speaks of the giving of the Torah, R. Jose bar Judah says: '... And what did Moses answer the *Gĕvûrā*?'[8] ' "And all the people perceived the thunderings" ... R. Akiba said: They saw and heard that which was visible; they saw a word of fire issue from the mouth of the *Gĕvûrā* and become hewn out upon the Tables' (*Mekhilta de-R. Ishmael*, Massekhta de-Ba-ḥodesh, ix, p. 235). When R. Ishmael b. R. Jose was asked whether he was worthy of learning Torah from Rabbi, he replied: 'Was Moses then worthy to learn Torah from the mouth of the *Gĕvûrā*?' (*T.B. Yevamot* 105b). In the name of the Amora R. Joḥanan it is reported: 'What is the meaning of the Scripture, "The Lord giveth the word: They that publish tidings are a great host"? — Each word that issued from the mouth of the *Gĕvûrā* was divided into seventy tongues' (*T.B. Shabbat* 88b). 'No break is made in (the public reading of) the curses... Said Abbaye: This was taught only with regard to the curses in Leviticus, but in (the reading of) the curses in Deuteronomy a break may be made. What is the reason? The former are formulated in the plural, and Moses pronounced them in the name of the *Gĕvûrā*, but the latter are formulated in the singular and Moses pronounced them in his own name.'[9] 'The Holy One, blessed be He, said to him (Moses): By thy life, all the prophets prophesy each inspired by [literally, 'from the mouth of'] the other. Thus the spirit of Elijah rested upon Elisha, the spirit of Moses rested upon the seventy elders... but thou dost prophesy by the inspiration of the *Gĕvûrā*. "The spirit of the Lord God is upon me, because the Lord hath anointed me to bring tidings to the humble" ' (*Pesiqta de-Rav Kahana*, Naḥamu, Buber 125b–126a; ed. Mandelbaum, p. 270).

It seems that the expression occurs in this context also in the Gospels, only the translators and commentators have not understood its meaning. In Mark i, 22 it is stated: ὡς ἐξουσίαν ἔχων καὶ οὐχ ὡς οἱ γραμματεῖς. The accepted translations — 'as one who had authority' [English versions], Macht begabt, gewaltsam [German], Delitsch 'as a man of dominion' [Hebrew]—are incorrect.[10] The true interpretation is: not like the scribes who report the statements of others, but 'as one who speaks from the mouth of the *Gĕvûrā*'.[11] Thus we find that the epithet *Gĕvûrā* was used in connection with revelation already at the end of the first century. What is the significance of this use, and is it merely fortuitous that the epithet *Gĕvûrā* was widely used in the second and third centuries, particularly in this context? In order to answer this question, we should consider the conception of *Gĕvûrā* that obtained in the environment of the Sages. Without doubt, this epithet corresponds to the term δύναμις that occurs also in Matthew xxvi 64. Jesus declares: 'Hereafter shall ye see the son of man sitting on the right hand of the *Gĕvûrā* (ἐκ δεξιῶν τῆς δυνάμεως).[12]

The concept 'dynamis' played an important role in the moulding of religious views in the ancient world, beginning with the third century B.C.E. It derives from the sciences. Aristotle distinguished between 'dynamis', that is potential power, and 'energia', actual power. The doctrine of sympathy, which originated in the discovery of natural forces in objects, forces that could be used in medicine and in magic, was widely current in the first century B.C.E. It was adopted by astrologers, who made use of it in order to explain the influence of the heavenly bodies, and was given a central place in Stoic physics.[13] The force was depicted as a form of breathing. πνεῦμα, πνοή, and the concept of power, with all its obscurities, developed into the miraculous and the mysterious. About two hundred B.C.E. an occult literature began to burgeon in Egypt in the form of physical explanations, whose object was to reveal the miraculous powers of various objects in the organic and inorganic world, their hidden characteristics and the sympathies and antipathies attaching to them. This pseudoscience had a great influence on the conception of the term 'power' in religious literature, and also affected religious life at the end of the age of antiquity. At the close of the Hellenistic epoch the gods no longer appeared personally to perform miraculous deeds; the theophany was a manifestation of δυνάμεις or ἐνέργειαι. The deities were no longer revealed in natural phenomena but in their underlying powers.[14] At the close of the pagan era, those who had not abandoned their gods were reconciled to the monotheistic concept with the help of the doctrine of power. Thus, it was possible to describe the various gods as powers of the sungod. In *Poimandres*, the principal hermetic work, we find a description like this: When the soul ascends to the planetarian spheres and is stripped of its corporeal powers, it approaches the eighth sphere equipped with its own power, and it joins those who exist there in a song of praise to the Father. It hears the powers above the eighth sphere praising God. They ascend to the Father and deliver themselves to Him in order to be changed into powers, and when they become powers they are in God. That is the happy end of those who possess the highest illumination — the gnosis.

The worship of images received a new meaning (see above, p. 23). Even the philosopher Plotinus (the third century C.E.) was of the opinion that although the deities do not actually dwell in the idols, yet their powers reside in them. With the help of complicated rituals the worshippers sought to bring down the divine power to the image. In this notion is also to be found the explanation of the vast dissemination of acts of sorcery and magic arts, which is evidenced by the magical amulets, inscriptions, and papyri. Underlying them all was the concept of power.

Even the worship of the kings, as it was practised and accepted in Egypt with respect to the Ptolemies and in the Roman empire from the time that Octavian received the title *Divus*, was primarily a cult of force. The power found expression in the assurance of order and a secure régime for the social structure, particularly after periods of wars and disturbances, whether it was after the death of Alexander or the protracted civil wars of the first century B.C.E.[15] It is necessary to remember all these facts and to consider all the religious ideas bound up with the concept of power in the ancient world in the environment of the Talmudic and Midrashic Sages, in order to understand why this subject exercised them so much and why they devoted so much attention to it. Stories, conversations, and dicta, which at first appear to be devoid of value and meaning, assume significance and the reality underlying them becomes apparent, when they are read in the light of these facts.

The might of the Lord is underscored in contrast to that of a human king:

> 'I will sing unto the Lord, for He is highly exalted.' To what can this be compared? To a human king who entered a country,

and all praised him, saying that he was mighty, whereas he was weak; that he was rich, whereas he was poor; that he was wise, whereas he was foolish; that he was compassionate, whereas he was ruthless; that he was just and faithful, whereas he had none of these virtues, only everyone flattered him, but He who spoke and the world came into being is not so. However great the praise given Him, He transcends His praises. 'I will sing unto the Lord' that He is mighty, as it is said 'The great, the mighty, and the terrible God' (Deuteronomy x 17); and it says 'The Lord strong and mighty, the Lord mighty in battle' (Psalms xxxiv 8); and it says 'The Lord will go forth as a mighty man, He will stir up His fury like a man of war; He will cry, yea, He will shout aloud, He will prove Himself mighty against His enemies' (Isaiah xlii 13); and it says 'There is none like unto Thee, O Lord; Thou art great, and Thy name is great in might' (Jeremiah x 6). 'I will sing unto the Lord' that He is rich, as it is said 'Behold, unto the Lord thy God belongeth the heaven' etc. (Deuteronomy x 14); and it says 'The earth is the Lord's and the fulness thereof' etc. (Psalms xxiv 1); and it says 'The sea is His, for He made it' (*ibid.* xcv 5); and it says 'Mine is the silver, and Mine the gold' etc. (Haggai ii 8); and it says 'Behold, all souls are Mine; as the soul of the father, so also the soul of the son is Mine; the soul that sinneth, it shall die' (Ezekiel xviii 4)....' (*Mekhilta de-R. Ishmael*, Massekhta de-Shira, i, p. 119; see *Mekhilta de-R. Simeon b. Yoḥai*, p. 73).

In accordance with the practice of the Sages, their ideas are conveyed in a homiletical manner, and the concatenation of verses found here shows that we have before us a Tannaitic exposition, dating at least from the second century. Here is a new hymn on the Lord's might, which stands in absolute contrast to that of a human king, for the latter requires the eulogy. It signifies the recognition of his power, and those who laud him flatter him, his might not being according to their panegyrics. But the might of the Holy One, blessed be He, who is the One who spoke and the world came into being, is beyond all praise, it is absolute, and is not dependent on eulogy. This might connotes dominion over the whole world — over life and death. This is the meaning of the riches, wisdom, compassion, justice and splendour.

The second benediction of the *ʿAmida prayer* [the Eighteen Benedictions; literally 'Standing prayer'], which is called in the Mishna (*Rosh Ha-Shana* iv 5) *Gĕvûrôt* ['Mighty Deeds'], epitomizes Rabbinic teaching on *Gĕvûrā*. When the Sages saw the need to emphasize the belief in the resurrection of the dead (below, chapter xv), they gave it a central position in the blessing of *Gĕvûrôt* and made it begin and end with 'the resurrection of the dead', for death, too, is one of *the mighty deeds of the Lord*, but it is not the boundary — He rules over it, reviving the dead. With reference to the Mishna 'We make mention of the mighty deeds of rain in [the benediction of] The Resurrection of the Dead' (*M. Berakhot* v, 2), the Amoraim asked why rain is mentioned in this benediction, and they explained: 'Because it is equivalent to the resurrection of the dead' and 'just as the resurrection of the dead means life to the world, so rainfall means life to the world' (*T.B. Berakhot* 33a; *T.P. ibid.* v, 2, p. 9a). God is 'the Author of mighty deeds', and there is no power apart from His. 'Blessed be He with whose strength and might the world is filled' (*M. Berakhot* iv, 2). The anthropomorphic metaphors in the Bible that speak of God as a warrior, girded with a sword and wearing a coat of mail and helmet, provided an excuse for the deification of the warrior king, and, on the other hand, also paved the way for a dualistic interpretation, which saw in God the man of war, the intermediate deity, the demiurge. Answers to arguments of this kind are to be found in sources of the second century:

> 'The Lord is a man of war, the Lord is His name' — He wages war with His name, and needs none of these attributes... for He appeared at the sea like a Warrior who did battle, as it is said, 'The Lord is a man of war'; He appeared at Sinai as an Old Man full of compassion... so as not to give an excuse to the Gentile nations to say that *there are two divine powers*; hence (it is written) 'The Lord is a man of war, the Lord is His name' — it is He who was in Egypt, it is He who was at the sea... (above, p. 38).

To this polemic against the believers in two divine powers the redactor of the *Mekhilta* contributes a kind of hymn on the Lord's might, stressing the contrast between it and that of a national hero:

> There is sometimes a hero in a country, and he is equipped with

> every weapon, but he has no strength and no power, no strategy and no ability for warfare; but the Holy One, blessed be He, is not so: He has strength and power and strategy and ability to make war... There is sometimes a hero in a country who has strength; but his strength at the age of forty is not like that which he has at fifty, nor is his strength at fifty like that at the age of sixty, nor is his strength at sixty like that of seventy, for the older he gets the more his strength diminishes; not so, however, is He who spoke and the world came into being, but 'For I the Lord change not'... There is sometimes a hero in a country, but once the arrow leaves his hand, he can no longer recall it; but the Holy One, blessed be He, is not so: for when Israel do not do His will, an edict, as it were, issues from Him... as soon, however, as they repent, He withdraws it... When a human king goes to war and provinces approach him and petition him for their needs, they are told: He is troubled, he is going to war; when he is victorious in battle and returns, then come with your petitions to him. But the Holy One, blessed be He, is not so: 'the Lord is a man of war', for He fights against Egypt; 'the Lord is his name', for He hears the cry of all mankind...[16]

Clearly, we have here a polemic directed against the conception of the hero emperor as a manifestation of power, the difference between this earthly phenomenon and the Divine revelation being brought into relief. The ending is actually based on historical realities: when a rebellion broke out in one of the provinces of the empire, or when the emperor went forth to war against the Persians and he passed through the various provinces, the representatives of the provinces would come to present their petitions. As a rule the answer was: When the emperor returns victorious from his wars, you can present to him your petitions.

The might and power of God are incomparable and illimitable. The contrast is emphasized in order to negate the worship of kings and of idols, both of which, as we have seen, are linked to a certain conception of power. In the light of these circumstances, the expositions of the Tannaim become comprehensible; for example, ' "Who is like unto thee, O Lord, among the gods?" — who is like unto Thee among those who call themselves divinities? Pharaoh called himself a god... Sennacherib called himself a god... Nebuchadnezzar called himself a god... the prince of Tyre called himself a god....' (*Mekhilta de-R. Ishmael*, Massekhta de-Wa-yĕhî, viii, pp. 142–143; *Mekhiltā de-R. Simeon b. Yoḥai*, p. 91). To this list of kings could be added 'the emperors of Rome who called themselves gods'. Every listener understood that this was the intention. The Sages were able to continue the polemic against the belief in the power of the idols — 'those which others called gods' — when they interpreted and carried forward the Biblical debate, like that in the last chapters of Isaiah. This disputation concerning the omnipotence of Israel's God assumed particular practical significance when the Temple was destroyed and Israel was deprived of its independence. We have testimony for it from both sides. That the teachers of the people whose independence had been taken away, whose land had been conquered, and whose Sanctuary laid in ruins should stand and proclaim that their God was all-powerful and 'the Lord of all creation' (*Mekhilta de-R. Ishmael*, Massekhta de-Wa-yissaʿ, vi, p. 175) could arouse only astonishment and derision among Gentiles. These are reflected in the words of Nebuchadnezzar, when he addressed Hananiah, Mishael, and Azariah: 'If your God has power and strength [dynamis], He will deliver you from my hand.'[17] The most drastic expression given to them is found in the famous Haggadah concerning Titus, who, upon entering the Temple, 'took a sword and cut down the curtain (of the Holy of Holies)... he dragged a harlot into the Holy of Holies and began to blaspheme, and revile, and insult, and spit at God on high, saying: "Is He the One of whom ye said that He slew Sisera and Sennacherib? Behold, I am in His house and in His domain; if He has power, let Him go forth and stand against me... he made a kind of enclosure and dismantled the lamps therein, and he collected the Temple vessels, and filled three ships with men, women, and children, that he might go and glorify himself overseas (i.e. in the triumphal procession in Rome)... he embarked, (thereupon) a billow arose (to drown him) in the sea; so he stood on (the) ship's deck and began to blaspheme, and revile, and insult, and spit at, (God on high). He said: "When I was in His house and in His domain, He had no strength to come and stand against me, yet now He confronts me here! Apparently (the) power of the God of the Jews resides in water: the generation of the Flood — it was only by water that He punished them; even as He did to Pharaoh so He seeks to do to me (that is to say, their God is only the God of the water and the sea). The Omnipresent then intimated to the sea and it ceased raging....' Thereafter it is related how a gnat caused the death of Titus (*'Avot de-R. Nathan*, Recension II, vii; it is also found in other sources). Here the doctrine of God's absolute power is expounded in contrast to the accepted polytheistic conception.

Titus's argument was not invented by the Sages. It was adduced by many. We shall cite it — on account of its clear formulation — from the work of one of the church writers, Minucius Felix, who wrote at the beginning of the third century. A representative of the pagans, called Caecilius, argues: 'Who is the One God who is unknown to a free people, to a kingdom, or at least to a faith known in Rome? Only the hapless Jewish people also served One God, but they did so in public, in temples with altars, sacrifices and rituals. But the One is so lacking in strength and power (here we have the explicit argument: a God, but lacking power and might) that He as well as His people are captive in the hands of the Romans.'[18]

This is the argument that the Sages also put into the mouth of Titus, at the time when he destroyed the Temple,[19] and without doubt they heard this contention in public. It seems that the other legends, parables, and dialogues concerning power likewise had an actual significance.

Special interest attaches to the 'marginal' note added to the main narrative by the Tanna Abba Ḥanan, the disciple of R. Eliezer b. Hyrcanus: 'Abba Ḥanan said: "O Lord God of hosts, who is mighty as Thou art, O Lord?" (Psalms lxxxix 9 [8]) — Thou art mighty in that Thou dost hear the blasphemy and reviling and insults of that wicked man and dost remain silent.'[20] Obviously, Abba Ḥanan did not make his observation with reference to the narrative in the form in which we have quoted it, for in it Titus is punished; thus the Almighty was not silent. Possibly Abba Ḥanan is also the author of the following anonymous dictum in the *Mekhilta*:[21] ' "Who is like unto Thee among the *'ēlîm* [literally, 'gods'], O Lord?" — who is like unto Thee among the dumb [*'illĕmîm*], who, like Thee, hears the humiliation of His sons and remains silent?...' At any rate, the two dicta transcend the entire debate about power, since according to them God's might exists even when it is not demonstrated and visible. It was actually this view, as we shall see, that gained the acceptance of the Amoraim.[22]

But before we consider their teachings, let us revert to the epithet *Gěvûrā*. We have found sources in which this designation appears specifically in connection with the revelation of God. The influence of this fact is discernible even in homilies in which the epithet *Gěvûrā* is not expressly mentioned. The verse 'O Lord, my strength [ᶜuzzî]' and my stronghold [*māᶜuzzî*], and my refuge, in the day of affliction'[23] is expounded in the *Mekhilta* thus: ' "The Lord is my strength [ᶜozzî] and song" — "my strength" means nothing else but Torah... Another explanation is, "my strength" is but another expression for sovereignty... "my strength" means only my power. Now all the nations of the world utter the praise of the Holy One, blessed be He, but mine is pleasanter and more beautiful before Him than theirs' (*Mekhilta de-R. Ishmael*, Massekhta de-Shira, iii, p. 126, and the parallels referred to there). ' "Thou hast guided them in Thy strength" — on account of the Torah, which they are destined to accept, "Thy strength" being but another designation for Torah...' (*ibid.*, ix, p. 146). 'But the Holy One, blessed be He, is giving His people and His loved ones the Torah, as it is said: "The Lord will give strength unto His people" ' (*ibid.*, Massekhta da-ᶜAmalek, Jethro, i p. 188). In parallelism with the use of *Gěvûrā* as a term for Divine revelation, the words 'strength' [*ᶜoz*] and 'stronghold' [*māᶜoz*] are expounded in the above-mentioned Tannaitic homilies in the sense of Torah, namely the revelation of God. Similar expositions are to be found also in the Amoraic homilies, for example: 'The Holy One, blessed be He, will have put on seven robes from the time that the world was created until He will punish wicked Edom... When He gave the Torah, He clothed Himself with strength, as it is said "The Lord hath girded Himself with strength" (Psalms xciii 1)...'[24]; ' "A wise man scaleth the city of the mighty": "the city of the mighty" — this means the heavens, which are the city of the angels. "A wise man scaleth" — this is Moses, who ascended to Heaven. "And bringeth down the stronghold wherein it trusteth" — this refers to the Torah. And how do we know that the ministering angels are called "mighty"? For it is said "Ye mighty in strength, that fulfil His word" (Psalms ciii 20). And how do we know that Moses ascended on high [to Heaven]? For it is said... And whence do we know that the Torah is called strength, for it is said "The Lord will give strength unto His people" (Psalms xxix 11)...' (*Midrash Tehillim* xxi 22).

The view that the Torah and its revelation are to be regarded as an expression of God's might and power finds parallels in *The Wisdom of Solomon* and in the writings of Philo. The author of *The Wisdom of Solomon* says of wisdom that it is 'the breath of the might of God' (τῆς τοῦ θεοῦ δυνάμεως). Thus God's might is expressed in wisdom, and wisdom is the product of this might. Philo, too, declares: 'Wisdom is the highest and chiefest of His powers'.[25] The powers are not visible in their essence, just as God, to whom they belong, cannot be thus perceived, but their work leaves an impress and effect, even as a wax seal leaves its impress without being in the least altered. Hence they are also called 'ideas'. We have here a complete identification of the powers with the ideas, with a play upon words: ἰδέας ἐπειδὴ ἕκαστα τῶν οὐτῶν εἰδοποιοῦσι (= give shape).[26] The whole universe exists by means of invisible powers, which the Creator has made to encompass existence from the ends of the earth to the ends of the heavens. These powers are unbreakable chains. What is the might of the Lord? His goodness and His lovingkindness.[27] Elsewhere he states: 'For He and His beneficent powers ever make it their business to transmute the faultiness of the worse wherever it exists and convert it to the better.'[28]

Both in *The Wisdom of Solomon* and in Philo's writings, the powers became something spiritual and immaterial, in contrast to the view prevailing in the non-Jewish Hellenistic world, which was unable — as one scholar put it — to think of power except in material terms. 'All power is material'[29]; hence even when they spoke of spirit, they depicted it as a celestial substance, as material of another kind. In *The Wisdom of Solomon* and in Philo these powers are presented as ideas, spiritual entities. In the light of this, we can also understand what the Sages did. The Divine power finds expression in Revelation, in the Revelation of the Torah. Thereby, the question of power and might is removed from the notions prevalent in the world with regard to power, and in this way we can understand the Rabbinic interpretations of the words עז *'ōz* ['strength'] and מעוז *mā'ōz* ['stronghold'], as well as the use of the term *Gĕvûrā* in the expression *mi-pî ha-Gĕvûrā* ['from the mouth of the Omnipotent'], when the revelation of the Lord is spoken of. These statements were not made in a vacuum. They form part of a complete system of thought, as reflected in the cited dicta.

But there is a difference between Philo's view and that of the Sages; for the latter could not be content with the theoretical interpretation only, which in the course of polemic and discussion led to exaggeration and the spiritualization of the concept of power — 'strength means Torah' — and to the paradoxical statement of Abba Ḥanan that God's silence is His might: 'Who is like unto Thee among the dumb?' God, who governs His world, also governs His people and congregation, protecting and preserving it. The question 'Is it fitting to give the name "Mighty" to One who sees the destruction of His House and remains silent... whose children are in chains — where is His might?'[30] never left them or ceased to trouble them. Hence they preached faith in the revelation of the Lord's strength in time to come, after the manner of the anonymous expositor of the verse 'Verily Thou art a God that hidest Thyself, O God of Israel, the Saviour' (Isaiah xlv 15): 'Isaiah said to the Holy One, blessed be He: Sovereign of the universe, verily [*'ākhēn*] Thou art a God that hidest Thyself. What is the meaning of *'ākhēn*? How canst Thou be a God that hidest thyself? Verily Thou hast power (δυνάμις in the original) and yet Thou dost hide thyself! He answered him: The God of Israel is a Saviour; I shall return and avenge' (*Canticles Rabba* iv, 8). The homilist asks here the same concrete question that had already been asked by Abba Ḥanan: How canst Thou stand and hear the blasphemy of that wicked one and remain silent? Only the preacher was not content with the Tanna's answer, to wit, that God's silence was His strength. The power and might of God exist absolutely, only their manifestation is a promise.

An eschatological orientation was given to the concept of power also by Paul, but he stresses the value of 'power' in contradistinction to the 'word'.[31] Its manifestation likewise became absolute and unconditional with the advent of 'the son of God with power according to the spirit of holiness...'; he is 'Christ the power of God, and the wisdom of God'.[32] In complete antithesis to this view, the Sages make the manifestation of the Divine power dependent on the conduct of the people and their attitude to the historic revelation of His strength, namely the Torah. We have already heard in one of the homilies that when the people repent, the Lord reveals His power. We have noted the analogy of the king, who cannot recall the arrow that has been shot, whereas God, even when He has decided to punish, withdraws His arrows, so to speak, if the people return in penitence. In one homily on the verse 'Of the Rock that begot thee thou wast unmindful, and didst forget God that bore thee' (Deuteronomy xxxii 18), the Rabbis do not argue 'Verily Thou art a God that hidest Thyself; Thou hast power and yet Thou dost hide Thyself', but they turn the argument against the people, who compel God, so to speak, to hide Himself and to withhold from them the manifestation of His might: ' "Of the Rock that begot thee thou wast unmindful" — whenever I wish to bestow good upon you, you weaken Heaven's power. You stood by the sea and said "This is my God, and I will glorify Him"; thereupon I wished to bestow good upon you, but you retracted, saying "Let us make a captain, and let us return into Egypt." You stood before Mount Sinai and said "All that the Lord hath spoken will we do, and obey"; I then wished to bestow good upon you, but you retracted and said of the calf "This is thy god, O Israel". Alas! whenever I wish to bestow good upon you, you weaken the power of Heaven' (*Sifre*, Ha'azinu, § 319, p. 365). This dictum is directed against oversimplified faith. The non-manifestation of God's power is not indicative of the absence of that power, and one must not come to God with the complaint 'where is Thy power?', but there is a nexus between the revelation of this power and the actions of human beings. Men's actions are able, as it were, to weaken His power and to prevent its being exercised; in the words of the Amora R. Judah b. R. Simon: 'So long as the righteous do the will of the Omnipresent they increase the strength of *Gĕvûrā*... but if not, then, so to speak, "they are gone without strength before the pursuer" (Lamentations i 6).'[33] We have already seen that evil deeds and transgressions can banish the Shekhina, as it were, from the world. In the view of the Sages, the ethical and religious conduct of man determines both the manifestation of God's presence in the world and the revelation of His power and might.

CHAPTER VI

MAGIC AND MIRACLE

The Rabbinic doctrine concerning God's all-embracing power has a bearing on other concepts. It excludes the possibility of the existence of magic power capable of influencing the laws of nature and the decrees of God. We have referred to the problem that confronted the Greeks in regard to the question of fate and the deity: if fate has independent and separate power, over which the gods have no control, what then is the nature of the divinities? If, on the contrary, the gods determine fate, what is the significance of fate as an independent force? The same reasoning applies to magic — it is impossible to reconcile it with the existence of an All-Powerful God. The Tanna R. Nathan, who flourished in the second half of the second century, said: 'If all the magicians of the world were to come together and seek to change morning to evening, they could not do so' (*Tanḥuma*, ed. Buber, Qoraḥ, § 6). Opposition to sorcerers is in keeping with the spirit of the Torah, only in Rabbinic literature it is much more detailed and is discussed with emphasis, indicating the actuality of the issue. Indeed R. Simeon b. Eleazar's appraisal of the matter in the Mishna is: 'fornication and sorceries have made an end of everything' (*M. Soṭa* ix, 13); and in the Tosefta (*Soṭa* xiv, 3): 'When the number of "whisperers" in court increased, wrath came upon the world and the Shekhina departed from Israel.' The Amoraim of the first generation, in the third century, held similar views: 'R. Joḥanan said: Why are they called *kashshāfīm* ['sorcerers']? Because they contradict the heavenly household [*KashshaFiM* is regarded as an abbreviation of *Kaḥash, Familia (shel) Maʿala*]' (*T.B. Sanhedrin* 67b). On the verse 'There is none else beside Him' (Deuteronomy iv 35) R. Ḥanina commented: 'Even in respect of sorceries' (*T.B. loc. cit.*). Rashi gives the explanation with precision: 'They are impotent before His decree, for there is no power besides Him.'

But this was not the accepted view among the broad masses of the people, and hence the prolonged debates and discussions on these questions. Magical practices and sorcery were widespread in the ancient world in the areas where the Sages lived, that is, throughout the Orient. The power manifested in sorcery and also the means employed in connection with it are called δύναμις.[1] The name of the God of Israel, as the God of power and might, is extensively used in magical papyri and invocations.[2]

In truth, there is a clear distinction regarding the concept of power between the prophetic-Biblical-Jewish ideology and the magical-mystic belief of the Hellenistic world. The might of God is revealed, in the Bible, in the act of creation, and in the historical Providence with which He watched over His people, which serves as a source of hope to those who love and revere Him. The power remains even when He manifests Himself — the power of an invisible God, who is immaterial. On the other hand, in the Hellenistic world the power was conceived as something impersonal, which was found in people and substances. It was a visible and material power. Magical acts were a concomitant of the nature of idolatry. Idolatry, in all its forms, believed in the existence of a source of power apart from the godhead, for it did not recognize a god who transcended the existential system that controlled everything and whose will was absolute. Magic flows from the desire to utilize these forces, and idolatry associates man with the deity in the need for magic.[3] Nor does the fact that there was also opposition to sorcery and sorcerers affect the position. Idolatry forbade injurious magic, especially in the case of a rejected and defeated religion.

To what extent the ancient world took the existence of magic for granted may also be deduced from the interesting story about R. Joḥanan b. Zakkai and the red heifer. The narrative is found, it is true, in a relatively late source, in an Amoraic account, but it may be assumed that it is older. 'A certain Gentile questioned Rabban Joḥanan b. Zakkai, saying to him: "These things that you do seem like magical practices. A heifer is brought and slaughtered and burnt and pounded and its ashes are collected, and when one of you is defiled by the dead, two or three drops are sprinkled upon him and you say to him: 'You are clean' ". He [Rabban Joḥanan b. Zakkai] answered him: "Has the spirit of *Tĕzāzît* [demon of madness or epilepsy] never entered you?" He replied: "No!" The (Sage) then said to him: "Have you not seen any one else into whom the spirit of *Tĕzāzît* has entered?" He replied: "Yes!" Thereupon (Rabban Joḥanan b. Zakkai) said to him: "And what do you do?" He replied: "We bring roots and fumigate under him and spray water upon it [the demon-spirit], and it flees." Said (the Rabbi) to him: "Do not your ears hear what your mouth speaks! Such, too, is this spirit—it is the spirit of uncleanness, as it is said: 'And also the prophets and the unclean spirit', etc. (Zechariah xiii 2)." When (the Gentile) had left, (Rabban Joḥanan b. Zakkai's) disciples said to him: "O Master, him you have thrust aside with a reed [i.e. dismissed with a paltry reply]; but what explanation will you offer us? Said he to them: "By your life! neither the dead person defiles nor does the water purify; only this is the decree of the Holy One, blessed be He. The Holy One, blessed He, hath said: I have ordained a statute, I have issued an edict, and thou hast no right to transgress mine edict." '[4] This narrative is instructive from many aspects. The enquiring Gentile wishes to show that in Israel's Torah, too, there are magical practices like those accepted in the ancient world round about. But the exorcism of the evil spirit is for him a fact not open to doubt; and when Rabban Joḥanan b. Zakkai explains to him that the sprinkling of the water mingled with the ashes is a form of exorcism, the explanation appeals to the Gentile. But to his own people, Rabban Joḥanan b. Zakkai reveals his true opinion, namely that this ritual of the sprinkling of the water of purification, which was prepared with the ashes of the heifer, has only a ceremonial significance. A corpse defiles, for this is the Halakhic rule, but this uncleanness is not an independent power, nor has the water any magical force; however, it is a precept, and by virtue of the precept, the corpse defiles and the water purifies.

We have here complete sublimation and demythologization of the heifer ritual, which served, of course, as an example of a statute [without stated reason], as it is said 'I have ordained a statute, I have issued an edict, and thou hast no right to transgress mine edict.' Whether the story was authentic — that is to say, belonged to the time of Rabban Joḥanan b. Zakkai — or not, it shows to what extent the problem was real and a subject for discussion.

But the Halakha, too, was compelled to take a stand with regard to the widespread magical practices. The Mishna defines who is a sorcerer. 'The sorcerer that performs an act is culpable,[5] but not he that (merely) creates an illusion. R. Akiba said in the name of R. Joshua: If two were gathering cucumbers (by sorcery), one may gather and not be culpable, and the other gather and be culpable: he who performs an act is culpable, (but) he who creates an illusion is not culpable (*M. Sanhedrin* vii, 11; *T.B. ibid.* 68a). According to this Halakha, which goes back to the generation of Rabban Joḥanan b. Zakkai's disciples, only one who performs a real act of magic is guilty; whereas one who creates an illusion — 'who merely pretends' — he is actually not held culpable.[6] A mere conjuror, who performs such conjuring tricks without being serious about the matter, is not guilty. The decisive condition is that the sorcerer who performs the magical act should treat his actions seriously, that is, that he should regard sorcery as something real.

Philo's approach was different from that of the Halakha; he distinguished between 'true magic', 'the visual science (ὀπτικὴ ἐπιστήμη) that examines the works of nature on the basis of clear concepts' — a most honoured science — and the delusive jugglery of itinerant magicians, who deceive and exploit the ignorant multitude. He is influenced by the Stoic definition of divination as 'the science of speculation (ἐπιστήμη θεωρητική) and of the interpretation of signs'. While the Mishna upholds the law of the sorcerer only with regard to one who performs a magical act, but not in respect of 'one who creates an illusion', Philo's entire opposition is directed principally against the latter.[7] This doctrinal attitude did not, of course, prevent the spread of magical practices — for which there is considerable evidence — especially among women. Simeon b. Sheṭaḥ ordered eighty women to be hanged in Ashkelon (*M. Sanhedrin* vi, 4). In the Palestinian Talmud (*Ḥagiga* ii, 2, 77d; *Sanhedrin* vi, 9, 23c) it is narrated at length that these women were witches. Referring to the verse 'Thou shalt not suffer a sorceress to live' (Exodus xxii 17), the

Baraita states: 'The Rabbis taught: (The law of the) sorceress applies to both man and woman. If so, why is "sorceress" specifically mentioned? Because mostly women engage in witchcraft' (*T.B. Sanhedrin*, 67a; cf. *T.B. Berakhot* 53a). R. Simeon b. Yoḥai testified: 'in the later generations when the daughters of Israel were addicted to magical practices' (*T.B. ʿEruvin* 64b); and in his name was reported the following dictum, phrased with the extremism characteristic of this Sage: 'The best of women is a sorceress' (*Tractate Soferim*, xv, end). But there is ample evidence of the widespread practice of sorcery, not only among women and simple folk, but also among the scholars in Eretz-Israel and even more so in Babylon.

In actuality, even the Sages of the Talmud and Midrash — despite their fundamental recognition that there is none besides God and that consequently witchcraft does not exist — could not ignore the facts, to wit, that broad masses of the people believed in and made use of these practices. They sought to find a compromise, in accordance with the teaching of R. Eliezer b. Jacob: ' "Neither shall ye practise divination nor soothsaying" — although there is no divination there are signs' (*T.P. Shabbat* vi, 10, p. 8c). Nor was any clear distinction drawn between science and magic, especially in the field of medicine. Among magical practices were included medicaments that originated in scientific experimentation. Hence the Sages, who prohibited an entire series of customary practices on account of 'the ways of the Amorite' [i.e. superstition],[8] were compelled to qualify their opposition. R. Samuel and R. Abbahu (said) in the name of R. Joḥanan: 'Anything that heals does not fall under the head of "ways of the Amorite" ' (*T.P. ibid.*, and *T.B. ibid.*, 67a in the name of Abbaye and Rava). We know that even Sages, especially in Babylon, used remedies that were obviously of a magical character.[9] Knowledge of witchcraft is attributed to R. Eliezer and R. Joshua (*T.B. Sanhedrin* vii, 4, 25d; *T.B. ibid.*, 68a). Rav recounted, as a fact, that 'a certain Arabian traveller' killed a camel and dismembered it [and that subsequently, it became alive again], while his uncle R. Ḥiyya told him that it was an illusion, and nothing more.[10] Of Rav himself it is said: 'He went up to a cemetery and performed certain acts', and Rashi explains what he did thus: 'He knew how to utter incantations over the graves and to comprehend, at each grave, by what kind of death (the occupant) had died, whether he had died at his proper time or through the evil eye.'[11] R. Ḥanina used to rely, in cases of inheritance, on the tradition that the spittle of the firstborn of a father heals.[12] R. Simeon b. Laqish did not refrain from allowing witchcraft to play a part in Halakhic argument.[13] There were Amoraim who endeavoured to make their curses against their enemies coincide with the moment of God's wrath, and even took steps to prevent the effects of sorcery.[14] Practices that were extremely widespread among the people were not always disallowed, but the attempt was sometimes made to give them a religious character consonant with the spirit of Israel's faith, although it was clear that the custom stemmed from a magic-mythological source. It is stated in a Baraita: 'If a tree casts its fruit, it should be painted with *siqra* [a red paint] and loaded with stones. Thereupon the Gemara asks: 'Granted that it should be loaded with stones so as to lessen its strength, but what remedy is effected by painting it with *siqra*?' The answer given is: 'So that people may see it and pray for it, as it is taught: "And he [the leper] shall cry, 'Unclean, unclean' " — he must make his grief known to the public, so that many may make supplication for him.'[15] Obviously, the original reason for the red paint derives from a popular belief in the power of the red colour. This is an example of the extrusion of magical aspects from widely current customs and their replacement by religio-ethical explanations.

A much more difficult problem than the spread of magical practices among the people was the question of legitimate miracles.

Undoubtedly, the religion of Israel, like every other religion and faith, postulates the possibility of miraculous acts. The problem is how to distinguish between miracles, which break nature's barrier and laws and accentuate the absolute power of God, and acts of magic, which likewise appear as wondrous deeds. This problem has confronted many religions, and it also challenged the Sages. Elijah's prayer on Mount Carmel, 'Hear me, O Lord, hear me' (I Kings xviii 37) was interpreted by the Amoraim of Eretz-Israel in the third century as follows: 'Hear me, that fire may come down from heaven; and hear me, that it should not be said these things are witchcraft.'[16]

Already in the Bible we find miraculous deeds — signs and portents — alongside acts of magic. The means are the same and common to both, but there is a clear, basic difference. God in the Bible does not employ, in contrast to the other gods, magical devices. Those who make use of them are only His messengers. The wonders of the Egyptian sorcerers emanate from their magical arts, which influence supradivine forces. Moses' wonders are a finger of God, who commanded him to perform them; they thus stem from His will. It is God who works miracles. The miracle serves in Scripture as a sign to the prophet-messenger, but the supreme criterion remains the same — whether it occurs by the command of the Lord. If a prophet comes and gives a sign or a portent, saying 'Let us go after other gods, which thou hast not known, and let us serve them; thou shalt not hearken unto the words of that prophet.'[17] Elisha, who seeks to heal Naaman by enjoining him to bathe seven times in the water of the Jordan, employs a means that has its parallel in Babylonian lore, but his object is to prove not only 'that there is a prophet in Israel', but also, and primarily, 'that there is no God in all the earth, but in Israel' (II Kings v 15).

The Sages of the Talmud and Midrash followed in this sphere, too, the Biblical lead, but, characteristically, they broadened and deepened their perception by viewing Biblical teaching as a whole, and by taking up an attitude towards manifestation of sorcery close to them, while controverting the beliefs and notions of their time. The common people were, of course, interested in one thing only — in the result of the action, without differentiating its source. On the other hand, the interest of the Sages was focused on emphasizing the fact that it was God who wrought the miracle[18] rather than on the miraculous act. Hence we find that their attitude to miracles, without which, as we have stated, religion cannot be envisaged, is ambivalent. The point is brought into relief in the well-known story about Ḥoni ha-Meʿaggel ['the Circle-Drawer'] and the attitude of Simeon b. Sheṭaḥ to his actions. Ḥoni ha-Meʿaggel worked a great miracle; he uttered a decree and the Holy One, blessed be He, fulfilled it and brought down rain when it was most needed. But Simeon b. Sheṭaḥ sent word to him: 'Were you not Ḥoni ha-Meʿaggel, I would pronounce a ban against you'.[19] One cannot fail to sense in Simeon b. Sheṭaḥ's words an expression of concern lest the language used by Ḥoni ('I swear by Thy great Name that I will not stir from here') and the act that he performed ('He drew a circle and stood inside it') should be misconstrued; only Ḥoni's personality and the veneration in which he was held by the people saved him from being banned. The same Simeon b. Yoḥai, who was opposed to the practice of witchcraft, was 'well-versed in miracles', and upon leaving the cave together with his son, he reduced men with a glance to heaps of bones,[20] and also exorcised an (evil) spirit from the emperor's daughter (*T.B. Meʿila* 17b). Both Talmuds and the Midrashim are full of miracles wrought by Ḥoni ha-Meʿaggel, Naqdimon b. Gorion, the Tannaim R. Ḥanina b. Dosa, R. Simeon b. Yoḥai, his son-in-law R. Phinehas b. Jair, and other wonder-workers down to the time of the last Amoraim.[21] However, Rav Papa enquired of Abbaye: 'Why is it that miracles happened to the former generations, but to us no miracle happens' (*T.B. Berakhot* 20a). This question testifies to a feeling of decline in miraculous deeds. But those who experienced miracles did not wholly come to an end; there are accounts of wonders that happened even to the last of the Amoraim (*ibid.* 54a).

In the interpretations that the Sages give to the Biblical miracles there is apparent the desire to emphasize the proof that they provide of God's strength and might. 'R. Simeon the Sidonite expounded:[22] When the wicked Nebuchadnezzar cast Hananiah, Mishael, and Azariah into the fiery furnace, Yurqamu,[23] the Prince of Hail, stood before the Holy One, blessed be He, and said to Him: "Sovereign of the Universe, let me go down and cool the furnace and deliver those righteous men from the fiery furnace." Said Gabriel to him: "The might of the Holy One, blessed be He, will not be (revealed) thereby, for thou art the Prince of Hail and all know that water extinguishes fire. But let me, the Prince of Fire, go down and cool it from within and heat it from without, and thus perform a miracle within a miracle." The Holy One, blessed be He, then said: "Go down!" At that moment Gabriel began (to praise God) and said: "And the truth of the Lord endureth for ever...." ' (*T.B. Pesaḥim* 118 a–b). Here emphasis is given to the greatness of the miracle with its inherent wonder, and *pari passu* the might that finds expression therein is demonstrated. In a parallel Midrash (*Canticles* vii 9) the practical outcome of the miracle is also mentioned: 'When the nations of the world saw the miracles and mighty deeds that the Holy One, blessed be He, had wrought for Hananiah and his companions, they took their false idols and broke them in pieces and made them into pairs of bells and hung them on their dogs and asses, and clappered them, saying: "Ye see now what we were worshipping." ' The miracle must lead to but one result, and therein lies its importance, namely the recognition of God's might and uniqueness, resulting in the breaking of the idols. Stories of this kind, which have a mythological aspect, preserve the essential principles held by the Sages. The importance of the miracle lies not in itself, but in the extent to which it accords with the faith in Him who performs the miracle. Thus R. Eleazar of Modiʿim expounded the verse 'And Moses built an altar, and called it Adonai-nissi [the Lord is my banner or miracle]': 'The Omnipresent called it "My miracle"... as long as Israel is in the miracle, so to speak, the miracle is before Him.'[24]

Most instructive is the following narrative, which has been preserved in a late Midrash, but its source is ancient. There the ethical aspect of miracles is made expressly clear to us:

> R. Phinehas said: It once happened in Damascus, where there was an idol-shrine, which had a priest called Abba Gulish, who ministered to the idol many years. Once trouble [*'ăninqê* (ἀνάγκη) *shel ṣaʿar*] came upon him. He cried to the idol many days, but to no avail. Thereafter he went out at night, and said: 'Sovereign of the universe, hearken unto my prayer and redeem me from my trouble.' Forthwith (God) hearkened to his prayer and he was healed; he then stole away and came to Tiberias and was converted to Judaism; he zealously kept the commandments and was appointed administrator of the poor. Now when money came into his custody, the hands that were accustomed to pilfer in the idol-house pilfered also the sacred funds; immediately one of his eyes began to hurt him and it went blind. Once again he misused the sacred funds, and his other eye began to pain and become blind. When compatriots of his came to Tiberias and saw that he was blind, they said to him: 'Abba Gulish, to what purpose did you mock the idol and forsake him?...' what did he do? He said to his wife: 'Arise, that we may go to Damascus. She took hold of his hand and they went. When they reached the hamlets in the vicinity of Damascus, people gathered about

him and said: 'Lo, it is Abba Gulish.' And they further said: 'The idol was right to blind your eyes'. Said he to them: 'I, too, have come only to entreat him and to make my peace with him; perchance he will restore my sight. Go and gather together all the people of the state.' They went and multitudes upon multitudes assembled in the idol-house and (even) went up on the roofs. When the place was full, he asked his wife to stand him upon a pillar that he knew there. He went and stood upon it and said to the assembly: 'My brethren, citizens of Damascus, when I was a priest and ministered to the idol, people used to leave deposits with me, and I subsequently denied receiving them, because the image has neither eyes to see nor ears to hear, so that he might punish me. Now I went to a God whose eyes roam the whole world, and no plot is hidden from Him, and my hands wished to pilfer and take as they were accustomed to do, but I scarcely managed to carry out my intention when he punished me; hence He blinded my eyes.' R. Phinehas ha-kohen bar Ḥama said, and R. Abbun also reported in the name of our teachers: Before ever he descended from the pillar the Holy One, blessed be He, gave him better sight than he had enjoyed before, so that His name might be sanctified in the world; and thousands and myriads of Gentiles were converted through him.[25]

R. Phinehas bar Ḥama belonged to the Amoraim of Eretz-Israel of the second half of the fourth century. This narrative, whose motif reminds us of the story of the conversion of Achior in the Book of Judith xiv 10, and whose language testifies that it was translated from Aramaic, makes it clear that the purpose of the miracle was to demonstrate the truth of Israel's faith and of his Torah, which forbids the misappropriation of charity or Temple funds. To the priest who was guilty of embezzlement while he was still ministering to the idol nothing happened, but once he was converted — and the conversion itself was the result of a miracle — then he was punished for his peculation. In Damascus he demonstrated this difference between idolatry and the worship of God, and the further miracle led to mass conversion.

Tales of this sort, which give expression to the purpose of the miracle in general terms, emphasizing at the same time the concept of power, are not many. More numerous are the dicta that use a miracle for the purpose of justifying the value of the commandments or of religious institutions. Of R. Akiba it is reported that he told Tineius Rufus that the River Sa(m)bation proved which was the Sabbath day.[26] Noteworthy for our subject is the story of the beast [cow] of a Jew that was sold to a non-Jew, and she refused to work on the Sabbath under the ownership of the Gentile, until her former owner came and whispered to her that she now belonged to a Gentile and is allowed to work on the Sabbath. The non-Jew said to the Jew: ' "I shall not let you go till you tell me what you did to her in her ear. I wearied myself with her and beat her, yet she would not get up." Thereupon the Jew began to console him, saying: "I performed no witchcraft nor sorcery; I merely told her thus and thus, and she stood up and ploughed." The Gentile was immediately seized with fear, saying: "Now if a cow, which has neither speech nor understanding, recognized her Creator, shall not I, who have been made by my Maker in His image and have been endowed by Him with understanding, go and acknowledge my Creator? Forthwith he went and was converted and studied and acquired knowledge of the Torah, and he was named Judah b. Torta, and to this day our teachers cite Halakha in his name.'[27] The non-Jew interpreted the whispering in the ear as an act of magic, but the Jew denied this. Undoubtedly we have a miracle here in the fact that the cow reacted to the whispered information that she had been transferred from the ownership of the Jew to that of the non-Jew, but this miracle is a consequence of the Halakha and confirms its truth; the Gentile was converted and merited the privilege that Halakha should be cited in his name. Miracles also serve to affirm the piety and virtue of the righteous in the past and in the present, as the Roman general said to Naqdimon b. Gorion 'I know that your God has brought this commotion upon the world only for your sake'.[28] Most of the miracles take place in order to deliver and save individuals or a community in times of trouble and distress, but the different motifs are frequently interlinked. The miracles and salvations that are wrought for the public are dependent upon their merit and deeds. The contradiction between the belief that God performs miracles and the difficult and depressed position of the nation served as a starting point for homilies of reproof; for example, on the verse 'Unto thee, O Lord, belongeth righteousness' (Daniel ix 7) the Midrash states:

> R. Eleazar asked, who said this verse? — Hananiah, Mishael, and Azariah uttered it. When they rose up from the furnace, all the nations of the world assembled, as it is stated, 'And the satraps, the prefects, and the governors, and the king's ministers, being gathered together,' (*ibid.* iii 27). And they stood up and spat in Israel's face, saying to them: 'You knew that your God performs such miracles and wonders, yet you brought it upon yourselves that He should destroy His house.' They spat into their faces, until they made all their bodies a mass of spittle, and Hananiah and his companions lifted their faces to heaven and justified the judgment, declaring: 'Unto Thee, O Lord, belongeth righteousness, but unto us confusion of face'.[29]

The argument put into the mouth of the Gentiles 'You knew that your God performs miracles and wonders' was derived from actual life. The belief of the Jews in miracles was well known. When Horace heard the story of the lamp that burnt without oil, he said: 'That the Jew Apella believes, not I.'[30] He was undoubtedly right in saying that Jews believed this, as the words of R. Ḥanina b. Dosa testify: 'He who commanded the oil to burn will likewise command the vinegar to burn' (*T.B. Taʿanit* 25a). But while Horace and other Greek and Roman writers regarded such tales as *Superstitio Judaica*, it was accepted in the time of R. Eleazar that the God of Israel wrought miracles and wonders, and the readiness to believe in miracles was exceedingly widespread. The problem was to reconcile this belief with the nation's destiny and with other elements of faith.

The religious value of the miracle is not absolute; it is controlled by and subject to other principles, and this is done, it appears, in various ways.

The former generations were vouchsafed miracles, because they gave their lives for the sanctification of God's Name. Precisely on account of the conception that a miracle served only to prove God's greatness and might — that is, the sanctity of his Name — the entire reason for the miracle is negatived if there is no willingness to sanctify God's Name on the part of those who perform miracles or wait for them. But whoever offers his life for the sanctification of the Divine

Name must not do so with a view that a miracle should be wrought for him. When Trajan was about to have Pappus and Lulianus executed in Laodicea, 'He said to them: "Are you not of the people of Hananiah, Mishael, and Azariah? Let your God come and deliver you from my hand." They replied: "Hananiah, Mishael, and Azariah were righteous men, and Nebuchadnezzar was worthy of having a miracle performed through him; but you are a wicked king and you are unworthy that a miracle should be wrought through you, and we are deserving of death unto Heaven...." '[31]

The best example of this standpoint, which regards the miracle as a means of sanctifying the Divine Name and makes it conditional on the other deeds of him who wishes to be vouchsafed the wonder, is to be found in the tales concerning R. Ḥanina b. Dosa, 'who was once praying when an *ʿarwād* [venomous lizard] bit him, but he did not interrupt his prayer. His disciples went and found the reptile dead at the mouth of its hole. Said they: Woe to the man whom an *ʿarwād* bites; but woe to the *ʿarwād* who bites Ben Dosa!' (*Tosefta Berakhot* iii, 20). In the Babylonian Talmud the story is recounted with differences of detail. There it is added: 'He put it on his shoulder and brought it to the House of Study, saying to them [the disciples]: "See, my sons, it is not the *ʿarwād* but sin that slays"' (*T.B. Berakhot* 33a). Here the moral drawn from the miracle is expressly stated. The miracle points to an act sanctifying the Divine Name: by placing himself in danger and not interrupting his prayer, although the *ʿarwād* had bitten him, R. Ḥanina b. Dosa was vouchsafed a miracle. The miracle, which came in the wake of the act of self-sacrifice, still further enhanced the sanctification of the Divine Name by being instrumental also in others' regarding the miracle as a consequence of R. Ḥanina b. Dosa's devotion to prayer.

The connection between the miracle and the law of recompense is clearly brought out in another story about R. Ḥanina b. Dosa. 'The Rabbis taught: It once happened that the daughter of Neḥunia, the well-digger, fell into a large cistern and people came and informed R. Ḥanina b. Dosa. The first hour he said to them: "All is well." The second hour he (likewise) said: "All is well." The third hour he said to them: "She has come up..." So the people said to him: "Are you a prophet?" He replied: "I am neither a prophet nor the son of a prophet, but is it conceivable that in the work in which the righteous man is engaged his seed should come to grief?..." '[32] The miracle was necessary in order to prove God's righteousness.

The problem of the relationship between the laws of nature and miracles did not greatly exercise the minds of the Sages. Changes in the natural order are mentioned in Tannaitic sources in relation to the generation of the Flood — 'the Omnipresent changed for them the order of the universe, so that the sun rose in the west and set in the east'[33]; nevertheless they persisted in their rebellion. The changing of the order of the universe was not a miracle. Express differences of opinion in relation to change in the natural order is first found in the days of the Amoraim. 'The Rabbis taught: It once happened that a man's wife died and left a sucking son, and the father had not the means to pay for a wet-nurse; then a miracle happened to him and he developed breasts like the two breasts of a woman, and he suckled his son. Rav Joseph said: Come and see how great is this man that such a miracle was wrought for him! Said Abbaye to him: On the contrary, how inferior is this man, that the natural order was changed for him' (*T.B. Shabbat* 53b). Abbaye discerns an indication of inferiority in the change of the natural order that was wrought for the man, not only because 'he did not merit that the gates of remuneration should be opened to him' (Rashi), but primarily because we do not hear of any act of his warranting the miracle. The happening thus remained a breach of the order of nature[34] and was not a miracle.

Corresponding to Elihu's invitation to Job to stand and consider the wonders of God in natural phenomena (Job xxxvii 11), the view is current among the Sages that the order of creation — that is, the order of nature — bears greater testimony to the Lord's mighty deeds than the miracles that breach this law-bound system. When R. Akiba came to the verses in Leviticus xi, in which the names of beasts, birds, and crawling creatures are mentioned, 'he used to say: "'How manifold are Thy works, O Lord!' etc. Thou hast creatures that live in the sea and that live on land. If those that live in the sea go on to the land, they die; and if those that live on dry land go into the sea, they die. There are creatures that live in fire and creatures that live in the air. If those that live in fire go into the air, they die; if those that live in the air go into the fire, they die. The place of life of the former spells death for the latter; and the place where the latter live spells death for the former. Thus Scripture declares: 'How manifold are Thy works, O Lord!' etc." '[35]

Similarly, Philo argues 'that these extraordinary and seemingly incredible events are but child's play to God' in comparison with the truly great things, namely the marvels of nature and existence.[36] At first blush it seems as though this view represents a return to primitive thinking, but it is precisely comparison with the latter that serves only to accentuate the difference. Primitive man lives in a world of miracles. Every event contains magical elements, and the sorcerer can perform miraculous deeds whenever he wishes,[37] but these miracles create no sense of wonder, nor do they serve as a sign or proof of God, who reveals His power through them and forms no part of nature. However, it is not only in nature but also in everyday life that the boundaries dividing the normal and natural from the miraculous are blurred. It once happened that 'two men went forth to do business, and a thorn got lodged in one of them; he thereupon began to blaspheme and revile (the Lord). After a time he heard that his companion's ship had sunk in the sea, whereupon he began to thank and praise (the Lord)... and this illustrates R. Eleazar's teaching: What is the meaning of the verse "Who doeth wondrous things alone; and blessed be His glorious name for ever"? — Even the one to whom the miracle happens is not conscious of the miracle vouchsafed him.' (*T.B. Nidda* 31a). R. Eleazar's statement, on the basis of which we say in the 'Prayer of Thanksgiving' [Singer's Prayer Book, p. 53] the words 'and for the miracles, which are daily with us', are explained in *Midrash Tehillim* (Psalms cvi, 1) thus:

> Many miracles and wonders dost Thou perform for us every day and no man knows. Then who does know? — Thou, O Lord. R. Eleazar b. Pedat said: See what is written: 'To Him who doeth great wonders alone' — He alone knows. And what is written thereafter? 'To Him who divided the Sea of Reeds in sunder' — the piece of bread [*pĕrûsā*, literally: 'the divided', i.e. livelihood][38] is equal in importance to the sea, which was divided in sunder. Just as the world cannot do without the piece of bread,[39] so it is not possible for the world to do without miracles and wonders. How are we to envisage this? A man is lying on a

bed, and a serpent is on the ground before him. When he seeks to rise, the serpent becomes aware of him. When he is about to put his feet on it, the serpent flees from him. And (the man) does not know what wonders the Holy One blessed be He performs for him...

Other Amoraim went even further than R. Eleazar and said that (the problem of) livelihood is greater than that of redemption and harder than the partition of the Sea of Reeds.[40] Although it is possible to argue that the miraculous construction put on earning one's livelihood is to be explained in the light of the difficult economic position obtaining in the third century in Eretz-Israel, yet this problem could have been solved by withdrawing the question of livelihood from the realm of miracles, in the spirit of Rav Naḥman bar Isaac's dictum[41]: 'Note that miracles are wrought ("by Heaven for the salvation of many human lives" — Rashi), yet food is not created' ('but that food should be created for the righteous in their homes, i.e. that they should find wheat growing in their houses, is not a common miracle' — Rashi). Hence it see msthat the sayings of the Amoraim of Eretz-Israel stem from their tendency to regard the natural order and normal occurrences as miracles. The bringing down of rain is accounted as equivalent to the resurrection, and according to R. Ḥiyya bar Abba and R. Abbahu 'The day of rain is greater than that of the resurrection of the dead.'[42]

The influence of this view is discernible also in the sphere of Halakha. With reference to the ruling in the Mishna (*M. Yevamot* xvi, 3) that evidence may be given of a man's death, in order to permit his wife to remarry, 'only after his soul has departed, even though he was seen amputated, or crucified, or being devoured by a wild beast', it is stated in the Palestinian Talmud (*ibid.* 5, p. 15c): ' "Even if he was seen amputated", for I presume that he was burnt with a heated blade and lived. "Crucified", in the case of a crucified person I presume that a Roman matron passed by and redeemed him. "Or being devoured by a wild beast", for I presume that Heaven had compassion on him. If he fell into a pit of lions, no testimony (concerning his death) is given, for I presume that he was vouchsafed miracles, as was Daniel. If he fell into a fiercy furnace, no evidence (of his death) is given, for I presume that miracles were wrought for him, as for Hananiah,

Mishael, and Azariah.' The explanations of the ruling of the Mishna are not essentially different from those given in regard to the statements of the Baraita:[43] 'If he fell into a pit of lions, if he fell into a fiery furnace.' Both sets of interpretations emanate from the presumption that we must take into account the possibility that 'Heaven would compassionate him', and that an unusual happening — in other words, a miracle — would occur to bring about the deliverance of the person in peril. The Mishna that we have cited — and also the additional Halakhot of the Baraita — is in accord with R. Meir's view, as we can infer from the next Mishna: 'If a man fell into the water, whether it has (a visible) end or not, his wife is forbidden (to remarry). R. Meir said: It once happened that a man fell into a large cistern and came up again after three days.' In the Baraita[44] the Sages dispute R. Meir's view and declare that (if a man fell) into water that has (a visible) end, his wife is permitted (to remarry), and concerning his story they said to R. Meir, 'miracles are not cited'. According to the interpretation of the Palestinian Talmud, we must conclude that they disagreed with R. Meir in regard to the other cases, too. They do not deny that the miracle occurred or the possibility of its recurring, only it may not be cited for the purpose of establishing the Halakha, because it does not belong to the permanent order. This view found its general formulation in the words of R. Jannai: 'A man should never stand in a place of danger, assuming that a miracle would be wrought for him, for perhaps it will not be wrought.'[45] R. Zera expressed himself in similar vein: 'A miracle does not happen every time'[46]; and after him Rava declared: 'We may not rely on miracles'.[47] Abbaye differed from him, saying that we may rely on a miracle. This is also related of Rav, at least when he was in the company of a scholar 'whose merit was great'. Those Sages who did not rely on miracles also did not wish to make use of their merits in order to effect a miracle. R. Jannai said: 'And if you should say that a miracle is wrought for him, his merits are reduced.' Rav Joseph also thought 'lest it be deducted from my merit in the world to come'.[48] Underlying the Sages' unwillingness to rely upon miracles is the tendency to restrict miracles. We also find a trend to limit the miracles of the past. The Mishna that informs us that the mouth of the earth that swallowed up Korah, the mouth of Balaam's ass, the rainbow, the rod, and the cloud were all created on Sabbath eve at twilight (*M. 'Avot*, v, 6) wishes to incorporate these miracles within the confines of nature. When the world was created, the universe was given the power to produce things that are outside the natural order. In the spirit of this Mishna is also the exposition of R. Jonathan, who belonged to the last of the Tannaim: 'The Holy One, blessed be He, stipulated with the sea that it should be rent asunder; this is the meaning of the verse "and the sea returned *lĕ-'ĕtānô* [E.V. 'to its strength']" (Exodus xiv 27) — that is, *li-tĕnāô* ['to its stipulation']' (*Gen. Rabba* v, 3, p. 35). R. Jonathan interprets the word *lĕ-'êtānô* in the sense of *li-tĕnāô* apparently with the intention to set the miracle within the bounds of the natural order. The passage continues there as follows: 'R. Jeremiah b. Eleazar said:[49] Not with the sea alone did the Holy One, blessed be He, make a condition, but with everything formed in the Six Days of Creation. This is the significance of the verse "I, even My hands, have stretched out the heavens, and all their host have I commanded" (Isaiah xlv 12) — I commanded the sea to be cleft, and the heavens to be silent before Moses, as it is said "Give ear, ye heavens", etc. (Deuteronomy xxxii 1); I commanded the sun and the moon to stand still before Joshua; I commanded the ravens to feed Elijah; I commanded the fire not to harm Hananiah, Mishael, and Azariah; I commanded the lions not to hurt Daniel, the heavens to open before Ezekiel, the fish to vomit out Jonah' — the entire gamut of Biblical miracles is included in the act of creation.

This view that the miracle was implanted in nature since the six days of creation is found also in Philo's writings. Although he holds that God fixed immutable laws of nature, to which powers (δυνάμεις) were given, yet, in opposition to Plato's teaching, which allows no room for miracles, Philo takes the view that these powers are not independent or autocratic. The qualities revealed in objects by miraculous acts — the sweetening of the water by means of the rod, the well in the rock — were inherent in their nature. The miracle consisted in the fact that God made them available to Moses at the requisite time. In a similar way the Stoics explained the existence of divination and astrology.[50]

It is difficult to say whether the Rabbinic dicta that we have cited on the subject resulted from extraneous influence, but it is clear that the incorporation of past miracles in the natural order is a form of rationalization that served the aim to restrict miraculous acts in the present. Just as the accentuation of God's might by means of analogies that compared Him with a human king, and by stories about miracles in the past and in the present, was explained by us against the background of religious life in the milieu of the Talmudic and Midrashic Sages, so, too, the restriction and limitation of miracles are to be understood against the background of the existing reality. Immanental tendencies and polemical aims in relation to other faiths are interlinked in this restriction. We have already stated that all faiths claim miracles in proof of their truth. That the miracle corroborates the truth and existence of God was an accepted principle in the ancient world. Stories about miracles close with the words 'Great is god so-and-so'. 'What is god? — That which is strong' is stated in a catechism preserved in a papyrus.[51] Every religion, especially one that raised the banner of proselytization, was confronted by the problem of what attitude to take towards miracles — the miracles of its own tradition and of those of other religions. Ancient Christianity adopted the principle that 'The mracle is legitimate magic, while magic is an illegitimate miracle.' On the one hand, the Apostles were opposed to magic and sorcery, and the Fathers of the Christian Church regarded the founders of sectarian groups as sorcerers, whilst the antagonism to Simon Magus (The Acts viii 9) is well known. But on the other hand, miracles occupied such an important place in the new faith that the Apostles and the Fathers of the Christian Church were caught up by the general prevailing trend and became integrated in it, while differentiating between permissible and forbidden magic. Without doubt miracles played a great role in the propagation of Christianity in the ancient world.[52] Instances of the exorcism of spirits, which occur very frequently in the Gospels, served as proof of the power of the new faith. Although it is easy to cite parallels to the miracles in the Gospels, both from the Bible and Rabbinic sources and from Graeco-Roman literature,[53] yet the importance ascribed to them by Christianity is to be explained against the background of the Messianic consciousness and the realization of the prophetic promises.[54] It is noteworthy that in the scant reports about Jesus and his disciples in Rabbinic literature they are primarily described as enchanters and sorcerers. 'It once happened that R. Eleazar b. Dama was bitten by a snake, and Jacob of Kefar Samma came to heal him in the name of Jesus b. Panṭera, but R. Ishmael did not permit him. They said to him: "You are not permitted, Ben Dama." He answered him: "I shall bring you proof that he may heal me." But before he was able to bring such proof, he died. Said R. Ishmael: "Happy are you, Ben Dama, that you departed in peace, and did not breach the fence of the Sages, for whoever breaches the fence of the Sages suffers retribution in the end, as it is said: "He who breaketh through a fence, a serpent shall bite him." '[55] '... And a master said: Jesus practised magic, and enticed and led Israel astray.'[56] Needless to say, Christians denied this, but, on the other hand, they spoke of the power that inhered in the name 'Jesus' to exorcise evil spirits. Justin maintains (*Dial, c. Tr.*, 1, 2, 85) that the Jews cannot exorcise a single spirit by virtue of the names of their kings, saints, prophets, or patriarchs. In the light of this, we can understand the story about R. Eleazar b. Dama, which we cited above, and likewise the claim that the books of the Minim are diviners' books, that is, works on witchcraft.[57] Minim here denotes Christians or Gnostic sects. Past enemies of Israel — Pharaoh, Balaam, Amalek — appear as sorcerers. 'The Pharaoh who lived in the days of Moses was a Magus' (*T.B. Moʿed Qaṭan* 18a). On the other hand, we find that Roman writers, including Pliny,[58] speak of Moses as a magician; his name also appears in magical papyri. It is noteworthy that, in the Midrash to the Scroll of Esther, Haman — he is the spokesman of all the revilers and blasphemers of Judaism, and sometimes the reference is not to the historical Haman — is made to say: 'There arose a sorcerer unto them called Moses the son of Amram, and he took his rod in his hand and muttered an incantation over the sea and it became dry, and he took them [the Israelites] across the seabed, but I do not know by what means he made it dry....'[59] Similarly, the victories of Joshua and David are there depicted as acts of magic. R. Jonathan and those who adopted his doctrine said, in reply to all this argumentation, that the miracles related in the Scriptures were not acts of Moses, Joshua and Elijah, but conditions made by the Holy One, blessed be He, with the work of creation.

An outstanding feature of the miracle stories in Rabbinic literature is the fact that the personality of the miracle-worker is not emphasized. The Sages were careful not to turn the person himself, who performed the miracle, into a wonder and marvel. The prayer 'He who answered Abraham' (*M. Ta'anit* ii, 4) is evidence of this. We do not pray to Abraham, our father, but to Him who answered Abraham. This point established a difference of principle between these stories and the tales about the miracles of Jesus, whose entire purpose is to accentuate his might and power. It will suffice to set side by side the following two narratives, which are similar in detail, but differ in their basic aim:

John iv 46–54

And there was an official, whose son was ill at Capernaum. When he heard that Jesus had come... he went and begged him to come down and heal his son... Jesus therefore said to him: 'Unless thou seest signs and wonders thou wilt not believe.' The man said to him... 'Sir, come down before my child dies.' Jesus said to him, 'Go, thy son will live.' The man believed the word that Jesus spoke to him and went his way. And as he was going down, his servants met him, and told him that his son was living. So he asked them the hour when he began to mend, and they said to him, 'Yesterday at the seventh hour the fever left him.' The father knew that was the hour when Jesus said to him 'Thy son will live'; and he himself believed, and all his household.

T.B. Berakhot 34b

Our Rabbis taught: Once the son of R. Gamaliel fell ill. He sent two scholars to R. Ḥanina b. Dosa to ask him to pray for him. Upon seeing them, he [R. Ḥanina b. Dosa] went up to an upper chamber and prayed for him. On coming down, he said to them, 'Go, for the fever has left him'. Said they to him: 'Are you a prophet?' He answered: 'I am neither a prophet nor the son of a prophet; but I have this tradition: if my prayer is fluent in my mouth, I know that he [the sick person] is accepted, and if not, I know that he is rejected. They sat down and wrote down the exact moment; and when they came to R. Gamaliel, he said to them: 'I swear by the Temple Service! you have stated the time neither too soon nor too late, but so it actually happened. At that moment the fever left him and he asked us for a drink of water.'

The Christian story seeks to confirm 'that this is indeed the Christ, the saviour of the world' (*ibid.*, v. 45), while the Jewish narrative puts into the mouth of R. Ḥanina b. Dosa — and also in the story that we cited above (p. 109) — the words 'I am no prophet, nor the son of a prophet'.

Even the line of demarcation drawn between the miracles of the pious and saints within the Jewish camp and the miracles of others, by proclaiming the latter witchcraft, did not satisfy everyone. There were those who preferred to regard the miraculous acts as due to the operation of God's edict, despite the fact that idolaters proclaim them to be miracles of their idols. This approach is clearly seen in the story that we cited in another connection,[60] according to which R. Akiba said to Zonin that 'when afflictions are sent upon a man, they are adjured to come upon him only on a given day and to leave him only on a given day, and through the medium of such-and-such a person[61] and such-and-such a medicine. When their time came to depart, (the sick person) happened to go to his idolatrous shrine. Thereupon the afflictions said: Rightly we should not leave. Then they added: But because[62] this fool acted improperly shall we break our oath?' R. Akiba's views in regard to Providence we shall discuss later on (ch. xi). At any rate, the reply he gave was acceptable to the questioner, who was apparently a follower of the popular Stoic philosophy, which taught that Fate decides the incidence and disappearance of suffering. This philosophy is also consonant with R. Akiba's inclination to regard God's miracles as forming part of the order of nature and creation (above, p. 110). The Sages were able to come to terms with miracles. Undoubtedly, personal leanings and experiences motivated each Sage either to emphasize or minimize miraculous happenings. There were always Sages who would not forgo miracles that transcended the bounds of nature, and did not refrain from relating and transmitting such occurrences even about Sages who themselves are seen to belong to those who reduced and limited all miraculous deeds. Even in regard to the role of transcendental forces and proofs, instead of logical reasoning, in the field of Halakha, there is no unified opinion. As against dicta and rules such as 'we pay no heed to a Heavenly Voice' (*T.B. Pesaḥim* 114a, and the parallels cited there), 'A prophet is not permitted from now on to introduce anything new' (*Sifra*, end of Leviticus; *T.B. Temura* 16a), 'Even if Elijah were to come and say... he would not be listened to' (*T.B. Yevamot* 102a), Talmudic tradition knows of the intervention of such forces in the Halakhic sphere, and R. Eliezer b. Hyrcanus was not alone in saying 'If the Halakha accords with my view, let this carob-tree prove it; thereupon the carob-tree was torn away a hundred cubits from its place... If the Halakha accords with my view, let the water-canal prove it; thereupon the water flowed backward... If the Halakha accords with my view, let the walls of the schoolhouse prove it; thereupon the walls of the schoolhouse inclined to fall... Again he said to them: If the Halakha agrees with me, let proof be given from heaven; thereupon a Heavenly Voice came forth and said: "Why do you dispute with R. Eliezer, for the Halakha accords with his view in all matters ....'[63]

Despite all the divergences of opinion, the essential premise that miracles are possible cannot be doubted; to believe in miracles is to believe in a Living, Omnipotent God. This omnipotence is beyond all doubt and is not subject to argument. Noteworthy from this standpoint is the criticism levelled by Galen against the Jewish concept of God's omnipotence: 'For Moses it sufficed to say that God willed the ordering of matter and forthwith it was set in order, for he believed that everything was possible to God, even if He should wish to form a horse or a bull out of dust. But we do not hold this view; we say that certain things are impossible by their nature, and God does not attempt to do them. He chooses the best of the creative possibilities.'[64] The Tannaim, who were contemporaries of Galen, strenuously rejected his viewpoint, for the actual belief in the unrestricted power of God was of primary importance in their estimation, and not the miracle. 'Like the case of R. Joḥanan, who sat and expounded: The Holy One, blessed be He, will bring precious stones and pearls, thirty (cubits) by thirty, and He will make an engraving within them ten (cubits broad) by twenty (cubits) high, and will set them up in the gateways of Jerusalem, as it is said: "And I will make thy windows of agates, and thy gates of carbuncle", etc. (Isaiah liv 12). A certain disciple derided him, saying: "Nowadays we do not find a gem the size of a dove's egg, shall we then find (precious stones) of such size?" After a time, he went on a sea-voyage and saw the Ministering Angels sawing precious stones and pearls. Said he to them: "What are these for?" They replied: "The Holy One, blessed be He, is due to set them up in the gateways of Jerusalem." Upon returning, he found R. Joḥanan sitting and expounding. Said he to him: "Master, teach, for it is fitting that you should teach; exactly as you have said, so have I seen." He (R. Joḥanan) replied: "Wretch!, *if you had not seen, you would not have believed!* You deride the words of the Sages!" He set his eyes upon him, and turned him into a heap of bones.'[65] The paradox in the story is that the disciple in question, called in one source 'a sectarian' [*Mîn*], believes in signs and wonders, but only if he sees them with his own eyes. Complete understanding of the mighty deeds and wonders of the Lord are in the end vouchsafed only to one who realizes his inability to conceive and depict these wonders, as the Amora R. Aḥa expressed it: 'We are unable to recount thy wonders and thoughts, which Thou dost execute; He is beyond praise. The case may be compared to two men, one of whom is strong and the other weak. Can the weakling relate the praise of the strong man? No! Why? Because he has no inkling of the strong man's prowess. But the strong man, who knows his own power, is able to tell the praise of (another) mighty one. This is the meaning of David's words: "Who can express the mighty acts of the Lord?" ' (*Midrash Tehillim* cvi 1). Here bounds are set to the praises of God's might.

We have before us a phenomenon similar to that which we observed when we spoke of the immanence of the Deity. In the feeling of God's nearness there is present religious explosive material; there lurks within it the danger of the identification of God with nature, just as in extreme transcendentalism there exists danger of removing God from the world. Praising God and stressing His might, that is, the fact that man is filled with wonder at His mighty deeds and miracles, contains much that is positive, but the attempt to express all His mighty acts and leaving this expression to human ability are liable to destroy our sense of distance and sublimity in regard to God, and thereby to detract from His greatness and majesty. Hence the Halakha proceeded to fix the praises of the Omnipotent. After they had been drawn up in proper order, 'it was forbidden, from then on, to relate the praise of the Holy One, blessed be He, for R. Eleazar said: 'What is the meaning of the verse "Who can express the mighty acts of the

Lord, or make all His praise to be heard (Psalms cvi 2)?" For whom is it fitting to express the mighty acts of the Lord? For one who can make all His praise to be heard. Rabba bar Ḥana said in the name of R. Joḥanan: Whoever eulogizes the Holy One, blessed be He, to excess is uprooted from the world.'[66] So, too, they acted in practice: 'R. Joḥanan and Jonathan went to establish order and harmony in certain cities of the South; on coming to one place, they found the superintendent saying "The great, mighty, and awe-inspiring, the eminent and the valiant God", and they silenced him. They said to him: "You are not permitted to add to the formula fixed by the Sages for the benedictions..." R. Jacob of Kefar Nibburaya interpreted in Tyre: "Praise is due to Thee, O God in Zion" (Psalms lxv 2 [1])... the case is comparable to a priceless pearl, the more one praises it one devalues it....'[67] The danger inherent in the free recitation of the Creator's praises is given its most original expression by the Amora R. Phinehas[68]: 'Moses formulated the wording of the prayer "The great, mighty and awe-inspiring God" (Deuteronomy x 17); Jeremiah said "The great, the mighty God" (Jeremiah xxxii 18), but he did not say "awe-inspiring". Why? He said: "the mighty" — it is fitting to call Him "mighty", because He sees the Temple in ruins and is silent. But why did He not say "awe-inspiring"? Because He inspires awe only in the Temple [*bĕ-ēt ha-miqdāsh*],[69] as it is said "Awe-inspiring is God out of the holy place". Daniel said: "The great and awe-inspiring God" (Daniel ix 4), but he did not say "the mighty". His children are held in chains — where then is His might? But why did he say "awe-inspiring"? It is fitting to call Him "awe-inspiring", because of the awe-inspiring things He did unto us in the fiery furnace. But when the men of the Great Assembly arose, they restored the greatness to its former estate, (saying): "The great, the mighty and the awe-inspiring God".' In this homily the question of giving expression to God's greatness is connected with that of theodicy. While the expositor ascribes to Jeremiah and Daniel a diminution of God's praise, corresponding to the reduced manifestation of Divine righteousness and power, the men of the Great Assembly restored the crown (of the Lord's attributes) to its former estate and fixed it for future generations out of absolute faith in God's unlimited power and in His righteousness, which transcends all human questions.

Like Job (xliii 1–3), who declares after the Lord's answer:[70] 'I know that Thou canst do all things... Therefore I have uttered what I did not understand, things too wonderful for me, which I did not know', the act attributed to the men of the Great Assembly ascribes an intrinsic value to the realization that God is inconceivable, a realization that is both calming and attractive to man, and, at the same time, a justification of the Godhead. However, this answer, which released the sovereign will of God from the ethical yardstick of man, and reaffirmed His mighty and awe-inspiring deeds in a world that appeared to deny them did not satisfy everyone, as can be seen from the explanation given for the action of the men of the Great Assembly in the Babylonian Talmud: 'They came and said: On the contrary, these are His mighty acts, these are His awe-inspiring deeds. Therein lies His might, that He suppresses His anger and is long-suffering towards the wicked. Therein lie His awe-inspiring deeds, for were it not for the awe-inspiring deeds of the Holy One, blessed be He, how could one nation maintain its existence among the (other) nations!'[71] According to this recension there is no difference in principle between the approach of the men of the Great Assembly and that ascribed to Jeremiah and Daniel. The latter formulated His praise according to the extent to which His power and might were felt, according to its actual manifestation, and they were not afraid 'to set a limit in these matters', for, as R. Isaac b. Eleazar expressed it, 'The prophets know that their God is truthful; hence they do not flatter Him'.[72]

The designation of a multiplicity of praises as flattery and the silencing of the superintendent who multiplied such eulogies in one of the towns of the South, seem to allude to mystic circles, which, like the literature of the *Hĕkhālôt* ['Heavenly Palaces'] in our possession, created hymns and prayers, basically composed of praise and glorification of God, by repeating and duplicating the honorific epithets, and the monotony of their rhythm was intended to induce in the worshipper a state of enthusiasm and ecstasy, and to arouse in him the *mysterium tremendum* towards the Holy King. In prayers of this kind the emphasis is primarily placed on the sublimity of the might and majesty of God, other aspects, such as the Lord's love and nearness to man, being set aside. Holiness transcends all ethical meaning, and is none other than the glory of His majesty.[73] Despite the opposition expressed in Halakhot, in the course of time the prayers formulated in these circles penetrated the established liturgy,[74] and it would appear that the prohibition was already relaxed in the days of the Amoraim. Thus R. Abbahu reports in the name of R. Lazar 'Wherever a worshipper has transgressed and said "glorious in majesty" [instead of "the Holy God"] he has not fulfilled his obligation, except if he substituted it for "the Holy God" in the New Year liturgy, and then only in Musaph ["Additional Prayer"].'[75] The use of this benedictory ending 'glorious in majesty' instead of 'the Holy God' emanates apparently from these circles. Outside the house of prayer, praises of God free from all restrictions used to be composed at gatherings of joy or mourning. Resh Laqish once invited the Meturgeman Judah bar Naḥmani to say words of praise to the Holy One, blessed be He, and the latter 'began and said "The God who is great in the abundance of His greatness, majestic and strong in the abundance of His awe-inspiring deeds, who by His word revives the dead, does great things that are unsearchable and wonders that are numberless" ' (*T.B. Ketubbot* 8b).

CHAPTER VII

THE POWER OF THE DIVINE NAME

The psalms and hymns that lauded the gods at length went hand in hand, in the ancient world, with oaths and adjurations whose purpose was to exert influence and pressure upon the gods to fulfil the will and aspirations of human beings. The formula of the adjuration, the knowledge of which was in the possession of sorcerers, enchanters, and miracle-workers, was primarily based on knowledge of the Divine Name. The Name was endowed with power. The Name and the Power were synonyms.[1] The discovery of the secret name of the god, which implied control of the divinity, occupied an important place both in Egyptian mythology and in the magical practice of the diviners and sorcerers, whose magic arts consisted of the muttering of names.[2] Such concepts and practices were prevalent both in the Hellenistic and in the Roman periods not only in Egypt but also in Eretz-Israel.

It is true that in the Bible itself the magical element is excluded from the faith.[3] There is no adjuration by God's name, nor is use made of it. God's name is called, it is mentioned, when there is a desire for His blessing, for His response; but He that responds and blesses is God, not the priest by mentioning the Name.[4] But the Name itself, even if it is not an instrument or implement that works and achieves miracles and wonders, reflects the presence of the Deity and expresses His power and might; and it may be assumed that in the popular consciousness this distinction was not strictly maintained. Indeed we have many testimonies from the era of the Hasmoneans and after of the prevalence of the view that there was latent power in the Name and of its use in adjurations. In *I Enoch* (lxix 14), the Prince of Oaths tells Michael 'to show him the hidden name in order that he might enunciate it in the oath, so that those might quake before that name and oath'; and in the *Book of Jubilees* (xxxvi 7) Isaac adjures by 'a great oath... by the name glorious and honoured and great'. Ḥoni Ha-meʿaggel [the Circle-Drawer], who lived in the days of Simeon b. Sheṭaḥ and Alexander Jannaeus, 'drew a circle and stood within it and said... I swear by Thy great name that I will not stir hence until Thou have pity on Thy children' (*M. Taʿanit* iii, 8).

The Jewish Hellenistic writer Artapanus[5] narrates in the style of Egyptian stories that Pharaoh fell into a dead faint when Moses muttered the Name in answer to his question 'Who is the Lord?' Moses revived him, but the priest to whom Moses delivered the Name inscribed on a tablet died in great agony. Although Josephus does not cite the whole story of Artapanus, yet he also says 'Then God revealed to him (= Moses) His name, which ere then had not come to men's ears, and of which I am forbidden to speak.'[6] That the Name was used when Moses met Pharaoh is not mentioned in Josephus' writings nor in Rabbinic sources, but it is actually in the latter that there is a reference to Moses' use of the Name in other contexts. In one of the versions of the story about the raising of Joseph's coffin, which the Egyptians had sunk in the Nile, it is stated that 'Moses took a tablet of gold and engraved thereon the Ineffable Name and cast it therein [into the Nile].'[7] Güdemann already noted the resemblance between the legend about Joseph's coffin and the Egyptian legend of Osiris in Plutarch's account.[8] Possibly the Haggada about Joseph's coffin originated in Egypt, and it is not surprising that it mentions Moses' use of the Name. From there it reached Eretz-Israel and found a place in the Rabbinic homilies. On behalf of the Tanna R. Nehemiah it is reported that Moses pronounced the Name against the Egyptian and slew him. The same thought is expressed by R. Levi in other words: 'He slew him with Israel's mysteries'.[9] On the verse 'The sea saw it and fled' (Psalms cxiv 3) the Tanna R. Nehorai said: 'It saw the Ineffable Name engraved upon the rod and it was rent asunder'.[10] In the Apocryphal work designated *The Prayer of Manasses*, the author of which was apparently a Greek Jew, the worshipper says to God: 'Who hast bound the sea by the word of Thy command, who hast shut up the Deep and sealed it with Thy terrible and glorious Name.'[11] The first part of the verse recalls the Midrash that states that God sealed, with the Torah, 'the Okeanos that it should not issue forth and flood the world'.[12] Without doubt, in the second part the reference is to sealing with something on which the Name was written, resembling the legend transmitted by 'a certain Rabbi, who was arranging Haggadic material before R. Joḥanan',[13] concerning David, to wit, that when he dug the foundations of the Temple and the Deep threatened to flood the world, 'he wrote the Name on a sherd and threw it into the Deep'. The use of the Name, which is attributed here to David and to his counsellor Ahitophel, is also known from the Haggada about Solomon and Ashmedai (*T.B. Gittin* 68a). Unquestionably, the authors of the Haggadot regarding David and Solomon transmitted ancient legends that gained currency in circles that used the Name themselves. The Amora Rabba relates that certain seafarers smote the stormy sea with clubs on which was engraved the sentence 'I am that I am, Yah, the Lord of hosts', and it ceased its raging (*T.B. Bava Batra* 73a). When Josephus describes the great wisdom of Solomon — his knowledge, for example, of the way to wage war against the evil spirits — he adds that he left behind him formulas of exorcisms, and appends to this statement a story concerning one Eleazar, a fellow countryman and contemporary, who knew this wisdom and 'adjured the demon never to come back into him, speaking Solomon's name and reciting the incantations which he had composed' (*Ant.* viii, 2, 5). Circles that made use of names and adjurations fostered traditions and Haggadot about the acts of earlier generations in this sphere. In magical Greek papyri there are mentioned 'the holy secret book of Moses, which is called the Eighth or the Sanctified' and 'the secret book about the Great Name' by Moses.[14] In these papyri there occur Hebrew Names in Greek transcription, such as Αδωναΐε ['*Ādonay*, 'Lord'], Ιάω [*Yāhô* (part of the Tetragrammaton)], βασημμ, and also the phrase βεσεν βερειθεν βεριο, which represents *bĕshēm Bāryā*(*tha*)*n Bāryā*, 'In the name of our Creator, the Creator'.[15] These Names, most of which are only epithets, found their way into the Greek papyri after they had long been used in amulets and Hebrew invocations, and it appears that their use in lieu of the Tetragrammaton is the result of a lengthy process that led to the restriction of the writing of the Ineffable Name and to its substition by other sigla or various names and epithets[16], as well as to stringent limitations on its enunciation. The Name remained in its original spelling only in the Bible, but in the later books there are clear indications that it was pronounced *'Ădonay*,[17] just as it was rendered in the Septuagint by ὁ Κύριος;[18] and there are Greek MSS. in which the Tetragrammaton is written in ancient Hebrew letters, without being translated at all.[19] In this form the Name is written both in the Habakkuk Commentary and in the chapters of the Psalms recently discovered.[20] When Philo mentions the Name inscribed on the *ṣîṣ* [the golden plate in front of the high priest's turban], he adds that it 'shows a name which only those whose ears and tongues are purified may hear or speak in the holy place, and no other person, nor in any other place at all. That name has four letters, so says that master learned in divine verities [the *theologus*], who, it may be, gives them as symbols of the first numbers, one, two, three and four.'[21] Also in Synagogue worship the Name was not pronounced, and in blessing the people outside the Temple the priests used only a Divine epithet. In the Temple, however, they pronounced the Ineffable Name[22] in the benediction, and on the Day of Atonement the high priest used to mention the Name ten times: 'six times in connection with the bull, three times in connection with the he-goat, and once in connection with the lots' (*Tosefta Yoma* ii, 2). He likewise enunciated it in the confession in the version *'ānnā ha-shēm* ['O Lord'], and in the prayer in which he besought atonement: *'ānnā' ba-shēm kappēr nā'* ['I beseech Thee by Thy Name make Thou atonement'] — an oath that seems like an adjuration.[23] But we have clear evidence of the care that was taken in mentioning the Name even in the Sanctuary: 'At first he used to utter it aloud; when unruly men increased, he used to utter it softly. R. Ṭarfon said: I was standing among my brother priests in the line and I inclined my ear towards the high priest and I heard him muffle [literally, 'swallow'] it [the Name] in the melody of the priests. At first it was entrusted to all men; but when unruly men increased, it was confided only to those who were worthy.'[24] An example of the muffling of the Name is perhaps to be found in the testimony of R. Judah, that when they went in procession round the altar they used to say "*Ănî wā-Hô*, save us we pray!' (*M. Sukka* iv, 5). *'Ȧnî wā-Hô* is simply a mumbled version of *'Ānnā* and the Name.[25] It would appear that also in the sentence they uttered upon departing '*Yfy lĕkhā mizbēaḥ*', the word *yfy* is not an expression of eulogy ['beauty'] addressed to the altar but a Divine epithet, reminiscent of the enunciation of the Name (*yfy–ywy*),[26] and the meaning of the utterance is 'O Lord, the altar is Thine', as in R. Eliezer's phrase 'To *Yah*, yea to Thee is the altar!'[27] The testimonies to this caution that the high priest observed on the Day of Atonement, and which the priests certainly practised during the rest of the year when reciting the priestly benediction, belong to the close of the Temple area; there is reason, however, to suppose that it was not adopted instantaneously, but was undoubtedly the result of a long process. There is a tradition, it is true, that declares 'when Simeon the Just died, they ceased to use the Name in the benediction'[28] but in another version it is merely stated that 'after the festival he was ill for seven days and died, and his colleagues refrained from using the Name in the benediction'. The meaning may simply be that on account of their grief and mourning the priests refrained for some time after his death from using the Name in the priestly benediction.[29] At any rate, we must not regard this tradition as fundamental and infer from it, in contradiction of all other sources, that a law was promulgated forbidding the use of the Name in the priestly benediction in the Temple.[30] And undoubtedly this tradition did not antedate the enactment ordaining 'that a man should use the Name in greeting his fellow' (*M. Berakhot* ix 5). This Mishnaic text, which has been given various interpretations,[31] must not be deprived of its literal sense nor sundered from the preceding statement: 'At the close of every benediction in the Temple they used to say *min hā-ʿōlām* "From everlasting" [literally, "From the world", world in Hebrew meaning also "eternity"];[32] but when the sectarians corrupted their teaching, saying "there is but one world", the (Sages) enacted that one should say *min hā-ʿōlām wĕ-ʿad hā-ʿōlām* "from everlasting to everlasting [literally, 'from world to world']".' The expression *mē-ʿōlām wĕ-ʿad ʿōlām* 'from everlasting to everlasting' occurs several times in the Bible (Psalms xc 2; ciii 17) and also in benedictory formulas, as, for example, in the prayer attributed to David 'Blessed art Thou, O Lord, the God of Israel our father, for ever and ever' (I Chronicles xxix 10). At the close of the first section of the Book of Psalms we find 'Blessed be the Lord, the God of Israel, from everlasting to everlasting! [*mē-hā-ʿōlām wĕ-ʿad hā-ōlām*] Amen and Amen' (Psalms xli 14; and in analogous phrasing in Psalms cvi 48), and in Nehemiah ix 5 'Then the Levites... said, "Stand up and bless the Lord your God from everlasting to everlasting", etc.' This formula simply means 'through all generations', 'for ever' and the like, just as *mēʿattā wĕ-ʿad ʿōlām*, 'from now and for ever'.[33] The sectarians who corrupted their teaching and declared that there was only one world are apparently the Sadducees. Their corruption caused the Sages to insist that at the close of every benediction in the Temple one should say 'from everlasting to everlasting'. Before this reform this closing benedictory formula was not used at all.[34] Similarly, when the sectarians corrupted their teaching, the Sages enacted that a man should use the Name in greeting his fellow. Here it is not stated with regard to which corrupt teaching this enactment was made, but if the same sectarians are spoken of, we can infer from the remedial regulation that in this case, too, the reference is to Sadducees, who denied Divine Providence.[35] The reform, which renews an ancient benedictory formula of the Bible — 'The Lord be with you', 'The Lord bless thee' — was intended to instil the belief in Divine Providence, and is not at all concerned with the pronunciation of the Name. It is improbable that only at such periods as the priests employed an epithet exclusively in the priestly benediction when pronounced outside the Temple, the Name was not used in greetings but merely a Divine title; for we observed that in ancient times, going back to the early Hasmoneans, care was taken not to mention the Name, and other designations were substituted for it. If the exact date when caution began to be exercised in respect of the pronunciation of the Name in the Temple and it commenced to be muffled is unknown to us, the reason at least for the change is stated: 'when unruly men increased', and these unruly men are none other than people who used the Name irresponsibly; compare the expression 'be profuse in vows or levity' (*M. Demai* ii, 3).

The use of amulets was extremely widespread; this is attested both by the Halakhot that mention them incidentally, as for example, 'a man should not go out [on the Sabbath]... either with phylacteries or with an amulet' (*M. Shabbat* vi, 2), 'He that takes out [on the Sabbath] leather to make an amulet...' (*ibid.* viii, 2–3),[36] and by popular parables, such as: 'R. Ḥunya in the name of R. Benjamin b. Levi said: This is comparable to a king who said to his son "Go and do business". He replied "Father, I am afraid to journey on land because of bandits, and to travel by sea because of pirates. What did his father do? He took a rod and hollowed it out and placed an amulet in it and warned his son, saying to him: "Let this rod be in your hand and you shall not fear any creature".'[37] The very secrecy and fear that enveloped the Ineffable Name and its pronunciation strengthened the belief in its power and in the value of its use, and people did not refrain from employing it both in amulets and in enchantments. It is significant that to the statement of R. Akiba, who numbered one that uttered a charm over a wound among those who have no share in the world to come, Abba Saul added 'Also he that pronounces the Name with its proper letters' (*M. Sanhedrin* x, 1). It is probable that this pronunciation of the Name with its proper letters was connected with the utterance of charms. It was to this, apparently, that the Amora R. Mana referred in his comment on Abba Saul's ruling: 'like the Cutheans, when they take an oath' (*T.P. ibid.* x, 5, p. 28b), that is, like the Samaritans who swear by the Name when an oath is imposed.[38] Although we know that the earlier Samaritans, in contrast to the later Samaritans,[39] pronounced the Name with its proper letters, and made use of it for magical purposes, yet it is clear that Abba Saul, like R. Akiba, referred to Jews. Mention should be made in this connection of the teaching 'whoever makes use of the Ineffable Name has no share in the world to come', which is cited in *'Avot de-R. Nathan* (Recension I, xii, p. 56) as an explanation of Hillel's saying 'whoever uses the Crown perishes' (*M. 'Avot*, i, 13).[40]

The writing of the Names in amulets and for magical purposes was performed according to the usual practice in this art. The Name of twelve letters, mentioned in a Babylonian Baraita, and the Name of forty-two letters, of which Rav speaks (*T.B. Qiddushin* 71a), and the Name of seventy-two letters, with which, R. Avin tells us, the Holy One, blessed be He, redeemed the children of Israel from Egypt[41] — none of these is explained either in the Talmud or in the Amoraic Midrashim. On the other hand, there are numerous philosophical and mystical explanations.[42] But undoubtedly the discovery of the magical papyri has served to clarify the subject of these Names, as M. Gaster and L. Blau[43] have shown. In these papyri the sounds of the Greek alphabet are used for the combination of names ἑπτᾶγράμμᾶτον ὄνομα in various patterns. This combination of letters, which is called ἀναγραμματίζειν, was achieved by Jews by means of the Tetragrammaton. Writing it three times produced the Name of twelve letters. A triangular structure, whose base consists of twelve letters — that is, three times the Tetragrammaton — and the succeeding lines contain progressively one letter less, until at the apex the Tetragrammaton is attained, comprises a total of seventy-two letters. The first four rows form the Name of forty-two letters. Since these Names, which were called the 'Great Name', were based upon the Tetragrammaton, it is not surprising that the same rules of caution were applied to their transmission. In a Babylonian Baraita it is stated, in parallelism with what we learnt about the Tetragrammaton: 'The Rabbis taught: At first the twelve-lettered Name was entrusted to all men; but when unruly men increased, it was confined only to the pious members of the priesthood....' Even clearer restrictions are found in the statement of Rav Judah, who said in the name of Rav: 'The Name of forty-two letters is entrusted only to one who is pious and humble, is middle-aged, is not irascible, is not given to drunkenness, and is not insistent on his rights. And he who knows the Name, and uses it with due care, and keeps it in purity, is beloved in Heaven and cherished on earth, and his fellow creatures stand in awe of him, and he inherits two worlds — this world and the world to come' (*T.B. Qiddushin, ibid.).* All the conditions that those worthy to have the Name entrusted to them were required to fulfil have as their object that the one who knows the Name should be careful of it and keep it in purity, not using it for any unworthy purpose. The Halakha prescribes the penalty of flogging for whoever uses the Name in cursing his fellow. This is an ancient Halakha. It is taught in an anonymous Baraita (*Tosefta Makkot* v, 10, p. 444, and *T.P. Shevuʿot* iii, 12, p. 35a), which is transmitted in the name of R. Jose the Galilean.[44] It is noteworthy that in *The Manual of Discipline* it is stated with regard to one who curses, using the Name, 'that he may never return to the council [formal membership] of the Community' (*Serekh ha-yaḥad*, 7, 1, ed. Licht, p. 160).

As regards the use of the Name for cursing, it is related by the Amoraim: 'Samuel once heard, as he was passing, a Persian cursing his son by the Name and he died' (*T.P. Yoma* iii, 7, p. 40d). The effective power lies in the Name itself, and it does not matter whether the Divine designation is uttered by a Persian man or woman (*Eccles. Rabba* iii, 11). Whoever is not careful in using it may kill people; hence the condition not to entrust it to an irascible person. Another stipulation is that the Name may not be confided to one who is dependent on others, as we learn from the following story: 'A certain physician in Sepphoris said to R. Phinehas bar Ḥama: "Come! I will entrust it [the Name] to you." He replied: "I am unable to receive it." "Why?" (the physician) asked him. He replied: "Because I eat tithe, and one who is familiar with it [the Name] may partake of nothing given him by any man" ' (*T.P. loc. cit.*). The reason is more fully explained in the parallel source: 'Lest he ask something of a man, and if he does not give it to him, he will become angry with him and slay him.'[45] The inherent power in the Ineffable Name also serves to explain why it is concealed and unknown: 'Thus said the Holy One, blessed be He: Now if when I have concealed the Ineffable Name from them, they slay by using an epithet, how much more so would they do so, if I openly entrusted to them the Ineffable Name!' (*Eccles. Rabba, loc. cit.*). Those Sages who knew the secret of the Ineffable Name regarded its concealment from the general public as a punishment. Thus R. Joshua b. Levi in the name of R. Phinehas b. Jair replied to the question: Why are the Jews not answered when they pray? — 'Because they do not know the secret of the Ineffable Name'.[46] Knowledge of the Name is regarded as the privilege of certain generations. R. Abba bar Kahana said: 'Two generations used the Ineffable Name — the men of the Great Assembly[47] and the generation of the Hadrianic persecutions... and some say that also in the generation of Hezekiah and in that of Zedekiah the Ineffable Name was known, as it is said: (Therefore) "Thus saith the Lord [the God of Israel]: 'Behold, I will turn back the weapons of war that are in your hands' " (Jeremiah xxi 4). What are the weapons of war? The reference is to the Ineffable Name, for they used to go forth to war, but did not wage war, yet their enemies fell; when, however, their iniquities caused the Temple to be destroyed, they [the Israelites] fell into the hands of their enemies. R. Aibu and the Rabbis expressed different views. R. Aibu said: The angels scraped off the Name that was upon them [the soldiers]; while the Rabbis declared: It peeled off of its own accord' (*Midrash Tehillim* xxxvi 8). These Amoraim of the third century, who tell us that the soldiers of Zedekiah used the Ineffable Name by inscribing it on their bodies, limit the intrinsic power of the Name, since the sins caused it to be annulled. Similarly, it is stated that the Tanna R. Ḥanina b. Teradion, one of the heroes of the generation of the Hadrianic persecutions, who knew the secret of the Ineffable Name, was punished because he uttered the Name with its proper letters (*T.B. ʿAvoda Zara* 18a), apparently with a view to using it. Clearly, the view that R. Ḥanina b. Teradion was punished is that of the Amoraim. Noteworthy is the fact that in the narratives dealing with men who knew the secret of the Name there appear a 'physician' and an almost unknown Sage, while those to whom it is desired to reveal the secret — and in the end the knowledge is not imparted — are the leaders of the generation. On the one hand, knowledge of the Name was regarded as indicative of a high religious and spiritual degree, and on the other, the dangers involved in the revelation of the Name, and even more so in its use, were recognized. Hence, restraint, which implied a forgoing of privilege, was decided upon. R. Joḥanan ruled: 'the Tetragrammaton may be confided by the Sages to their disciples once in a septennate.' When Rava 'proposed to expound it at a public lecture, a certain old man [elder] said: it is spelt [Exodus iii 15] *lĕʿallēm*.'[48] He alluded thereby to the exposition transmitted by Rav Naḥman bar Isaac: ' "This is My name for ever [*lĕʿōlām*]"; but it is spelt *lĕʿallem* ["to conceal"]'.[49] A solution to the contradiction between this exposition and the continuation of the verse 'and this is My memorial unto all generations' can be found in another teaching of the same Amora: 'The world to come is not like this world; in this world (the Ineffable Name) is written with *Yôd Hē'* [the initial letters of the Tetragrammaton] and read *'Āleph Dālet* [the initial letters of *'Ădōnay*], but in the world to come it will all be one — (His name) will be read with *Yôd Hē'*, and written with *Yôd Hē'* '(*T.B. Pesaḥim* 50a). In this saying the Sage resigns himself to a religiously imperfect world: the knowledge of the Name and its pronunciation shall be complete only in the world to come, when

God's name will be one, and there will be no danger of its being contaminated by other names and used in a polytheistic-syncretistic sense, a practice that was widely current in the magical literature, in amulets, and in invocations. The sources that refer to the use by wicked people of the 'name of impurity' are few.[50] For such a concept opens the way to a dualistic outlook. Even Balaam is said to have used the Ineffable Name.[51]

It seems to me that the account we have given above suffices to refute the view of Christian theologians who sought to discover in the non-enunciation of the Name and the substitutic n of epithets for it a fundamental difference between Judaism and Biblical religion. Equally unacceptable is the view that the desistance from the pronunciation of the Name had its origin in the Babylonian Exile,[52] and that it resulted from fear of the Gentiles' mockery and blasphemies of the type mentioned in Ezekiel (xxxvi 20) and Psalms (xl 5 [4]; lxxiv 10). It appears that actually the discontinuance of the enunciation and mention of the Name was intended to prevent the blurring of the distance between God and man and the use of the Name for magical purposes. But this fact does not indicate a 'decline' in Israel's faith or the estrangement of Judaism from God, for it was precisely the sense of God's nearness that found expression, as we have seen, in the designations that are indicative of it; only in them and in their interpretations — as in relation to the Ineffable Name — there is also manifest that tension between the feeling of aloofness and nearness, which characterizes the attitude of the Sages to God.

CHAPTER VIII

THE CELESTIAL RETINUE

The epithets coined by the Sages for the designation of their Sovereign reflect the range of relationship between God, on the one hand, and the world and man on the other. They reveal His attributes and at the same time describe His actions. The question that emerges is: To what extent did the concepts and beliefs that we discovered in these epithets influence the attitude of the Sages to the angels that fill the space of the Biblical world? They include, to begin with, those simple messengers that are created, as it were, to carry out given assignments and to vanish from the world as soon as these have been completed, then the Temple ministers — the Seraphim and Cherubs — who appear in the visions of the seers, angels that multiply in their thousands and myriads, until we come to the Guardian Angels, who are permanently appointed over entire peoples, and finally the angels, with personal names, who have a fixed place in the Celestial Retinue and fulfil a permanent role in the world below.

Upon examining the Biblical verses, the Sages clearly realized that neither in the Pentateuch, nor in the Prophets, nor in the Hagiographa, is there a uniform and consistent angelology; on the contrary, we find there varied and dissimilar approaches. Thus the Rabbis felt that in many passages in which an angel is mentioned the reference is to the Lord Himself; but because of its disinclination to employ corporeal expressions, the Bible transferred the task to an angel. Hence there were Tannaim who did not hesitate to extrude the angels from verses whose purpose was actually to stress the nearness of the Lord to His people, or when they feared that the task assigned to the angel might raise him to the level of an independent power, a kind of demiurge. Because they possessed the epithet 'Shekhina', which expresses the presence of God, they had no difficulty in deducing from the verse 'And the angel of God, who went before the camp of Israel' (Exodus xiv 19): 'When they went down to the sea the Shekhina was with them'.[1] As a result of this outlook, the Sages often completely ignored in their homiletical expositions the word 'angel', as though it did not appear in the text at all. When R. Nathan asked R. Simeon b. Yoḥai: '(Why is it that) everywhere you find "the angel of the Lord": ["And the angel of the Lord found her"] (Gen. xvi 7), "And the angel of the Lord said unto her" (*ibid.*, v 9), whereas here it is said "And the angel of God ['*Ĕlōhîm*]... removed" (Exodus xiv 19)', R. Simeon b. Yoḥai answered in the spirit of the teaching of his teacher R. Akiba[2]: "*Ĕlōhîm* everywhere means nothing else but Judge. Scripture tells us that the Israelites were at that moment *sub judice* — whether to be succoured or to be destroyed with the Egyptians.'[3] In this exposition the word 'angel' in the text is voided of all meaning. Nay more, at times the concept 'angel' was introduced into the text, although the term does not appear there at all, in order to make it a peg on which to hang a homily on the relationship of the Shekhina to Israel, as, for example: ' "Even the selfsame day it came to pass, that all the hosts of the Lord went out" — these are the Ministering Angels. Thus you find that so long as the Israelites are in bondage, the Shekhina, so to speak, is in bondage with them, as it is said: "and they saw the God of Israel; and there was under His feet the like of brick work of sapphire stone" (Exodus xxiv 10). But when they were redeemed what does the text say? — "And like the very heaven for clearness". And it is further stated "In all these afflictions He was afflicted" (Isaiah lxiii 9).'[4] The tendency to take away the role of the angel from Biblical passages where the importance of Israel and its redemption are spoken of goes back to early times, and the very verse in Isaiah cited above, which the Sages interpreted according to the *Qrê*, is translated in the Septuagint according to the *Kĕtîv*: Οὐ πρὲσβυς οὐδὲ ἄγγελος ἄλλ' αὐτὸς κύριος ἔσωσεν αὐτοῦς that is to say, the translators read: 'not an ambassador [*ṣir* for *ṣar*] nor angel, (but) His presence saved them'.[5] This interpretation corresponds to the Tannaitic exposition 'not by means of an angel, nor by means of an emissary', which is frequently found when there is a reference to God's vengeance on His people's foes and His salvation of Israel,[6] only the Sages went even further and associated the Shekhina directly with Israel's distress, servitude, and exile.

A special problem was engendered by the verses: 'Behold, I sent an angel before thee, to keep thee by the way, and to bring thee into the place which I have prepared. Take heed of him, and hearken unto his voice; be not rebellious against him; for he will not pardon your transgression; for My name is in him. But if thou shalt indeed hearken unto his voice, and do all that I speak; then I will be an enemy unto thine enemies, and an adversary unto thine adversaries' (Exodus xxiii 20–22). The Targumim have left the word 'angel', but have rendered 'for My name is in him' by 'for in My name is his word'.[7] No Tannaitic exposition of these verses have come down to us.

In the Amoraic interpretations there are to be found two lines of exegesis. The one moderates the words by establishing the rule: 'Wherever the angel appears the Shekhina appears';[8] other expositors connected these Scriptures with the verse 'behold, Mine angel shall go before thee', etc. (Exodus xxxii 34) and with Moses' challenging request 'If Thy presence go not with me, carry us not up hence' (*ibid.* xxxiii 15). The sending of the angel was construed as a punishment after the episode of the calf: 'The Holy One, blessed be He, said to Israel "If you had been worthy, I Myself would have become your Messenger, as I did in the wilderness (for it is said 'And the Lord went before them by day' [*ibid.* xiii 21]); but now that you have proved unworthy, I shall hand you over to a messenger (as it is stated 'Behold, I send an angel')." When were they put in charge of a messenger? When they worshipped idols. Whence do we learn this? For thus the Holy One, blessed be He, said to Moses: "Go, lead the people"; Moses replied: "If Thy presence go not with me, carry us not up hence." Moses further said: "Sovereign of the universe! What difference is there between us and the idolaters? We have prophets, and they have prophets; we have a Guardian Angel, and they have a Guardian Angel!' According to R. Levi, the Holy One, blessed be He, did indeed promise 'that the Israelites would not be put in the charge of a Guardian Angel in the lifetime of Moses', but when Moses died that Guardian Angel was restored to his place, for Joshua saw him, as it is said "And it came to pass, when Joshua was by Jericho... And he said: 'Nay, but I am captain of the host of the Lord; I am now come" (Joshua v 14). Therefore, it is said: "Behold, I send an angel before thee." '[9] Thus the verse tells of the punishment: 'Just as the Gentile nations are in the charge of Guardian Angels, so are you in the charge of Guardian Angels' (*Exod. Rabba*, *ibid.* § 7).

In Daniel the Sages encountered the Guardian Angels of the pagan nations, the Guardian Angel of Persia and of Greece among the heavenly host. Basing themselves on Isaiah xxiv 21 'And it shall come to pass in that day, that the Lord will punish the host of the high heaven on high, and the kings of the earth upon the earth', the Tannaim already expounded 'that the Holy One, blessed be He, will not punish the kingdoms in the time to come, until he has punished their Guardian Angels first'. Thus the Israelites actually saw, when standing by the sea, the Guardian Angel of Egypt fall[10]; only at the sea the Holy One, blessed be He, Himself punished the Guardian Angel of Egypt, and so it shall also be in the time to come.

The contrast between the Gentile peoples, who are ruled over by Guardian Angels, and Israel is reflected already in the Septuagint to Deuteronomy xxxii 8, where the words 'He set the borders of the peoples according to the number of the children of Israel' are rendered: κατὰ ἀριθμὸν ἀγγέλων θεοῦ, '...according to the number of the angels of God'. This is also the view of Ben Sira in the verse 'He appointed a ruler [i.e. Guardian Angel] for every nation, but Israel is the Lord's own portion'.[11] A similar notion is held by the author of *The Book of Jubilees* and is also expressed in *The War of the Sons of Light with the Sons of Darkness*,[12] and it was only Israel's sin that brought it about that they, too, were put in the charge of a Guardian Angel. This conception of the angel's task opened the way — but provided at the same time an opportunity of replying — to the arguments of the sectarians. A Sage called Idit or Rav Idi, of whom Rav Naḥman said 'He who knows how to answer the sectarians as Rav Idi let him do so, but if not let him not reply', was asked by a sectarian: 'It is written "And unto Moses He said: 'Come up unto the Lord' " (Exod. xxiv 1); it should have said "Come up unto Me"! He [R. Idi] replied: It is Meṭaṭron (who said this), and his name is the same as his Master's, as it is written "For My name is in him".

If so [said the sectarian], worship him! [R. Idi:] It is written "Be not rebellious [*tammēr*] against him", that is, exchange Me [*tĕmîrēnî*] not for him. — [The sectarian:] If so, why is it written "He will not pardon your transgression"? He [R. Idi] answered: We hold the belief that we did not accept him even as a messenger, for it is written: "If Thy presence go not, etc." '[13] Who was this sectarian who debated with Rav Idi, and what was the special reason for the praise accorded the latter? The sectarian's question clearly alludes to the belief in two divine powers, that is, in a demiurge or son of God, who fulfils an independent role beside the God Most High; it seems to me most likely that the reference is actually to a Christian sectarian. R. Idi's answer was that the angel referred to was the angel who was destined to be the guide — Meṭaṭron, who went before them[14] — in other words, that he was only a messenger, nothing more, and his power derived from the fact that the Lord's Name was in him. When the sectarian expressed the thought that he [Meṭaṭron] should be worshipped, R. Idi drew his attention to the admonition in the verse *'al tammēr bô*, which is interpreted to mean 'do not exchange Me for him'. By the question, Why did the Torah see fit to emphasize that 'He will not pardon your transgression', the *Min* revealed the identity of the angel; He that spoke to Moses was the one who had the power to forgive transgressions. To this came the sharp riposte of Rav Idi 'that even as a messenger' Moses did not wish to accept him; hence, we are to understand that the whole episode came as a punishment upon Israel. The words 'for My name is in him' are not an explanation of the name Meṭaṭron. It is doubtful if Rav Idi himself knew exactly the etymology or significance of this name. He was only interested to tell us that he who spoke to Moses was an honoured angel, who derived his power of action from the fact that his Master's name was upon him or within him. The name itself Rav Idi took from the onomasticon of angels current in his Babylonian environment.[15]

In the detailed acts of redemption wrought during the Exodus from Egypt and the parting of the Sea of Reeds tasks were assigned to angels, and at the same time corporeal expressions were thereby obviated. The Tannaim were able to do this by applying parallels to clearly-stated verses.

Moses' words 'Fear ye not, stand still, and see the salvation of the Lord' are explained in the *Mekhilta* (Massekhta de-Wa-yĕhi, ii, p. 94) in expanded dialogue form: 'They [the children of Israel] said to him: "When?" — He [Moses] answered them: "Tomorrow." They then said to him: "Moses, our teacher, we have not the strength to endure more." — Thereupon Moses prayed, and the Holy One, blessed be He, showed them legions upon legions of Ministering Angels standing by them, as it is stated in Scripture "...And his servant said unto him: 'Alas, my master! how shall we do?' And he answered: 'Fear not: for they that are with us are more than they that are with them!' And Elisha prayed, and said: 'Lord, I pray Thee, open his eyes, that he may see.' And the Lord opened the eyes of the young man; and he saw; and, behold, the mountain was full of horses and chariots of fire round about Elisha" (II Kings vi 15–17).' So, too, it is taught, on the basis of the verse in Ezekiel xxxviii 22, that the Ministering Angels threw arrows and hailstones, fire and brimstone upon the Egyptians. The verse 'And the Lord overthrew [*wa-yĕnaʿēr*] the Egyptians' the Sages explained thus: 'He delivered them, as it were, into the hands of youthful angels [*nĕʿārim*], as it were, into the hands of cruel angels, for it is said "And a cruel angel shall be sent against him" (Prov. xvii 11); and it says "Their soul shall perish at the hand of youth" etc. (Job xxxvi 14).'[16] In the stories about the miracles wrought for the Hebrew wives in the rearing of their children, it is stated: 'And the Holy One, blessed be He, used to send from the heavens on high one who cleaned and beautified them in the manner of a midwife, who makes the infant beautiful' (*T.B. Soṭa* 11b). However, a similar statement is transmitted in the name of R. Levi 'The Holy One, blessed be He, assigned to each of them two angels, one to wash him and the other to clothe him', but it appears that this Haggada is earlier than his time, for R. Ḥiyya the Great, already, reacted to it from the viewpoint that excludes angels from everything connected with Israel's redemption; it is he who said 'This was done not by angels but by the Holy One, blessed be He, Himself, as it is said "Then I washed thee" (Ezekiel xvi 9). Had the text said "Then I caused thee to be washed", I might have thought: Possibly by means of an angel; but it is written "Then I washed thee", and not by means of an angel. Praised be the name of the Holy One, blessed be He — He himself rendered them this service.'[17]

In the literature of the Tannaim — and the Amoraim followed their example — these angels remain anonymous and are not given names. R. Samuel bar Naḥman, the author of the saying that sustenance is greater than redemption — 'For redemption is (wrought) by an angel, whereas sustenance is (vouchsafed) by the Holy One, blessed be He, Himself; redemption is wrought by means of an angel (as it is said) "the angel who hath redeemed me"'[18] — did not specify the name of the angel. In this regard there is a great similarity between Rabbinic teaching and the *Books of the Maccabees*. Judas Maccabeus recalls in his prayers the salvations of the Lord in past wars (*I Maccabees* iii 18; iv 9, 30), and before the battle with Nicanor he supplicates 'when they that came from the king [i.e. Sennacherib] blasphemed, Thine angel went out and smote among them one hundred and eighty-five thousand. Even so crush this army before us today' (*ibid.* vii 41–42). It is obvious that the expression 'Thine angel went out' derives from the verse (II Kings xix 35) 'that the angel of the Lord went forth'; but in the continuation he forgot the angel as it were, and said 'Even so crush this army'. Yet even the author of *II Maccabees*, whose style is less restrained, is not immoderate, but phrases the prayer in parallel language 'So now... send a good angel before us' (xv 23). In another passage he prophesies, as it were, in language used by the Tannaim in relation to the Exodus from Egypt, when he describes how 'the enemy saw five resplendent men from heaven on horses... they also showered arrows and thunderbolts on the enemy...' (*ibid.* x 29–30).

Although the author of *I Maccabees* knew the story of Hananiah, Mishael and Azariah, who 'were saved out of the flame' and about Daniel, who was delivered from the mouth of the lions (ii 59), it is doubtful if he knew the visions concerning 'Michael, one of the chief princes, came to help me' (Daniel x 13), or those concerning 'Michael... the great prince who standeth for the children of Thy people' (*ibid.*, vii 1). In the case of the Tannaim there can be no doubt that they knew these verses; nevertheless they assigned no part to Michael in the past wars of Israel. Only in late Midrashim does Michael take his place as the Guardian Angel of Israel, who fights their battles, as in the apocalyptic works themselves.[19] Thus we find: 'From the day that the Holy One, Blessed be He, revealed Himself to Moses, He appeared to him only through an angel, as it is said "And the angel of the Lord appeared unto him in the flame of fire" etc. (Exodus iii 2) — that is Michael. At that moment he watched over Moses and Israel at the sea, for it is said ..."in Egypt"....'[20] Unlike the Books of Kings and the *Books of the Maccabees*, it is stated in the Midrash that Michael went forth to fight against Sennacherib. The apocryphal character of this Midrash, which attributes its dicta to Tannaim, will become clear in the continuation of our chapter. Also traces of the views opposed to this Midrashic statement, with which the author seeks to come to terms, are still quite evident:

> R. Nehemiah said: Come and see the love of the Holy One, blessed be He, towards Israel, for the Ministering Angels, who are the mighty of strength that do his bidding were appointed by the Holy One, blessed be He, as the guardians of Israel. And who are they? — Michael and Gabriel, for it is said 'I have set watchmen upon thy walls, O Jerusalem' (Isaiah lxii 6); and when Sennacherib came, Michael went forth and smote them, and Gabriel, by the command of the Holy One, saved Hananiah and his companions. Why was this? — The Holy One, blessed be He, made certain stipulations with them. When? — When He sought to go down to deliver Abraham from the fiery furnace, Michael and Gabriel said to Him: 'We shall go down to deliver them.' Said He to them: 'Had he [Abraham] gone down to the furnace for the sake of one of you, you would have delivered him; but since he has gone down for My sake, I shall go down and save him, for it is said "I am the Lord that brought thee out of the furnace ['*ûr*, in the sense of 'fire'] of the Chaldees" (Genesis xv 7). But I shall give you a time when you can go down, because you undertook to save him in honour of My name. You Michael (shall go) against the camp of Assyria, and you Gabriel against the camp of the Chaldees'... and Michael did as He told him, as it is said 'And it came to pass that night, that the angel of the Lord went forth' (II Kings xix 35). It has been taught: All the generals and commanders were drinking wine and they left their vessels lying about. The Holy One, blessed be He, said to Sennacherib: 'Thou hast done what thou didst wish, as it is said "By thy messengers [the same word as for angels] thou hast taunted"

(*ibid.* v. 23); I, too, shall act through My messenger.' What did He do to him? — 'And under his glory there shall be kindled a burning like the burning of fire' (Isaiah x 16)... the Holy One, blessed be He, said to Michael 'Leave their garments and burn their souls...' And just as the Holy One, blessed be He, wrought in this world by the hand of Michael and Gabriel, so He will act through them in the time to come, for it is said (Obadiah i 21): 'And saviours shall come up on mount Zion to judge the mount of Esau' — this refers to Michael and Gabriel. But our holy master [R. Judah ha-Nasi] said: This refers to Michael by himself, for it is said 'And at that time shall Michael stand up, the great prince who standeth for the children of thy people', for he pleads for Israel's needs and speaks concerning them, as it is said 'Then the angel of the Lord spoke and said: "O Lord of hosts, how long wilt Thou not have compassion on Jerusalem" (Zechariah i 12)'; and it is further said 'And there is none that holdeth with me against these, except Michael your prince' (Daniel x 21). R. Jose said: To what can Michael and Samma'el be compared? To a defending counsel and prosecutor standing in court; the one speaks and the other speaks. When the one finished speaking and the other finished speaking, the counsel for the defence knew that he had won the case. Thereupon he began to praise the judge, (asking him) to announce the verdict. Now the prosecutor wished to add a word; said the defending counsel to him: 'Hold thy peace and let us hear (the verdict) of the judge.' So Michael and Samma'el stood before the Shekhina, and the Satan was accusing and Michael was defending Israel. Then the Satan came to speak (again), and Michael silenced him. Wherefore? — As it is said (Psalms lxxxv 9 [8]): 'I will hear what God the Lord will speak; for He will speak peace unto His people.' This then is the meaning of the verse 'In the night I will call to remembrance my song' — for the miracle of Hezekiah (*Exodus Rabba* xviii 5).

Since the sources, out of which the expositor composed his exposition, are available to us, we can easily discern the interpolations and inventions of the author. With regard to the rescue of Abraham from the fiery furnace, a story that is first mentioned in the era of religious persecution by the disciples of R. Akiba,[21] the opinion was expressed by R. Eliezer b. Jacob: 'Michael went down and rescued Abraham from the furnace. The Rabbis declared: The Holy One, blessed be He, delivered him... And when did Michael go down? In the time of Hananiah, Mishael and Azariah.'[22] The succinct statement of the Sages was dramatized in the *Midrash Tanḥuma*: 'When our father Abraham was cast into the fiery furnace, the angels quarrelled among themselves. Michael said: "I shall go down and rescue him"; and Gabriel said: "I shall go down and rescue him." Thereupon the Holy One, blessed be He, said: "I Myself shall go down and rescue him", as it is said: "that brought thee out of Ur [i.e. the fiery furnace] of the Chaldees" (Genesis xv 7). He [God] said to them: "His [Abraham's] descendants you will deliver." When Hananiah, Mishael and Azariah went down into the fiery furnace, the angel came down and rescued them, as it is said "Nebuchadnezzar spoke and said: 'Blessed be the God of Shadrach, Meshach, and Abed-nego, who hath sent His angel, and delivered His servants...' "[23] In the rescue of Hananiah, Mishael and Azariah only one angel is mentioned, nor does the expositor explain who the angel was that rescued them. The argument between the two angels he composed, apparently, out of two sources: *Genesis Rabba*, according to which Michael was the rescuing angel, and a source in which Gabriel suggested that he should deliver Abraham, but the Holy One, blessed be He, rejected his suggestion and said to him: 'I am Unique in My world, and he is unique in his world; it is fitting that the Unique should deliver the unique.'[24] The author of the Midrash in *Exodus Rabba* harmonized the two expositions. Both Michael and Gabriel wished to save Abraham, only 'Had he [Abraham] gone down to the furnace for the sake of one of you, you would have delivered him; but since he has gone down for My sake, I shall go down and save him', but as compensation for this he added: 'You Michael (shall go) against the camp of Assyria, and you Gabriel against the camp of the Chaldees', that is, to save Hananiah, Mishael and Azariah.

However, the homilist did not refrain from citing a Baraita[25] — which is in fact a statement by R. Joshua b. Qorḥa — that justifies the use of angels in the war with Sennacherib, in contrast to the first action of the Lord against Pharaoh,[26] but he omitted the antithesis to Pharaoh, for actually he saw nothing objectionable in redemption by means of angels. On the contrary, to the words (which are not known from any other source) 'Come and see the love of the Holy One, blessed be He, towards Israel, for the Ministering Angels, who are the mighty of strength that do His bidding, were appointed by the Holy One, blessed be He, as the guardians of Israel', he added 'And who are they? — Michael and Gabriel', and in the continuation of the homily he assigned them a decisive role in the redemption of the time to come, and cited the divergent view of 'our holy master', who transfers the entire action to Michael, Israel's defending counsel, and he relies on the words of R. Jose, who describes the struggle between Michael and Samma'el. The very mention of Samma'el in a Tannaitic statement suffices to invalidate the trustworthiness of the entire tradition.[27] Whereas the later, anonymous homilist takes the angel mentioned in the story of Sennacherib and identifies him with Michael and raises him to the level of a redeeming angel in the past and in the future, we actually possess a contrary tradition! It reduces the stature of the angel and his role even in the war with Sennacherib, which it likens to the redemption from Egypt: 'R. Eliezer said: He smote them with His hand, as it is said "And Israel saw the great hand"; it was the same hand that was destined to punish Sennacherib. R. Joshua said: He smote them with His finger, for it is said "Then the magicians said unto Pharaoh: 'This is the finger of God' "; it was the same finger that was destined to punish Sennacherib. R. Eliezer, the son of R. Jose the Galilean, said: The Holy One, blessed be He, said to Gabriel: "Is thy scythe sharpened?" Said he to God: "Sovereign of the universe, it is sharpened and ready since the Six Days of Creation", as it is said: "For they fled away from the swords, from the sharpened sword..." (Isaiah xxi 15). R. Simeon b. Yoḥai said: It was the season when the fruits ripen; so the Holy One, blessed be He, said to Gabriel "When thou goest forth to ripen the fruits, deal with them", as it is said "As he passeth he shall take you; for morning by morning shall he pass by, by day and by night, and it shall be a sheer terror to understand the report" (*ibid.* xxviii 19)... And some say: He breathed into their nostrils....'[28] The starting point for the Tannaitic homily is the passage II Chronicles xxxii 21–22, and especially, apparently, the words 'Thus the Lord saved Hezekiah', which recall the verse (Exodus xiv 30) 'Thus the Lord saved Israel that day out of the hand of the Egyptians, and Israel saw....' In the dicta of R. Eliezer and R. Joshua, the angel disappears altogether.[29] Likewise in the homilies of R. Eliezer b. R. Jose the Galilean and R. Simeon b. Yoḥai the angel plays only a limited role; and the latter Sage identifies him particularly with Gabriel and not with Prince Michael! Many Amoraim, too, followed in the path of the Tannaitic homilies, and of special interest is the statement of R. Isaac Nappaḥa, who describes the end of Sennacherib's army thus: 'He opened their ears and they heard the song of the Living Creatures and died.'[30]

Whereas in the account of the Revelation on Mount Sinai in the Book of Exodus angels are not mentioned, they appear in their myriads in the allusions to the event in the other books of the Bible.[31] The Tannaim in their homilies wove, of course, the verses in Exodus into those of other passages. However, they also noted the difference, in this respect, between the theophany at the Sea of Reeds and that on Mount Sinai and said:

> The Holy One, blessed be He, does not act like a human being. When a human (king) goes forth to war, he issues forth with many men; and when he goes in peace he goes with but few retainers. But He who spoke and the world came into being is not so; when he goes out to war He goes alone, as it is said 'The Lord is a man of war, the Lord is His name' (Exodus xv 3), and when he returns in peace, he comes with thousands and myriads, as it is said 'The chariots of God are myriads, even thousands upon thousands' (Psalms lxviii 18).[32]

But the sayings and expositions of the Tannaim with reference to the Revelation on Mount Sinai are not essentially different from their utterances about His manifestation at the partition of the Sea of Reeds. They speak of direct revelation, without refraining from corporeal expressions, and of His appearing alone without retinue: 'Because He revealed Himself at the Sea as a Warrior doing battle, as it is said "the Lord is a man of war"; He revealed Himself at Sinai as an Elder full of compassion, for it is said "and they saw the God of Israel" (Exodus xxiv 10).'[33] R. Akiba rejected Pappus's attempt to interpret the verse 'To a steed in Pharaoh's chariot' (Canticles i 9) in a manner reminiscent of a chariot.[34] Also in the expositions, reported in R. Akiba's name, of the verses in Canticles that allude, in his view, to the Revelation on Mount Sinai,[35] there is no reference to angels or a chariot. Of primary importance in the estimation of the Sages was the fact of the direct manifestation in both theophanies: '"In the sight of all the people" — this teaches that they saw at that moment what neither Isaiah nor Ezekiel saw.'[36] The verse 'And when the people saw it, they trembled, and stood afar off' (Exodus xx 15) they interwove with Psalms lxviii 13 [12] and expounded: 'This teaches us that the Israelites retreated twelve miles and then went forward again twelve miles, thus making twenty-four miles for each commandment; altogether, therefore, they walked that day two hundred and forty miles. At that time, the Holy One, blessed be He, said to the Ministering Angels: "Lead away and help your brethren", as it is said: "Kings of armies flee, they flee" (Psalms lxviii 13 [12]), they flee walking away and they flee coming back. Nor was it the Ministering Angels only, but also the Holy One, blessed be He, ...'[37] The participation of the angels in the Biblical passages is confined to the task of aiding and encouraging the Israelites.

A totally different attitude to the role of the angels at the Revelation on Mount Sinai is to be found in the Midrashim of the Amoraim. There, too, verses from Exodus are woven into those of Psalms lxviii, but it is the latter that are dominant:

> 'I am the Lord thy God' etc. — this is to be understood in the light of the verse 'The chariots of God are myriads, even thousands upon thousands; the Lord is among them, as in Sinai, in holiness.' R. Avdima of Haifa said: I learnt in my Mishna that there came down with the Holy One, blessed be He, to Sinai twenty-two thousand Ministering Angels... Another explanation is: 'The chariots of God are myriads, even thousands upon thousands' — He came down with twenty-two thousand chariots... chariots of God. In the name of the group that came up from Babylon they said that there came down with the Holy One, blessed be He, to Sinai twenty-two thousand chariots. So taught Elijah, may he be remembered unto good. 'The chariots of God are myriads, thousands upon thousands': R. Tanḥum b. Ḥanilai said: As far as the arithmetician (Sophist) can calculate — thousands upon thousands, myriads upon myriads.[38]

In another source, the words of R. Tanḥum b. Ḥanilai, who was the disciple of the celebrated Haggadist R. Joshua b. Levi,[39] are reported as follows: 'Thousands upon thousands, myriads upon myriads, up to the point where the arithmetician can no longer calculate'[40]; that is to say, in antithesis to R. Avdimi's view, R. Tanḥum said that the number of angels that came down was so great that even a σοφιστής could not count them. A similar exposition is given by R. Eleazar b. Pedat: 'When the Holy One, blessed be He, came, a thousand thousand and a myriad myriads (of angels) came down with Him.'[41] The Mishna in which R. Avdimi learnt the number of the angels, which amounted to twenty-two thousand, is reported in the name of 'the group that came up from Babylon' as a Mishṇa taught by Elijah, may his name be for blessing, in the following version: 'There came down with the Holy One, blessed be He, twenty-two thousand chariots; each chariot like the chariot seen by Ezekiel.'[42] The group that came up from Babylon were Amoraim, possessed of a mystic tradition, who went to Eretz-Israel, just as R. Eleazar b. Pedat also emigrated from Babylon, only he had a different version of the tradition, while R. Avdimi followed the Mishna of those 'Babylonian Rabbis' who were contemporaries of R. Eleazar b. Pedat.[43] At any rate, when the Tannaitic Midrashim speak of thousands and myriads being present at the manifestation of the Shekhina, the reference is not to angels but to the Children of Israel. 'R. Jose says: Had (only) two thousand and two myriads been present, they would have been worthy to receive (the Torah).'[44] Even when the exposition is centred on the verse Psalms lxviii 18, its intention and purport are different. It comes to teach 'that just as the Shekhina abides in heaven above only among thousands and myriads, so the Shekhina abides on earth below only among thousands and myriads'.[45] The number of the angels that descended on Mount Sinai is mentioned also in a homily of R. Joḥanan, but he linked this number with a given task to be fulfilled by the angels with respect to Israel — a motif that is found, without the number, in a Tannaitic homily:[46] '..."What shall I take to witness for thee?" (Lamentations ii 13) — with how many adornments did I adorn you! for R. Joḥanan said: On the day that the Holy One, blessed be He, came down to Sinai to give the Torah to Israel, sixty myriads of Ministering Angels came down with Him, and each one of them held a crown in his hand with which to crown the Israelites. R. Abba bar Kahana said in the name of R. Joḥanan: A hundred and twenty myriads, one (angel) to put a crown upon each Israelite, and one to gird him with weapons.'[47] In a late source R. Joḥanan's homily is reported in the name of the Tanna R. Eleazar b. Arakh.[48] However, the motif that the people of Israel were vouchsafed arms or special raiment or crowns, when they stood at Mount Sinai, is old. But in all the early sources in which the Haggada is reported in the name of Tannaim, it is not the angels who do the girding, clothing, and crowning, but the Holy One, blessed be He, Himself. This is how the verse 'And that is the sword of thy excellency' (Deuteronomy xxxiii 29) is expounded: 'The Holy One, blessed be He, said to him: "Moses, I shall in future give (back) to the Israelites the weapon that I took away from them at Horeb," as it is stated "And the children of Israel stripped themselves of their ornaments from mount Horeb onward" (Exodus xxxiii 6). "I have taken an oath that I shall return it to them," as it is said "As I live, saith the Lord, thou shalt surely clothe thee with them all as with an ornament, and gird thyself with them, like a bride" (Isaiah xlix 18).'[49] It seems that there is an allusion here to the following Baraita: 'R. Simeon b. Yoḥai taught: The weapon that God gave to the Israelites at Horeb had the Ineffable Name engraved upon it; and when they sinned in connection with the calf, He took it away from them. How did He take it from them? R. Aibu and the Rabbis disagree on the matter. R. Aibu said: (the Name) peeled off of its own accord; but the Rabbis declare: An angel came down and peeled it off.'[50]

In the source in which the motif ' "graven [*ḥārût*] upon the tables" — according to R. Neḥemiah — (means) freedom [*ḥērût*] from the angel of death' is connected with the raiment vouchsafed to the Israelites at Mount Sinai there is no mention of angels: 'R. Phinehas b. Ḥama in the name of R. Joḥanan, in the name of R. Eleazar the son of R. Jose the Galilean, stated: The Holy One, blessed be He, said: If the Angel of Death should come and ask "Why was I created?" I shall answer him "a *stationarius* have I created thee over the nations, but not over my children". For when they accepted the Torah, the Holy One, blessed be He, clothed them with the splendour of His majesty.'[51]

Apparently, the change that occurred in the homilies of the Amoraim was intended to avoid undue corporealization; hence the task of putting on and taking off, of dressing and stripping was assigned to the angels. But there were Amoraim who felt concern at the prominence given to the appearance of angels at the giving of the Torah in Biblical verses, and saw the need to stress even in this context the sovereignty of the Holy One, blessed be He, over them: ' "The Lord is among them" (Psalms lxviii 18). Said Resh Laqish: There is a tablet on the heart of each angel, and (on it) the name of the Holy One, blessed be He, is combined with the angel's name — Michael, Gabriel, Raphael. "The Lord is among them" — the text has *Adonay* [not the Tetragrammaton], (signifying that) My sovereignty is within them.'[52]

However, no fundamental differences are to be found among the Sages, when they come to consider the attitude of God to the angels on the one hand, and to Israel on the other. Both the Tannaim and the Amoraim have given expression in various ways to His preference for the people of Israel. Apparently, this preference serves to explain R. Akiba's exposition, which, however, R. Ishmael rejected as far-fetched and contradicting an express verse: 'The Rabbis taught: "Man did eat the bread of the mighty" (Psalms lxxviii 25) — bread eaten by the Ministering Angels; this is the view of R. Akiba. When the exposition was reported to R. Ishmael, he said to them: "Go, say to Akiba: Akiba, you are mistaken. Do angels eat bread? Has it not already been said 'I did neither eat bread nor drink water?' " (Deuteronomy ix 9). How then is (the verse) "Man did eat the bread of the mighty" to be explained? It was absorbed by the two hundred and forty limbs.'[53] R. Akiba did not reply to R. Ishmael's criticism, because he held that Moses' status transcended that of the angels, and he did not mind portraying them as eating manna.[54] In keeping with the teaching of R. Akiba, his disciple R. Me'ir stated in regard to the angels' eating at Abraham's house: 'The proverb has it: When you come to a city conform to its mores. In heaven where there is no eating, Moses, when he went up there, behaved like them (the angels), (as it is written) "Then I abode in the mount forty days and forty nights"; on earth where there is eating — (it is written) "And he stood by them under the tree, and they did eat." '[55]

R. Akiba's disciples continued to expound their master's teaching 'Beloved are Israel' (*M. 'Avot* iii, 14) and said: 'O Israel, you are more beloved of Me than the Ministering Angels... [O Israel] you are more honoured in My sight than the Ministering Angels... you are greater in My sight... holier in My sight... more praiseworthy than the Ministering Angels.'[56] The author of the homily 'The Israelites are more beloved than the Ministering Angels' is R. Me'ir. Actually, we find another homily in his name informed by similar sentiments: 'Who is greater, the guardian or the guarded? From the verse "For He will give His angels charge over thee, to keep thee" it is to be inferred that the guarded is greater than the guardian. R. Judah said: Who is greater, he that carries or he that is carried? From the verse "They shall carry thee upon their hands" (*ibid.* v. 12), we see that the one carried is greater than the carrier. R. Simeon said: Who is greater, the sender or the messenger? From the Scripture "Here am I: send me", we learn that the sender is greater than the messenger.'[57] An anonymous Baraita explains the dictum 'The Israelites are more beloved than the Ministering Angels' as follows: 'For the Israelites utter song (of praise to God) at all times, whereas the Ministering Angels utter song only once a day; others say, once a week; and others again, once a month... nor do the Ministering Angels utter song in heaven until the Israelites have said it upon earth' (*T.B. Ḥullin* 91b). The passage appears to be directed against the apocalyptists, who transferred the main praise of God to the world of the angels.[58] The preference accorded to Israel is linked to the idea of election, although in R. Me'ir's view the Israelites are called 'sons' even when they do not behave as such.[59] But even he admits that there is a difference in their status when they perform God's will and when they do not. The concept of the absolute election is the outcome of the certainty that the chosen people will again choose to fulfil the Almighty's will. This view is reflected in the answer given to the arraignment of the angels at the time of the parting of the Sea of Reeds: 'When the children of Israel walked on dry land in the midst of the sea, the Ministering Angels expressed astonishment: People who worship idols (are allowed to) walk on dry land in the midst of the sea! And how do we know that the sea, too, was filled with wrath against them? For it is said "and the waters were a *ḥōmā* ['wall'] unto them"; read not *ḥōmā* but *ḥēmā* ['wrath']. And what caused Israel to be delivered on their right hand and on their left? "On their right hand" — by virtue of the

Torah, which they were destined to receive on their right hand, as it is said "At His right hand was a fiery law unto them" (Deuteronomy xxxiii 2); "and on their left" — this means prayer.'[60] The angels' arraignment of the creation of Adam found its answer when the Israelites uttered a song at the sea: 'And as for the angels who had said "What is man, that Thou art mindful of him?"... at that moment the Holy One, blessed be He, said to the Ministering Angels: "Come and behold the song that My children are hymning to Me." When they beheld, they, too, uttered song...'[61] When the people of Israel is spoken of, many of the Sages have almost no scruples in using anthropomorphic expressions to describe God's love for his people, or His distress and suffering at their calamities and troubles. In so far as love is concerned, it will suffice to point to the homilies that regarded Canticles as an allegorical portrayal of the pattern of relationship between the Shekhina and the Congregation of Israel from the time of the Exodus onward. R. Akiba, who proclaimed that Canticles was 'most holy'[62], did not hesitate to express part of the praise of the Holy One, blessed be He, in the language of the Song of Songs (v 10) 'My beloved is white and ruddy, pre-eminent above ten thousand'. The readiness that we found among some Amoraim, and especially in the case of R. Joḥanan, to transfer certain tasks to angels, in order to avoid corporeal expressions, also appears as a solution in the explanations of Canticles. Referring to the verse 'Let him kiss me with the kisses of his mouth', 'R. Joḥanan said: An angel brought forth the commandment from before the Holy One, blessed be He (in the case of each commandment), and presented it to every Israelite, saying: "Do you accept this commandment? It contains so-and-so many laws, and so-and-so many penalties..." And the Israelite answered, "Yea, yea!" Forthwith the angel kissed him on the mouth. This is the meaning of the verse: "Unto thee it was shown, that thou mightest know" — through a messenger.'[63]

However, the trend to avoid anthropomorphic interpretations by the introduction of angels did not stand the test of the polemic with Christian exegetes, who also expounded Canticles homiletically, only in their homilies the Church took the place of the Congregation of Israel. The Church Father Origen put an unfavourable interpretation on the mediation of angels and stressed the superiority of the Church, which was vouchsafed the kisses of Jesus.[64] It is not to be supposed that the Amoraim of the fourth century were less sensitive to anthropomorphic homilies, but the polemical need decided the issue; hence they did away with the role of the angels, and transferred it to the commandment itself, which visited every Israelite and said to him '"Do you accept me? I contain so-and-so precepts..." and it taught him Torah.' Others adopted the view of R. Joshua b. Levi, who held that 'the Israelites heard two commandments from the mouth of the Holy One, blessed be He',[65] and on this basis the Sages interpreted the verse 'Let Him kiss me with the kisses [literally 'of the kisses'] of His mouth' to mean 'and not with all the kisses' but 'only with two commandments: "I am the Lord thy God..." and "Thou shalt have no other gods before Me..."'; thus there is no room left for 'a son of God' nor for 'the first-born of creation'. The Tannaitic dicta relating to the Almighty's participation in the troubles of His people — to the exile of the Shekhina together with them[66] — contain the most corporeal expressions among the Amoraic statements. R. Isaac b. Samuel said in the name of Rav: 'The night comprises three watches, and at every watch the Holy One, blessed be He, sits and roars like a lion, saying: "Alas for Me, that I have destroyed My house, and burnt My Temple and exiled My children among the nations of the world."[67] And even an Amora like Rav Qaṭṭina,[68] who himself was granted the vision of an angel, heard a voice that explained to him the meaning of the word זועות *zĕwāʿôt* ['earthquakes'] in the Mishna — which he rendered גוהא *gûhā'* [rumbling of the earth] — as follows: 'At the moment when the Holy One, blessed be He, remembers His children who abide in travail among the nations of the world, He sheds two tears into the Great Sea, and His voice is heard from one end of the world unto the other; and this is גוהא *gûhā*.' When he proceeds to add another explanation of his own, which is no less anthropomorphic, to wit, '[God] claps His hands', Qaṭṭina bases himself on the verse in Ezekiel xxi 22. In the name of other Amoraim we find similar expressions: '[God] heaves a sigh', 'He kicks at the heavens', 'He presses His feet beneath the Throne of Glory'.[69] The extent to which the Amoraim were undeterred by corporeal phrases, when their theme was the distress and salvation of their people, is brought home to us when we read the commentary of Rabbenu Ḥananel. He is, indeed, aware that all these things were said 'only with a view to showing Israel that the Holy One, blessed be He, had not forsaken them or forgotten them or abandoned them, but is destined to restore them; all this was intended to encourage them, so that they should not despair of redemption'. Yet at the same time he protects his Maker's honour by saying: 'Heaven forfend! that an (actual) tear welled from the eye; they were only drops that looked like tears... the Holy One, blessed be He, commands an angel and he claps his hands... He sighs — Heaven forfend! that the Almighty should sigh; it means only that the Holy One, blessed be He, enjoins an angel to utter a sigh... He orders an angel and he kicks at the heavens...'[70] Rav Qaṭṭina and other Amoraim, who were familiar with angels, nevertheless assigned them no place in the theme of Israel's troubles and redemption; in respect of this theme they were like Jonah and insisted on 'the honour of the son rather than that of the Father'.[71]

The attitude to the angels' place and status changes when the reference is not to the people of Israel but to individuals. Not only are the angels not ousted from the passages where they expressly appear in Holy Writ, and their actions not minimized, but they are given a role even when they are not mentioned in the Biblical stories and episodes; thus angels are added in order to avoid anthropomorphic expressions. In this regard there is a resemblance between the approach of the Septuagint and the Aramaic Targumim, on the one hand, and the Rabbinic homilies on the other. The verse Exodus iv 24 'that the Lord met him and sought to kill him' is translated by the Septuagint: συνήτησην αὐτῷ ἄγγελος κυρίου καὶ ἐζήτει αὐτὸν ἀποκτεῖναι — 'the angel of the Lord met him...'; also the Targum of Onkelos and the Targum Yerushalmi render in the same way. In similar vein R. Jose declared '...Because he (Moses) neglected his duty, securing his lodging before he performed the circumcision, therefore the angel sought to slay him.'[72] Likewise Rabban Gamaliel said 'The angel did not seek to kill Moses but the child.'[73] But both Sages were anticipated by R. Joshua in his exposition of the verse 'And the name of the other was Eliezer; for the God of my father was my help and delivered me from the sword of Pharaoh': 'At the moment when Dathan said to him "Who made thee a prince and a judge over us? ...Now when Pharaoh heard this thing" (R. Joshua) said: 'They seized Moses and brought him up to the scaffold and bound him and laid the sword upon his neck. At that moment an angel came down and appeared to them in the likeness of Moses; so they seized the angel and left Moses alone.'[74] The Tanna R. Eleazar b. R. Simeon enunciated the rule: 'We do not find that the Holy One, blessed be He, spoke with a woman save with Sarah alone.' The verses that contradict this rule the Amoraim reconciled by resorting to angels.[75] But the Sages did not see fit to appoint angels in all instances. When they deemed it necessary, they added details to the Pentateuchal narrative, and felt no concern that they had interpolated corporeal expressions. The story relating how Miriam 'was shut up seven days' was expounded in an anonymous Baraita as follows: 'Who shut Miriam up? Should you say Moses shut her up, but then Moses was not a priest, and a non-priest may not inspect symptoms of leprosy! And should you say Aaron shut her up — but Aaron was a relative, and a relative may not inspect symptoms of leprosy! The Holy One, blessed be He, however, accorded Miriam at that moment great honour. [He said:] "I am a priest, and I shall shut her up; I shall pronounce her definitely leprous and I shall free her." '[76] This account was apparently due to a desire to emphasize Miriam's righteousness despite her sin and the punishment inflicted upon her. It finds expression also in the following homily: 'Miriam waited a while for Moses, as it is said "And his sister stood afar off" (Exodus ii 4); therefore the Omnipresent delayed for her the Shekhina, the Ark, the priests, the Levites, and the Israelites.[77] The question whether the angels were higher than man was a matter of dispute, and we have already mentioned the views of those who placed man, as the élite of Creation, above the angels.[78] While the Septuagint translated the verse 'For Thou hast made him a little lower than *'Ĕlōhîm*' (Psalms viii 6), βραχύ τι παρ' ἀγγέλους, that is, 'less than the angels', the Tannaim and the Amoraim used this and the verses that follow as evidence of man's pre-eminence, whenever the angels argue against the Holy One, blessed be He. When man was created, He said to the angels that man's wisdom exceeded theirs, and Adam gave proof of this by giving names (to the animals).[79] Rav Judah reported in the name of Rav that the companies of angels who said 'What is man that Thou art mindful of him?' were punished by the Holy One, blessed be He, who 'put forth His little finger among them and burnt them' (*T.B. Sanhedrin* 38b). Rav and Samuel both stated 'Fifty gates of understanding were created in the world, and all were given to Moses except one', and they based their statement on the verse 'For Thou hast made him a little lower than *'Ĕlōhîm*.'[80] R. Joshua b. Levi taught that when Moses ascended to receive the Torah, the angels argued 'The hidden treasure that Thou didst keep concealed nine hundred and seventy-four generations[81] before the world was created, dost Thou wish to give to a human being?... Said the Holy One, blessed be He, to him [Moses] "Give them an answer." ' Thereupon Moses proceeded to show that it is not in the power of the angels to keep the Torah, and they 'retracted and acknowledged that the Holy One, blessed be He, was right, as it is said "O Lord, our Lord, how glorious is Thy name in all the earth!", whereas "(whose) majesty is rehearsed above the heavens" is omitted. Forthwith each one became his friend and transmitted something to him, for it is said "Thou hast ascended on high, thou hast led captivity captive; thou hast received gifts for man [באדם *bā'ādām*]" — in recompense for their having called thee man, thou has received gifts. Even the angel of death communicated a secret to him, as it is said "And he put on the incense and made atonement for the people", and it is further stated "And he stood between the dead and the living" etc. Had he [the angel of death] not told him [Moses], how would he have known?'[82] When the Holy One, blessed be He, wished to let His Shekhina dwell among men, the angels again objected, and David deduced from the phrasing of the verse 'O Lord, our Lord, how glorious is Thy name in all the earth! Whose majesty is rehearsed above the heavens' that the earth takes precedence over the heavens.[83] However, not only was 'the Shekhina primarily among the denizens of earth' (see above, p. 48), but the destruction of the Temple led to 'the diminution of the heavenly household' (*T.B. Ḥagiga* 13b). Nevertheless, man's high status and superiority over the angels is not immutable. The fulfilment and observance of the Torah, which he was privileged to receive on account of his virtues, are prerequisites of this eminence as of every other position of distinction. In an anonymous homily in the *Sifre* (Numbers § 119, p. 143), it is stated: 'Beloved are Israel, for when He calls them by a byname, He uses only the title "priests", as it is said "But ye shall be named the priests of the Lord..." (Isaiah lxi 6). Beloved are the priests, for when He calls them by a byname, He uses only the epithet of the Ministering Angels, for it is said "For the priest's lips should keep knowledge, and they should seek the law at his mouth; for he is the messenger [מלאך *mal'ākh*, rendered elsewhere angel] of the Lord of hosts" (Malachi ii 7). When the Torah issues from his mouth, he is like the Ministering Angels, but if not he is like the beasts or cattle, who know not their Creator.' This rule applied to all righteous men and even to Moses. The prophets were called angels. R. Joḥanan said 'They were called angels ['messengers'] from their father's house [origin], that is, by virtue of their essential task, for they are messengers of the Omnipresent. Verses that according to their simple sense referred to angels of the Most High, were interpreted by the Sages as relating to Moses and Phinehas.[84] But even so, R. Tanḥum b. R. Ḥanilai, the disciple of R. Joḥanan, expounded the verse 'Bless the Lord, ye angels of His, ye mighty in strength, that fulfil His word, hearkening unto the voice of His word' (Psalms ciii 20) as speaking of the earthly beings, whereas the continuation 'Bless the Lord, all ye His hosts' speaks of the celestial beings, for, since,the celestial beings are able to carry out the missions of the Holy One, blessed be He, it is said 'Bless the Lord, all ye His hosts', but in the case of the inhabitants of earth, seeing that they are unable to fulfil the tasks assigned to them by the Holy One, blessed be He, it is said 'Bless the Lord, ye angels ['messengers'] of His'.[85] Moses' triumph over the angels puts him in a unique position, which transcended even Jacob's struggle and victory. According to an anonymous Midrash, 'Jacob said to Moses "I am greater than you; I encountered an angel and conquered him." Said Moses to him "You encountered the angel in your domain, but I ascended to the Ministering Angels in their domain, and they were afraid of me, as it is said 'The angels [מלאכי *mal'ăkhê*; but the Masoretic text has מלכי *malĕkhê* ('kings')] of hosts flee, they flee' (Psalms lxviii 13 [12])" '.[86]

Moses' superiority over the angels stemmed from the fact that he was a righteous man who fulfilled the Lord's word[87], but since he was also an intermediary between Israel and their Father in heaven, 'he was affected by the sin' of the people, which lowered his standing *vis-à-vis* the angels. This was inferred from the same verse that testified in the preceding homily to the angels' fear of Moses: ' "Kings of hosts flee, they flee." R. Judan in the name of R. Aibu said: The text does not read "angels of hosts" but "kings of hosts", that is, the kings of the angels. Even Michael, even Gabriel, were unable to look at Moses' face. When Israel sinned, however, Moses could not even look at a *galearius* [subordinate angel], "For I was in dread of the anger and hot displeasure" (Deuteronomy ix 19).'[88]

The author of The Epistle to the Hebrews accepted the idea that the righteous were greater than the angels and transferred it to the 'Son', linking it up with his Christological doctrine. Of the 'Son' he says 'For unto which of the angels said He at any time, "Thou art my son, this day have I begotten thee" (Psalms ii 7)? And again, "I will be to him a Father, and he shall be to me a son"? And again, when He bringeth in the first-begotten into the world, He saith, "And let all the angels of God worship him..." But to which of the angels said He at any time "Sit on My right hand, until I make thine enemies thy footstool..."? For unto the angels hath He not put into subjection the world to come, whereof we speak. But one in a certain place testified, saying "What is man that Thou art mindful of him? or the son of man, that Thou visitest him? Thou madest him a little lower than the angels... Thou hast put all things in subjection under his feet." For in that He put all in subjection under him, He left nothing that is not put under him. But now we see not yet all things put under him. But we see Jesus, who was made a little lower than the angels for the suffering of death, crowned with glory and honour: that he by the grace of God should taste death for every man.'[89] The author of the epistle, who knew no Hebrew, cited Psalms viii 6 [5] according to the Septuagint,[90] and in agreement therewith he taught that Jesus in his lifetime was a little lower than an angel, for he came to save the children, who are flesh and blood, 'and he partook of flesh and blood like them, that through death he might destroy him that had the power of death, that is, the devil'. But when he died, he was exalted and became 'faithful to Him who appointed him, as also Moses was faithful in all His house. For this man was counted worthy of more glory than Moses... And Moses verily was faithful in all His house, as a servant... But Christ as a son over His house...'[91] The writer of the epistle argues against the view of those who wish to regard Jesus as a messenger, angel or archon, a view that was apparently widespread and against which Christian writers polemized even in the second century.[92] He made use of the motif 'The righteous are greater than angels', and especially of what was said concerning Moses, but in a Christological direction. It appears that it is against homilies of this type that the words of the Palestinian Amora of the fourth century, who knew Greek[93] and added to the dicta of his predecessors regarding the Ministering Angels and angels, were aimed: 'Rabbi Berechia said in the name of R. Abba bar Kahana: The Holy One, blessed be He, is destined to set the domain of the righteous in front of the domain of the Ministering Angels, and the Ministering Angels will ask them, saying "What hath God wrought?" "What hath the Holy One, blessed be He, taught them?" R. Levi bar Ḥayyuta said: Has He not already done so in this world? This is the meaning of the verse "Nebuchadnezzar answered and said: 'Lo, I see four men loose, walking in the midst of the fire, and they have no hurt' "... Scripture does not state "and the appearance of the first" but "and the appearance of the fourth". They were quenching the fire before him. "Like a son of God" — R. Reuben said: At that moment an angel descended and struck him on his mouth. He said to him: "Wicked man! amend thy words. Has He a son?" (Thereupon) he retracted and said "Blessed be the God of Shadrach, Meshach, and Abed-nego" — Scripture does not say here "who hath sent His son" but "who hath sent His angel, and delivered His servants that trusted in Him". '[94]

The views that we have thus far cited concerning the relationship between men and angels are based on the independence of the righteous man of angels. He casts his dread over all of them irrespective of whether they are good or bad angels. But alongside these dicta and homilies there are others that reflect a different outlook, which is to a large extent common also to the apocryphal literature and is likewise widely current in the Greek and Iranian worlds. Everywhere angels accompany man and guard him.[95] The problem, on the one hand, of the existence of evil in the world, and, on the other, the driving power that manifests itself in man to win through and do great things, called forth similar solutions in different places and periods. The Tanna, the Haggadist R. Eliezer the son of R. Jose the

Galilean, adopted the concept of the accompanying angels, but distinguished between righteous and wicked men. He said 'If you see a righteous man about to set out on a journey and you wish to proceed on the same journey, start out three days earlier (than you intended) because of him, or three days later on account of him, so that you may journey with him. What is the reason? Because the Ministering Angels accompany him, as it is said "For He will give His angels charge over thee" (Psalms xci 11). And if you see a wicked man about to set out on a journey and you wish to proceed on the same journey, start out three days earlier (than you intended) because of him, or three days later on account of him, so that you may avoid journeying with him, since angels of Satan accompany him, as it is stated "Set Thou a wicked one over him; and let Satan stand at his right hand" (Psalms cix 6).'[96] The angels minister to the righteous and help them to fulfil their good intentions. Of R. Ḥanina b. Dosa it is related: 'He once saw the men of his town taking up votive and freewill offerings. Said he: They are all taking up votive and freewill offerings to Jerusalem, and I shall not bring anything? What did he do? He went to the city and saw there a stone, which he cleaned, chiselled and painted. (Then) he said: I vow to bring it up to Jerusalem. (Thereupon) five men appeared. Said he to them: Will ye bring up this stone for me to Jerusalem? They replied: Give us five *selas*, and we shall bring up your stone for you to Jerusalem; only you must lend us a finger. So he gave them a hand, and lo! they were standing in Jerusalem. When he wished to pay them the five *selas*, he did not find them. So he went into the Hewn Chamber. They [the Sages] said: Perhaps they were Ministering Angels? They then applied to him the following verse: "Seest thou a man diligent in his business? he shall stand before angels" [מלאכים *mal'ākhîm*, the Masoretic text has מלכים *mĕlākhîm* ("kings")].[97] The humble and natural task of the angels accords with the stylistic simplicity and freshness of the narrative, which belongs to the category of miracle tales, with which we have dealt earlier. (p. 118).

The concept of the angels who accompany a person penetrated deeply into the religious consciousness and left its mark on the Halakha: 'Upon entering a privy' — it is stated — 'a man pronounces two benedictions, one on entering and one on leaving.' While the blessing on leaving constitutes a thanksgiving for the creation of man and praise for the wisdom of the Creator, 'what does he say on entering? Honour to you, you honoured ones, who minister in the holy place; this is the way of nature. Make way; blessed be the honoured God.'[98]

It is true that alongside of the saving angel we find the destroying angel, and a cruel angel,[99] and among the host of heaven the enticing spirit[1] and the Satan ['Adversary']; but they are all engaged in the Lord's mission. In Rabbinic sources, too, both the ministering and destroying angels do the Lord's mission and belong to His household.[2] But the expression 'angels of Satan' in the dictum of R. Eliezer b. R. Jose the Galilean refers to the special 'familia' of Satan.[3] The statement of this Tanna on our subject has a distinct apocalyptic character.[4] However, the expression does not recur[5] even in the sayings of the Amoraim that accepted the motif of differentiation between the angels accompanying the righteous man and those escorting the wicked one. R. Eleazar said: 'When a righteous man passes from the world, three groups of Ministering Angels go forth to meet him... when a wicked man perishes from the world, three groups of Destroying Angels go forth to meet him...'[6] Contrariwise R. Zeriqa states 'The two Ministering Angels who escort him testify against him,'[7] and no distinction is drawn by this Sage between the wicked and the righteous. Although even in R. Eleazar's dictum it is not specifically stated that the angels of destruction are the same as the angels of Satan, yet his words are very similar to those of R. Eliezer b. R. Jose the Galilean. He also interpreted the events of the past as a conflict between Samma'-el and Gabriel (*T.B. Soṭa* 10b), and it appears that the role he assigned to Samma'el and to the angels of destruction is connected with the concept that denies all evil to the Almighty, for he is the author of the dictum that 'the name of the Holy One, blessed be He, is not mentioned in relation to evil, only in relation to good.'[8] It is indeed also stated in the name of R. Joḥanan the teacher of R. Eleazar: 'Before the Holy One, blessed be He, there stand only angels of peace and mercy, but the angels of indignation are far from Him, as it is said "They come from a far country, from the end of heaven, even the Lord, and the weapons of His indignation, to destroy the whole earth" (Isaiah xiii 5).'[9] But the angels of indignation are not the angels of Satan; it is thus clear that R. Joḥanan did not go as far as R. Eliezer b. R. Jose the Galilean or R. Eleazar in removing evil from God. When he himself reports in the name of R. Eliezer the son of R. Jose the Galilean, he states: 'Even if nine hundred and ninety-nine angels arraign a man, and but one angel pleads in his favour, the Holy One, blessed be He, decides in his favour. Nor, in the end, need it be the whole of that angel, but even if nine hundred and ninety-nine facets of that angel indict him and but one facet of that angel pleads in his favour, the Holy One, blessed be He, decides in His favour.'[10] Although the accusers are only ordinary angels, yet R. Joḥanan kept them also far from the Holy One, blessed be He. As we shall see in our discussion regarding Creation,[11] the Sages included in that which was created by Him who spoke and the world came into being also darkness and evil, but despite their desire to avoid the slightest taint of dualistic belief they did not overlook the problem of the relationship between God — who is the God of good, lovingkindness and compassion — and evil. The existence of angels, including prosecutors and destroying angels, headed by Satan, the Angel of Death, sufficed to conjure up custodians of evil in the world; but bounds were always set to their independence and power of action. R. Joḥanan said in the name of R. Eliezer the son of R. Jose the Galilean: 'When the Israelites stood at Mount Sinai and said "All that the Lord hath spoken will we do, and obey" (Exodus xxiv 7), at that moment the Holy One, blessed be He, called the Angel of Death and said to him: "Although I have made you Cosmocrator (κοσμοκράτωρ) over My creatures, you must have nought to do with this nation. Why? Because they are My children." This is the meaning of the verse "Ye are children of the Lord your God" (Deuteronomy xiv 1). It further says "And it came to pass, when ye heard the voice out of the midst of the darkness" (*ibid.* v. 20). But is there darkness on high? Lo, it is written "And the light dwelleth with Him" (Daniel ii 22)! The meaning is that the Angel of Death, who is called Darkness...'[12] The significance of this homily now becomes perfectly clear against the background of the dualistic doctrine, according to the extreme formulation it receives in the Scroll of *The Manual of Discipline*, which states 'In the hand of the Prince of Lights is dominion over all the sons of righteousness; in the ways of light they walk. And in the hand of the Angel of

Darkness is dominion over the sons of wickedness; and in the ways of darkness they walk.'[13] Against views of this kind, R. Eliezer b. R. Jose the Galilean emphasizes that not only was the cosmocrator, the Angel of Death called Darkness, created by the Holy One, blessed He — this is admitted also by the author of *The Manual of Discipline* — but his very dominion is not a decree that cannot be changed, annulled, or restricted. On the contrary, the giving of the Torah served to annul his dominion over Israel, and only when they acted corruptly and made the calf were they again delivered into his power.[14]

However, not only the non-recurring episode of the receiving of the Torah, but the very possibility of the observance of the precepts diminishes the reality of the force of evil in the world — the danger and the menace connected with the angels of destruction and demons; nay more, it also lessens the need of protection by the good angels and intercessors. Not just two angels accompany man, but their number grows with the number of precepts; and sometimes it seems that the precepts themselves are the good angels. The Tanna R. Eliezer b. Jacob taught 'He who performs one precept acquires for himself one intercessor, and he who commits one transgression acquires for himself one accuser.'[15] This dictum was developed, through integration with other ideas and motifs, into the following homily:

> '...For He will give His angels charge over thee, to keep thee in all thy ways' (Psalms xci 11): If a man performed one precept, he is given one angel; if he performed two precepts, he is given two angels; if he did all the precepts, he is given many angels... And who are these angels? They who guard him against the demons, as it is said 'A thousand may fall at thy side, and ten thousand at thy right hand.' What is meant by 'fall'? They make peace with him... 'And ten thousand at thy right hand' — why a thousand at the left side and ten thousand at the right side? Because the left does not need many angels, for the name of the Holy One, blessed be He, is inscribed in the phylacteries and the phylacteries are placed on the left hand... Said R. Ḥanina to him: It is not written in Scripture 'may *be* at thy side' but 'may *fall*'. The left, which is not steeped in precepts, causes only a thousand demons to fall; but the right, which is steeped in precepts, causes ten thousand demons to fall. R. Joshua b. Levi

said: What is meant by 'A thousand may fall at thy side'? The Holy One, blessed be He, assigns to each Israelite a myriad and one thousand angels, to guard him and make a way for him, and one of them proclaims before him, saying: 'Grant honour to the image of the Holy One, blessed be He', for the entire world is full of spirits and demons. R. Judah bar Shalom said in the name of R. Levi: There is not a *bêt rōva*ʿ [an area of ground capable of producing a quarter of a *qav* of seed] in the space of the world that does not contain nine *qav* of demons. What form do they take? R. Levi said: They have a mask (*forma*) over their faces, like the millers' asses, and when sins warrant it, the mask is removed, and the person becomes insane. So long as the angel utters the proclamation, a man is safe; but as soon as he is silent, the man is immediately injured, and the angel declares 'so-and-so's end has come', as it is said "Yea, his soul draweth near unto the pit, and his life to the destroyers" (Job xxxiii 22)'. Scripture does not say here 'to the dead' [*la-mēthîm*] but 'to the destroyers' [*la-mĕmîthîm*] — to those angels of destruction to whom he is delivered. And how do we know that the angel proclaims before him? For it is stated 'If there be for him an angel, an intercessor, one among a thousand' — if there is of those thousand (angels) one who proclaims before him 'to vouch for man's uprightness', then at that moment 'He is gracious unto him, and saith: "Deliver him from going down to the pit, I have found a ransom." ' From this we may infer that if a man is rich in precepts, a myriad and a thousand angels keep guard over him; but if he is flawless in Torah and good deeds, the Holy One, blessed be He, (Himself) guards him, as it is said 'The Lord is thy keeper, the Lord is thy shade upon thy right hand' (Psalms cxxi 7). And thus you find in the case of Jacob of whom it is written 'a perfect [*tam*] man, dwelling in tents' (Genesis xxv 26) — 'a perfect man' in good deeds; 'dwelling in tents', occupying himself with the Torah and growing rich in precepts — camps of angels were assigned to him to guard him, as it is said (*ibid.* xxxii 2): 'And Jacob went on his way, and the angels of God met him...' and it is further stated 'And, behold, the Lord stood beside him, and said... And, behold, I am with thee, and will keep thee whithersoever thou goest' (*ibid.* xxviii 13–15). R. Hoshaiah said: Happy is he that, born of woman, saw the King of kings and His household guarding him, and sending angels to perform his mission, as it is said (*ibid.* xxxii 4) 'And Jacob sent angels before him to Esau.'[16]

This homily has as its main object to exhort people to keep the commandments. The preacher accepted the prevailing view that the whole world was full of demons;[17] but the Torah had the power to confine the sphere and compass of their activity. On account of the merit of R. Ḥanina b. Dosa and his Torah-learning, the time when Igrat, the daughter of Mahalat, and her armies of destroyers have dominion was restricted to the nights of the Sabbaths and the nights of Wednesdays, and Abbaye even succeeded in banishing her from settled areas.[18] It is reported, however, in the name of Rava that he attributed dreams that have a prophetic character to an angel, whereas vain dreams he ascribed to demons. But Rava himself also said that 'a man is shown (in his dream) only the thoughts of his own mind.'[19]

It is not without interest to point to parallels in the sources of the Persian religion from the Sassanian era. The presence of Ahriman in the world is not an ontological fact; the created world is wholly the work of Ahura Mazda, only it serves as an easy sphere of activity for the destructive and negative groups of Ahriman. In the Sixth Book of the *Dēnkart*, which is an ethical treatise, the author wishes to persuade his readers that the struggle against the negation of the demons is not one against real creatures, but is primarily a conflict between man and himself, and every individual bears responsibility. For if they are not allowed to dwell in man, the demons cannot exist.[20] Similarly, but more profoundly, Plotinus developed his doctrine of the demon. In his opinion, we choose the demon for ourselves by the way of our lives, for by our conduct we select the supreme directing power.[21]

So far our discussion about the world of the angels was linked and subject to theological, historical, national, and ethical questions. The concepts concerning the relationship of God to man, whom He had created, and to His chosen people, the problem of the righteous and the wicked, the source of evil in the world — it was these that determined and regulated the acts and portrayal of the angels. But even within the restrained dicta and homilies there burgeoned motifs and expressions that did not grow out of the soil of reflective thought or religious-ethical preaching, but had its source in the imagination, motivated by the desire to penetrate into hidden worlds and the impulse to relate and convey what happens in them. The apocalyptic literature is characterized by descriptions of this kind, and even includes works that were actually dictated by angels. Undoubtedly these books and their like were popular in various circles. However, the Sages understood the difference between the visions of Daniel and those of the prophets. 'R. Simeon b. Laqish said: Also the names of the angels were brought by him from Babylon. At first (Scripture states) "Then flew unto me one of the seraphim" (Isaiah vi 6), "Above Him stood the seraphim" (*ibid.* vi 2), thereafter (we find) "the man Gabriel" (Daniel ix 21), "except Michael your prince" (*ibid.* x 21).'[22] But not only were the names of the angels in Daniel accepted; they were also augmented by the names of many other angels. They all constitute the Court of the Holy One, blessed be He, like the court of a king. In this Court there have occurred and there continue to take place acts and episodes that are revealed to those who are worthy; these are akin to mythological tales of various cultures. Stories of this nature are found not only in the apocryphal literature, but also in the Midrashic homilies and in the Talmuds. When these are anonymous, bearing the name of no Sage, they present us with a panoramic picture, emphasizing characteristics, names, attributes and conflicts. Although we find Tannaim and Amoraim who do not hesitate to mention 'the angels of Satan' or a struggle between 'Samma'el and Gabriel',[23] yet their remarks are always brief and colourless, lacking mythical characteristics. They serve to testify that ampler and more detailed accounts relating to the themes that have reached us through the apocryphal writings were also known to them, only they purposefully avoided transmitting them. But many of their colleagues did not proceed at all along the path of absorption and adaptation, but chose the way of interpretation, which led to eradication and nullification. Just as we have seen that there were Sages who, in consequence of their conception of the Torah and the precepts, eventually not only nullified the influence of the demons and angels upon earth, but, in effect, negated their reality, so there were scholars who turned the

Heavenly Court into a Heavenly Court of Law and Academy, which are a reflection of an earthly law court and academy, and thus they emptied the idea of its original content. The views and aim of the latter did not remain without influence on the sources that ostensibly appertain to the former category, and only by positing this influence are we able to understand their significance and intent. Also conversely, the trend towards eradication and reversal of the position likewise did not achieve perfection, and traces of early strata are still to be detected without difficulty.

To project clearly the phenomena that we have discussed, we shall cite conspicuous examples for each one of them. The story of the serpent in the Book of Genesis — on account of whom death came into the world — which left no further trace in the Biblical books, received extensive treatment in the apocryphal literature and in the Haggada. In the *Book of Adam and Eve* (xvi 1–7) Satan stands behind the serpent and says to him: 'Be only my instrument, and I shall speak by your mouth a word whereby you shall beguile him.' According to the Revelation to John (xii 9; xx 2) 'that ancient serpent' is called Devil and Satan, and Justin Martyr even found etymological proof for this identification. The word σατανάς is just a combination of סטה *sāṭā* ['deviate'] and נחש *naḥash* ['serpent'], i.e. 'a faithless, heretical serpent'.[24] In the early Midrashim there is no trace of such an identification, and Satan does not appear at all during the episode of the serpent; but the creation of the serpent itself is connected with that of Eve. On the verse 'And closed up the place with flesh instead thereof' (Genesis ii 21), R. Ḥanina the son of Rav Ada commented: 'From the beginning of the Book up to this point there is no *Samekh*; but as soon as she [Eve] was created, Satan was created with her.'[25] It is not to be supposed that this Amora was not thinking of Satan's rôle in the incident of Eve's sin. R. Jeremiah b. Eleazar, who called the serpent an 'Epicurian'[26], regarded him as a heretic. The angel standing behind the serpent is identified in *Pirqe de-R. Eliezer* as 'Samma'el', and his action is depicted as a sequel to the angels' denunciation of the creation of man, which we found in the early Midrashim. But whereas in them the angels become reconciled to man's creation and recognize his wisdom[27], in the Midrash that was edited later — but into which there infiltrated descriptions and stories current in apocalyptic literature — the denunciation marks the beginning of man's downfall, and indirectly of the rebellion against God. After Adam had given names to all the creatures, the angels said: 'If we cannot devise a plan to make man sin before his Creator, we shall not prevail against him. Now there was Samma'el, the great prince of heaven, as well as the Living Creatures and the Seraphim, who have six wings, but Samma'el has twelve wings. He [Samma'el] took his company and went down and inspected all the creatures that the Holy One, blessed be He, had created, and he found none more cunning to do evil than the serpent... who had the appearance of a camel, and he [Samma'el] went up and rode on him, while the Torah cried aloud, saying: Samma'-el, the world was only just now created, is this a time to rebel against the Omnipresent, will you at this juncture stir up revolt on high?... As for the serpent, every act that he performed and every word that he spoke, he spoke and did only at the will of Samma'el.'[28] The resemblance to the account that we cited from the *Book of Adam and Eve* requires no stressing; only Satan's place is here taken by Samma'el. In addition to the penalty imposed in the Torah narrative on the serpent and on Adam and Eve — the *dramatis personae* of the Biblical drama — in the mythical story of *Pirqe de-R. Eliezer* Samma'el, too, is not exonerated and his punishment fits the crime. The Holy One, blessed be He, 'cast down Samma'el and his followers from their holy place in heaven'.[29] In the meantime 'Samma'el took hold of Michael's wing to force him down, but the Holy One, blessed be He, saved him [פלטו *pĕlāṭô*] from his hands'.[30] However, the matter did not end with the downfall of Samma'el's host. In the name of Rabbi the Midrash declares: 'The angels who fell from their holy place, from heaven, saw the daughters of Cain walking about with uncovered *pudenda* and with painted eyes like harlots, and they went astray after them, taking from among them wives, as it is said 'that the sons of God saw the daughters of men' (Genesis vi 1). Other sayings of the same *genre* are cited in the name of R. Joshua b. Qorḥa and R. Zadok.[31] Although the names of the Tannaim mentioned are apocryphal, the interpretation itself, that by 'the sons of God' angels are meant, is old, since R. Simeon b. Yoḥai already reacted to it. After his own explanation 'sons of judges' had been cited, it is stated 'R. Simeon b. Yoḥai used to curse all those who called them "sons of

God" '.[32] Samma'el's followers walked in the footsteps of their prince, for the author of *Pirqe de-R. Eliezer* relates of him, when he comes to the story of Cain's birth: 'A serpent-rider came to her [Eve] and made her pregnant; thereafter Adam came to her and made her conceive Abel, as it is said "And Adam knew Eve his wife". What is meant by "he knew"? — that she was pregnant and he saw, from its [the foetus's] likeness, that it belonged not to earth's creatures but to the celestial beings;[33] and she prophesied and said "I have gotten a man with the help of the Lord". '[34] Although the name of the 'serpent-rider' is not expressly mentioned, yet it is obvious that the reference is to Samma'el.[35] The erotic theme is old. The motif of jealousy is alluded to in *The Wisdom of Solomon* (ii 24) 'but through Satan's envy death entered the world', but the nature of the envy is not described.[36] In the Tosefta[37] it is stated: 'So, too, we find in the case of the serpent, who set his mind on killing Adam and taking Eve to wife.' In the name of R. Joshua b. Qorḥa it is reported: 'Because he saw them engaged in sexual intercourse and he lusted for her.'[38] According to the Amora R. Joḥanan, who was familiar with the apocalyptic sources, the desire and lust were implemented, and he says 'When the serpent went into Eve, he injected contaminating lust into her.'[39] However, the primary teaching of the dictum is found in the continuation, to wit, that 'The Israelites who stood at Mount Sinai lost their contaminating lust', and it seeks, as we shall see later, to refute the idea of original sin. But R. Joḥanan's statement and the dicta of the Tannaim testify that they knew the last-mentioned motif, which we have cited in a version similar to that of *Pirqe de-R. Eliezer* and Targum Pseudo-Jonathan; and it seems that R. Joshua b. Qorḥa and the anonymous Tanna of the Tosefta were also acquainted with it (only they tempered it), just as we find other testimonies to the Sages' familiarity with the myth of the Serpent-Satan-Samma'el, as it appears in the apocryphal literature. In the Slavonic *Enoch*[40] there stands at the head of the Watchers, who defected from the Lord, their 'chieftain' Satanail, and 'upon fleeing from heaven he became Satan'.[41]

But little is left of the original rebellious character of Satanail in Rabbinic literature. In a Baraita the role of Satan is defined thus: 'He goes down to earth and incites, he ascends to heaven and arraigns, and he has permission to speak. From this we learn that permission has been given to Satan to arraign.'[42] In addition to his task as inciter in the form of the serpent, he is also the accuser, as he appears in the prologue of the Book of Job. Influenced by the account in Job, R. Joḥanan makes the Almighty, so to speak, the object of the incitement and declares: 'Were it not written in Scripture, it would be inconceivable to say it — He was like a man who is incited and falls a prey to the incitement.' And even Resh Laqish, who identifies Satan with the evil inclination in man,[43] does not deprive him at the same time of the role of Satan-Accuser or that of the Angel of Death.[44] However, no distinction is drawn in the various sources between these functions; thus even Samma'el sometimes appears also as the inciting evil inclination.[45] But Samma'el's main influence is felt in the struggles against the supremacy of man, and therein he retains his rebellious character. Only the name Samma'el is not preserved in all the sources; at times his place is taken by Satan, without further qualification, or by another angel. The verse 'And there wrestled a man with him' (Genesis xxxii 25) was explained by R. Ḥama b. R. Ḥanina thus: 'It was the Guardian Angel of Esau; it was to him that he [Jacob] said "I have seen thy face, as one seeth the face of God, and thou wast pleased with me" (Genesis xxx 10). It is like the case of an athlete who was standing and wrestling with the king's son; on looking up and seeing the king standing over him, he allowed himself to be vanquished [literally 'trodden down'] by him [the son]' (*Genesis Rabba* lxxvii 3, p. 912). Nor is it surprising that Esau's Guardian Angel is identified in a later source with Samma'el;[46] especially as there were Midrashim that equated the man who wrestled with Jacob actually with Michael, the Guardian Angel of Israel,[47] and this identification also finds support in ancient sources.[48] But it seems that these, too, were preceded by a source that considered the man to be God Himself. Traces of this mythological Midrash are to be found in early and in late Midrashim. Thus it is stated in *Genesis Rabba* (lxxvii, 3, p. 921): ' "For thou hast striven with God and with men"... with celestial beings, that is, an angel. R. Ḥama b. R. Ḥanina said: It was the Guardian Angel of Esau... Another explanation is: "For thou hast striven with God" — thou art he whose image is engraven on high.' From the same source undoubtedly emanates also the daring homily on Genesis xxxiii 20: ' "And he erected there an altar, and called it

El-elohe-Israel." He said to Him: Thou art God among the celestial beings; I am god among the earthly inhabitants.' To this homily R. Simeon b. Laqish reacted sharply: 'Even the superintendent of the Synagogue does not assume authority unto himself, but you have taken authority unto yourself! Tomorrow your daughter will go out and be raped; this is the meaning of the verse "And Dinah... went out".'[49] Obviously the identification of the angel with Michael, the Guardian Angel of Israel, is an attempt to moderate this homily, while the exposition of R. Ḥama b. R. Ḥanina, like the comments of Resh Laqish, is an expression of opposition. The Guardian Angel of Edom — Samma'el — serves to oust here a grosser myth. We possess clear evidence that similar traditions were known in Jewish circles before the time of R. Ḥama b. R. Ḥanina and Resh Laqish. Origen cites from a work, current among the Jews under the title 'The Prayer of Joseph': 'Jacob, however, said: I am called Jacob by men, but my name is Israel, for by God I am called Israel, that is, a man that sees God (Yśr-'el), for I, behold I am the first-born of all the prophets who were created by God.' He adds: 'I came from across the River [Euphrates] in Syria, and behold the angel of the Lord Uriel appeared and said that I had come down and dwelt among the children of men, and therefore I was called Jacob. He was envious of me, and fought and wrestled with me, saying *that his name was above my name*, and above that of the angel appointed over all. And I told him his name and his place among the sons of God: Art thou not Uriel, the eighth after me, whereas I, behold I am Israel, the captain of the angels of the hosts of the Lord and the captain of the myriads of the sons of God? Am I not Israel, the first minister before the Lord (ὁ ἐν προσώπῳ θεοῦ λειτουργός πρῶτος ἐν ὀνόματι ἀσβέστῳ), and I called my God by a name that is inerasable.'[50]

Against this myth is directed the homily attributed to R. Ḥiyya Rabba or to R. Yannai about the angels who found Jacob, whose image is engraven on high, asleep and they began to 'sport with him [*aliter*: 'dance round him'], to leap on him [or: 'round him'], to scoff at him [or: 'encompass him']' (*Genesis Rabba* lxviii, 12, p. 788). The angels who 'discovered the secret of the Holy One, blessed be He' were demoted in Jacob's dream by the Sages who expounded the subject. Bar Qappara, R. Joshua b. Levi and the Rabbis interpreted his dream as referring to the altar, to Mount Sinai, and to the Exiles (*ibid.*, pp. 781–785). R. Joḥanan completely nullified the dream and taught ' "And Jacob awaked out of his sleep [משנתו *mi-shĕnātô*]", that is, from his study [ממשנתו *mi-mishnātô*]'.[51] R. Joḥanan's disciple, R. Abbahu, commented on the words ' "And he dreamed": dreams neither make nor mar' (*Genesis Rabba*, *ibid.*, p. 784). The Scripture 'And, behold, the Lord stood beside him' alone remains unaffected, and R. Abbahu himself drew attention to the difference between this verse and that which precedes it: ' "And, behold, the Lord stood beside him" (Genesis xxviii 13). What is stated earlier? — "And behold the angels of God ascending and descending on it" (*ibid.* v. 12). R. Abbahu said: This is like a prince who was sleeping in his cradle and flies were resting on him; but as soon as his nurse came, she bent over him and suckled him and the flies flew away from him. Even so (it was with Jacob): at first (we read) "And behold the angels of God ascending and descending on it", but as soon as the Holy One, blessed be He, appeared, they fled from him!' In the opinion of R. Joḥanan and R. Abbahu, the Almighty spoke with Jacob when he was awake, and this view also underlies apparently the homily of R. Ḥama bar Ḥanina: ' "Iron alone with [usually rendered 'sharpeneth'] iron; so a man is alone with the presence [literally, 'countenance'] of his friend" (Proverbs xxvii 17) ...as soon as our father Jacob arose, "a man alone with the presence of his Friend" — the Shekhina communed with him alone!'[52] It is also R. Ḥama b. R. Ḥanina who said that the angel who wrestled with Jacob 'was the Guardian Angel of Esau' (above, p. 170).

The introduction of Samma'el into the episode of Jacob bears a secondary character, and despite the struggle with the celestial beings, which is expressly mentioned in the Bible, we have seen that this story took the place of another ancient motif, and is in this respect different from the account of Satan-Samma'el in the episode of Adam.

Akin to it is the story of the passing of Moses. The primary motif, that it was not the Angel of Death who took his soul, is found in the Sifre:[53] 'At that moment, the Holy One, blessed be He, said to the Angel of Death: "Go, bring me Moses' soul." So he went and stood before him (Moses). Said Moses to him: "Where I dwell you are not allowed to stand, yet you say to me 'surrender your soul'!" Thereupon he (Moses) rebuked him (the Angel of Death) and he went forth reprimanded. The Angel of Death accordingly went and reported Moses' answer to the Almighty. The Omnipresent then said (again) to the Angel of Death: "Go and bring me his soul...".' The Angel of Death searched high and low for Moses but could not find him, until the mountains and hills[54] revealed to him 'that God had concealed him for life in the world to come.' The version given here, according to which the Angel of Death is deceived, appears to be an abridgement of a detailed narrative, and we actually possess such a narrative, although it is clear that it is not the source of the *Sifre*. To a certain extent it seems like the continuation of the angels' arraignment of the giving of the Torah to Moses, only the roles are changed. Whereas when Moses ascended to heaven, he struggled with angels and Seraphim who opposed him and sought to consume and destroy him, and the Holy One, blessed be He, shielded and sheltered him from them,[55] in the Midrash before us Moses himself is refractory, and Samma'el, as an angel, becomes a messenger. The version of the story that I cite well reflects the apocalyptic orientation in the description of the heavenly sphere, which, being powerful and concrete, also became popular. Hence I reproduce it in full; it will also serve as a frame of reference for pointing up the opposite trend, which is interpretative and speculative.

In this Midrash[56] it is stated:

> When Moses saw that his decree was sealed, he arose and drew a small circle and sat within it, saying: I shall not move from here until Thou dost abrogate that decree. What did Moses do at that time? He put on sackcloth and wrapped himself in sackcloth and rolled himself in the dust, and stood praying and supplicating before the Holy One, blessed be He, until heaven and earth and the natural order of the universe were in commotion, and they said 'Has the time come when the Holy One, blessed be He, wills (to destroy the world)?' Thereupon a Heavenly Voice went forth and declared: 'The time when the Holy One, blessed be He, wills the destruction of the world has not yet arrived,[57] only He holds in His hand the soul of every living thing, and the spirit of all the flesh of man [usually rendered: "the breath of all mankind"]', and 'man' refers to Moses, as it is said 'And the

man Moses was very meek'. What did the Holy One, blessed be He, do at that time? He proclaimed in every gate, and in every heaven, and in all the gates of every court of justice, that Moses' prayer should not be accepted, or brought before Him, because the Divine decree concerning him had been sealed. Now the angel appointed to make proclamations is called Akhraziel. At that moment the Holy One, blessed be He, called urgently and said to the Ministering Angels: Arise and lock the gate of every heaven. Until the voice of prayer prevailed and rose upward, seeking to ascend to heaven on account of Moses' prayer, which was like a sword, and rent and cut without cessation, for his prayer was like the Ineffable Name, which he had learnt from Zagza'el, his teacher, the scribe of all the heavenly beings.[58] Of this (moment) it is said 'and I heard behind me the voice of a great רעש *ra'ash*'; now *ra'ash* connotes commotion, and 'great' alludes to Moses, as it is said 'Moreover the man Moses was (very) great'. What is meant by 'Blessed be the glory of the Lord from His place'? When the Wheels of the Chariot and the flaming Seraphim[59] perceived that the Holy One, blessed be He, said 'Do not accept the prayer of Moses' and He showed no favouritism and did not grant him life and did not bring him into the Land, they cried 'Blessed be the glory of the Lord from His place', for He shows no favouritism either to small or great. And how do we know that Moses prayed 515 times? For it is stated 'And I besought [ואתחנן *wā-'etḥannān*] the Lord', and the numerical value of *wā-etḥannan* amounts to this. At that time Moses said before the Holy One, blessed be He: 'Sovereign of the universe, Thou knowest full well the toil and travail and distress that I endured on their [Israel's] account in connection with the precepts, until I established Torah and precepts among them. I thought that just as I had witnessed their distress so I should behold their prosperity. But now that the time of Israel's prosperity has come, Thou dost say to me "Thou shalt not go over this Jordan!" Thus, Thou dost falsify Thy Torah, for it is written "In the same day thou shalt give him his hire". Is this the recompense for the forty years that I toiled until they became a holy people? as it is said: "but Judah still ruled with God and was faithful to the

Holy One" (Hosea xii 1).' The angel Samma'el, the head of the demons [literally, 'satans'], was waiting every moment for Moses' death, saying: 'When will the moment come when Moses will die, when I shall go down and take Moses' soul from him?' Of him David said 'The wicked watcheth the righteous, and seeketh to slay him' (Psalms xxxvii 32). Among all the demons there is none so wicked as Samma'el, and among all the prophets there is none so righteous as Moses... Thus, the wicked Samma'el waited for the soul of Moses, saying: When shall Michael weep and I fill my mouth with laughter... At one time Moses said before God: 'Sovereign of the universe, if Thou wilt not permit me to enter the Land of Israel, let me be like the beasts of the field, which eat grass and drink water, but see the world; let me be even as one of them.' Said (God) to him: 'Enough unto you!' Then (Moses) said to Him: 'Sovereign of the universe, if not, let me be in this world like a bird, which flies in the air in all directions and daily gathers its food, and in the evening returns to its nest; let me be even as one of them.' Said (God) unto him: 'Enough unto you!' (Again Moses) said to Him [God]: 'Sovereign of the universe, leave one of my eyes beneath the door, and let the door be placed upon it three times a year, so that I may live and not die.' (God) answered him: 'Enough!'[60] When Moses saw that no creature could deliver him from death... What did Moses do? He took the scroll and wrote thereon the Ineffable Name, and before he had completed writing the Book of the Song the moment arrived for Moses to die. At that moment the Holy One, blessed be He, said to Gabriel: 'Go and fetch Moses' soul.' Said he before Him: 'Sovereign of the universe, he who is equal to the sixty myriads (of Israel) — how can I see him die? And he who possesses these things — how can I vent my anger upon him?' Then He said to Michael: 'Go and fetch Moses' soul.' Said he before God: 'I was the teacher and he was my disciple — how can I see him die?' Thereafter He said to Samma'el: 'Go and fetch Moses' soul'. Forthwith he donned his anger, and girded on his sword, and wrapped himself in ruthlessness, and went to meet Moses. When, however, Samma'el saw him sitting and writing the Ineffable Name, and the radiance of his countenance was like that of the sun, and he resembled an angel of the Lord of hosts, he was afraid of Moses. He thought: Verily, the angels are not able to take Moses' soul...[61] and Samma'el could not open his mouth to speak to Moses until Moses said to him: ' "There is no peace" saith the Lord "concerning the wicked"; what are you doing here?' He replied: 'I have come to take your soul.' Said (Moses) to him: 'Who sent you?' He replied: 'He that created the whole world.' Said (Moses) to him: 'you shall not take my soul...[62] Begone from me!...' Samma'el immediately returned and reported to the Almighty. Said the Holy One, blessed be He, to him: 'Go and fetch Moses' soul.' Forthwith he drew his sword from its scabbard and made ready to attack Moses. At once Moses became wroth with him and took in his hand the staff of God on which was engraved the Ineffable Name and smote Samma'el with it with all his might, until he fled before him, and (Moses) pursued him with the Ineffable Name and took a ray from between his eyes and blinded his eyes.[63] Thus far success attended Moses. A moment later a Heavenly Voice came forth and said: 'The moment of your death has at last arrived.' Said Moses before the Holy One, blessed be He: 'Sovereign of the universe, remember unto me the day when Thou didst reveal Thyself unto me in the thorn bush... I beg of Thee, deliver me not into the hand of the Angel of Death.' A Heavenly Voice went forth and declared unto him: 'Fear not, I Myself shall attend to you and to your burial.'[64] At that moment Moses arose and sanctified himself like the Seraphim, and the Holy One, blessed be He, descended from the highest heavens of the heavens to take away the soul of Moses, and the three Ministering Angels — Michael, Gabriel and Zagza'el — with him...' After they had attended to his body, 'the Holy One, blessed be He, called upon the soul to leave his body'. But she [the soul] still refused and countered with the question: 'Is there a purer body than that of Moses?' When the Holy One, blessed be He, said to the soul 'Go forth, tarry no more, and I shall raise you up to the highest heavens of the heavens, and cause you to dwell beneath the Throne of My Glory beside the Cherubim and Seraphim and Legions', she said before Him: 'Sovereign of the universe, from beside Thy Shekhina on high two angels, 'Azza and 'Azza'el, descended and lusted for the daughters of the earth, and they corrupted their way upon earth, until Thou didst suspend them between earth and heaven. But the son of Amram, from the day that Thou didst reveal Thyself to him in the thorn bush, did not visit his wife, as it is said "And Miriam and Aaron spoke against Moses". I beg of Thee, let me stay in Moses' body.' At that moment, the Holy One, blessed be He, sought out and took his soul with a kiss.

To the author of this Midrash the world of the angels was palpable and real, in whose lore and history he was well versed. There were even Tannaim and Amoraim with whom angels walked and in whose name they transmitted Halakhic and Haggadic dicta.[65] The last motif — that of the angels 'Azza and 'Azza'el — also reveals the nature of the sources with which the author of our Midrash was familiar.[66] He lived in the world of the apocalypse, but at the same time he exercised his imagination in the service of faith, holding that the world of the Torah conquers and subdues the world of the angels of the Most High. There is a difference between the two parts of the drama 'Moses and the Heavenly Retinue': While in the first part — 'Moses Ascends on High' — he does indeed defeat the angels, and according to one version brings about their surrender and subjugation, nevertheless he is in need of the help of the Holy One, blessed be He, in order to withstand the angels on high and to be protected from 'being harmed by them'. In the second part, on the other hand — 'The Death of Moses' — all the angels, including the Angel of Death, Samma'el, are afraid of him, and are unable to prevail against him, and only the Holy One, blessed be He, treasures his soul. Moses' power derives from the Torah, with which he occupied himself. The high status of this Torah is recognized even by those circles whose words are steeped in vision and fantasy, and here and there we also find an echo[67] of the activity of the Sages, who made the 'Heavenly Retinue' in the image, as it were, of the 'Earthly Retinue', transferring their academies and law courts to the celestial sphere.

The use of the word *familia* ['Retinue'] to denote the angels found in the entourage of God is peculiar to the Rabbis, and has no parallel in the Hellenistic or Christian literature.[68] The Tanna Abba Saul, the first who is known to have used this loan-word, likens Israel to the retinue of a king, and thus expounds the verse ' "ye shall be holy."... the retinue of the King. And what must they do? Do as the King does.'[69] But already in the Midrash of the Tannaim the discrepancy between Job xxv 3 'Is there any number of His armies' and Daniel vii 10 'Thousand thousands ministered unto Him...' is resolved by the conjecture 'The Heavenly Retinue was, as it were, diminished'.[70] The fact that God is the Judge of the whole earth and passes judgement on His creatures easily led to His *familia* being pictured as a law-court. Although the Holy One, blessed be He, is called in Tannaitic literature 'Bet Din' ['Law-Court'],[71] yet the actual use of the term Bet Din in a context in which the Ministering Angels are to be found, whose existence no one doubted — either among the Sages or in the academies of the various schools of philosophers — opened the way to their being included in this Bet Din. R. Eleazar said 'Wherever there is no judgement there is judgement', and his words were interpreted to mean 'If justice is executed on earth, judgement is not executed in heaven; but if judgement is not carried out on earth, judgement is carried out in heaven.' There is also the following version: 'When the Bet Din execute judgement... and when the Bet Din do not execute judgement... There is judgement in heaven, and the Holy One, blessed be He, sits over them in judgement and exacts from them [i.e. punishes them].'[72] Although R. Ishmael b. R. Jose still emphasizes in his admonition 'Judge not alone, for none may judge alone save One' (*M. 'Avot* iv, 5), yet R. Akiba is already concerned to stress not the actual fact that God judges alone, but that His judgement is righteous and not arbitrary. When Pappos 'expounded the verse "But He is at one with Himself and who can turn Him? And what His soul desireth, even that He doeth" (Job xxiii 13) — He judges all mankind alone and there is none to reply to His words, R. Akiba said to him: "Enough, Pappos!" Rabbi Pappos countered: "And how do you explain the words 'But He is at one with Himself and who can turn Him'?" Said (R. Akiba) to him: "We do not argue against Him who spoke and the world came into being; but He judges all in truth and all with justice." '[73] R. Simeon b. Yoḥai, R. Akiba's disciple, did not refrain from associating the heavenly Bet Din with the making of man, in order to emphasize how perfect was the work of man's creation and to refute the arguments of the Gnostics. He did not hesitate to expound 'It is not written here "whom He has already made" but "whom they have already made". As it were, the King of the kings of kings, blessed be He, and his Bet Din voted for each part of you and set you up on your proper basis (as it is written) "Hath He not made thee and established thee?" (Deuteronomy xxxii 6).'[74] The earliest Amoraim — possibly also with the aim of discouraging even experts from judging alone[75] — also attributed to the Holy One, blessed be He, irreproachable judicial procedure. Thus we find 'R. Joḥanan said: The Holy One, blessed be He, never does aught in His world without first consulting the Bet Din on high. What is the reason? "And the word was true, even a great host" (Daniel x 1) — when is the seal of the Holy One, blessed be He, true? When He consults the Bet Din on high.'[76] In a parallel source we find in R. Joḥanan's dictum the expression 'the Heavenly Retinue [פמליה שלמעלא *pamalyā shĕlĕma'ălā*]'.[77] R. Eleazar, the colleague and disciple of R. Joḥanan, formulated the rule 'wherever it is stated "the Lord God", the reference is to Him and His Bet Din. The Scriptural determinant is: 'And the Lord hath spoken evil concerning thee' (I Kings xxii 23).[78] R. Eleazar apparently also used the fact of the heavenly Bet Din's existence in order to dissociate evil from the Holy One, blessed be He — a trend that we find clearly expressed in his teaching.[79] In this spirit, about two generations later, R. Judah b. Pazzi formulated the statement 'Even the Holy One, blessed be He, does not judge alone, as it is said "And all the host of heaven standing by Him on His right and on His left" — these arguing in favour and the others in condemnation. But although He does not judge alone, He seals alone ...'[80] The Amora R. Judan b. Polia gave the following interpretation to the words of Job (i 21): ' "The Lord gave and the Lord hath taken away..." — when He gave, He consulted no creature, but when He took away He consulted His Bet Din.'[81] The Heavenly Court (*familia*) operates only as God's agents, and R. Joḥanan indeed explained the word מכשפין *mĕkhashshĕfîn* ['sorcerers'] to mean 'they contradict [מכחישין *makhḥîshîn*] the Heavenly Court'.[82] But in the Heavenly Court, as in the earthly Bet Din, there are differences of opinion. The Palestinian Amora R. Alexandri, who was a contemporary of R. Joḥanan, and transmitted many dicta in the name of R. Joshua b.

Levi,[83] said: 'Whoever occupies himself with the Torah for its own sake makes peace in the Heavenly Court and in the Earthly Court, as it is said "Or else let him take hold of My strength, that he may make peace with Me; yea let him make peace with Me" (Isaiah xxvii 5).'[84] R. Safra said after his prayer: 'May it be Thy will, O Lord our God, to make peace in the heavenly *familia* and in the earthly *familia* and among the disciples who occupy themselves with Thy Torah, whether for its own sake or not; and may it be Thy will that all who occupy themselves (with the Torah) not for its own sake may eventually do so for its sake.'[85] R. Alexandri made peace in the heavenly *familia* depend on study of the Torah in the earthly *familia*, and he followed in the footsteps of his teacher R. Joshua b. Levi, who was able to report that, in respect of three matters, 'the earthly Bet Din retracted and the heavenly Bet Din concurred with them'.[86] Now while R. Joshua b. Levi spoke of past acts, the celestial concurrence in which was deduced from verses, his great contemporaries made similar observations about contemporary matters. In the name of R. Ḥama b. R. Ḥanina — or R. Hoshaiah — it is stated: 'In human procedure, when the governor announces that the court will sit today and the bandit says the court must sit tomorrow, who is obeyed? Is it not the governor? But in the case of the Holy One, blessed be He, it is not so. If the Bet Din declare that today is New Year, the Holy One, blessed be He, tells the Ministering Angels: "Set-up the platform [for holding court], let the prosecuting and defending counsel take their stand, for My children have announced that today is New Year." But if the Bet Din reconsidered the matter and decided to postpone it to the following day, the Holy One, blessed be He, says to the Ministering Angels: "Remove the platform, let the prosecuting and defending counsel leave, for My children have decided (upon reconsideration) to postpone it [the New Year] till tomorrow."'[87] A statement that appears to contradict this view is nevertheless explained in conformity with it. It is taught in the Mishna 'R. Eleazar b. R. Zadok said, if it [the new moon] was not seen at its proper time, it is not sanctified because it has already been sanctified by heaven.' In regard to this R. Ba b. R. Zavda said in the name of Rav: 'The reason for R. Eleazar b. R. Zadok's ruling is that since the Bet Din on high see that the Bet Din below are not sanctifying it [the new moon], they sanctify it.'[88] In place of 'Heaven'[89] we have here 'the Bet Din on high'. The Amora R. Abbahu introduces the motif of the envy of the angels,[90] when they see that the Holy One, blessed be He, prefers the Bet Din below. He explains the verse "Happy is the people that know the joyful shout; they walk, O Lord, in the light of Thy countenance" (Psalms lxxxix 16 [15]) with reference to the five elders, when they enter to intercalate the year. What does the Holy One, blessed be He, do? He leaves His counsellors (σύγκλητοι) and descends and causes His Shekhina to dwell below. The Ministering Angels declare: 'Behold, it is God, it is God! Behold, it is the Almighty, it is the Almighty! Behold, it is Truth, it is Truth! Should He of whom it is written "A God dreaded in the great council of the Holy ones, and feared of all of them that are round about Him" (Psalms *ibid.* v. 8 [7]) leave His counsellors and descend and cause His Shekhina to dwell with the inhabitants of the world below? Why then was all this done? — In case they erred, the Holy One, blessed be He, would illuminate the Halakha for them. This is the meaning of the verse "They walk, O Lord, in the light of Thy countenance.'[91] The role of the heavenly Bet Din is made subsidiary to that on earth, and the cultivation of the Halakha in the academy of heaven is like that in the earthly academy, but the final decision is in the hands of the latter.[92] The principle of the supremacy of the study of the Torah and the freedom the Rabbis took for themselves in its study made the heavenly *familia* subject thereto. Even one of the explicit and central tasks assigned by the Bible to the angels — namely, the uttering of song and praise — was greatly restricted by the increased importance given to the prayers and praises of Israel, to the point where the Sages said that 'The Ministering Angels on high utter no song until Israel do so below'.[93] Nay more, particularly in connection with this function there are to be found Baraitot and dicta of the last of the Tannaim and the first of the Amoraim which completely deny the angels' continued existence. R. Samuel bar Naḥman said in the name of R. Joḥanan: 'No company of angels utters praise more than once.' R. Ḥelbo explains his words to mean 'Every day the Holy One, blessed be He, creates new angels, who sing a new song and depart.'[94] Samuel transmitted to R. Ḥiyya, the son of Rav, the following saying of his father: 'Every day the Ministering Angels are created from the River of Fire [נהר דינור *Nĕhar Dînûr*] and they utter song and cease to exist.' R. Samuel bar Naḥman, on the other hand, said in the name of R. Jonathan: 'From every utterance that proceeds from the mouth of the Holy One, blessed be He, an angel is created.'[95] According to one account R. Joshua b. Hannaniah gave the Emperor Hadrian an answer similar to the view held by Rav.[96] Indeed, there is external evidence of the antiquity of this conception. Justin Martyr, the younger contemporary of R. Joshua, cites the view that 'the Father, if He so wills, causes a force to manifest itself, and, if He so wills, He brings about its extinction, and in this way — they teach — the angels, too, are created.' But he adds: 'There are angels who exist for ever, without returning to the source whence they came into existence.'[97] Likewise the Amora R. Ḥelbo excluded from the community of angels 'Michael and Gabriel; it is they who are the Princes of heaven. All of them [i.e. the angels] are replaced, but they are not replaced'. All these dicta and discussions are not different from the formulations of prayers, which have incorporated verses that speak of the praise and glory offered up by the angels, Serafim and Ofannim. It appears that in the sphere of the popular religion the worshippers were not content merely to mention the names of angels in hymns and praises, but did so also in prayers and supplications for the fulfilment of human needs, even of a very material nature. In condemnation of the worship of angels a Baraita teaches: 'If one slaughters... to Michael, the Prince of the Great Host... it is as flesh offered to idols.'[98] The following teaching of the Amora R. Judan is directed against prayers recited to angels: 'If a human being has a patron, then if he finds himself in trouble he does not enter his house suddenly, but he comes and stands at his patron's door and calls his slave or a member of his household, and he says: So-and-so is standing at the door of your court. Now he (the patron) may or may not invite him in. But the Holy One, blessed be He, is not so. If trouble comes upon a person, let him not cry either to Michael or to Gabriel, but let him cry unto Me, and I shall answer him forthwith. This is the meaning of the verse: "whoever shall call on the name of the Lord shall be delivered".'[99] Still stronger opposition than that evoked by prayer to, and worship of, the angels was aroused by the views that made the angels partners in the creation of the world; and, needless to say, the tradition that the whole world was created by angels, inculcated by various Gnostic doctrines,[1] appeared even to apocalyptic circles (which assigned a considerable role to Princes, and angels, and even to angels of destruction, and angels of Satan, Belial and *Masṭēmā* [hatred]) to be in conflict with Israel's Torah. But we shall discuss these problems in the chapters devoted to the creation of the world and of man.

CHAPTER IX

'HE WHO SPOKE AND THE WORLD CAME INTO BEING'

From the Bible the Sages received the belief in God as the Sole and Omnipotent Creator of the world. But the story of creation in the Book of Genesis, with its obscurities and discrepancies, presented them with problems and difficulties. There were still current among the people legends that resembled the remnants of the mythical epics that are to be found in the Scriptures themselves.[1] Ideas and motifs borrowed from the cosmogonic teachings of the Persians, Greeks and Gnostic sects infiltrated into the circles that came in contact with them. All these were sufficient to make the study of the 'Work of Creation' an esoteric doctrine, which can be transmitted only to individuals. Indeed, we learn in the Mishna (*M. Ḥagiga* ii, 1) that the 'Work of Creation' may not be expounded before two. Only the Palestinian Talmud states that this Mishna 'is by R. Akiba, but according to R. Ishmael we may expound (in the presence of two)'.[2] The significance of this dispute is to be explained in the light of another difference of opinion between these Sages regarding the interpretation of the first verse of Genesis: '[את השמים ואת הארץ *'et ha-shāmayim wĕ-'et hā-'areṣ* — 'the heaven and the earth'] — R. Ishmael asked R. Akiba a question: Seeing that you have studied twenty-two years under Nahum of Gimzo, (who taught that) אך *'akh* ['but'] and רק *raq* ['only'] are limitations of the text, and את *'et* and גם *gam*, are amplifications, how do you explain *'et* of this verse? He replied: Had Scripture written בראשית ברא אלהים שמים וארץ *bĕ-rēshît bārā' 'Ĕlōhîm shāmāyim wā-'āreṣ* ['In the beginning God heaven and earth created'], we might have thought that heaven and earth were also deities. Said [R. Ishmael] to him: "For it is no vain thing for you" (Deuteronomy xxxii 47), and if it be vain — it is due to you [literally 'from you', rendered above 'for you'], because you do not know how to expound the Scripture. This is the meaning: את השמים *'et ha-shāmayim* comes to include the sun and the moon, the stars and the planets; and ואת הארץ *wĕ-'et ha-'āreṣ* comes to include trees and herbage and the Garden of Eden.'[3] R. Ishmael asked R. Akiba the meaning of the verse according to the latter's method of exegesis, namely that of Nahum of Gimzo, who interpreted every את *'et*. But R. Akiba's reply sought to controvert a Gnostic explanation.[4] Thus, the particles את *'et* do not serve to amplify but to separate between God and heaven and earth, and to teach us that the last two are not creators but created things, and that the Holy One, blessed be He, had no partners in the work of creation. An exposition of this kind was of interest only to individuals that engaged in disputation with sectarians and were familiar with their views. It was out of place to give this exposition in public. R. Ishmael, who according to his exegetical method regarded את *'et* in the verse as part of its grammatical structure,[5] argues, contrary to the opinion of R. Akiba, that those who expound the particle את *'et* can find an amplification in this verse, too, namely that heaven and earth were created already on the first day together with all their host. This exposition could be given in public. Exegetical explanations of this kind were taught in the School of R. Ishmael, and possibly it was from this source that there emanated the dispute between the School of Shammai and the School of Hillel concerning the order in which heaven and earth were created: 'The School of Shammai said: The heavens were created first; the School of Hillel said: The earth was created first.' The School of Shammai and the School of Hillel seek to reconcile the contradiction between the verse 'In the beginning God created the heaven and the earth' and the verse 'in the day that the Lord God made earth and heaven.' The School of Shammai regard the verse 'The heaven is My throne, and the earth is My footstool' (Isaiah lxvi 1) as a third passage that harmonizes the first two, and they illustrate their viewpoint with an example: 'It is like the case of a king, who made a throne for himself and thereafter the footstool (ὑποπόδιον).' The School of Hillel, on the other hand, gave as an example 'The case of a king who built a palace — after building the lower floor, he builds the upper storey'[6] and their harmonizing verse was apparently 'Yea, My hand hath laid the foundation of the earth, and My right hand hath spread out the heavens' (Isaiah xlviii 13).[7] This dispute also falls within the category of explicatory expositions that reconcile conflicting verses by employing illustrations that are intended to make the matter comprehensible to simple folk. Another note is struck by R. Simeon b. Yoḥai, the disciple of R. Akiba. He reacts to this debate as follows: 'I am surprised that the Fathers of the world should differ on this subject; they were both created together like a pot and its lid, (as it is written) "when I call unto them, they stand up together" (Isaiah *ibid.*). He, too, uses an illustration and cites a verse as proof of his interpretation. But his illustrative example is not related to the Scriptural text, which is merely the conclusion of the passage in which the School of Hillel found support for their views. R. Simeon limits the duration of the work of creation: heaven and earth were not created one after the other but simultaneously — 'they are equal'.[8] Primacy is given not to the verses but to knowledge.[9]

R. Simeon b. Yoḥai reacts, with the same expression of surprise, to another dispute between the School of Shammai and the School of Hillel on the subject of creation. 'There is a difference of opinion between the School of Shammai and the School of Hillel. The School of Shammai say: The plan was formulated during the night, and the work was carried out by day. The School of Hillel said: Both the planning and the execution took place during the day. Said R. Simeon b. Yoḥai, I am surprised that the Fathers of the world, the School of Shammai and the School of Hillel, should differ about the creation of heaven and earth. The planning took place both by day and by night, and the execution was carried out at sunset.'[10] The dispute between the School of Shammai and the School of Hillel is not specially based on Scriptural exposition, but is linked to the verse 'These are the generations of the heaven and of the earth when they were created, in the day that the Lord God made earth and heaven' (Genesis ii 4). According to the School of Shammai the designing of creation took place at night, and the implementation during the day. According to the School of Hillel both of them occurred in the day time. It is obvious that in our case it was not the interpretation of the verse that led to the distinction between thought and act, since there is no basis for it in the Biblical text. On the contrary, it appears that the concept that the plan of creation preceded the execution was used to explain the verse: since the expression 'when they were created' comes before 'in the day', the School of Shammai posit that the planning was in the night, while the School of Hillel combine the two. R. Simeon b. Yoḥai accords primacy to the thought, declaring that it took place both by day and by night, while the act was restricted to sunset. In the Septuagint verses ii 4–5 are linked together. The words 'in the day that the Lord God made' are related also to 'no shrub of the field' and to 'no herb of the field'. On the basis of this translation, Philo asks 'What is the meaning of the words "God made every shrub of the field before it was upon the earth and every herb of the field before it had sprung up"? These words contain a reference to the Incorporeal Ideas, for the expression "before it was" alludes to the perfection of every shrub and herb, of the plants and trees. Since Scripture states that, before they had sprung upon the earth, He had made shrubs and herbs and other things, it is evident that He had formed Incorporeal Ideas.'[11] It might be argued that the dicta of the School of Shammai and the School of Hillel were intended to solve the same difficulty in the verses as that noted by Philo, but just as Philo's concept of the 'Ideas' was already to hand for him, so, too, the concept of the creation in thought was already in the possession of the School of Shammai and the School of Hillel, only the two are not to be identified, and there can be no question of attributing to the Schools of Shammai and Hillel knowledge of the doctrine of Ideas. The similes, by which they likened the creation of the world to the erection of a house and the making of a throne, brought in their train the premise of planning in thought. Philo also uses the illustration of a king who wishes to build a city and invites an architect who designs its buildings.[12] It is quite possible that such illustrations were employed by preachers both in the Land of Israel and in Alexandria even before the time of Philo and the disciples of the Schools of Shammai and Hillel; they actually have a basis in the metaphorical expressions of the Bible, only Philo introduces the simile to explain that the world of Ideas does not exist in a given 'place'. R. Simeon b. Yoḥai by his expression of surprise and his reply makes God's way of creating the world far different from man's method of construction, and he restricts the entire implementation to sunset alone. The dating of the exposition concerning the 'Work of Creation' to the time of the disciples of Hillel and Shammai accords well with the Haggada about Alexander the Great and the Sages of the South, according to which Alexander asked the Sages of the South ' "Were the heavens or the earth created first?" They answered: "The heavens were created first, as it is stated in Scripture 'In the beginning God created the heaven and the earth.' " He (then) asked them: "Was the light or the darkness created first?" They replied: "It is an insoluble question." '[13] To the first question the answer of the Sages of the South was in agreement with the view held by the School of Shammai, and in truth we know that 'There were Edomite disciples in the School of Shammai', Edomite signifying 'southerner'.[14] To the second question, the speculations in regard to which, as we shall see later, exercised the Sages of the subsequent generations to no small extent, they replied that there was no solution. Since nothing is stated in the story of Genesis concerning the creation of light, this question is connected with the problem of the existence of eternal matter and opened the way to the belief in two divine powers. The declaration that 'there was no solution' already failed to satisfy Rabban Gamaliel, who gave an unequivocal answer, when he was questioned on a similar subject. 'A certain philosopher once raised the following question before Rabban Gamaliel, saying to him: "Your God was a great Artist, but He had at His disposal fine ingredients to help Him." The (Patriarch) asked him: "What were they?" The philosopher replied: "*Tōhû* and *Bōhû* [usually rendered: 'without form and void'] and darkness and water and wind and deeps." Said Rabban Gamaliel to him: "Perish the thought! creation is stated in respect of all of them". '[15] In this reply there is a clear rejection of the conception of the creation of the world out of uncreated matter. We do not know who the philosopher was. However, he not only maintains the doctrine of eternal matter,[16] but even attempts to find support for it in the Bible; hence a Jewish sectarian is probably referred to.

Rabban Gamaliel's reply and likewise R. Akiba's homily on the meaning of את *'et* in the first verse of Genesis are clear evidence that these Tannaim were familiar with various doctrines on the subject of the 'Work of Creation'. Despite all the caution that the Rabbis exercised by transmitting their words to individuals and their avoidance of expounding these problems in public, it was impossible to prevent some traces of the views and concepts that they controverted from clinging to themselves, and there were some Sages who did not completely reject the alien views, but sought to harmonize what they absorbed with Biblical teaching. The following story about R. Joshua b. Ḥanania and Ben Zoma sheds light on our subject, if we correctly understand the meaning of its obscurities: 'Once Simeon b. Zoma was standing lost in wonderment. R. Joshua passed by and greeted him once and twice, but Ben Zoma did not answer him. At the third time he replied agitatedly. Said (R. Joshua) to him: "What is the matter Ben Zoma? What preoccupies you [מאיין הרגלים *mē'ayin hā-raglayim*, literally: 'Whence the feet', i.e. 'Whence do you come?']?" (Ben Zoma) replied: "לא מאיין *lō' mē 'ayin* [literally: 'Not from nothing', 'Not from where or whence'], Master." Said (R. Joshua) to him: "I call heaven and earth as my witnesses that I shall not stir from here until you tell me what the trend of your thoughts is." He replied: "I was contemplating the work of creation and (I found that) there is hardly two or three fingers' breadth between the upper and the lower waters. It is not written here 'And the spirit of God was blowing' but 'was hovering' — like a bird flying with fluttering wings, its wings all but touching." R. Joshua turned round and said to his disciples: "Ben Zoma is gone." Before many days were out Ben Zoma departed this world.'[17] An acute and interesting interpretation was recently advanced by S. Lieberman[18] for this obscure and difficult story. In his view, Ben Zoma's reply to R. Joshua's innocent question 'What preoccupies you?' hints that he was occupied with the questions that exercised the Gnostics. Ben Zoma's answer לא מאין *lō' mē'ayin* is explained by Lieberman to mean 'nought that comes from the "where?" '. The Gnostics used to ask 'From where do you come, and whither are you going?' However, they were accustomed to reply 'I have come from the place of light, from the place where the light was created,'[19] while Ben Zoma's answer is more reminiscent of the answers given by Israel's Sages,[20] namely that man originates in a place of darkness, a place of impurity, and proceeds to a place of darkness and impurity. Ben Zoma's reply was orthodox, only it showed that he was preoccupied with the question that constantly engrossed the attention of the sectarians. But according to this explanation we cannot understand R. Joshua's insistence or the transition to the subject of the Work of Creation. It therefore seems that the reply לא מאין *lō' mē'ayin* is already directed to the focal point of the narrative. When R. Joshua turned to Ben Zoma, who was so lost in thought that he did not return his greetings, with the question מאין לאן *mē'ayin lĕ'ān* ['whence — whither?'] or מאין הרגלים *mē'ayin hā-raglayim* [literally: 'Whence the feet'; rendered above: 'What preoccupies you?'], the surprised Ben Zoma understood that the question was directed to the subject of his thought, 'Whence, from what was the world created?' At first he denied that he was engaged in studying this question, and replied 'Not from whence', that is, I am not occupying myself with this question of 'whence?'. Needless to say, this formulation could be interpreted to mean that he wished to say that the world was not created out of nothing [*mē'ayin* may also mean 'ex nihilo'], and hence it is not to be wondered at that R. Joshua repeated his question in the form of an adjuration. Ben Zoma revealed to him the content of his contemplation of the Work of Creation[21], and R. Joshua found it to contain alien doctrine. It is difficult to identify Ben Zoma's account with one of the cosmologies current in the second century, and it is greatly to be doubted if Ben Zoma actually had in mind a definite Gnostic conception.[22] At most we can say that his words contain ingredients of a dualistic myth, which presupposes the existence of eternal matter.[23] The description of the spirit of God as 'all but touching' is in keeping with two other statements of Ben Zoma in which he limits the Divine work in the act of creation and preserves the distance between God and matter. With regard to the verse 'And God made the firmament' (Genesis i 7) it is stated: 'This is one of the Scriptures with which Ben Zoma set the world in commotion... "And He made" — how is this possible! Surely the world was created by a word, (as it is written) "By the word of the Lord were the heavens made; and all the host of them by the breath of His mouth!" (Psalms xxxiii 6).'[24] The commotion caused by Ben Zoma was due to the fact that in this verse 'And it was so' occurs after God's creative act, and not as in the account of the other days, where 'And it was so' appears after the Divine utterance. The wording 'This is one of the Scriptures with which Ben Zoma set the world in commotion' deserves attention. It indicates that many of Ben Zoma's homilies set the world of the Sages astir. At any rate Ben Zoma's portrayal sufficed to produce R. Joshua's reaction. Indeed R. Joshua rejected every interpretation and homily that contained the slightest hint of a dualistic conception, even though they were innocent in their formulation and content. R. Eliezer held that 'Everything existing in the heavens was created from the heavens; everything upon earth was created from the earth.' Contrariwise R. Joshua declared 'Everything in heaven and on earth was created from heaven only.'[25] This sensitivity on the part of R. Joshua is to be explained by the fact of his stay in Alexandria.[26] There he came to know the prevailing philosophical systems, and there too, it appears, he held those debates that are transmitted by the formula: 'Hadrian asked R. Joshua b. Ḥanania'. One of the questions was 'How did the Holy One, blessed be He, create His world?'[27] The answer has not been preserved in its original wording, but in the garb of an Amoraic dictum, which we shall discuss later. At all events it appears that the restrictions imposed upon occupying oneself with the 'Work of Creation' could not stand up to the pressure of questions, whether from within or without. The journeys of the Sages to Egypt, Syria, and Asia Minor, as well as the proliferation of sects in Eretz-Israel, intensified the need to know what answer to give. The circle of those who knew grew larger, and a Sage like Ben Zoma was not inclined to preserve this knowledge as purely esoteric teaching. But in most Tannaitic dicta there is no support to be found for overstepping the bounds of Scriptural expositions, although they considered it right to reply to questions that the earlier authorities refrained from even meditating upon. Whereas the Elders of the South proclaimed that the question 'What was created first, the light or the darkness?' cannot be resolved, we find the disciples of R. Akiba, R. Judah, and R. Nehemiah discussing it and offering solutions according to the method of R. Ishmael, by having recourse to Biblical texts and refraining from speculative and mythological thought. 'R. Judah said: The light was created first. The case may be compared to that of a king who wished to build a palace, but the site was in darkness. What did he do? He kindled lights and a lantern (φανός) in order to know where to lay the foundation (θεμέλιος).

Thus the light was created first. R. Nehemiah said: The world was created first. The case may be compared to a king who built a palace and adorned it with lights.'[28] R. Judah remains consistent in his view that 'The world was created in six days, for in the account of each day it is written "and it was so" '.[29] Hence he says that the light was created first, but — as we may infer from the simile, 'but the site was in darkness' — the darkness was not created, it was there already. In another version the point is more fully explained: '...but the site was in darkness... Even so was it when the Holy One, blessed be He, built the world — it was all in darkness.'[30] On the other hand, R. Nehemiah follows the view of R. Ishmael, who holds that 'The world was created on the first day'; thus there was a single act of creation, and hence the question of precedence does not arise. The creation of the light was only like decorating with lights. R. Judah draws no inference whatsoever from the existence of darkness, nor does he refer to the light as *materia prima*, from which the world was created; he presents it only as the first created entity.[31] To my mind, the Tannaitic dicta contain no trace of any discussion about primeval matter. The dispute of R. Eliezer and R. Joshua, which we cited above, is not concerned with the matter from which the heavenly bodies and the earth were created, but with the place from which they were formed. This is made clear by a parallel Baraita: 'R. Eliezer says: It was created from the middle... R. Joshua states: The world was created from the sides' (*T. B. Yoma* 54b). The world spoken of here is simply the earth. R. Eliezer, who holds that the offspring of the earth were created from the earth, sees this creation as taking place from the middle, from one central point. R. Joshua, on the other hand, in whose opinion even the progeny of the earth were created from heaven, declares: The earth was created from the sides, and not from a central point. Only this interpretation of their dispute enables us to understand the saying of the Sages 'Both were created from Zion', that is, both the issue of heaven and the issue of the earth were created from a central point in the earth — from Zion. According to one version[32] the author of the dictum is actually R. Judah, and the proof of the creation of the world from Zion is to be found in Psalms i 2 ' "Out of Zion, the perfection of beauty, God hath shined forth"... and "shined forth" refers to light.'[33] This means to say that the original creation of light was from Zion. At any rate, the Tannaim do not expressly deal with the question 'Whence was the light created?', just as there is no reference to be found in their teachings to *materia prima*. It is true that in the past century scholars[34] have endeavoured to find a reference to primeval matter in the warning given by R. Akiba upon entering Pardes ['Garden', 'Paradise']: 'When you come to the stones of pure marble, say not "Water, water"!' (*T.B. Ḥagiga* 14b). But this dictum has no connection with the Work of Creation[35]; it is only a warning — as has been shown — to those who speculate on the Chariot.

All that is stated in the name of the Tannaim with reference to the 'Work of Creation' contains nothing that may not 'be expounded'. They do not enquire what was 'before the world was created', nor 'What is above? What is beneath? What was beforetime? What will be hereafter?'[36], a formulation that bespeaks — like the warning of Ecclesiasticus (iii 21–22) 'Seek not (to understand) what is too wonderful for thee, and search not out that which is hid from thee' — the avoidance of mystic speculations. This opposition is not only directed to exposition in public or before disciples, but to any study of the subject, as is stated in the Mishna of *Ḥagiga* (ii, 1): 'Whoever meditates upon four things, it were better for him if he had not come into the world.'[37] This sentence emanates from a different source[38] from that of the first part of this Mishna, which permits exposition before one disciple.

A marked change took place in regard to speculation on the Work of Creation at the close of the Tannaitic period and the beginning of the Amoraic period. In the name of Rav, the foremost of the Babylonian Amoraim, there are transmitted, without any reservation, mythological teachings concerning the creation of the world. Basing himself on Job xxvi 12 'By His power He stilled the sea; by His understanding He smote Rahab', he elaborates the account and declares: 'When the Holy One, blessed be He, wished to create the world, He said to the Prince of the Sea: "Open your mouth and swallow all the waters of the world." He replied: "Sovereign of the universe, suffice it for me that I remain with my own." Thereupon, He struck him with His foot and slew him' (*T.B. Bava Batra* 74b]. In a late Midrash a parallel myth is found in the following form: 'Why did the Holy One, blessed be He, create His world in Nisan and did not create it in Iyyar? Because when the Holy One, blessed be He, created His world, He said to the Prince of Darkness: Depart from Me, because I wish the world to be created in light.'[39] The difference between the two narratives does not consist in the fact that Rav speaks of the Prince of the Sea, whom he identifies with the Scriptural Rahab, while the anonymous account refers to the Prince of Darkness. In point of fact, it may even be said that the world that contains Sea only is also a world of darkness. The fundamental distinction between them is that the Holy One, blessed be He, slays the Prince of the Sea, whereas the Prince of Darkness only departs from Him, but does not disappear altogether. The very independence of both the Prince of the Sea and the Prince of Darkness recalls the Iranian creation stories, like that of the first chapter of the *Bundahišn*,[40] but whereas in Rav's dictum the removal of the Prince of the Sea took place before the creation of the world and thereby the struggle came to an end and dualism was ousted from the world, the request of the Holy One, blessed be He, to the Prince of Darkness in the anonymous legend 'Depart from Me, for if you do not do so, I shall rebuke you...' brings to mind the Iranian legend, according to which Ahriman, beholding the power and might of Ahura Mazda, 'runs back into the darkness', but the conflict continues there until the eschatological end arrives. It is not without reason that Rav introduced the remnants of the ancient Biblical myth about the rebellion of the sea and its helpers[41] and related them to the account of the creation of the world. His aim was to rebut other creation stories, such as that in the anonymous Midrash, which found currency in his area and absorbed new and contemporary mythical elements, although even in their case manifest dualistic myths were eschewed. When the Prince of Darkness asks God in the anonymous Midrash 'And what wilt Thou create after the light?', he receives the reply 'darkness'. Darkness is not formed by the Prince of Darkness but by the Creator of light.

Also in other teachings of Rav that deal with the Work of Creation there is found the theme of disobedience and rebellion on the part of the creatures. Rav Judah transmits in his name: 'When the Holy One, blessed be He, created the world, it continued to expand like two warp clews, until the Holy One, blessed be He, rebuked it and brought it to a halt, as it is said: "The pillars of heaven were trembling, but were astonished at His rebuke" (Job xxvi 11).'[42] What these two clews were we learn from another teaching of Rav: 'The Holy One, blessed be He, took fire and water and kneaded them into each other, and therefrom were the heavens made.'[43] R. Joḥanan combined, as it were, the two dicta and formulated them as follows: 'The Holy One, blessed be He, took two clews, one of fire and one of snow, and kneaded them into each other, and from them was the world made.'[44] But his statement lacks the motif of expansion, like the warp, and of rebuke; the fire is simply the light created on the first day. Rav Judah transmitted in the name of Rav:[45] 'Ten things were created on the first day, namely: heaven and earth, תהו *tōhû* [E.V. 'unformed'] and בהו *bōhû* [E.V. 'void'], light and darkness, wind, water, the nature of day and the nature of night.' All these created entities are mentioned in the first five verses of the Book of Genesis. But what is the meaning of the creation of תהו *tōhû* and בהו *bōhû*? In the verse it is stated 'Now the earth was תהו *tōhû* and בהו *bōhû*'! The explanation given by Rav[46] is: 'תהו *Tōhû* is a green line that surrounds the whole world, out of which darkness[47] proceeds, for it is said "He made darkness His hiding-place round about Him" (Psalms xviii 12 [11]). בהו *Bōhû*, this means slimy[48] stones that are sunk in the deep, whence issued the water, as it is said "And He shall stretch over it the line of תהו *tōhû* [E.V. 'confusion'] and the plummet of בהו *bōhû* [E.V. 'emptiness']" (Isaiah xxxiv 11).' The order of creation according to Rav is therefore as follows: the creation of תהו *tōhû* and בהו *bōhû*, from which, in turn, the darkness and water were formed; thereafter light was created — fire, and out of the fire and water the heavens were made. The creation of the land resulted from the withdrawal of the water, which was described in mythological terms. Rav's exposition seeks to remove the difficulty of the initial verses of the Torah, with reference to which Rav Huna said in the name of Bar Qappara: 'If Scripture had not stated it, it would not be possible to say it: "God created the heaven and the earth" — out of what? From "Now the earth was תהו *tōhû*" etc.'[49] These dicta of Rav differ from the simple and sharp answer given at the time by Rabban Gamaliel to the philosopher (above, p. 188). Rav not only declares that the term creation applies in Scripture to all of them, but he examines and expounds the order and development of creation. In the last dictum are to be found the beginning of the doctrine of the primordial elements and the emanations, as we find it in a later Midrash and as it appears in *Sefer Yeṣira* ['Book of Creation'].[50] Rav's teachings contain no Gnostic speculations. On the contrary, it seems that Rav's account of the 'Work of Creation' is expressly aimed against the doctrines of the 'Knowers' [Gnostics]. It appears that we possess the exordium of Rav's 'Work of Creation', which reads:[51] ' "Let the lying lips be dumb" (Psalms xxxi 19 [18]) — let them become deaf-mute, bound together, silenced...[52] "which speak *'ātāq* [E.V. 'arrogantly'] against the Righteous" (Psalms *ibid.*) — which tell, with pride and contempt, of the Righteous One of the world matters that He has hidden [העתיק *he'tîq*] from His creatures. This refers to one who exalts himself saying: I expound the Work of Creation. He thinks he is as one who exalts, but he is only as one who contemns... What is written thereafter? "Oh how abundant is Thy goodness, which Thou hast laid up for them that fear Thee!" (*ibid.* v. 20 [19]) — may he not have[53] "Oh how abundant is Thy goodness"! Normally[54] if a human king builds a palace on a site of sewers, and a dunghill and garbage, then if any one comes and says: This palace is built on a site of sewers, a dunghill and garbage, surely he will be guilty of disparagement! Even so if anyone comes and says: This world was created out of תהו *tōhû* and בהו *bōhû* and darkness, surely he is guilty of disparagement!' For a long time already scholars have noted the anti-Gnostic character of the analogy.[55] It is not ruled out that the exordium, which in effect is a curse, was initially intended against anyone who boasted of expounding the Work of Creation, but it was changed by Rav and directed towards those who expound with pride and contempt, that is the Gnostics, who used to begin their expositions with arrogant declarations, such as 'And the hidden way, the holy way called Gnosis, do I make known'.[56] They expounded with contempt, for their aim was to show the created world to be defective, and their knowledge to be arcane and esoteric wisdom. Not so is the account of the Creation in the Torah. To Rav is also attributed the saying 'By ten things was the world created: by wisdom, understanding, knowledge, strength, rebuke, might, righteousness and judgement, lovingkindness and compassion.'[57] Although all 'the things' are supported by verses in which they occur in connection with the creation of the world or its parts, yet not only is this nexus not always sufficiently clear, as, for example, in the case of 'Righteousness and judgement are the foundation of Thy throne' (Psalms lxxxix 15 [14]) or 'Remember, O Lord, Thy compassions and Thy mercies; for they have been of old' (*ibid.* xxv 6), but their very inclusion in the number of 'things by which the world was created' elevates them to the status of Divine attributes and forces.[58]

W. Bacher[59] wished to find in the ten things, by which the world was created, the Divine Name of forty-two letters, and connected this teaching of Rav with another dictum of his (*T.B. Berakhot* 55a): 'Bezalel knew how to combine the letters by which heaven and earth were created. It is written here "And He hath filled him with the spirit of God, in wisdom, in understanding, and in knowledge" (Exodus xxxv 31); and it is written elsewhere "The Lord by wisdom founded the earth; by understanding He established the heavens" (Proverbs iii 19); and it is further written "By His knowledge the depths were broken up (*ibid.* 2)".' We have already dealt above (p. 131) with the correct interpretation of the Name of forty-two letters and we have seen that it has no connection with the 'ten things'; and it seems that there is also no relationship between it and Rav's statement about the letters. The ten things, which are the forces and attributes that were active at the time of Creation, do not annul the ancient Mishna[60] 'By ten sayings the world was created' (*M. 'Avot* v, 1), but found their expression in them. These ten sayings are 'letters' in the sense that they are elements of speech and utterance, and not numbers or physical elements of the universe, and Rav states that Bezalel knew how to combine them, because he possessed three of the powers by which the world was created. Rav does not say that the world was created by a combination of letters, nor does his statement comprise the doctrine of Creation expounded by the *Sefer Yeṣira*, which is based on mutations and arrangements of the letters,[61] nor yet the numerical system of Pythagoras.[62] God created the universe only with an utterance. It appears that express opposition to the doctrine that attributes to God creation by the manipulation of letters is to be found in a dictum of R. Joḥanan, the younger contemporary of Rav in Eretz-Israel: ' "when they were created" — R.

Abbahu said in the name of R. Joḥanan: He created them a *Hē'*. Just as the *Hē'* — unlike all the other letters, which require the use of the tongue — does not need the tongue (for its enunciation), even so the Holy One, blessed be He, created His world without toil or effort, but only "By the word of the Lord" (Psalms xxxiii 6), which was no sooner uttered than "the heavens were made".' In conformity with this teaching, R. Joḥanan's colleague and disciple, R. Eleazar, interpreted the verse כי ביה ה׳ צור עולמים *kî bĕ-Yah, YHWH, ṣûr ʿōlāmîm* [usually rendered: 'For the Lord [*YH*] is God, an everlasting Rock' (Isaiah xxvi 4)] as follows: 'With these two letters [*YH*] the Holy One, blessed be He, created [*ṣûr* = *ṣār*, 'formed'] ...this world was created with a *Hē'*..., and the next world was created with a *Yôd* [*ʿōlāmîm*, plural, indicates two worlds]'[63] — with two letters, which involve no toil and no effort, and not by combinations of letters or the use of the Divine Name.[64] At first blush, these dicta seem to contradict R. Akiba's teaching in the Mishna: 'Beloved are Israel for unto them was given the instrument by which the world was created; still greater was the love that it was made known to them that to them was given the instrument by which the world was created.'[65] The entire Torah, therefore, served as the instrument of Creation. Obviously, this idea posits the existence of the Torah before the creation of the world.

The notion of the pre-existence of the Torah is rooted in the mythological conception of the image of wisdom that prevailed in the ancient East and traces of which are discernible in the metaphors of the book of Proverbs[66], such as 'The Lord made me as the beginning of His way, the first of His works of old' (viii 22), 'Then I was beside Him, like a master markman ['*āmôn*]; and I was daily His delight' (*ibid.* v. 30). The identification of wisdom with the Torah[67] is old, and is alluded to in 'the praise of wisdom' of the Book of Sirach, where wisdom declares: 'Then the Creator of all things gave me a commandment... And He said, Make thy dwelling in Jacob, and in Israel receive thine inheritance' (xxix 8–9). Wisdom became Torah 'a possession for the assembly of Jacob', and in accordance with this concept the Amora R. Hoshaʿia expounded the verse in Proverbs thus: "*ʾĀmôn* – *'Ûmān* [artisan, architect]; the Torah says: "I was the instrument of the Holy One, blessed be He." As a rule, when a human king builds a palace, he does not build it by himself, but calls in an architect, and the architect does not plan the building in his head, but he makes use of rolls and tablets, to know how to make the rooms and wickets. Even so the Holy One, blessed be He, looked in the Torah and created the world. And the Torah declares, "With *rē'shît* [E.V. 'In the beginning'] God created, and *rē'shît* means none other than Torah, as it is said "The Lord made me *rē'shît* [E.V. 'as the beginning'] of His way." '[68] In this homily the significance of the view that the Torah was the instrument of the Holy One, blessed be He, in the creation of the world is explained, to wit, 'He looked [מביט *mabbîṭ*] in the Torah and created the world.' Maimonides[69] wondered at the expression הסתכל *histakkēl* ['to look at', 'contemplate'], which corresponds to הביט *hibbîṭ*, and wrote: 'for Plato uses this very expression when he states that God contemplates the world of Ideas and thus produces the existing beings'. It is not surprising, therefore, that modern scholars[70] discovered the doctrine of Platonic Ideas in the saying of R. Hoshaʿia, and found a parallel to the Amora's analogy in that employed by Philo[71] concerning the architect who was invited to build a city. But actually a careful comparison of the analogies and the points illustrated shows us the difference between Philo and the Sages and enables us to grasp the significance of their teaching. In Philo's analogy, the architect 'first sketches in his own mind well nigh all the parts of the city that is to be wrought out, temples, gymnasia, town-halls, market-places, harbours, docks, streets, walls to be built, dwelling-houses, as well as public buildings to be set up. Thus after having received in his own soul, as it were in wax, the figures of these objects severally, he carries about the image of a city which is the creation of his mind. Then by his innate power of memory, he recalls the images of the various parts of this city, and imprints their types yet more distinctly in it: and like a good craftsman (δημιουργὸς ἀγαθός) he begins to build the city of stones and timber, keeping his eye upon his pattern (παράδειγμα) and making the visible and tangible objects correspond in each case to the incorporeal ideas.' Similarly, Philo declares, God acted when He came to create the world. 'He conceived beforehand the models of its parts, and out of these He constituted and brought to completion a world discernible only by the mind, and then, with that for a pattern, the world which our senses can perceive.' Philo states in his introductory remarks that He adduces an illustration from our world in order to refute the erroneous view that the World of Ideas exists in a given place. In the analogy he emphasizes repeatedly that the forms are engraven on the soul of the Demiurge[72], and in accord with this he states, with reference to the point illustrated by the analogy, that 'the universe that consisted of Ideas would have no other location than the Divine Reason (θεῖον λόγον)'. On the other hand, R. Hoshaʿia's homily contains not the slightest reference to the world of Ideas or to the location of the Ideas. In the analogy, 'the architect does not plan the building in his head, but he makes use of rolls and tablets' — a fact that Philo carefully refrained from mentioning,[73] because it contradicted his purpose in adducing the analogy. Like the architect who looks at the rolls and tablets, so the Holy One, blessed be He, looked in the Torah, but it contains no forms and sketches of temples, gymnasia, markets and harbours, and this Torah is not a concept but the concrete Torah with its precepts and statutes, which are inscribed in letters. Out of those letters and not from numbers — their combinations and mutation — are the utterances with which the Almighty created the world constructed. It is precisely those who are of the opinion that the analogy in the Midrash reached the Palestinian Amoraim from Philo, directly or through intermediatory processes,[74] that must wonder at the absence of any substantial influence by Philonic thought. In truth, the analogy of the Midrash is only a literary embellishment, and in antithesis to Philo's analogy, whose purpose is to facilitate our understanding of the world of Ideas, which lacks a location of its own, the architect's study of his plans does not explain God's contemplation of the Torah. Indeed, in another — anonymous — Midrash the concept of R. Hoshaʿia's homily finds expression in a different form, which actually stresses the contrast between a human being and the Holy One, blessed be He: ' "My hand laid the foundations of the earth" (Isaiah xlviii 13) — said the Holy One, blessed be He: "For My thoughts are not your thoughts... For as the heavens are higher than the earth..." (*ibid.* lv 8–9) — a man sits and calculates, saying: This is how I shall build, this is how I shall make it; he thinks out in a little while what he does not accomplish in a decade. But the Holy One, blessed be He, is not so; for (what) He thinks out in a thousand years He builds in one day, as it is said: "Remember His covenant for ever, the word which He commanded to a thousand generations" (I Chronicles xvi 15). The heavens were created in one day, for it is said: "By the word of the Lord the heavens were made" (Psalms xxxiii 6). And when He created the world, the Torah, as it were, gave Him light, for the world was without form and void, as it is said: "For the commandment is a lamp, and the Torah is light." Said the Holy One, blessed be He, I seek workmen. The Torah answered Him: I shall put at your service twenty-two workmen, namely the twenty-two letters of the Torah....'[75] The whole Torah is written with twenty-two letters, including the account of Creation. However, the letters do not combine only to describe the work after the event, but it is they themselves that wrought at the time of Creation. The dicta concerning the part played by the Torah and its letters in the creation of the world are devoted more to the praise of the Torah than to the cosmogony and 'Work of Creation'. The homilies on the individual letters, their form and sound, serve paradoxically either to limit the study of the 'Work of Creation' in general, or to contradict the teachings of Gnostic sectarians. We have already cited the expositions of R. Joḥanan and R. Eleazar, whose aim was to emphasize that the world was not created with toil but by an utterance. Anonymous homilies came to explain why the story of creation begins with the letter *Bêt*[76]: 'Why was (the world) created with a *Bêt* [that of בראשית *Bĕ-rē'shît*]? Because it is an expression of blessing [ברכה *bĕrākhā*, 'blessing', begins with a *Bêt*]. And why not with an *'Ālef*? Because it belongs to an expression of cursing [ארור *'ārûr*, 'cursed', begins with an *'Ālef*]. Another explanation is... in order not to give the sectarians an excuse to say: How can the world stand, seeing it was created by a locution of cursing.' A different homily explains that the shape of the letter *Bêt*[77] implies that 'He that is above created us... and He... the Lord is His name.' The sectarians are Gnostics, who claimed that the created world was evil, for, according to Simon Magus,[78] it was not the work of the Good Most High God but of the Demiurge, who was originally sent by the Good God to create the world, but he rebelled against him and proclaimed himself the supreme god. Marcion[79] argued that the transcendental god of lovingkindness stands facing the god of judgement and righteousness, who is the god of the world and is evil, and hence the world is also evil. Clearly the second homily is likewise directed against such views, and stresses that the God of Israel, whose name is the Lord [the Tetragrammaton], is 'He that is above', and there is none superior to Him, and He is also the Creator of the world. The letters of the Torah, with which the world was created, were used by the Amoraim as symbols and intimations, in which they found support for the basic concepts, which were the heritage of generations, concerning the Creator and the created world, but they were forced to defend these ideas anew against sectarians and deviationists. The testimony of the verse 'And God saw everything that He had made, and behold, it was very good' (Genesis i 31) is reiterated in the Prophets and mentioned again in the Hagiographa. Although Philo[80] relies on Plato when he declares that the cause of Creation was the wish of God to vouchsafe of His goodness to the world and to make it more perfect, yet it is obvious that he could have based his words on the Holy Scriptures. It is not at all surprising, therefore, that the Sages reiterated this thought in various forms. The verse 'The Rock, His work is perfect' (Deuteronomy xxxii 4) is expounded in the Sifre[81]:

> His work is perfect in regard to all the inhabitants of the world, and there is not the slightest reason[82] for questioning his works. There is not one of them who would speculate and say: If I had three eyes, or three hands, or three legs, or if I walked on my head, or if my face were turned backwards, how it would befit me!

The homily appears to be directed against people who did, in truth, question 'the perfection of the work' in the creation of the world. Indeed, in a parallel source[83], where the dictum is attributed to R. Simeon b. Yoḥai, the polemical aim is underscored by 'An analogy to a human king who built a palace, and people entered it and said: If the pillars were taller it would have been more beautiful; if the walls were higher, it would have been more beautiful; if the ceiling were loftier, it would have been more beautiful.'

The question why insects and reptiles were created was put to the Sages just as to the Stoics.[84] Like Chrysippus, who lived 280 B.C.E., they also endeavoured to show the usefulness and purpose inherent in all creatures and beings, as Rav stated:[85] 'Of all that the Holy One, blessed be He, created in His world, He created nothing without a purpose. He created the snail (as a remedy) for a scab; He created the fly for the hornet's (sting); the mosquito for a serpent's (bite)...' This and similar sayings also contained an implicit answer to those who criticized the perfection and goodness of the world. There is also not wanting an isolated attempt to exclude certain creatures from the original creation. Thus it is stated in a Baraita in the name of R. Nathan:[86] 'Three were tried and four were declared guilty: Adam, Eve, and the Serpent (were tried), and the earth was punished together with them; (as it is said) "Cursed be the ground!" (Genesis iii 17) — that it should produce unto him cursed objects like gnats and fleas and flies....' Upon this the Amora R. Isaac Magdela'a remarked 'It, too, has its use'. This observation is in the spirit of the teaching of the Rabbis who differed from R. Nathan and said: 'Even creatures that seem to you wholly superfluous in the creation of the world — such as fleas, gnats, and flies — are also an integral part of the creation of the world, and they all fulfil the mission of the Holy One, blessed be He....'[87] The anti-Gnostic trend is conspicuous in the sayings of the Amoraim of the end of the third century and of the fourth century. R. Isaac bar Marion, the contemporary of R. Eleazar, declared 'This is the story of the heavens and the earth' — their Creator praises them, who then shall condemn them? Their Creator lauds them, who then shall find fault with them? We must conclude, therefore, that they are beautiful and praiseworthy.'[88] R. Levi bar Ḥayeta, the author of the famous statement that the Jews recited the שמע *Shĕma*' at Caesarea in Greek (*T.P. Soṭa* vii, 1, p. 21b), who lived one generation after R. Isaac, applied an analogy to the subject that resembles the one that we have already encountered (above, p. 196) in another context, and whose anti-Gnostic character is manifest: 'If a human king builds a palace and puts a gutter at the entrance, it is not befitting. But the King of the kings of kings, blessed be He, created man, and placed his 'gutter' at his 'entrance', yet it constitutes his beauty and his excellence.'

The anti-Jewish and antinomian element found expression in the common and immutable principle, present in all Gnostic doctrines, that the world was created by angels.[89] Against this view are directed numerous polemical homilies of the Amoraim, which expressly negate all participation on the part of the angels in the act of Creation. This polemic manifested itself even in sayings dealing with the creation of the angels. Nothing is stated in the Pentateuch concerning the creation of the angels, but in the *Book of Jubilees* ii, 2, we find, 'For on the first day He created the heavens above and the earth and the waters and all the spirits which serve before Him — the angels of the presence and the angels of sanctification and the angels (of the spirit of fire)' etc. In the Slavonic *Enoch* xi, 8, the Creation begins with the statement: 'And I commanded the celestial beings that one that is visible should go forth from those who are invisible and Uriel, the exceeding mighty, went forth...' In the name of R. Joshua b. Qorḥa it is reported: 'When the Holy One, blessed be He, created the world on the first day, He created the Angel of Death.'[90] On the other hand, a different answer was given to the question 'When were the angels created?'[91] by the Palestinian Amoraim at the beginning of the third century. 'R. Joḥanan said: They were created on the second day... "who hast laid the beams of Thy chambers on the waters" (Psalms civ 3), and it is written "who makest the winds Thy messengers" (*ibid.* v. 4). R. Ḥanina said: They were created on the fifth day, for it is written, "And let birds fly above the earth" (Genesis i 20), and it is written "And with two he flew" (Isaiah vi 2).' The polemical purpose of these views was stressed by R. Joḥanan's disciple, R. Isaac, who said:

> Both according to R. Ḥanina and according to R. Joḥanan it is agreed that none [of the angels or active beings] was created on the first day, that you should not say[92] Michael was pulling in the south and Gabriel in the north, and the Holy One, blessed be He, was stretching in the middle, but 'I am the Lord, who made all things, who stretched out the heavens alone, who spread out the earth מאתי *mē'ittî* [*Qrê* (Masoretic reading): 'by Myself']' (*ibid.* xliv 24). The written text [*kĕtîv*] has מי אתי *mî 'ittî* ['who was with Me?'] — who was My partner in the creation of the world? In the ordinary course of events, when a human king is praised in a country, the great men of the country are praised with him. Why? Because they help him bear the burden (of state). But the Holy One, blessed be He, is not so — He alone created His world, He alone is glorified in His world.

Not only did the angels not create the world, but they did not even assist in its creation, for the created world is not evil and its Creator glories in it. The sectarians were given a handle by the plural in the Scripture 'Let us make man in our image' (Genesis i 26). The homilies of the Amoraim on this verse reflect various aims, and some of them are rooted, apparently, in an ancient exegetical tradition. The Baraitot that report the changes made by the Sages [in rendering the Pentateuch into Greek] for King Ptolemy[93] include also the emendation: 'I shall make man in an image and likeness.' Philo, who was puzzled by the wording of the passage, used it to find a solution to the problem of the existence of evil in the world. Although he expresses himself with great caution, stating that the true reason for creating man in cooperation with others is known only to the Creator, yet he advances the theory that God Himself created the plants and cattle, which have no intellect and hence are free from sin and iniquity. So, too, He created by Himself the celestial beings, which are living creatures possessed of intellect (ζῷα νοερά) but unaffected by evil. On the other hand man is subject to good and evil, righteousness and wrongdoing, beauty and ugliness; hence God was assisted by others in the creation of man. Only the good in man comes from God, whereas the evil in him emanates from others who are subservient to Him.[94] It was not only the debate in which the Sages were engaged with the sectarians that made it impossible for them to adopt Philo's explanation in its entirety and to make the angels partners in the creation of man; the very idea of making the angels responsible for the evil in man was unacceptable to them.[95] It is true that R. Ḥanina, who postponed the creation of the angels to the fifth day (of Creation), did not refrain from saying 'When (God) came to create the first man, he took counsel with the Ministering Angels.'[96] Thus while the Gnostics made the angels responsible for the creation of man in general, and Philo attributes to them the creation of the evil in man, the earliest Amoraim limited the association of the angels to consultation only. The nature of this consultation is described in the words of R. Simon as follows: 'When the Holy One, blessed be He, came to create the first man, the angels formed themselves into groups and factions; some said, "Let him be created", others said, "Let him not be created". This is the meaning of the verse "Lovingkindness and truth are met together; righteousness and peace have kissed each other" (Psalms lxxxv 11 [10]). Lovingkindness said, "Let him be created", for he performs acts of lovingkindness; Truth said, "Let him not be created", for he is wholly false...' However, the evil part of man was not created by the angels, but as R. Huna Rabba of Sepphoris stated: "While the Ministering Angels were arguing with one another, were wrangling with one another, the Holy One, blessed be He, created him, saying to them: "What can you do about it? Man has already been made." It was actually the angels who continued to argue 'Why was this trouble created?'[97] It was none other than the angels who were opposed to the creation of man on account of the evil in him, and it was God who created man, with all his evil, against the view of the angels. This was also the opinion of Rav, and it was transmitted by his pupil Rav Judah in drastic terms (*T.B. Sanhedrin* 38b):

> When the Holy One, blessed be He, sought to create man, He created a company of Ministering Angels and said to them: 'Is it your wish that we should create man in our image?' Said they before Him: 'Sovereign of the universe: What will his deeds be?' He replied: 'Of such and such a nature shall his deeds be.' Said they before Him: 'Sovereign of the universe, "What is man that Thou art mindful of him, and the son of man that Thou dost care for him?" (Psalms viii 5 [4]?' He thereupon put forth His little finger among them and burned them. The same happened with the second company. The third company said before Him: 'Sovereign of the universe, when the former angels spoke to Thee, what did they achieve? The whole world is Thine; whatever Thou dost will to do in Thy world, do!' When it came to the men of the generation of the Flood and the men of the generation of the Tower of Babel, who acted wickedly, they (the angels) said before Him: 'Sovereign of the universe, did not the former angels speak rightly before Thee?' He replied: 'Even to old age I am He, and even to grey hairs will I carry you' etc. (Isaiah xlvi 4).

These narratives are conspicuously antithetic to the Gnostic doctrines. But there were Amoraim who completely negated the consultation with the angels. R. Joshua b. Levi said: 'He consulted the work of heaven and earth... R. Ammi said: He took counsel with His heart....' R. Hilla[98] rejected the concept of consultation: 'There was no consultation here, but it was like a king who was strolling in front of his palace and saw a boulder (βωλάριον) lying on the ground. Said He: "What shall we do with it?..." ' — that is to say, this is the way kings speak. R. Abbahu also ignored the difficulty presented by the plural 'Let us make' and from the verse (Isaiah xl 14) 'Whom did He consult for His enlightenment?', he proved, with the help of an analogy, the absurdity of the notion of consultation. In the spirit of his teaching the author of the following anonymous Midrash declared: 'It is a foolish error to say that He took counsel with another.'[99] At any rate it is doubtful if, in disputations with sectarians and Christians, they made use of the interpretation 'He took counsel with the Ministering Angels.' R. Joḥanan said generally 'Wherever the sectarians advanced heretical interpretations, their refutation is near at hand: "Let us make man in our image" — "So God created man in His own image" ' (*T.B. Sanhedrin* 38 b). When the sectarians asked R. Simlai concerning this verse, he replied 'Read what follows: "Scripture does not write, *wa-yivrĕ'u 'Ĕlōhîm* ['So God created' (*plural*)] the man", but "*wa-yivrā' 'Elōhîm* ['So God created' (*singular*)]."'[1] This occurrence is corroborated also by the exegesis of the Church Fathers, who found support for their doctrine in the verse in Genesis. Justin Martyr, who wrote the *Dialogue with Trypho* in the years 155–161 C.E., interprets the word 'Let us make' (ποιήσωμεν) as referring to 'Christ, the Logos, and Wisdom,' and rejects the interpretations of the Jewish Sages, who say that God spoke to Himself or that He addressed the elements (τὰ στοιχεῖα) of which man was formed. Regarding the interpretation that the plural alludes to the angels, he states that this is the explanation of 'what you call sectarianism (παρ' ὑμιν... αἵρεσις).'[2] We thus learn that the expositions of R. Joshua b. Levi and R. Ammi were already known in the middle of the second century C.E. as 'the interpretations of the Jewish Sages'; on the other hand the introduction of the angels into the verse was regarded as a sectarian-Gnostic interpretation. The Church Fathers, Theophilus of Antioch[3] and Irenaeus[4] disallowed the Gnostic idea of the association of the angels with the making of man and adopted the Jewish interpretations, namely that God addressed Himself, His heart, or in their terminology, His Sophia, Logos, or 'hands' — expressions that they identified with the 'son' or the 'holy ghost'. Tertullian[5] states expressly that those who argue that God consulted the angels do so from anti-Christian motives, in order to contradict the view that by the plural Scripture refers to the Trinity. In the light of these statements it is not surprising, therefore, if, in debates with Christians, Jewish homilists, who engaged in polemics with Christians and with Gnostics, did not refrain from using the specific form that they assigned to the Gnostic view, namely that God consulted the angels. The Church Father Basil[6], who lived in the fourth century, attributed truly to the Jews the opinion that God consulted the angels when He came to make man. None of the exegetical and polemical requirements changed in the least the basic concept of the Sages obtaining at all periods, which found expression in the words of the prophet 'I am the Lord, who made all things, who stretched out the heavens alone, who spread out the earth *mē'ittî*' (Isaiah xliv 24). This was interpreted by R. Ḥanina, as we have seen (above, p. 204), according to the *kĕtîv*: 'The written text was *mî'itti* ['Who was with Me?'] — Who was My partner in the creation of the world?', and he rejected, by virtue of his interpretation, all thought of the angels' taking part in the creation of the world.

The question of the creation of the light occupies a special place in the doctrine of the 'Work of Creation' of the Amoraim. We have already seen that the Tannaim wrestled with the question of the order of the creation of light and darkness (above, p. 191), but the Pentateuchal narrative also confronted them with the problem of the relationship between the light, which was created on the first day, and the luminaries, which were created on the fourth day. The Tanna R. Jacob, the teacher of the Patriarch R. Judah, distinguished between the two of them, saying 'By the light that the Holy One, blessed be He, created on the first day one could look and see from one end of the world to the other.' The Sages disagreed with him, declaring: 'They are the very same luminaries that were created on the first day, but they were not hung (in the sky) until the fourth day.' The Amora R. Eleazar accepted R. Jacob's opinion and added an explanation of the fate of the light of the first day: 'When the Holy One, blessed be He, observed the generation of the Flood and the generation of the Tower of Babel and saw that their deeds were corrupt, He arose and concealed it from them, as it is said "From the wicked their light is withheld" (Job xxxviii 15). And for whom did He hide it away? For the righteous in the time to come....'[7] While the dispute between the Tanna R. Jacob and the contemporary Sages is concerned with the removal of a Biblical difficulty, and only incidentally did R. Jacob reveal his view of the specific character of the light, we learn from the homilies of the Amoraim that the creation of light was bound up with esoteric teaching, only they made it — as in other instances — exoteric. R. Simeon b. R. Jehozadak asked R. Samuel b. R. Naḥman: 'Since I have heard that you are an authority on Haggada, (tell me): Whence was the light created? He replied: The Holy One, blessed be He, wrapped himself in it as in a garment and the splendour of His majesty shone from one end of the world to the other. He imparted this information in a whisper. Said (R. Simeon b. R. Jehozadak) to him: It is fully stated in the Bible, "who coverest Thyself with light as with a garment" etc. (Psalms civ 2), yet you speak in a whisper! The latter replied: Just as I heard it in a whisper so I transmitted it in a whisper.'[8] The whisper implies a mystic meaning,[9] other than the simple sense of the Scripture. This fact did not prevent R. Isaac, the younger contemporary of R. Samuel bar Naḥman,[10] from delivering this homily in public, and R. Berechiah, who lived about two generations later, observed: 'If R. Isaac had not expounded it,[11] would it be possible to say it?' He also transmitted the answer given before R. Samuel b. Naḥman and R. Isaac to the question: 'Whence was the light created?' — 'From the place of the Sanctuary was the light created....' In the early homilies of the Amoraim[12] the question, to which R. Samuel bar Naḥman gave an answer, is reported in the version that we have cited. However, in the homilies of the *Tanḥuma*[13] the text reads: 'How did the Holy One, blessed be He, create the world?' A number of scholars[14] have regarded this recension as the primary one, and have construed it as though the questions asked were 'Out of what did the Holy One, blessed be He, create the world?' Hence they have also interpreted the answer of R. Samuel bar Naḥman as if he meant to say that the primeval matter from which the world was created was the light. But the meaning of the question in the second version is simply 'In which way and in which order did the Holy One, blessed be He, create the world?'[15] and the answer puts the creation of the light first. But what in truth did R. Samuel bar Naḥman and those Sages who transmitted the teaching to him in a whisper have in mind? It seems that the scholars of the last century[16] were right in seeing a parallel to the Midrashic statement in the words of Philo[17]: 'The ruling faculty (τὸ ἡγεμοντκόν) is illumined by a brilliant light, so that it appears as though clothed in garments. The first being created by the True Being — the Logos (πρεσβύτατος τοῦ ὄντος λόγος) — wears the world as a garment.' In another passage he states:[18] 'Now that invisible light perceptible only by mind (ἀόρατον καὶ νοητὸν φῶς) has come into being as an image of the Divine Logos, which brought it within our ken: it is a supercelestial constellation, fount of the constellations obvious to sense. It would not be amiss to term it "all-brightness" (παναύγειαν), to signify that from which sun and moon, as well as fixed stars and planets draw, in proportion to their several capacity, the light befitting each of them.' The light that seems like a garment is only the emanation of the Logos. In similar vein R. Samuel bar Naḥman said that the first light issued forth when the Almighty wrapped Himself in light as with a garment. Indeed we find in one source[19] the wording of the question and answer in the following form: 'Whence did the light issue into the world? He replied: The Holy One, blessed be He, wrapped Himself in a white mantle[20] and the whole world shone from the radiance of His majesty.' Support for this interpretation of the dictum of R. Samuel bar Naḥman is to be found in another Midrashic exposition of this Amora: 'Because in this world people walk by the light of the sun by day and by the light of the moon by night, but in the time to come they will not walk by the light of the sun by day nor by the light of the moon by night... By whose light will they walk? By the light of the Holy One, blessed be He.'[21] The light in the time to come is the first emanation of light.

Among the ten things that were created on the first day, Rav included 'the nature of day' and 'the nature of night' (above, p. 195), that is, the creation of time. Contrary to this view, R. Judah b. R. Simon[22] said, with reference to the verse 'And there was evening and there was morning' (Genesis i 4): 'From this is to be inferred that there was an order of times before this.' It appears that R. Judah b. R. Simon, who lived three generations after Rav,[23] acquired the concept from his predecessors, for R. Abbahu, the contemporary of R. Simon, the father of R. Judah, stated with reference to the same verse, 'From this is to be inferred that the Holy One, blessed be He, created worlds and destroyed them, until He created these, declaring, "These please Me, those did not please Me".'[24] This exegetical approach is followed by the author of the Midrashic exposition of Psalms iv 13: ' "Thou carriest them away as with a flood; they are as asleep" — these are the nine hundred and seventy-four generations that existed before the creation of the world, and were swept away in the twinkle of an eye because they were wicked.'[25] This is a variant version of the 'Baraita' that R. Simeon the Pious[26] taught relative to the verse 'Who were snatched away before their time, whose foundation was poured out as a stream' (Job xxii 16) — 'These are the nine hundred and seventy-four generations who pressed forward to be created before the world was created and were not created; the Holy One, blessed be He, arose and planted them in every generation, and they are the insolent ones of each generation.'[27] There is reason to believe that the anonymous homilist who asserted that the generations did exist and were swept away was a contemporary of R. Joḥanan and Resh Laqish,[28] and apparently R. Simeon the Pious already sought to contradict him.

The view that the existing world came after a series of worlds that had been created and destroyed is attributed by Philo to the majority of the Stoic philosophers. He rejects this view, for he states that no reason can be found for the destruction and creation of worlds. We cannot attribute to God either the desire to destroy or the wish to create new worlds. The former militates against His attribute of goodness, while the second can only be explained if the new world were more perfect than its predecessor, a supposition that is inconsistent with the perfection of the Creator's works.[29] Indeed Philo expressly states that 'Time there was not before there was a world.'[30] Whence did the aforementioned Sages derive the idea of a sequence of times prior to the world and of worlds that preceded our world?[31] It seems that the postulate that worlds and generations of inferior quality and degree existed before the creation of our world had as its purpose the enhancement of the value and perfection of the present world and its creatures and the contradiction of the views concerning the imperfection and defectiveness of the existing world, in accordance with the doctrine of Gnostics of the type of Valentinus[32] in the second century, who followed the teachings of Plato[33] regarding the relationship between eternal being (αἰὼν) and the Cosmos. The latter stated '...just as the model continues to subsist for ever. He wished to implant this quality, as far as possible, also in this our world. But the nature of that which lives is eternal and could not be vouchsafed in its entirety to something that came into being. Therefore He thought to make a kind of moving image of eternity. At the very time when He arranged the heavens, He made this eternity that abides in unity... it is this that we call "time".'[34] 'Eternity' is the world of ideas that stands in antithesis to time. Plato already identified the ideas with numbers. In the doctrine of the eternal beings of Valentinus, the aeons are the models of the times that are fixed by the stars. They unite to form 'a fullness' (πλήρομα), a spiritual world. The aspiration of the Gnostic was to be redeemed from the defective world and to attain to the world of the 'eternal beings'. In opposition to these views there was set up a series of worlds that preceded the more perfect one in the sequence of times.[35]

Our discussion of the concepts of the Sages concerning the creation of the world was based on dicta of the Tannaim and Amoraim, that is to say, on teachings that might be expounded. These homiletical expositions were partly derived from the section of Creation in the Pentateuch and from verses in the Prophets and the Hagiographa, in which the subject of Creation is mentioned. We have seen that in the days of the Amoraim the perspective was widened, and views that were at first regarded as esoteric and were transmitted only in a whisper percolated into the Midrashic expositions that were given in public and into the instruction of the academies. We find an unambiguous polemic against sectarian views and alien cosmogonies, but this polemic, too, did not remain without influence or consequences. Ideas that were prevalent in the Hellenistic world found lodgement in the world of the Sages, and it may apparently be assumed that not a few of the homiletical expositions of the Sages on the subject of the 'Work of Creation' are merely crumbs of cosmogonic and cosmological speculations that were cultivated in 'a whisper' in restricted circles of the Sages who 'knew' and mediated upon the 'Work of Creation'. It is also related of famous Babylonian Amoraim[36] of the fourth century that they combined study of the Halakhot of Creation with theurgical and magical practices. We do not know whether the esoteric teachings at the time of the Amoraim reached a stage of literary consolidation. At any rate, in so far as the Talmuds and Midrashim are concerned, even the dicta that bear a distinctly esoteric stamp are interwoven with the usual Midrashic expositions and are embellished with the customary analogies and images. Only in the circles of 'those who delve into the Chariot' and the authors of the *Hekhalot* [Books of Divine Palaces] literature was there an efflorescence of works of the type of *Sefer Yeṣira* [Book of Creation][37] and the 'Baraitot' of the 'Orders of Creation'.[38] It will suffice to compare the themes that are common to these works and to the Talmuds and Midrashim[39] in order to grasp the differences between them in both style and presentation and the atmosphere enveloping them. Whoever reads the various 'doctrines of creation', from that of Plato to those of the neo-Platonists, the cosmogonic 'dramas' of the Gnostics or the Pahlavi creation literature, and assumes that these theories were partly known to the Sages, will be surprised at the paucity of their influence, for despite the fact that the Sages broadened the canvas of the picture of creation in Genesis, adding to its details and explaining its obscurities, they still remained true to its fundamentals. God Himself and alone — without the help of Demiurge, angels or forces — created the world. Notwithstanding the emphasis they gave to the fact that the world was created by an utterance,[40] this utterance did not receive the connotation of 'Logos' in the Philonic sense.[41] It was not hypostatized and no independent existence was attributed to it, just as no such meaning can be assigned to the מימרא *Mêmrā'* of the Targumim.[42] The Rabbinic viewpoint in regard to the creation of the world found succinct expression in the epithet 'He who spoke and the world came into being', which according to one tradition was already used by Simeon b. Shetaḥ,[43] and in the use of the word בראשית *bĕ-rē'shît* ['In the beginning'] in the sense of 'world'.[44] The principle of faith that God created the world was incorporated in the wording of the *ʿAmida* prayer [Eighteen Benedictions] in the formula coined by the patriarch Abraham: 'God Most High, Maker of heaven and earth'.[45]

CHAPTER X

MAN

The ultimate purpose of the creation of the world was man. 'For one man is equal to the entire work of creation'[1], since it has been granted only to man to recognize Him who spoke and the world came into being. The interest of the Sages in man and his problems — in his person, his spirit, and his soul — is infinitely greater than in the order of nature and of the world. In a homily on the words of Jeremiah (ix 22) 'Let not the wise man glory in his wisdom', an anonymous homilist expressed this preference in the words: 'Human beings who have recognized the sun and the moon and the planets... they have the wisdom to instal this great device in order to know the work of God in the sky... they have the wisdom to improve others, but they lack the wisdom to improve themselves.'[2]

Before we begin discussing the views of the Sages concerning man, let us briefly summarize what there is to be learnt on the subject from the Bible.[3]

In the Bible a monistic view prevails. Man is not composed of two elements — body and soul, or flesh and spirit. In Genesis (ii 7) it is stated 'and man became a living soul [נפש *nefesh*]', but the term *nefesh* is not to be understood in the sense of *psyche*, *anima*. The whole of man is a living soul. The creation of man constitutes a single act. The *nefesh* is in actuality the living man, and hence *nefesh* is also used in place of the word אדם *'ādhām* ['man']. When the Lord says to Moses 'For all the men who were seeking thy life are dead' (Exodus iv 19), the reference is not to his *psyche* but to his whole being, and the same applies to the words of Elijah, when he states '...And they seek my life, to take it away' (I Kings xix 10). But on the other hand *nefesh* also expresses all the feelings and sentiments of a person. In the verse 'for ye know the heart [*nefesh*] of a stranger' (Exodus xxiii 9), and in similar verses, the word *nefesh* is used in the sense of 'existence', 'feeling', 'attitude' — in brief, what is called today the 'human condition'.

What is the essential nature of the *nefesh*? Although the Bible states 'for the blood is the *nefesh*' (Deuteronomy xii 23), yet the verse does not mean to say that the essence or material of the *nefesh* is blood. It merely informs us that when blood is shed human life grows weak and comes to an end. Blood is here only a manifestation of life like breathing, which is a symptom of life, or like flesh and spirit. In actuality the *nefesh* is constantly in man and is to be found in all his actions, and there is no difference between it and the flesh. 'O God... my *nefesh* thirsts for Thee; my flesh faints for Thee...' (Psalms lxiii 2), the poet sings. *Nefesh* is in parallelism here with 'flesh'. Hence it is possible to have an expression like 'he shall not go near a dead *nefesh*, that is, a dead person. Here *nefesh* stands in the place of *'ādhām*. Similarly **רוח** *rûaḥ* ['spirit', 'breath'] is only a manifestation of life. 'In whose hand is the soul [*nefesh*] of every living thing, and the breath [*rûaḥ*] of all mankind' (Job xii 10). The *rûaḥ* is not part of the components of man, but the form in which he finds expression; consequently it is possible to coin phrases like **מורת רוח** *môrat rûaḥ* ['bitterness of spirit'], **רוח קנאה** *rûaḥ qin'ā* ['spirit of jealousy'], **רוח זנונים** *rûaḥ zĕnûnîm* ['spirit of harlotry'], and others. Pedersen[4] rightly perceived that the *rûaḥ* is not the centre of the *nefesh* but the power that moves it, the force that acts on the centre and thrusts it forward in a given direction. Every organ of the body serves as a substitute for the entire body. Thus the heart stands for the whole body. *Nefesh*, **גוף** *gûf* ['body'], and *rûaḥ* form an indivisible entity, and it may be said that man is a psycho-physical organism. This unity finds expression in lack of differentiation between the word and the substance in the Hebrew tongue, and the relationship between the word and the substance is like that between *nefesh* and *gûf*. In order to denote the absence of existence, non-being, the Hebrew says: as 'naught' [**לא דבר** *lō' dābhār*] = non-existent. For the existent finds expression only in action and movement, and if there is no action or movement, there is nothing [literally 'no word']. The *dābhār*, word, pertains only to that which exists; hence there is no difference between theory and practice, and there is no abstraction. Actuality is the fact of power and action, which are life. Life is conceived as power. Disease weakens this power. 'To heal' [רפא *rappē*'] means to revive, to restore to power, to bring life back. Hazael was sent by the king of Aram to ask Elisha 'Shall I live from this sickness?' (II Kings viii 8), that is to say, shall I recover [literally 'return to my strength']?

Sleep is the narcotization of this power, and even death is not the antithesis of life but its extreme enfeeblement; hence the dead are also called רפאים *rĕphā'îm*, that is, the weak. And to the king of Babylon, who descends to Sheol, the dead say: 'Thou, too, hast become weak as we!' (Isaiah xiv 10), as though life continued in Sheol, only in a weak form.

In the light of this interpretation, we may also understand the first story in Genesis concerning the tree of knowledge and the tree of life. Man may eat of the tree of life, which vitalizes him, whilst upon eating of the tree of knowledge, this power is taken away from him, and his life, as it were, grows weak. It is noteworthy that this narrative finds no further echoes in the Bible itself. Nor is it interpreted as an explanation of the nature of man or of the origin of evil, as in other doctrines. On the contrary, Scripture continues to speak of death as an integral part of life. Joshua declares 'And now I am about to go the way of all the earth' (Joshua xxiii 14) — as a fact. It is of interest to observe that Moses, too, does not argue against the actual decree of death. He knows that he must die, only he is unable to realize a portion of his life — to see the land. The dead person is gathered unto his fathers. The Bible's interest is in life upon earth, and this earth is the land of the living — the land that makes life possible, consequently there is no romantic nostalgia for the wilderness. If the prophet says 'O that I were in the wilderness' (Jeremiah ix 1 [2]), he does so only in a spirit of disappointment. On the contrary, the desert is an accursed place, and if the period of the wilderness is mentioned, it is only as a preparation for entrance into the Land.[5]

A man lives among his brethren, and isolation is an abnormal condition. The people is not merely an assemblage of a number of persons, but is a personality. The name of the people is the 'Children of Israel', and Israel is a personality. Hence it is sometimes difficult to decide whether the Bible refers to the individual or to the people.

The views of the Sages concerning man are linked to and hinge upon the Scriptures, and the spirit of the Bible informs them. But at the same time they result from the contemplation of human existence, with all the contradictions that manifest themselves in man's character and actions, and in particular they flow from a consideration of the paradox in man, in whom there is, on the one hand, existence and being, and, on the other, nothingness and void. Therefore they were very interested in probing into the creation and formation of man. The Sages found a basic principle in the verse 'In the image of God made He man'. In his dictum 'Still greater was the love in that it was made known to him that he was created in the image of God' (*M. 'Avot* iii, 14), R. Akiba declared that the election of man consists in the fact that it was made known to him that he was created in God's image. His disciple and colleague, Ben 'Azzai, pointed to the verse 'This is the book of the generations of Adam. In the day that God created man, in the likeness of God made He him'[6] as the great principle of the Torah. The function of man is to know the acts of God. The starting point is God, not man. In the way man was created and in the form that the Creator gave him, two principles find expression — that of human unity and that of the individual worth of each man. 'Hence man was created a single individual... and for the sake of peace among men, that one should not say to his fellow: My father was greater than yours... and to declare the greatness of the Holy One, blessed be He, for a man stamps many coins with one seal, and they are all identical, but the King of the kings of kings stamped every man with the seal of the first man, and none is identical with his fellow. Therefore it is the duty of every one to say: For my sake the world was created' (*M. Sanhedrin* iv, 5). This Mishna states, on the one hand, that no man is identical with his fellow, but is a separate personality, possessing his own worth and bearing responsibility for the existence of the world, but at the same time all men are stamped with the one seal, and no one can say to his fellow that he is unique. The Baraita[7], which elaborates the theme of the Mishna, also adds the question why 'man was born last'. The first answer, 'That the sectarians should not say that he was a partner with Him in His work', seeks to contradict dualistic conceptions (see above, p. 155). The second answer, 'Another explanation is: Why was he created last? So that if he becomes overweening, one can say to him: A gnat preceded you in the work of creation'[8], comes to emphasize the antithesis in man. On the one hand he is stamped with the seal of the Holy One, blessed be He, and on the other a gnat came before him. The awareness of man's greatness and nothingness, which the poet expressed in the verses 'What is man that Thou art mindful of him... Yet Thou hast made him little less than the angels' (Psalms viii, 5 [4]–6 [5]) the Tannaim discovered, even before Philo's time,[9] in the section of Creation in Genesis. The fact that death deprives man of the faculty of speech and of the ability to move, but leaves the body with all its organs, strengthened the sense of duality.

Man appeared to the Tannaim as composed of various parts. The first man was entirely created by God, but the making of a man that is born is shared by partners: 'The white is from the male, out of which brain and bones and sinews are formed; and the red is from the female, out of which the skin and the flesh and the blood are made; and the spirit and the life and the soul are from the Holy One, blessed be He. Thus all three have a share in him' (*T.P. Kil'ayim* viii, 4, p. 31c). In a Baraita in a parallel source (*T.B. Nidda* 31a) the division is more detailed: 'And the Holy One, blessed be He, endows him with spirit, soul [or, breath], beauty of features, eyesight, capacity to hear, speech, ability to walk, understanding, and discernment; and when his time arrives to leave the world, the Holy One, blessed be He, takes His share and leaves the portion of his father and mother before them. Said Rav Papa: This is the meaning of the folk saying 'Shake off the salt and throw the meat to the dog.' The popular adage quoted by Rav Papa, which declares in effect that 'Once you shake off the salt from the meat it is only fit for dogs', seeks to liken the soul to salt, which preserves the body. The superiority of God's share over those of the other partners is brought out clearly in a third source, in the analogy of R. Judah the Patriarch, which informs us incidentally that the idea of the threefold division was actually known before his time. It is stated there:

> And when his [man's] time to depart (from this world) arrives, the Holy One, blessed be He, takes His share and leaves that

of his father and mother before them, and his father and mother weep. The Holy One, blessed be He, says to them: 'Why do you weep? Have I taken ought of yours? I have taken only that which is Mine.' They answer Him: 'Sovereign of the universe, so long as Thy portion was integrated with ours, our share was preserved from worms and maggots; but now that Thou hast taken away Thy share from ours, our portion is lying exposed to worms and maggots.' R. Judah the Patriarch illustrated this with the help of an analogy: To what can the matter be compared? To a king who had a vineyard, which he leased to a tenant farmer [for a share of the crop]. The king (one day) instructed his servants: 'Go, hold vintage in my vineyard, taking my share and leaving that of the tenant in its place. Forthwith they went and carried out the king's command, whereupon the tenant began to cry aloud and weep. Said the king to him: 'Have I taken anything of yours? Is it not my own that I have taken?' He replied: 'O my lord, the king! so long as your portion was with mine, my share was preserved from spoliation and theft. But now that you have taken your share, mine lies exposed to spoliation and theft.

The king (of the analogy) represents the King of the king of kings. The tenant symbolizes a man's father and mother. So long as the soul is in man, he is protected: but once he dies, he is subject to worms and maggots... (*Ecclesiastes Rabba* v, 10). The *nefesh* includes all the vital parts of man, all his senses; they are the portion of the Creator in man, without which the other parts cannot exist. Nevertheless the other parts of man are not disparaged. This truth finds expression in the special emphasis given to the precept to honour father and mother, which is equated with the honour to be shown to the Omnipresent. This equation is explained by the fact that all three are partners in man.[10] This idea which was already known to R. Simeon b. Yoḥai, has an analogue in Philo's writings.[11] The latter bases it on the Stoic view that parents have a human aspect, for they die, but also a Divine aspect, in that they bring to birth. Philo did not approve the worship of parents inculcated by the Stoics, and even opposed it[12]; and needless to say the honouring of parents, which the Sages preached and explained on the basis of the share of the father and mother in the birth of the child, was far removed from the Stoic conception. For it was they [the Sages] who taught ' "Ye shall fear every man his mother, and his father, and ye shall keep My sabbaths; I am the Lord" — you are all duty-bound to honour Me.'[13]

The concept of the three parts of which man is constituted and the explanation of the partnership of the three posit the existence of a schism between the parts. On the basis of this postulate the question was raised: When do body and soul become integrated. This question became a subject of discussion between the Sages and Gentiles. 'Antoninus asked Rabbi: "At which stage is the evil inclination [יצר הרע *yēṣer hā-rāʿ*] instilled in man?" He replied: "From the moment that he is formed." Thereupon (Antoninus) said to him: "If so, (the embryo) would dig its way through (the mother's) womb and go forth! The answer must therefore be when (the child) has gone forth." Rabbi admitted to him (Antoninus) that his view was in accord with that of the Bible: "For the imagination [יצר *yēṣer*] of man's heart is evil [רע *raʿ*] from his youth...". He further inquired: "At which stage is the soul instilled in man?" Said (Rabbi) to him (Antoninus): "As soon as he leaves his mother's womb." He replied: "Leave meat without salt for three days, will it not become putrid? The answer must be: From the moment that he (the child) is commanded (to come into existence)." And Rabbi admitted to him that Scripture also supports him: "[As long as my breath is in me] and the spirit of God is in my nostrils (Job xxvii 3), [and Thy command hath preserved my spirit]" (*ibid.* x 12) — when didst Thou give me the soul? From the moment that Thou didst command me.'[14] Rabbi accepts the answer of Antoninus that the soul is instilled the moment the embryo comes into being, and it is noteworthy that it is stated here explicitly that Rabbi received the idea from Antoninus, that is to say, the source itself testifies that the concept was of non-Jewish origin.[15] The emperor-philosopher,[16] the representative of Hellenistic culture, and the Jewish Patriarch both adhere to the view that draws a line of demarcation between the body and the soul. This was not merely the personal opinion of Judah the Patriarch, but a widely held notion. His contemporary, R. Simai, who belonged to the Ḥasidim ['Pietists'] and is designated 'the most holy'[17], said: 'All created beings that were created from heaven, their soul and body are from heaven; and all creatures that were created from the earth, their soul and body are from the earth, except man, whose soul is from heaven and his body from the earth. Therefore, if he observed the Torah and did the will of his Father in heaven, he is like the beings (of heaven) above, for Scripture states "I said: Ye are godlike beings, and all of you sons of the Most High" (Psalms lxxxii 6). But if he did not observe the Torah nor do the will of his Father in heaven, he is like the creatures of (earth) below, as it is said (*ibid.* v. 7): "Nevertheless ye shall die like man" ' (*Sifre*, Ha'azinu, § 306, pp. 340–341). Man accordingly holds a position between the higher beings (of heaven) and the lower creatures (of earth), but he is able wholly to exalt himself and be among the higher beings, if he deserves the Torah and does the will of his Heavenly Father. Contrariwise, if he does not observe the Torah, he becomes like the lower creatures. In another Baraita stress is laid on the difference between man's spiritual attributes and his bodily needs: 'Six things have been stated of human beings: in respect of three they are like the Ministering Angels, and in regard to three like beasts. In respect of three they are like the Ministering Angels: they have understanding like the Ministering Angels, and walk erect like the Ministering Angels, and speak the holy tongue like the Ministering Angels. In regard to three they are like beasts: They eat and drink like beasts, and they propagate like beasts, and they ease themselves like beasts' (*T.B. Ḥagiga* 16 a). The Palestinian Amoraim in the fourth century provided a Scriptural basis for these ideas: ' "So God created man in His own image, in the image of God He created him; male and female He created them" (Genesis i 27). R. Joshua bar Nehemiah in the name of R. Ḥanina bar Isaac, and the Rabbis in the name of R. Lazar said: He created in him [man] four features [literally, 'creations'] from (heaven) on high and four from (earth) below. He eats and drinks like a beast, he propagates like a beast, and relieves himself like a beast, and dies like a beast. From (heaven) on high: he stands (erect) like the Ministering Angels, he possesses understanding like the Ministering Angels, and he sees like the Ministering Angels' (*Genesis Rabba* viii, 11, p. 64). These concepts resemble those of Philo[18], only he, following Plato[19], distinguishes in man not two but three parts: the body that is fashioned from clay, the animal vitality that is linked to the body, and the mind that is instilled in the soul, this being the Divine mind. Man is a synthesis of earthly substance and the spirit of God (γεώδους οὐσίας καὶ πνεύματος θείου). Man has been created both mortal and immortal — mortal in respect of his body, immortal in regard to his mind.[20]

The mind is part of the blessed soul, something of that first mould, of the first man, who was wholly idea. A dualistic anthropology similar to Philo's in its extremism, but enunciated in rhetorical, homiletical fashion rather than in philosophical style, is presented by Josephus. In his speech in Galilee, in which he explains his refusal to put an end to his life, he declares 'All of us, it is true, have mortal bodies, composed of perishable matter, but the soul lives for ever, immortal: it is a portion of the Deity housed in our bodies' (*Wars* iii, 8, 5). This concept lies at the heart of the oration that Josephus puts into the mouth of the leader of the Zealots at Masada, but seeing that it seeks to serve the opposite purpose, namely to persuade the heroes of Masada to commit suicide, it is worded even more drastically:

> For from of old... we have been continually taught by those precepts, ancestral and divine — confirmed by the deeds and noble spirit of our fathers that life, not death, is man's misfortune. For it is death which gives liberty to the soul and permits it to depart to its own pure abode, there to be free from all calamity; but so long as it is imprisoned in a mortal body and tainted with all its miseries, it is, in sober truth, dead, for association with what is mortal ill befits that which is divine. True, the soul possesses great capacity, even while incarcerated in the body; for it makes the latter its organ of perfection, invisibly swaying it and directing it onward in its actions beyond the range of mortal nature. But it is not until, freed from the weight that drags it down to earth and clings about it, the soul is restored to its proper sphere, that it enjoys a blessed energy and a power untrammelled on every side, remaining, like God Himself, invisible to human eyes (*ibid.* vii, 8, 7).

The residence of the soul in the body is a downgrading, and its release from the chains of the body is freedom. The formulation here is more extreme than in the dicta of the Sages, for they assess this partnership positively, and man's ascent is achieved not by the liberation of the body from the soul, but by the performance of good deeds and precepts, whereas Josephus makes the severance of the bond between the body and soul the primary factor, a view that largely resembles that of Philo. Undoubtedly, the unusual circumstances[21] in which Eleazar uttered his speech help to explain the pungency and extremism of the wording, but at the same time Josephus' words testify to what extent the dualistic anthropological view was prevalent at the end of the Second-Temple epoch, before the time of R. Judah the Patriarch and R. Simai. The separation between body and soul gave rise to a problem in regard to the doctrine of requital: Who is responsible and to whom are reward and punishment due? If man is divisible and not a monolithic whole, what bearing has this position on the principle of reward and punishment, and how is it operated?

This question, too, is raised in the debate between Antoninus and Rabbi, which is reported in the *Mekhilta de-R. Ishmael* (Massekhta de-Shira, ii, p. 125): 'Antoninus asked our holy teacher [R. Judah the Patriarch]: When a man dies and the body disintegrates, does the Holy One, blessed be He, make him stand in judgement? He replied: Instead of asking me about the body, which is unclean, ask me about the soul which is pure. The case is analogous to that of a human king who had a beautiful orchard' etc. The question is more explicitly stated and the analogy is more complete in the Babylonian Talmud (*Sanhedrin* 91a–b): 'Antoninus said to Rabbi: The body and soul can free themselves from judgement. How? The body can say: It is the soul that sinned, for since the day that it left me, I lie still as a stone in the grave. And the soul can say: The body has sinned, for since the day that I left it, I fly in the air like a bird.[22] Said (Rabbi) to him: I shall give you an analogy. To what can the case be compared? To that of a human king who had a beautiful orchard that contained fine early fruit, and he posted two watchmen there, the one lame and the other blind... so the lame man was carried pick-a-back by the blind man, and they took them and ate them. After a time the owner of the orchard came. Said he to them: Where are the fine early fruits? Said the lame man to him: Have I then feet to walk with? Said the blind man to him: Have I then eyes to see? What did (the owner) do? He put the lame man astride the blind man and judged them as one. Even so the Holy One, blessed be He, takes the soul and casts it into the body and judges them as one....'[23]

Despite all the elements in dualistic anthropology that are common to the teachings of the Sages and the Stoic-Platonic views, which were prevalent in the Hellenistic world, the conception of dualism and the antithesis between flesh and spirit in Rabbinic dicta are less drastic. We do not find a distinction drawn by the Sages between souls that were never attached to a body and are the pure souls that serve the Creator and act as supervisors, on the one hand, and the souls that have an inclination towards matter and descend into the body, on the other, as Philo holds.[24] Concepts derived from foreign sources, and for which there is no Biblical authority, were bounded by the belief in reward and punishment and by the postulate of free will. Developments that occurred in these beliefs left their mark on the anthropological conception, just as the latter, in turn, influenced the former. Instructive in our context is the saying of the Tanna ʿAqavia b. Mahalal'el, who lived about the time of Hillel and Shammai, and possibly was still a contemporary of Philo: 'Reflect on three things, and you will not come within the power of sin: know whence you have come, and whither you are going, and before whom you are destined to give account and reckoning. Whence you have come: from a putrefying drop; whither you are going: to a place of dust, worms, and maggots; and before whom you are destined to give account and reckoning: before the Supreme King of kings, the Holy One, blessed be He.'[25] The Tanna does not mention body and soul, but addresses himself to the whole man, to whom he gives the answer: you come from a putrefying drop; and this whole man — as in the analogy that we have cited, but without stressing the dualism — will have to give account and reckoning. The words of the Tanna recall those of Job (x 9–22) 'Remember that Thou hast made me like clay; and wilt Thou turn me to dust again? Didst Thou not pour me out like milk and curdle me like cheese?...' But whilst Job is devoid of any unsavoury expression, and contains only the statement that man is like clay in the hand of the potter, the phrase 'putrefying drop' has an unpleasant significance. Job declares 'I should have been as though I had not been; I should have been carried from the womb to the grave'; but thereafter comes 'a land of gloom as darkness itself; a land of deep darkness without any order'. The question of reward and punishment appertains to life upon earth, which he regards with perplexity. In contrast to this, ʿAqavia b. Mahalal'el declared that after man has gone to the place of dust, worms, and maggots, he is destined to give account and reckoning. ʿAqavia does not seek to repeat the thought of Job (xxxiv 14–15) 'If He set His heart upon man, if He gather unto Himself his spirit and his breath... and man shall return unto dust', or that of Ecclesiastes (xii 7) 'And the dust returneth to the earth as it was, and the spirit returneth unto God who gave it'. Neither verse speaks of a sequel linked to human life. On the other hand ʿAqavia wishes to emphasize the responsibility and status of man, who is due to give account and reckoning before 'the King of the kings of kings', and he is the same man who emanates from a putrefying drop and goes to a place of dust, worms, and maggots, and the account and reckoning concern man's deeds when he was body and spirit. Only the outcome of this account and reckoning determines whether the soul shall return to Him that gave it. In this sense R. Samuel bar Naḥmani expounded in the name of R. Avdimi of Haifa the aforementioned verse of Ecclesiastes: 'Thus saith the Holy One, blessed be He, to man: Behold, I am pure, and My abode is pure, and My servants are pure, and the soul that I give you is pure. If you will give it (back) to me as I give it to you, well and good; but if not, I shall burn it before you.'[26] The purity of the soul is not something immutable but the outcome of the life of the whole man, both body and soul; hence the interest of the Sages in the human body.

The creation of man's body was discussed by the Tannaim, and their views were mostly transmitted by Amoraim. 'R. Ḥanina bar Pappa gave the following interpretation: What is the significance of the verse 'Thou measurest my going about and my lying down, and art acquainted with all my ways' (Psalms cxxxix 3)? It teaches that man is not formed from the whole (putrefying) drop, but from the purest part of it. The School of R. Ishmael taught: This may be compared to a man winnowing in the threshing floor: he takes that which is edible and leaves the refuse.'[27]

This conception of the formation of the child from the drop was known in antiquity since the days of Aristotle.[28] Philo[29] writes thus:

> Now in particular creatures the order we find is this, that they begin at what is lowest in its nature, and end in the best of all;

what this best of all is we must go on to show. Now seed is the original starting-point of living creatures. That this is a substance of a very low order, resembling foam, is evident to the eye. But when it has been deposited in the womb and become solid, it acquires movement, and at once enters upon natural growth. But growth is better than seed, since in created things movement is better than quiescence. But nature, or growth, like an artificer, or (to speak more properly) like a consummate art, forms living creatures, by distributing the moist substance to the limbs and different parts of the body, the substance of life-breath to the faculties of the soul, affording them nourishment and endowing them with perception. We must defer for the present the faculty of reasoning, out of consideration for those who maintain that it comes in from without, and is divine and eternal.

In estimating the drop of semen there is no difference between ʿAqavia and Philo. In regard to the formation of the various parts of the body there is a resemblance between the view of Philo and that of the Amoraim, only while Philo uses abstract concepts, the Amoraim, addressing themselves to simple people, employ images that are comprehensible to them. Philo, in speaking of the creation of man, uses the concept nature (φύσις), which he portrays as a craftsman (τεχνίτης), and does not speak, in the context of man's creation, about God, for man's body is earthly and transient, given to sin, and there is no connection between it and God, just as there is no nexus between the Deity and any form of evil, for evil does not emanate from the Godhead; from Him stems only good. Therefore He handed over the creation of the body to others, and consequently Scripture states with reference to the creation of man: 'Let us make man.'[30] All this applies to the first man, whereas relative to his descendants Philo's view is even more pessimistic, for Adam, the father of the whole human race, was more perfect both in body and in soul, and differed greatly from his offspring in his two constituent parts. In his scions a decline set in; in every generation there was further deterioration, and their powers and attributes of body as well as soul, became continually weaker.[31] It never entered the minds of the Sages, however, to say that the body was not created by God. The words 'In the image of God made He man' applies to man as a whole, as is apparent from the narrative about Hillel the Elder, which is the complete antithesis of Philo's view. ' "A man who is kind benefits himself" — this refers to Hillel the Elder. When Hillel the Elder took leave of his disciples, he continued to walk. Said his disciples to him: "Master, whither are you going?" He replied: "to perform a *miṣwa* ['precept', 'good deed']". Said they to him: "And what is the *miṣwa* that Hillel is going to perform?" He replied: "To bath in the bathhouse." Said they to him: "Is this a *miṣwa*?" He answered them: "Yea! If now in the case of the images of the kings, which are set up in their theatres and circuses, the superintendent in charge of them cleanses them and washes them and he is provided with sustenance [literally 'portions']... how much more so we, who have been created in the (Divine) image and likeness, as it is written "In the image of God made He man"!'[32] Hillel's view that the verse 'In the image of God made He man' refers to man as a whole was upheld by the Tannaim who came after him. R. Akiba did not hesitate to say 'Whoever sheds blood destroys the image', and his disciple Ben ʿAzzai even added 'Whoever does not engage in propagation of the species is deemed by Scripture to diminish, as it were, the likeness.'[33] In preserving the human race we preserve the 'image of God' in the world; and this is not achieved by the release of the soul from the body. This thought found expression in *Midrash Tannaim* in an analogy similar to that cited by Hillel: 'This may be likened to a human king who entered a country, and set up images of himself, and made statues of himself, and coins were struck with his likeness. Subsequently his images were overturned, his statues were broken and his coins were annulled; thus the likeness of the king was diminished. Even so, whoever sheds blood is deemed by Scripture to diminish, as it were, the likeness of the King.'[34]

We have seen that Philo distinguished between Pristine Man and the first historical man, and between him and his descendants.[35] Such a differentiation is not to be found in the teaching of the Tannaim. When Pappas interpreted the verse ' "Behold, the man is become as one of us" (Genesis iii 22) — as one of the Ministering Angels', R. Akiba said to him: 'Enough! Pappas.'[36] Although man was created from the ground, and Eve from Adam, and now 'It is impossible for man (to propagate) without woman, and for woman without man', yet even now 'It is not possible for both of them without the Shekhina.'[37] Dicta that describe the first man in a manner stressing the differences between him and other human beings, and representing him as a kind of 'macroanthropos', are enunciated by the Amoraim only from the beginning of the third century. Rav Judah said in the name of Rav[38]: 'The first man extended from one end of the world to the other... when he sinned, the Holy One, blessed be He, placed His hand upon him and diminished him.' R. Jeremiah b. Lazar said: 'When the Holy One, blessed be He, created the first man, He created him a hermaphrodite (ἀνδρόγυνος)...' And R. Samuel bar Naḥman said: 'When the Holy One, blessed be He, created the first man, He created him with two faces (διπρόσωπος); then He sawed him asunder and made him with a back on each side.'[39] Already a century ago and more scholars[40] pointed to the similarity between these descriptions and the story narrated in Plato's *Symposium*.[41] But it seems that actually this 'resemblance' does not shed light so much on itself as on the entire principle of comparisons and resemblances of this kind. In the *Symposium* we have a mythological tale, told by Aristophanes in order to explain the nature of Eros as a craving for the completeness of man, who is only a part of what he once was. In the Midrash no inference is drawn from the dictum. The notion of the hermaphrodite the Amora bases on the verse 'male and female created He them' (Genesis v 2), and R. Samuel bar Naḥman resolves the contradiction between his statement and the verse 'And He took one of his ribs', but no attempt is made there to invest the dictum with any implications whatsoever. We are confronted by a phenomenon similar to that which we found in the Amoraic exposition of the creation of the world.[42] Remnants of myths and legends, which had gained currency in various circles, were absorbed and Judaized and deprived of their hurtful mythological characteristics. We do not know if the myth became known to the Amoraim in its Platonic or another form, but what remains in their expositions is an altogether soulless myth. The hermaphrodite and the man with two faces are not represented as ideal or perfect forms; and when the Holy One, blessed be He, saws the man with two faces in half, this is not done in order to prevent an attempt on the part of the creatures to make war against the gods, and in the view of the Amora there is no difference between 'He sawed him in half' and 'He took one of his ribs'.

This man, who was a hermaphrodite, became a male and female, while Philo held that God first created 'man as a genus' (τὸν γενικὸν ἄνθρωπον), who was bisexual, and only subsequently did he form the special species known as 'Adam' (τὸ εἶδος... τὸν 'Αδάμ). [43] Even the homiletical expositions of the Amoraim that speak of the enormous proportions of the first man and thus resemble the statements of Philo lack the differentiation customary in the latter's writings between the heavenly man (οὐράνιος ἄνθρωπος), who was not fashioned but was 'stamped' with the likeness and image of God (οὐ πεπλάσθαι κατ' εἰκόνα δὲ τετυπῶσθαι θεοῦ),[44] and Adam who was formed out of the dust of the ground. On the contrary, it appears that they actually seek to contradict this conception.[45] Rav and R. Eleazar themselves not only declare that the stature of the succeeding generations was reduced, but they state of the first man that 'When he sinned the Holy One, blessed be He, placed His hand upon him and diminished him.'[46] A similar trend is to be found also in the Haggada that speaks of the beauty and radiance of Adam: 'R. Levi in the name of R. Simeon b. Menasia (said): The apple of the heel of the first man outshone the disk of the sun. And be not surprised at this; it is customary that a man makes two salvers (δισκάριον), one for himself and one for the son of his house. Whose does he make the more beautiful? Is it not his own? Even so was Adam created for the service of the Holy One, blessed be He, and the disk of the sun was created for the service of mankind. Does it not follow *a fortiori* that the apple of Adam's heel should outshine the disk of the sun?'[47] Despite all the radiant beauty of the first man he was only the servant of the Holy One, blessed be He. In the various Gnostic doctrines the gods, and in particular the supreme deity, bore the names 'the Complete Man' (ὁ τέλειος ἄνθρωπος), 'the First Man', 'the Man of Light', and also just 'Man' ('Άνθρωπος).[48] Apparently the Amoraim at the beginning of the third century knew of such doctrines. The dictum of R. Hoshaiah bears testimony to this: 'When the Holy One, blessed be He, created the first man, the Ministering Angels mistook him [for God] and wished to say before him, 'Holy!' To what can the matter be compared? To a king and a governor who were driving in a carriage (καρρούχα), and the citizens wished to cry 'domine!' to the king, and they did not know which was he. What did the king do? He pushed him [the governor] out of the carriage; then the people knew (who was) the king. So, too, when the Holy One, blessed be He, created the first man, the angels mistook him [for God]. What did the Holy One, blessed be He, do? He put him to sleep, and all knew that he was man. This is the meaning of the verse, 'Cease ye from man' etc. (Isaiah ii 22).'[49] In another Midrash the connection between Adam's size and his identification as a god is explained. '"And God said: 'Let us make man in our image'" — He created him from one end of the world to the other. How do we know that this was so? It is written: "Since the day that God created man upon the earth, and from the one end of heaven unto the other" (Deuteronomy iv 32). When the angels beheld a new figure, they wished to prostrate themselves to it, but Michael, who is familiar with the Inner Sanctum, cried out to them: "It is man...." '[50] It seems that Rav himself, in his dictum 'The first man was a sectarian'[51], had in mind 'the first man' as envisaged by those sectarian groups. It is not impossible that in Rav's days the Jews in Babylon were also acquainted with the Iranian myths about the Pristine Man — the *gayōmard* — and about the first human pair — *mašyē* and *mašyānē* — 'who were joined to each other and were of the same stature. The splendour (*Xuarra*) came upon them. They were so like each other that it was not clear which of them was male and which female.'[52] It may well be that these speculations were linked to the Pentateuchal narrative and were integrated with it in Jewish circles, just as they left their impress on Christian Gnostic works.[53] Although the Iranian myth has reached us in sources of a late date, yet there is no reason to suppose that, having regard to all its complexities, it is merely the product of the influence of the isolated sentences of the Midrash.[54] On the contrary, the Amoraim absorbed remnants of the myths about the creation of man that were current in their neighbourhood, voided them of their mythological content, and superimposed upon them the principles of their faith. But in the process they were also influenced to no small extent. The very recognition that the First Man was different and unique reduced the importance attributed to the fact recorded in the section of Creation that he was the last of the created beings. Obviously, the Sages could not deny the express statement of the Bible, but a compromise was found. Adam was both the first man and the last.

R. Simeon b. Laqish, to whom too is attributed the view that Adam was created with two faces, explained the verse in Psalms (cxxxix 5) thus: אחור וקדם צרתני *'āḥôr wāqedem ṣartānî* [to be rendered according to the Sage: 'Last and first Thou didst form me']: *'āḥôr* ['last'] — of the work of the last day, *wāqedem* ['first'] — of the work of the first day... "And the spirit of God hovered over the face of the waters" — that was the spirit of the First Man, as Scripture states, "And the spirit of the Lord shall rest upon him" ' (Isaiah xi 2). The verse that was cited as proof could lead to an identification of the spirit of the First Man with that of the Messiah; and actually we find an eschatological exposition by Resh Laqish that is based on this verse. But the very possibility of the identification was sufficient for the exposition of Resh Laqish to be rejected. His colleague R. Eleazar negated the interpretation of the word *qedem* as referring to the first day, and gave instead the forced explanation to the verse 'Let the earth bring forth a living soul' (Genesis i 24) — 'this refers to the spirit of the First Man.'[55] In the fourth century R. Berechiah found another compromise solution: 'When the Holy One, blessed be He, wished to create the world, His first work of creation was none other than man, whom He made a lifeless body. When He came to instil a soul into him, He declared: If I set him up now, he will say that he was My partner in the work of Creation; I shall therefore leave him as a lifeless body until I create everything. When He had completed all things, the Ministering Angels said to Him: Art Thou not going to make man, as Thou didst say? He answered them: I have already made him, and he lacks nought but the infusion of a soul. So He set him up and completed with him the world — with him He began and with him He ended, as it is written: "Last and first Thou didst form me." '[56] The homilist used a mythological dictum concerning the creation of man: 'He [God] created him [man] as a lifeless body, which extended, as he was lying down, from one end of the world to the other,' and he linked the notion to the motif that we found in Tannaitic teaching — the fear of the sectarians — 'lest they say that he [man] was God's partner in His work [of Creation]' (above p. 217). The contemporary of R. Berechiah, the Amora R. Jeremiah b. R. Eleazar, who transmitted the dictum that man was created a hermaphrodite, did not refrain from giving the Tannaitic exposition of Proverbs ix 1–4, which begins with the analogy cited above (p. 218) and ends with the words: 'and thereafter: "She hath sent forth her maidens, and she calleth upon the highest places of the city: 'Whoso is thoughtless, let him turn in hither'; and to him who is without sense" — this refers to Adam and Eve. "Upon the highest places of the city" — (this connotes) that the Holy One, blessed be He, enabled them to fly and called them gods... this is the meaning of the Scripture, "and ye shall be as God". (Yet) after all this praise — "Whoso is thoughtless, let him turn in hither"; they forsook the will of the Holy One, blessed be He, and did the will of the serpent....'[57]

The primary interest of the Sages was focused on the offspring of the First Man — on living man. He was no less than Adam the work of God's hands. It is actually in the Midrashic expositions of the Tannaim[58] that emphasis was given to the miracle of the development of the child in its mother's womb as a work of the Creator that has no parallel: 'A human being is by nature incapable of forming a figure in darkness, but the Holy One, blessed be He, did form a figure in the dark[59], as it is said: "My frame was not hidden from Thee, when I was being made in secret, intricately wrought in the depths of the earth" (Psalms cxxxix 15). A human being, when he seeks to form a figure, naturally begins with its head or with one of the limbs, and then completes it; but the Holy One, blessed be He, forms the entire figure at once, as it is said, "for He forms everything at once" [E.V. "for He is the former of all things"], and it is further said "and there is no צור *Ṣûr* [E.V. "Rock"] like our God" (I Samuel ii 2) — there is no Artist [צייר *Ṣayyār*] like our God. A human being goes to an image maker and says to him: "Make me the figure of my father", and he (the image maker) says to him: "Let your father come and stand before me", or "Bring me his portrait and I shall make his figure". But the Holy One, blessed be He, gives man a son from a drop of water [i.e. semen] and he resembles the form of his father.' Not all the Tannaim hold that the Holy One, blessed be He, formed the figure of the child at one stroke. In the name of R. Joḥanan b. Zakkai[60] it is stated that the form of the embryo is completed at the end of forty days; and while he does not differentiate in this regard between male and female, R. Ishmael was of the opinion that the male was completed in forty-one days and the female in eighty-one.[61] In the argumentation on this theme the Sages based themselves on a story about Cleopatra, the queen of Alexandria, whose maidservants were sentenced to death by royal decree, and they were examined.[62] This fact shows that these views were acquired from non-Jewish sources. Like Aristotle, Pliny, Galen, and others[63] the Sages also differed on the question as to which part of the embryo's body is formed first. Abba Saul held that the embryo developed from the navel, whilst others declared that the process began with the head.[64]

The view of man as 'a small world'[65], a microcosm, is likewise found already in Tannaitic teaching. R. Jose the Galilean said:[66] 'All that the Holy One, blessed be He, created upon earth He created in man... He created thickets in the world and He created thickets in man, that is, man's hair....' Thus the Sage continues to find parallels for all man's bodily parts among the created things of the world. Philo[67] also regarded man as a microcosm. He states that God is the supreme and most perfect Planter. His plant is the world, which is both soil and tree; even so is man, who is a miniature world. Taking as his basis the verse (Psalms xciv 9) 'He who planted the ear, does he not hear? He who formed the eye, does He not see?' he states: 'He (God) took our body, as though He were taking some deep-soiled plot of ground and made the organs of sense as tree-beds in it.' He then proceeds to describe the planting of the spiritual and intellectual powers. While the Tanna likens the parts of the body to the created things of the world, Philo is not interested in the body and its parts, but in the spiritual powers and the senses. The comparison of God to a planter, and the world and man to a tree, is not found in Rabbinic teaching. It is true that R. Jose the Galilean uses the analogy of sowing in his homily: 'What is the significance of the verse, "I will give thanks unto Thee, for I am fearfully and wonderfully made, wonderful are Thy works, and that my soul knoweth right well" (Psalms cxxxix 14)? Come and see that the ways of man are not like those of the Holy One, blessed be He. In the case of a human being, if a man puts (diverse) seeds in a garden bed, each one grows into its own kind (of produce); whereas the Holy One, blessed be He, forms the embryo in a woman's womb, and all of them grow into the same species' (*T.B. Nidda* 31a). But the analogy seeks to emphasize the difference between man the sower and the Holy One, blessed be He, who forms a figure. Nor did the Sages expound, in the manner indicated above, either the verse cited by Philo or the verse 'The branch of My planting, the work of My hands, wherein I glory' (Isaiah lx 21). Hence it is difficult to find in Philo's statement, mentioned earlier, 'a Hebrew mystic tradition'.[68] This tradition knows nothing of the 'Cosmic Tree',[69] and the images used by Jose the Galilean are not of a mystical character. Their purpose is solely to stress the wonder inherent in the formation of the embryo and its unfoldment in its mother's womb. The form given to it in forty days is that of the entire human being — both body and soul. Indeed there are sources that, in place of 'form' [צורה *ṣûrā*] or 'embryo' [ולד *wālād*], employ the terms 'soul' [נשמה *nĕshāmā*] and 'life' [נפש *nefesh*].[70] It is evident that the authors of these dicta, or their formulators, posited the separate existence of the soul before it entered the body. But there were scholars who stated categorically, on the basis of various Rabbinic sayings, that the concept of the pre-existence of the soul was also widespread in Judaism, both in that of the apocryphal writings and in that of Rabbinic literature itself. Plato's concept of the pre-existence of souls[71] — and as it was taught by Philo[72] under his influence — is part of the general dualistic doctrine, which counterposed matter and spirit, that is to say, the corporeal world, which we see, and the world of Ideas — the forms and forces that existed before they materialized, before they became visible entities. These Ideas are completely independent of the material phenomena of the world, for they preceded the latter. The evil in the world is connected with matter, and man's sin is linked to the body. Sin can be conquered only by fighting the body and by separating the soul from it. In the words of Plato: 'This is precisely the business of the philosophers — to pry the soul loose and isolate it from the body.'[73] Pre-existence implies immortality, whereas the existent and visible is not endowed with immortality, but is transient. Such an antithesis between matter and idea is not to be found in Rabbinic teaching. In the Greek conception the rational soul, which is pre-existent, forms the human personality. The distinction between the rational and irrational soul is unknown to the Sages. The soul is only a part of the man who was to be created — the spirit of life, which God breathed into man, who was formed from the ground. Greek thought found its most perfect expression in the dialogue *Phaedo*, which states that the task of philosophy is the liberation of the soul from the body. Unlike Greek thought, Rabbinic teaching does not speak of the immortality of the soul, but of the resurrection of the dead. Man dies, but he is destined to rise again to life. The term 'immortality' [אלמות *'almāwet*] is not to be found in the dicta of the Sages, and when they cite Aquila's translation of Psalms xlviii 15, על מות *'al māwet* — ἀθανασία', they interpreted it with reference to the future world, 'where there is no death'.[74] Philo also held the belief in metempsychosis; the soul is eternal and passes from man to man or from man to beast. On the other hand, the sayings of the Sages contain no reference to the transmigration of souls. The philosophers Pythagoras and Plato understood this concept of the soul's donning various bodies as a punishment, and the ideal was to be found in eternal separation, that is to say, in the cessation of this process of the soul's clothing itself in a body. Since in Plato's view the kingdom of eternal Ideas is of primary importance, man's ability to comprehend these Ideas is proof of that fact that the soul belongs to this realm. Moreover, since the Ideas cannot be grasped by the senses but only by memory, their pre-existence is thereby confirmed, for memory derives from the state wherein the soul itself existed as an Idea. The eternal soul undergoes metempsychosis until it attains its complete purification, and only absolute separation entitles it to the world of truth.

Let us now turn our attention to those sources in which it was supposed that the idea of the pre-existence of the soul could be discovered. But before we examine the teaching of the Sages, let us open the *Book of the Wisdom of Solomon*, whose author was influenced by Stoic philosophy, and possibly also by Plato, and in which it was thought that the concept of pre-existence[75] could be found. It states 'Because wisdom will not enter into a soul that deviseth evil, nor dwell in a body held in pledge by sin' (i 4), 'For a corruptible body weigheth down the soul, and the earthly frame lieth heavy on the mind that is full of cares.' (*ibid.* ix 15). Thus the author of *The Wisdom of Solomon* does indeed point to the antithesis between the corruptible body and the earthly frame, on the one hand, and the soul and mind, on the other, the former weighing down and lying heavy on the latter. There is a word-play here that recalls the σῆμα σῶμα (the body is the grave of the soul) of Plato. But actually the harmonizing verse (*ibid.* viii 19–20) 'Now I was a child good by nature and a good soul fell to my lot, nay rather, being good, I came into a body undefiled' speaks of 'a body undefiled', the personality being linked to the body. A pure soul fell to his lot, and no distinction is drawn between the body and the soul; it is an undivided personality — 'Now I was a child good by nature'. The writer speaks here equally of the pre-existence of the body as of the soul, as Yitzhak Heinemann[76] has noted. Thus even the author of *The Wisdom of Solomon* is still more of a Jew than a Platonist or Hellenist, and does not allude to the concept of pre-existence. The verse 'Because wisdom will not enter into a soul that deviseth evil' etc. does not express, according to Heinemann, flight from the body, but the conclusion that only a pure body and a pure soul can hope for wisdom. Scholars also sought to discover the concept of pre-existence in the exposition of R. Eleazar of Modiʿim: 'Why do you cry unto Me? Do I require a command where My children are concerned? "Concerning My sons, and concerning the work of My hands, command ye Me?" (Isaiah xlv 11). Lo, they have already been prepared before Me since the six days of Creation, as it is said "If these ordinances depart from before Me, saith the Lord, then the seed of Israel also shall cease from being a nation before Me for ever" (Jeremiah xxxi 36)'.[77] But in truth the Tanna only states that the election and eternal existence of the people of Israel were foreseen since the six days of Creation. The foreknowledge of God is referred to here, not the pre-existence of the soul.

Support for this concept is to be found only in the dicta of the Palestinian Amoraim of the second half of the third century: ' "But with him that standeth here". R. Abbahu said in the name of R. Samuel bar Naḥmani: Why is it written "But with him that standeth here... and also with him that is not here"? — Because the souls were there, but the body was not yet created; hence standing is not mentioned in connection with them.'[78] 'Scripture does not say "that standeth with us" but "with us this day" — this refers to the souls that were still to be born — with regard to whom standing is not mentioned — for they, too, were included.' The homilist asks: Why is it written in the first instance 'that standeth this day', whereas in the clause 'and also with him that is not here' the word 'standeth' does not occur? The answer is that all the souls destined to be born were there, only the Torah distinguishes between souls that were already clothed in bodies, with regard to which Scripture says 'standeth this day', and those that had not yet donned bodies. This dictum posits the pre-existence of the souls, but its primary concern is not with this concept *per se*; rather it seeks to stress the presence of all the souls of Israel throughout the generations at the time of the giving of the Torah. Rav Assi, a contemporary of R. Abbahu, said: 'The son of David will not come until all the souls in גוף *Gûf* have come to an end, for it is said, "For the spirit that enwrappeth itself from Me [and the souls which I have made]" (Isaiah lvii 16).'[79] The expression *Gûf* is explained by Rashi thus: 'There is a Treasure-house called *Gûf*, and at the time of Creation all the souls destined to be born were formed and placed there.'[80] However, Rav Assi's statement can be interpreted differently, in the light of the parallel dictum: 'R. Tanḥum bar Ḥiyya — others cite it in the name of the Rabbis — said: King Messiah will not come until all the souls that were originally planned (by God) to be born will be born, and these are the souls recorded in the Book of the First Man.'[81] It is not stated here that the souls exist in a given place. Accordingly it is possible that even the words 'all the souls in *Gûf* [literally 'body']' of Rav Assi's dictum refer to the souls that were predestined to be clothed in bodies. At any rate we also learn from R. Tanḥum's statement that the souls were fated for this since the days of Creation. Special significance, going beyond the subject of our discussion, attaches to R. Levi's homily on the Scripture 'Let us make man': 'R. Joshua of Sikhnin in the name of R. Levi said: He (the Almighty) took counsel with the righteous. This is the meaning of the verse "These were the 'creators' [usual rendering: 'potters'] and those that dwelt among plantations [i.e. Paradise] and hedges; there they dwelt occupied with the King's work" (I Chron. iv 23)... "They dwelt occupied with the King's work" — with the King of the kings of kings, the Holy One, blessed be He, dwelt the souls of the Righteous, with whom He took counsel and created the world' (*Gen. Rabba* viii, 7, p. 61). Here we have a reference to the existence of the souls before the creation of the world. We shall revert to the differentiation between the souls of the righteous and those of the wicked and discuss it in another context.

Several scholars imagined that they could find the theme of 'the Treasure-house of souls' that are due to be born in the dicta of the Tannaim who express, in their view, divergent opinions regarding the number of firmaments; but they achieved this only by not paying attention to the correct text, and in truth this source also corroborates our statement that the concept is not found before the third century, the reference being to the dispute in the Babylonian Talmud (*Ḥagiga* 12b): 'R. Judah said: There are two firmaments, as it is said... Resh Laqish stated: Seven... *ʿAravot*, in which there are right, judgement and righteousness, the treasures of life and the treasures of peace and the treasures of blessing, and the souls of the righteous and the spirits and the souls that are yet to be born, and dew wherewith the Holy One, blessed be He, will revive the dead. Right and judgement, for it is written... righteousness, for it is written... the treasures of life, for it is written... and the treasures of peace, for it is written... and the treasures of blessing... for it is written... the souls of the righteous, for it is written "Yet the soul of my lord shall be bound up in the bundle of life with the Lord thy God"; the spirits and souls that are yet to be born, for it is written "For the spirit that enwrappeth itself is from Me, and the souls which I have made".' Assuming that R. Judah is the Tanna R. Judah bar Ilʿai, Bacher[82] noted the difficulty that ר״ל 'R. L' [i.e. Resh Laqish] appears as his debating opponent; hence he conjectured that 'R. L' was a corruption of ר״מ 'R. M' [i.e. R. Me'ir], the chief disputant who engaged in controversy with R. Judah. The scholars[83] who dealt with this controversy relied on Bacher, but in the Munich MS. of the Babylonian Talmud[84] and in *Haggadot ha-Talmud* (Constantinople 1481) it is explicitly stated 'Rav Jehuda [יהוד׳] said in the name of Rav: There are two firmaments... Resh Laqish said: Seven...'; also in the first edition of *ʿEn Yaʿaqov* 'Rav Judah' is expressly named, and in the continuation 'Resh Laqish'. Likewise in the parallel sources[85] these dicta are attributed to Amoraim.

The 'Treasure-house of souls' is indeed mentioned already in the period of the Tannaim, but only in the sense of a place where the souls of the righteous are kept after their death. The Tannaim were not exercised by the question of the soul's source and the way it became attached to the body, but by the question of the fate of the souls of the righteous and the wicked. These Midrashic expositions are linked to verses from which, it would seem, we may infer that all the souls have one destiny, for example: ' "Who knoweth the spirit of man...?" (Ecclesiastes iii 21); it was taught: Both the souls of the righteous and the souls of the wicked ascend on high, only the souls of the righteous are placed in the Treasure-house, whereas the souls of the wicked are cast to the ground, for Abigail said to David under inspiration of the Holy Spirit (I Samuel xxv 29) "Yet the soul of my lord shall be bound in the bundle of life." Should I think that this applies also to the wicked? Therefore the Bible teaches "And the souls of thine enemies, them shall he sling out, as from the hollow of a sling." A Roman lady once asked R. Jose b. Ḥalafta, saying: "What is the meaning of the Scripture 'Who knoweth the spirit of man whether it goeth upward?' " He answered her: "These are the souls of the righteous, which are enshrined in the Treasure-house." She then asked him: "And what is the meaning of the verse 'And the spirit of the beast whether it goeth downward to the earth?' " He replied to her: "These are the souls of the wicked, which go downward, as it is said (Ezekiel xxxi 15), 'In the day when he went down to the netherworld I caused the deep to mourn and cover itself for him' " ' (*Ecclesiastes Rabba* iii, 21). R. Jose b. Ḥalafta reconciles the sceptical verse in Ecclesiastes with the doctrine of reward and punishment. This intent also underlies the homily of R. Eliezer b. R. Jose the Galilean: ' "Let the Lord, the God of the spirits of all flesh..." R. Eliezer b. R. Jose the Galilean said... that so long as a man is alive, his soul is in the charge of the Creator... when he dies, it is enshrined in the Treasure-house, as it is said "Yet the soul of my lord shall be bound in the bundle of life"... I might thus infer that this applies to both righteous and wicked; therefore the Scripture teaches "And the souls of thine enemies, them shall he sling out, as from the hollow of a sling." '[86] Also the Baraita that speaks of the introduction of the soul into the body and uses the analogy of the 'royal raiment' for the souls, mentions the word Treasure-house only with reference to the souls that have been separated from the bodies after death, and not before the birth of the child. 'The Rabbis taught: "And the spirit returneth unto God who gave it": Give it (back) to Him as He gave it to you — in purity; you, too, (return it) in purity. This is comparable to a human king who distributed royal raiment to his servants. The wise among them folded the garments and laid them in a chest; the fools among them went and did their work in them. After a time the king demanded (the return of) his garments. The wise among them returned them to him in immaculate condition; the fools among them returned them in a soiled state. The king was pleased with the wise, but was angry with the fools. Regarding the wise he said: "Let my apparel be deposited in the treasure-house, and they may go to their homes in peace"; with regard to the fools he said: "Let my garments be given to the fuller, and let them be detained in prison." So, too, the Holy One, blessed be He, declares concerning the bodies of the righteous: "He entereth into peace, they rest in their beds" (Isaiah lvii 2); and regarding their souls He says: "Yet the soul of my Lord shall be bound up in the bundle of life". But with regard to the bodies of the wicked He declares: "There is no peace, said the Lord, unto the wicked" (Isaiah xlviii 22), and of their souls He says: "And the souls of thine enemies, them shall he sling out, as from the hollow of a sling." '[87] An interesting parallel to the Baraita that we have cited is to be found in the *Book of Ezra* IV,[88] which was originally composed in Hebrew, and all scholars are agreed that its date is not later than the nineties of the first century C.E., that is, shortly after the destruction of the Temple:

> And concerning death [this] is the teaching: When the decisive decree has gone forth from the Most High that the man should die,
> as the soul from the body departs
> that it may return to Him who gave it,
> to adore the glory of the Most High, first of all: if one of those that have scorned,
> and have not kept the ways of the Most High,
> that have despised His law,
> and that hate those who fear God —
> Such souls shall not enter into habitations, but shall wander about henceforth in torture, ever grieving and sad, in seven ways...
> Of those, however, who have kept the ways of the Most High this is the order,
> when they shall be separated from the vessel of mortality...
> wherefore the matter as it relates to them is as follows... the fourth order (is):

they understand the rest which they now, being gathered in their habitations,
enjoy in profound quietness guarded by angels....

The 'Habitations' and the 'Treasure-house' are a location for the souls after man's death. At any rate, the dicta quoted earlier are far removed from the teaching of the Amora R. Levi, which we cited (above, p. 237), for they speak of the souls of the righteous, which come to the Treasure-house only after they have proved in their lifetime that they are righteous, whereas in the saying of R. Levi they have not yet been clothed in the body. R. Levi approaches the Platonic view, as we found it expressed in Philo's writings, but even he did not say that the ideal state of the souls is when they are unattached to the body; in his view, too, the function of all the souls is to be joined to bodies. The concept of pre-existence as it appears in the teaching of the Amoraim in the third century, and even in the form and formulation that it received at the end of the first century or the beginning of the second century C.E., in the Slavonic *Book of Enoch* and in the Syriac *Book of Baruch*[89], remained fundamentally different from the Greek philosophic view;[90] it does not stem from the conception of the basic antithesis between spirit and matter. The souls in *Gûf* are not actually lowered in status or changed by their attachment to the body. In Rabbinic lore the concept of pre-existence is integrated with that of the all-embracing knowledge of God, which includes the whole of man, his body and his soul, in the sense of 'Thine eyes did see mine unformed substance, and in Thy book they were all written' (Psalms cxxxix 16). At the same time, the speculations concerning the pre-existence of the soul led to a certain change in the appraisement of the relationship between the soul and the body and of the measure of their responsibility for human actions. While R. Ishmael uses the analogy of the lame man and the blind man in order to infer that the Holy One, blessed be He, 'restores the soul to the body and judges them together', at the beginning of the Amoraic epoch we find the analogy: 'It is like the case of a priest [Kohen] who had two wives, one was a priest's daughter and one was the daughter of an Israelite, and he handed to them dough of heave-offering and they defiled it; he thereupon blamed the priest's daughter, but left the Israelite's daughter alone. Said she [the priest's daughter] to him: "Our lord, priest, you gave (the dough) to both of us together; why then do you blame me and leave her alone?" He answered her: "You are a priest's daughter, and have been trained in your father's home; but she is an Israelite's daughter and was not trained in her father's home. Hence I blame you." In the same way the Holy One, blessed be He, will in the hereafter say to the soul: "Why did you sin before Me?" She will answer him: "Sovereign of the universe, the body and I have sinned together, why then dost Thou blame me and leave it alone?" He will reply to her: "You hail from the celestial beings on high, from a place where no sin is committed; whereas the body comes from among the earthly creatures below, from a place where sin is committed. Hence I blame you." '[91] The main responsibility rests on the soul, for it transcends all parts of the body.[92]

These views concerning the pre-existence of the soul and its status raised anew the question of the time when the soul becomes united with the body. It is true that in the Halakhot of the Tannaim opinions are to be found on the legal status of the embryo in its mother's womb, and similarly there exist Haggadic dicta based on the premise that the embryo possesses an active soul. But an explicit and elucidated discussion on this question comes down to us only from the time of R. Judah the Patriarch in a dialogue that he had with Emperor Antoninus, which we have cited earlier, and according to which Rabbi conceded that the soul was placed in man from the moment of conception. The ancient view of the Tannaim was that the embryo was not an independent being but a part of the mother's body, or, in Talmudic terminology, 'The embryo is the thigh [i.e. an integral part] of its mother'.[93] The Septuagint, followed by Philo, interpreted the verses Exodus xxi 22–23 as referring[94] to the embryo, and they distinguished between an embryo whose form is incomplete — in which case the person who caused its death pays a fine — and one whose form is complete, in regard to which Scripture prescribes 'But if any harm follow, then thou shalt give life for life'. On the other hand, the Tannaim explain that this verse speaks of 'harm' to the mother; only if she dies is the smiter liable to death, but there is no death penalty on account of the child.[95] In conformity with this view it is taught in the Mishna: 'If a woman is in hard travail, the child is cut up in her womb and brought out member by member, because her life has priority over that of the child. But if the greater part of it is already born, it is not to be touched, for one life may not be set aside on account of another.'[96] But before 'it goes forth into the atmosphere of the world, it is not a living being.'[97] Thus 'If a woman is due to be executed, we do not wait for her to give birth, but if she was (already) sitting on the birthstool, we wait for her to give birth.'[98] Only at the beginning of parturition is the embryo deemed a separate person.[99] Undoubtedly the Tannaim were acquainted with the view that considered the embryo a living creature, and, indeed, expressly sought to contradict it: 'I might have thought that if she was pregnant they would postpone (the execution) until she gave birth. Therefore, the Bible teaches "He that smote him shall surely be put to death." I might have thought that if she was three months pregnant, they should not postpone (the execution) until she gives birth; but if she was nine months pregnant, they should postpone (the execution) until she has given birth. Therefore Scripture teaches: "He shall surely be put to death." '[1] In the light of our knowledge that it was customary, where non-Jews were involved, to inflict the death penalty for the killing of an embryo, we can also understand the Halakha, transmitted in the name of R. Ishmael, that the Noachides are put to death even for killing embryos.[2] Among the Tannaim we do not find any one who upholds, in the field of Halakha, the view that the embryo, while still in its mother's womb, is a separate body, and regards it as a living being. The statement in the Babylonian Talmud concerning a Tanna who maintains that an embryo is not its mother's thigh is just a conjectural observation.[3] The attempts, too, of modern scholars[4] to discover this conception in Halakhot of the Tannaim have proved abortive.[5] It would appear that in the sphere of Halakha this opinion is not earlier than the time of the Amora R. Joḥanan,[6] although traces of it are already to be found in the Haggada of the Tannaim. In the name of R. Jose the Galilean the following interpretation is reported: ' "Out of the mouth of babes and sucklings hast Thou founded strength" (Psalms viii 3). "Out of the mouth of babes" — these are the embryos in their mothers' womb, as it is said "Or as a hidden untimely birth I had not been; [as babes that never saw light]" (Job iii 16).' So, too, R. Me'ir said,

'Even the embryos in their mothers' womb opened their mouth and uttered song unto the Omnipresent.' Rabbi, however, did not expound the verse thus, but declared ' "babes" means the infants that are out (of their mothers' body), as it is said "to cut off the children from without [usually rendered: 'from the street']" (Jeremiah ix 20); "sucklings" — these are the children at their mothers' breast... both the former and the latter opened their mouths and uttered song unto the Omnipresent....'[7] But the Haggada was not content until it had attributed the other view also to Rabbi. Whereas he ruled anonymously in the Mishna 'If a pregnant woman smelled (food and craved for it), she may be given food until she recovers herself' (*M. Yoma* viii, 5), and there is no indication that the 'will' of the embryo is taken into consideration, it is narrated in the Talmud that 'Once a pregnant woman smelled (food and craved for it); when people came to Rabbi (to ask for his ruling), he said: "Go, whisper to her that it is the Day of Atonement." They whispered to her, and she was dissuaded (from eating). (Rabbi) thereupon applied to her the verse, "Before I formed thee in the womb I knew thee" etc. R. Joḥanan was born of her.'[8] The Haggada comes, as it were, to stress the new teaching of R. Joḥanan, that while he was still in his mother's womb he observed the Halakha that 'The embryo is not its mother's thigh.' The extent to which the view that the embryo is 'alive' prevailed among R. Joḥanan's contemporaries is reflected in the dicta that express consternation at unethical phenomena by emphasizing the reaction of the embryos. For example, 'R. Eleazar said: A man in whom there is hypocrisy, even the embryos in their mothers' womb curse him' (*T.B. Soṭa* 41b). And 'Rav Ḥana bar Bizna said in the name of R. Simeon the Pious: Whoever withholds a Halakha from a disciple, even the embryos in their mothers' womb curse him' (*T.B. Sanhedrin* 91b). Both Sages refer, for support, to verses in which the word לאם *lĕ'ōm* [usually rendered, 'people'] occurs and they explained that '*lĕ'ōm* specifically connotes embryos, for it is said 'And the one embryo [*lĕ'ōm*] shall be stronger than the other.' This interpretation is based on the homiletical expositions of the Scripture 'And the children struggled together within her' (Genesis xxv 21), which portray the wars between Esau and Jacob and their political and religious conflicts as taking place while they were still in their mother's womb.[9] The movement of the embryo also served as proof that the embryo is a living creature.[10] The homilies on 'And they struggled together', which attribute conscious life to the embryo, are by R. Joḥanan, Resh Laqish and R. Levi. The diffusion of this conception, which became general, left its impress also in the sphere of Halakha. Characteristically it cleaves to the ancient principle long after it had been abandoned by the Haggada — that is, in reality — and the old Mishna remained unchanged. Since no explicit dispute is to be found among the Tannaim on the question of 'The embryo is its mother's thigh', we may explain various debates as centring on this subject and conclude that one Tanna or another is of the same opinion as R. Joḥanan, namely that 'The embryo is not its mother's thigh'[11]; nevertheless indications are to be discerned in the Talmudic discussions that a change of view had taken place.[12]

It would appear that the compilation of a whole tractate on "The Formation of the Child" is to be ascribed to the school of R. Joḥanan. Although the text of this tractate has reached us in late sources[13], yet almost all its ideas and motifs belong to the contemporaries of R. Joḥanan and his disciples. The Midrash begins with the words: 'R. Joḥanan said: What is the meaning of the verse "Who doeth great things past finding out; yea, marvellous things without number" (Job ix 10)? Know, that all the souls, those that existed since Adam and those that will still come into being until the end of the whole world, were created in the six days of Creation, and are all in the Garden of Eden, and were all present at the giving of the Torah.' Here the doctrine of the pre-existence of the souls is ascribed to R. Joḥanan in a form that seems to combine the sayings of R. Samuel bar Naḥman, R. Abbahu, R. Levi, and R. Tanḥum bar Ḥiyya, which we have cited above (p. 236). The motif of the angel who is in charge of conception belongs to R. Ḥanina bar Papa: 'The angel in charge of conception is called "Night". He takes a drop (of semen) and places it before the Holy One, blessed be He, saying to Him: Sovereign of the universe, what shall be the destiny of this drop? Shall (the person) be strong or weak, wise or foolish, rich or poor?'[14] The description of the state of the foetus and its behaviour in its mother's womb is derived from the homily of R. Simlai[15]: 'What does the foetus resemble in its mother's womb? A writing tablet lying folded: its hands rest on its two temples, its two elbows on its two legs, its two heels on its two buttocks, its head lies between its knees, its mouth is closed, its navel is open, it eats of that which its mother eats, it drinks of that which its mother drinks, it does not defecate lest it kill its mother... a lamp burns on its head, and it looks and sees from one end of the world to the other, as Scripture states "When His lamp shined above my head, and by His light I walked through darkness" (Job xxix 3)... and it is taught the whole of the Torah[16], for the Bible declares "And He taught me and said unto me: Let thy heart hold fast my words, keep my commandments and live" (Proverbs iv 4)... but as soon as it comes into the world, an angel arrives and slaps it on its mouth and causes it to forget the whole of the Torah... and it does not go forth until it is made to take an oath... and what kind of oath is imposed upon it? Be righteous and be not wicked; and even if the whole world says unto you "You are righteous", be wicked in your own estimation, for the Holy One, blessed be He, is pure and his ministers are pure, and the soul that He placed within you is pure. If you guard it in purity, well and good; but if not, I shall take it away from you.'

In the motif of the unborn child's knowledge of the Torah and his forgetting it upon being born, scholars, since Jellinek[17], have discerned the ἀνάμνησις of the Platonic myth.[18] In our time, too, Yitzḥak Baer[19] found in the dictum of R. Simlai a doctrine that is 'patently Platonic... and it becomes wholly comprehensible if we extrude the references to the child's stay in its mother's womb, a feature that was interpolated by peculiar and late copyists, for it is not possible to say of the child in its mother's womb that it "looks and sees from one end of the world to the other"; this ability can only be ascribed to the soul, when it abides above the arch of heaven as in the descriptions of Plato's *Phaedrus*, and it is understandable that in its pre-existent life in the celestial world the soul learnt the whole of the Torah.' The very need to declare, without giving any reason, that the basic subject-matter of the source was a feature 'that was interpolated by peculiar and late copyists' shows the weakness of the argument. What appeared to Baer as 'not possible' was considered by R. Simlai as highly feasible. R. Simlai aimed to describe the formation of the child in the mother's womb. The child with its temples, elbows, legs, and head is the one that looks from one end of the world to the other, and is also the one that learns Torah. This portrayal is far removed from the Platonic myth, whose theme is the doctrine of recompense, and its central motif is metempsychosis. The choosing soul is not *tabula rasa*, but it has behind it the experience of former incarnations and its choice is influenced by that experience. From this is to be inferred that the life of man is a preparation for the future existence of the soul in its new incarnation. Therefore man must strive to live a good life in order that his soul may choose well. There is no mention or indication of the doctrine of metempsychosis either in the discourse of R. Simlai, or in the long account of 'The Formation of the Child', although motifs that appear in the Platonic myth[20] have been added to it, but again with significant changes. In the Jewish Midrash the angel in charge of conception — לילה *Laylā* ['Night'] — takes the drop of semen and brings it before the Creator and 'forthwith the Holy One, blessed be He, decrees what shall happen to the drop in the end, whether it should be male or female, weak or strong, poor or rich, short or tall... and similarly He decrees its history. But whether the person is to be righteous or wicked, (God does) not (predetermine); this He leaves solely to man...' This choice is implemented after birth. In Plato's myth the souls choose, from among the various types of life, the way of life 'that will necessarily be the person's lot', and this choice is made 'according to what the soul was used to in its previous existence'. Those who err in their choice sometimes realize their error and lament their choice, but this plaint has nothing in common with the disinclination of the spirit to enter the 'drop', as portrayed in the Midrash: 'The spirit opens its mouth and declares before Him: "Sovereign of the universe, sufficient unto me is the world in which I have dwelt since I was created. Why is it Thy will to inject me into this foetid drop, for I am holy and pure, and I am hewn from the substance of Thy glory!" The Holy One, blessed be He, immediately answers the soul: "The world into which I bring you will be better for you than that in which you dwelt (hitherto); moreover, when I formed you I did so only for this drop." Forthwith the Holy One, blessed be He, compels it to enter therein.' The motif of the burning lamp above the head of the child, and likewise the theme of the angel who slaps the child on its mouth, which are featured in R. Simlai's exposition,[21] have no parallels in the Platonic myth. Furthermore, in the Talmudic account the forgetfulness is general and the same for all, whereas in Plato's myth 'Everyone is obliged to drink a certain measure of this water, but the one whose understanding fails to save him drinks more than the prescribed quantity, and in so doing he forgets everything.' It is unthinkable that R. Simlai or the anonymous author of the tractate on 'The Formation of the Child' knew the Platonic myth in the written form as we find it today in *The Republic*. The story, which originated according to Plato in Asia Minor, reached them from folk-sources voided of Plato's ideas and clothed in a Jewish garb. Its absorption into the world of the Sages occurred after the views regarding the pre-existence of the souls and the independent existence of the embryo in its mother's womb had become crystallized. However, this very combination of concepts and motifs attests the absence of an absolute dichotomy, 'body—soul', which is characteristic of Platonic thought.

Although there is a great gulf between the teaching of the Amoraim concerning man and the thought of the early Tannaim, and the amalgam of body and soul had disintegrated, yet the Amoraim never went so far as to negate the body altogether. In the dicta and homilies in which the soul and the body form an antithesis, this contraposition is not intended to underscore opposition, but to point to the division of functions, which, in combination, sustain man. Ten things in the human body serve the soul,[22] but the soul also serves the body. It pervades and nourishes the body,[23] and when a person is asleep, 'it ascends and draws life for him from on high.'[24] The soul also works for the body when it is asleep, and the bond between them is not severed. This teaching contradicts the statement about sleep that Josephus[25] puts into the mouth of Eleazar: 'Sleep, in which the soul, undistracted by the body, while enjoying in perfect independence the most delightful repose, holds converse with God by right of kinship, ranges the universe and foretells many things that are to come.' This description is intended to serve as 'convincing proof' of the rightness of the notion that upon death 'the soul is freed from the weight that drags it down to the earth.'

The fundamental difference between the Rabbinic view and the Hellenistic and Gnostic concepts is actually seen most clearly when the former and the latter are expressed apparently in identical images and phraseology, and yet do not convey the same idea. The comparison of the place and function of the soul in the human body with the relationship of God to the world is found in various formulations in the Midrashic expositions of the Amoraim and also in Philo's writings. But in the Midrashim the comparison leads to the conclusion: 'Let the soul, which permeates the body, come and praise the Holy One, blessed be He, who fills the universe... Let the soul, which bears the body, come and praise the Holy One, blessed be He, who bears His world... Let the soul, which is pure in the body, come and praise the Holy One, blessed be He, who is pure in His world... Let the soul, which sees but is not seen, come and praise the Holy One, blessed be He, who sees but is not seen....'[26] Contrariwise, Philo speaks in the style of Plato. The status of the human mind (ἀνθρώπινος νοῦς) in man is like that of the Great Ruler (ὁ μέγας ἡγεμὼν) in the Cosmos. It sees, but is not seen. The love for wisdom sweeps it beyond the entire palpable world; it is drawn to the loftiest height of all the concepts and it is comparable to one who goes to the Great King Himself.[27] This portrayal, which is nearer to that of Eros in Plato's *Phaedrus* than to the Midrash, is based *au fond* on the view of the body as a prison, a view that also pervades Philo's allegorical interpretations, like his commentary, for instance, on Exodus xxxii 27: 'Go to and fro from gate to gate throughout the camp, and slay every man his brother, and every man his companion, and every man his neighbour.' 'Brother' means the brother of the soul, that is, the body. 'Neighbour' [literally, 'near one'] denotes the senses that appertain to the soul, but are nevertheless its enemies; the Levites must remove from their soul all that is near to the flesh. Life constitutes a prison sentence for the soul.[28] Actually, Philo has no interest in this life, but in that which preceded it and in that which is to come after it. The whole course of history is a negative phenomenon, since it is only a product of decline and sin. The concepts of the Sages, even when they give expression to the anthropological dualism, and even when they stress the hereafter and the world to come, do not ignore 'this world'. God is the God of history and all that happens in it, and in the course of history the whole of man — both body and soul — is active. These principles were conducive to the fact that even those Sages who maintained the dualism 'body—soul' did not draw extremist inferences from it. Fundamentally, Talmudic Judaism retained, despite all influences and deviations, the concept of the unity of body and soul.

Like the Tannaim[29], the Amoraim also used the word 'body' to denote the whole of man. 'Body' was even substituted for 'soul'. The expression 'healing of soul' in the Mishna is interpreted by the Amoraim as healing of the body.[30] R. Judah b. R. Ḥiyya declares that the Torah is the elixir of life for the whole body of man.[31] Man is praised not only for his pure soul but also for his pure body. Thus even when Rabba bar Naḥmani died, a heavenly voice proclaimed 'Blessed are you, Rabba bar Naḥmani, that your body is pure and your soul went forth in purity.'[32] The Babylonian Talmud uses the same phraseology in reporting R. Ishmael's exclamation at the death of his sister's son, Ben Dama, while in the Tosefta he is quoted as saying 'Blessed are you Ben Dama, that you left the world in peace.'[33] But in Eretz-Israel, when the highest encomium was bestowed by the Sages upon a saintly Tanna, they also spoke of 'that holy body'.[34] The sinful man defiles both his body and his soul.[35]

A parallel to this conception of the relationship between the body and the soul is found in the teaching of Zarathustra, as it is reflected in the sources of this religion from the period of the Sassanids.[36] According to the Persian conception, which is common to all the sources, the body and soul, contrary to the teaching of Mani, form a unity, both fighting the power of falsehood. The body is the instrument, the garment of the soul. The soul works by means of the body, for without it no action is conceivable. The body was not created as the Manichaeans held, out of darkness, but is composed of material similar to that of the soul. The body is as necessary to the soul as a garment to the body, and if it is unseemly to walk about undressed, how much more so is it unbecoming to appear before the Creator naked; hence the soul must arise at resurrection clothed in a new and shining body. Falsehood fights against the body, defiles it, and thereby seeks to destroy the integrity of the human personality. The motif of the garment recalls the dictum, quoted earlier[37], that compares the body to clothes. Only the man who is privileged to have a healthy body is also granted a healthy soul; hence man must cultivate health of body and of soul at the same time. The soul is free and responsible to its Maker. Man, who has donned a garb of flesh, has free will, and he can impose his will on others. Ahura Mazda created the free will, which means man's control over his desires. The soul was created for the purpose of fighting against the powers of darkness, and the body serves as a weapon in this struggle; hence it is an act of folly not to guard its fitness and ability. The body is likened to a horse that carries one to battle, and no man goes to battle riding on a hungry steed. In this doctrine there is no room for the veneration of suffering and asceticism.[38] The views of the Sages on asceticism we shall discuss further on. For the time being we shall cite only an example that brings into sharp relief the nexus between the doctrine of asceticism and the conception of man and his essential nature, and shows to what extent it threatens our actual faith in the Creator and the created. In a sermon of an Ophite sect, as preserved in the writings of the Church Father Hippolytus,[39] it is stated that the secret of man was revealed only to a few individuals — the Gnostics. The beginning of perfection is gnosis. The gnosis of God is the goal of perfection. Primordial Man is actually the transcendental quintessence of man; and he is beyond sex differentiation — he is a hermaphrodite. When Primordial Man begot a human being, he begot himself. The essence of man is in the seed and in the Logos, but it also finds expression in the spirit and the will, and his essence as spirit is 'the word of the Lord' or 'the utterance of the Lord'. Man enshrines within himself the totality of the gods and the worlds and the ages. All nature yearns for the luminous spirit, in order to be incorporated in the life of light. Needless to say, this is only the inner man, but he exists within man, who descended into the abyss, a descent that finds expression in the fact that he — the outer man — was created by the Demiurge. And this abyss is the chaos and void. The true man, that primary will, exists in a chaotic world, namely the body, which comes from the dust, and the soul that gives it life is bound to it and does not break out of the body, but is incarcerated in it as in a grave. The whole of existence, with all its aspirations, including the vital and procreative power, is like the dream of a captive. The redemption of man is to be found only in ἀναγένησις, in rebirth, which means returning to oneself. The redeemer and the redeemed are identical;

man can attain selfhood by means of spiritual rebirth, that is extreme ascetism, which means the abolition of sexual life. Flight from the body implies escape from cosmic birth. The man who redeems himself opens the portals of spiritual existence by forgoing the mystery of birth. Man becomes a god, or, more correctly, the extreme abstraction of existence annuls both the man and the god. There is god only in so far as he is a form of man, and there is man only in so far as he is a form of god.[40] It is hardly necessary to say how far removed are speculations of this nature from the mode of Rabbinic thinking, which is wholly based on the distinction between God, the Creator, and man, the created,[41] and since man is a creature of God's making, he can regard his creation only as of positive value.

The following Baraita apparently contradicts what has been stated here: 'Our Rabbis taught: For two and a half years the School of Shammai and the School of Hillel engaged in debate, the former declaring that it had been better for man not to have been created than to have been created, and the latter maintaining that it was better for man that he was created rather than not created. They decided, upon voting, that it had been better for man not to have been created, but now that he has been created, let him examine his (past) deeds; others say, let him consider his (future) actions' (*T.B. ʿEruvin* 13b). This Baraita has been cited by many as the source of an entirely pessimistic outlook, and parallels to it from Graeco-Roman literature have been noted.[42] The very indication of the fact that the dispute lasted 'two and a half years'[43] and that it ended in a decision by vote calls for elucidation. We find nowhere else a Halakhic decision in respect of a dispute of this kind, and *a fortiori* there is no vote taken. The Baraita itself is known from no other source of Rabbinic teaching — only from the Babylonian Talmud; and even there its subject-matter is not discussed and there is no comment on its theme.[44] Strangely enough just that decision decided by majority vote leaves no traces, and there is not the slightest indication of its influence on Tannaitic doctrine. It does not accord with Hillel's attitude to the human body (above, p. 227), nor with the story told of Rabban Gamaliel the Elder, to wit, 'that he was once strolling on the Temple Mount, when he saw a non-Jewish woman and he pronounced a benediction regarding her' — the reference being to the blessing 'Blessed be He that He created such beatiful creatures in His world.'[45] And unquestionably it cannot be harmonized with the dictum of R. Akiba 'Beloved is man, for he was created in the image of God' (*M. 'Avot* iii, 14), or with his saying 'Whatever the Holy One, blessed be He, does is all for good' (*T.B. Berakhot* 60b), or with R. Jacob's aphorism 'Better is one hour of repentance and good deeds in this world than the whole life of the world to come' (*M. 'Avot* iv, 17). Nay more, it contradicts the Halakha jointly maintained by the School of Shammai and the School of Hillel: 'A man shall not abstain from procreation unless he already has children' (*M. Yevamot* vi, 6); and it was the School of Shammai that taught 'And was not the world created only for fruition and increase, as it is said (Isaiah xlv 18) "He created it not a waste; He formed it to be inhabited"?', and the School of Hillel retracted and taught according to the view of the School of Shammai, and both Schools regarded the propagation of the species as 'for the good of the social order' (*M. Giṭṭin* iv, 5). The formula 'It had been better for him not have been created' was applied by R. Ḥiyya[46] to one who studied (Torah) without the intent to observe it. Its concrete meaning is: It would be better for him not to exist, if only not to commit this sin. In similar vein it is reported in the name of R. Simeon b. Yoḥai — and, in the opinion of others, in the name of R. Simeon the Pious, or in the name of Rav: 'It were better for a man to cast himself into a fiery furnace rather than shame his fellow in public';[47] and they deduced this principle from Tamar, who was prepared to be burnt rather than put Judah to shame. Among the Amoraim who transmitted this dictum mention is made of R. Joḥanan; now R. Joḥanan is also the author of a parallel teaching to that of R. Ḥiyya: 'If a man studies (Torah) without the intent to observe, it had been better for him if his placenta had turned over on its face, and he had not emerged into the world.'[48] These dicta are a kind of curse upon those who commit transgressions or fall into sin, and was already used by Jesus when he said: 'But if a man is a cause of stumbling to one of these little ones who have faith in me, it would be better for him to have a millstone hung round his neck and be drowned in the depths of the sea.'[49] When the grandson of R. Joshua b. Levi had a choking fit, and there came a man and whispered an incantation for him in the name of Jesus b. Pandera and he recovered, R. Joshua b. Levi said: 'It would have been better for him if he had died.'[50] In a more general form it is stated in the Midrash:[51] 'It would have been better for the wicked to have been blind, for their eyes bring a curse upon the world'; and the preacher mentions in support of his view the case of 'the sons of God', of Ham, of the princes of Pharaoh, of Shechem, and of Balak, who were led into sin by what they saw. At any rate, the expression 'It were better for him not to have been created' in the aforementioned sources does not embody a pessimistic philosophy. Even if we wish to maintain the authenticity of the dispute, lasting two and a half years, between the School of Shammai and the School of Hillel, it is apparent that it was concerned not with the evaluation of human existence, but with the attitude to be adopted towards the wicked man, who studies but does not observe (of whom R. Ḥiyya speaks), or of one who neither studies nor observes. We may conjecture that the School of Hillel, who were 'gentle and submissive', undoubtedly maintained, in the spirit of their teacher, that even of such people it should not be said that 'it had been better for them not to have been born', and if they finally reached the conclusion — as R. Ḥiyya and R. Joḥanan held — that 'it had been better for them not to have been created', in the sense that 'The death of the wicked is beneficial to them and beneficial to the world' (*M. Sanhedrin* viii, 5), the edge of this assent was blunted by the addition 'But now that he has been created, let him examine his (past) deeds.' It certainly did not occur to them to assert that the very creation of man is a failure, for 'All that the Holy One, blessed be He, created in His world He created only for his glory, as it is said (Isaiah xliii 7): "Everything that is called by My name, it is for My glory I have created it, I have formed it, yea, I have made it."' Not only is man included in 'all that He created', but as R. Nehemiah declared 'One man equals in importance the whole work of creation.'[53] And this is the sense of the Mishna itself: 'Whoever saves alive a single soul, it is accounted to him as though he had saved a whole world.' It is in the saving alive of man that the relationship between the Creator and His world finds expression, and it is through him that His kingdom and providence are implemented.

CHAPTER XI

ON PROVIDENCE

The question of fate and choice was, according to the testimony of Josephus, one of the religious dogmas regarding which the sects in the time of the Second Temple differed. He declares that the Pharisees 'attribute everything to fate (εἱμαρμένη) and to God; they hold that to act rightly (i.e. do good) or otherwise (i.e. do evil) rests, indeed, for the most part with men, but that in each action fate cooperates'.[1] On the other hand the Essenes maintained that all human actions were predestined by providence, and that a man does naught of his own free will; while the Sadducees denied fate and the Creator's providential care for his creatures and argued that all acts lie within the power of human beings.[2] In *Antiquities* xviii, 1, 3, he adds the Pharisees' explanation of their doctrine: they state that 'It was God's good pleasure that there should be a fusion and that the will of man with his virtue and vice should be admitted to the council-chamber of fate.' In the past certain scholars cast doubt on Josephus, asserting that he equated, in his account, the concepts of the sects to those of the philosophical schools: the Pharisees were likened to the Stoics, the Essenes to the Pythagoreans.[3] But now, it seems, the modes of thought of the Qumran Sect and its doctrine of predestination have come to refute the sceptics, at least so far as the Essenes are concerned. The generally accepted identification of the Sect with the Essenes is borne out by Josephus, while Josephus' account finds corroboration in the teaching of the Sect.[4] But do his observations regarding the Pharisees truly cover all that the Sages taught on this subject? And does his general summary accord with the views of the Sages as a whole, or does it perchance represent only a single school of thought,[5] whereas actually there were divergences of view between different authorities at different periods?

The term *Hashgaḥa* ['Providence'] was, as we know, invented by the Tibbonides; the Sages did not coin a similar word, but found the theme of Providence mentioned in the Torah and iterated in the Prophets and mentioned yet again in the Hagiographa, and they devoted much time to studying its ways, to discerning its quiddity and to probing its significance. There are two aspects to Providence: one involves the government of the world, the control of nature, and the provision of the needs of all mankind.[6] This aspect of Providence comprises all human beings, including the wicked and the idolatrous nations.[7] The other aspect of Providence consists of scrutinizing the ways and deeds of mortals,[8] as stated by the prophet Jeremiah (xxxii 19): 'Great in counsel and mighty in deed; whose eyes are open to all the ways of men, rewarding every man according to his ways and according to the fruit of his doings.' God is a God who dispenses justice and does righteousness; hence He necessarily scrutinizes the actions of His creatures and takes cognizance of their deeds, and only an unbeliever would declare 'There is neither judgement nor Judge.'[9]

This belief in a twofold Providence gives rise to a number of questions. What is the relationship between the Divine concern to provide the needs of mankind and the supervision of their acts? Do these actions of theirs, which bring in their train punishment or reward, influence the processes of the government of the world, and does man, who is free to choose his ways, determine the ways of Providence, which reacts to his deeds? Or are human actions, too, perhaps only component details of the processes of the world, which is conducted by the will of the Creator, both the deeds of the righteous and those of the wicked being decided by Him, together with their reward and retribution, and is the twofold Providence only 'dual fate' — not, it is true, the edict of destiny or the law of nature, but the decree of the Creator? Let us now see if, and when, the Sages asked questions of this kind upon accepting the belief in Biblical Providence, and what answers they gave to them.

We shall begin with R. Akiba's teaching, not merely because his dictum is quoted by all who are concerned with our problem, but because his observations on the subject of Providence is on the one hand a summation of the view prevailing in the circle of the Sages up to his time, and on the other hand marks a new conception, which is linked, apparently, to a change in their understanding of other religious ideas. Since the days of Maimonides, R. Akiba's aphorism in *Mishna 'Avot* (iii, 15), 'Everything is seen and freedom of choice is given', has been interpreted as treating of the contradiction between God's omniscience and human free will. Maimonides himself also found therein the reconciliation of the contradiction, according to his method of interpretation. Others regarded it not as a solution of the difficulty but the postulation of two principles of faith and the duty of maintaining them together.[10] However, several of the earliest commentators of the Mishna already did not understand the phrase הכל צפוי *ha-kōl ṣāfûy* in the sense of 'Everything is revealed and known from the outset', but in the connotation 'All that a man does in the innermost chambers, the Holy One, blessed be He, watches and observes',[11] and as Rabbi said, 'Know what is above you — a seeing eye' (*M. 'Avot* ii, 1); this explanation accords with the use of the stem צפה *ṣāfā* in the idiom of the Tannaim. This verb does not signify knowledge of the future, but seeing that which exists and is present, like the Biblical usage 'The eyes of the Lord keep watch [צפות *ṣōfôt*] upon the evil and the good' (Proverbs xv 3). R. Akiba himself said: 'I was watching [צופה *ṣôfe*] Rabban Gamaliel and R. Joshua, (and I saw) that whereas all the people were waving their palm-branches, they waved them only at "We beseech Thee, O Lord" ' (*M. Sukka* iii, 9); Rabban Gamaliel also used the verb in a similar sense: 'I was watching [*ṣôfe*], and (I observed that) we were within the (Sabbath) limits before nightfall.'[12] The use of *ṣāfā* in the signification of 'to know beforehand', 'to see beforehand', as, for instance, 'He foresaw by the holy spirit [i.e. prophetic spirit] that they would...', The 'Holy One, blessed be He, foresaw that they would...' I found only in Amoraic sayings.[13] The content of the Mishna likewise shows that R. Akiba's intention was not to resolve the contradiction between [God's] foreknowledge and [man's] freewill, but to make man realize his responsibility for his actions.[14] This responsibility is grounded in two factors: in the permission given to man to choose his own way and in the realization that man is destined to account for his actions before Him who sees and examines his ways. It is on this responsibility that R. Akiba establishes his doctrine of recompense (*M. 'Avot* iii, 16).

R. Akiba walked in the footsteps of Hillel, who, on returning from a journey and hearing an outcry in the city, said 'I am confident that this does not come from my house' (*T.B. Berakhot* 60a). This attribute of confidence is linked to the clear realization of man's freedom of choice and his absolute responsibility for his deeds. And thus Hillel proclaimed at the rejoicing marking the ceremony of Water-Drawing: 'If I am here everything is here... to the place that I love there my feet lead me.'[15] In the spirit of these words the Sages also interpreted Hillel's dictum 'If I am not for myself, who is for me?' as aimed against the belief in the beneficent influence of ancestral merit: 'If I am not for myself, who shall be for me? If I have not acquired merit for myself in this world, who will endow me with the merit to enjoy life in the hereafter? I have no father, I have no mother, I have no brother; our father Abraham cannot redeem Ishmael, our father Isaac cannot redeem Esau....' (*'Avot de-R. Nathan* xii; *Sifre Deuteronomy* § 329). However, R. Akiba does not negate the value of the influence of ancestral merit; on the contrary, he is of opinion that the father dowers his son with wisdom, beauty, and wealth (see below, p. 265), and he declared 'Happy is he whom his forebears endowed with merit; happy is the man who has a peg to hang on!'[16] But even ancestral merit merely helps; it does not affect man's choice, nor diminish the extent of his responsibility. This responsibility is the great principle that R. Akiba inculcates in the Mishna in *'Avot* with which we are concerned. There is not to be found in it the belief in predestination nor foreknowledge (*Praescientia*). On the contrary, it is not inconceivable that it is actually directed against those who profess this belief.

A polemic of this nature contains no novelty. Sirach already argued against those who deny Divine reward and retribution because of a deterministic outlook: 'Say not: "From God is my transgression", for that which He hateth made He not...' (xv 11), 'He commanded no man to sin, nor gave strength to men of lies' (*ibid.* v. 20).[17] But R. Akiba's words are, in my opinion, directed against a conception akin to that which is represented in the doctrine of Paul. His theology of destiny teaches: 'For those whom he foreknew he also predestined... And those whom he predestined he also called; and those whom he called he also justified...' (Romans viii 29–30). He negates the value of deeds: 'In order that God's purpose of election might continue, *not because of works* but because of his call' (*ibid.* ix 11). Obviously there is no room for choice or permission, and therefore the matter 'depends not upon man's will or exertion, but upon God's mercy' (*ibid.* v. 16). Paul's doctrine of predestination is connected with his views on original sin, which cleaves to man, and on God's grace, which works through Jesus Christ upon those who believe in him, 'For sin will have no dominion over you, since you are not under law but under grace' (*ibid.* vi 14). It has already been shown that the ancient doctrine of predestination and of grace, which raises the elect above the sphere of flesh and sin, is also found — without the Christological elements — in the works of the Qumran Sect,[18] and that it is possible to restore many concepts of Paul's writings to the phraseology of the scrolls. Nevertheless there is an important difference. Despite all the emphasis laid on God's grace, the Covenanters scrupulously observed the precepts, though at the same time they regarded themselves alone as 'Israelites who walk blamelessly' (*Manual of Discipline* fol. 9, l. 11) and denied the election to Israel as a whole. For the Covenanters believed that the world, including the people of Israel, are divided into 'Children of Light', to whom has been granted the spirit of truth, and 'Children of Darkness', to whom has been given a spirit of wickedness.[19] From the doctrine of immutable predestination and election by grace Paul drew more far-reaching inferences, namely the annulment of the commandments and the separation of Christianity from the Congregation of Israel. It is not our task to determine in what ways Paul and the Qumran Sect were in touch with each other, but it is manifest, beyond any doubt, that the views that they held in common were prevalent in various circles at the end of the Temple period.

R. Akiba's teaching contradicts every single article of the aforementioned creed. The gulf between the two doctrines is also reflected in the phrasing and style. The Scrolls and Paul's writings are marked by prolixity and verbosity, charged with pathos and ecstasy; R. Akiba's Mishna is characterized by a succinct and lapidary style, which possibly indicates that we have here not an individual expression of opinion, but the final crystallization of a belief endorsed by generations of scholars. This doctrine is seen in its entirety, if we combine the Mishna of which we have been speaking hitherto with the preceding Mishna.[20] In complete contrast to the partition of the world into a realm of light and a realm of darkness, the unity of the human species is stressed in the saying 'Beloved is man, for he was created in the image of God.' In antithesis to individual election by Divine grace[21] stands the election of the whole people of Israel as a relationship of son to Father. The grace of election does not find complete expression in itself but in the giving of the Torah, the vessel whereby the world was created. Its observance is incumbent not only upon 'all the children of truth', who were vouchsafed an abundance of acts of grace (*Manual of Discipline* fol. 4, l. 5). Freedom of choice is given to all Israel. God looks upon the wicked and the good and judges the world by goodness, for He is the God of righteousness and justice as well as the God of grace and compassion, but it is not 'only through His goodness that a man shall be right' (*Psalms of Thanksgiving* fol. 13, l. 17: 'only through Thy goodness shall a man be right'), nor 'Those whom He called He also justified' (*Romans* viii 30), but 'all is according to the amount of work'. In fine, the dictum of R. Akiba under discussion does not seek to resolve, nor even to present, the problem of the contradiction between God's foreknowledge and man's freedom of choice, but to underscore the latter. A similar expression to 'Everything is seen and freedom of choice is given', in accordance with our interpretation, is also found in *The Psalms of Solomon* (ix 1–4): 'Where, then, can a man hide himself from Thy knowledge, O God? Our works are subject to our own choice and power (ἐν ἐκλογῇ καὶ ἐξουσίᾳ) to do right or wrong in the works of our hands; and in Thy righteousness Thou visitest the sons of men.'

However, the question is asked: If punishment and reward are dependent solely on the deeds of man, who is free to act according to his will, do they not influence God's providential care for the world and His governance? An answer to this question is apparently given in R. Akiba's observations about afflictions: 'When they are sent upon a man, they are adjured to come upon him only on a given day and to leave him only on a given day, and through the medium of such-and-such a remedy. When their time came to depart, (the sick person) happened to go to his idolatrous shrine. Thereupon the afflictions said: Rightly we should not leave, but because this fool acted improperly shall we renounce our oath?'[22] However, as we have seen, this story does not seek to give a ruling on the question of Providence and predestination, but contains a discussion concerning miraculous occurrences that are ascribed to the gods and which are used as evidence of their existence and power. Zonin,[23] the enquirer, who represents himself as an enlightened philosopher who does not believe in the reality of idols, nevertheless took cognizance, like most of the Stoics, of popular belief and its widespread experience of miracles that took place in the temples of the gods.[24] R. Akiba's reply accorded with the spirit and understanding of the Stoic enquirer, who conceded the nullity of idolatry,[25] but maintained the view that εἱμερμένη ['fate'] determined the time when the pains would come on and when they would cease, and likewise the remedy by which the cure would be effected. The conduct of the person concerned is unable to change anything in the chain of causation or in the natural order of the events. The future is necessarily predetermined. Also the personification of the afflictions, which remain under oath, conforms to the Stoic concept that the world is full of divine 'powers'. By means of this conception the Stoics attempted to draw closer to the world of popular polytheistic faith, while ignoring the difference between the gods, who possess personality and are closely related to human beings, and impersonal forces, which are related to the cosmos only. We may state that R. Akiba's reply belongs to the category of answers that are given to the disciples' question 'But what explanation will you give us?' (*Pesiqta de-Rav Kahana*, Para, p. 40b). The reply was able to satisfy Zonin, but was this the view of R. Akiba, namely that the afflictions that were due to go were compelled to do so, and that the sin committed by the ailing person could not change this 'compulsion'? However, in a later version of the narrative its character is wholly changed. The ailing or mutilated person who enters an idolatrous shrine is 'a worthy man who performs the precepts', and his cure is explained as follows: 'He was due to receive from the hand of the Holy One, blessed be He, the reward of the commandments standing to his account, and since he left his world (i.e. denied the fundamental principle of faith), the Holy One, blessed be He, said "Why should I retain this man's reward?" Forthwith the Holy One, blessed be He, paid him his reward by healing him, so that no recompense should be due to him from the Holy One, blessed be He, together with that of the righteous; hence he went forth cured.'[26] In this version *a man's deeds* are the determinant factors, and the surprising phenomenon of healing being effected in an idolatrous temple finds an explanation in the sphere of the law of requital and the ways of God in bestowing reward and inflicting punishment according to R. Akiba's doctrine: 'The Holy One, blessed be He, deals strictly both with the former and the latter: He is strict towards the righteous and punishes them for the few wrongful acts that they perpetrated in this world, so that He may send them an unreduced recompense in the world to come, and He bestows well-being upon the wicked and rewards them for the few good deeds that they have performed in this world.'[27]

The dictum that we cite next, which was transmitted by אחר *Aḥer* ['Other'] — that is, Elisha b. Avuyah — in the name of R. Akiba, teaches apparently, by its formulation, the doctrine of immutable fate, but an examination of its content shows that this is not the case. Aḥer asked R. Me'ir the meaning of the verse Ecclesiastes vii 14: 'God has made the one as well as the other.' Apparently Aḥer wished to find an allusion in this verse to fate, which determined the righteous and the wicked in the world. R. Me'ir diverted the verse to another homily, to which Aḥer reacted by saying: 'R. Akiba, your teacher, did not expound it thus, but (God) created righteous men (and) He created wicked men; He created the Garden of Eden (and) He created Gehenna. Every man has two portions, one in the Garden of Eden and one in Gehenna. The righteous man, having been found worthy [by the Heavenly Court], receives his own portion and that of his fellow in the Garden of Eden; the wicked man, having been found guilty, receives his portion and that of his fellow in Gehenna' (*T.B. Ḥagiga* 15a). To each one a portion is allocated both in the Garden of Eden and in Gehenna, and which of these falls to a man's lot depends purely on his actions. Were the righteous and the wicked predetermined, it would only be necessary to prepare for each one the place due to him. This view of R. Akiba regarding the unrestricted freedom of man's choice also underlies his controversy with R. Pappos concerning the interpretation of the verse 'Behold, the man hath become like one of us' (Genesis iii 22). R. Pappos explained it to mean 'like one of the Ministering Angels. Said R. Akiba: "Enough, Pappos!" Pappos retorted: "And how do you explain 'The man hath become like one of us'?" [Said R. Akiba to him]: "The Holy One, blessed be He, put two ways before him, one of death and one of life, and he chose the way of death." '[28] R. Pappos' exposition alludes to a concept that makes a fundamental distinction between man before and after he had sinned. The sphere of primordial man was interior to that of the Ministering Angels [i.e. nearer to God]. He was like the Only One (as it were) of the universe, and God thought to give him dominion over His world and to make him king over all His creatures. 'Said the Holy One, blessed be He: "I am King over the celestial beings, and man shall be king over the earthly creatures." ' These and similar dicta[29] are transmitted by Amoraim and are found in late sources, but they clearly recall the words of Philo about the First Man, who takes second place after God, as viceroy and ruler over all things;[30] he is the 'heavenly man' (οὐράνιος ἄνθρωπος) and the divine logos.[31] This First Man was, of course, perfect (τέλειος) and had no need of commandments and prohibitions. The first commandment was not given to this man, who was created in the image of God, but to the man who was taken from the ground.[32] It was not difficult to continue and say that man, after his fall, after he had erred in his choice, lost this potentiality and was placed under the dominion of sin. However, Philo did not draw this conclusion, which negates man's freedom of choice and repentance; but Paul came to that conclusion when he incorporated therein the Christological element: 'One man's trespass led to condemnation for all men' (Romans v 18), 'As was the one man of dust, so are all those who are of the dust' (I Corinthians xv 48). It is not possible to be redeemed save again by the help of the heavenly man: 'Just as we have borne the image of the man of dust, we shall also bear the image of the man of heaven' (*ibid.* v. 49).[33] R. Akiba rejected utterly the comparison of the first man to the Ministering Angels, and by implication all that flowed from this elevation. Man was placed from the outset beneath the yoke of the commandment, and he was given permission to choose between the way of life and the way of death. This right was not taken away from him after he had sinned and the penalty of death was imposed upon him. It remains within the power of every man to this day.

We have thus found so far in the teaching of R. Akiba a clear emphasis on the principle of the freedom of choice, but we have not discerned an antithesis between this principle and that of Providence presiding over the world and its natural order, which R. Akiba meditated and which aroused his wonderment (*Sifra*, Shemini, Sec. 5). Of his disciple, R. Simeon b. Yoḥai, it is related that he saw a fowler laying a snare with which to trap a bird, and behold, he heard a Heavenly Voice saying, 'Demos!' ['pardon!'], and the bird was saved. Thereupon the Tanna said: 'A bird, unless Heaven wills it, is not caught, how much more so a human being!'[34] Clearly neither R. Akiba nor his colleagues and disciples completely evaded the question of the relationship between the two principles, and if not explicit then implicit expression was given thereto. However, the belief in Providence is essentially different from that in fate, for it posits the free Will of God as a basic and fundamental verity, and thereby it also differs from both astrology and Stoic teaching. But this Will and its decisions perforce determine man's fate and the ways and circumstances of his life. On the other hand, they are also determined by the free choice of man.

It seems that neither the Tannaim in the first and second centuries, nor the Amoraim who followed them, produced a solution to the problem. Belief in the two principles — both in Providence and in freedom of choice — is common to them all, but they differ in fixing their boundaries and in the ways of reconciling them. The differences are to be understood in the light of their divergent experiences of life — for we are not dealing here with speculative thought but with pragmatic reflection — and also as due in no small measure to external influences, emanating from astrology and widely current popular beliefs on the one side, and from the solutions to the problem of predestination and freedom of choice, as advanced by the Stoics in the course of centuries, on the other. Both approaches came to the knowledge of the Sages, by diverse channels, at the end of the Tannaitic period only, and especially in the days of the Amoraim. The answers are reflected at times in the attitude they adopted towards other questions.

To R. Akiba is attributed the homiletical exposition of the verse ' "And righteousness delivereth from death" — not from violent death but from death itself' (*T.B. Shabbat* 156b). This is the reading in our printed editions, but in *Haggadot ha-Talmud* ['Talmudic Legends'] (Constantinople 1511) and in *ʿEn Yaʿaqov* ['Fountain of Jacob'], editio princeps (Salonica 1515), the text has: 'and not from death itself but from violent death.'[35] The importance and correctness of this reading becomes clear in the light of R. Akiba's express teaching in the Baraita on the predetermination of the number of years of a man's life. 'It is taught: "The number of thy days I will fulfil" — these are the years of the generations [i.e. the allotted span of life]. If a man is worthy, he is vouchsafed the full period; if he is unworthy, his years are reduced. This is the view of R. Akiba. But the Sages declare: If he is worthy the years of his life are increased, if he is unworthy they are reduced. They said to R. Akiba: Now Scripture states "And I will add unto your days fifteen years"! He answered them: The added years were of his own. Know now that this is so, for a prophet arose and prophesied "Behold, a son shall be born to the house of David, Josiah by name", although Manasseh had not yet been born....'[36] The length of the days of a man is predetermined, only his wicked deeds may lead to their reduction. 'If a man dies under the age of fifty, he dies by כרת *kārēt* ['cut off'] (*T.P. Bikkurim* ii, p. 1; *T.B. Moʿed Qaṭan* 28a). A man's good deeds bring about only the completion of his days and his delivery from violent death. Accordingly R. Akiba said (*M. ʿEduyot* ii, 9) that a father endows his son with years only in the framework of 'the number of the generations that have gone before him, and of them he [the son] is the end, as it is said: "Calling the generations from the beginning" (Isaiah xli 14).' In other words, the (ancestral) merit cannot prolong a man's years beyond the years of the generations that the Almighty allotted to him.[37] R. Akiba's doctrine is briefly summarized by Naḥmanides in his commentary on Exodus xxiii 26: 'As it is said "The number of thy days I will fulfil" — this means that he will not die in battle or through plague or change of weather, but only through old age, that is, that he will complete his days according to the number that forms the life of man in his generations.' Death is part of the order of the universe, and accordingly measured spans have been allotted to human life, and when the appointed time arrives it cannot be postponed, for new generations wait to take their place. When Moses wished to cross the Jordan, God said to him 'I created My world as a series of eras. Had Abraham then committed a sin that he died? The reason was that the age of Isaac was pressing to enter history, and Isaac passed away only because Jacob's epoch was pressing to begin; and now Joshua's term of office presses to commence.'[38] Although the Sages differ from R. Akiba and declare that good deeds are conducive to length of days, yet their teaching does not imply that 'There is no death without sin'. This doctrine appears only in the time of the Amoraim.[39]

Thus in the case under discussion a limit has been set to the influence of human free choice on the one hand, and on the other a certain segment has been removed from the area of fate's dominion. A similar compromise is found relative to other subjects in the answer given by R. Joshua b. Ḥananiah to the Alexandrians. They asked him: ' "What shall a man do to become wise?" He replied: "Let him devote more time to study and less to trade." Said they to him: "Many have done so without success!" — "Rather must they supplicate Him to whom wisdom belongs, as it is said 'For the Lord giveth wisdom, out of His mouth cometh knowledge and discernment' (Proverbs ii 6)..." "What shall a man do to become rich?" Said he to them: "Let a man engage in trade and deal honestly." They replied: "Many have acted thus without success!" — "Rather let a man supplicate Him to whom (all) wealth belongs, as it is said 'Mine is the silver and Mine is the gold' (Haggai ii 8)..." "What shall a man do that he may have male offspring?" He replied: "Let him take a woman meet for him and sanctify himself at the time of intercourse." They answered: "Many have done so without success!" — "Rather let him supplicate Him to whom children belong..." ' (*T.B. Nidda* 70b). The Gemara deduces from the remarks of R. Joshua that 'the one without the other was insufficient,' that is to say, that the deeds of man that are performed with understanding and in conformity with the laws of ethics and the precepts of religion can assure the desired results only if they accord with the designs of Providence, 'which knoweth what the future holds in store', in accordance with R. Joshua b. Ḥananiah's answer to the Romans (*T.B. Sanhedrin* 90b).

A kind of sequel to R. Joshua b. Ḥananiah's dicta is provided by the following dialogue: 'A Gentile (once) asked R. Joshua b. Qorḥa, saying: "Do you not aver that the Holy One, blessed be He, foresees that which will happen?" He replied: "Yea!" He then retorted: "But it is written 'And it grieved Him at His heart' (Genesis vi 6)." Said R. Joshua to him: "Has a male child ever been born to you?" He answered "Yea!" "And what did you do?" The Gentile replied: "I rejoiced and I gave a celebration for all to rejoice." Thereupon R. Joshua said to him: "But did you not realize that in the end he would die?" The Gentile answered: "In the hour of joy we must rejoice, in the time of mourning we must mourn" ' (*Genesis Rabba* xxvii, 4). Foreseeing an event is not conceived here as an arbitrary determination of the future event, just as in the analogy a man does not determine his son's ultimate death. On the contrary, it contains the possibility of choice, and in God's reaction there is an expression of grief at man's not having chosen the right path.

This integration of man's freedom of choice with the ways of Providence provides the rationale of numerous Halakhot of the School of R. Ishmael. The Torah enjoined: 'When thou buildest a new house, then thou shalt make a parapet for thy roof, that thou bring not blood upon thy house, when the faller falls from thence' (Deuteronomy xxi 8). In a Baraita the Sages stated: 'The School of R. Ishmael taught: "When the faller falls from thence" — this man was destined to fall since the time of Creation, for he had not (yet) fallen, yet Scripture calls him 'faller'; for good is brought about through the good and guilt [i.e. punishment] through the guilty' (*T.B. Shabbat* 32a; *Sifre Deuteronomy* Sect. 229). The fall had been decreed upon the falling man by Providence, but it was the house-owner's sin that caused him to fall through his neglect. A similar explanation was given of the verse 'And if a man lie not in wait, but God cause it to come to hand' (Exodus xxi 13): 'If one man killed a person accidentally, and another slew a person intentionally, the willful murderer — it comes about — falls by the hand of the innocent homicide' (*Mekhilta Mishpaṭim*, § 4; cf. *T.B. Makkot* 10b). This interpretation was already known to Philo, who concludes his annotation with the words: 'God uses as His ministers those whose sins are few and easily remedied, though He does not show approval of them but merely takes them as suitable instruments of vengeance. For He would not wish that anyone whose whole life is stainless and his lineage also should set his hand to homicide however justly deserved.'[40]

What we have finally shown corroborates to a certain extent Josephus' statement that the Pharisees, in asserting that everything is decided by fate, do not negate man's will to aspire after anything he desires. Since it is God's decree, He willed that there should be a synthesis and that the human will, which chooses between good and evil,[41] should also participate in the determination of fate. Nor is it surprising that this approach should bring to Josephus' mind the Stoic doctrine that teaches that the εἱμαρμένη does not nullify the intended and purposive action of man. Contrariwise, this is included in the εἱμαρμένη, and without it the outcome foreseen from the beginning would not be achieved. The wise man is distinguishable from the fool in that he discerns in fate προνοία ['foresight'], which seeks his good, and therefore he accepts it gladly and acts in conformity with it.[42] However, Josephus overlooked the fundamental difference between the Stoic εἱμαρμένη, which is only the law of nature and the chain of causation, and God, who has free will. But the factual account is correct at any rate in so far as a section of the Pharisaic Sages of his time is concerned.

Already in R. Akiba's generation there is discernible still another way of defining the relationship between Providence and free choice, namely the complete separation between man's religio-ethical conduct and his external life and its circumstances. Ben ʿAzzai said: 'Precept leads to precept and transgression to transgression. For the reward of a precept is a precept and the reward of a transgression is a transgression' (*M. 'Avot* iv, 2). This saying apparently refers to the view that in this world there is no reward except that which inheres in the actual observance of the precepts. Ben ʿAzzai does not state that a man is helped by Heaven to perform additional precepts, if he has fulfilled one. This idea, which we shall encounter soon, did not accord with his outlook. In *Mekhilta* (Wa-yassaʿ, Sec. i) we learn: 'Simeon b. ʿAzzai said: "שמוע *Shamoaʿ* ['Hearken']", why then does Scripture add "תשמע *tishmaʿ* ['thou shalt hearken']"? From this is to be inferred that if a man desires to hearken, he is given the opportunity to do so; to forget, he is (likewise) enabled to do so. But perhaps this means after a time? Hence Scripture teaches: "And it shall be if hearken thou shalt hearken" [usually rendered: 'And it shall come to pass, if thou shalt hearken diligently'] (Deuteronomy xxviii 1), "[and it shall be] if forget thou shalt forget" [usually rendered: 'And it shall be, if thou shalt forget'] (Deuteronomy viii 19). ["And it shall be"] — forthwith! How is this to be envisaged? If a man wishes to hearken, he is afforded the opportunity to hearken at once; to forget, he is enabled to forget at once. He (further) said: If a man wishes to hearken בטובתו *bĕṭôvātô* [literally, 'for his good'], he is granted to hearken שלא בטובתו *shellō' bĕṭôvatô* ['not for his good']; to forget *bĕṭôvātô*, he is enabled to forget not *bĕṭôvātô*. Freedom of choice is given, "If it concerneth the scorners, He scorneth them, but unto the humble He giveth grace" (Proverbs iii 34).' The earlier dicta stress that man is granted freedom of choice, and that Heaven does not stand in his way or hinder him, but his desire to hearken or to forget is immediately fulfilled. The commentators found it difficult, however, to explain the second dictum, and some emended the text. Saul Horovitz (*Mekhilta*, p. 158) gives this interpretation: 'That if a man learns voluntarily, the Holy One, blessed be He, brings it about that he should learn even where he himself had not intended to learn.' But this interpretation makes the word *bĕṭôvātô* redundant. Although we find the expression *shellō' bĕṭôvātô* used in the sense of 'perforce' (*T.B. Sanhedrin* 7b), yet in most Mishnayot and Baraitot the signification of *bĕṭôvā* and *shellō' bĕṭôvā* is 'for benefit' and 'and not for benefit'.[43] Here, too, it appears to me, this is the meaning to be given to the words: If a man wishes to hearken with a view to his benefit, that is to say, for the sake of the hoped-for reward, he is, indeed, vouchsafed to hearken but not for his benefit — without receipt of reward. On the other hand, if he wishes to forget for his benefit — out of a desire to gain thereby, he is allowed to forget, but the advantage is not granted him. A man's good is not dependent on his choice, nor is the welfare of the righteous.

A similar significance attaches also to his following dictum: 'When does the Holy One, blessed be He, show them (i.e. the righteous) the reward in store for them? Near their death' (*Genesis Rabba* lxii, 2, p. 672), and the dictum is akin to the view expressed in a subsequent generation by the Tanna R. Jacob: ' "That it may go well with thee" — this refers to the world that is wholly good; "And that thy days may be prolonged" — this refers to the world that is wholly long.' In other words: 'There is no reward for (the fulfilment of) precepts in this world'[44] — a doctrine that contradicts the ancient Mishna 'If a man performs but a single precept, he is granted good and length of days.'[45] As we have seen, R. Akiba disagreed with this Mishna, for he severed the connection between the length of a man's life and his actions. Although in regard to a man's livelihood he said: 'Whoever gives alms to the poor knows no dearth',[46] yet without doubt both his teaching and the example that R. Akiba set in his life by his death led to the conclusion that precepts are not rewarded in this world. He expressed the view that 'suffering is precious', and when his flesh was combed with iron combs, he declared that all his days he had prayed for that moment. Clear expression is given to the effect of R. Akiba's death on the concept of reward and punishment and on that of Providence in the Haggada about Moses, attributed to Rav. After Moses had been shown R. Akiba's eminence in Torah-knowledge, he said: ' "Show me his reward"... he beheld his flesh being weighed at meat stands. So he said unto God: "Sovereign of the universe, such is Torah and such its reward!" The Lord replied: "Silence! Thus was it decreed by Me" ' (*T.B. Menaḥot* 29b). Rav made the death of R. Akiba the pivot of his Tannaitic predecessors' view that not only death but even 'violent death' does not depend on human actions alone. However, Ben ʿAzzai already placed all the other benefits of man in this world under the absolute control of Providence, human conduct having no effect thereon, and thus Ben ʿAzzai declared: 'Of that which belongs to you you will be given, and by your name you shall be called, and in your place you shall be seated, and there is no oblivion before the Omnipresent, and no man touches that which is prepared for his fellow.'[47]

Such a doctrine concerning the reward given for the fulfilment of the precepts could be held by a few individuals only. In instructing the general public, in preaching the observance of the commandments, even Ben ʿAzzai could not forgo the principle that 'The disciples of Abraham our father enjoy (their reward) in this world and inherit the world to come' (*M. 'Avot* v, 19). And the same Ben ʿAzzai, when he warned the people to answer 'Amen' correctly — and this admonition was directed to the common folk, for whom this constituted their primary participation in congregational prayer — he said: 'Whoever answers an 'orphaned' Amen [i.e. in response to a benediction he himself has not heard], his children will be orphaned; a 'curtailed'

(Amen) [i.e. the *Nûn* not distinctly pronounced], his days will be curtailed; a 'prolonged' (Amen), his days and years will be prolonged.'[48]

The restriction of reward to the next world obviated the need to observe the ways of Providence in all that related to man's material life, but it did not solve the problem of the extent of his freedom in making religious and ethical decisions. Nay more, this very distinction between the holy and the profane enabled one to see the problem clearly. Was there then no connection between a man's piety and his wealth, or his beauty or ugliness? Indeed, we learn in a Baraita that if a poor man argues before the Heavenly Court 'I was a poor man and preoccupied with my livelihood', they say to him: 'Were you poorer than Hillel?' Similarly, R. Eleazar b. Ḥarsom condemned the rich, and Joseph condemned the wicked (*T.B. Yoma* 35b).[49] But perhaps these righteous men were vouchsafed attributes and virtues that were not granted to other people, and they were chosen to be righteous? In truth such a conclusion was actually reached at the close of the Tannaitic period: 'And there were three who were named by the Holy One, blessed be He: Isaac, and Solomon, and Josiah. What does Scripture say of Isaac? "Nay, but Sarah thy wife shall bear thee a son; and thou shalt call his name Isaac" (Genesis xvii 19). And what is stated with regard to Solomon? "Behold, a son shall be born to thee, who shall be a man of rest; and I will give him rest from all his enemies round about; for his name shall be Solomon, and I will give peace and quietness unto Israel in his days" (I Chronicles xxii 9). What is said of Josiah? "Behold, a son shall be born unto the house of David, Josiah by name" etc. (I Kings xiii 2). Some say: Also Ishmael among the Gentiles. We find the names and deeds of the righteous are revealed before the Omnipresent even before they are born, as it is said: "Before I formed thee in the belly I knew thee" (Jeremiah i 5). We thus find that the names of the righteous (are known to God beforehand); whence (do we know that this is also true of) the names of the wicked? Therefore Scripture teaches: "The wicked go astray from the womb" (Psalms lviii 4 [3]).' This exposition, which is found in the *Mekhilta* (Pisḥa § 16, ed. Horovitz, p. 60), resembles in meaning the observation in *The Manual of Discipline* (iv, 22) concerning the upright, 'For them God chose for an everlasting covenant', and the statement in *The Zadokite Document*[50] (ii, 12) regarding 'those who abominate the ordinance': 'For God disapproved of them from the beginning of the world, and ere their foundations were laid, He knew their deeds.' The first part of the passage in the *Mekhilta* occurs in *Genesis Rabba* in the name of R. Isaac, and he is, apparently, the Tanna from the School of R. Ishmael, who is often mentioned in the *Mekhilta* and in the *Sifre*. It seems that R. Isaac stated only of three righteous men that their names were designated before they were formed, but not of all the righteous. This differentiation finds support in another Midrashic exposition of R. Isaac. ' "The Lord bless thee..." — R. Nathan said: May He bless thee with property and keep thee in (health of) body. R. Isaac said: And keep thee from evil inclination' (*Sifre Numbers* § 40). Preservation from the evil inclination does not signify the foreordained election of the preserved, but it has at least the value of the active help of Providence in man's struggle against temptation. This view of the help afforded by Providence to man in making his choice was not the opinion of an individual but that of the entire School of Ishmael. Freedom of choice was limited to the initial decision. This is the meaning of the exposition in the *Mekhilta de-R. Ishmael* (Wa-yassa' i, p. 157): ' "And He said: 'If thou wilt diligently hearken' " [literally: 'If hearken thou wilt hearken'] — from this the Sages inferred: If a man hearkened to one precept, he is enabled to hearken to many precepts, as it is said, "If thou wilt diligently hearken". If a man forgot one precept, he is made to forget many precepts.' Not only does one precept lead to another, and if a man seeks to hearken, he is given the opportunity of doing so — as Ben 'Azzai taught — but his desire and resolve are augmented. In another Baraita we find: 'The School of R. Ishmael taught: Transgression dulls the heart of man, as it is said: "Neither shall ye make yourselves unclean with them, that ye should be defiled thereby" (Leviticus xi 43). Read not ונטמאתם *wĕniṭmē'tem* ['that ye should be defiled'] but ונטמטם *wĕniṭṭamṭem* ['that ye should become dull-hearted']. The Rabbis taught: "Neither shall ye make yourselves unclean with them, that ye should be defiled thereby" — this means, if a man defiles himself a little, he is defiled much... The Rabbis taught: "Sanctify yourselves therefore, and be ye holy" (*ibid.* v. 44) — if a man sanctifies himself a little, he is sanctified much....'[51] This doctrine may be the result of meditation and experience; but it is difficult to consider it fortuitous that, both in the conception of free choice as in the explanation of Providence, there exists a certain similarity between the approach of R. Ishmael and his School, on the one hand, and the Stoics and Philo of Alexandria, on the other. From the first century B.C.E. onward the Stoics ascribe a decisive practical value to the recognition of man's freedom of decision and to the responsibility implicit in this decision.

The concepts of good and evil are inherent in man; decision means correct use of these ideas. For this purpose a *prior decision* (προαίρεσις) is necessary. Philo regarded freedom of choice as a gift from God, which was vouchsafed to man in order to nullify the laws of nature that rule him. Freedom of choice applies to both good and evil, but man is not left on his own in opting for good. After he has proved his power in subduing the evil inclination and preferring the good, and after he has realized that this power comes to him from God, God comes to his aid and helps him. This Divine grace is granted to all men, but there are some who are vouchsafed this even before they are born. On the other hand, the choice of evil is wholly in man's hands.[52] One cannot overlook the contradiction and difficulty of Philo's thesis. On the one hand, free will is a gift of God, and thereby man becomes most like Him,[53] but, on the other hand, it comes only to explain the choice of evil, which cannot emanate from God, from whom only good can issue.[54] Reasoning of this kind is completely absent in Tannaitic teaching. If Divine intervention is posited in the wake of man's choice, it is not restricted only to the option of those who choose good ('If a man hearkened to one precept, he is enabled to harken to many precepts'), but includes also the case of those who prefer evil ('If a man forgot one precept, he is made to forget many precepts'). But even when the issue is actually not man's choice of good or evil, but God's choice of man, we find that not only the names of the righteous and their deeds are revealed before the Omnipresent prior to their birth, but also the names and acts of the wicked. The wicked are not subject to the dominion of Belial, and the idea of the creation of the righteous and the wicked is not linked to a dualistic theology, as we know from the writings of the Qumran Sect. The view shared by the Tannaim is that all the creatures are subject in their lifetime to the rule of the Holy One, blessed be He. A Tanna of the

School of R. Ishmael expounded: '"Let the Lord, the God of the spirits of all flesh, set..." — this teaches us that all the spirits go forth only from before Him.' R. Eliezer b. R. Jose the Galilean added: 'Grasp this verity, that so long as a man remains alive, his soul is in the keeping of his Maker, as it is said: "In whose hand is the soul of every living thing, and the breath of all mankind" (Job xii 10)'; the differentiation between the place of the righteous and that of the wicked obtains only after their death (*Sifre Numbers* § 139).

Even the Tanna R. Isaac only intended to say that certain righteous men were privileged to be chosen before their birth. However, a general deduction was drawn from this dictum, namely that all the righteous and all the wicked were named before they were formed, but it was not yet explained when the designation of the names took place, and it even seemed a probable inference from the verse in Jeremiah i 5, 'Before I formed thee in the belly I knew thee', that it refers to a recurring act. Finally, R. Yannai, one of the earliest Palestinian Amoraim came and gave the following interpretation: 'From the beginning of the creation of the world, the Holy One, blessed be He, saw the deeds of the righteous and the deeds of the wicked. "Now the earth was unformed and void" — this refers to the acts of the wicked; "And God said: 'Let there be light' " — this alludes to the acts of the righteous; "And God saw the light, that it was good" — this is a reference to the deeds of the righteous; "And God divided the light from the darkness" — (that is) the works of the righteous from those of the wicked. "And God called the light Day" — this connotes the deeds of the righteous; "and the darkness He called Night" — this is an allusion to the actions of the wicked.'[55] Thus the passage speaks of a determination that took place once only and of the division of humanity into two camps: the righteous who are 'children of light' and the wicked who are 'children of darkness'. But neither of these groups leaves the sphere of God's jurisdiction, as is stated at the end of this allegorical exposition: '"One day" — this means that the Holy One, blessed be He, gave them a unique day. Which was that? — the Day of Judgement.'

R. Joḥanan, the contemporary and disciple of R. Yannai, went much farther in his formulation, saying: 'The name of the Holy One, blessed be He, is not mentioned relative to evil, but only in connection with good'[56]; he did not, however, state that evil was not created by the Holy One, blessed be He. Their aversion to the notion that evil does not emanate from God led the Amoraim to give an emphatic interpretation, in the reverse sense, to every Biblical verse in which any support or basis for this idea could be discerned. R. Eleazar,[57] the disciple of R. Joḥanan, who transmitted in his master's name the dictum that we have cited, expounded the verse 'Out of the mouth of the Most High proceedeth not evil and good' (Lamentations iii 38) thus: 'From the moment that the Holy One, blessed be He, said[58] "See, I have set before thee this day life and good, and death and evil" (Deuteronomy xxx 15), good has not gone forth to him who does evil nor evil to him who does good, but only good to the doer of good and evil to the doer of evil.' This exposition follows upon the interpretation of the verse 'Who is he that saith, and it cometh to pass, when the Lord commandeth it not?' as referring to the wicked men Pharaoh and Haman, who acted as they did not at the command of the Lord but on their own account, and it seeks to contradict the view that evil has its own domain; hence it emphasizes man's freedom of choice, and, in another version of R. Eleazar's dictum, even assumes an extreme form: ' "Behold, I set before you..." (Deuteronomy xi 26) — since the Holy One, blessed be He, proclaimed this at Sinai, from that moment evil and good do not issue (from God), but evil comes of its own accord upon those who do evil, and good comes to those who do good.'[59] But just as evil comes of its own accord as a result of human actions, so good also comes of its own accord, for the choice of good is not a necessity in the development of man, which flows from the very fact that he is endowed with a power that draws him near to God. This latter doctrine, which several of the Church Fathers adopted, restricts human freedom and limits it to a given period.[60]

The fear of the belief in dualism, which aims to solve the problem of the source of evil and militates against the ancient doctrine of predestination, thus led to the limitation of the area to which Providence applied and to the special emphasis laid on man's freedom of choice. This restriction served also to obstruct the influence of the belief in astrology, which was widely current in the epoch of the Amoraim. In the Roman era astrology was no longer a religion, although it originated in the late Babylonian cult, and it must be distinguished from the worship of the host of heaven, in the form, for example, of sun-worship, which was a kind of official religion of the Empire. Astrology posited a game involving a fixed number of abstract powers, that obeyed unchanging and enduring laws, and controlled all existence. The value of the sun and the heavenly host consisted not, as in natural religion, in their appearance and action, but in their role in the deterministic array of forces. Astrology was incorporated in various systems of thought — Pythagorianism, Stoicism, and Gnosticism — and for the very reason that it was not a religion, the various faiths felt the need and possibility of coming to terms with it.[61]

From the time of R. Me'ir and his contemporaries there has come down to us a discussion on the significance of eclipses: 'When the luminaries are eclipsed, it is an evil omen for the whole world... R. Me'ir said: When the luminaries are eclipsed, it is an evil omen for Israel's "enemies" [a euphemism, meaning: for the Israelites themselves], because they are accustomed to calamities... When the sun is eclipsed, it is an evil omen for the Gentiles; if the moon is eclipsed, it is an evil omen for the "enemies" of Israel, for the Gentiles regulate their calendar by the sun, but Israel by the moon[62]... R. Josiah said: When the planets are eclipsed in the east, it is an evil omen for the inhabitants of the east; in the west, it is an evil omen for the inhabitants of the west. R. Joḥanan said: Both sets of omens are intended for the Gentiles, as it is said: "Thus saith the Lord: Learn not the ways of the nations, and be not dismayed at the signs of heaven" (Jeremiah x 2).' Phenomena that are seen but infrequently among the heavenly bodies are interpreted here only as a sign and omen for evil to come; in another Baraita the phenomena are themselves regarded as a punishment for certain sins. But neither view ascribes the eclipses of the luminaries to independent forces; they are considered signs or messengers of Providence, and hence the aforementioned dicta are not to be regarded as astrology. But even in the sphere of this restricted meaning, a special place was assigned to Israel by almost all the Tannaim treating of the subject, and R. Jonathan even excludes the Jews completely by referring to the verse in Jeremiah. In a Baraita in the *Sifra* astrology is included in the prohibition 'Ye shall not practice divination.'[63] R. Jonathan's contemporary, R. Jose of Huṣal,[64] said: 'Whence do we know that we may not consult the Chaldeans, for it is stated "Thou shalt be whole-hearted with the Lord thy God" ' (*T.B. Pesaḥim* 113a).

This prohibition does not imply the denial of the actual value of astrology and its reality. This belief was shared by Tannaim and Amoraim alike.[65] The early Amoraim dispute over the question whether the planets and Chaldean lore affect the Jews. In R. Joshua b. Levi's notebook were recorded the indications of a man's character according to the day on which he was born, as, for example, 'He who is born on the second day of the week will be irascible'; R. Ḥanina, on the other hand, was of opinion that not the constellation of the day but that of the hour is the determining factor. Hence 'He who is born under the planet Venus will be rich and unchaste... he who is born under Jupiter (צדק *Ṣedeq*) will be a man who acts rightly...', in other words: 'The constellation makes wise, the constellation makes rich, and Israel is subject to planetary influence' (Rashi: 'This means that neither prayer nor alms-giving changes the planetary influence'). Contrariwise, Rav and Samuel held that the fulfilment of the precepts is able to nullify the influence of the planets, and R. Joḥanan deduced — as did R. Jonathan in his day — from Jeremiah x 2 that Israel does not stand under planetary influence.[66] He also stresses the question of freedom of choice. The verse '*I am that I am... I am* hath sent me unto you' (Exodus iii, 15) was thus expounded by R. Joḥanan: ' "I am that I am" applies to individuals, but in the case of the many [i.e. the people as a whole] I rule over them perforce, against their will, though their teeth be broken...'[67]; to the individual freedom of choice is granted. Thereon depends also the possibility of repentance, of which R. Joḥanan said 'Great is repentance, for it rends asunder the decree imposed upon a man' (*T.B. Rosh Hashana* 17b).

Astrology not only contradicted the freedom of human choice, but also impaired the concept of Providence, that is, the doctrine of the free will and unrestricted power of God. Apparently R. Ḥanina did not overlook this problem, but even the Amoraim who excluded Israel from the influence of the constellations and transferred them to the domain of Providence[68] stressed the ways of Providence in fullest detail and described them in expressions and images derived from the sphere of astrology. Rav Judah said in the name of Rav: 'Forty days before the formation of a child a heavenly voice goes forth and declares: The daughter of So-and-so is (to be married) to

So-and-so; such and such a house (shall belong) to So-and-so; such and such a field (shall belong) to So-and-so' (*T.B. Soṭa* 2a), and, on the other hand, he reports in the name of Samuel: '*Each day* a heavenly voice goes forth and declares: The daughter of So-and-so (is to be married) to So-and-so; such and such a field (shall belong) to So-and-so' (*T.B. Moʿed Qaṭan* 18b). Rav, therefore, speaks of a decree that is determined before birth,[69] while Samuel is able to make the decision depend on human action, and R. Joḥanan and Resh Laqish agree with him, at any rate in so far as marriage is concerned (*T.B. Soṭa, loc. cit.*).

Belief in Providence makes man the focal point of the universe, and like Chrysippus[70], the most important representative of the ancient Stoics, Rav and the Amoraim who follow his view reach the conclusion that there is a benefit and purpose attaching to all beings and creatures: 'Said Rav Judah in the name of Rav: Of all that the Holy One, blessed be He, created in His world, there is naught that He created without purpose' (*T.B. Shabbat* 77b). And the Rabbis said: 'Even things that appear to you wholly superfluous in the creation of the world — like fleas, gnats and flies — also form an integral part of the world-creation, and the Holy One, blessed be He, uses them all in His service.'[71] The central position of man is not to be understood in the sense of 'Thou hast put all things under his feet' (Psalms viii 7 [6]). Everything is directed only towards him, but he himself directs nothing, not even his limbs. R. Joḥanan did not declare with Hillel 'To the place *that I love* thither my feet lead me', but he said 'A man's feet are responsible for him; they lead him to the place where *he is wanted*.'[72] Even a man's religious integrity is not entirely in his own hands. Following upon the ideas that we found expressed by the Tannaim, R. Joḥanan said: 'When the majority of a man's years have passed without his sinning, he will not sin thereafter, for it is said "He will keep the feet of His holy ones" ' (I Samuel ii 9).[73]

The last of the Amoraim, the Palestinian Haggadists, applied the inferences that they drew from this conception of Providence also to the question of reward and punishment and its relationship to human actions. In *Tanḥuma*[74] the following daring homily is cited: 'Come and see, when the Holy One, blessed be He, created the world, He created the angel of death already on the first day. Whence do we know this? Said R. Berechiah: Because Scripture states "And darkness was upon the face of the deep" (Genesis i 2) — this means the angel of death, who darkens the face of mankind; whereas man was created on the sixth day, yet he was blamed for having brought death into the world, as it is said "For in the day that thou eatest thereof thou shalt surely die" (*ibid.* ii 17). To what can the matter be compared? To a man who wished to divorce his wife. When he decided to go home, he wrote a bill of divorcement; then he entered his house, with the divorce in his possession, seeking a pretext for giving it to her. He said to her: "Mix me a cup (of wine) to drink." She mixed his cup. When he took the cup from her hand, he said to her: "Here is your divorce." Said she to him: "What sin have I committed?" He replied: "Go from my house, for you have mixed me a lukewarm cup (of wine)." She retorted: "You already knew beforehand that I should mix you a tepid cup (of wine), for you wrote the divorce and brought it with you!" Even so did Adam argue before the Holy One, blessed be He: "Sovereign of the universe, two thousand years before Thou didst create Thy world, the Torah was by Thee as an אמון *'āmôn* [variously rendered: 'nursling' or 'master-workman'] (Proverbs viii 30), and in it is written 'This is the law: when a man dieth in a tent' (Numbers xix 14); if Thou hadst not prepared death for mankind, wouldst Thou have written thus? Only Thou hast come to put the blame on me; this is the meaning of the verse 'He is terrible in His doing toward the children of men' (Psalms lxvi 5)." ' The passage merely states that man's sin did not cause death to come into the world; the decree of death would have existed even without him, and man's act served only as an instrument for implementing it. The homilist says the same with regard to Moses' death, and he cites in the name of R. Judan a similar explanation of Joseph's being brought down to Egypt, and finally R. Tanḥuma summarizes the thought with the analogy: 'To what can the matter be compared? To a cow on whose neck they (the owners) wish to put a yoke, but she prevents the yoke from (being placed on) her neck. What did they do? They took her son away from following her and drew him to the place that they wished to plough, and the calf lowed. When the cow heard her son lowing, she went reluctantly for her son's sake. So was it with the Holy One, blessed be He: He wished to fulfil the decree of

"Know of a surety", so He found a pretext for all those events, and they (Jacob's family) went down to Egypt and they "paid the debt"; hence Scripture declares "And Joseph was brought down to Egypt". This is the meaning of the verse: "He is terrible in His doing" etc.' Human deeds that appear to man as the decisions of his own will are in truth only links in a chain of events whose purpose is to realize what Providence has decreed. This concept is actually implicit in the aphorism 'A man's feet are responsible for him; they lead him to the place where he is wanted', and this is the position arrived at even by those Amoraim who excluded Israel from the rule of the planets. The gulf between them and the Amoraim who held that 'Israel is subject to the constellations' narrowed, especially when we take into consideration the fact that it was precisely the latter who felt it their duty to raise expressly the subject of human free will.

Even though he accepted the influence of the planets upon Israel. R. Ḥanina did not restrict the extent of the influence of Divine Providence. In opposition to the view of R. Joḥanan, who said that the sorcerers 'lessen (the power of) the Council [*Familia*] on High' (Rashi: 'For they slay those whom (Heaven) decreed to live'), R. Ḥanina proclaimed ' "There is none else besides Him" — even where sorcery is concerned' (Rashi: 'They [the sorcerers or sorceries] have not the power to *resist His edict*, for there is no power besides Him')[75]; sorcery and the planets are likewise subject to the Creator's Providence, 'For if it has not been decreed by Him, they cannot hurt the person.'[76] Hence R. Ḥanina said: 'A man does not bruise his finger below [upon earth] unless it be announced concerning him (Rashi: 'decreed concerning him') on high, for it is said: "A man's goings are of the Lord; how then can man look to his way?" (Proverbs xx 24).'[77] This emphasis placed on the all-embracing power of Providence does not nullify the value of man's deeds, nor does it exempt him from taking reasonable care in his conduct and actions. In the field of Halakha, too, the postulate that it lies within a man's power to act according to his decision forms the basis for rulings; thus 'All that is within a man's power (to do) is not regarded as though the act were lacking.'[78] It was none other than R. Ḥanina who said: 'All (ailments) are in the power of Heaven except cold and draughts, for it is said: "Cold and draughts [usually rendered: 'thorns and snares'] are in the way of the froward; he that doth keep his soul holdeth himself far from them" (Proverbs xxii 5).'[79] There are also everyday occurrences that happen to a person on account of his transgressions; undoubtedly R. Ḥanina did not mean only 'cold and draughts' and he mentioned them solely on account of the verse. Or in the words of the Palestinian Talmud:[80] 'Rav who lived where the evil eye was common, used to say: "Ninety-nine die of the (evil) eye, and (only) one by (the decree of) Heaven." R. Ḥanina, because he lived in Sepphoris where cold prevailed, used to say: "Ninety-nine die of cold, and (only) one by (the decree of) Heaven." ' If this is the position with regard to everyday occurrences, a man must surely not rely on his constellation or on Providence alone in all that appertains to his conduct. Although R. Ḥanina said 'Everything is in the power of Heaven except the fear of Heaven, for it is said: "And now, Israel, what doth the Lord thy God require of thee, but to fear [the Lord thy God] (Deuteronomy x 12)', yet alongside this dictum stands the analogy used by R. Ḥanina: 'This is comparable to a man who is asked for a big article and he has it; (in which case) it seems to him but a small article. (If he is asked for) a small article and he does not possess it, it appears to him like a big article.'[81] Thus the attainment of the 'fear of Heaven' [i.e. piety] is not vouchsafed to every person in equal measure and as a result of the same effort. 'He who is like a man who has a big article' — that is to say, by nature and character he was born under the constellation of a righteous and pious man — the achievement of piety is a small matter for him, but for one born under another planet it is a difficult task.

The ultimate conclusion resulting from an exhaustive investigation of the various dicta of R. Ḥanina is not different from that which we reached from a study of the teachings of Rav and R. Joḥanan, despite the divergent starting point and postulates. Nor is it different from what their contemporary, the philosopher Plotinus, taught on this subject, notwithstanding the gulf between the former and the latter's thought and methods of thinking. According to Plotinus, the causes of our deeds lie within us and not in Providence; their consequences, however, are not in our power, but irresistibly follow the course designed by Providence. We may compare Providence and our relationship to it with the advice of a physician and our attitude to it. If we follow his advice, the action is in truth our own, but we act according to the understanding of the medical expert. If we act contrary to his advice, then, too, it is we who perform the deeds, but in opposition to the supervision [= providence] of the doctor. The fault is ours, and we must bear the consequences.[82] The experience of life and the compulsion of faith lead them to a complementary approach. A portion of the second principle combines with the first; the differences are of extent and degree of emphasis. This approach remains basically also the heritage of the later Amoraim, who never ceased meditating on the problem of Providence and to wonder about the significance of free choice. Rava proclaimed: 'Children, (length of) life, and sustenance do not depend on merit but on destiny [*mazzala*, 'planetary influence'].'[83] He based himself on the respective destiny of his teachers, Rav Ḥisda and Rabba. The former lived to the age of ninety-two and was wealthy, while the latter lived only forty years and his house lacked even barley bread. This realization did not prevent Rava from praying that he should be vouchsafed the wisdom of Rav Huna, the riches of Rav Ḥisda and the humility of Rabba bar Huna; and he adds that the first two requests were granted him, but not the third. Although it is possible to say that this prayer was not based on merit and righteous deeds, but was a supplication for the grace of Providence, which alone rules over fate, nevertheless Rava expressly attributed decisive importance to deeds, even though he did not overlook the contradiction between Providence and free choice, and even questioned the extent of man's responsibility for his actions. In the course of interpreting the words of Job (x 7), Rava said: 'Job sought to exempt the whole world from judgement; he said to Him [God]: "Sovereign of the universe, Thou hast created the ox with cloven hoofs and Thou hast created the ass with closed hoofs; Thou has created the Garden of Eden [Paradise] and Thou hast created *Gêhinnôm* [Gehenna]; Thou hast created righteous people and Thou hast created wicked people. Who hinders Thee?" But what did Job's companions answer him? "Yea, thou doest away with fear and restrainest devotion before God" (*ibid.* xv 4) — the Holy One, blessed be He, has created the evil inclination and He has created the Torah, its antidote.'[84] Thus, despite everything, he who has been created wicked can be made righteous by virtue of the Torah, which enables him to control his inclination,[85] and there is no argument capable of releasing man from judgement. The responsibility of man, who must account for his actions, set definite limits to the decrees of Providence; and as the feeling of responsibility and the frequency with which man is judged grew, so did the power of fate diminish, and man's mastery and his sense of freedom and the possibilities of his influence over his destiny increase. R. Simeon b. Yoḥai taught: 'If the Israelites were worthy on New Year, and abundant rains were decreed for them, and subsequently they sinned, then to reduce the rains is impossible, since the decree has already been issued. What does the Holy One, blessed be He, do? He scatters them over seas and deserts and rivers, so that the land does not benefit from them... If now they were not worthy on New Year, and scanty rains were decreed for them, and subsequently they repented, then to augment the rains is impossible, since the decree has already been issued. What does the Holy One, blessed be He, do for them? He sends the rains down for the needs of the land and causes dew drops to fall, and winds to blow with them, so that the land may benefit from them.'[86] Here the inference is drawn from the view, which is also held by most of the Tannaim, and forms the basis of our prayers on New Year and the Day of Atonement, namely that the sentence that receives the seal of finality on the Day of Atonement cannot be changed. Rava[87], indeed, asked why we pray the whole year round, and answered that we do so in accordance with the view of R. Jose that man is judged every day, 'for according to the Rabbis, who maintain that man is judged on New Year, once his judgement has been completed, (further) prayer is futile.'[88] If man is judged each day, he can influence his destiny by his prayer, and this is the view of Rava, who attributed, as we have observed, man's benefits to his constellation. The Torah, which, in Rava's opinion, the people of Israel accepted voluntarily,[89] set bounds to the rule of fate. By virtue of the Torah man became free and could pray to God and entreat His favour and grace. An anonymous Palestinian homilist expressly differentiated between two kinds of benefits: 'The Holy One, blessed be He, created three gifts in the world—wisdom, might, and wealth; if a man is vouchsafed one of them he takes all that is desirable in the whole world. This is true, however, (only) when the gifts come from the Holy One, blessed be He, and come through the power of the Torah. But the might and wealth of man are valueless, for thus said Solomon: "That the race is not to the swift, nor the battle to the strong, neither yet bread to the wise, nor yet riches to men of understanding" etc. (Ecclesiastes ix 11); and so, too, said Jeremiah (ix 22): "Thus saith the Lord: Let not the wise man glory in his wisdom neither let the mighty man glory in his might, let not the rich man glory in his riches"; and these gifts, since they do not come from the Holy One, blessed be He, are ultimately destined to leave him.'[90] But from whom derive 'the gifts that do not come from the Holy One, blessed be he'? It seems that this expositor was prepared to ascribe benefits to fate, as did Rava above, only he explicitly terms these benefits as imaginary and lacking value and durability in the estimation of one who believes in the power of the Torah, which bestows true benefits upon man.[91]

To sum up: We must state that we have found a multifaceted struggle extending over generations of Sages, which cannot be summarized in a dictum formulated by one or other scholar — not even in the formulation of Josephus, with which we commenced our discussion. We have seen that the Tannaim and Amoraim were divided in their views. The latter did not rely on the former, but renewed the discussion and study, at times even with greater daring and depth. We noted the influence of trends, from within and from without, on the extent of the emphasis placed both upon man's freedom of choice and upon his dependence on Providence. It seems to me that in the light of our account the views expressed in the scroll of the *Covenant of Damascus* [= Zadokite Document] and the Qumran Scrolls are less surprising than is generally supposed. One thing we did not find: the elevation of a single principle to the level of a systematic doctrine that imposed itself upon everything and endeavoured to reconcile the conflicting facts speculatively. Even those among the Sages — in particular the Amoraim — who were inclined to come to extreme conclusions in the direction of one principle, did not completely forsake the other. The bounds that the Sages set themselves were determined by other fundamentals in their religious thinking. They did not retreat from contradiction, for their aim was not to find a smooth philosophical solution, but to activate all man's powers

— both the potency inherent in the consciousness of freedom and the will to do good and that which flamed from the feeling of the nullity of man and his complete dependence on Divine Providence, for their religious thought was directed, in equal measure, towards God and towards the world and society.

CHAPTER XII

THE WRITTEN LAW AND THE ORAL LAW

In the two oldest traditions of the Oral Law the word 'Torah' is used in two different connotations. The Men of the Great Synagogue said three things: 'Be deliberate in judging, and raise up many disciples, and make a fence for the Torah' (*M. 'Avot* i, 1). The dictum is directed to the teachers and judges of the people, counselling them how to act in giving judgement and instruction. 'Torah' signifies here the teaching of precepts and Halakhot as in the ancient Mishna: 'They both came to the Great Court that was in the Chamber of Hewn Stone, whence *Torah* goes forth to all Israel' (*M. Sanhedrin* xi, 2). On the other hand, when Simon the Just declared: 'Upon three things the world is based: upon the *Torah*, upon Temple service, and upon deeds of loving-kindness' (*M. 'Avot* i, 2), he refered to Torah study[1], in which Temple service and deeds of loving-kindness are included. These three things are also enumerated in II Chronicles (xxxi, 21). It is stated of Hezekiah 'And in every work that he began in the service of the house of God, and in the Torah, and in the commandments....' In the saying of Simon the Just the Torah is placed first. Possibly this difference reflects a certain development. For the Chronicler 'the service of the house of God' was not yet implicitly included in the general term 'Torah'; it was the theme of תורת כהנים *Tôrat Kohănîm* ['the Torah of the priests'], as is evident also from the name of the third book of the Pentateuch, *Torat Kohanim*, which is undoubtedly early.[2] Contrariwise the term 'Torah', as used by Simon, includes both the law of the Temple service and the practice of loving-kindness. The study of the Torah is one of the pillars of the world. Torah alone is the covenant between God and His people, and the presence of the Shekhina among His people depends on the fulfilment and study of the Torah.[3] The study of the Torah implies also its expansion, and therefore the term 'Torah' in the mouth of Simon the Just is not confined to the Mosaic Torah. Whereas in Proverbs and in Job there is no mention of Torah and precepts on the basis of which a covenant has been made, and the term 'Torah' refers to the teaching of the father, the mother, the sage, and the teacher, or to the counsels of Wisdom itself, in Sirach the two concepts of Torah — that of Moses and that of Wisdom — are merged into a single idea. While in Jeremiah (ii 8) 'they that handle the Torah' correspond to the 'priests', in Sirach (xv 1) 'he that taketh hold of the Torah' is in parallelism with 'he that feareth the Lord'. The remnants of the Wisdom myth referring to Wisdom's pre-existence and its presence at the creation of the world, found in Proverbs (viii 22 ff)[4], were transferred to the Torah, and it was said that it existed before the creation of the world[5], while R. Eliezer b. R. Zadok and R. Akiba spoke of the Torah as 'an instrument wherewith the world was created'[6], although this myth militates against the doctrine of Revelation. It may be said that in the Hellenistic period, before the Maccabean Revolt, the word 'Torah' comprised the corpus of precepts, the teaching of the prophets, and the wisdom of the elders. But at the same time the term denotes particularly the Torah of Moses in all its parts and not just the section treating of the commandments and ordinances. Although it is stated in the Mishna in which the first classification of the precepts is found: '(The laws concerning) civil cases and Temple services, levitical cleanness and uncleanness, and the forbidden relations have what to rest on, and it is they that are the essentials of the Torah' (*M. Ḥagiga* i, 8), yet they are not the whole of the Torah. Echoes and traces of the twofold meaning of the term 'Torah' are still encountered in a later period, when the threefold division 'Torah, Prophets, and Hagiographa' had become a fact that also reflected the relative degree of holiness of each of them. Verses from the Prophets and the Hagiographa are cited in answer to the question 'Whence do we prove this from the Torah?' not only in Tannaitic but also in Amoraic dicta,[7] although the rule was already known that 'No inference may be drawn concerning Torah laws from statements in the post-Pentateuchal books of the Bible.'[8]

This fact shows to what extent the conception of the word 'Torah' in its broad and general connotation was perpetuated; it explains the fact that Paul and the author of the Gospel according to John refer to verses from the Prophets and from the Hagiographa as νόμος and is not to be regarded merely as a consequence of the use of νόμος as the translation of Torah.[9] They were only continuing an ancient tradition, as reflected in Daniel's words 'the Torah of Moses the servant of God' and 'His תורות *Tôrôt* ['laws'], which He set before us by His servants the prophets' (Daniel ix 10–13; see II Chronicles xxix 25; Ezra ix 10–14). The inclusion of prophecy and wisdom in the term Torah disproves the view that was current among theologians — and is still to be found today — which ascribes to Judaism, in the period following the destruction of the First Temple, a legalistic and unhistorical conception of 'Torah'.[10] But, on the other hand, it must be admitted that the replies given to the accounts of Weber, Bousset, and others are not altogether free from an apologetic undertone[11], and consequently helped somewhat to blur the distinctive connotation of the term 'Torah'. Principally they blamed the Septuagint, which rendered the word 'Torah' by νόμος and thus influenced the other Biblical translations. Even a scholar like C. H. Dodd, who well understood the meaning of 'Torah' in Hebrew in its various semantic nuances, writes:[12] 'It is clear that for the Jews of Egypt in the Hellenistic period the developed meaning of תורה as a code of religious observance, a "law" for a religious community, was the normal and regulative meaning, and they made this meaning cover the whole use of the word in the Old Testament. Thus the prophetic type of religion was obscured, and the Biblical revelation was conceived in a hard legalistic way. In thus rendering the term the translators are no doubt reflecting the sense in which their community read the Hebrew Bible, but their rendering helped to fix and stereotype that sense.' But the question is: Those communities were certainly not more legalistic than the local Jewry in Eretz-Israel, and if the latter continued to understand the word 'Torah' in a wider sense than that implied in the concept Halakha, why then did just Hellenistic Jewry deviate in comprehending it in its restricted sense? Dodd even attributes the very course taken by Hellenistic Judaism and Paulinian Christianity to the unfortunate translation of the word 'Torah':

'Where thinkers bred in Hellenistic Judaism sought to escape into a religion of greater spiritual freedom and spontaneity, it was not by any way of return to the prophetic idea of תורה, but by taking up a fresh attitude to religion conceived as Law. Philo accepted the Law as such and allegorized it: Paul declared that Judaism, being a legal religion, was superseded by the religion of the Spirit.'

This view actually characterizes Hellenistic Jewry as more legalistic than Palestinian Jewry, and overlooks Philo's testimony regarding the extreme allegorists in Alexandria, who maintained a Paulinian standpoint before Paul himself.[13]

Instead of decrying the Septuagint and charging it with distortions and misunderstandings belonging to later generations, it seems preferable to learn from it, and if we understand thoroughly the signification and development of the Hebrew term, we shall see that νόμος actually fits it. In the period with which we are concerned 'Torah' includes 'the commandment, and the statutes, and the ordinances' (αἱ ἐντολαὶ καὶ τὰ δικαιώματα καὶ τὰ κρίματα), whether they deal with a particular subject — such as 'the Torah ['law'] of the burnt-offering', 'the Torah of the sin-offering', 'This is the statute of the Torah', or 'This is the Torah: when a man dieth in a tent' — or whether they constitute a combination of heterogeneous statutes and ordinances that the Lord commanded by the hand of Moses, as in Deuteronomy (xvii 18). If now the concept of Torah was extended so as to include therein the admonitions regarding the observance of the precepts, the history of Israel, the biography of the Patriarchs and the story of Man,[14] this was all directed towards the making of the covenant and the acceptance of the commandments and statutes and ordinances and was centred on them. Without difficulty it was also possible to include in the definition of Torah the reprimands and promises of the prophecies and the ethics of the Wisdom books, while the enactments serving as a fence to the Torah themselves became Torah[15] viewed as δόγμα δ'ανθρώπων φρονίμων ('the instruction of wise men'). It would appear that for the Jews of Alexandria, too, the term 'Torah' was not a word but an 'institution', embodying the covenant between the people and its God, and reflecting a complex of precepts and statutes, customs and traditions linked to the history of the people and the acts of its rulers, kings, and prophets. If this was the connotation of 'Torah', it could not be translated διδαχή or διδασκαλία, but only νόμος, in the sense in which it was interpreted also by Pindar, Νόμος ὁ πάντων βασιλεύς, and as Plato understood it, namely as 'The constitution and living régime of a people, which is not comprised of a number of agreements and treaties, but is an institution of customs and traditions that are linked to one another by innumerable threads that tie them to the past of the people.'[16] In this sense the Greek translator of Isaiah i 10 understood the word Torah in the verse 'Give ear unto the Torah of our God, ye people of Gomorrah', when rendering it νόμος, since 'I cannot endure iniquity along with the solemn assembly' and 'Wash you, make you clean, put away the evil of your doings' are Torah. He also translated Isaiah xxiv 5 'Because they have transgressed the *Tôrôt*, violated the statute, broken the everlasting covenant' by διότι παρέβησαν τὸν νόμον and not by ἄγραφος νόμος[17], for νόμος is not φύσις, the law of nature[18], but Torah, which comes to master nature and the impulses.

The Greek word νόμος from the outset signified to the Jews of Alexandria neither more nor less than the word 'Torah', and there is no ground for assuming that it did not also comprehend the oral traditions, which were not written down. However, in the course of the constant contact with Greek culture, deviations occurred from the original conception of 'Oral Law', and at the same time a change took place in the actual attitude to the significance and meaning of Torah.

The term תורה שבעל פה *Tôrā she-bĕ-ʿal-pe* ['Oral Law'] first appears in the story about the proselyte who asked Shammai 'How many *Tôrôt* have you?' and the latter answered 'Two: the Written Torah and the Oral Torah'.[19] It is similarly related that Rabban Gamaliel gave the same reply to the general Agnitus.[20] This answer given to Gentiles who were candidates for conversion is evidence of the fact that they knew that alongside the Written Torah was to be found 'the tradition of the fathers' and apparently they also knew that this 'tradition of the fathers' was regarded as Torah. Otherwise the question 'How many *Tôrôt* have you?' is incomprehensible. The important point in the answer that was given is that the oral tradition is also Torah. The reply contains not the slightest indication that the two *Tôrôt* were differently evaluated. 'Just as you have accepted the one in faith so accept also the other in faith', said Hillel to the proselyte.[21] The tradition of the fathers is Torah. But at the same time it is clear that the term the 'Oral Torah' has not the signification of a Torah that preceded the Written Torah and transcends it in value, as is the case in the concept ἄγραφος νόμος — the Unwritten Law. For the unwritten law is in fact 'a law not given' by a divine or human lawgiver, but one that exists like nature, and it is of no consequence whether it was or was not written down, whereas the distinctive character of the 'Oral Torah' lies in the fact that it was not put in writing, yet it is also, like the written Torah, not a natural law, but one that was given, be its provisions fences made by the Men of the Great Synagogue and their successors, or interpretations given at Sinai, as R. Akiba held. Philo accepted the Greek view and identified himself with it. In his exposition of the verse 'Thou shalt not remove thy neighbour's landmark, which they of old have set' (Deuteronomy xix 14) he states: 'Now this law, we may consider, applies not merely to allotments and boundaries of land in order to eliminate covetousness but also to the safeguarding of ancient customs. For customs are unwritten laws (ἄγραφοι νόμοι), the decisions approved by men of old, not inscribed on monuments nor on leaves of paper, which the moth destroys, but on the souls of those who are partners in the same citizenship. For children ought to inherit from their parents, besides their property, ancestral customs which they were reared in and have lived with even from the cradle, and not despise them because they have been handed down without written record. Praise cannot be duly given to one who obeys the written laws, since he acts under the admonition of restraint and the fear of punishment. But he who faithfully observes the unwritten deserves commendation, *since the virtue which he displays is freely willed*' (*De spec. legibus*, iv, 149). Most important is the conclusion: the 'unwritten law' is kept voluntarily. As Yitzhak Heinemann has shown,[22] Philo's statement is derived from Aristotle's *Rhetoric*, despite its being based on a verse in Deuteronomy, and not withstanding that the exegetical tradition of the verse relative to the Torah was known in Palestine. The word ὅρος, 'boundary', whose signification also comprised, as we know, decision, rule, and canon[23], provided Philo with the opportunity for his exposition, just as the Hebrew 'Thou shalt not remove

(תסיג *tassîg*) thy neighbour's landmark' brought to mind the סיג *sĕyāg* ['fence'], and led to the teaching: 'Whence do we learn that one who interchanges the words of R. Eliezer for those of R. Joshua etc. transgresses a negative commandment? For Scripture teaches "Thou shalt not remove thy neighbour's boundary" ' (*Sifre Deuteronomy*, § 188, p. 227). But the very comparison of the two expositions underlines the difference between them. The Tannaitic Midrash does not speak of 'laws inscribed on the soul', but of the words of the Sages. The prohibition discovered by the Sages in this verse enjoins accuracy in giving the names of those who transmit the Halakhot and forbids us to change them, while Philo in his interpretation equates ἄγραφος παράδοσις with ἄγραφος νόμος and approximates it to the connotation it bore in his environment.[24]

The νόμος comes close to being φύσις. The higher law cannot be opposed to nature, as Aristotle taught. The author of the Hellenistic homily, called *IV Maccabees* (v 7), which represents a kind of synthesis of Judaism and Hellenism, not only attributed to Antiochus the argument 'For most excellent is the meat of this animal [the pig] which nature has graciously bestowed upon us, and why should you abominate it?', but Eleazar's answer was made in the same spirit: 'Therefore do we eat no unclean meat; for believing our Law to be given by God, we know also that the Creator of the world, as a Lawgiver, feels for us according to our nature' (*ibid.* v. 25). This conception of 'Torah' not only opened the way to allegorical exegesis, but also to the conclusion that the allegorical interpretation is the primary one, since it enables us to prove that *quod scriptum est* cannot be opposed to nature.[25] The dictum of R. Eleazar b. Azariah was against such a view: 'How do we know that a man should not say "I have no wish to wear mingled stuff [שעטנז *shaʿaṭnēz*], I have no desire to eat the flesh of swine" ... but (he should say) "I do desire it, (but) what can I do, seeing that my Father in Heaven forbade it" ' (*Sifra*, Qedoshim, ch. xi). The Torah is not according to Nature, whereas Hellenistic Judaism transformed the Written Law into ἄγραφος νόμος, an unwritten law according to the inner meaning of the concept. At the same time the opposite development occurred in the understanding of the term 'Oral Law' in the Rabbinic world up to the time of the destruction of the Temple. The tradition of the fathers, the enactments, and the decrees became Torah alongside the Written Torah. It was not the exegetical dialectic nor the discussion that decided, but the authority of the institutions. The institutional character of the ancient Halakha is confirmed also by the two features that characterize it — the absence of controversy and anonymity. The expositions of the Scribes were recognized as Halakhot only in so far as they corroborated and validated traditions and enactments, testimonies and practices in the possession of the Sages.[26] But these, too, formed only a part of the Oral Law, which was indeed Torah, but contrary to the view of the Sadducees — who had 'a Book of Decrees written down and deposited' — it was forbidden to write it and to turn it into a Written Torah. The Written Law remained unchanged. Its interpretations and expositions formed the instruction of this Torah in all its parts. Its teaching embraced the law 'If an ox gored a cow' (*M. Bava Qamma* v, 1), the 'Work of the Chariot', the rules of defilement applying to the shield 'with which they sport in the arena' (*M. Kelim* xxiv 1), and those affecting the head-net 'of a harlot' (*ibid.* xvi), as well as the Halakhot relating to repentance and atonement.

Our account of the development of the conception of Torah, both that of the Tannaim and that of Hellenistic Judaism, may serve as a background to the understanding of the antithesis that Paul established between the letter (γράμμα) and the spirit (πνεῦμα), which aimed at the annulment of the Torah, 'For when the Gentiles, which have not the law, do by nature what the law requires, are a law unto themselves, even though they do not have the law. They show that what the law requires is written on their hearts...' (Romans ii 14). He addresses himself also to those who know the Torah, using the metaphor 'the law being dead', and hence 'We are discharged from the law, dead to that which held us captive, so that we serve not under the old written code but in the new life of the spirit' (*ibid.* vii 6). It is difficult to find in Tannaitic literature a dictum more opposed to Paul's teaching than that of Matthew[27] 'For truly, I say to you, till heaven and earth pass away, not an iota, not a dot, will pass from the law until all is accomplished. Whoever then relaxes one of the least of these commandments and teaches men so, shall be called least in the kingdom of heaven.'[28] It is not the observance of the precepts that is spoken of here, for in that case it is difficult to explain this wording even from a polemical aspect. At any rate the Tannaim were more moderate; R. Joshua said: 'If a man learnt two Halakhot in the morning and two in the evening, and the rest of the day he is engaged in his work, it is accounted unto him as though he had fulfilled the whole of the Torah.' R. Eleazar of Modiʿim said the same thing concerning 'Whoever transacts his business honestly and is popular with his fellow creatures' (*Mekhilta*, Wa-yissaʿ, i, p. 158, and *ibid.* ii, p. 161); and it is also reported in the name of R. Akiba that 'If a man fulfils one precept, it is as though he fulfilled them all' (*T.B. Sanhedrin* 81a; *Midrash Tehillim* xv, 3).[29] Hence it seems that Matthew's statement actually refers to the annulling in principle of the obligatory character of the Torah and precepts, including the instruction of others to do likewise, in the sense: 'If a man says, I accept upon me the whole Torah except this one thing', we apply to him the verse 'Because he hath despised the word of the Lord, and hath broken His commandments' (*Sifre Be-midbar*, § 112, p. 121).

Subsequently Jesus, too, makes statements in his sermon that go beyond the Written Torah. The formula is 'It was said... but I say to you'. 'It was said' refers to what is expressly stated in the Torah, 'but I say to you' marks his 'expansion', the outcome of the inner interpretation. The parallel text to that of Matthew is the Baraita of R. Ishmael: 'With respect to three passages the Halakha overrides the Scriptural instruction... *the Torah said* (the bill of divorcement should be written) on a "book" [i.e. parchment], *whereas the Halakha said* "on anything" (detached)', etc.[30] Sometimes the breaking of the law is in effect its observance, as R. Joḥanan and Resh Laqish taught when they expounded the verse ' "It is time to work for the Lord, they have made void Thy law" (Psalms cxiv 126), saying: Rather let a letter of the Torah be uprooted than the Torah should be forgotten in Israel'[31]; and their words are but another version of the interpretation contained in the dictum of Hillel the Elder: 'when you see that the Torah is forgotten in Israel and none pay attention to her, gather in [i.e. be withdrawn in your study], as it is said "It is time to work for the Lord, they have made void Thy law." '

There is not much point in citing parallels, be it from Rabbinic teaching or from other legal systems, that distinguish between 'the attribute of justice' and 'the attribute of mercy' or 'beyond the strict requirement of the law', or between λόγος and διάνοια, in order to explain Paul's standpoint. The question confronting him was not that of 'the spirit of the law', or of justice in antithesis to law. He went beyond the contrast between spirit and content, and when he declared 'For the letter kills, but the spirit gives life' (II Corinthians iii 6), he was not thinking of inner interpretation,[32] which reveals the letter, 'For the Lord is the Spirit, and where the Spirit of the Lord is, there is freedom' (*ibid.*, v. 17). Although he does not say that the Torah is sin, yet he declares that 'Apart from the law sin lies dead' (Romans vii 7–9). The time had arrived for the annulment of the Torah, 'For Christ is the end of the law, that every one who has faith may be justified' (*ibid.* x 4). It was the Messianic fulfilment that led Paul to arrive at the last conclusion: the annulment of the Torah. With the advent of the Messiah man is no longer in need of being liberated from sin and from thoughts of the flesh with the help of the spiritual-allegorical interpretation of the Torah. Freedom came to him from the power of faith in the Messiah. The function of the allegorical interpretation was only to provide corroboration and testimony to this fundamental fact.

Do we find any reactions in the Rabbinic world, be it to the extreme allegorization of the Torah and the reduction of its precepts to nullity, or to the eschatological reasons advanced for the abolition of the Torah? It seems that such reactions not only are to be found, but they also show that the alien, revolutionary approaches were not, despite the struggle against them, without influence, and that it behoves us to trace their effects. Our first information about the Sages' taking a stand against the Christians and about any contact with them dates from the time of Rabban Gamaliel of Jabneh. Indeed, we possess a dictum from this period that seems to be a reaction to Paul's teaching. The contemporary of Rabban Gamaliel, R. Eleazar of Modiʿim, said: 'If a man profanes the hallowed things, and despises the festivals, and gives (a wrong) interpretation of the Torah [Hebrew: מגלה פנים בתורה *mĕgalle pānîm ba-Tôrā*, literally: 'discloses a face (= aspect, meaning) in the Torah'], and makes void the covenant of Abraham our father, and puts his fellow to shame, even though he has good works to his credit, he has no share in the world to come.'[33] The expression *mĕgalle pānîm ba-Tôrā* is difficult and has received many interpretations,[34] because its simple meaning is 'one who discloses (= gives) an interpretation of (a passage of) the Torah, and this cannot be regarded as wrong. In order to overcome this difficulty there have been added in the Mishna the words 'which is not according to the Halakha'.[35] Although they are an addition, yet this interpretation alone shows us the correct way of understanding the expression, which is not to be dissociated from the other parts of the dictum: the interpreter of the Torah, referred to by the Mishna, is one who expounds the Torah in an allegorical sense, leading to the annulment of the festivals, the contemning of the hallowed things, and the abolition of the covenant of Abraham. Such an interpreter of the Torah has no portion in the world to come. Do not the words read like a riposte to Paul's teaching: 'Nor is true circumcision something external and physical. He is a Jew who is one inwardly, and real circumcision is a matter of the heart, spiritual and not literal' (Romans ii 28–29)? Although Philo polemizes against the extreme allegorists, who likewise explained circumcision symbolically and contented themselves with its inner significance (*De migratione*, 92), yet it appears from Philo's own statement that these were but few (*ibid.* 93), and certainly did not constitute a sect or a movement.[36] It is very doubtful if R. Eleazar of Modiʿim knew anything about them. On the other hand, it is probable that he, like Rabban Gamaliel, was acquainted with the Judeo-Christians against whom it was enacted that they should be expressly mentioned in one of the blessings of the Eighteen Benedictions, which includes an imprecation against those who withdraw from the Community[37]; it is to them that the expressions 'who makes void the covenant of Abraham our father and gives a (wrong) interpretation of the Torah' refer.[38] In the Baraita attached to the Mishna in Sanhedrin that enumerates those who have no share in the world to come, it is also stated: 'They added to them one who casts off the yoke [of Judaism], and one who makes void the covenant, and one who gives a (wrong) interpretation of the Torah.'[39] The verse 'Because he hath despised the word of the Lord, and hath broken His commandment' is expounded in the *Sifre* thus: '"Because he hath despised the word of the Lord" — this refers to one who gives a (wrong) interpretation of the Torah; "and hath broken His commandment" — this means one who makes void the covenant of flesh' (*Sifre*, *Be-midbar*, § 112, p. 121). The contemptuous attitude adopted by the Christians towards the Temple and its hallowed things and towards the observance of the Sabbath and the festivals led to the association of offenders in these two respects with the 'one who makes the covenant void'. The expression 'He who puts his fellow to shame' is wanting in the recensions of the Mishna, and also in the parallel sources[40]; and even in the texts in which it occurs its position is not fixed,[41] and it is not impossible that the original dictum of R. Eleazar of Modiʿim also did not include 'one who profanes the hallowed things and despises the festivals'. The sting in the saying lies in the denial of a share in the world to come to 'one who gives a (wrong) interpretation of the Torah, and one who makes void the covenant', whereas Paul connects the beginning of the New Order specifically with (wrong) interpretation of the Torah and with the abolition of the covenant.

Is there to be found in Rabbinic teaching prior to Paul a basis for the view that the advent of the Messiah would lead to the annulment of the Torah, or to its exchange for a new Torah? This question is the subject of much discussion in the scholarly literature, both that dealing with Paul and that which treats of the problems of Jewish eschatology, and even special monographs have been devoted to the theme.[42] There are actually dicta that ostensibly do not belong to the subject and yet shed more light on it than sayings that speak expressly of 'the annulment of the precepts', and which are frequently cited, like the statement of Rabban Simeon b. Gamaliel 'When a man dies, he is exempt from (the observance of) the precepts.'[43] The Tanna does not come to inculcate a new teaching — namely that a dead man is exempt from keeping the commandments — but seeks to explain by this fact, which is well known — as Paul states — to all who have knowledge of the Law (Romans vii 1), the Halakha that we desecrate the Sabbath for the sake of a living person, but not for the dead. Rabban Simeon b. Gamaliel's statement is without any eschatological significance; on the other hand the words 'that the law is binding on a person only during his life' serve in Paul's mouth as the proem of his homily that with the death of Christ the authority of the Torah had ceased.

The oldest source pertaining to the subject of the Torah in the End of Days already clearly shows the difference in viewpoint between the close of the Temple era and that of Usha. 'R. Joshua said: I have received as a tradition from Rabban Joḥanan b. Zakkai, who heard it from his teacher, and his teacher from his teacher, as a Halakha given to Moses at Sinai, that Elijah will not come to pronounce unclean or clean, to remove (families) afar or to bring (them) nigh, but to remove afar those (families) that were brought nigh by violence and to bring nigh those (families) that were removed afar by violence... The like of these Elijah will come to pronounce unclean or clean, to remove afar or to bring nigh... R. Simeon said: To compose disputes, and the Sages said: Neither to remove afar nor to bring nigh, but to make peace in the world, as it is written "Behold I will send you Elijah the prophet... and he shall turn the heart of the fathers to the children and the heart of the children to their fathers." '[44] The starting point for Rabban Joḥanan b. Zakkai's statement was the passage at the end of Malachi concerning the mission of Elijah 'before the coming of the great and terrible day', and he regarded the purpose of the prophet's mission to be the imposition of his authority on the violent men who, in matters of family lineage, had been accustomed to remove afar and to bring nigh arbitrarily. This testimony of R. Joshua concerning Rabban Joḥanan b. Zakkai's exposition is linked to his other testimony that the widow of (a man belonging to) a family of doubtful purity — that is, a family of which a suspected *ḥālāl* [the male issue of a priest's illegitimate connection, who as such, is unfit for priesthood] was a member [and who might have been the widow's husband] — was eligible for marriage to a priest. To this Rabban Gamaliel reacted: 'We accept your evidence, but what shall we do, for Rabban Joḥanan b. Zakkai decreed that courts should not be set up for such cases? The priests would hearken to you if you ruled to remove afar, but not (if you ruled) to bring nigh.'[45] The words of the prophet 'And he shall turn the heart of the fathers to the children and the heart of the children to their fathers' are interpreted by the Tanna as referring to the settling of questions of family and peace. Modern commentators have also linked the verse to Malachi's rebuke (ii 11–15) to those who dealt treacherously with the wives of their youth and put them away.[46] The coming of Elijah is in no way connected with giving decisions and declaring doubtful cases permissible, but with imposing of authority to circumvent those who seek to undermine them. The reference, of course, is to the advent of Elijah before the coming of the Messiah, for in the world to come the question of family purity is not relevant. It is thus evident that R. Simeon's statement also has this period in view, but the task that he assigns to Elijah is different. In his opinion Elijah will come to decide which of the disputing Sages is right. At first there were no disagreements in Israel. One Torah went forth from the Chamber of Hewn Stone to all Israel, but when the Sanhedrin was abolished and the number of the disciples of Shammai and Hillel that did not wait sufficiently upon the scholars increased, the disputes in Israel multiplied (*Tosefta Sanhedrin* i, 1) 'and two Torahs were formed' (*Tosefta Soṭa* xiv, 9). This dictum is preceded there by a parallel saying 'When the proud [זהורי *zĕhûrê*] of heart increased, the disputes multiplied in Israel and became two Torahs.'[47] Although Rabban Joḥanan b. Zakkai attempted to organize anew the centre in Jabneh and Rabban Gamaliel aspired to invest the Patriarch and his court [*Bêt Dîn*] with decisive authority, yet these efforts did not suffice to renew the previous position and to restore 'the crown to its former estate'. R. Akiba drew the necessary inference from the changed circumstances and chose the way of his teachers, Nahum of Gimzo and Neḥunya b. Haqana, and weighed down the scales in favour of untrammeled freedom of exposition. On the one hand, Halakhot that originated in traditions, customs, acts, and testimonies found their validation in Scripture, and on the other, 'the niceties of Rabbinical exegesis and what the scribes are due to originate' had already been handed down — it was held — to Moses at Sinai and are only tradition. Even with regard to a certain formulation of a dispute between the School of Shammai and the School of Hillel, R. Eleazar b. ʿAzariah took an oath, which was worded as follows: 'I swear by the Torah! These are the things that were said to Moses at Sinai.'[48] R. Akiba incorporated the Oral Law in the Written Law, in its words, and in its letters. It is in this sense that his exposition in the *Sifra* is to be understood (Be-ḥuqqotay, viii, p. 112 c): ' "These are the statutes and ordinances and Torahs" — this teaches that two Torahs were given to Israel, one in writing and the other orally. Said R. Akiba: Did

Israel then have (only) two Torahs [literally: 'laws']? Behold many Torahs were given to Israel: "This is the Torah of the burnt-offering", "This is the Torah of the meal-offering", "This is the Torah of the guilt-offering", "This is the Torah of the sacrifice of peace-offerings", "This is the Torah: When a man dieth in a tent... in Mount Sinai by the hand of Moses" — this teaches us that the Torah with its Halakhot and details and interpretations were given by Moses at Sinai.' The giving of the Torah at Sinai is renewed, as it were, every day through the study of the Torah and its expositions. The verse 'And all the people perceived the thunderings' (Exodus xx 15) was interpreted by R. Akiba thus: 'They saw a word of fire issuing from the mouth of the Almighty and hewn out upon the tablets' (*Mekhilta de-R. Ishmael*, Ba-ḥodesh, ix, p. 235). R. Akiba's disciple, Ben ʿAzzai, stated concerning himself: 'I thread words of the Torah onto the prophets and words of the Prophets onto the Hagiographa, and the words of the Torah are as joyful as when they were given at Sinai.' The fact that fire flamed around him when he expounded words of Torah he explained as follows: 'Primarily when they [the words of the Torah] were given at Sinai they were given only in fire, (as it is written), "and the mountain burned with fire unto the heart of heaven." '[49] While Ben ʿAzzai transferred the experience of the Revelation at Mount Sinai to the study of the Torah in his days, Rabbi found that the verse ' "And all the people perceived the thunderings" came to tell us the praise of Israel, to wit, that when they all stood before Mount Sinai to receive the Torah, they heard the Divine word and expounded it' (*Mekhilta, ibid.*). The Revelation included not only the Torah and its interpretations, but also the bestowal of the authority to interpret. In accordance with this conception, Rav was able to sum up the view of R. Akiba and his disciples concerning the Oral Law with the following extraordinary story about Moses: When he ascended to Heaven and the Holy One, blessed be He, showed him R. Akiba sitting and expounding, Moses did not understand what he was saying, but nevertheless 'his mind was set at ease' when he heard that, in reply to a question of his disciples: 'Master, how do you know this?' R. Akiba answered: 'It is a Halakha of Moses given at Sinai' (*T.B. Menaḥot* 29b).

However, the freedom and multiplicity of the expositions cast doubt on the unity of the one Torah, for the disputes increased and the authority to decide declined. R. Simeon, the disciple of R. Akiba, insisted on laying down clear limits and fixed times [with reference to ploughing in the year preceding the Seventh Year], so that it could not be said: 'You give the law for each man into his own hand' (*M. Shevi'it* ii, 1). To his colleagues he said 'All the standard measures of the Torah are fixed' (*Tosefta Menaḥot* xiii, 8). Although he cited as examples of Torah standards forty *se'ah* for ritual immersion, and the size of an egg for uncleanness of food, that is to say, measures that are not explicitly stated in the Torah, but were accepted by the Sages as a whole, yet in regard to matters that were in dispute among the scholars themselves the fear remained 'that no regulation of the Torah would be like another' (*Tosefta 'Eduyot* i, 1, p. 454). Despite all efforts to achieve unity it was none other than R. Simeon who came to the conclusion that only Elijah would compose the differences of opinion and integrate the Torah again into a single whole. R. Simeon's statement is not to be equated with those passages in the Mishna and the Talmuds that declare 'Let it remain (undecided) until the coming of Elijah' or 'When Elijah comes he will say'; there Elijah is not depicted as deciding between different opinions, but as revealing the true position with regard to a certain set of facts of which human beings have no knowledge.[50] A similar instance is cited in the Book of Ezra (ii 62–63), where it is stated that the priests who were excluded as unclean from the priesthood had not found the record of their genealogy. 'And the governor said to them that they were not to partake of the most holy food, until a priest with Urim and Thummim should arise.'[51] R. Simeon's dictum, however, is to be understood in the light of the viewpoint of those Sages, like R. Eliezer b. Hyrcanus and others, who did not discount the possibility of the vouchsafement of a heavenly revelation, whether in the form of a *Bat Qôl* [Heavenly Voice] or a prophet, that would appear and decide in matters concerning which we could not, and never would, reach a conclusion by the force of our argumentation and reasoning; in the same way the Sages transmitted Halakhot that had been promulgated and enacted by the prophets through the power of their prophecy. Nay more, the prophets were invested with the authority to revoke temporarily a law of the Torah. The verse 'A prophet will the Lord thy God raise up unto thee, from the midst of thee, of thy brethren, like unto me; unto him ye shall hearken' (Deuteronomy xviii 15) was expounded thus: 'Even if he says to thee: Transgress temporarily one of the precepts ordained by the Torah, as did Elijah on Mount Carmel, hearken unto him' (*Sifre Deuteronomy*, § 175). On the other hand, R. Joshua and those who followed his views were opposed to the intervention of heavenly powers in deciding matters of Halakha. The Torah is not in Heaven, and we do not hearken to a *Bat Qôl*. In accordance with this standpoint the rule was formulated: ' "These are the commandments" — this implies that no prophet is permitted to originate any new ruling from now on',[52] and the Amora Rav inferred from this doctrine that in the hereafter, too, prophecy would not be able to intervene in Halakhic matters, and should Elijah come and decide against accepted custom, he would not be listened to. Matters of Halakha do not depend on the decision of the prophet who brings tidings (*T.B. Yevamot* 102a; *T.B. ʿAvoda Zara* 36a).

In the light of what has been stated above, it can clearly be seen that Paul found no existing view concerning the abolition of the Torah or its replacement by a new Torah in the Messianic era. At most a prophet could claim that by virtue of his prophecy he came to annul, as a temporary measure, a law of the Torah, or to promulgate an enactment, or to establish a custom that was prophetically revealed to him. But such was not the claim of Paul. In the person of Jesus as Messiah and redeemer Paul saw the fulfilment of prophecy and the realization of the Messianic promise: 'For Christ is the end of the law, and only he that believes in him shall be justified' (Romans x 4). Undoubtedly, Paul's remark about 'the end of the law' is bound up with his Messianic outlook. But this Messianic doctrine was moulded by his view that 'no human being will be justified in his sight by works of the law, since through the law comes knowledge of sin' (*ibid.* iii 20). His attitude to man and his concept of sin are the source of his antinomianism.[53]

Traces of Christian views on the place of the Torah in the new faith are to be found in the teaching of the Tannaim and Amoraim, but here, too, the difference between the reactions at the end of the first century and the beginning of the second and those of a later period is conspicuous. The first response in our possession also dates from the time of Rabban Gamaliel. In the neighbourhood of his sister,

Imma Shalom, the wife of R. Eliezer, there lived a philosopher, who also acted as a judge and had the reputation of not taking bribes. They wished to play a hoax on him and to put him to the test. Imma Shalom brought him a golden lamp and subsequently said to him: 'We wish to divide our (deceased) father's estate'; he replied 'Divide!' 'Said he (Rabban Gamaliel) to him: "It is written in the Torah that where there is a son, a daughter does not inherit." The latter replied: "Since the day that you were exiled from your land, the Law of Moses has been revoked and the Evangel has taken its place, wherein it is written: a son and a daughter inherit equally." ' The following day Rabban Gamaliel gave him a Libyan ass, and when he appeared before him, 'He said to them: "Look at the end of the Evangel, where it is written: 'I have come not to abstract from the Law of Moses, but I have come to add (thereto)'; and therein it is written: 'Where there is a son, a daughter shall not inherit.' " ' When Imma Shalom cried 'Let thy light shine forth like a lamp', Rabban Gamaliel said 'The ass has come and extinguished the lamp.'[54] Ninety years ago Güdemann showed[55] that we have here a sarcastic parody of onc of the λόγια according to the Hebrews, which was used also by the author of Matthew (v 15–16): 'Nor do men light a lamp and put it under a bushel (τὸν μόδιον), but on a stand, and it gives light to all in the house. Let your light so shine before men.' This saying gave rise to the motif 'The ass has come and knocked the lamp over' by substituting חמור *ḥămôr* ['ass'] for חומר *ḥômer* ['bushel'].[56] But of greater interest to us is the ambivalent attitude to the Torah, which finds expression in the story that confirms the view that in the ancient Christian community they had not yet freed themselves from the yoke of the Torah, and seemingly they were afraid to draw inferences in the spirit of Paul's preaching; this is the background to the passage in Matthew (v 17–19).[57] The Jews saw no need to engage in a serious controversy with the New Testament and were content to underscore the hesitancy and inconsistency of those who professed it. Hence it is not surprising that we find no signs of struggle against Paulinian ideas, and certainly not of the influence of his views, before the end of the Tannaitic era and the beginning of the Amoraic period, that is to say, until the ideological crystallization of Christianity in the spirit of Paul's teaching and its popular expansion and diffusion. The following exposition of R. Joshua b. Levi is directed, apparently, against Paul's view that the Torah has been superseded by grace: 'To what do these twenty-six (verses of) "Give thanks" correspond? To the twenty-six generations that the Holy One, blessed be He, created in His world, and did not give them the Torah, but sustained them by His grace.'[58] There was need of grace so long as the Torah had not been given.

Development occurred in the conception of the Torah in two directions. On the one hand the Torah was completely removed from all dependence on supernatural forces — on prophecy inspired by the Holy Spirit, or on a *Bat-Qôl.* Not only was a Prophet not permitted to originate (laws), as several Tannaim stated, but R. Isaac and Resh Laqish said that all that the Prophets prophesied they received from Sinai. For the Voice that was heard on Mount Sinai already included the words of the Prophets throughout the generations, and only when the time arrived for proclaiming a given prophecy and the generation was fit for it to be made public, did there arise the Prophet assigned to the task, who had received the appropriate prophecy on Mount Sinai. Hence there is nothing really new in the utterances of the Prophets; the words existed from of old, and it is their publication that occurs at different times. But not only 'did all the Prophets receive their prophecy from Sinai, but also the Sages that have arisen in every generation received their respective teaching from Sinai.'[59] Similarly R. Joshua b. Levi taught: 'Bible, Mishna, Talmud, and Haggada, even what a senior disciple is due to teach in the presence of his master, was already stated to Moses at Sinai.'[60] The sole difference between the utterances of the Prophets and those of the Sages is that the former may be written down, whereas the latter must remain oral, and this distinction does not necessarily favour the former. Only Israel's sinfulness caused the Prophets to appear, as R. Ada b. R. Ḥanina taught: 'Had not Israel sinned, they would have been given only the Five Books of the Torah, and also the Book of Joshua, which desciibes the disposition of the Land of Israel (among the tribes). What would the reason for this be? "For in much wisdom is much vexation." '[61] If only they had listened to the words of the Holy One, blessed be He, they would not have needed the words of the Prophets. But the Oral Law is not so. The expositions of the Sages possess decisive authority and deserve at least the same place in the scale of religious values as the Written Torah, and in truth transcend it. According to R. Joḥanan the covenant was made at Mount Sinai only on account of the Oral Teaching (*T.B. Giṭṭin* 60b; *T.B. Shevuot* 39a). The dependence of the Written Law on the Oral Law is pungently expressed by R. Simeon b. Laqish: 'There are many verses that deserve to be burnt, yet they are basic parts of the Torah',[62] that is to say, there are verses that appear to their readers to be unnecessary and need never have been written in the Torah, but the Sages are able to show that they are essential elements of the Torah, 'and important concepts derive from them.'

R. Samuel b. Naḥman, who was one of the leading Amoraim of Eretz-Israel in the middle of the third century, taught: 'Oral [בפה *bĕ-fe*, literally 'by mouth'] laws have been proclaimed, and written laws have been proclaimed and we cannot tell which of these is more precious; but since it is written, "For in accordance with [על פי *ʿal pî* literally 'by the mouth of'] these words I have made a covenant with thee and with Israel", we may infer that the oral precepts are more precious' (*T.P. Pe'a* ii, 4, p. 17a). This dictum intimates that primarily the covenant is based on the Oral Law. But the reason for the preference to be given to the Oral Torah was differently explained by one of the last of the Palestinian Amoraim. 'R. Judah bar Shalom stated: When the Holy One, blessed be He, said to Moses "Write down!", Moses asked for the Mishna to be in writing. But because the Holy One, blessed be He, foresaw that the Gentiles would translate the Torah and read it in Greek, and thereupon they would declare "We are Israel", and so far the scales would be even, so the Holy One, blessed be He, said to the nations: "You aver that you are My children? I cannot tell; only they who possess My arcana (מסטורין *misṭôrîn*) are My children." Which are these?—the Mishna.'[63] It is clear that this dictum explains the superiority of the Oral Torah as an answer to the claims of Christianity following upon Paul's statement concerning the Church as the true heir of Israel, since it is the son of the free woman, while Israel according to the flesh is at most the son of the bondwoman (Galatians iii 26, iv 21; Romans ii 28). The Fathers of the Christian Church, from Justin to Augustine, claimed that the Book of Books is no longer the property and heritage of the Jews.[64] The authors of the Apostolic writings and the Church Fathers based most of their teachings on passages from the Prophets, whom they regarded as their spiritual ancestors. Contrariwise, the Amoraim came and elevated the Sages of the Oral Torah to the level of the Prophets and even gave the former precedence over the latter. At the close of the third century R. Avdimi of Haifa declared: 'Since the destruction of the Temple, prophecy was taken away from the Prophets and given to the Sages' (*T.B. Bava Batra* 12a). The underlying reason for this view was transmitted at the beginning of the fourth century in the name of R. Tanḥum b. R. Ḥiyya: 'To what are a Prophet and Elder comparable? To a king who sent two of his agents σημαντήριον to a province. Concerning one he wrote: If he does not show you my seal and my signet, do not believe him! Concerning the other he wrote: Although he does not show you my seal and my signet, believe him! Thus, too, it is written of the Prophet: "and gives thee a sign or a wonder" (Deuteronomy xiii 2); but here (it is stated): "according to the instructions which they give thee" (*ibid.* xvii 11).'[65] As a result of this approach they denied the Prophets who were active in the past the possibility of initiating or amending anything in the conduct of life by Divine injunction, and if we find that innovations and enactments were ascribed to them, these were not only given at Mount Sinai together with all 'that a senior disciple was due to originate', but just as the disciple innovates by dint of his reasoning, so, too, the Prophets established what they did as a result of their argumentation (*T.B. Temura* 16a); and even Elijah offered up sacrifices on a high place only after he had expounded a given Scripture, but not by Divine injunction.[66] The teachings of prophecy are included in the Torah, and they, too, are Torah. Hence the Amoraim were able to polemize against sectarian groups that belittled the utterances of the Prophets. Evidence of such a polemic has survived in an anonymous homily: 'When Asaph came, he began to say: "Give ear, O my people, to my Torah" (Psalms lxxviii 1)... Said Israel to Asaph: "Is there then another Torah that you say 'Give ear, O my people, to my Torah'? We have already received it at Mount Sinai!" He answered them: "The transgressors of Israel say that the Prophets and the Hagiographa are not Torah and that they do not believe in them, as it is stated: 'Neither have we hearkened to the voice of the Lord our God, to walk in His laws, which he set before us by His servants the prophets' (Daniel ix 10) — thus we see that the Prophets and Hagiographa are Torah. Hence it is said 'Give ear, O my people, to my Torah.' " '[67] It seems that the homilist's polemic was directed against a Judeo-Christian sect that, although it was devoted to the 'New Testament', identified Jesus with Moses, but in its struggle against the antinomistic orientation of Paul refused to recognize the Prophets, who came after Moses and whose words were used by Paul and Barnabas and their followers to reject the Torah.[68] It is noteworthy that the author of the *Epistle of Barnabas* proceeds in the opposite direction. He endeavours to raise the teachings of the Torah to the plane of prophecy and to prove that the statutes upon which Paul vented his wrath are really words of prophecy, which allude to the life and work of Jesus.[69] Against both these views the homilist that we have cited argues that the Prophets and Hagiographa are Torah. The three of them form a threefold Torah. The compass and bounds of this Torah, as well as its significance, were determined by the Sages. It was already stated in an ancient Mishna that 'The laws concerning the Sabbath, Festal-offerings and acts of trespass are as mountains hanging by a hair, for they have scant Scriptural basis but many laws' (*M. Ḥagiga* i, 8), and the greatest of the last Babylonian Amoraim, Rav Ashi, following his predecessors, declared: 'Do not lightly regard a גזרה שוה *gĕzērā shāwā* [an analogy drawn between two laws based on verbal congruities in Scriptural verses], for the cases to which death by stoning applies are essential laws of the Torah, yet Scripture teaches (most of them) by *gĕzērā shāwā*' (*T.B. Keritot* 5a). Even Halakhot that were not based on verses were designated by the Amoraim 'Torah law'.[70] The realization of the difference between written and oral regulations finds expression in the appraisal that 'The Sages safeguarded their own enactments more than those of the Torah'[71] and in the hyperbolical statements concerning the supreme authority of the expositions and decisions of the Rabbis. The Almighty Himself is bound by them. God sits and occupies Himself with the section of the Red Heifer, and He cites a Halakha in the name of R. Eliezer, despite the astonishment of Moses, who cries: 'Sovereign of the universe, Thou dost hold in Thy power the creatures of heaven and earth, yet Thou dost sit and cite a Halakha in the name of a human being!' (*Pesiqta de-R. Kahana*, Para, ed. Mandelbaum, p. 73).

The Lord sits and recites the dispute between R. Abiathar and R. Jonathan, while Rabbah decides the controversy between God and the heavenly academy (*T.B. Giṭṭin* 6 b; *T.B. Bava Meṣiʿa* 86a). Nor is it surprising that to R. Akiba was attributed the dictum: 'Just as they debate Halakha on earth, so they debate Halakha in Heaven' (*Tanḥuma*, Exodus xviii).[72]

The Sages who professed these views allowed no possibility of change in the validity, compass, and nature of the Torah. The advent of the Messiah is incapable of altering anything therein, for 'It [the Torah] does not belong to [literally, 'is not in'] Heaven'. 'Moses warned them [i.e. Israel]: Say not another Moses will arise and bring us another Torah from Heaven. I declare to you now "It is not in Heaven" — nothing thereof was left in Heaven' (*Deuteronomy Rabba* viii, § 6). The expression 'another Moses' in this anonymous dictum is noteworthy, for its visualization of the Messiah as 'another Moses' was also likely to bring in its train the sequel that this 'other Moses' would bring another Torah. Actually Jesus was described as *Moses redivivus* or as *Moses novus*. However, these similitudes have their origin in Biblical similes and became a stereotyped motif in a considerable portion of the Messianic Haggadah.[73] It seems, therefore, that the homily that we have cited was directed against Messianic concepts that were current among the Rabbis, and to which the homilist was opposed. Underlying his exposition and those of the Amoraim that we have discussed so far is a Messianic conception not unlike that of the Sage Samuel, namely that 'the only difference between this world and the days of the Messiah will be (the termination of) the bondage of the kingdoms' (*T. B. Berakhot* 34b, and the parallel passages listed there). But there were Sages who envisaged the Messiah differently, and apparently their views concerning the Torah and the position occupied by prophecy were also different. Whereas Rav held that the world was created only for the sake of David, 'who would compose many hymns and praises (to God)' (Rashi), and Samuel was of the opinion that the creation was due to the merit of Moses 'who would receive the Torah' (*ibid.*), R. Joḥanan, on the other hand, considered that 'the world was created on account of the Messiah' (*T. B. Sanhedrin* 98b). Now R. Joḥanan testifies, concerning many a Halakha, that 'It was based on tradition deriving from Haggai,

Zechariah and Malachi', that is to say, that these laws were 'of the nature of prophecy and their plain reason is not known.'[74] It was he who said 'The rite of the willow-branch is an institution of the Prophets',[75] and the verse 'These words the Lord spoke unto all your assembly... with a great voice and it did not cease' (Deuteronomy v 19) he did not interpret like Resh Laqish 'that from it prophesied all the prophets that arose', but that 'One voice broke up into seven voices, and these were divided into seventy languages.'[76] On the other hand, he held: 'In all things if a prophet should say to you "Transgress the precepts of the Torah!" listen to him, except in the case of idolatry' (*T.B. Sanhedrin* 90a), and he left it to Elijah to come and elucidate passages of Scripture that we do not know how to interpret.[77] At the same time R. Joḥanan said 'The Prophets and the Hagiographa will be annulled, but the Five Books of the Torah will not be abolished' (*T.P. Megilla* i, 1, p. 70d). He did not disclose to us whether he meant the days of the Messiah or the world to come. At any rate it appears that he refers to a time when the prophetic promises will have been fulfilled and there will be no need for words of rebuke and comfort, in the spirit, as it were, of the dictum of one of the last of the Tannaim, R. Simeon b. Eleazar, whose exposition R. Joḥanan had heard in his youth (*T.P. Maʿasrot* i, 2, p. 48d): 'the days of the Messiah, when there will be neither merit nor guilt.'[78] R. Joḥanan was one of the transmitters of the dictum of the Tanna R. Menaḥem of Gallia [or Galatia], the contemporary of R. Simeon b. Eleazar: 'In the hereafter all the sacrifices will be abolished, but the thanksgiving offering will not be abolished; all prayers will be abolished, but thanksgiving will not be abolished.'[79] In a world where there is neither merit nor guilt there is no place for sacrifices, which are brought to make atonement for sins, nor for prayers for human needs. Nevertheless the Five Books of the Torah will not be annulled. R. Joḥanan's statement 'The generation in which the son of David will come the number of scholars will decrease...' is possibly based on the apocalyptic Baraita that contains an account of the septennium in which the son of David will come, and where it is said: '... In the third year there will be a great famine... and the Torah will be forgotten by Israel... in the fifth year there will be great abundance, and people will eat and drink and rejoice; the Torah will return to its pristine state and renew itself unto Israel.'[80] That means that the Torah, which will have been forgotten, will be restored to them. It is not stated here by whom this will be achieved, but in early Midrashim already the Messiah is allotted a role in the teaching of the Torah. A homily is transmitted in the name of the Rabbis on Genesis xlix 11: 'When he of whom it is written "Lowly, and riding upon an ass" etc. (Zechariah ix 9) comes, "he will wash his garments in wine", that is, he will compose for them Torah teachings; "and his vesture in the blood of grapes", that means, he will correct all their errors.' To this R. Ḥanin reacted by saying: 'Israel will have no need of king Messiah's teaching in the hereafter, for it is stated, "unto him shall the nations seek" (Isaiah xi 10) — but not Israel. In that case, why will king Messiah come, what will he come to do? — to gather the exiles of Israel and to give the Gentile Nations thirty commandments.'[81] The point about the thirty commandments is derived from Zechariah (ix 12), 'So they weighed for my hire thirty pieces of silver', which also serves as a basis for the thirty pieces of silver of Judas Iscariot (Matthew xxvii 9). Possibly the homilist wished to say that the Messiah will not come to remove the yoke of the commandments from Israel, but to impose their observance upon the Gentiles. The dictum of R. Ḥanin, who apparently held that God Himself would teach Torah to Israel in the world to come,[82] only serves to underscore the purpose of the Rabbis' homily. Concerning the Torah-instruction of the Messiah we are informed in another saying: 'The Torah that a man learns in this world is as nought compared with that of the Messiah' (*Ecclesiastes Rabba* xi, 8). The author of the dictum is mentioned in a parallel passage, which is, however, somewhat milder, and reads as follows: 'R. Hezekiah said in the name of R. Simon bar Zavdi: all the Torah that you learn in this world is as nought compared with that of the world to come, because in this world a man learns Torah and forgets, but in the hereafter lo, it is written (Jeremiah xxxi 33), "I will put My law in their inward parts" ' (*Ecclesiastes Rabba* ii, 1). It is difficult to regard the second part of the dictum, which begins with 'because', as an explanation of the first part; apparently it is another saying, which was attached here as an explanation,[83] while in truth its meaning is different. In asserting that the Torah of this world is as nought compared with the Torah of the world to come,

R. Simon was referring, as the commentators of the Midrash have also indicated,[84] to the quality of the Torah, in the sense of R. Avin's teaching 'The lowest form [נובלת *nôvelet*] of heavenly wisdom is Torah.'[85] The Torah that the Messiah would teach is heavenly wisdom, while the earlier Torah is like *nôvelet*, that is, fruit that drops from the tree before it has ripened. The Amoraim in the fourth century who created their vision of the Messianic era, and did not, like Samuel, regard it only as a time devoid of the bondage of the kingdoms, but gave it a Utopian and apocalyptic[86] character, came, as a result of these portrayals, to endow the Messiah also with authority to give decisions and expound Halakhot transcending the existing Torah. R. Simeon b. Judan describes a beast contest (κυνήγιον, literally: 'hunt') witnessed by the righteous in the hereafter, and in the course of it it is stated: 'Behemoth strikes Leviathan with his horns and slaughters him by piercing, and Leviathan hits Behemoth with his fins and tears him.' The Midrash makes the righteous ask in surprise 'Is this ritually correct slaughter?' and R. Abba bar Kahana attributes to God the answer: ' "For Torah shall go forth from Me" (Isaiah li, 4) — new Torah law [חידוש תורה *ḥiddush Tôrā*] shall come forth from Me.'[87] Although the 'hereafter' and Torah taught by the 'Holy One, blessed be He,' are spoken of here, yet in these Messianic legends the terms 'the days of the Messiah', 'the Garden of Eden', and 'the world to come' approximate to one another and the distinctions between them are blurred.[88]

Combined with the difference between the Torah that God and the Messiah will teach and the existing Torah, there is also a certain conception of the reasons underlying the precepts. Alongside commandments for which rational, historical, ethical, or utilitarian explanations can be adduced are to be found precepts for which no such reasons could be ascertained. The Tannaitic explanation, already ascribed to Rabban Joḥanan b. Zakkai, was that these commandments are (Divine) decrees, which may not be questioned, or argued against.[89] But there were Amoraim who were not satisfied with this answer and postulated the existence of esoteric reasons not only for the statutes and decrees, but also for precepts the grounds for which are apparently evident.[90] They held that the reasons for the law of the red heifer, which for others is a statute [i.e. a law for which there is no apparent explanation], the Lord had revealed to Moses. But if the motives underlying the Torah precepts remained hidden in this world, they were destined to be revealed in the world to come.[91] Not only are there concealed reasons for the commandments, but the letters of the Torah could also be combined differently from their present sequence. Rav said 'Bezalel knew how to combine the letters by which heaven and earth were created' (*T.B. Berakhot* 55a). The words of Job xxviii 13 'Man knoweth not the order thereof' were expounded by R. Eleazar thus: 'The sections of the Torah were not given in their proper order, for if they had been given in the correct order, any one reading them would be able to revive the dead and perform wonders; consequently the true arrangement of the Torah was concealed, but it is known to the Holy One, blessed be He, as it is said (Isaiah xliv 7) 'And who, as I, can proclaim and declare it and set it in order for Me' (*Midrash Psalms* iii, 2, p. 33). It follows from R. Eleazar's statement that the Torah in our possession cannot, in its present arrangement, be used for the working of miracles. The revelation of its original textual order is in the power of God and only He can divulge it. The Cabalists, however, attempted to decipher the esoteric structure of the Torah.[92] They did this by giving the words of the Sages a meaning that did not accord with their simple sense and original intent.[93] The reasons and intrinsic attributes of the Torah, which are not disclosed in this world, have been reserved for elucidation in the hereafter. The Torah, which the Almighty will teach the righteous Himself or through the medium of His Messiah, will be, from these aspects, 'a new Torah'. In the mystical Midrash *Otiyyot de-R. Akiba* ['The Letters of R. Akiba'] (*Bate Midrashot*, Pt. II, p. 367) it is stated: 'The Holy One, blessed be He, will sit in the hereafter in the Garden of Eden and expound the Torah, and all the righteous of the world will sit before Him, while the whole of the heavenly court will be upstanding. On the right of the Holy One, blessed be He, will be the sun and the planets, and on His left the moon and all the stars, and the Holy One, blessed be He, will expound before them the reasons of the new Torah that the Holy One, blessed be He, will give them through the Messiah.'

Those Sages who regarded the prophets of the past not only as reprovers and comforters, but also as teachers of Halakha under

Divine inspiration, and posited the possibility that the Mind of the Most High would continue to be revealed to human beings even in matters of jurisprudence and law, of ritual prohibition and permissibility, undoubtedly linked to their Messianic expectation the renewal of the Torah and the elucidation of its obscurities and inner reasons. Although this opened the way to an antinomistic spirit,[94] yet so long as the Messianic faith continued to be engrossed in its Utopian vision, there was no immediate danger. It in no way changed the attitude of the homilists and apocalyptists of the Messianic era to Torah and precept in the present, and they even occupied themselves with Halakhot whose observance was connected with the days of the Messiah in the spirit of 'Expound and receive reward!' (*T.B. Zevaḥim* 45a). Obviously the Amoraim who maintained that the Torah was completely free from the control of transcendental powers, and were extreme in their insistence on the independent existence of the Torah and the autonomy of its students, rejected out of hand the concept of change or mutation in Israel's attitude to the Torah in the Messianic epoch. It is entirely unnecessary to augment the existing Torah. In antithesis to the words of the Psalmist, who declared, without further interpretation, 'I have seen an end to every purpose; but Thy commandment is exceeding broad' (Psalms cxix 96), Rav Ḥisda transmitted, in the name of Mari bar Mar, a precise calculation of the size of the Torah in relation to the world. On the basis of Zechariah v 2 he calculated and found that 'The whole universe is one three-thousand-and-twentieth of the Torah.'[95] It is clear that the reference is to the Torah in our possession. In so far as the Torah was concerned, the days of the Messiah were in the eyes of the Sages an age when the Torah could be fulfilled in its entirety, and hence they continued to occupy themselves with the laws relating to the Temple and the holy things, and even decided Halakhot in respect of these subjects;[96] thus many enactments and Halakhot were explained in the light of the possibility that 'the Temple would soon be rebuilt.'[97] The two approaches existed side by side, and the express testimony for the annulment of the precepts in the hereafter has reached us with the addition of remarks by the other side: ' "The Lord permitteth forbidden things" [Psalms cxlvi 7, usually rendered: 'The Lord looseth the prisoners']. What is meant by "permitteth forbidden things"?

Some say: Every beast declared unclean in this world the Holy One, blessed be He, will declare clean in the hereafter... but others say: He will not permit them in the hereafter...' (*Midrash Psalms* cxlvi § 4, p. 535). So long as the Messianic expectation did not claim that it was in the process of being fulfilled, the two views — even if they were not integrated — could at least dwell in peace side by side. But when this claim was made, the clash came.

CHAPTER XIII

THE COMMANDMENTS

I. *Their Source and the Ways of Their Observance*

Despite all the expansion of meaning that the term 'Torah' underwent in Rabbinic literature, the precept remained its basic element; without commandments there could be no Torah. The spectrum of relationships between God and the individual Jew or the Jewish people, as it emerges from the Bible, is closely linked to the theme of the precept. God's first revelation to man is marked by the *commandment* 'And the Lord God commanded the man, saying: "Of every tree of the garden thou mayest freely eat; but of the tree of the knowledge of good and evil, thou shalt not eat of it; for in the day that thou eatest thereof thou shalt die"' (Genesis ii 16–17). God reveals Himself to man as the *commanding* God, who permits and forbids. Man is allowed to choose whether he will observe the precept or not, but to transgress it spells death. The election of Abraham, the father of the people, was due to the fact that 'I have chosen him that he may command his children and his household after him to keep the way of the Lord by doing righteousness and justice' (*ibid.* xviii 19). The response of the people to the Divine Revelation was: 'All that the Lord hath spoken will we do, and obey' (Exodus xxiv 7). The word of the Lord must be made *deed* by man.[1] But the term 'commandment' includes also 'prohibitions' [literally, 'thou shalt not do'], as Scripture puts it 'And if any one of the common people sin through error, in doing any of the things which the Lord hath commanded not to be done [literally, 'one of the commandments which shall not be done'], and be guilty' (Leviticus iv 27). The commandment is indicative of the Commander's power to command. Indeed the Commanding Deity appeared on Mount Sinai accompanied by thunder and lightning. The people that received the precepts became a kingdom of priests and a holy nation of the God-King.[2] The commandments of the Lord constitute the content of the covenant made between Him and His people: 'And he wrote upon the tables the words of the covenant, the ten commandments' (Exodus xxxiv 28). Breaking the covenant means forsaking the precepts: 'And they rejected His statutes, and His covenant that He made with their fathers... and they forsook all the commandments of the Lord their God...' (II Kings xvii 15–16). The whole of Israel's history in the period of the First Temple, as it is described in the Former Prophets, and all the utterances of the Prophets of Israel centre on keeping or breaking the covenant. The covenant comprises all the commandments and, where any given transgression is referred to, there also occurs, as a parallel to the 'breaking of the covenant', the expression 'breaking of the precept'.[3] The pact made by Ezra with the people was 'with a curse and an oath, to walk in God's law, which was given by Moses the servant of God, and to observe and do all the commandments of the Lord our Lord, and His ordinances and His statutes' (Nehemiah x 30). To this general declaration is attached a series of detailed precepts, which are particularly stressed on account of their importance at the time when the pact was made. The place of prophetic rebuke and preaching, which warn against transgressing the Torah and the commandments in general, is taken by the exact definition of the commandments and the admonition to observe their details. Continuing the Biblical concept of the Kingdom of God,[4] the Sages portray the relations between God and His people in images taken from the actual circumstances of the Roman empire, and the analogies do not always come to emphasize the differences between the King of the kings of kings and a human sovereign. An anonymous dictum in the *Mekhilta*, which forms the exordium of the Rabbinic interpretation of the Decalogue, includes the following comparison: ' "I am the Lord thy God" — why were the Ten Commandments not cited at the beginning of the Torah? The Sages explained the matter with the help of a parable: To what can the matter be compared? To one who entered a country and said to the inhabitants "Let me reign over you". They replied: "Have you done anything for our welfare that you should reign over us?" What did he do? He built the (city) wall for them, introduced the water (supply) for them, and waged wars on their behalf. He (then) said (again): "Let me reign over you." They answered him: "Yea, yea!" In the same way the Omnipresent brought out the Israelites from Egypt, divided the sea for them, sent down for them manna, raised up for them the well, brought them a flight of quails, and waged for them the war with Amalek. (Then) He said unto them: "Let Me reign over you". They responded: "yea, yea!"' (*Mekhilta de-R. Ishmael*, Massekhta de-Ba-ḥodesh, v, p. 219).

The very question 'Why were the Ten Commandments not cited at the beginning of the Torah?' flows from the view that the whole concern of the Torah is the precept, and that the entire election of Israel took place only that the Torah might be accepted. All that preceded — the history of the Patriarchs, the bondage of Egypt and the Exodus — is not of primary importance. All these are to be understood as preparatory events leading to the Revelation. On the face of it, it appears from the homily cited above that the acceptance of the yoke of God's Kingdom is the result of the people's assent, but closer scrutiny reveals that this consent was not a matter of free choice, but a decision that was enforced and directed by God's will to impose the yoke of the Torah and commandments on the people chosen for this purpose. Undoubtedly this homily cannot serve as proof of the autonomous character of Jewish ethical teaching. Since the publication of Moritz Lazarus' work on 'The Ethics of Judaism',[5] there has been no halt to the attempts to point to various Rabbinic dicta as evidence of the correspondence between the fundamental principle of Kant's ethical system and the religious ethic of Judaism. However, Lazarus' hypothesis has been rejected in unambiguous terms by Hermann Cohen[6], who made it clear that an autonomous ethic means one that emanates from man and from him alone, that is to say, man is the source of the ethic and God is not its source but only its principle, whereas in all religions, and undoubtedly this is the case in the Jewish faith, God is the source of the ethical law. Hermann Cohen's criticism deals with the general conception. He did not enter into an analysis of the dicta of the Sages on which Lazarus relied[7], and which, as well as similar sayings, continued to form the basis for the arguments of scholars[8] whose main object was to prove the supremacy of the Jewish ethic, and in whose estimation there was no higher corroboration or imprimatur than approximation to the system of Kant. In the light of their contentions many scholars of standing have become accustomed to read and explain Rabbinic dicta and homilies not in consonance with their simple meaning, or according to the intent of their authors, by taking them out of their historical context.

One of the principal sources of the idea of the 'autonomy of ethics' was provided by the dicta concerning the recognition of God and the observance of the Torah by the Patriarch Abraham, such as those in the Mishna at the end of Tractate Qiddushin: 'We find that Abraham our father had kept the whole Law before it was given, for it is written "Because that Abraham obeyed My voice and kept My charge, My commandments, My statutes, and My laws". '[9] But this Mishna only states that Abraham observed the Torah before it was given to Israel. It does not state that he had arrived of his own accord at the recognition of the Torah. The very proof derived from the verse 'Because that Abraham obeyed My voice' precludes the possibility of such an interpretation. Indeed at the end of *Tosefta Qiddushin* it is stated: 'And the Omnipresent blessed him [Abraham] and magnified him in his old age more than in his youth, because he kept the Torah before it was promulgated, as it is said: "Because that Abraham obeyed My voice and kept My charge, My commandments, My statutes, and My laws" — this teaches us that the ordinances of the Torah and the enactments of the Scribes were disclosed [נגלו *niglû*][10] to him.' Thus it is expressly stated here that the ordinances of the Torah were disclosed to him, that is to say, that he was vouchsafed a prior revelation and not that he attained to the Torah of his own accord. In a figurative manner this concept is expressed in a saying attributed to R. Simeon b. Yoḥai: 'R. Simeon b. Yoḥai said: No father taught him; he had no teacher. Whence, then, did he learn the Torah? The Holy One, blessed be He, appointed unto him his two reins as two teachers, and they poured forth and taught him wisdom,[11] as it is written: "I will bless the Lord, who hath given me counsel; yea, in the night seasons my reins instruct me"...' (*Genesis Rabba* lxi, 1, pp. 457–658). It is true that R. Simeon b. Yohai's dictum is followed by the statement of the Amora R. Levi: 'He taught himself Torah, as it is said: "The dissembler in heart shall have his fill from his own ways; and a good man shall be satisfied from himself" (Proverbs xiv 14)...' (*Genesis Rabba* xcv, 3, p. 1189). But even this saying only avers that Abraham learnt Torah, but it may well be that this Torah was given and revealed to him. Even when Abraham proves the existence of One God to Nimrod empirically (*Genesis Rabba* xxxviii, 13, p. 363), it is not stated that Abraham came by himself in this way to recognize the Creator, but, on the contrary, 'R. Isaac said: The case could be compared to one who travelled from one place to another and saw a castle on fire. Said he: "Is it possible that the castle has no governor?" Thereupon the owner of the castle looked out and said to him: "I am the owner of the castle." Thus, because Abraham our father said: "Is it possible that the world has no governor, the Holy One, blessed be He, looked out and said to him: I am the Governor, the Sovereign of the whole world"' (*ibid.* xxxiv, 1, p. 345). Here, when the recognition of God is referred to, the matter is described as an actual act of revelation. 'The Holy One, blessed be He, looked out and said to him: I am the Governor, the Sovereign of the whole world.' Likewise in the apocryphal work 'The Apocalypse of Abraham',[12] Abraham's recognition of the One God comes as a result of revelation. Of his own accord he came to a negative conclusion only, namely the realization of the nullity of the idols.

Only in later Midrashim is the spontaneity of Abraham's recognition of God emphasized, as, for example, in the *Pesiqta Rabbati*: ' "...Thou hast loved righteousness" (Psalms xlv 8 [7]) — this refers to Abraham, for the Holy One, blessed be He, saw that while all those generations were idolaters, Abraham rose up and left them and was not like them. Whereas all of them were idolaters, Abraham arose and *gained wisdom by his own efforts* and served the Holy One, blessed be He...' (*Pesiqta Rabbati*, xxxiii, p. 150a). In one of the late Midrashim the group of men who learnt to recognize God of their own accord was even enlarged; thus we read: 'Another explanation is: "Who hath given Me anything beforehand, that I should repay him?" (Job xli 3 [11]): the verse speaks of Abraham, who of his own accord recognized the Holy One, blessed be He, as it is written: "The dissembler in heart shall have his fill from his own ways..." (Proverbs xiv 14;

this verse, as we have seen, was already expounded in *Genesis Rabba*). What is meant by "The dissembler [סוג *sûg*] in heart shall have his fill from his own ways"? R. Abba Kahana said: The heart that is full of dross [סיגים *sîgîm*] because of its ways is destined to have its fill. "And a good man shall be satisfied from himself" (*ibid.*) — this refers to Abraham, who of his own accord recognized the Holy One, blessed be He, for there was no one, but himself, to teach him how to know the Omnipresent. And he was one of the four human beings who spontaneously learnt to know the Holy One, blessed be He: Job of his own accord recognized the Holy One, blessed be He... Hezekiah, king of Judah, also recognized the Holy One, blessed be He, by himself... and King Messiah likewise recognized the Holy One, blessed be He, by intuition.'[13] In *Seder Eliyyahu Rabba* (ed. Friedmann, vii, p. 35) it is said with regard to Adam, Noah, Abraham, Isaac, Jacob, Judah, and Joseph: 'The Torah was not given to them, but they kept it of their own accord. Therefore the Holy One, blessed be He, loved them completely and he likened their name to His own great name.'[14] In all the ancient sources, however, in the statements of the Tannaim and early Amoraim, referring to the observance of the precepts by those enumerated above, it is not stated 'that they kept them of their own accord'.[15]

Before we suggest an explanation of the difference that we find between the early sources and the later Midrashim in regard to the Patriarchs' recognition of God and their observance of the commandments, let us deal with the other proofs derived from the statements of the Tannaim and early Amoraim respecting autonomous ethics. Repeated reference has been made to the anonymous dictum in the *Sifra*: ' "Mine ordinances shall ye do" — these are the laws written in the Torah that, if they had not been written, should by right have been written, such as the laws concerning robbery, forbidden relations, idolatry, cursing God, and bloodshed, for if they were not written (in Scripture) they should by right have been written.'[16] Are we in truth permitted to state on the basis of this dictum that the Talmudic Sages 'entertained the idea that the content of this ideal of holiness is uniform, and is to be found in the human consciousness in simple form and as something that is self-understood'?[17] Only tendentious reading that pays no attention to the continuation of the homily can lead to such a conclusion. Otherwise we cannot explain how one could attribute to a homilist of the second century the view that the laws of forbidden relations, idolatry, and cursing God constitute an ideal of holiness that is inherent in the consciousness of humanity Indeed, it is not this that the homilist had in mind. When he states that משפטים *mishpāṭîm* ['ordinances'] are laws 'that, if not written (in Scripture), should by right have been written,' he wishes to stress that the reasons underlying these precepts are known and can be explained, whereas חקים *ḥuqqîm* ['statutes'] are commandments 'against which the evil inclination argues, and the Gentile peoples argue, such as (the prohibition) to eat pig, and to wear a garment of two kinds of stuff; the law of removing the sandal of the brother of the deceased by the widow, of the purification of the leper, and of the he-goat that is to be sent away, against which the evil inclination argues, and the Gentile peoples argue. Therefore Scripture teaches "I am the Lord" — I have ordained these statutes, and you are not permitted to challenge them.' There is no other difference between the two categories of commandments. The observance of both of them is obligatory, because they are written in the Torah. Just as the latter are called 'My statutes', so the former are termed 'My ordinances'.

Lazarus thought that he had traced a very early source for the idea of the autonomy of ethics in the Targum of Onkelos to Genesis iii 22. The Scripture 'Behold, the man is become as one of us, to know good and evil' is translated there 'Behold, man has become alone in the world by himself to know good and evil.' Lazarus discovers in the Targum 'profound ethical understanding', for he finds it expressly stated therein that 'man recognizes good and evil of his own accord'.[18] But anyone conversant with the methods of the Targum knows that Onkelos seeks to remove here the anthropomorphic expression in the biblical phrase 'as one of us', and apparently in order to obviate the interpretation that he is referring to autonomous ethics, which is attributed to him, he rendered, after מניה *minnēh* ['by himself'], למידע טב וביש *lĕ-mîdaʿ ṭāv û-vîsh* ['to know good and evil'] and not (as *ibid.* iii 5: ותהון כרברבין חכמין בין טב לביש *û-tĕhôn kĕ-ravrĕvîn ḥakkîmîn bên ṭāv lĕ-vîsh* ['And ye would become like the great ones wise to distinguish between good and evil']) למיחכם בין טב לביש *lĕ-miḥkam bên ṭāv lĕ-vîsh* ['to be wise to distinguish between good and evil']. The reference is to the knowledge of the fact that good and evil exist, and not to discerning, by his own powers, between good and evil.[19]

As proof of the correctness of their view, Lazarus[20] and those who follow him have also cited the Baraita on wronging by means of words: 'The Rabbis taught: "Ye shall not therefore wrong one another" (Leviticus xxv 17) — Scripture speaks of verbal wrongs... How is this to be understood? If a man was a penitent, one must not say to him: "Remember your former deeds" ... If ass-drivers wanted (to buy) grain from him, he must not say to them: "Go to so-and-so, who sells grain", though he knows that he has never sold any. R. Judah said: A man should not feign interest in a purchase, when he has no money, for the matter is left to the heart [i.e. conscience], and of anything left to the heart it is stated "And thou shalt fear thy God" ' (*T.B. Bava Meṣia'* 58b). 'Matters left to the heart' — they argue — are things that a man himself discovers; but clearly this is not the correct interpretation, and undoubtedly we must not deviate from Rashi's explanation that R. Judah seeks only 'to give the reason why the precept to fear God is mentioned in this connection... and this is what he means: For in all these cases the good or bad intent is known only to the heart of the person concerned — he alone knows whether he spoke sincerely or perversely, and he can say: I acted only for the best; I thought that you had grain to sell, or, I did wish to buy this commodity. And in regard to every matter that is left to a man's heart it is stated: Be afraid of Him who knows our thoughts, if they be for good or for deception' (Rashi, *ad loc.*, s.v. *Shĕhărê* ['For']; see *Sifra*, Be-har, iv, 2, p. 107d). The prohibition 'that one should not say "How much does this article cost?", when one does not wish to buy' does not emanate from a man's heart, but it is left to his heart 'that he should fear Him who commanded us concerning these things'; the same applies to the other commandments in regard to which it is written 'And thou shalt fear thy God'.[21] Only in the light of this interpretation can we understand the statement of R. Simeon b. Yoḥai, transmitted by R. Joḥanan: 'Verbal wrong is more reprehensible than financial wrong, because of the former it is said "And thou shalt fear thy God", but of the latter it is not said "And thou shalt fear thy God".' [22]

In the Tannaitic sources that we have cited so far, it is possible to discover the idea of moral autonomy at best by an exegetical method that, as we have seen, does not interpret them according to their natural sense, but imputes to them notions that the Sages never intended to convey. On the other hand, some scholars supposed that express statements about the sovereignty of the moral law and its independence of the Divine Commander could be found in the dicta of the early Amoraim, and they even injected into them the doctrinal dispute between the heteronomous and the autonomous conception. The latter is represented, in their view, by the saying of R. Joḥanan: 'Had the Torah not been given, we could have learnt modesty from the cat, (the prohibition of) robbery from the ant, and (the prohibition of) forbidden relations from the dove' (*T.B.* *ʿEruvin* 100b). Thus it is stated here explicitly, as it were, that even without revelation man can attain, by contemplating the life of nature, to moral conduct. The diametrically opposite view was found by scholars in the dictum of R. Ḥanina; 'Greater is he who is commanded and fulfils (the precept) than he who is not commanded yet fulfils it' (*T.B.* *Qiddushin* 31a), which expresses in the clearest terms the primacy of theonomy. Felix Perles[23] does not deal generally with 'the idea of the autonomy of the Jewish ethic';[24] following Hermann Cohen, he recognizes the theonomous basis of Judaism, but he seeks an explanation of those Rabbinic teachings that contradict this principle, and he proposes to solve the problem by positing Hellenistic influence wherever views in favour of autonomy are apparent. Primarily he had in mind Philo of Alexandria and his view concerning ἄγραφος νόμος, the unwritten law.

In another context[25] we have already pointed out that 'the unwritten law' is not the Oral Law. The classic example of the unwritten law is that upheld by Antigone against the law of Creon. Actually both were unwritten, but the difference was that one was a law promulgated by the king and the other was a law that had never been promulgated — it was a law of Nature — and as such it was also divine, and older than any written statute. Philo accepted these Greek views, and thus he was able to say: 'The Patriarchs went to no school; selftaught they loved to follow Nature, for they regarded Nature as the most venerable law' (De Abra. 6). This is the Stoic view concerning the place of law in nature, which is opposed to Jewish teaching regarding supernatural revelation.[26] Such concepts infiltrated also, according to Perles, into the world of the Sages, and because in their innocence they did not grasp the extreme conclusions implicit in the concept of autonomy, they adopted them as their own. But there is no proof that the Sages were indeed acquainted with the theory of 'the natural law', nor is there any need to recruit this idea in order to reconcile the antithesis between the teaching of R. Joḥanan and that of R. Ḥanina, if we comprehend their true meaning from their context. In the dictum preceding that of R. Joḥanan, R. Ḥiyya explains the words addressed by Elihu to Job (xxxv 11) 'Who teacheth us through the beasts of the earth, and maketh us wise through the fowls of heaven' as referring to certain attributes of living creatures from which man can learn. In conjunction with this verse he merely declares that God endowed the creatures with these qualities, 'that He instilled wisdom in them' (Rashi, *ibid.*), in order that man may learn from them.[27] R. Joḥanan limits R. Ḥiyya's teaching by stating 'Had the Torah not been given, we could have learnt...'; but since it was given, there is no need for this.[28] R. Joḥanan's saying is no more related to the subject of autonomy than to the verse in Job; in the same way R. Ḥanina, too, does not come to teach the doctrine of heteronomy, when he asserts that the one who is commanded and fulfils (the commandment) is superior to him who is not commanded, yet fulfils (the precept). For the latter also did not attain to fulfilment of the commandments as a result of intellectual cognition; he merely belongs to the category of people whom the Torah exempted from the observance of the precepts. This is made explicitly clear by the context in all the passages in which R. Ḥanina's dictum is cited. In *Tractate Qiddushin*, it follows upon the story of how a certain Gentile acted towards his father in Ashkelon. 'Rav Judah said in the name of Samuel: R. Eliezer was asked; To what extent is the honouring of parents (to be observed)? Said he to them: Go forth and see how a certain Gentile acted towards his father in Ashkelon; his name was Dama son of Nethina. The Sages wished to buy from him jewels for the ephod at a profit of 600,000 (gold denars) — Rav Kahana taught: 800,000 — but the key was lying beneath his father's pillow, and he would not disturb him. The following year the Holy One, blessed be He, gave him his reward: a red heifer was born to him in his herd. (Thereupon) the Sages of Israel came to him (to buy it). Said he to them: I know that if I were to ask all the money in the world, you would give it to me; but I ask of you only the money that I lost through honouring my father. Said R. Ḥanina: Now if one who is not commanded yet fulfils (the commandment) is so (rewarded), how much more so will he who is commanded and fulfils (the commandment be rewarded)! For R. Ḥanina said: Greater is he who is commanded and fulfils (the precept) than he who is not commanded yet fulfils (the precept).' If we examine the narrative and the dictum linked to it, we shall observe that it is not stated here that the deeds of one who is not commanded do not merit reward, nor is their value negated. Only their relative value is emphasized. The question whether the Gentile had come to observe the commandment of honouring one's father so meticulously as a result of his own thinking[29], or through having learnt it from his Jewish acquaintances, just as he derived from them his knowledge of the ephod and the red heifer, is irrelevant in the context of our story and likewise as regards the inference that R. Ḥanina drew from the incident. Furthermore, in the other passages where the saying of R. Ḥanina is cited the reference is to a Gentile who studies the Torah (*T. B. Bava Qamma* 38a; *T. B. ʿAvoda Zara* 3a), or to a Jew who is exempt from keeping the commandments, as in the statement of Rav Joseph: 'At first I thought: If one would tell me that the Halakha is according to R. Judah, who said "a blind man is exempt from (the observance of) the commandments", I would give a banquet for the Rabbis, for I am not enjoined yet I observe. But now that I have heard the teaching of R. Ḥanina "Greater is he who is commanded and fulfils (the commandment) than he who is not commanded yet fulfils (the commandment)", on the contrary, if one would tell me that the Halakha is not according to R. Judah, I would give a banquet for the Rabbis' (*T.B. Qiddushin, loc. cit.*; *T.B. Bava Qamma* 87a). When Rav Joseph regarded himself as one who is not commanded yet fulfils (the commandment) and consequently thought that he transcended one who kept (the commandments) because he was so enjoined, it never occurred to him to claim that he had discovered the precepts independently, but only that he was exempt from performing the precepts that had been ordained, yet kept them voluntarily. We must not, therefore, speak of autonomy but of free decision.

Even within the ambit of the theonomic conception and the observance of the commandments as one who keeps them because he is enjoined to do so, a man is enabled to make use of attributes and methods of observance that are related to his temperament, his will, and his nature. It is actually the fulfilment of the commandments as one who observes them because he is enjoined — with devotion and meticulous exactitude — that can give the religious observer the right, as it were, of regarding himself as joint-author of those precepts, and this is the significance of R. Joḥanan's dictum: 'Whoever performs one precept truly is accounted as though he had promulgated it from Mount Sinai, for it is said: "Thou shalt therefore observe and do" (Deuteronomy xxvi 16). What then is the meaning of the words "and (ye) shall do them"? It signifies that whoever observes the Torah and performs it truly is accounted as though he had enacted it and promulgated it from Mount Sinai. R. Joḥanan said further: Whoever keeps the Torah truly is accounted by Scripture as though he had made himself, for it is said: "And the Lord commanded me at that time to teach" etc. The text does not say "to do them" [לעשות אותם *laʿăśôt 'ôtam*] but "to make yourselves with them" [לעשתכם אתם *laʿăśōtkhem ôtām*] (Deuteronomy iv 14) — this implies that he is accounted as though he had made and created himself.'[30] The second dictum is not only intrinsically instructive, but also helps to elucidate the meaning of the preceding saying. Just as by the hyperbolical expression 'as though he had made and created himself' R. Joḥanan did not intend to detract in any way from the fact that man was God's creation, but sought to stress that in the proper fulfilment of the precepts there is, as it were — this qualifying phrase must be emphasized — an element of additional creation and fashioning of man, who becomes a partner of the Almighty in the work of creation,[31] so, too, when he declares that he who performs a precept truly is accounted as though he had promulgated it from Sinai, it did not enter R. Joḥanan's mind to detract from the source of the precept, which is in the Self-revealing and commanding God, but to emphasize that by keeping the Torah truly man is elevated to the status of becoming a revealer by his innate power.[32] The non-recurring Revelation on Mount Sinai is renewed by him, and he becomes a partner therein. In the manner of R. Joḥanan, and even in his very words, homilies are transmitted in the name of other Amoraim, both of Eretz-Israel and of Babylon, based on expositions of other verses[33], to the effect that one who fulfils the commandments willingly renews the Revelation at Mount Sinai. The Tanna R. Eliezer b. Jacob already taught: ' "And Moses and the priests the Levites spoke unto all Israel, saying: 'Keep silence, and hear, O Israel, this day thou art become a people" (Deuteronomy xxvii 9) — but did they receive the Torah this day? Surely they had received the Torah forty years ago, yet the verse says "this day"? This teaches us that when Moses taught them the Torah and they accepted it gladly, Scripture accounted it unto them as though they had received it this day from Sinai. Therefore it is said: "This day thou art become a people unto the Lord thy God" ' (*Canticles Rabba* ii, 5). But it is this very homily that brings into relief the specific significance of the Amoraic teachings that we have cited. R. Eliezer b. Jacob merely declares that when the Israelites accepted the Torah after the lapse of forty years, it was as though the Revelation at Mount Sinai had been renewed; he does not say that it was as though they themselves had promulgated the Torah from Sinai, as R. Joḥanan and R. Ḥama b. R. Ḥanina had stated. They express in their dicta the paradox that the reward of theonomy is the feeling of autonomy, and is the privilege only of one who accepted the Torah and its commandments as they were revealed, and fulfils them in truth. This acceptance is the result of the choice and free decision of each individual, and indeed R. Joḥanan received and transmitted the Haggadah that was current in the academies of the Tannaim[34] to the effect that God had offered the Torah in turn 'to every nation and tongue, but they did not accept it until He came to Israel and they accepted it' (*T.B. ʿAvoda Zara* 2b). But he was not content with the willing acceptance of the people as a whole; he emphasized: 'An angel brought forth the commandment from before the Holy One, blessed be He [in the case of each commandment] and presented it to every Israelite, saying: "Do you accept this commandment? It contains so-and-so many laws..." And the Israelite answered: "Yea!...." '[35]

A view that is diametrically opposite to the concept of choice is to be found in the dictum of R. Avdimi bar Ḥasa, apparently a Babylonian Amora of the second generation,[36] who expounded ' "And they stood at the nether part of the mount"... This teaches that the Holy One, blessed be He, tilted the mountain over them like a cask and said unto them: "If you accept the Torah, well and good; and if not, there shall be your burial." ' This homily of R. Avdimi is an individual view, which has no parallel. The image, however, of the Israelites' actually standing beneath the mountain is already to be found in the *Mekhilta*, but it is precisely there that the phrasing emphasizes that they did this voluntarily: 'This teaches us that the mountain was plucked up from its place and they [the Israelites] drew near and stood under the mountain, as it is stated: "And ye came near and stood under the mountain" (Deuteronomy iv 11). Concerning them it is stated in post-Mosaic Scriptures (*Canticles Rabba* ii, 14): "O my dove, that art in the clefts of the rock... for sweet is thy voice, and thy countenance is comely." '[37] In an anonymous Talmudic passage (*T.B. ʿAvoda Zara* 2b) it is already pointed out that R. Avdimi's homily not only contradicts that of the Mekhilta, which states that the Gentile peoples were given an opportunity to accept the Torah, but also deprives it of its underlying reason: 'Hence the Gentile peoples were called upon to accept the Torah, so that they should not be able to argue before the *Shekhina* ['Divine Presence'], saying: Had we been asked, we should certainly have accepted the obligation (of the Torah)' — and the Talmud offers the explanation it thinks fit. Some of the Geonim and *Risho'nim* [the post-Geonic authorities] attempted to reconcile R. Avdimi's dictum with the Scripture 'We will do, and obey'.[38] But the Amoraim of his generation and the next did not accept his view. R. Aḥa bar Jacob's reaction, 'This provides a powerful protest against the Torah', expresses opposition, declaring, in effect, that the view that the Torah was accepted under coercion nullifies the demand for its observance.[39] Apparently in an attempt to justify the attitude of the people to the Torah in the period of the First Temple, Rava is inclined to leave R. Avdimi's homily in its place, only he adds to it: 'Even so the generation in the days of Ahasuerus accepted it (anew).' 'The voluntary acceptance of the Torah' is a fundamental principle in the estimation of Rava.[40] Indeed, we find him maintaining the view of those Amoraim who hold that the free decision of man does not find complete expression in the acceptance of the yoke of the Torah and commandments alone, but continues in the course of their observance, and it not only has the power to elevate man 'as though he had made himself',[41] but also to give him a share in the ownership of the Torah and the moulding of its nature. Thus said Rava: 'A man should always study that part of the Torah that his heart desires, as it is said "But whose desire is in the Law of the Lord". Rava further said: At first (the Torah) is named [i.e. in the verse] after the Holy One, blessed be He, but in the end it is called after him [i.e. the student], as it is said "Whose desire is in the Law of the Lord and in his [i.e. his own] Law doth he meditate day and night." '[42] It is noteworthy that Rava's dictum in the Talmudic discussion is preceded by another exposition of the same verse, namely: 'R. Avdimi bar Ḥama said: The Holy One, blessed be He, fulfils the desires of everyone who occupies himself with the Torah, as it is said "If he (occupies himself) with the Law of the Lord, his desire (is granted)." ' In the view of R. Avdimi, the revelation of a man's desire to study the Torah is not a decisive factor, for the study is incumbent upon him. In his exposition he detaches the words 'his desire' from 'the Law of the Lord'. To this Rava reacts, when he declares that a man's desire (to occupy himself) with the Torah transforms it from the Lord's Torah into the Torah of the one who studies it. It seems that this doctrinal difference between the two Amoraim also lies at the root of their different homilies on Deuteronomy xxx 11–13: 'For this commandment which I command thee this day... It is not in heaven... Neither is it beyond the sea....' R. Avdimi bar Ḥama bar Dosa expounded: ' "It is not in heaven", for if it were in heaven, it would be incumbent upon you to go up after it; and if it were "beyond the sea", it would be incumbent upon you to cross (the sea) after it.' On the other hand, Rava, like R. Joḥanan, declares: ' "It is not in heaven" — it is not to be found in one who, on account of it, allows his conceit to soar to the heavens; nor is it to be found in one who, on account of it, allows his arrogance to grow vast as the sea.'[43] While R. Avdimi deduces from the verse the duty to keep the Torah and to study it in all circumstances, Rava predicates this upon a man's attributes and qualities.

Our analysis has, we believe, made it amply clear that Rava's view summarizes the prevailing opinion in the academies of the Amoraim. Nor is this surprising, since it is consonant with the history of the Halakha, which is based on the authority of the Sages to extend and restrict the application and ambit of the precepts. It is true that R. Akiba and his disciples held that 'The Torah with its laws and subtle distinctions and interpretations was promulgated through Moses at Sinai'[44], and we have already seen (above, p. 300) that this theory of a general and comprehensive Revelation nullifies in fact the difference between the two Torahs; but in this very extremism emphasis is given to the freedom of the Sage to interpret the words of the Torah, to expound, to enact, and to decree (prohibitions), secure in the knowledge that he is realizing the Revelation, transforming the potential into actuality, and revealing to his generation that which it needs.[45]

But there also remained a sphere, transcending the law and Halakha of the Oral Torah, in which man could introduce innovations and additions by his own initiative; this sphere is called 'beyond the strict letter of the law'. R. Eleazar of Modiʿim expounded the verse 'And thou shalt show them the way wherein they must walk, and the work that they must do' (Exodus xviii 20) as follows: ' "and the work" — that means the strict letter of the Law; "that they must do" — that connotes beyond the strict letter of the Law' (*Mekhilta de-R. Ishmael*, Massekhta da-ʿAmalek, Yitro, ii, p. 198). He thus learnt from the Scripture the duty to act beyond the strict requirements of the Law. R. Joḥanan even said 'Jerusalem was destroyed only because they judged therein (strictly) according to Torah law'; and the meaning, as the Talmud explains there, is 'that they based their judgements (strictly) on Torah law and did not act beyond the requirements of the Law'.[46] The requirement of the law is actually the Halakha, according to which the judge must give his decision, but sometimes the Halakha itself ordains that the judge is not obliged to act according to 'the letter of the Law', and they are the cases in which the strict requirement of the Law is not consonant with, and even runs counter to, 'the public weal'.[47] But the detailed nature of that which is 'beyond the requirement of the Law' has not been determined and is left to the human heart, and this is also borne out by the stories in the Talmuds about acts that were 'beyond the requirement of the Law',[48] from which it is clearly to be seen that what is defined as 'beyond the requirement of the Law' is not prescribed by law. This needs to be emphasized in the light of what has been said on this subject on the basis of the following narrative in the Babylonian Talmud (*T.B. Bava Meṣiʿa* 83a): 'Certain porters broke a barrel of wine belonging to Rabbah bar bar Ḥanan; so he seized their cloaks. Thereupon they went and told Rav. Said he (to Rabbah bar bar Ḥanan): 'Give them their cloaks." "Is this the law?" the latter inquired. (Rav) replied: "Yea, (as it is written) 'That thou mayest walk in the way of good men' " (Proverbs ii 20). So he returned to them their cloaks. (The porters) then said (to Rav): "We are poor, and we have toiled all day and we are hungry, and we have nothing. Said (Rav) to (Rabbah bar bar Ḥanan): "Go, pay them." The latter rejoined: "Is this the law?" (Rav) replied: "Yea, (as it is written:) 'and keep the paths of the righteous' (Proverbs *ibid.*)." ' The word 'Yea' fired the imagination of the homilists and scholars and led them to proclaim that 'beyond the requirement of the Law' became law.[49] But unfortunately the word 'Yea' is missing in the MSS. and the works of the *Risho'nim*[50], just as it is wanting in the version of this story cited in the Palestinian Talmud: 'Once a potter delivered his pots to a man, who broke them; so the potter seized his cloak. Thereupon the man went (and complained) to R. Jose bar Ḥanina. The latter said to him: "Go, tell him: 'That thou mayest walk in the way of good men.' " He went and told the potter, and he returned his cloak. Subsequently (R. Jose bar Ḥanina) asked the complainant: "Did he pay you?" The man replied "No". So he said to him: "Go, tell him: 'And keep the paths of the righteous.' " So he went and told the potter, and the latter gave the man his pay.'[51] R. Jose bar Ḥanina and the Amora in the Babylonian Talmud advised the potter, or the owner of the wine casks, to act beyond the requirement of the Law, and they based themselves on the verse in Proverbs ii 20 and not on the verse in Exodus xviii, because they did not accept the exposition of R. Eleazar of Modiʿim, but agreed with R. Joshua (*Mekhilta loc. cit.*): ' "That they must do" — that means the good deed', i.e., the good deeds that are the Torah precepts, and which R. Eleazar of Modiʿim deduced from the beginning of the verse. On the other hand, the Scriptures 'the way of good men' and 'the paths of the righteous' implied acts to which the good men and the righteous attained of their own accord.

If a Sage instructed someone else to act according to this standard, he felt the need to inform him that his instruction was not based on law. Although in the story that we have cited, Rav explained the position only in reply to Rabbah bar bar Ḥanan's question 'Is this the Law?', it is possible that he supposed that Rabbah would understand of his own accord that he was referring to the way of good and righteous men and not to strict law. When R. Eleazar wished to give a practical decision and to rule that daughters be given alimentation from moveable property (of their deceased father's estate), 'R. Simeon b. Eliakim said to him: "Master, I know full well that you are not acting according to the strict requirement of the Law but in accordance with the principle of compassion; but (there is the danger) that the disciples may note (your ruling) and fix it as a Halakha for the future" ' (*T.B. Ketubbot* 50b). Not only are these good deeds not identifiable with the Law, but not even with what is accepted as right and good in the estimation of most people. The Sages of Nehardea had this last point in mind when they ruled with regard to 'a person who takes possession (of an estate situated) between brothers or partners... He is removed even on account of the right of pre-emption, for it is said "And thou shalt do that which is right and good in the sight of the Lord" (Deuteronomy vi 18).'[52] Apparently they expounded the verse in the same way as R. Akiba: ' "That which is good" — in the sight of Heaven, and "That which is right" — in the sight of man.'[53] And man must fulfil his duty in both directions; hence matters that fall within the category of 'And thou shalt do that which is right and good' may also be Halakha[54]; whereas the things that are beyond the requirement of the Law[55] are not Halakha[56], but acts of piety.[57] The pious man forgoes his rights (*M. 'Avot*, v, 10), and acts beyond the requirement of the law, and this is the attribute of piety.[58] Similarly the Palestinian Talmud explains the contradiction between the decision Rav gave to 'a certain man' and his own conduct by the antithesis: 'There (in the case of the man, he ruled) according to strict law, but in his own case Rav acted according to the quality of piety' (*T.P. Shevi'it* [end], p. 39d). The Mishna does, indeed, teach (*Shevi'it* [end]): 'All moveable goods are acquired (only) by the act of drawing (the article towards oneself); but whoever keeps his word (alone), the spirit of the Sages finds pleasure in him', and accordingly one who does not keep his word, 'the spirit of the Sages does not find pleasure in him'. But from the context and from the *Mishna Bava Meṣiʿa* iv, 2, we see that the reference is to one who received money, without the act of drawing having taken place, and retracted, or, at least according to Rava (*T.B. Bava Meṣiʿa* 48a), to a case of 'words unaccompanied by money', that is to say, where one had agreed to sell, but had not received any money, and in such circumstances 'the Sages find no satisfaction in this man's conduct' (Rashi, *ibid.*).[59] Rav, however, said: 'When I tell my household to give a gift to a person, I do not retract' (*T.P. Sheviʿit* [end]). Rav did not say anything to the recipient of the gift but to his household[60], yet even so he did not wish to retract, and this constitutes 'pious conduct'. Of a Sage of the calibre of R. Joshua b. Levi it is expected that he would act beyond legal requirements; hence his argument 'But did I not fulfil the ruling of a Mishna?' is countered by Elijah with the remark, 'But is this a Mishna-ruling followed by the pious?' (*T.P. Terumot* viii, 5, p. 44b; see also *T.B. Bava Batra* 7b).

While the opinions of the Tannaim were divided, in the case of man's duties to God, as to whether every man has a right to act with special stringency where he himself is concerned, and R. Simeon b. Gamaliel declared 'Not every one that wishes to assume the name (of a pious personage) may proceed to do so' (*M. Berakhot* ii, 8), for 'if he has not the reputation of a Sage and a pious man in the public estimation, this is only a form of arrogance' (Rashi, *T.B. Berakhot* 17b), and people react with displeasure;[61] yet in all that appertains to the precepts to be observed by a man towards his fellow, such a restriction cannot, of course, apply. Without doubt, when the Sages urged people to go beyond the letter of the law, they also employed the argument that a man prays to God to act towards him in accordance with the attribute of compassion. In the name of Rav it is reported that the Almighty Himself prays: 'May it be My will that My compassion may conquer My anger, and that My compassion may prevail over My (other) attributes, so that I may deal with My children mercifully and act towards them with charity that goes beyond the requirement of the law' (*T.B. Berakhot* 7a). On the other hand a man is not truly pious unless he observes the 'laws of damages' [i.e. of *Neziqin*], that is to say, the practice of the Early Pious Men in this sphere.[62]

The dicta that we have cited relative to 'beyond the requirement of the law' and 'pious conduct' indicate how wide is the range of matters, even for the person who keeps the precepts because he is enjoined, that remain subject to his desire and will, to his temperament and attributes. There is no autonomy. In contrast to Kant's ethical system, in which God is no more than an Idea that serves to complete the science of ethics, in the doctrine of the Sages God ever remains the Source and Giver of the commandments. But even the man who does good, because he regards it as a precept and law, is allowed to determine his own ways of fulfilling the observance, so that he may achieve perfection through them and also introduce innovations and augment them. For freedom of decision, which marked the acceptance of the Torah, whether at Sinai, or at a later period — in the sense of 'the generation accepted it' — was not taken away from those who keep the Torah and fulfil its commandments. The Amora Rava, who, we found, maintained the merit of the voluntary acceptance of the Torah, likewise praised Israel's uttering 'we will do' before 'we will hear' (*T.B. Shabbat* 88a–b), and he regarded the linking of 'the enactments of the Scribes', which are 'new regulations ordained in each generation to provide a hedge and a fence', to the old laws of the Torah as a corollary to them both. In the same spirit he expounded the verse ' "New and old, which I have laid for thee, O my beloved" (Canticles vii 14) — the Congregation of Israel declared before the Holy One, blessed be He: "Sovereign of the universe, I have imposed more restrictive edicts upon myself than Thou hast, and I have fulfilled them" ' (*T.B. ʿEruvin* 21b and Rashi *ad loc.*). Rav ʿAwira, a contemporary of Rava, attributes, in the name of his teachers — R. Ammi and R. Assi — a similar appraisement to God. To the contention of the angels that He shows favouritism towards Israel, 'He answered: Why should I not favour Israel? For I enjoined them in the Torah "And thou shalt eat and be satisfied and bless the Lord thy God" (Deuteronomy viii 10), yet they are so meticulous as (to say grace) for food the size of an olive or of an egg' (*T.B. Berakhot* 20b). When the Amoraim contemplated the image of the precepts in their generation after they had become studded with the minutest detailed regulations introduced by the 'fence'-makers and ordinance-ordainers and the acts of the pious, and when they considered, again, the image of the observers of the precepts, they could — with complete conviction — declare that whoever fulfils a commandment correctly 'it is as though he had promulgated it from Sinai' and 'as though he had created himself' (see above, p. 326).

These and similar dicta, which serve as an appraisal of the role of the human personality in the fulfilment of the precepts, explain the change that had taken place in the consciousness of the past, that is to say, in the evaluation of the observance of the commandments by the Patriarchs, with which we dealt above (p. 320). We are confronted by a phenomenon that may be termed 'the acts of the scions are a sign to their sires'. The tradition is common to the ancient sources — both to the apocryphal literature, like the *Book of Jubilees* and the *Testaments of the Twelve Patriarchs,* and to the Haggadot of the Tannaim and early Amoraim — that the Patriarchs kept the Torah and the commandments, be it that they were directly enjoined concerning them by God, or that they received the laws as an oral or written tradition from their predecessors. The other way (to account for the patriarchal observance of the Torah), which is preferred by the pseudepigraphic literature, in which Enoch fulfils the central role in the transmission of the Torah and commandments,[63] is also not altogether wanting in the homilies of the Sages.[64] The function of Enoch, who is not mentioned in Tannaitic literature at all — and even in the Amoraic homilies the attitude to him is not positive[65] — is, however, fulfilled by Shem and Eber. In their academy Jacob studied fourteen years, and they transmitted to him Halakhot, which he in turn handed down to Joseph[66]; but primarily the observance of the precepts by the Patriarchs is conceived, as in the case of the Torah itself, as the outcome of direct revelation.[67] There were also Tannaim who were disinclined to attribute to the Patriarchs the observance of more commandments than those expressly mentioned in the Torah. This emerges from the following Mishna that treats of the law of the sinew of the hip: 'It applies to clean but not to unclean beasts. R. Judah said: (It applies) also to unclean beasts. R. Judah argued: Was not the sinew of the hip forbidden from the time of the sons of Jacob, when unclean beasts were still permitted to them? They replied: It was enjoined at Sinai, but it was recorded in its (due) place.'[68] Neither the Sages nor R. Judah, however, solve the question by positing that the Patriarchs observed the prohibition not to eat unclean beasts.

While we found neither in the apocryphal literature nor in the dicta of the Tannaim and the Amoraim the view that the Patriarchs came to observe the commandments of their own accord,[69] this is expressly stated in later Midrashim. However, it is not, as some scholars have thought[70], the result of Philo's influence,[71] but flows from the internal development in the evaluation of man's part in the performance and moulding of the precepts. If the Sons were allowed to act 'as though they had created the commandments' and as though 'they had promulgated them from Sinai', how much more so was this permitted the Fathers![72] The role assumed by the observers of the precepts and the glory with which they had been crowned were linked to a qualitative change that had taken place in the actual connotation of the term 'precept', and hence they also conduced to a new appraisal of the range and number of the commandments. The Rabbinic use of the term 'precept' became greatly extended. It not only comprises the positive and negative precepts explicitly mentioned in the Torah,[73] which are also called עשה *ʿăśē* [literally 'do'] and לא תעשה *lō' taʿăśe* [literally 'do not'], but every verse of the Torah is called a precept. R. Joḥanan said 'in the name of R. Simeon b. Yoḥai: Moses wrote for us three sections in the Torah, and each one contains sixty precepts; these are: the Section of the Passover Sacrifice, the Section of Damages, and the Section of *Qĕdôshîm* ['Be ye holy']'.[74] Whoever examines these sections will readily see that they do not contain sixty commandments each, but that each comprises sixty verses. We learn from the statements of the Tannaim that they scrutinized the compass and content of the precepts from many aspects. The very multiplicity of the commandments in the Torah leads them to the view that man is obliged to perform a precept with everything given him by God. 'There is not a thing in the world that is not subject to precepts to be performed in the name of the Omnipresent. Produce entails many commandments: the heave-offerings, the tithes, the dough-offering, the first-fruits, the gleanings, the forgotten sheaf, and the corner of the field. To the gates of houses and cities pertains a precept dedicated to the Omnipresent, as it is said: "And thou shalt write them upon the door-posts..." (Deuteronomy vi 9). To the cloak and garments belongs a precept ordained by the Omnipresent, as it is said: "Thou shalt not wear a mingled stuff... Thou shalt make the twisted cord..." (*ibid.* xxii 11–12). Clean beasts embrace a precept enjoined by the Omnipresent, as it is said: "All the firstling males that are born of thy herd and of thy flock thou shalt sanctify unto the Lord thy God; thou shalt do no work with the firstling of thine ox, nor shear the firstling of thy flock" (*ibid.* xv 19). Unclean beasts are affected by a precept of the Omnipresent, as it is said: "And the firstling of an ass thou shalt redeem with a lamb; and if thou wilt not redeem it, then thou shalt break its neck" (Exodus xxxiv 20). With regard to beasts that grow up wild and birds that fly in the air, Scripture ordained that when they come into your possession they should not lack a precept, as it is said: "that taketh in hunting any beast or fowl that may be eaten..." (Leviticus xvii 13); and other kinds of cattle and beasts that Scripture does not specify by name are combined together so that they should not be devoid of a precept, as it is stated: "Notwithstanding, no devoted thing, that a man may devote unto the Lord of all that he hath, whether of man or beast..." (*ibid.* xxvii 28). The holy things of the Sanctuary, though they are all holy, are classified in numerous degrees.'[75] 'A man performs ten precepts before ever he eats a piece of bread' (*T.P. Ḥalla* i [end], p. 58a).

In the light of what has been stated about matters that belong to the heart, about acting beyond the requirements of the law, and about the way the commandments are to be fulfilled, it is not surprising that in the term מצוה *miṣwā* ('precept', 'religious act', 'meritorious deed') were included even things that are not obligatory. Not only acts of charity are called *miṣwā*.[76] While R. Ile'a reports in the name of R. Eleazar b. R. Simeon that 'A man may deviate from the truth for the sake of peace, as it is said "Thy father did command... so shall ye say unto Joseph: Forgive, I pray thee now..." (Genesis l 16–17)', R. Nathan disagrees with him and maintains that it is a *miṣwā* [a religious act] to do so in the interests of peace;[77] that which is a matter of free choice has thus become a *miṣwā*. In a similar manner R. Joḥanan explained the dispute between the first quoted authority and R. Judah in the Mishna in *Soṭa* (viii, 7): 'To what does the foregoing refer? To an optional war [רשות *rĕshût*], but in a war waged in a religious cause [*miṣwā*] all go forth, even the bridegroom from his chamber and the bride from her bridal chamber. R. Judah said:

To what does the foregoing refer? To a war waged in a religious cause, but in an obligatory [חובה *ḥôvā*] war all go forth, even the bridegroom from his chamber and the bride from her bridal chamber.' While Rav Ḥisda differentiates between an optional war and a war waged in a religious cause and an obligatory war, 'R. Joḥanan said: There is a semantic difference between them; R. Judah called an 'optional war' a 'war waged in a religious cause', but in an obligatory war every one goes forth....'[78] The enlargement of the sphere to which *miṣwā* applied and the upgrading of optional matters to the status of *miṣwā* reduced the original obligatory character of the term and it bifurcated into a precept that is optional and one that is obligatory. When Samuel formulates the point of dispute in regard to the evening service, he states that 'Rabban Gamaliel says: It is obligatory; R. Joshua says: It is optional.'[79] For the term *miṣwā* could be interpreted as 'an optional precept', which was what R. Joshua actually had in mind, for it is clear that he, too, considers that one who recites the evening prayers performs a *miṣwā*[80], only this precept is not of an obligatory nature, so that a person would be liable to punishment for failing to observe it. Since an optional religious act was also called just *miṣwā*, it became necessary to designate an entirely obligatory religious act *ḥôvā* ('duty'). Thus R. Abba is not satisfied with the formulation of 'R. Ile'a in the name of R. Eleazar b. R. Simeon: Just as it is a meritorious act [*miṣwā*] for a man to say that which will be listened to, so is it meritorious for a man not to say that which will not be listened to,' and he declares 'It is a duty [*ḥôvā*], for it is said: "Reprove not a scorner, lest he hate thee; reprove a wise man and he will love thee" (Proverbs ix 8)' (*T.B. Yevamot* 65b). The meaning is: Just as one who reproves a wise man fulfils a precept, so one who rebukes a scorner and says something that is not listened to commits a transgression. The use of the term *miṣwā* in two senses sometimes caused misunderstanding. When Abbaye declares that 'It is a *miṣwā* for orphans to pay their father's debt', he meant to say, as Rashi states, 'On account of their father's honour, only the court must not compel them to do this, because it is not an express positive commandment like that of the "Tabernacle" and "palm branch", but merely a meritorious act [*miṣwā*] prescribed by the Rabbis.'[81] Hence, when Rav Papa, using the same expression, said 'Payment of the debt due to a creditor is a *miṣwā*', Rav Kahana raised an objection: 'In view of your statement that payment of the debt due to a creditor is a *miṣwā*, what is the position if he says "I have no desire to perform a meritorious deed [*miṣwā*]?" ' Thereupon Rav Papa replied that he had in mind a positive commandment, that is, one whose observance is obligatory and concerning which it has been taught in a Baraita: '...But in the case of a positive commandment, for instance, if he is told "Make a tabernacle!" and he does not do so, (or carry) a "pa'm branch" and he does not do so, he may be beaten till he expires. [82] From our previous remarks, it is clear that Rav Papa's statement and Rav Kahana's objection do not involve a disagreement in principle on the question whether payment of a creditor is a religious duty or an obligation under civil law.[83] Such a distinction was far from the mind of the Amoraim. Undoubtedly even Rav Kahana did not recognize an obligation under civil law that did not fall within the category of the commandments. That which is not a commandment (*miṣwā*) is certainly not obligatory but optional; yet within this option it was possible, as we have seen, to upgrade and approximate certain acts to the status of commandment, even acts not included in the concept of 'an obligation under civil law'.

The idea that even human actions that are related only to man's bodily needs are to be regarded as having religious merit [*miṣwā*] is attributed to Hillel the Elder. The dictum of R. Jose in the Mishna ('*Avot* ii, 12) 'And let all your deeds be for the sake of Heaven' is glossed in '*Avot de-R. Nathan* (Version II, xxx, p. 66): 'Like Hillel, for when Hillel went anywhere (and) he was asked: "Whither are you going?" (he would answer): "I go to perform a precept." — "What precept, Hillel?" — "I am going to perform my needs." — "Is this then a religious act?" He replied: "Yea, so that the body be not impaired." (Or on another occasion they might say to him:) "Whither are you going, Hillel?" — "I go to perform a precept." — "What precept, Hillel?" — "I am going to the bathhouse." — "Is this then a precept?" — He replied: "Yea, in order to cleanse the body. Here is proof that this is so: If now in the case of the statues (εἰκόνιον) that stand in the royal plazas, the officer appointed to cleanse and polish them is given an annual state salary, and furthermore is raised to the status of the nobility of the kingdom, how much more so we, who have been created in the Divine image and likeness, as it is said 'For in the image of God made He man!'" (Genesis ix 6). Shammai expressed a different view: 'Let us fulfil our obligations with this body.'[84] Shammai also recognized a man's duty to care for his body, so that it should not become impaired and should be clean. Man must maintain his body in the sense of 'perforce you live', and he does not require the verse 'For in the image of God made He man.' A man's duty towards his body is to be differentiated from the precepts between man and God and between man and man, and is not included among the acts to be performed for the sake of Heaven. In the light of the foregoing we can explain another dispute between Shammai and Hillel, which scholars have found difficult to understand:[85] 'It is taught, It was said of Shammai the Elder: All his days he used to eat in honour of the Sabbath. If he found a fine beast, he would say: This is for the Sabbath. If he (subsequently) found another that was still better, he would set aside the second (for the Sabbath) and eat the first. But Hillel the Elder had another attitude, for all his works were for the sake of Heaven, as it is said "Blessed be the Lord day by day."'[86] It appears that the words 'all his works were for the sake of Heaven' have the same meaning as in *M. 'Avot* and in the story in *'Avot de-R. Nathan*, namely that Hillel regarded even eating on week days as an act to be dedicated to Heaven, and in this sense he interpreted the verse 'Blessed be the Lord day by day.'[87] Shammai said otherwise; concerning eating during the week-days, which he considered necessary, he declared: 'Let us fulfil our obligations with this body.' He considered that the direction of thought to Heaven found fulfilment in the observance of commandments not necessary to the body: 'It was said of Shammai the Elder that he never ceased speaking of the Sabbath; if he bought anything good, he would say: This is for the Sabbath; a new vessel, he would say: This is for the Sabbath' (*Mekhilta de-R. Simeon b. Yoḥai*, p. 148). We are confronted by a doctrinal dispute. In Hillel's view a man is able — and consequently he is so enjoined — to dedicate all his acts, even where natural functions are concerned, to Heaven; whereas Shammai posits such a possibility only in the case of acts that are precepts. In the spirit of Hillel's approach it was taught in a Baraita 'A man should wash his face, hands and feet every day for the sake of his Maker, for it is said "The Lord hath made everything for His own purpose" (Proverbs xvi 4).'[88] Similarly Bar Qappara expounded: 'Which is the short Scriptural passage on which the fundamentals of the Torah are dependent? — "In all thy ways acknowledge him" (Proverbs iii 6)'; and Rava further inferred from his words: 'even where a transgression is involved'.[89] At first blush Rava's remark recalls the dictum of R. Naḥman bar Isaac 'More meritorious is a transgression performed with good intent [i.e. for the sake of Heaven] than a precept fulfilled with an ulterior motive',[90] but, as we shall see below (p. 398), it is doubtful if the thought is the same. At all events committing a transgression for the sake of Heaven only means doing it in order to fulfil a precept, as is to be inferred from the statement of ʿUlla: 'Tamar was guilty of adultery (and) Zimri was guilty of adultery. Tamar committed adultery and kings and prophets were descended from her; Zimri committed adultery, and myriads of Israelites fell on his account.'[91]

One cannot overlook the danger to the observance of the precepts from the standpoint of Hillel, for if every act can be done in the name of Heaven, then something is abstracted from the absolute value of the precept and a way is opened for the nullification of the worth of the ritual laws whose connection with the knowledge of the Lord is not clear or simple. In truth, Jesus reached such extreme conclusions in his polemic against the Halakha, as is reported in the Gospels.[92] The danger was evident to Hillel himself, and in the light of it we must understand the Baráita: 'Hillel the Elder said: When (the scholars) draw in, scatter, when they disseminate, draw in. When you see that the Torah is beloved of all Israel, and all rejoice in it, scatter it abroad, as it is said "There is that scattereth and yet increaseth" (Proverbs xi 24). When you see that the Torah is being forgotten by Israel, and not all take heed of it, draw it in, as it is said: "When it is time to work for the Lord" (Psalms cxix 126).'[93] The scattering that finds expression in the demand that all one's actions should be in the name of Heaven, and regards the washing of the body as a religious act, is suited to a time when the Torah is beloved of all Israel, and all rejoice therein; but when all do not take heed of the Torah, it is a 'time to work for the Lord'. I have deviated from the interpretation of the commentators who have explained Hillel's statement to refer to 'Torah study', and I have interpreted it to relate to the observance of the precepts. It would seem that R. Me'ir already interpreted in this way the saying of Hillel 'They have made void Thy law — it is time to work for the Lord'[94], referring it to times when the observance of the precepts was prohibited, and many indeed did not stand up to the test. Thus 'R. Me'ir used to say: There is not a man in Israel who does not perform a hundred precepts each day... there is not a man in Israel who is not encompassed by precepts....' Noteworthy is the addition to the Baraita that parallels the dictum of R. Me'ir: 'The Rabbis taught: Beloved are Israel, for the Holy One, blessed be He, encompassed them with precepts — phylacteries on their head, and phylacteries on their arms, and fringes on their garments, and *mĕzûzôt* on their portals, and concerning them David said: "Seven times a day do I praise Thee, because of Thy righteous ordinances" (Psalms cxix 164); and when David entered the bathhouse and saw himself naked, he said: "Woe is me, for I am naked, without precepts"; but when he remembered the circumcision in his flesh, his mind was set at rest' (*T.B. Menaḥot* 43b). At a time when the observance of the commandments was forbidden, including circumcision, it was inappropriate to say that the very entry into the bathhouse was in itself a religious act, but primarily it was necessary to emphasize the value and importance of the precepts, in accordance with the teaching of R. Me'ir's contemporary R. Simeon b. Yoḥai: 'If you see that people have grown very lax in matters of the Torah, arise and be strong therein.'[95] On the other hand it seems that the dicta of Bar Qappara, Rava, and Rav Naḥman bar Isaac are to be understood against the background of the feeling of generations in which 'the Torah was beloved of all Israel and all rejoiced therein', a feeling that found expression in the words that Rava attributed to the Congregation of Israel.[96]

II. *The Number, Classification, and Evaluation of the Precepts*

The consciousness that Israelites were encompassed every moment by precepts, and that the Lord 'Left nothing in the world unendowed by a precept',[97] serves as a background to the homily of R. Simlai: 'Six hundred and thirteen precepts were given to Moses — three hundred and sixty-five of them are negative commandments, like the number of the days of the solar year, and two hundred and forty-eight are positive commandments, corresponding to the parts of the human body' (*T.B. Makkot* 23b). It is the idea that there is a precept for every day of the year and every part of man's body[98] — 'each part says to man: pray, perform this precept through me... each day says to man: pray, do not commit this transgression on me'[99] — that led to the fixing of the exact number six hundred and thirteen. In the Tannaitic sources this number is unknown, and in the passages where it appears in the printed editions it is only an interpolation that is wanting in the MSS; for instance: '...Now it is surely an argument from minor to major: If they (the Gentiles) failed to observe the seven precepts enjoined upon the Children of Noah, how much less (would they be able to keep) the six hundred and thirteen commandments!' But in the MSS the reading is: '...how much less all the commandments of the Torah!'[1] The other Amoraim that speak about the number of the precepts, including those who find support for the number 613 in the numerical value of the word Torah [תורה TWRH, which adds up in Hebrew to 611] plus the first two commandments of the Decalogue, which were uttered by the Almighty,[2] based themselves on the homily of R. Simlai. We know of no attempt to count the precepts in the Talmudic era, but the enumerators of the commandments from the time of the compiler of the *Halakhot Gedolot* onward encountered many difficulties. Maimonides severely criticized the enumerators of the precepts who preceded him, he shows lack of method and system in their ways of enumeration. However, even the principles and rules that he set forth as the basis of his Book of Precepts[3] aroused much criticism; it is worthwhile citing the summary remarks of R. Simeon b. Ṣemaḥ Duran at the end of his work *Zohar ha-Raqiaʿ* ['Splendour of the Heaven'][4]: 'And now, O reader, note carefully what I have written: both in the case of the positive and negative precepts there are many differences of opinion and much confusion in respect of the number of the commandments... and if all the leading authorities could not find their way in this regard, how can the least of them hope to work out the calculation where one builds and the other demolishes, one fences in and the other breaches the fence, one raises an objection and the other resolves it...

and perhaps the consensus of opinion that the number of the precepts is 613 — 345 and 248 — conforms to the view of R. Simlai and his interpretation of the precepts, but we do not rely on his interpretation in deciding the Halakha, but on the Talmudic study of the subject. The reason why this number is mentioned everywhere is that we find no other Sage who counted them, and so we have taken his enumeration, and even if the number is too low or too high, it is approximately correct, and as the Sages often say (*T.B. Sukka* 8a; *T.B. Bava Batra* 27a): "It is a small amount, and a small amount is disregarded." ' This epitome supports our observations about the beginning of R. Simlai's homily and its purpose.[5] The matter becomes clear if we consider the continuation of the exposition: 'David came and reduced them to eleven, as it is written: "A Psalm of David. Lord who shall sojourn in Thy tabernacle..." (Psalms xv 1–5); Isaiah came and reduced them to six, as it is written: "He that walketh righteously, and speaketh uprightly..." (Isaiah xxxiii 15); Micah came and reduced them to three, as it is written: "It hath been told thee, O man" (Micah vi 8); Isaiah further reduced them to two, as it is said: "Thus saith the Lord, keep ye justice and do righteousness" (Isaiah lvi 1); Amos came and brought them down to one, as it is said: "Thus saith the Lord unto the house of Israel, Seek ye Me and live" (Amos v 4).'[6] Although an Israelite has been given precepts corresponding to each day of the year and every part of his body, yet the prophets already came and reduced them to a few commandments, even to one. Only these precepts are really principles, which, if you wish to fulfil them, you must particularize and interpret them, and consequently you observe many commandments.[7] R. Simlai's homily is cited in the Talmudic discussion on the teaching of the Tanna R. Hananiah b. Gamaliel in the Mishna: 'If now he that commits a single transgression forfeits his soul thereby, how much more so shall he that fulfils a precept be granted his soul!'[8] It is possible that R. Hananiah derived his teaching from the reply given by R. Akiba to Rabban Gamaliel, the father of R. Hananiah: ' "He is just, he shall surely live" (Ezekiel xviii 9) — when Rabban Gamaliel reached this verse, he wept and said: Only he that does all these things shall live; but not if he does one of them! R. Akiba answered him: If so, when Scripture enjoins "Defile not yourselves in all these things" (Leviticus xviii 24), does it also mean only in all of them, but not in one of them? Surely it means in one of these things! Likewise here the sense is that by (doing) one of these things (he shall live).'[9] R. Simlai's statement is thus in the nature of a comment that dissociates itself from both R. Ḥananiah's saying and R. Akiba's reply. It is true that a man may become meritorious by virtue of a single precept, but only if this precept has special and all-embracing significance.

The question of the relative value of the commandments found expression in many varied forms in the teaching of the Sages. On the one hand we find dicta that proclaim the absolute equality of all the precepts, and on the other we encounter clear distinctions drawn between more important and less important commandments, and methods of classifying precepts and transgressions according to various criteria. An exhaustive study of the sources shows us that they do not indicate so much disagreement between the Sages over principles as they reflect the result of reciprocal influence between doctrinal approaches and the experiences of the Rabbis regarding the realities of observing the precepts. The formulation and style of the evaluative dicta were largely determined by the desire to influence these realities and the possibility of directing them. The Mishna (*Shevuot* i, 6) 'And for all other transgressions specified by the Torah, light or grave... involving positive or negative commandments, the penalty of "extinction" [Divine punishment through premature or sudden death], or of death by sentence of the court, the scapegoat makes atonement' is interpreted by the Amora Rav Judah thus: 'This is the meaning... the light (transgressions) are those involving positive or negative commandments; and the grave (transgressions) are those punished by "extinction" or death by sentence of the court.'[10] The differentiation between light and stringent precepts is based, therefore, on the severity of the penalty that the transgressions entail.[11]

The distinction between stringent and light commandments was differently understood by Ben ʿAzzai. On the verse ' "Only be steadfast in not eating the blood..." R. Simeon b. ʿAzzai remarked: Now there are three hundred similar positive precepts in the Torah! It comes to teach us, therefore, that if in regard to blood, than which there is no lighter precept among all the commandments, Scripture admonished you thus, how much more so in the case of the other precepts.'[12] The eating of blood is something repulsive; consequently it is easy to abstain from it. Lightness and stringency are not measured by the extent of the reward or punishment involved in doing the precept or transgression, but according to the effort required to fulfil the commandments or to refrain from the transgressions. So, too, a precept not entailing expenditure of money, or involving danger to life, is called 'a light commandment'. The criterion of reward and punishment is disregarded and does not determine the issue. Indeed, Ben ʿAzzai maintained the principle of 'The reward of a precept is a precept, and the reward of a transgression is a transgression.'[13] In a similar manner R. Simeon b. Yoḥai explained the stringency of the commandment to honour parents. The effort required to keep it elevates this precept to an especially high plane: 'For it is taught, R. Simeon b. Yoḥai said: Great is (the precept of) honouring father and mother, for the Holy One, blessed be He, put it above the honour due to Him. It is stated "Honour thy father and thy mother", and it is said "Honour the Lord with thy substance" (Proverbs iii 9). With what should you honour Him? With the substance that He graciously bestows upon you — setting aside the gleanings, the forgotten sheaf, the corners of the field; separating the heave-offering, the first tithe, the second tithe, the poorman's tithe, and the dough-offering; preparing a booth, a palm-branch, a ram's horn, phylacteries, and fringes; feeding the poor and the hungry, giving drink to the thirsty. If you have, you are obliged to do all these things; but if you have not, you are not obliged to do any of these things. But when we come to the commandment of honouring parents, whether you have substance or not, you must "honour thy father and thy mother", even if you have to go begging.'[14] The duty is absolute, and the effort required is great. It is noteworthy that R. Simeon b. Yoḥai's homily is cited in relation to a Mishna that particularly specifies a series of precepts in the light of reward: 'These are things whose fruits a man enjoys in this world, while the capital is laid for him in the world to come: honouring father and mother, the practice of loving kindness, and making peace between a man and his fellow; but the study of the Torah is equal to them all' (*M. Pe'ah* i, 1). The Mishna groups all these precepts together on the basis of reward. R. Simeon's statement in the Baraita lacks the criterion of reward; in its place he makes the measure of personal sacrifice required for the fulfilment of the commandments the yardstick of their importance.

Alongside the formal scale used to determine the relative significance of the precepts, there are not wanting sources that employ an individual measuring-rod that discovers in this or that commandment characteristics that raise the importance of the precept; for example, ' "the Lord will pass over the door, and will not suffer... (Exodus xii 23)" — a conclusion *a minori* may be drawn from this: If now in the case of the blood of the passover sacrifice offered up in Egypt, which was a light precept, and was of a temporary character, and was not to be observed day and night, and was not enjoined for all times, Scripture declares "and He will not suffer the destroyer", then in the case of the *mĕzûzā*, which is a weighty commandment, containing the Tetragrammaton ten times, and is to be kept day and night, and is enjoined for all times, how much more so that He will not suffer the destroyer!...' (*Mĕkhilta de-R. Ishmael*, Massekhta de-Pisḥa, xi, p. 39). It appears that the Tannaim adopted this method with a view to endearing certain precepts to the people, and for this purpose they did not refrain from hyperbole, particularly in respect of commandments that were lightly esteemed by the public. In one Baraita it is stated that the precept of fringes is 'a light commandment'[15], whereas in another Baraita the opposite is asserted: 'This precept is equal to all the precepts put together, for it is written: "that ye may look upon it, and remember all the commandments of the Lord" ' (*T.B. Menaḥot* 43b). R. Simeon b. Yoḥai expounded: 'Whoever is meticulous in the observance of this commandment is privileged to receive the Divine Presence; for here it is written "that ye may look upon it ['*ōtô*]" (Numbers xv 39), and elsewhere it is stated "Thou shalt fear the Lord thy God, and Him ['*ōtô*] shalt thou serve" (Deuteronomy vi 13)' (*T.B. Menaḥot, loc. cit.*). R. Me'ir found an internal proof of the importance of the precept based on its nature: 'It is not said here "that ye may look upon them" but "that ye may look upon Him" — thus Scripture teaches that whoever observes the commandment of fringes is deemed as though he had received the Divine Presence, for תכלת *tĕkhēlet* ['blue' of the cord inserted in the fringes] resembles the (colour of the) sea, and the sea resembles the sky and the sky resembles the Throne of Glory.'[16] Concrete evidence of the punctiliousness with which the precept of fringes was observed is in our possession from the time of Bar Kokhba. In the caves of Bar Kokhba there have been found bundles of fringes and even a woollen fleece dyed blue [*tĕkhēlet*][17]; this shows that even the remaining fighters living in the caves scrupulously observed the commandment of fringes. Possibly this strict observance actually developed after the destruction of the Temple as a remedy for the crisis emanating from Israel's inability to receive the Divine Presence in the Temple. The precept of the fringes served as a surrogate: whoever kept this easy commandment 'received, as it were, the Divine Presence'. The edicts prohibiting the observance of the precepts, which followed the rebellion, made it particularly hard to keep the commandment of fringes, for it was difficult to conceal them. The sayings of R. Simeon b. Yoḥai and R. Me'ir were intended to encourage and stimulate the observance.

We also find a similar evaluation of the precept of the Sabbath and of that of circumcision. 'Rabbi said: This (is) the commandment of the Sabbath, which is equal to all the commandments of the Torah. R. Eleazar bar Avina said: It is written, (Nehemiah ix 14) "And madest known unto them Thy holy Sabbath, and commandments and statutes". [Why is מצוות *miṣwôt* ('commandments') written *plene*?] To teach you that it [the Sabbath] is equal to (all) the precepts of the Torah.'[18] Similarly it is taught 'In the Pentateuch and the Prophets and the Hagiographa we find that the Sabbath is equal to all the commandments of the Torah....' Concerning the precept of circumcision it is stated that since this commandment supersedes the Sabbath, it is necessarily of greater importance: 'It is like the case of two noble ladies who proceed side by side, so that you cannot tell which is the greater of the two. But when one steps down on account of the other, you know that the other is the greater of the two' (*T.P. Nedarim* xiii, 14, p. 38b).

The extent to which the evaluations of the ordinances by the Sages were liable to changes due to social and political circumstances is particularly manifest in their dicta concerning the precept of charity. On the one hand we have sayings and homilies, in uninterrupted succession, from the time of R. Joḥanan b. Zakkai and his disciples to that of the Amoraim R. Eleazar and R. Jose, that extol charity and elevate it to the level of the Temple service and the reception of the

Divine Presence; and on the other, there are enactments against dissipation of all one's wealth in giving charity and dicta that encourage a person to spare his possessions. Both the former and the latter are to be understood against the background of political, religious, and social conditions: the destruction of the Temple, taxes, and forced labour. The charitable deeds of the Christian communities influenced, separately or jointly, the dicta evaluating charity and the practice of loving kindness.[19] The saying 'Dwelling in Eretz-Israel is equal to all the commandments of the Torah' is found incorporated in a narrative about a journey of Sages abroad after the revolt of Bar Kokhba, at the time of the Ḥadrianic persecution (*Sifre Deuteronomy* § 80).

The emphasis given to the inner worth of the precepts restricted, in no small measure, the concept of reward as the criterion of the appraisal of the precepts, but it did not entirely nullify the need to stress the idea of reward for the precepts — not only in the world to come, but also in this world — in exhortations to observe the commandments. Not all accepted the view of Ben ʿAzzai (above, 249), nor was everyone prepared to be content with 'The reward of a precept is another precept', or to agree with the opinion of R. Jacob that 'There is no reward for precepts in this world.'[20] R. Nathan taught: 'There is not a single precept, even a light one, enjoined in the Torah whose reward is not given in this world; as to the world to come, I have no conception how great the reward is there.'[21] But even R. Nathan equated the commandments from the viewpoint of their reward, much as Rabbi taught in the Mishna (*'Avot* ii, 1): 'And be heedful of a light precept as of a weighty one, for you know not the reward given for the precepts.' The precepts are conceived in their entirety as a single body, and the individual commandments are, as it were, organs of equal value that sustain this body. In one analogy we are told: 'R. Ḥiyya taught: To what can the case (of the precepts) be compared? To a king who had an orchard, into which he brought workers, but he did not disclose to them the (respective) recompense for the saplings to be planted in the vineyard. For had he revealed to them the (respective) reward for his plantings, they would see which sapling carried a high recompense and plant that; thus the work of the orchard would be partly left undone and would (only) partly be accomplished.'[22] The Torah is compared here to an orchard containing various plants, and it is necessary to maintain all the plants without distinction.[23] This view that the commandments are of equal importance has a bearing also upon the Halakha, for the law is that 'He that is occupied with a precept is exempt from (performing another) precept' (*T.B. Sukka* 25a), and irrespective of the precept with which he is occupied, he is not obliged to interrupt its observance in order to fulfil another.

From the homily of R. Simeon b. Yoḥai on the stringency of the commandment to honour father and mother, and from the fact that the reward of longevity mentioned in connection therewith is the reward promised in the Torah also for fulfilling the command to let the mother-bird go (before taking the young), the Amora R. Abba bar Kahana inferred that 'Scripture equated... the lightest of precepts, namely that of letting the mother-bird go, and the weightiest of precepts, to wit, that of honouring father and mother' (*T.P. Pe'a* i, 1, p. 15d; *T.P. Qiddushin* p. 61b [end]). Not only the promise of equal reward for these two precepts, but also the absence of any mention of reward in respect of other precepts, makes the evaluation of the commandments by the measure of their reward nugatory. Thus the same Abba bar Kahana expounded: 'It is written: "Lest תפלס *tĕfallēs* the path of life, her ways wander so that thou shouldst not know" (Proverbs v 6) — the Holy One, blessed be He, made the bestowal of reward to those who fulfil the precepts irregular, so that they should perform them באמונה *be-'ĕmûnā*.'[24] He interprets the Scripture 'Lest *tĕfallēs* the path of life': Lest thou come to weigh (connecting the verb with *peles*, 'a balance' [literally, 'make level']) the commandments, which are the path of life. In order to obviate this — i.e. that you should not choose which precept to keep and which not — 'her ways wander so that thou shouldst not know', the Torah concealed their reward, and 'so that they should perform them *be-'ĕmûnā*' — that is, 'in faith'. A similar exposition (of another verse) is given by 'R. Aḥa in the name of R. Isaac: It is written "Of every charge keep thy heart; for out of it are the issues of life" (Proverbs iv 23) — of all that you are told in the Torah take heed; for you do not know from which of the precepts life will issue forth unto you.'[25]

However, it was just this comparison of the precepts from the aspect of their reward that did not prevent the Amoraim from promising the reward of longevity for commandments whose observance was lax, like phylacteries, for example: 'Resh Laqish said, He who puts on phylacteries lives long.'[26]

What we have stated so far related to positive precepts. The question now arises whether negative precepts, where the penalties, in the case of transgression, were disclosed by the Torah — e.g. flogging, 'extinction', death by order of the court — were also subjected to changes in the criteria of evaluation. Are there indications here, too, that the appraisal of a transgression is independent of the punishment inflicted for it? In truth we find in this respect as well that the gravity of certain offences was emphasized without regard to the penalty. The need for differentiation crystallized at times of oppressive religious decrees and ordeals, when the Sages had to decide for which offences a man was required to give his life rather than transgress, and a concrete Halakha emerged that specified, out of the entire corpus of precepts, three things — idolatry, incest, and murder — for which alone a man should prefer death to sin. Although each of these three iniquities carries the penalty of death, yet the form of execution is not alike. Forbidden relations include transgressions that are punished by extinction, and others that involve execution by order of the court. But the penalty of death is to be found for other wrongful acts, regarding which it was not ordained 'Let him be slain and not transgress'. Thus these three offences were singled out not on account of the punishment they involve, but because they rest on fundamental principles the abolition of which could undermine the entire existence of Judaism. The source treating of this is the teaching of R. Joḥanan: 'In the name of R. Simeon b. Jehozadak it was reported that it was decided by vote in the upper chamber of the house of Nitza in Lydda: In respect of any law of the Torah, if a man is ordered "Transgress and be not slain!", let him transgress rather than be slain, except in the case of idolatry, incest and murder.'[27] But where the Sabbath is concerned, for example, a man should desecrate it rather than be put to death, even though the Sabbath, too, involves death by order of the court. The Amoraim extended the obligation of the maxim 'Let a man be slain and not transgress' to particular circumstances: 'When Rav Dimi came back (from Eretz-Israel) he said in the name of R. Joḥanan:

This was taught only in regard to a time when there is no religious persecution, but at a time of persecution a man should suffer death rather than violate even a minor law.[28] When Rabin came back he reported in the name of R. Joḥanan: Even when there is no religious persecution, the law that we have stated [limiting the obligation of martyrdom to three precepts] applies only (when the transgressions are committed) in privacy, but publicly a man should face death and not infringe even a minor commandment[29].' Thus the dicta of these Amoraim add considerably to the stringency of the principle, in that one should suffer martyrdom and not transgress even a minor precept in public; and what is meant by a minor precept is explained in the name of Rav as 'Even to change one's shoe strap'.[30] At first glance it might seem that the explanation represents a later interpretation in the direction of greater severity, but we have evidence that it is precisely this interpretation that reflects the actual position. In *IV Maccabees* (v 19–22), which was composed near the time of the destruction of the Temple, Eleazar declares: 'Think it not, then, a small sin for us to eat the unclean thing, for the transgression of the Law, be it in small things or in great, is equally heinous; for in either case equally the Law is despised.' On the Scripture 'of them that love Me and keep My commandments' (Exodus xx 6) we find the comment: 'R. Nathan said: "Of them that love Me and keep my commandments" — these are the Israelites who dwell in the Land of Israel and give their lives for the precepts. Why are you going forth to be executed? Because I circumcised my son. Why are you going to be crucified? Because I ate unleavened bread. Why are you being scourged? Because I performed the palm-branch ritual.'[31] Here we have practical corroboration of the Halakha transmitted by the Amoraim, to wit, that in times of persecution Jews gave their lives not only for the three laws on which a vote was taken at the house of Nitza in Lydda, but for every precept, if transgression in public was involved. Indirect evidence for this is to be found also in the following story related by R. Me'ir: 'We were once sitting before R. Akiba and we were reading the *Shĕma'*, but we did so inaudibly on account of a quaestor who was standing at the entrance.' R. Me'ir wished to infer from this that the *Shĕma'* need not be recited audibly, but the Sages 'said to him: A time of peril is no proof' (*Tosefta Berakhot* ii, 13, p. 4), that is to say, they acted thus in privacy at a time of danger. But even in public Jews did not give their lives for all the commandments, as we learn from the following Baraita: 'R. Simeon b. Eleazar said: Every precept for which Israel submitted themselves to death at the time of the Roman persecution — for example, idolatry and circumcision — is still scrupulously observed by them; but every precept for which they did not give their lives at the time of the Roman persecution — like phylacteries, for instance — is still laxly observed.'[32] In the parallel passages to this Baraita the examples of the precepts, both those for which the Jews gave their lives and those for which they did not submit to death, vary. Thus it is stated that 'the Sabbath, circumcision, study of the Torah, and ritual ablution, for which they laid down their lives, are retained by them'; and that, on the other hand, such institutions as 'the Temple, the civil courts, the Sabbatical year, and the Jubilee, for which the Jews did not submit to death, have not been preserved by them.'[33] These differences are not to be regarded as just *variae lectiones*; they appear to reflect differences of fact, for not all the actual — or proximate — periods of persecution were alike, nor were all places treated equally, as R. Isaac noted: 'There was a city in Eretz-Israel... for the wicked kingdom once promulgated an edict (prohibiting Jewish religious observances) against the Jewish people, but against that city it did not promulgate the decree.'[34] Although it was stated that the people did not give their lives for the precepts of the year of Release, and hence they remained lax in observing them, yet it is stated: 'In the district of R. Judah the Sabbatical year was strictly observed.'[35] Even when there was no religious persecution, the avoidance of given transgressions did not correspond to their gravity or to the punishment incurred by the transgressors. There were times and places in which greater heed was taken not to commit minor sins than graver ones; and contrariwise there were those who treated minor transgressions and Rabbinic prohibitions lightly.[36]

The attitude to prevailing transgressions affected also the adoption of preventive measures and safeguards in Halakhic matters,[37] but primarily it influenced the homilies and preaching of the Sages. For example, 'Rava expounded: What is the meaning of the verse "And furthermore, my son, take heed: of making many books..." (Ecclesiastes xii 12)? My son, pay greater heed to the words of the Scribes than to those of the Torah. For the injunctions of the Torah contain positive and negative commandments; but as regards the enactments of the Scribes whoever transgresses them is worthy of death. Should you argue: If they (the Rabbinic laws) have real substance, why were they not written down? Therefore Scripture declares: "Of making many books there is no end; and much study is a weariness of the flesh" (*ibid.*).'[38] The concluding remarks of Rava imply that in his initial statement, too, he had in mind one who transgresses the enactments of the Sages by denying the principle of the Oral Law, holding that it is valueless. It appears that this is also the purport of the following Baraita, which may have been the source of Rava's exposition: 'R. Ishmael taught: In the case of Torah ordinances, there are things that are prohibited and things that are permitted, there are light and weighty precepts; but all the injunctions of the Scribes are stringent.'[39] R. Ishmael declares that in contrast to the precepts of the Torah, which contain light and weighty commandments, the enactments of the Scribes are all equally strict, for transgressing them implies denial of the authority of the Oral Law. With regard to this R. Eleazar, or R. Samuel bar Naḥmani, said that the case resembles 'a heap of stones—if one of them is disturbed, they are all disturbed.' This analogy and those like it seek to explain the consequences of the disrespect shown to the Sages by those who say 'that scribe' or 'those Rabbis'; these detractors exemplified, in the opinion of R. Joḥanan and R. Eleazar, the 'Epicurean' who, the Mishna[40] declares, has no share in the world to come.[41] The enactments of the Rabbis are of equal stringency, for in implementing them one fulfils, according to Abbaye, the principle 'It is a precept to hearken to the injunctions of the Sages'[42], and in transgressing them one transgresses, in the view of Rav Ivya — the younger contemporary of Rava — the prohibition 'Thou shalt not turn aside from the sentence which they shall declare unto thee, to the right hand, nor to the left' (Deuteronomy xvii 11)[43], while Rav Kahana declares: 'All Rabbinic enactments are based on the prohibition "Thou shalt not turn aside".'[44] The homilies of the Palestinian Amoraim on the endearing character of the Rabbinical ordinances and Rava's remarks about their stringency[45] have as their purpose the reinforcement of the Oral Law as against those who assail it and its foundations. However, these expositions did not aim to abolish the difference in principle between Torah and Rabbinical legislation, which found expression in the rule 'A doubtful case involving Torah-law must be decided stringently; a doubtful case involving Rabbinical law is decided leniently.'[46] The differentiation in principle between prohibitions carrying the penalty of death by order of the court and those bearing the penalty of 'extinction', as well as ordinary negative commandments, also remained unchanged. The transgressions that were subject to the rule 'Let a man submit to death rather than transgress' were regarded, of course, as transgressions that could wholly undermine the Torah and precepts; as the Tanna R. Simeon b. Eleazar expressed it: 'He who blasphemes and worships idols has no precept left (to keep).'[47] But the recognition of basic differences and distinctions did not prevent the Sages from conjoining light and weighty precepts, when the times called for this. In antithetic parallelism to the first Mishna of *Tractate Pe'a*, which enumerates 'things whose fruits a man enjoys in this world while the capital is laid up for him in the world to come', the Tosefta states: 'For which things is a man punished in this world, while the fundamental retribution is kept in store for him in the world to come? For idolatry, incest, murder, and also for slander, which is accounted equal to all of them put together.'[48] To the three transgressions that come under the rule 'Let a man submit to death rather than transgress', and for which one is punished in both worlds, the Sages not only added slander, but said that it is as grave as all of them put together. The extreme gravity ascribed to slander and the retribution attached to it[49] simply testify that this sin was very widespread at all times. In similar vein to the statement in the Tosefta concerning slander, R. Joḥanan expounded the subject of larceny: '...R. Yudan said in the name of R. Joḥanan: It may be compared to a basket full of iniquities — who lays the charge against them all? Larceny! R. Phinehas in the name of R. Joḥanan said: It is comparable to a number of people that included idolaters, murderers, and the incestuous; yet it is the larceny inherent in them all that is as grave an iniquity as all of them put together.'[50] It is clear that from the aspect of punishment larceny is less heinous than the other crimes enumerated with it in the same homily. But R. Joḥanan's statement concerning the gravity of the sin of larceny is to be understood in the light of his comments on another verse: ' "...He that killeth an ox is as if he slew a man" (Isaiah lxvi 3)... R. Joḥanan said: Whoever robs his fellow to the value of a *peruṭa* is deemed to have killed him. And there are many verses (that prove this): "He that killeth an ox is as if he slew a man" (Isaiah *ibid.*); "And he learned to catch the prey, he devoured men" (Ezekiel xix 6); "So are the ways of every one that is greedy of gain; it taketh away the life of the owners thereof" (Proverbs i 19); "For the violence against the children of Judah, because they have shed innocent blood" (Joel iv 19); "And they said unto the king: 'The man that consumed us' " (II Samuel xxi 5). But did he slay them or plan to destroy them? Rather the meaning is that because he destroyed Nob, the city of priests, which provided them with food, it is accounted to him by Scripture as if he had slain them.' Another reason for the gravity of the sin of robbery is given in the homily of R. Joḥanan's contemporaries following the preceding exposition: 'R. Lazar asked R. Ḥanina... saying to him: What is the meaning of the verse "Two things have I asked... falsehood and lies... lest I be full, and deny" (Proverbs xxx 7–9) — which is the worse, the first or the second? He replied: The second, adding: We find that the Holy One, blessed be He, overlooked idolatry, but not חילול השם *Ḥillûl ha-Shēm*, "Desecration of the Divine Name" [i.e. disgracing the Jewish religion].'[51] To explain the homily it is necessary to cite the verses in full: 'Two things have I asked of Thee; deny me them not before I die: remove far from me falsehood and lies; give me neither poverty nor riches; feed me with mine allotted bread; lest I be full, and deny, and say: "Who is the Lord?" Or lest I be poor and steal, and profane the name of my God.' Riches are apt to lead to heresy, and poverty to theft, and the last to desecration of the Divine Name.[52] The greater gravity of the sin of robbery is thus to be understood as due to *Ḥillûl ha-Shēm*, which is liable to result therefrom.

The motive of profanation of the Divine Name can transform a light transgression into the gravest, just as קידוש השם *Qiddûsh ha-Shēm*, 'Sanctification of the Divine Name' [an act that redounds to the glory of Heaven and the Jewish religion] is able to elevate an act of but slight import to a religious deed of the highest significance. That *Ḥillûl ha-Shēm* is a graver transgression, from the punitive aspect, than offences involving 'extinction' and death by order of the court was already taught by R. Ishmael in the Baraita stating that 'There are four categories of persons with respect to atonement... if a man committed a transgression entailing 'extinction' or death by order of the court and repented, (penitence) and the Day of Atonement suspend (the punishment), and suffering makes atonement... But if one profaned the name of Heaven, and repented, penitence has not the power to suspend (the retribution), nor the Day of Atonement to expiate (completely); but repentance and the Day of Atonement atone one third, and suffering throughout the other days of the year atones a third, while the day of death purges it, for it is said: "surely this iniquity shall not be expiated by you till ye die" (Isaiah xxii 14); this teaches us that the day of death cleanses it away.'[53] The exposition of this Tanna implies that *Ḥillûl ha-Shēm* is a graver sin than idolatry, and so the Palestinian Amoraim actually taught: 'We find that the Holy One, blessed be He, overlooked idolatry but not *Ḥillûl ha-Shēm*'; and they based their exposition on the verse in Ezekiel (xx 39) 'As for you, O house of Israel... Go ye, serve every one his idols, even because ye will not hearken unto Me; but My holy name shall ye no more profane.'[54] The desecration of Heaven's name occurs in public acts, and thus R. Abbahu stated in the name of R. Ḥanina the Babylonian: 'Rather let a man transgress in secret than profane Heaven's name in public.'[55] R. Ḥanina's teaching is in accord with that of the following Baraita: 'For it is taught, R. Ileʿai the Elder said: If a man sees that his evil inclination is getting the better of him, let him go to a place where he is unknown, and put on sordid clothes and wrap himself in a sordid cloak, and do what his heart listeth, but let him not desecrate the name of Heaven in public.'[56] This view of R. Ileʿai is disputed by the Tanna R. Joḥanan b. Beroqa, the disciple of R. Joshua, who says: 'He that profanes the name of Heaven secretly shall be requited openly; in profaning the Name it is all one whether it be done inadvertently or wantonly.'[57] The purport of this Mishna is that if a man 'committed a transgression in secret', which, if known to the world, would have constituted desecration of the Divine Name, then 'the Holy One, blessed be He, punishes him openly by doing something to him that discloses to all that he committed the wrong and thus makes his shame public'[58], as is stated in a Baraita: 'Hypocrites are exposed on account of the Name.'[59] In keeping with the view of R. Joḥanan b. Beroqa concerning *Ḥillûl ha-Shēm* perpetrated in secret, R. Isaac declared: 'When one commits a transgression in secret, it is as though he thrust aside the feet of the Divine Presence'; and Rav Joseph said that the dictum in the Mishna (*Ḥagiga* ii, 1) 'Whosoever takes no thought for the honour of his Maker, it were a mercy if he had not come into the world' referred to 'one who commits transgression in secret'.[60] Even harsher words were uttered by R. Benjamin. He interpreted the verse 'But I returned and considered all the oppressions that are done under the sun; and behold the tears of such as were oppressed, and they had no comforter' (Ecclesiastes iv 1) as alluding to 'the hypocrites of the Torah: all the people think that he is a Bible scholar, but he is not; (that he is) a Mishna authority, but he is not; he is wrapped in his cloak and wears phylacteries on his head, "and behold the tears of such as were oppressed, and they had no comforter." Said the Holy One, blessed be He: I must bring them to account, as it is said (Jeremiah xlviii 10) "Cursed be he that doeth the work of the Lord deceitfully." '[61] In a certain sense the statement of R. Joḥanan b. Beroqa and the dicta of the Amoraim mentioned above may be regarded as a reaction to the overemphasis on *Ḥillûl ha-Shēm* in public, which implied the diminution of the gravity of sins and iniquities performed in secret, a view that in truth found expression in the teaching of R. Ile'ai the Elder.

It is manifest, however, that the primary and decisive factor in *Ḥillûl ha-Shēm* is the public performance of the acts; hence the matter does not depend on the gravity of the offences alone, but on the circumstances of the time and place, such as a period of harsh decrees and persecution directed against religious observance.[62] Consequently the factor of *Ḥillûl ha-Shēm* exerted considerable influence on the framing of laws relative to non-Jews. Rabban Gamaliel decreed that an object robbed from a Gentile should be forbidden because it involves desecration of the Divine Name;[63] R. Akiba said that Jewish judges, before whom a Gentile and Jew came for judgement, 'may not circumvent him [the Gentile], on account of *Ḥillûl ha-Shēm*'[64]. Some Sages regarded it as a profanation of the Name to refrain from a public act of *Qiddûsh ha-Shēm* in the presence of Gentiles, even if the deed itself was lawful and was not generally known, nor liable to cause *Ḥillûl ha-Shēm.* A case in point is the story told about Simeon b. Sheṭaḥ, that he returned the lost property of a Gentile, and when his disciples expressed surprise and questioned his action, seeing that the lost property of a Gentile may be kept, he replied: 'What do you think, that Simeon b. Sheṭaḥ is a barbarian? Simeon b. Sheṭaḥ prefers to hear "Blessed be the God of the Jews!" to receiving the reward of this whole world.' This is an anonymous account of the Palestinian Talmud, but stories similar to that about Simeon b. Sheṭaḥ are also cited about Amoraim who acted in a given way in order that Gentiles might bless the God of the Jews.[65] R. Abba bar Zemina used to work as a tailor for a Gentile in Rome. The latter wished to compel him to eat the flesh of נבלה *nĕvēlā* [an animal not slaughtered according to Jewish ritual law], and threatened to kill him, if he did not do so. Said R. Abba to him 'If you wish to kill, kill; for I shall not eat the flesh of *nĕvēlā*.' Subsequently the Gentile said to him: 'Now I can tell you that if you had eaten, I should have killed you. If one is a Jew, let one be a Jew; or if one is an Aramean [= Gentile], let one be an Aramean.'[66] R. Mana remarked on this story that if R. Abba bar Zemina had known of the Rabbinic teaching that when a man is compelled to infringe any of the precepts of the Torah in private, he should transgress rather than be killed, he would not have refrained from eating. But R. Abba bar Zemina was faithful to the principle that he transmitted in the name of R. Hoshaiah: 'Greater is *Qiddûsh ha-Shēm* than *Ḥillûl ha-Shēm*',[67] and the words of the Gentile constituted *Qiddûsh ha-Shēm.*

Notwithstanding the great store that the Amoraim set by the outward aspect of their conduct, they nevertheless regarded their duty in its inward aspect as of primary importance, and the stringency of their demands was linked to the personality of those concerned and to the position that they occupied in the social order. To the question 'What constitutes *Ḥillûl ha-Shēm*?' Rav answered 'In my case, if I took meat from the butcher and did not pay at once.' Rashi annotates: 'When I am late in paying, he (the butcher) thinks that I am a robber, and he learns from me to view robbery lightly.'[68] Instead of adducing an example of an act of *Ḥillûl ha-Shēm*, Abbaye cites the following Baraita: ' "And thou shalt love the Lord thy God" — this means that Heaven's name should become beloved through you; that a man should study Scripture and Mishna and attend upon the scholars, and conduct his business courteously with people in the market-place. What will people then say of him? Happy is this person who has learnt Torah, happy is his father who taught him Torah, happy is his teacher who instructed him in Torah. Woe to the people who have not learnt Torah! This man who has learnt Torah — see how noble are his ways, how perfect his actions! With respect to him Scripture declares: "And He said unto Me: Thou art My servant, Israel, in whom I will be glorified" (Isaiah xliii 3). But if one studies Scripture and Mishna, and attends on the scholars, and does not know how to conduct his business (properly) in the market-place, and does not speak courteously to people, what do people say of him? Woe to this man who learnt Torah, woe to his father who taught him Torah, woe to his teacher who instructed him in Torah! This man who learnt Torah — have you seen how bad are his ways, how ugly his deeds? Of him Scripture says: "In that men said of them: These are the people of the Lord, and are gone forth out of His land" (Ezekiel xxxvi 20).'[69] The Tanna R. Simeon b. Eleazar said: 'When Israel do the will of the Omnipresent, then His name is magnified in the world... and whenever they do not do His will, His name is profaned in the world.'[70] He is called 'one that does the will of his Father in Heaven' who fulfils the Torah and studies it.[71]

Despite all the distinctions that we find in their relative assessment of the precepts and the emphasis given to one or other commandment, the Sages never attained to a permanent classification of the precepts, either according to their inner character, or on the basis of the source of their revelation and the ways of their promulgation. This is particularly noticeable in their attitude to the Decalogue and in the difference between their conception of the Ten Commandments and that of Philo of Alexandria. In Philo's view all the precepts of the Torah are the detailed regulations of the Ten Commandments, which he calls roots, principles, or sources. He treats of the matter in his works *De Decalago* and *De Specialibus Legibus*,[71a] and arranges the individual precepts in groups according to the 'roots', i.e. classifies them according to the Ten Commandments.

Wolfson, in his big work on Philo of Alexandria,[72] observes simply that in Rabbinic literature, just as in Philo, it is stated that the Decalogue includes all the commandments. He bases himself on the dictum in *Canticles Rabba* (v, 14): 'Hananiah the son of R. Joshua's brother said: Between each commandment (of the Decalogue) the sections and detailed interpretations of the Torah were indited. When R. Joḥanan expounded the Scriptures and reached the verse "set with Tarshish" (Canticles v 14. Tarshish is apparently taken here to be the Sea of Tarshish; cf. Jonah i 3) he said: The son of the brother of R. Joshua gave me a beautiful interpretation of this: "Just as in the case of waves, between one big billow and another there are small waves, so between one commandment and another (of the Decalogue) the sections and detailed interpretations of the Torah were indited."' The source of this dictum is in the Palestinian Talmud: 'Hananiah the son of the brother of R. Joshua said: Just as in the case of the sea there are small waves between one big billow and another, so between one commandment and another came the detailed interpretations and signs of the Torah' (*T.P. Sheqalim* vi, 1, p. 49d [end]). But these expositions merely intend to state that between one commandment and another the interpretations and detailed regulations of the commandment in question were written down, as R. Joḥanan observed in the passage quoted (above, p. 336). In these homilies it is not asserted that the Ten Commandments incorporate all the precepts of the Torah; only that every commandment forms the basis of interpretations and subtle inferences, detailed laws and general rules, and deductions by argument from minor to major and by analogy, in other words, all that the Halakha originated in the Oral Law was, as it were, written beside each commandment.[73] It seems that for very definite reasons the Sages refrained from introducing the concept that all the precepts were enshrined in the Decalogue. With reference to the Mishna[74] that states that in the Temple it was customary to read the Ten Commandments every day, the Palestinian Talmud declares: 'Rightly the Ten Commandments should be read every day. Why then are they not read? On account of the contention of the Minim; that it should not be said: These alone were given to Moses at Sinai.'[75] Obviously the Sages were concerned not to give prominence to the Ten Commandments and not to accord them a special status, in order not to provide sectarians with the opportunity to assert that only these commandments were promulgated at Sinai, but not the other precepts. In reply it was stated that alongside the Ten Commandments were written their interpretations. The 'sectarians' mentioned in the Palestinian Talmud are undoubtedly members of sects close to Christianity, who, in their antinomian approach, repudiated the observance of the precepts, and confined themselves to keeping the moral commandments only.[76]

The concept of the special status of the Ten Commandments, in its Philonian form, first appears only in late Midrashim, beginning with the eleventh century. The clear language employed by these Sages also demonstrates the difference between Philo and these works on the one hand, and the views of the Tannaim and Amoraim on the other. In *Bereshit Rabbati*,[77] which emanated from the circle of R. Moses ha-Darshan, it is stated: '...corresponding to the Decalogue, which the Holy One, blessed be He, uttered at Sinai, in which the whole Torah is comprised, the 613 precepts....' Here it is explicitly asserted that all the commandments are included in the Decalogue, and this concept occurs also in other Midrashim that belong to this circle.

It seems that the idea reached these works from R. Saadia Gaon. In his *'Azhārôt* he declares at the beginning of the First Commandment: '...And His word is like fire, whose sparks are many precepts shining in each Commandment / In His wisdom, which incorporated in the Ten Commandments six hundred and thirteen precepts to teach....' At the end of the first commandment he sums up thus: 'The wisdom of the first commandment is that I have included therein eighty honoured precepts....' In the case of the other commandments, too, the number of implicit precepts and a summary are given. Finally it is stated: '...I have laid up in the Ten Commandments the six hundred and thirteen precepts of the Law of Thine adherents... corresponding to the six hundred and thirteen letters from אנכי *'ānōkhî* ["I"] to אשר לרעך *'ăsher lĕ-rē'ekhā* ["that is thy neighbour's"] ....'[78]

This is the basis on which the *'Azhārôt*, the liturgical poems composed on the theme of the 613 precepts, are constructed, including those in R. Saadia Gaon's Prayer Book, and thence the concepts reached R. Judah Albarceloni in Spain, and apparently also the circle of R. Moses ha-Darshan and other writers. It is noteworthy that R. Saadia Gaon does not base himself on any internal source. Rashi, again, in his commentary on the Pentateuch (Exodus xxiv 12) simply relies on R. Saadia Gaon, stating: ' "The tables of stone, and the law and the commandment, which I have written that thou mayest teach them" means that all six hundied and thirteen precepts are implied in the Ten Commandments, and R. Saadia explained, in the '*Azhārôt* that he composed for each of the commandments, the precepts connected therewith.' Needless to say the sources that we first cited from the Palestinian Talmud and the Midrashim were known to Rashi, but he did not base himself on them, because apparently he, too, interpreted them in the way that I have explained, and did not regard them as a source for R. Saadia's doctrine. Precisely the verse to which Rashi attached the interpretation of R. Saadia Gaon is expounded by Resh Laqish in a form that entirely precludes the opinion that the whole Torah was implied in the Decalogue: 'R. Levi bar Ḥama said in the name of R. Simeon b. Laqish: What is the meaning of the verse: "And I will give thee the tables of stone, and the law and the commandment, which I have written, that thou mayest teach them"? "Tables" signifies the Decalogue, "law" the Pentateuch; "and the commandment" the Mishna; "which I have written" the Prophets and Hagiographa; "that thou mayest teach them" the Talmud. This teaches us that they were all given to Moses at Sinai.'[79] Rashi himself refrained from introducing R. Saadia Gaon's view into the Talmudic sources, even when their formulation was anachronistic. It is stated that Moses broke the tables because he argued from minor to major as follows: 'If now in the case of the passover offering, which is but one of the 613 commandments, the Torah enjoined: "there shall no alien eat thereof", how much more so when the entire Torah is involved and the Israelites have apostatized.'[80] The expression 'one of the 613 commandments' put into the mouth of Moses is anachronistic; but 'the entire Torah' means only the 'whole Torah' existing at the time, namely the Decalogue. Rashi, too, glossed 'the entire Torah is dependent upon these tablets', and not that the whole Torah is comprised in the Decalogue.[81]

The difference between the two conceptions is to be seen in two commentaries on *Tractate Sheqalim*. In a commentary composed by a native of Ashkenaz it is stated: ' "With Tarshish"... and my teacher told me in the name of his uncle R. Samuel Ḥasid ["the Pious"] "set with תרשיש — Tarshish", that is, with 600 [ת״ר] and 6 [שש] precepts, plus the seven Noahide laws, which make 613.'[82] He thus found an allusion to the fact that all the precepts are dependent on the Ten Commandments. On the other hand it is stated in another commentary, attributed to a disciple of R. Samuel b. R. Shneor:[83] 'Between one commandment and another of the Decalogue were its details, reasons, and signs; the explanation of *scriptio defectiva* and *plena*...' (*ibid.*), that is to say, that the explanations and details of the precepts that were linked to each commandment were inscribed on the tables.[84]

The early Midrashim do not distinguish between the importance of the Decalogue and of the other commandments, although they, too, endeavour to concentrate the Divine revelation throughout the generations into that of Mount Sinai. But they do this in a different way: 'R. Isaac said: That which the prophets were destined to prophesy in each generation they received at Mount Sinai. For thus Moses said to Israel: "But with him that standeth here with us this day before the Lord our God, and also with him that is not here with us this day" — (the end of) the verse does not read "that standeth here with us this day", but "with us this day"; this refers to the souls that were still to be born... for, although they were not in existence at the time, each one received his due. So, too, Scripture says "The burden of the word of the Lord of Israel by the hand of Malachi" (Malachi i 1) — the text does not state "in the days of Malachi", but "by the hand of Malachi", because the prophecy was already in his hand since Sinai, but he was not given permission to prophesy till that moment. Similarly Isaiah... nor was it only the prophets who were vouchsafed their prophecy at Sinai, but also each of the Sages, as they arose in their respective generations, received that which was due to him from Sinai...' (*Exodus Rabba* xxviii, 6). These matters were not incorporated in the Decalogue, but were revealed at the moment in the One Revelation. The concentration of the revelation was due to two motives, which have polemical overtones. The first arose from the fact that the Oral Law was held in light esteem; the amalgamation aimed to give it equal importance with the Written Law. The second reason was to obviate the claim of an additional revelation, for all was revealed at that time. But there is no attempt here to elevate the value and distinctive character of the Ten Commandments; on the contrary all the precepts are equated here with the Decalogue.

III. *The Reasons of the Precepts*

When the question of heteronomy and autonomy and the term 'precept' were discussed, it was seen that the Sages did not adopt a one-sided stand on these problems. Although the precepts are heteronomous, yet there remained ample opportunity for man to exercise his creative power, which is, as it were, autonomous, in the sphere of the observance of the commandments. The precept is obligatory, but it extends also to the domain of will. The Sages regard the commandments as of equal importance, but do not refrain from magnifying or emphasizing the value of one or other precept, either for educational reasons or for motives connected with prevailing circumstances. It is obvious that if the commandments are decrees that are not to be questioned, and there is no difference between them, the question of the reasons of the individual precepts has no basis whatsoever. Also to the question as it concerns the entire body of precepts the heteronomous view has apparently only one answer: the will of the commanding God.[85] But the picture that emerges from the sources is not simple or unambiguous, either in regard to the reason of the commandments as a whole or in respect of the purpose of the individual precept. One reason of the precepts is the reward. 'R. Hananiah b. ʿAqashya said: The Holy One, blessed be He, wished to grant merit to Israel, therefore he multiplied for them Law and commandments, as it is written: "The Lord was pleased, for His righteousness' " sake, to make the teaching great and glorious" (Isaiah xlii 21).'[86] If we read the dictum in its present context, the purport appears to be that the Holy One, blessed be He, vouchsafed precepts to Israel in order to grant them reward, for in the preceding Mishna in *Tractate Makkot* it is stated: '...R. Simeon b. Rabbi said: (Scripture enjoins) "Only be steadfast in not eating the blood; for the blood is the life" etc. (Deuteronomy xii 23). If now a man that abstains from blood, which fills one with a sense of loathing, is rewarded, how much more so shall a man who refrains from robbery and incest, which a person lusts after and craves, gain merit for himself and his generations and the generations of his generations to the end of all generations!' But R. Ḥananiah b. ʿAqashya expresses the view (incidentally this is the only saying by this Sage known to us)[87] that all the precepts were given with a view to granting Israel reward.[88] But if this dictum is a later addition to the Mishna, and is to be read by itself, its intent may be that the multiplicity of Torah and precepts brings merit to those who observe them, for the Divine Commander has no need of the commandment, but the commandment subserves only the benefit of man. The sole purpose of the precept is to endow man with righteousness. Indeed R. Hananiah b. ʿAqashya's teaching was thus interpreted by the Amora R. Aḥa: ' "The Lord was pleased for his righteousness' sake" — "for his righteousness' sake", that means, for your righteousness' sake; in order to grant you merit did I enjoin it upon you.'[89]

The concept that the commandments were given for the sake of man was expressed by Rav in his interpretation of the verse 'As for God, His way is perfect; the word of the Lord is tried...' (Psalms xviii 31). 'Rav said: The precepts were given only for the purpose of trying [i.e. refining, disciplining] people thereby. For what difference does it make to the Holy One, blessed be He, whether one slaughters at the neck or at the nape? This proves that the purpose is to try mankind.'[90] Rav formulated his principle on the basis of what Tannaim before him had said concerning individual precepts, namely that their observance preserves a man from sin. Thus R. Eleazar b. Jacob said: 'Whoever has phylacteries on his head, phylacteries on his arm, fringes on his garment, and a *mĕzûzā* on his door (post) is entirely secured against sinning, as it is said "And a threefold cord is not quickly broken", and it is further said "The angel of the Lord encampeth round about them that fear Him, and delivereth them" (Psalms xxxiv 8)' (*T.B. Menaḥot* 43b).

The two explanations of the reason for the precepts — that of reward and that of the refining of mankind — are to be found in two interpretations of the term חוקים *ḥuqqîm* ['statutes']. 'R. Levi said in the name of R. Ḥama b. R. Ḥanina: *ḥuqqîm* (are so called) because they are engraven חקוקים (*ḥăqûqîm*) upon the evil inclination... R. Abba b. Eliashiv said: *ḥuqqîm* (are so called) because they bring man to life in the world to come...' (*Leviticus Rabba* xxxv, 5–6, pp. 822–823). The first dictum states that the precepts strengthen man in his fight against temptation — 'in order to refine mankind thereby'; while the second saying stresses the thought of reward.

The precepts constantly test man. The very testing constitutes the refining process and suffices to save a person from making mistakes, and there is no need for him to add thereto other tests. Rav, who said that the precepts were given 'in order to refine mankind thereby', is also the author of the dictum 'A man should never offer himself to be tested, for David king of Israel offered himself for testing and failed. He said unto God: "Sovereign of the universe! why do we say (in the *Amida* prayer) 'the God of Abraham, the God of Isaac, and the God of Jacob', but not 'the God of David?' He answered: "They were tried by Me, but you were not." Thereupon he (David) said to Him: "Sovereign of the universe! examine and try me", as it is said: "Examine me, O Lord and try me" etc. (Psalms xxvi 2). Said He "I shall try you and yet vouchsafe you a privilege, for whereas I did not apprise the Patriarchs (beforehand how they would be tested), I tell you (now) that I shall put you to a test of chastity...." ' When David had failed to stand up to the test, he declared: "...Thou hast proved mine heart; Thou hast visited me in the night; Thou hast tried me, and shalt find nothing; I am purposed (זמותי) that my mouth shall not transgress." He said (in effect): "Would that a bridle had fallen in mine enemy's [i.e. my] mouth, and he [i.e. I] had not spoken thus"[91], that is to say: Would that my mouth had been bridled, so that my word could have been restrained and this request "Examine me" obviated.'

The precepts are intended to augment man's strength, so that he can stand up to the test; and if he succeeds then the observance of the precepts also gives him added holiness. This concept, that the observance of the commandments brings greater sanctity, is already to be found in Tannaitic literature. Of the Sabbath it is said ' "for it is holy unto you" — this teaches us that the Sabbath enhances Israel's holiness.'[92] R. Judah the Prince said with regard to the precept of fringes: '...What is the meaning of the Scripture "and be holy unto your God"? This refers to the holiness of fringes. It teaches us that the fringes add to Israel's sanctity.'[93] Similarly all the commandments serve to heighten Israel's sanctity, as is stated by the Babylonian Tanna: 'Issi b. Judah said: When the Omnipresent enjoins a new precept upon Israel, He endows them with new holiness.'[94] Holiness means abstinence, as is stated in the Sifra: ' "Ye shall be holy" means: Ye shall be abstinent.'[95] The Amora R. Levi did not refrain from explaining in this way the precept of offering sacrifices in the Tent of Meeting: 'Because the Israelites were avid idolaters in Egypt, and offered their sacrifices to demons... and the Israelites used to transgress the prohibition of high places in offering up their sacrifices... (therefore) the Holy One, blessed be He, said: Let them offer their sacrifices to Me at all times in the Tent of Meeting, and so they will abstain from idolatry....'[96] The general applicability of this reason for the commandments is borne out by the formulation of the benediction 'who sanctified us by His commandments and commanded us....'[97] The sanctity is, as it were, withdrawn from the precept itself and transferred to the act of the precept and to him that performs it. The commandment is thus voided not only of any magical-mythical quality, but also of its very ritual-cultic basis.

In the Torah, too, the Sabbath day is not intrinsically holy; it is God who blessed and sanctifies it.[98] The Tannaim, however, gave special emphasis to the verse 'Ye shall keep the sabbath therefore, for it is holy unto you' (Exodus xxxi 14), as does R. Simeon b. Menasya in the following exposition: 'The Sabbath is delivered to you, but you are not delivered to the Sabbath.' The Sages regarded the Sabbath as given over to them not only to decide the nature of its rest, the way to honour it, how to fill it with delight and hallow it, but even how to annul it. Thus we find that 'Once R. Ishmael and R. Eleazar b. Azariah and R. Akiba were going on a journey, and Levi ha-Saddar ['systematizer'; or, reading סרד *sārād*, 'net-maker'] and R. Ishmael the son of R. Eleazar b. Azariah were walking behind them, when the following question was put to them: Whence do we learn that the saving of life supersedes the Sabbath?' and each one endeavoured to find a Scriptural basis for this principle, which had undoubtedly already been accepted before their time.[99] When Rabbi expounded the verse ' "And be holy unto your God", (saying:) This refers to the sanctity of the fringes', or when the Sages interpreted the same Scripture with respect to 'the sanctity of all the precepts', these expositions have no mythical-magical connotation, as in the Cabbala[1], nor do they allude to holiness emanating from the substance of the ritual observance that is linked to the object of the precept. When Samuel heard Rav Assi declare 'It is forbidden to assort coins in front of the Ḥanukka lamp', he asked in surprise 'Has a lamp sanctity then?' Rav Joseph explained that the reason of Rav Assi's Halakha was 'that the precepts should not appear contemptible.'[2] However, not only the Ḥanukka lamp, but also the sanctity of the Torah scroll and phylacteries is linked to the observance of the commandments connected with them, and it is thus taught in a Baraita: 'A Torah scroll, phylacteries and *mĕzûzôt* that were written by a sectarian, an informer, a Gentile idolater, a slave, a woman, a minor, a Samaritan, or an apostate Jew are invalid, for it is said "And thou shalt bind them", "and thou shalt write them" — this implies that those enjoined to bind might write, but those not thus enjoined might not write.'[3] In other words, a Torah scroll and phylacteries, although written and prepared according to law, are devoid of sanctity, if they were written by one who does not observe the relevant precept or by one who is not obliged to do so. Furthermore, their sancity depends also on their having been written with proper intent.[4] The commandments enhance Israel's sanctity, but this sanctity has its source only in the observance of the precepts themselves, not beyond it. Hence even if the original reason for the precept's promulgation no longer obtains, the motive for its observance and the sanctity belonging to its performance are not abolished. Consequently it was possible for R. Levi to continue to extol the sacrifices and even to find[5] grounds for their detailed regulations, although the original reason had ceased to apply.

Insofar as symbolic reasons are given, they refer to details in the observance of rituals that are not mentioned in the Torah. Thus 'Rav Judah said: The knot of the phylacteries must be placed high and not low, so that Israel may be high and not low, and it must face frontwards, so that Israel may be in front and not behind' (*T.B. Menaḥot* 35b). Similar reasons are transmitted in the name of R. Joḥanan and in the name of R. Jose b. Ḥanina for the waving of the meal-offering, as it is described in the Mishna: 'He swings them forward and backward and upward and downward.'[6] Following on R. Me'ir's teaching concerning the importance of the commandment of the fringes (above, p. 347), the number of the windings in the segments of the fringes was explained symbolically :'One should not make less than seven [segments; *aliter*, windings], corresponding to the seven heavens', and if one makes more, he should not exceed thirteen, corresponding to the seven heavens and the six intervening spaces.[7]

The Sages noted the fact that apart from the general reasons there are precepts whose grounds are explained in the Torah itself, such as love of the proselyte and the prohibition of wronging him, the reason for which is immediately stated: 'For ye were strangers in the land of Egypt' (Exodus xxii 20). In regard to the Sabbath Scripture declares: 'For in six days the Lord made heaven and earth' etc. (Exodus xx 11), and 'That thy man-servant and thy maid-servant may rest as well as thou. And thou shalt remember that thou wast a servant in the land of Egypt' (Deuteronomy v 14–15). With respect to the restoration of a pledge that is a night covering, it is said 'And it shall come to pass, when he crieth unto Me, that I will hear; for I am gracious' (Exodus xxii 24). For the prohibition that no Ammonite or Moabite shall marry into the community of Israel the explanation given is: 'Because they met you not with bread and with water... and because they hired against thee Balaam the son of Beor...' (Deuteronomy xxiii 5). The educational motive is also not wanting: 'to fear the Lord our God' (Deuteronomy vi 24; xiv 23), especially where punishments are concerned: 'And all the people shall hear, and fear' (*ibid.* xvii 13) and similar expressions. Both Tannaim and Amoraim continued this approach, when they asked with regard to various laws and precepts 'For what reason did the Torah say', 'Why did the Torah say?', or 'Why is this matter different?' The tradition of questions of this kind bears, to begin with, the name of Rabban Joḥanan b. Zakkai. In his replies he advances an ethical educational idea, which goes beyond the explicit law; his interpretation, however, is not allegorical, but is based on a close examination of the language of Scripture, or on deep analysis of the nature of the deeds and the doers. For example, ' "For if thou lift up thy tool upon it" etc. — Rabban Joḥanan b. Zakkai comments: Scripture enjoins: "Thou shalt build... of unhewn stones" (Deuteronomy xxvii 6), that means stones that bring peace. Now we may argue from minor to major: If in the case of the stones of the altar, which neither see, nor hear, nor speak, the Holy One, blessed be He, commanded "Thou shalt lift up no iron tool upon them", because they make peace between Israel and their Father in heaven, how much more so shall no retribution be visited upon one who makes peace between one man and another, between a man and his wife, between city and city, between nation and nation, between government and government, or between family and family!'[8] To the question why the Torah saw fit to be more stringent in the case of a thief, who has to pay twofold, whereas a robber has only to restore the value of the robbed article, R. Joḥanan b. Zakkai replied: 'The robber put the honour of the servant on the same level as that of his master; the thief apportioned greater honour to the servant than to his master. The thief acted, as it were, as if the Eye on high does not see, and as if the Ear does not hear, as it is said "Woe unto them that seek deep to hide their counsel from the Lord, and their works are in the dark..." (Isaiah xxix 15), "And they say: 'The Lord will not see, neither will the God of Jacob give heed' " (Psalms xciv 7).'[9] In the law of the thief and the robber, R. Joḥanan b. Zakkai discovers a reason that amounts to a principle: The punishment of hypocrites, who act secretly, is severer than that of those who commit transgressions openly.'[10] The principle that the Holy One, blessed be He, has consideration for people's dignity R. Joḥanan b. Zakkai learnt from the law that the thief who slaughters an ox pays fivefold, 'because (the ox) walks by himself; for a sheep, however, since he [the thief] has to carry it on his shoulder, he pays (only) fourfold', if he slaughtered or sold it.[11] Similarly R. Joḥanan b. Zakkai's disciples down the generations explained the reasons of the laws and precepts. R. Akiba said that a thief who slaughtered or sold (a stolen animal) has to pay fourfold or fivefold 'because he has become rooted in sin'.[12] R. Me'ir differed from R. Joḥanan b. Zakkai in the inference he drew from the disparity in the penalties to be paid for stealing an ox and a sheep. 'Come and see — he said — how highly labour is esteemed by Him who spoke and the world came into being: for an ox who has work to do, he must pay fivefold; for a sheep, who has no work to do, he pays (only) fourfold!'

The principle of 'measure for measure', whose influence is discernible in very many spheres of Rabbinic thought, also played an important role in the elucidation of the reasons of the precepts and their details.[13] In this instance, too, the inaugurator was R. Joḥanan b. Zakkai, who said with regard to the ear-piercing of a Hebrew slave who refused to be freed: 'His ear had heard "Thou shalt not steal", yet he went and stole, therefore let it [his ear] of all his organs be pierced.'[14] By means of the principle of 'measure for measure' an entire series of details — down to the minutest particulars — of the laws of *soṭa* [a woman suspected of infidelity] has been explained, apparently by R. Me'ir.[15] Concerning the heifer whose neck is broken, R. Joḥanan b. Saul said: Why did the Torah ordain that a calf should be brought into a ravine? The Holy One, blessed be He, said: Let that which has produced no fruit come and have its neck broken in a place that yields no fruit, and atone for one who was not granted to produce fruit.'[16] A calf one year old has not yet calved, and its neck is broken in a rough ravine, which does not produce fruit, in order to atone for the murder of a man, who has been prevented from raising up seed. The answer given to the question 'Why is the leper different that the Torah enjoined "He shall dwell alone; without the camp shall his dwelling be"?' does not explain the isolation on hygienic grounds, but declares 'He caused a division between husband and wife, between a man and his fellow; therefore the Torah ordained "He shall dwell alone" etc.' (*T.B. ʿArakhin* 16b). This reason is based on the belief that leprosy serves only as retribution for slander[17], which causes disunity; hence part of the leper's punishment consists of isolation. In the course of a certain Talmudic explanation of the purpose of offering the incense in the innermost sanctuary on the Day of Atonement, expiation is also found for slander on the principle of 'measure for measure': 'The School of R. Ishmael taught: For what does incense atone? For slander; let the ritual performed in secret come and atone for the act committed in secret.'[18] This Baraita was unknown to R. Jonathan of Bet Guvrin, since R. Simeon reports in his name another form of atonement for slander, and this, too, conforms to the principle 'measure for measure', only the measure is different: 'For him that speaks slander there was no atonement, but the Torah appointed as his atonement the bells of the (high priest's) robe: "And it shall be upon Aaron to minister; and the sound thereof shall be heard" — let sound come and atone for sound.' R. Simeon himself found iniquities for which other priestly vestments served to atone.[19] The sin of the golden calf also provided an opportunity for discovering in details of the precepts an atonement for this misdeed. For example, 'R. Josa b. Ḥanina taught the following Baraita: "And thou shalt make an ark-cover of pure gold" — let the gold of the ark-cover come and atone for the gold of the calf.'[20] Although the law of the red heifer is considered a divine decree, which has no reason,[21] R. Levi explained one of the details of its laws as an expiation for the making of the calf: 'Why are (all) the congregational sacrifices males, and this one (the red heifer) alone is a female? R. Levi said: The case may be compared to the son of a female slave who dirtied the royal palace. Said the king: "Let his mother come and clean up the dirt." Even so the Holy One, blessed be He, said: "Let the heifer come and atone for the misdeed of the calf." '[22]

The attention paid to the reasons of the precepts emanated also from a practical need. Additions and adjustments were made to the laws and precepts in the course of their daily observance in ever-changing circumstances. Often it was explained that it was precisely these innovations and amendments that fulfilled the basic reason of the commandment, whereas its literal observance nullified its original intent. An instructive example is the enactment of *prosbol* [Jastrow: 'A declaration made in court, before the execution of a loan, to the effect that the law of limitation by the entrance of the Sabbatical year shall not apply to the loan to be transacted'] by Hillel the Elder: 'When he saw that the people refrained from giving loans to one another and transgressed the Scripture "Beware that there be not a base thought in thy heart, saying: 'The seventh year, the year of release, is at hand'; and thine eye be evil against thy needy brother, and thou give him naught" (Deuteronomy xv 9), Hillel enacted the *prosbol*' (*M. Shevi'it* x, 3). The Mishna rules: 'Compensation for damages must be assessed on the best land, a creditor (is paid) out of medium land, and a wife's marriage contract out of the poorest land' (*M. Giṭṭin* v, 1). The first Halakha was based on the Torah law concerning one who lets his beast loose and it feeds in another man's field: 'Of the best of his own field and of the best of his own vineyard, shall he make restitution' (Exodus xxii 4). 'R. Akiba said: The verse comes only to tell you that compensation damages must be assessed on the best land.'[23] R. Simeon, of whom it is said 'that he expounded the reasons of Scripture' gave the following explanation: 'Why did the Sages ordain that "Compensation must be assessed on damages of the best land?" On account of robbers and men of violence [i.e. those who take by force, though they pay], so that a man may say to himself: Why do I rob, and why do I take by violence? To-morrow the court of justice will seize my possessions and take my finest field, basing themselves on the verse "Of the best of his own field, and of the best of his own vineyard, shall he make restitution." Therefore they ordained: "Compensation for damages must be assessed on the best land"' (*T.B. Giṭṭin* 49b). The purpose of this stringent enactment[24] is prevention and deterrence — to discourage the greed of robbers and men of violence. While the law of payment for damages is expressly stated in the Torah — 'Of the best of his own field' etc. — the collection of a debt from land is only a Rabbinic law, which is based, however, on the underlying motive inherent in the precept to lend to the needy, on which Hillel grounded his enactment. In the continuation of the above Baraita R. Simeon says: 'Why did the Sages rule that "A creditor (is paid) out of medium land"? In order that a man, on seeing that his fellow has a fine field or dwelling, should not say to himself: "I shall hasten to give him a loan, so that I may take it [the field etc.] in repayment for my loan." Therefore the Sages said: "A creditor (is paid) out of medium land." But if so, why should he not collect his debt out of the poorest land? In that case you would lock the door before borrowers.' The Amora 'Ulla, following R. Ishmael's view, said[25]: 'Under Torah law a creditor should be paid out of the poorest land, for it is said: "Thou shalt stand without, and the man to whom thou dost lend shalt bring forth the pledge without unto thee" (Deuteronomy xxiv 11). What does a man as a rule bring forth without? The least valuable articles. For what reason then did the Sages say "A creditor (is paid) out of medium land"? In order not to lock the door before borrowers.' R. Simeon's view that the reasons of Scripture may be expounded is disputed in several passages by R. Judah. In the Mishna it is stated: 'A pledge may not be exacted from a widow whether she is poor or rich, as it is said "Thou shalt not take the widow's raiment in pledge" (Deuteronomy xxiv 17).' But in the Baraita there is a difference of opinion: 'A pledge may not be exacted from a widow whether she is poor or rich, as it is said "Thou shalt not take the widow's raiment in pledge" — this is the view of R. Judah. R. Simeon says: If she is rich she is subject to distraint, but not if she is poor, for you are required to restore (the pledge) to her, and you give her (thereby) a bad reputation among her neighbours. What does he mean? This is what he means: Since you exact a pledge from her, you are obliged to return it to her; and as a result of having to return it to her, you give her a bad reputation among her neighbours.'[26] According to the law of the Torah, if a lender has possession of a poor borrower's pledge and the latter needs the pledged article every day or every night, he is obliged to return the pledge each day: if it is a garment worn by day, he must return it every morning and may take it away (only) in the evening; and the reverse procedure applies if it is a night covering. R. Simeon is of the opinion that the reason of the prohibition 'Thou shalt not take the widow's raiment to pledge' is that to a poor widow the lender who has taken a pledge will have to return the pledge each day and will thereby bring her into disrepute; therefore the Torah referred in this verse only to a poor widow, but from a rich widow a pledge may be taken. In the discussion of the subject in the Babylonian Talmud the question is raised: 'Are we to infer that R. Judah does not expound the reasons of Scripture, whereas R. Simeon does? But we have learnt the reverse. For it is taught: "Neither shall he multiply wives to himself" — not more than eighteen. R. Judah says: He may multiply (wives) to himself, provided that they do not turn his heart away. R. Simeon said: Even if one is liable to turn his heart away he may not marry her. Thus we see that R. Judah expounds the reasons of Scripture, but R. Simeon does not.' The Sages answer: 'Generally R. Judah does not expound the reasons of Holy Writ, but this case is different, since its reason is stated: Why must he not multiply (wives) to himself? So "that (his heart) turn not away".' This means to say, here the reason is explicitly given in Scripture, and hence if there is no cause to fear that they will turn his heart away, the king is permitted to multiply wives to himself. 'But R. Simeon holds that generally we interpret the reasons of Scripture, but the present case is different, for the Bible could have stated "Neither shall he multiply wives", without having recourse (to the explanation) "that (his heart) turn not away", and I would have known that the reason underlying (the injunction) "Neither shall he multiply" was "that (his heart) turn not away". Why then did Scripture write "that (his heart) turn not away"? So that even if there be one who may turn his heart away, he may not marry her. If so, why does the Bible ordain "Neither shall he multiply wives to him"? Even such as Abigail.'[27] R. Simeon's view is, therefore, that the Torah did not reveal the reasons of its precepts, but left this matter to the Sages. If a reason is specifically stated, it becomes an additional commandment, and itself requires a reason. In the instance just cited R. Simeon says: I should, of my own accord, have concluded that the reason of the prohibition 'Neither shall he multiply wives to himself' is that they should not turn away his heart. Now that the Torah has added 'that his heart turn not away', we have here another law: 'Neither shall he multiply wives' in any circumstances, even if they be like Abigail, because many wives are liable to turn away his heart. 'That his heart turn not away' forbids him to take even a single wife who may turn away his heart. On the other hand R. Judah, understanding the stated motivation literally, makes it the primary factor, and consequently he limits the prohibition only to cases where the given reason applied.

R. Simeon employs the expository method of 'the reason of Scripture' even where only Rabbinic enactments are involved. In this way he raises them to Torah status and creates thereby new Halakhot. In the Mishna (*Yevamot* viii, 3) it is taught: 'An Ammonite or a Moabite is forbidden and forbidden for all time [to marry an Israelite], but their females are permitted forthwith.' R. Simeon adds the comment: Since the Torah explains that their sin lay in their not having met the children of Israel with bread and water, we may infer that the Torah intended to prohibit only the males, for it is not the way of women to meet guests with bread and water.

Undoubtedly this enactment based on the differentiation 'An Ammonite but not an Ammonitess' etc. is an ancient Halakha, dating, apparently, from as early as the Hasmonean period, from the time of the conquests, when the Jewish population spread to Transjordan. At any rate the ruling 'An Ammonite, but not an Ammonitess, a Moabite, but not a Moabitess' is not to be regarded as an exegetical inference, for if so we could also by the same token conclude 'an Egyptian man but not an Egyptian woman', 'a male bastard but not a female bastard', an argument, in truth, that is advanced in the Talmuds.[28] Now R. Simeon proceeds to expound the reason stated in the Torah 'because they met you not with bread and with water': 'It is the way of a man to meet (wayfarers), but it is not the way of women to do so.'[29] Thus the Torah itself excluded an Ammonitess and a Moabitess from the prohibition, and even explained the reason for the prohibition of the Ammonite and Moabite, for it made it possible thereby to deduce that Egyptian and Edomite women were also permitted: 'R. Simeon said: It is an inference from minor to major: if where the males are forbidden for ever, the females are permitted forthwith, how much more so, where the males are forbidden for but three generations, should the females be permitted forthwith!'[30] For the stringent prohibition of the Ammonites and Moabites [to marry an Israelite] — in contrast to the Egyptians and Edomites — R. Simeon also found a reason: 'R. Simeon said: The Egyptians drowned the Israelites in the sea, and the Edomites met the Israelites with the sword, yet Scripture forbade them for only three generations. The Ammonites and Moabites, because they took counsel to ensnare Israel in sin, were forbidden by Scripture for all time. This teaches you that he that causes a man to sin commits a graver crime than he who kills him; for he that slays him does not put him out of this world and the world to come, whereas he who makes him sin puts him out of both this world and the world to come' (*Sifre Deuteronomy*, § 252).

Not for all the precepts could there be found particular reasons of the kind that we have mentioned. Certain cultic ceremonies even astonished the Sages by their resemblance to cultic ceremonies current among Gentile idolaters. It is actually of Rabban Joḥanan b. Zakkai, who revealed the motivation of many precepts, that we are told that he preferred not to search for allegorical interpretations and occult reasons for the red heifer. He left the Gentile who asked him the meaning of the rite in the realm of belief prevailing in his environment, but to his disciples he said: 'By your life! the corpse does not defile nor does the water purify; it is simply a decree of the Holy One, blessed be He. The Holy One, blessed be He, declared: I have ordained a statute, I have decreed a decree, and you may not transgress my decree — "This is the statute of the law".'[31] There are pointers to the fact that the story was related about R. Joḥanan b. Zakkai, because he witnessed the preparation of the ashes of a red heifer in his day,[32] and his disciples asked him questions concerning the laws of the heifer.[33] We do not, indeed, find reasons for the rite of the heifer in the dicta of the Tannaim — either for its general laws or its particular regulations — but neither did they interpret the word חוקה *ḥuqqā* ['statute'], which is used by Scripture in connection with the heifer, as exceptional; they regarded it as signifying a rule in the same way as 'This is the ordinance of the passover' (Exodus xii 43). R. Eliezer formed an analogy between the word statute here and the verse 'And this shall be an everlasting statute unto you', which refers to the Day of Atonement (Leviticus xvi 34), and taught that the rites of the heifer must be performed in white vestments.[34] Not all the Tannaim held that חוקים *ḥuqqîm* ['statutes'] are גזרות *gĕzērôt* ['decrees'], and even those who adopted this interpretation did not consider גזרה *gĕzērā* ['decree'] to signify an injunction that has no rationale. R. Joshua expounded: ' "The statutes" mean decrees, and "the laws" [תורות *tôrôt*] mean injunctions'; but R. Eleazar of Modiʿim said: ' "The statutes" refer to incestuous relations... and "the laws" signify decrees.'[35] Irrespective of whether the dictum attributed to R. Joḥanan b. Zakkai was actually uttered by him in the version transmitted, or is merely ascribed to him, there is nothing to be found in Tannaitic teaching to indicate that they know more about the reasons of the rites of the heifer than they disclosed. It is true that in the preparation of the heifer, as in other sacrificial rites, we are confronted by ancient ritual ceremonies, for which it is not difficult to find parallels in temple practices and sacrificial laws that were current in antiquity.[36] Even if the Sages were aware that these rituals were shared by other cults,[37] they certainly did not know and did not think about the original significance of these customs in non-Jewish worship. Hence, if they compared the laws of the red heifer to those of the Day of Atonement, they did so only because they had already found a basis for this in the Pentateuchal sections, and because both rituals are distinctly ceremonies of purification, but they undoubtedly did not have in mind the well-known Greek antithesis between the Chthonian and Olympian gods.[38] The Amoraim are divided in their views regarding the underlying reason of the red heifer and the reasons of similar precepts. There were some who regarded these commandments as void of any rationale and found difficulty in understanding their details, but the word 'statute' determined their decretal character, even though the evil inclination criticizes them, as 'R. Joshua of Sikhnin said in the name of R. Levi: The evil inclination criticizes four laws, and in each case Scripture writes "statute". These concern: the wife of a brother, diverse kinds of stuff, the scapegoat, and the (red) heifer. Whence do we learn (that one is forbidden to marry) the wife of a brother? (The Bible enjoins) "Thou shalt not uncover the nakedness of thy brother's wife" (Leviticus xviii 16), yet it is written "her husband's brother shall go in unto her" etc. (Deuteronomy xxv 5). While the husband is alive, she [i.e. his wife] is forbidden (to his brother); but if the husband dies childless, she is permitted to the brother; and Scripture terms it a "statute": "Ye shall therefore keep My statutes, and Mine ordinances, which if a man do" (Leviticus xviii 5). Whence do we learn (the prohibition) of diverse kinds of stuff? "Thou shalt not wear mingled stuff" etc. (Deuteronomy xxii 11), yet a linen garment with (woollen) fringes is permissible; and Scripture terms it a "statute": "Ye shall keep My statutes" etc. (Leviticus xix 19). Whence do we learn (the law of) the scapegoat? "And he that letteth go the goat for Azazel (shall wash his clothes) (Leviticus xvi 26), although it itself makes atonement for others; and Scripture terms it a "statute": "And it shall be a statute for ever unto you" (*ibid*., v. 29). Whence do we learn (the law of) the (red) heifer? We have learnt there (in the Mishna): "All who engage in the (rite of the red) heifer, from the beginning to the end, defile their garments" (*M. Para* iv 4); yet the heifer itself purifies the unclean; and Scripture terms it a "statute": "This is the statute of the law" (Numbers xix 2).'[39] R. Levi, therefore, regarded the word 'statute' as referring to a decree concerning the observance of precepts that arouse astonishment, not from the aspect of the Scriptural ordinance — the general reason discussed above (p. 368) sufficed him to explain this — but actually from the viewpoint of the Rabbinic interpretation, as, for instance, a linen garment with (woollen) fringes.[40] The law of mingled stuff *per se*, and likewise the precepts of the scapegoat and the red heifer as such, require no explanation, except for enigmatic particulars of their detailed regulations. R. Joḥanan and R. Eleazar, like R. Levi, drew attention to laws and Halakhot that contain an inner contradiction and have no manifest reason, applying to them the verses: 'Who can bring a clean thing out of an unclean? Not one' (Job xiv 4) and (Ecclesiastes vii 23) 'I said: "I will get wisdom"; but it was far from me' (*T.B. Nidda* 9a). A similar note is struck by an anonymous homily, not unlike a poem in its language and form, in which the motif of the reasonless precept and decree constitutes a refrain:

' "Who can bring a clean thing out of an unclean? Not one" — like Abraham from Terah, Hezekiah from Aḥaz, and Mordecai from Shimei; Israel from among the nations, (and) the world to come out of this world.

Who did so? Who commanded so? Who decreed so? Is it not the One? Is it not the Only One of the universe?

There we have learnt (*M. Nega'im* viii, 2): A bright spot the size of a split bean (makes a man) unclean; (but) if it spread throughout his skin, he is clean.

Who did so? Who commanded so? Who decreed so? Is it not the Only One of the universe?

We have learnt there (*M. Ḥullin* iv, 3): If a woman's child died within her womb and the midwife put forth her hand and touched it, the midwife becomes unclean for seven days, but the woman remains clean until the child comes forth. So long as the dead (child) is within (his mother's womb) he is clean; (but) as soon as he goes forth, he is unclean.

Who did so? Who commanded so? Who decreed so? Is it not the One? Is it not the Holy One of the universe?

And we have learnt there (*M. Para* iv, 4): All who are engaged in the rite of the (red) heifer, from beginning to end, defile their garments, yet the heifer itself purifies the unclean.

The Holy One, blessed be He, however, said: I have framed a statute and issued a decree, and you may not transgress My decree.'[41]

Evidently the attempt to discover the reason of the precepts is completely relinquished here, and instead there is a sense of joy at their observance as decrees of the Only One of the universe. This was also the view of R. Jose b. R. Ḥanina. R. Aḥa says in his name: 'When Moses ascended to heaven, he heard the voice of the Holy

One, blessed be He, as He was sitting and studying the section of the red heifer, and citing a Halakha in the name of the one who said it: "R. Eliezer said: The calf (whose neck is broken) must be a year old, and the (red) heifer two years old." Said Moses to the Holy One, blessed be He: "Sovereign of the universe, the beings of heaven and earth belong to Thee, yet Thou dost sit and say Halakha in the name of a mortal!" Said the Holy One, blessed be He, to him: "Moses, a certain righteous man is due to arise in My world and he will commence his exposition with the section of the (red) heifer: 'R. Eliezer says: The calf (whose neck is broken) must be a year old, the (red) heifer must be two years old.' " Said Moses to God: "Sovereign of the universe, may it be Thy will that he come forth from my loins." (The Almighty) replied: "By your life, he shall issue from your loins...." '[42] The Lord does not reveal to Moses the hidden reason underlying the section of the (red) heifer, but 'teaches a Halakha' in the name of him who said it. In accord with this view, R. Jose b. R. Ḥanina explained the word 'thee' in the Scripture 'that they bring thee a red heifer' to mean 'He intimated to him: All the heifers will come to an end, but yours will remain'; He did not, however, reveal any secret to him. It is possible that this exposition is already directed against the homily that found in the word 'thee' a basis for the view that to Moses were revealed things that were not disclosed to others. In our sources, indeed, the following homily is transmitted in the name of R. Isaac: 'Moses, to you I reveal the reasons of the (red) heifer, but for others it is a "statute".'[43] But we find dicta, even by early Amoraim, concerning Torah reasons that were revealed to individuals. In the name of Rav a homiletical interpretation is transmitted of the verse 'And the prophet Ahijah the Shilonite found him in the way; now Ahijah had clad himself with a new garment; and they two were alone in the field' (I Kings xi 29), namely 'that all the reasons of the Torah were open to them like a field' (*T.B. Sanhedrin* 102a). R. Eleazar expounded the verse 'For her gain shall be for them that dwell before the Lord, to eat their fill ולמכסה עתיק *wĕ-li-mĕkhasse ʿatîq* [E.V. 'and for fine clothing'] (Isaiah xxiii 18): 'What is meant by *li-mĕkhasse ʿātîq*? This denotes one who reveals the things concealed [*mĕkhasse*] by the Ancient [*ʿattîq*] of days. What are these things? The reasons of the precepts.'[44] The reasons of the Torah are regarded as concealed, but they were revealed to individuals. R. Ṭarfon said to R. Akiba: 'Akiba, of you Scripture declares "He bindeth the streams that they trickle not; and the thing that is hid bringeth he forth to light" (Job xxviii 11)', and he explained the verse to mean: 'Things hidden from men R. Akiba hath brought forth into the light.'[45] R. Ṭarfon's interpretation undoubtedly refers to the Halakhot and homilies of R. Akiba, who 'expounded (Scripture) so that it accorded with the Halakha' (*Tosefta Zevaḥim* i, 8); but the Amoraim R. Ḥuna and R. Aḥa, echoing the words of R. Ṭarfon, said that the reasons of the Torah laws that were not revealed to Moses were disclosed to R. Akiba and his colleagues.[46]

The Amoraim who were opposed to the study and revelation of the reasons of the commandments could not ignore the fact that the reasons of many precepts are stated alongside of them in the Torah itself. Indeed R. Isaac, who depicted God as saying 'Moses, to you I reveal the reasons of (the rites of) the (red) heifer, but for others it is a statute', did not refrain from explaining the concealment of the rationale of the Torah laws to be due to the misjudgement caused by the revelation of expressly stated reasons. 'R. Isaac further said: Why were the reasons of the Torah precepts not revealed? Because the reasons of two Scriptures were made known and the greatest man in the world stumbled on account of them. It is written "He shall not multiply wives to himself". Said Solomon: I shall multiply and my heart shall not be turned away. Yet it is written: "When Solomon was old, his wives turned away his heart." It is further written "He shall not multiply to himself horses", but Solomon said: I shall multiply and not cause (the people) to return (to Egypt). Yet it is written: "And a chariot came up and went out of Egypt for six" etc.'[47] R. Isaac disagrees both with R. Simeon, who expounded the rationale of Scripture, and with R. Judah (see above p. 375), and it appears that his extreme statements were inspired by the fear that the quest for the reasons of the commandments was liable to undermine not only the observance of the precepts whose motives were not known, but also, in particular, the fulfillment of those for which reasons were found. The very question regarding the purpose of a thing attributes, to a certain extent, more importance to the reason than to the thing itself, and there is the danger that the reason will become the primary consideration and the actual matter subsidiary. Especially when the enquirer succeeds in finding a profound reason for a precept that appears to be of little significance, or of a strange and dubious nature, there is the danger that the observance of the precept will fall into desuetude and the reason itself will be regarded as sufficient. Actuated by an approach similar to that of R. Isaac, there were some Palestinian Amoraim who strongly objected to the motivation of commandments by God's attributes of compassion. In the Torah itself 'for I am gracious' (Exodus xxii 26) is expressly given as the reason for the law of the pledge, and the Tanna Abba Saul defined the imitation of God and the copying of His ways in the following terms: 'Just as He is compassionate and gracious, so you be compassionate and gracious.'[48] But the Amora R. Josa be R. Bun said 'They do not do right to interpret the attributes of the Holy One, blessed be He, as compassion, namely those who expound "My people, the children of Israel" to mean: Just as I am compassionate in heaven, so be you compassionate upon earth; whether it be a cow or a ewe you shall not slaughter it with its young in one day. They do not do right to evaluate the decrees of the Holy One, blessed be He, as compassion.'[49] This view, which does not accept Abba Saul's teaching as a reason for observing the commandments, follows upon the attempts of the Amoraim to interpret the Mishna: 'If a man says (in his prayer) "Unto [על *'al*] a bird's nest doth Thy compassion extend", or "May Thy name be remembered for well-doing", or "We give thanks, we give thanks", he is silenced.'[50] Whereas the formulas 'We give thanks, we give thanks' and 'May Thy name be remembered for well-doing' were regarded as allusions to a belief in dualism, opinion was divided as to why exception was taken to saying 'Unto a bird's nest doth Thy compassion extend',[51] nor was its wording certain.[52] Some read 'Up to [עד *'ad*] a bird's nest' etc., and according to this text R. Jose, in the name of R. Simon, explained that the defect of this prayer was that it set a limit to the attributes of God: 'Up to a bird's nest Thy compassion extends, but no further.' But even the first version was interpreted by R. Phinehas in the name of R. Simon as follows: 'He is as one who finds fault with the attributes of the Holy One, blessed be He. To a bird's nest Thy compassion extends, but to this man [i.e. himself] they do not extend.' The flaw in the prayer is not therefore, according to R. Simon, that it represents the attributes of the Lord as compassion, but, on the contrary, that this attribute is not sufficiently emphasized, or that the slightest doubt is cast upon its action. However, from the Mishna itself it is evident that this formula, like the others, was used by sectarians.[53] From this point of view it certainly appears that the citation of the reproachful dictum of R. Josa b. R. Bun was directed against the translators — to whom belonged the author of the existing Palestinian Targum (Leviticus xxii 28) — who assess 'the decrees of the Holy One, blessed be He, as compassion'[54] by making the reason of the precept '(ye shall not slaughter) it and its young' the basis for teaching the virtue of compassion. In quoting the observations of R. Josa b. R. Bun, the Sages intimated that one who said in his prayer 'Unto a bird's nest doth Thy compassion extend' likewise belonged to this category of translators, for they too give a similar reason for the commandment to let the dam go from the nest. In Babylon, where translators of the type we have mentioned did not exist, they did not object to additions being made to the text of the *Tefilla* ['Prayer', i.e. Eighteen Benedictions]. Thus it is related of Rabba, the contemporary of R. Josa b. R. Bun: 'A certain (reader) went down (before the Ark) in the presence of Rabba and said: "Thou hast taken pity upon the bird's nest, have Thou pity and compassion upon us; Thou hast taken pity on 'it and its young' [see Leviticus xxii 28], have Thou pity and compassion upon us." Said Rabba, How well this scholar knows how to placate his Master with praise!'[55] But in truth even in Eretz-Israel there were Amoraim who considered the Divine attribute of compassion to be the underlying reason of the commandments to send the dam away from the nest and not to slaughter on the same day both 'it and its young'. In the name of R. Levi, who, as we have seen, said with regard to only four laws 'that the evil inclination criticizes them, and in each case Scripture writes "statute" ', R. Berechia transmitted the following homily: 'It is written "The Righteous One regardeth the life of His beast" (Proverbs xii 10): "The Righteous One regardeth" denotes the Holy One, blessed be He, in whose Torah it is written "Thou shalt not take the dam with the young" (Deuteronomy xxii 6); "but the tender mercies of the wicked are cruel" (Proverbs *loc. cit.*) alludes to the wicked Sennacherib, to whom Scripture refers in the verse "The mother was dashed in pieces with her children" (Hosea x 14). Another interpretation: "The Righteous One regardeth the life of His beast" — this is the Holy One, blessed be He, in whose Torah it is written "And whether it be cow or ewe, ye shall not kill it and its young both in one day"; "but the tender mercies of the wicked are cruel" signifies the wicked Haman....'[56] R. Levi's homily is not far removed from the rendition of 'Those who translate'.

The story of the exodus from Egypt is mentioned in the Torah not only in connection with precepts of which it is expressly said that they are a reminder of this event, but also in association with commandments like 'Just balances, just weights, a just ephah, and a just hin shall ye have: I am the Lord your God, who brought you out of the land of Egypt' (Leviticus xix 36). In *Torat Kohanim* the verse is expounded by the Tannaim thus: 'On this condition have I brought you forth from the land of Egypt, namely that you accept the precept of measures; for whoever acknowledges the commandment of measures acknowledges the exodus from Egypt, and whoever denies the commandment of measures denies the exodus from Egypt.'[57] A similar exposition is given of the reference to the exodus from Egypt in connection with the prohibition of usury: '(I brought you forth from the land of Egypt) on condition that you accept the precept of usury, for whoever acknowledges the precept of usury acknowledges the exodus from Egypt, and whoever denies the commandment concerning usury denies the exodus from Egypt.'[58] This condition attaching to the exodus from Egypt is certainly not to be restricted only to weights and usury. Actually, in a third passage it is stated: 'On condition that you accept the yoke of the precepts, for whoever acknowledges the yoke of the precepts acknowledges the exodus from Egypt....'[59] However, this all-embracing version makes the mention of the exodus from Egypt specifically in relation to these and not to other commandments meaningless. Apparently the Sage who used the general formula 'Whoever acknowledges the yoke of the precepts acknowledges the exodus from Egypt...' in the context of the section dealing with reptiles does not follow the view that explains, in a similar way, the mention of the exodus from Egypt in connection with weights and measures and in relation to the prohibition of usury. The difference is made clear in Tannaitic expositions that elucidate the reference to the

Exodus in the Section of Fringes: 'What has the exodus from Egypt to do with (our subject) here? Its significance is this: that a man should not say: I shall put (threads of) coloured stuff or of *qĕlā' 'îlān* [wool treated with dye made of wood ash] (in the fringes), since they resemble *tĕkhēlet* ['blue', 'violet']; for who will inform against me publicly? "I am the Lord your God"—remember what I did to the Egyptians, whose deeds were wrought in secret and I made them known publicly.' Here a special reason is given for the mention of the Exodus in connection with fringes: it contains an admonition to those who perform the precept improperly, yet pretend to have observed it. But in the continuation of this homily it is stated: 'Another interpretation: Why is the exodus from Egypt mentioned in relation to every commandment? The matter may be compared to a king whose friend's son was taken captive, and when he redeemed him, he did so not to make him a free man but a bondman; so that if he issued a command and he (the former captive) should refuse to obey, he would say to him: "You are my bondman." Upon entering the country, he said to him: "Tie my sandals, and carry my belongings before me and bring them to the bathhouse." When the young man began to object, he produced a bond against him and said: "You are my bondman." So, too, when the Holy One, blessed be He, redeemed the descendants of Abraham, His friend, He did not redeem them to be His sons but His bondmen; so that if He issued a decree and they refused to obey, He could say to them: "You are My bondmen." When they had gone forth to the wilderness, He began to impose upon them some light precepts and some stringent commandments, like those pertaining to the Sabbath, incest, fringes and phylacteries. Thereupon they became recalcitrant; then said He to them: "You are My bondmen; it is to this end that I redeemed you, namely that I should decree and you should fulfil." '[60] Here it is explained that the condition laid down at the Exodus was that all the commandments should be observed as decrees, that Israel should carry them out as servants, and that there is no difference in practice between precepts in conjunction with which the Exodus is expressly mentioned and those unrelated to this event. The former come to teach us concerning the latter.[61] The acknowledgement of the exodus from Egypt means the acceptance of the yoke of the kingdom of Heaven;

the denial of the Exodus signifies the refusal to accept that yoke.

The difference between this conception and that of the first interpretation, which explained the reference to the Exodus in connection with the law of fringes by a particular feature of this precept, thus becomes perfectly clear. The Amora Rava, who, it was noted, adopted a voluntaristic view — namely that the yoke of the commandments is to be accepted willingly and that the proper fulfilment of the precepts implies their remaking — accepted the first interpretation of the mention of the Exodus in the Section of Fringes; he was not, however, content with this, but transferred it and adapted it also to other commandments. 'Said Rava: Why did Scripture mention the exodus from Egypt in connection with interest, fringes, and weights? The Holy One, blessed be He, declared: It is I who distinguished in Egypt between the seed that became a first-born and the seed that did not; it is I, too, who will exact retribution from one who nominally transfers his money to a Gentile and lends it to an Israelite on interest, and from one who steeps his weights in salt, and from one who inserts a thread dyed with *qĕlā' 'īlān* (in his fringes) and asserts that it is *tĕkhēlet*.'[62] The reference to the exodus from Egypt in connection with these precepts serves not only to remind us that the Israelites went forth from Pharaoh's bondage on condition that they should be the Lord's servants and accept the yoke of the commandments, but it points to the way that the precepts should be kept and to the duty to observe them truly. This homily of Rava fits in with his entire outlook regarding the precepts and accords with his view on acting for the sake of Heaven (see above, p. 329). The effect of his views can also be seen in his Halakhic decisions. We shall illustrate our observations by reference to one of the laws of interest: 'Our Rabbis taught: If an Israelite borrowed money on interest from a Gentile, who settled the sum [i.e. the principal and interest] on him as a loan and became converted, then if this settlement as a loan preceded the conversion, he [the proselyte] may collect both the principal and the interest. But if this settlement took place after the conversion, he [the convert] may collect the principal but not the interest. R. Jose said: If a Gentile borrowed money from an Israelite, the latter may in either case collect both the principal and the interest. Rava said in the name of Rav Seḥora in the name of Rav Huna: The Halakha is according to R. Jose. Said Rava: What is R. Jose's reason? So that it should not be said: This (Gentile) became converted because of his money.'[63] At first blush it seems that R. Jose's ruling is unfair to the proselyte, because if he settled the debt on the Israelite after his conversion, he does not receive the interest from him, but in the reverse instance, if the convert was the borrower, the Israelite can exact the interest from him. Furthermore, the decision of Rav Huna and Rav Seḥora is a halakhic pronouncement without a reason. Now Rava came and revealed the rationale of R. Jose's ruling and of the Halakha: 'So that it should not be said: This (Gentile) became converted because of his money', and the conversion will be discredited as not having been genuine.

Notwithstanding all the divergences that we have found between the Tannaim and Amoraim in their attitude to the motivation of the precepts, one view is common to all, namely that the reasons are not a condition of the fulfilment of the precepts.[64] Even those who sought to discover reasons do not consider the motive to have absolute value, but maintain the primacy of the precept and the observance. This is also the focal point of difference between them and the Hellenistic Jews, and not necessarily the extremists among them, who gave an allegorical interpretation to the commandments. Thus even Philo, who insisted on the practical observance of the precepts, maintained their fundamental thesis that the simple meaning of Scripture is analogous to the body and the esoteric reasons are comparable to the soul. Although he requires us to concern ourselves with the needs of the body in order that we may attain to the soul, to the hidden truth, yet it is (in his view) only the deep thinker who can achieve spiritual perfection.[65] It is inconceivable that Philo would have answered the question regarding the reason of the red heifer or of any other commandment with the words: 'I have ordained a statute, I have decreed a decree' etc. He could not have given this answer, because he did not recognize the yoke of the commandments, since he shared the view of the Greek autonomous ethical doctrine[66]; hence he has to find ethical and social reasons for every precept. Should those who discover the reasons of the precepts think for a moment that there is no need to fulfil the commandments practically, Philo has one answer: Even a person who attains to recognition of the truth, must take care of his good name, and this he cannot achieve unless he respects the statutes and customs that are generally accepted.[67] There is no need to stress how far this motivation is from the view of the Sages. To them the very observance of the commandments is of primary importance and the goal, and if the reason of a particular precept is not known, there still remains the motivation of the entire order of commandments, and this is valid for all sections of the nation. 'Beloved are Israel, for Scripture encompassed them with precepts — phylacteries on their heads and phylacteries on their arms, a *mĕzûzā* on their doors, fringes on their garments... The Holy One, blessed be He, said to Israel thus: "My children, be distinguished by your observance of the precepts, so that you may be pleasing to Me." '[68] The observance of the precepts is the link between God and the Israelite; and there is no difference between the Sages, who know the reasons of the precepts, and simple folk, or between precepts whose reasons have been disclosed and those whose rationale is concealed. It was actually Rava who formulated the rule 'The precepts were not given for enjoyment', that is to say, they were not given to Israel to afford them pleasure by their fulfilment, but to be a yoke upon their neck, for 'their observance is the King's decree imposed upon them'.[69] Even when the Sages interpret Scriptural passages allegorically, they give emphasis to the intrinsic importance of the precept and not to its motive. We shall illustrate the point by reference to a Midrashic exposition of the verse 'Behold, thou art fair, my love' (Canticles i 15), which was interpreted as a duologue between the Holy One, blessed be He, and the Congregation of Israel: ' "Behold, thou art fair, my love, thou art fair" — you are fair in (the observance of the) precepts; in acts of lovingkindness; in (keeping) positive precepts; in (keeping) negative precepts; in (the fulfilment of) domestic precepts, to wit, the dough-offering, the heave-offerings, and tithes; in (honouring) precepts of the field, namely gleanings, the forgotten sheaf, the corners of the field, the poor man's tithe, and ownerless property, in respect of the sowing of diverse kinds of seed....'[70] The motif of this homily is the same as that which we found already in the Tannaitic dicta[71] relating to the commandments that encompass man. Similar to it is the motif that the Lord left nothing in the world for which He did not ordain a precept: 'This is the meaning of Scripture "Light is sown for the righteous, and gladness for the upright in heart" (Psalms xcvii 11); and it further says "The Lord was pleased, for His righteousness' sake, to make the teaching great and glorious" (Isaiah xlii 21). The Holy One, blessed be He, sowed the Torah and the precepts for Israel so that He might enable them to inherit the life of the world to come. He left nothing in the world for which He did not ordain a precept unto Israel. When he [the Israelite] goes forth to plough (he is enjoined) "Thou shalt not plough with an ox and an ass together"; to sow — "Thou shalt not sow thy vineyard with two kinds of seed"; to reap — "When thou reapest thy harvest in thy field [etc.]"; if he kneeds — "Of the first of your dough ye shall set apart a cake for a gift"....'[72] Such homilies are, as it were, hymns to the precepts. Furthermore, the allegorical interpretations of certain verses form, so to speak, an addition to the precepts. 'Rav Aḥa bar Ḥanina expounded: What is the meaning of the verse "He hath not eaten upon the mountains, neither hath lifted up his eyes to the idols of the house of Israel, neither hath defiled his neighbour's wife, neither hath come near to a woman in her impurity" (Ezekiel xviii 6)? "He hath not eaten upon the mountains" (means) that he did not eat on account of his ancestors' merit; "neither hath lifted up his eyes to the idols of the house of Israel" (signifies) that he did not walk with haughty mien; "neither hath defiled his neighbour's wife" (denotes) that he did not harm (by unfair competition) his neighbour's trade; "neither hath come near to a woman in her impurity" (implies) that he did not benefit from the charity fund.'[73] Undoubtedly, the homilist did not intend to negate the simple sense of the verse, but since the prophet repeats, in different words, the prohibition expressly stated in the Torah, he set out to find in them an additional connotation, and added prohibitions that are not stated in the Torah.[74]

Although the precepts were not given for enjoyment, yet the discovery of their reasons and the very observance of the commandment can afford the one who fulfils it a feeling of gratification and joy. The Sages created the concept 'the joy of the precept'. Testimony to joy of this kind is to be found as far back as Temple times. It is stated in the Tosefta (*Pe'a* iii, 8): 'Once a certain *ḥasid* ['pietist'] forgot a sheaf in his field and he said to his son: "Go and offer up a bull as a burnt offering and a bull as a peace-offering." He (the son) asked:

"Father, why do you rejoice over this precept more than over any of the other precepts ordained in the Torah?" He answered: "All the other commandments of the Torah the Omnipresent gave us to perform consciously, but this one we perform unconsciously. For if we did it wittingly before the Omnipresent, we should not be fulfilling this commandment..." Now we can argue from minor to major: If in the case of one who did not intend to act meritoriously but did so, it is accounted to him as if he had earned merit, how much more does this apply to one who has the intention to act meritoriously and does so!' The joy of the pious farmer lay in the fact that a precept had been performed without his knowledge, and this is possible only in the case of the forgotten sheaf, which 'automatically becomes the property of the poor, and is acquired by the poor before it becomes known to the owner that he had forgotten it, and thus the entire precept is fulfilled without his knowledge', for if this were done intentionally, it is no longer the precept of the forgotten sheaf but ordinary charity.[75] It is possible that this story was already known to R. Eleazar b. Azariah, who said: 'Whence do we know that if a man dropped a *sela'* from his hand and a poor man found it and supported himself with it, Scripture accounts it to him as if he had performed a meritorious act? Because the Torah teaches: "It shall be for the stranger, for the fatherless, and for the widow, that the Lord (thy God) may bless thee." Now we may argue from minor to major', etc.[76] The syllogism in the *Tosefta* and in the *Sifre* is a note of the redactors, who hold, of course, that he who intends to perform a meritorious deed and does so, will certainly be vouchsafed blessing, and he has every right to rejoice at the fulfilment of the precept.

It is praiseworthy of a man to fulfil the commandments from a spirit of joy, and Rabbi already said: 'To make known the praise of Israel, that when they all stood on Mount Sinai to receive the Torah, they were all of one mind to accept the kingdom of Heaven with joy.'[77] On 'And Moses did as the Lord commanded him' or 'as Thou didst command me' the Halakhic Midrashim comment: 'He went and did (God's command) with joy.'[78] On 'And Aaron and his sons did' the Sages add 'They were as glad and joyful when they received instructions from the mouth of Moses, as if they had received them from the mouth of the Holy One, blessed be He....'[79]

The ascription to former worthies of joy in the observance of the precepts of the Lord is indicative of the high esteem in which this joy was held by the Tannaitic homilists themselves. This clearly emerges from the express statements of the Palestinian and Babylonian Amoraim. R. Isaac bar Marion said: 'The Torah teaches you proper conduct: when a man performs a commandment, he should do it with a joyful heart.'[80] R. Ileʿa said to ʿUlla that when he goes up to Eretz-Israel he should give his greetings to his brother Berona 'in the presence of the whole college, for he is a great Torah scholar and rejoices in the observance of the precepts'.[81] The contradiction in Ecclesiastes, which states 'Then I commended joy' (Ecclesiastes viii 15) and also 'And of joy: "What doth it accomplish?" ' (*ibid.*, ii 2), is harmonized thus: ' "Then I commended joy" — this refers to the joy of (observing) the precept; "And of joy: 'What doth it accomplish?' " — this alludes to joy that does not emanate from (the fulfilment of) a precept. Thus Scripture teaches you that the Divine presence does not rest (upon a person) either when he is in a melancholy, or indolent, or frivolous mood... but only when he is inspired by a joyful cause [דבר שמחה].'[82] Regarding the addition to the precepts[82a] made by one who is enjoined to observe them, it is stated in an anonymous homily on Leviticus xii 2: ' "And in the eighth day the flesh of his foreskin shall be circumcised": the Torah does not ordain here that one should incur expenses (on the matter). See, however, how much the Israelites cherish the precepts, how great is their outlay in order to observe them! Said the Holy One, blessed be He, "Since you augment the commandments, I shall also enhance your joy, as it is said (Isaiah xxix 19) 'The humble also shall increase their joy in the Lord.' " '[83] On the other hand the very observance in joy is regarded as an act of righteousness.[84]

But the Sages were not unaware that not every person is capable of achieving joy when performing a precept, and that not every one is able to fulfil the commandments at all times in a spirit of joy. Thus 'R. Samuel bar Naḥmani said R. Jonathan pointed out a contradiction: It is written "The precepts of the Lord are right, rejoicing the heart" (Psalms xix 9), and it is also stated "The word of the Lord tries [literally, 'is tried']" (*ibid.* xviii 31).' He replied: 'If he is worthy, it gives him joy; if he is unworthy, it tries him.'[85]

The whole subject of the joy of the precept is linked to the observance of the commandments for their own sake, that is to say, a man should observe the commandments not with a view to gaining thereby honour, status, and recognition, but because he was enjoined to do so and as an expression of his love of the Lord. The verse 'to love the Lord your God' (Deuteronomy xi 22) is thus expounded in the *Sifre*: ' "To love" — lest you say: I shall study the Torah that I may be called Rabbi, that I may sit in council, that I may enjoy length of days in the world to come, Scripture enjoins us "to love": study without thought of gain, and the honour will come in the end.'[86] 'R. Eleazar b. R. Zadok taught: Do things for the sake of doing them, speak of them for their own sake';[87] that is to say, do things for the sake of observing them. The reference here is to study of the Torah, for the verse also deals with that subject, but the principle applies equally to the keeping of the precepts themselves. If a man thinks of the reward of the precept when performing it, this is not considered observing the commandment for its own sake, and he certainly does not rejoice over the commandment itself but over the reward attaching to it. There were Tannaim who found manifestations in nature itself inculcating the observance of precepts for their own sake. Thus R. Dostai b. R. Jannai said: 'Why did the Omnipresent not create hot springs in Jerusalem like those of Tiberias? In order that a man should not say to his fellows: "Let us go up to Jerusalem, for if we go up for but a single dip, it is worth it." The pilgrimage in that case is not for its own sake.'[88]

As we have already indicated in another connection[89], the Sages realized that not every man was capable of attaining to this level of studying the Torah and observing the precepts for their own sake, and held that 'all were equal relative to the Torah' (*Sifre Deuteronomy* 48), which had not been given to the elders and prophets alone, but to the whole community of Israel. It is indeed stated in the name of R. Joḥanan: 'What is the meaning of the verse "For the ways of the Lord are right, and the just do walk in them; but transgressors do stumble therein" (Hosea xiv 10)? It is analogous to the case of two men who roasted their paschal lambs; one of them ate it for the sake of the precept, and the other for the sake of eating a full meal. To the one who ate it in order to fulfil the commandment (applies) "and the just do walk therein", while to him who ate it to enjoy a good meal (applies) "but the transgressors do stumble therein" ' (*T.B. Nazir* 23a). R. Joḥanan differentiates between those who consume the paschal lamb out of gluttony and those who eat it in order to fulfil a religious duty. To the former he applies the Scripture 'but the transgressors do stumble therein', but to the latter (the words) 'and the just do walk in them'. Resh Laqish, however, disagreed with him and countered: 'You call this man "wicked"? Granted that he has not fulfilled the commandment ideally, he has at least prepared the paschal lamb!' In other words, the precept was performed, even if the intent was invalid. R. Eleazar agreed with Resh Laqish. Torah studied for its own sake he designated 'Torah of lovingkindness', whereas Torah that is studied with an ulterior motive he called 'Torah that is not of lovingkindness' (*T.B. Sukka* 49b [end]), although he is also the author of the dictum ' "That delighteth greatly in His commandments" (Psalms cxii 1) — "in His commandments", but not in the reward of His commandments' (*T.B. ʿAvoda Zara* 19a). A favourite saying of Rava was: 'The goal of wisdom is penitence and good deeds. A man should not study much Scripture and much Mishna, and then kick at his father and mother and teacher, or at one who is superior to him in wisdom and authority, as it is said "The reverence of the Lord is the beginning of wisdom, a good understanding have all they that practise it" (Psalms cxi 10). The Bible does not say "all they that study it" but "all they that practise it", (that is,) practise it for the sake of the ideal, and not from other motives. All who practise it for other reasons, it were better that they had not been created.'[90] This drastic teaching is not directed against those who perform the precepts from ulterior motives, but against those who study Torah without the intention to observe and practise it, making the Torah a spade to dig with or a crown wherewith to magnify themselves, to use the expressions of R. Zadok and Hillel.[91] Indeed Rava employed strong language against scholars who studied Torah from other than religious motives. After the saying of R. Samuel bar Naḥmani in the name of R. Jonathan 'Woe betide the enemies of the scholars [a euphemism for the scholars themselves] who occupy themselves with the Torah, but have no reverence for Heaven' and the proclamation of R. Jannai 'Alas for him who has no courtyard, yet makes a gate for his court!', Rava's dictum is cited: 'He said... to the Rabbis: I beseech you, do not inherit a two-fold Gehenna!'[92] It seems, therefore, that, as Rashi explains, it was only with reference to those who do not study the Torah for its own sake that Rava said 'it were better that they had not been created', using the phraseology of R. Ḥiyya, who also taught 'that he who studies (the Torah) without the intention to practise it, it were better that he had not been created.'[93] On the other hand Rava adopted a more lenient attitude towards the observance of precepts from ulterior motives. The contradiction between the verse 'For Thy lovingkindness is great *unto* the heavens and Thy truth *unto* the skies' (Psalms lvii 11 [10]) and the verse 'For Thy lovingkindness is great *above* the heavens' (*ibid.* cviii 5 [4]; the Biblical text lacks the definite article, though inserted in the Talmud) is explained by Rava as follows: 'The latter verse refers to those who perform (the precepts) for their own sake, the former verse refers to those who perform them from other motives.' The Talmudic redactor states that Rava was of the same opinion as Rav Judah, who said in the name of Rav: 'Let a man ever occupy himself with (the study of the) Torah and (the observance of the) precepts, even though it is not for their own sake, for from doing these things from ulterior motives he will eventually come to do them for their own sake.'[94]

However, as we have seen, Rava agreed with him only as far as the precepts were concerned, but as regards Torah-study, he held the same view as R. Ḥiyya and R. Joḥanan. At any rate even to those who perform the commandments for ulterior reasons Rava applied the verse 'For Thy lovingkindness is great unto the heavens', and not 'it were better that they had not been created'. It appears that with regard to the observance of the precepts, he accepted the reasoning of Rav: 'for from doing these things from ulterior motives he will eventually come to do them for their own sake'.

The attitude to be taken in respect of precepts not performed for their own sake was not a theoretical issue only, but also had practical Halakhic bearings, for the question was raised whether a man who observed a commandment without the intention of fulfilling his religious duty actually discharged his obligation or not. However, the question of the principle whether the observance of precepts requires intention or not appears only in discussions of the Babylonian Talmud. Rava, who holds that one who blows the Shofar [ram's horn] to make music fulfils his religious duty, clearly represents the view that the fulfilment of the precepts does not require intent.[95] But the Amoraim and the redactors of the Talmud were also able to base themselves on Mishnayot and Baraitot, where the rule, though not explicitly stated, was at any rate implied, only it is not always possible to decide if the Tanna had in mind a general principle or a detailed regulation. In the Babylonian Talmud the following Baraita is cited on the subject of blowing the Shofar: 'The listener hears for himself, and the Shofar-blower does so with no one specifically in mind. Said R. Jose: This applies only to a congregational precentor, but a private individual does not discharge his obligations until both he that listens and he that blows the Shofar intended (the religious duty to be duly performed thereby, the former by hearing, the latter by causing him to hear the Shofar-blowing).'[96] From this it was inferred that R. Jose holds that the performance of the precepts requires intent; but the question arises whether such an inference is really justified, for possibly R. Jose's ruling applies only to the Shofar, in which case the precept consists primarily of hearing. Indeed, in another Baraita we find 'It is taught: An Israelite may circumcise a Cuthean [= Samaritan], but a Cuthean may not circumcise an Israelite, because the former is circumcised in the name of Mount Gerizim, this is the view of R. Juda. Said R. Jose to him: But where do we find it (ordained) in the Torah that circumcision needs intention? On the contrary, let him go on circumcising in the name of Mount Gerizim, till he perish!'[97] Nor is the Tanna's reason always clear; sometimes it is possible to find another explanation for his ruling, unconnected with the question of intention. In the Babylonian Talmud (*Pesaḥim* 114b) the Sages wished to infer from a Baraita that R. Jose was of the opinion that 'the precepts require intent', but subsequently they rejected the inference, arguing: 'Perhaps R. Jose holds that the precepts do not require intent.'[98] Often even the formulation of the statements is not unambiguous, and sometimes the dictum of an Amora, to whom the Babylonian Talmud ascribes the view that the precepts require intent, is reported in the Palestinian Talmud in a version that does not corroborate this conclusion.[99] But even the

Sages who took the view that precepts do not require intent, made an exception in the case of prayer, which is the 'service of the heart.'[1] Not only the pious men of old used to wait an hour before they said the תפלה *Tĕfillā* ['Prayer', i.e. Eighteen Benedictions], 'that they might direct their heart toward the Omnipresent' (*M. Berakhot* v, 1), but even artisans were forbidden to say the *Tĕfillā* 'on top of a tree or on top of a course of stones' (*ibid.* ii, 4), and a porter might not say the *Tĕfillā* until he had laid down his burden,[2] for 'he who says the *Tĕfillā* must concentrate his mind'.[3] Obviously a distinction must be drawn between כונה *kawwānā* ['devotion', 'concentration', 'intention'] in regard to *Tĕfillā* and *kawwānā* applied to the precepts, for in the former case it does not mean to fulfil one's obligation in respect of the precept of *Tĕfillā*, but concentration of the mind on the subject and content of the *Tĕfillā*. In view of this distinction it is possible to understand the differences of opinion concerning *kawwānā* during the recitation of the *Shĕma*ʿ. In the name of R. Akiba and in the name of R. Judah it was transmitted that if a man concentrated his mind in the first paragraph, he fulfilled his duty. According to R. Eliezer and Bar Qappara only the first three verses of the first paragraph require *kawwānā*, while R. Me'ir and R. Judah the Patriarch held that only the first verse requires concentration of the mind.[4] The matter was still the subject of dispute in the days of the Amoraim. Thus R. Mana, one of the last of the Palestinian Amoraim, said: 'Even if you say that the recitation of the *Shĕma*ʿ does not require *kawwānā*, the *Tĕfillā* does require *kawwānā*.'[5] Some Amoraim insisted on *kawwānā* also in the case of other commandments, if they involved hearing. In the Mishna (*Megilla* ii, 1) it is stated that if a man read the *Mĕgillā* [the Scroll of Esther] drowsily, he has discharged his obligation. But in the Palestinian Talmud it is related: 'Menasseh was sitting before R. Zeʿira and dozing (while reciting the *Mĕgillā*); said he [R. Zeʿira] to him [Menasseh]: 'Repeat the passage, because you were not concentrating.'[6] This was also R. Zera's attitude in respect of the blowing of the Shofar: 'R. Zera said to his attendant: "Put your mind to it and blow for me." '[7]

The problem confronting the Sages is known in every religion and in every system of ethics. What significance can a man's conduct have, if he observes the laws of ethics and religion as stereotyped, conventional acts without giving them an inner meaning? Some people declare: These are 'precepts learned by rote', and actions that are merely external and unaccompanied by inner feeling — inward devotion — only do harm, and it is better to dispense with them. On the other hand it is realized that not everyone is capable of being constantly in that high state of tension requisite to action intentionally and consciously performed for its own sake. Religions and sects professing strict ideals and demands — which set out with the clear intention to preserve the consciousness of their ideals in daily life, and did not accept the observance of acts that lacked inner faith — eventually suffered not only from apathy, but, in most cases, even from licentiousness. In the light of such experiences the question arises whether the absolute demand that, where people are unable to keep observances ideally, it is better for them not to keep them at all does not actually contain from the outset an encouragement and invitation, as it were, to those who seek a dispensation from the yoke of the commandments. Apparently such considerations presented themselves to the Sages and they enable us to explain the dictum of one of the later Amoraim — Rav Naḥman bar Isaac — which is sharply worded: 'A transgression committed with good intent is better than a precept performed from ulterior motives' (*T.B. Nazir* 23b). The saying occasioned surprise already in the Talmud, which emends it: 'Rather say "as good as a precept performed from ulterior motives", that is to say, a transgression committed with good intent is not better than a precept performed from ulterior motives, but is equal to it. From the context of the Talmudic discussion it is evident that 'a transgression with good intent' [literally 'a transgression for its own sake'] is taken to mean one that is committed for the sake of a religious principle [מצוה *miṣwā*: 'precept', 'religious duty', religious principle', 'good deed'].[8] Thus a good deed [*miṣwā*] 'resulting from a transgression is, as it were, a precept that is performed through a transgression committed with good intent.[9] It is surprising therefore that this should be termed עברה לשמה *ʿăvērā li-shĕmāh* [literally 'a transgression for its own sake']! Hence it seems that originally *ʿăvērā li-shĕmāh* signified a transgression committed with intent to transgress, just as מצוה לשמה *miṣwā li-shĕmāh* means a precept performed for the sake of the precept. Undoubtedly Rav Naḥman bar Isaac is not speaking in praise of transgression, but in dispraise of the observance of a precept from ulterior motives; and just as Rava worded his dictum strongly, saying 'it were better that they had not been born', so Rav Naḥman bar Isaac formulated his remarks in similar fashion. He who commits a transgression from a sense of religious idealism is better than one who fulfils a precept insincerely. In other words, the aphorism seeks to emphasize the importance of the spirit in which a deed is performed, and that intention and devotion transcend the action itself. This is an individual view, and it was not shared by Rav, Resh Laqish, R. Eleazar, or Rava. The observance of the precepts for their own sake was not less important in their estimation, but the inherent difficulty of the matter, which already found expression in the words of the Tanna R. Nehemiah, 'Whoever accepts one commandment in faith is worthy that the Holy Spirit should rest upon him',[10] made them realize that by keeping and performing many precepts a man may eventually attain the capability of fulfilling at least part of them for their own sake, in faith and with perfection.[11] A man may not, however, postpone the observance of a precept until such time as he can perform it perfectly, as is stated by the Tanna R. Josiah: 'Just as we may not allow מצה *maṣṣā* ['unleavened bread'] to become leavened (through delay), so we must not allow a *miṣwā* ['precept'] to become "leavened" [i.e. to delay its observance]; but if you have the opportunity to perform a precept do so forthwith.'[12] The reason is explained in an Amoraic homily on the verse 'Whatsoever thy hand attaineth to do by thy strength, that do' (Ecclesiastes, ix 10) — 'whatsoever precept you can perform whilst you still have the strength, do. Why? When a man is no more in the world, his intention is likewise no more. Grasp whatever precept you can, while you are still alive.'[13] The observance of a precept brings in its train love of the precepts, and 'He who loves the commandments is never sated with them.'[14]

CHAPTER XIV

ACCEPTANCE OF THE YOKE OF THE KINGDOM OF HEAVEN

Love and Reverence

The purpose of the Torah and the precepts is the acceptance of the yoke of the kingdom of heaven, which finds expression in the fear [i.e. reverence] and love of the Lord. But even when explaining the order of the Ten Commandments on Mount Sinai, and likewise the order of the sections of the *Shĕma*ʿ, the Tannaim ruled that the intended and desired procedure for a Jew is first to assume the yoke of the kingdom of heaven and then the yoke of the commandments. ' "Thou shalt have no other gods before Me": Why is this stated? Because Scripture said "I am the Lord thy God". The matter may be compared to a human king who entered a province. Said his servants to him: "Impose decrees upon the people." He answered them: "No; when they accept my sovereignty, I shall impose decrees upon them; for if they do not accept my sovereignty, they will not accept my decrees either..." '[1] To the question 'Why does the paragraph "Hear, O Israel..." precede the paragraph "And it shall come to pass, if ye shall hearken..."?' R. Joshua b. Qorḥa replied: 'So that a man should first take upon himself the yoke of the kingdom of heaven and thereafter the yoke of the commandments' (*M. Berakhot* ii, 2). The acceptance of the yoke of the kingdom of heaven means to acknowledge the God who is One and Unique, and to bear witness that there is no other god. Thus the section 'Hear, O Israel' is characterized in Tannaitic exegesis as 'a section containing the acceptance of the kingdom of heaven, while idolatry is diminished therein'.[2] The thought is elaborated in the Amoraic homily on the words of the Psalmist (lxxiii 25): 'Whom have I in heaven? And with Thee I desire none upon earth' [this is a literal rendering of the verse] — 'Israel said to the Holy One, blessed be He: Sovereign of the universe, whom have I in heaven? We recognize no other god, only the God of heaven. "And with Thee" — nor do we associate with Thee any god upon earth; but we declare Thy unity and proclaim "Hear, O Israel, the Lord, our God, the Lord is One".'[3] The assumption of the yoke of the kingdom of heaven by the recitation of the verse 'Hear, O Israel' finds expression in the response that follows it, 'Blessed be the name of the glory of His kingdom for ever and ever',[3a] which was the response recited in the Temple after the benediction[4] and after the utterance of the Divine Name by the High Priest on the Day of Atonement.[5] Undoubtedly this response also originated in the reading of the *Shĕma'* in the Temple[6], only the usage spread beyond its precincts. However, when the recital of the *Shĕma'* became an individual obligation, some Sages abolished completely the saying of 'Blessed be the name of the glory of His kingdom for ever and ever', because they were concerned not to make an unnecessary breach between two verses of the Torah[7]; but the majority continued to pronounce the response in a low voice.[8] This emerges from the tradition reported by R. Abbahu: 'In Usha they instituted that it (the response) should be said aloud on account of the heresies of the sectarians.'[9] This enactment was due to the fear that saying the response in a low voice would make it easy for people with Christian heretical tendencies to interpolate their credal professions. The enactment of Usha is therefore to be regarded as a kind of sequel to that of 'the benediction concerning sectarians' in the *Tĕfillā*, whose aim was to exclude those suspected of sectarian heresy.[10] Just as the Sages abolished the daily recitation of the Decalogue, which was customary in the Temple, 'because of the assertion [טענת *ṭa'ănat*] of the sectarians — that they should not say: These precepts only were given to Moses at Sinai'[11], so they maintained the saying of 'Blessed be the name of the glory of His kingdom for ever and ever' in a loud voice for a similar reason. Both the abolition of the one custom and the preservation of the other aimed to deny the views of the sectarians any purchase in the customs of Israel and to prevent the spread of their influence. But while attempts to restore the recitation of the Decalogue are known to us only in places where sectarians were not to be found[12], the enactment of Usha was disregarded and the response 'Blessed be the name of the glory of His kingdom for ever and ever' was said in an undertone not only in Nehardea, where no sectarians existed[13], but also in various parts of Eretz-Israel.[14] At all events the response 'Blessed be the name of the glory of His kingdom for ever and ever' lent emphasis to the acceptance of the yoke of the kingdom of heaven implicit in the utterance of 'Hear, O Israel'[15], only this utterance did not give it exhaustive expression. The Sages regarded it as merely a beginning or preamble, which was expressly continued in the second verse of the passage of the *Shĕma*ʿ, ' "And thou shalt love the Lord thy God" — act from love.' Although acting out of love is deemed in this homily the highest stage in man's relationship to God, yet it must be linked to fear [reverence], 'for love where there is fear and fear where there is love are only found in relation to the Omnipresent.'[16] The explanation of this nexus is given in another homily: 'Act from love and act from fear. Act out of love, for should you wish to hate, know that you love, and he that loves does not hate. Act out of fear, for should you wish to rebel, know that you fear, and he that fears does not rebel.'[17] Actually, we are presented here with an explanation of the fact that love and fear are found in close association in the Bible, especially in Deuteronomy[18] and Psalms — thus corresponding to the attribute of God, who is 'a jealous God' and at the same time 'shows lovingkindness'[19] — and in the prayer of Nehemiah (i 5), which begins 'I beseech Thee, O Lord, the God of heaven, the great and awe-inspiring God, that keepeth covenant and steadfast love *with those who love* Him and keep His commandments' and concludes (*ibid.* 11) '...let Thine ear be attentive... and to the prayer of Thy servants who delight *to fear* Thy name'.[20]

However, we still have to consider whether this appraisement of love and fear in relation to the Lord and the suggested reconciliation between them was a generally accepted view, and if so when it acquired this formulation. The expression מורא שמים *môra' shāmayim* ['fear of heaven'] first occurs in the saying of Antigonus of Sokho 'Be not like servants that minister to the master for the sake of receiving a reward (פרס *pĕrās*), but be like servants that minister to the master not for the sake of receiving a reward; and let the fear of Heaven be upon you' (*M. 'Avot* i, 3). Irrespective of whether 'not for the sake of receiving 'פרס'[21] refers to wages, or the maintenance [פרוסה *pĕrûsā*, literally 'piece of bread'] of the slave[22], or whether it means a gratuity as a token of the benefactor's appreciation[23], a servant who does not await a reward undoubtedly serves his master out of love, or at least out of gratitude. Antigonus, not yet satisfied with this attitude, adds 'and let the fear of Heaven be upon you'. In commenting on this Mishna, *'Avot de-R. Nathan* states: 'It is like a man who does the will of his master, but is presumptuous in regard to his master's will, (or like a man who does the will of his father) but is presumptuous in regard to his father's will. One that acts out of love cannot be compared with one who acts out of awe and fear... for we find that the Early Fathers served (God) in awe and fear... Of Abraham it is said "for now I know that thou art a God-fearing man" (Genesis xxii 12); of Joseph it is stated "I fear God" (*ibid.*, xlii 18); of Jonah it is written "and I fear the Lord, the God of heaven I fear" (Jonah i 9).'[24] Clearly this Baraita understood Antigonus' dictum to mean that the service of God which is inspired by awe and fear transcends that which is motivated by love alone, because a servant who serves his master without expectation of reward may possibly be presumptuous in regard to his master's will. This opinion is opposed to the view that we have indicated as generally accepted, but its strangeness is not sufficient ground for assigning to it a late date.[25] If, however, we re-examine the teaching of Antigonus, we shall see that actually it does not contain the differentiation between 'fear' and 'love' found in the Baraita, nor the preference given to the former over the latter, but the 'fear of heaven' of which it speaks enshrines as a precondition service of God out of love, for only by serving Him without expectation of reward can a man prove that the fear of Heaven rests upon him. Thus the author of the Baraita was justified in drawing his conclusions from the Sages' words. The new approach in Antigonus' teaching becomes evident when his dictum is compared with the words of Ben Sira:[26] 'With all thy heart fear God, and hallow His priests, With all thy strength love thy Maker, and His ministers do not forsake.' 'Fear' and 'love' are also used as synonymous verbs when he speaks of 'They that fear the Lord... and they that love Him'. There is no difference whatsoever to be found between the two categories;[27] on the other hand the motive of reward is prominent in the verses

'Ye that fear the Lord wait for His mercy; and turn not aside, lest ye fail. Ye that fear the Lord, put your trust in Him, and your reward shall not fail. Ye that fear the Lord hope for His benefits and for eternal gladness and mercy.'[28]

The impact of the personality of Abraham and his ordeal in the episode of the עקדה *'Ăqēdā* [the Binding of Isaac] had a decisive influence on the conception of the terms 'fear' and 'love'. The ancients pointed to Abraham's ordeal. Nehemiah referred to him in the words 'and foundest his heart faithful before Thee' (ix 8). Ben Sira wrote 'He established the covenant in his flesh, and when he was tested he was found faithful' (xliv 20). So, too, it is stated in *I Maccabees* (ii 52): 'Was not Abraham found faithful when tested?' But only the Tannaim proceeded to draw definite conclusions regarding man's relationship to his God. Antigonus defined the relationship of man to God as 'fear of Heaven', and this term included the love that was exemplified by the servant who served his Master not for the sake of receiving reward. His saying is unrelated to reward and punishment, and contains no allusion to God's attributes in His dealings with man. Philo of Alexandria also employed the analogy of a servant in his discussions about love and fear in man's relations with the Deity. However, comparison with Antigonus' dictum points up the difference between the doctrine of the Sage and that of Philo. The latter's[29] starting point is the Torah's teaching on God's jealousy, anger, and wrath. In speaking thus Moses does not address himself to those who do not overlay their conception of God with attributes of created beings; the lawgiver is also bound to take into account the multitude. Whether they are unintelligent or failed to receive a proper education, they are unable to see clearly, and consequently they are in need of physicians in the form of mentors who will provide them with treatment suited to their condition: 'Thus ill-disciplined and foolish slaves receive profit from a master who frightens them, for they fear his threats and menaces and thus involuntarily are schooled by fear. All such may well learn the untruth, which will benefit them, if they cannot be brought to wisdom by truth.' In this homily[30] Philo grasps the fear peculiar to untutored slaves, who need a master that strikes awe. Fear has a pedagogical justification merely for people who think of God in terms of the verse 'that, as a man chasteneth his son, so the Lord thy God chasteneth thee.'[31] Love of the Lord, on the other hand, is the heritage only of those 'into whose conception of the Existent no thought of human parts or passion enters, who pay Him the honour meet for God for His own sake only.'[32] Philo does not recognize 'fear of Heaven' as a true value, and certainly not as a supreme value. Love is linked to a correct understanding of the nature of God, and is not the portion of 'servants that minister to the master not for the sake of receiving a reward'. Philo's statement concerning the servants recalls the verses of the Odyssey: 'Servants, when their masters are no longer there to order them about, have little will to do their duties as they should' [translation by E. V. Rieu].[33] On the other hand, it is actually Seneca's view[34] that appears far removed from the course of Philo's thought. Seneca teaches that the master should implant in the hearts of his servants not a feeling of dread but of reverence, giving as his reason: 'For that which suffices for a god must necessarily suffice also for a human master.' Seneca does not transfer a concept belonging to the ethics governing human relations to the sphere of theology, but, conversely, he deduces from man's relationship to the deity what a servant's attitude to his master should be. In his view 'he that is revered is also loved; but love cannot be harmonized with fear.'[35] Seneca comes close to Antigonus' dictum. Possibly there is actually to be discerned in the observations of Seneca, who was almost a contemporary of Rabban Joḥanan b. Zakkai, the influence of the teaching of the Jewish Sages.[36] Undoubtedly Philo's arguments and Seneca's approach are completely congruent.[37] Philo does not distinguish between 'fear resulting from terror' and the fear which is reverence, and Seneca, again, does not connect his statement concerning fear and love with the attributes of Deity. Only where Philo freed himself, in the course of his discussion, from the nexus between the attributes of God and the two ways of serving Him, was he capable of grasping the concept of the fear of God more positively. A contributing factor, apparently, was also the transmission of Palestinian traditions, although he did not always cite them in their correct context.[38]

The words of the Lord to Abraham, following upon the incident of the *ʿĂqēdā*, 'For now I know that thou art a God-fearing man, seeing thou hast not withheld thy son, thine only son, from Me', show clearly that after the unconditional act of sacrifice and devotion Abraham was granted the designation of 'a God-fearing man'. Yet there is no more perfect expression of love of the Lord than the act of the *'Åqēdā*; moreover Abraham was the friend of the Lord, as was stated by the prophet Isaiah (xli 8): 'the seed of Abraham My friend'. Indeed, it appears that R. Me'ir's observation '(the term) "a God-fearing man" applied to Abraham (means that he was so) out of love'[39] was a generally accepted view. Thus we are told in *The Book of Jubilees* (xvii 18): 'And in everything wherein He had tried him, he was found faithful, and his soul was not impatient, and he was not slow to act; for he was faithful and a lover of the Lord.' In conformity with this view the disciples of R. Akiba attributed the observance of their teacher's exposition ' "With all thy soul" — even if He takes your soul'[40] to the Patriarch Abraham himself. R. Simeon b. Yoḥai taught that the Lord said to Abraham: 'By your life, I account it unto you as if, had I bidden you to slaughter yourself, you would not have resisted for My sake, but would have obeyed and allowed yourself to be slaughtered on My account.'[41] Another disciple of R. Akiba, R. Eliezer b. Jacob, even went so far as to represent Abraham as offering his life in the fiery furnace for the principle of God's Unity.[42] In accordance with this view the Sages expounded the verse 'of them that love Me and keep My commandments' as follows: ' "Of them that love Me" — this refers to the Patriarch Abraham and his like...', that is, those who sanctify the Divine Name through religious martyrdom.[43] It is even reported in the name of R. Judah, R. Akiba's disciple, that all the glory vouchsafed Abraham was only on account of the ordeal in the fiery furnace: '...Abraham's deeds were not known until he was cast into the fiery furnace; and just as anyone who gathers myrrh gets his hands gummed with the bitter myrrh, so Abraham embittered his life and afflicted himself with sufferings.'[44]

Although none could doubt that Abraham's fear of God was inspired by love, the Sages were nevertheless conscious of the existence of a type of fear that stemmed only from dread of punishment and the possibility of losing one's reward. This kind of fear is unable to stand up to the test of suffering and tribulation. Thus R. Joshua reported that his teacher Rabban Joḥanan b. Zakkai used to expound all his days: 'That Job served the Omnipresent only out of fear, as it is stated (Job i 8): "a whole-hearted and an upright man, one that feareth God, and shunneth evil" '.[45] Rabban Joḥanan b. Zakkai could not regard Job as 'a God-fearing man' in the same sense as Abraham, since, in contrast to the Patriarch, Job did not stand the test of suffering without uttering harsh reproaches against Heaven.[46] Hence he said that Job did not serve God out of fear flowing from love, but out of fear resulting 'from anxiety lest retribution be visited upon him'. Possibly the Scriptural proof is based on the fact that the words 'a God-fearing man' are followed by the phrase 'and shunneth evil'.[47] The subjoined homily of Rabbi Akiba reads like a commentary on Rabban Joḥanan b. Zakkai's dictum, but reflects a more extreme viewpoint:[48] 'A certain king had four sons: One remained silent when punished; another protested when punished; another pleaded for mercy when punished; and another, when punished, said to his father "Punish me (still more)". Abraham was silent when punished, as it is said: "Take now thy son, thine only son, whom thou lovest, even Isaac... and offer him there for a burnt-offering" (Genesis xxii 2). He could have answered: "Yesterday Thou didst tell me 'For in Isaac shall seed be called to thee' " (*ibid.* xxi 12). Yet it is stated "And Abraham rose early in the morning" etc. (*ibid.* xxii 3). Job remonstrated when punished, as it is said "I will say unto God: Do not condemn me; make me know wherefore Thou contendest with me" (Job x 2). Hezekiah begged for mercy when punished, as it is stated "and he prayed unto the Lord" (II Kings xx 2)... David said to his Father "Punish me (even more)", as it is said "Wash me thoroughly from mine iniquity, and cleanse me from my sin" (Psalms li 4).'[49] In accordance with this view of Job as a rebel, Akiba grouped him with the generation of the Flood, Egypt, Gog and Magog, and the wicked who are punished in Gehenna for twelve months.[50]

While Antigonus of Sokho included love in the term 'fear of Heaven', which is in consequence man's religious ideal as portrayed in the utterances of the Prophets and the Psalmist,[51] Rabban Joḥanan b. Zakkai's statement that we have elucidated demonstrates that the fear of Heaven was understood by others as a concept devoid of love; this was apparently an outcome of the undue emphasis placed on the principle of reward and retribution.[52] But the formulation of

Rabban Joḥanan b. Zakkai's dictum does not yet contain the antithesis 'fear-love'; underlying it is rather the contrast between fear out of love and fear from dread of punishment. This interpretation is also confirmed by another source. Before his death R. Joḥanan said to his disciples: ' "May it be the Divine will that the fear of Heaven be upon you like that of mortals." Said his disciples to him: "Is that all?" He answered: "Would that it were so! Observe when a man commits a transgression, he hopes: May no one see me!" '[53] The surprise of the disciples at the comparison of the fear of Heaven to that of human beings is to be understood on the basis of the identification of the 'fear of Heaven' with fear of Heaven's retribution, which is not present in the fear of men. In this reply Rabban Joḥanan b. Zakkai emphasizes that the fear of Heaven implies the consciousness of the awe-inspiring character of God at all times and in the performance of every human act. Just as the proximity of an honoured and beloved man will hold a man back from perpetrating a transgression out of a sense of shame, so the feeling of God's nearness, glory, and love should prevent a man from sinning, and not primarily the fear of punishment. Only after the meaning of the concept 'fear' had become restricted and was applied to one aspect — fear on account of reward and retribution — did the clear contrast 'love-fear' come into being. It first appears about two generations after Rabban Joḥanan b. Zakkai. R. Joshua b. Hyrcanus expounded: 'Job served the Omnipresent only out of love, as it is said "Though He slay me yet will I wait for Him" (Job xiii 15). The matter, however, is still undecided (for the *Kĕthîv* here is לא איחל *lō' 'ăyaḥēl*, whereas the *Qĕrê* is לו איחל *lô 'ăyaḥēl*): Is the sense "I wait for Him", or "I do not wait for him"? Therefore Scripture declares: "Till I die I will not put away my integrity from me" (*ibid.* xxvii 5) — this teaches that he acted from love.' R. Joshua b. Ḥananiah accepted his view and said: 'Who will take away the dust from your eyes, O Rabban Joḥanan b. Zakkai!... and has not Joshua, the disciple of your disciple, now taught that he acted from love?'[54] Two things must be noted in the homily of R. Joshua b. Hyrcanus. First, that he does not deny the fact that Job's words contain reproaches against Heaven, and there is no attempt here to expound all his utterances favourably. Even in regard to xiii 15 he observed that it was a moot matter, for one could also read 'Though

He slay me I will not wait for Him'. Secondly, the decisive proof that Job acted out of love is derived from the last chapter of Job containing a charge against God (*ibid.* xxvii 2): 'As God liveth, who hath taken away my right; and the Almighty who hath dealt bitterly with me.' He did not, however, interpret even this verse contrary to its plain meaning, but only noted that it is followed by Job's declaration 'Till I die I will not put away my integrity from me',[55] that is to say, despite his complaints Job preserved his integrity. Integrity connotes submission out of a sense of devotion and love.[56] Round about the time of R. Joshua b. Hyrcanus, a Sage called Ben Peṭuri also expounded the verse 'As God liveth, who hath taken away my right; and the Almighty, who hath dealt bitterly with me' in Job's favour. He argued that 'No one vows by the life of the king unless he loves him.'[57]

In the homilies of R. Joshua b. Hyrcanus — which were approved by R. Joshua b. Ḥananiah and by Ben Peṭuri — wherein Job is depicted as serving God from love, there is a change in the very conception of the term love. It is no longer just fear emanating from love, which accepts suffering with complete devotion without question or protest, but also love stemming from chastisement and even from reproach of Heaven. This view is summed up in R. Me'ir's homily: 'For the term "a God-fearing man" is applied to Job and it is also applied to Abraham. Just as the expression "a God-fearing man" when applied to Abraham means out of love, so, too, when applied to Job it signifies from love.' As for 'all the charges made in the Book, they were uttered only relative to the occasion'.[58] But not all the Tannaim and Amoraim agreed that Job was to be adjudged one who served God from love. On the contrary, there were some who criticized his 'fear of God', and even the Sages who defended him did so only by interpreting his reproaches in a manner that took the sting out of the complaint and indictment. The issue came to the fore already in the dispute between R. Eliezer and R. Joshua: ' "The earth is given into the hand of the wicked" (Job ix 24). R. Eliezer said: Job sought to overturn the Divine order. Said R. Joshua to him: Job was only referring to Satan.'[59]

The problem of the harsh words and reproaches of Job assumes special importance in the *Targumim* [translations of Scripture] of the Book. The question already troubled the Sages in ancient times.

R. Jose relates: 'Once R. Ḥalafta visited Rabban Gamaliel at Tiberias. He found him sitting at the desk of Joḥanan b. Nazif and in his hand was a *Targum* of the Book of Job, which he was reading. Said R. Ḥalafta to him: I remember that Rabban Gamaliel the Elder, your grandfather, was sitting on a step on the Temple Mount, when a *Targum* of the Book of Job was brought to him, and he ordered the builder to build it into the wall. At that time Rabban Gamaliel (II) sent instructions to withdraw it from circulation.'[60]

We do not know what translation was brought to Rabban Gamaliel the Elder — whether Greek or Aramaic; certainly not that which we have today.[61] But whether this was the Septuagint,[62] or a translation that rendered the Book quite literally,[63] the reason for its suppression is to be found in the very fact of translation — on the same principle as 'The incident of Reuben is read (in Hebrew), but is not translated' (*M. Megilla* iv, 9) — or at most in the manner of the rendition, which did not find favour with Rabban Gamaliel. But the blame is not to be put on the differences of opinion between the Pharisees and the Sadducees.[64] If in truth Rabban Gamaliel was afraid that the Sadducees could find support for their views in the Book of Job, his fears would have applied not only to the translation but to the original. But we do not find that the Sages sought to withdraw Job from circulation. On the contrary, according to the Mishnaic tradition (*M. Yoma* i, 6) it was customary to read before the High Priest, on the evening of the Day of Atonement, from the Book of Job, and this tradition probably dates back to the time of Rabban Gamaliel the Elder. Furthermore, it is hard to imagine that the Sadducees, who denied the doctrine of determinism, could have approved the rebellious conduct and charges of Job. It appears that until the time of Rabban Gamaliel the Elder a translation of Job was not current at all,[65] and that when a translation was brought to him, he found that it deserved only to be suppressed. But the withdrawal did not prevent a *Targum* from appearing in the days of his grandson Rabban Gamaliel of Jabneh, when he visited Tiberias. We do not know the nature of this translation, which apparently *per se*, without the story told by R. Ḥalafta about the action of his grandfather, would not have been suppressed by Rabban Gamaliel. At any rate it seems that the renderings that were not withdrawn were oriented towards the exegesis that explained away the harsh charges of Job and were therefore motivated by the desire to put his personality in a favourable light, after the manner of R. Joshua. This is also the attitude adopted, in many passages, by the translator of the Septuagint. His Job is much more long-suffering and humble than the Hebrew Job. In not a few passages the Greek Job speaks almost with composure, and his words lack that quality of self-assurance and protest found in the Hebrew original. He mitigates the indictments by means of interpretations, omissions, and interpolations.[66] To the verse at the end of the Book, 'So Job said, being old and full of days', the translator adds 'And it is written that he will rise to life again with those whom God will raise up'. This addition accords with the spirit of the translation of several verses that, in contrast to the original, express the hope in life after death.[67] The renditions that toned down Job's rebelliousness and contention facilitated the creation of a story about Job totally different from that of the Biblical book. In the Greek pseudepigraphical work called *The Testament of Job*, or *The Words of Job*,[68] not only are all Job's arguments and charges thrust aside, but he himself is depicted there in the image and character of the Patriarch Abraham; he is not merely a liberal host but an iconoclast who purges his area of idolatry, casts down the idols, and closes their temples. His struggle is entirely directed against Satan. The roles of Job and his friends are interchanged. It is they who lament and complain about his bitter fate, but he stands up to the trial and cries 'Shall I sin with my lips against the Lord? It shall surely not come to pass!' (xxxviii 2), even as he had undertaken at the beginning (v 1) 'to stand the ordeal, and not to weaken till the day of his death'.[69] Here the position is completely reversed. Needless to say, not a little must be attributed to the 'artistic' character of the composition. Imaginative, legendary works of this kind are accustomed to glorify the image of their hero to the point of overlooking other personalities. Hence it is interesting to note that in a book that strongly resembles in form *The Testament of Job*, namely the *Testament of Abraham*[70], the angel Michael says to God: 'There is none like him (Abraham) in the land, not even Job, that excellent man.'[71] The viewpoint of *The Testament of Job* is prevalent also in ancient Christian literature. 'The patience of Job and the end of the "Lord" ' are presented together as an example to sufferers in the Epistle of James (v 11), and this line of interpretation was followed by Tertullian and other church fathers in the Christian church.[72] But this approach was not accepted by the Sages, not even by those who argued in Job's favour.[73]

While R. Joshua saves Job by diverting his harsh words to Satan, R. Eliezer declares that he was a blasphemer. R. Ishmael, too, was far from comparing Job to Abraham, but said 'Job was one of Pharaoh's servants, one of his leading courtiers, as it is written "He that feared the word of the Lord" etc. (Exodus xi 2); and Scripture says of him "a wholehearted and an upright man, one that feareth God, and shunneth evil'.[74] Job was therefore only one that feared the Lord from fear of punishment. A similar statement is made by R. Ḥiyya concerning Job: 'I had but one righteous Gentile in My world, and I gave him his reward and dismissed him from My world.'[75]

This appraisal is still more evident in the wording of an anonymous Baraita: 'There was once a pious man among the Gentile nations called Job, and he came into the world only with the object of receiving his recompense. When the Holy One, blessed be He, brought upon him afflictions, he began to revile and blaspheme. So the Holy One, blessed be He, doubled his reward in this world, in order to exclude him from the world to come' (*T.B. Bava Batra* 15b). A Baraita that enumerates the various types of Pharisees and distinguishes between a 'God-fearing Pharisee' and a 'God-loving Pharisee' illustrates the two by observing: 'A God-fearing Pharisee is (exemplified) by Job, a God-loving Pharisee is Abraham; the noblest of them all is the God-loving Pharisee like Abraham.'[76]

In all these sources Job appears as one who fears God only on account of reward and punishment. The Amora R. Levi explains the difference between Abraham and Job actually on the basis of their reactions, which ostensibly appear alike: 'R. Levi said: Two men — Abraham and Job — said the same thing. Abraham said "far be it from Thee to do such a thing, to slay the righteous with the wicked" (Genesis xviii 25); Job said "It is all one — therefore I say: He destroyeth the innocent and the wicked" (Job ix 22). Abraham was rewarded for this, Job was punished for it. Abraham said it with due deliberation; Job spoke intemperately — "It is all one" ' (*Genesis*

Rabba xlix, §9, p. 509). Abraham made his statement with calm deliberation; he could not imagine that God would slay the righteous with the wicked, whereas Job made a definite and unqualified charge — 'It is all one'![77]

R. Levi enlarged the scope of Abraham's doubts. To the question 'Why did the Holy One, blessed be He, make the revelation to Abraham?' he replied: 'Because he questioned in his heart (the justice of destroying) the generation of the Flood, and thought: It is inconceivable that there were no righteous men among them.'[78]

It should also be noted that a similar conception of a confrontation between Abraham and God is to be found in Philo's work *Quis Rerum Divinarum Heres?* On the verse Genesis xv 2 he comments: 'When, then, is it that the servant speaks frankly to his master? Surely it is when his heart tells him that he has not wronged his owner, but that his words and deeds are all for that owner's benefit. And so when else should the slave of God open his mouth to Him who is the ruler and master both of himself and of the All, save when he is pure from sin and the judgements of his conscience are loyal to his master, when he feels more joy at being the servant of God than if he had been king of all the human race...'[79] 'For to whom should a man speak with frankness, but to his friend?.... But observe on the other hand that confidence is blended with caution. For while the words "What wilt Thou give me" (Genesis xv 2) show confidence, "Master" shows caution... He who says "Master, what wilt Thou give me?" virtually says no less than this, "I am not ignorant of Thy transcendent sovereignty; I know the terrors of Thy power; I come before Thee in fear and trembling, and yet again I am confident... Thou hast given me a tongue of instruction that I should know when I should speak... Why then shall I not take courage to say what I feel? Why shall I not inquire of Thee and claim to learn something more? Yet I, who proclaim my confidence, confess in turn my fear and consternation, and still the fear and the confidence are not at war within me in separate camps, as one might suppose, but are blended in a harmony.'[80] Undoubtedly these remarks of Philo contain a totally different appraisal of the fear of God from that which characterizes his other homilies. This indicates that Philo also absorbed something of the ancient Rabbinic conception of the fear of God that flows from love, and that echoes of their homilies on Abraham's confrontation with his God had reached him too. But the fact that Philo bases his homily specifically on the verse 'What wilt Thou give me?' and not on the daring verses uttered by Abraham when he came to pray for the men of Sodom is puzzling. Yet it is actually his exposition of these verses in other treatises[81] that enables us to understand his viewpoint; for he removes from these passages the daring characteristics that mark Abraham's questions, which, although asked unprovocatively, are nevertheless prompted by a sense of bewilderment that an entire city, which possibly also contains some righteous people along with the wicked, should be overturned. According to Philo, Abraham's concern was also extended to those people in whom elements of 'the righteous and the wicked' were intermingled. On the other hand, even the question 'What wilt Thou give me?' gave Philo the opportunity to interpret it as a request for added knowledge.[82]

Even those Sages who were most emphatic in their praise of Job and his virtues, irrespective of whether they considered him a Jew or a pious Gentile, confined their praise to the first period of his life, which preceded his ordeal. When R. Joḥanan said 'Greater tribute is paid by Scripture to Job than to Abraham' (*T.B. Bava Batra* 15b), he had in mind Job's earlier years, and it is he also who stated 'There was no more righteous Gentile than Job, yet he came only with reproaches... There were no greater prophets than Moses and Isaiah, yet both of them came only with entreaties' (*Deuteronomy Rabba* ii, 4). This assessment is not far removed from the differentiation between Job and Abraham reported in the name of R. Levi, who expressed his criticism of the comparison drawn between Job and Abraham in an original manner. He declared that Satan acted from pious motives, for when he saw that the Holy One, blessed be He, was inclined to favour Job, he said: 'Heaven forbid that He should forget Abraham's love.'[83] In the generation following R. Joḥanan, R. Ḥanina bar Papa said of Job: 'Had he [Job] not reproached (God) then just as we now say "The God of Abraham, the God of Isaac, and the God of Jacob", so we should have said "and the God of Job" ' (*Pesiqta Rabbati* 190a). God's name was not linked to Job's because of the charges he hurled against Him; hence we do not include his name when we mention the God of the Patriarchs in the

Tĕfillā. Rava, who applied to many of Job's utterances the words 'Dust to Job's mouth!', because he reviled, blasphemed, and denied God[84], found no other argument in Job's favour than 'a man is not to be held responsible for what he says in his distress', and Job spoke by reason of his distress and suffering.

The different evaluations of Job's religious personality are connected with the views of the Sages relative to the ways of fearing and loving God, and not with their attitude to the Gentile world and its pious men; and it would certainly be out of the question to represent the polarity between the views of Rabban Joḥanan b. Zakkai, R. Eliezer, and R. Ḥiyya, on the one hand, and of R. Joshua b. Hyrcanus, Ben Peṭuri, and R. Joshua, on the other, as based on the antithesis between the particularistic notion that a Gentile saint like Job could not attain to the spiritual plane of Abraham, and the universalistic conception that a Gentile could likewise reach such heights.[85]

The opinion of R. Joshua b. Hyrcanus, with which R. Joshua b. Ḥananiah agreed, that Job — despite his complaints and protests — served God out of love was not acceptable to the majority of Tannaim and Amoraim. The discussion on Job's personality and utterances indicates the way in which the concepts of 'fear of God' and 'love of God' had crystallized. Fear emanating from love is no longer fear but love; but love that induces a man to be presumptuous towards his master, to complain of his ways, and to be insolent to him, is not love, and fear due to dread of punishment is to be preferred to it. When Rabban Joḥanan b. Zakkai expressed to his disciples the wish that their fear of Heaven might be like their fear of human beings[86], he sought to convey to them two teachings on the subject. He had in mind, firstly, the abolition of the fear of men and the acceptance of the yoke of the kingdom of heaven in its place. Rabban Joḥanan b. Zakkai's answer to another question of his disciples supports our interpretation. When his disciples asked him 'Why should a slave have his ear bored rather than any of his other organs?' he answered them: '(The ear) had removed from itself the yoke of the kingdom of heaven and accepted the sovereignty of the yoke of a human being; therefore Scripture said 'Let the ear come and be pierced, because it did not keep what it had heard.'[87] The second thing that R. Joḥanan b. Zakkai wished to teach them was that the practical significance of this fear of Heaven, of the sense of the presence of God, to whom everything is revealed and known, was fear of sin. It meant primarily withdrawing from transgression. But clearly the compass of the term's meaning in Temple times was very wide. The name of the 'Chamber of Secrets', which was situated in the Temple, is explained in the Mishna (*M. Sheqalim*, v, 6) as follows: 'The God-fearing used to put (their gifts) there secretly, and the poor of good families received their support from it secretly.' Thus these God-fearing people scrupulously observed the precept to give charity in secret. In the story about the families that outwitted the guards stationed by Jeroboam the son of Nebat along the roads to prevent pilgrims from going up to Jerusalem reference is made to 'whoever was worthy and sin-fearing in that generation' and they were the people 'who risked their lives for the Torah and the precepts'.[88] It may also be assumed that the tribute paid to ʿAqavya b. Mahalalel, that the Temple court, when full and locked, did not hold anyone to compare with him in wisdom or the fear of sin, did not refer to the fear of transgressions only.

It seems that the sources we have cited suffice to show that before the Destruction, about the time of Rabban Joḥanan b. Zakkai, the designation 'sin-fearing' was specifically applied to men who in the same measure as they were careful to avoid transgressions were scrupulous in the observance of the commandments with devotion and love, just as the expression 'fear of Heaven', when used by Rabban Joḥanan b. Zakkai, denoted fear out of love and piety and not from dread of punishment or hope of reward. As we have seen, already in the days of the Tannaim 'love' was differentiated from 'fear' (*Sifre Deuteronomy* § 32), a distinction being drawn between a 'Pharisee from love' and a 'Pharisee from fear'.[89] But an extreme connotation, which is quite distinctive, is given to the term 'love' in R. Akiba's teaching. Love assumes both a martyrological and mystical character. The ideal son among the King's four sons is, according to R. Akiba, David, who is punished yet says to his Father 'Punish me still more!'[90] His watchword is 'suffering is precious',[91] completely severing the nexus between 'suffering' and the doctrine of retribution in this world or in the world to come, and regarding it as a supreme good for the servant of the Lord. This constitutes, according to Ben ʿAzzai (*Sifre Deuteronomy* § 32), love 'until the draining of life', and this R. Akiba observed at the moment of his death, when he declared: 'All my life I was troubled about the verse "with all thy soul", (which means) even if He takes your soul. I said: When will it be granted me to fulfil it?'[92] At that moment he did not think of suffering as conducive to repentance, as an indication of atonement, or even as a sign of the Lord's love for His righteous ones, ideas that find expression in Psalms (xciv 12), Proverbs (iii 11–12) and Job (v 17–20). Likewise the author of *The Psalms of Solomon* approximates[93] more closely to the concepts of the Biblical verses referred to than to R. Akiba's approach.[94] The portrayal of the overpowering love of man's soul in its yearning for God's fellowship, for entry into *Pardes*, and for knowledge of the 'Work of the Chariot', R. Akiba found in the Song of Songs, which he proclaimed to be 'most holy' (*M. Yadayim* iii, 5). To him is likewise attributed the saying 'If the Torah had not been given to us, the Song of Songs would have sufficed to guide the world.'[95] When R. Akiba entered *Pardes* in peace and left it in peace, the Sages applied to him the verse from the Song of Songs 'Draw me, we will run after Thee'; and when he died sanctifying God's name as a martyr, his disciple Joshua b. Jehonathan applied to him the verse from the Song of Songs מישרים אהבוך *mĕshārîm 'ăhēvûkhā* [usually rendered: 'rightly do they love Thee'], which he interpreted to mean: 'They loved Thee far more than the righteous of old' [reading מִישָׁרִים *mîshārîm* for מֵישָׁרִים *mĕshārîm*].[96] This mystical-martyrological conception of love could only be adopted by a few, and just as in explaining the dictum 'suffering is precious' the Sages already in the generation following R. Akiba began to resort again to reasons, both old and new, linked to the principle of reward and punishment[97], so too they explained the difference between love and fear as one reflected in the measure of the reward. The Tanna R. Simeon b. Eleazar said: 'Greater is he that acts from love than he that acts from fear, for the merit of the latter remains for a thousand generations, whereas that of the former endures for two thousand generations.'[98] The early Amoraim — R. Ḥama b. R. Ḥanina, Rav Judah, and R. Joḥanan — explained away contradictions between the assurances and promises in various verses by stating that 'in the one case (the penitence) was from love, in the other from fear'.[99] Even for the ten ordeals with which Abraham was tested an explanation is offered that declares:

'And why so many? In order that when our forefather comes to receive his reward, the nations of the world may say: "More than all of us, more than any one, is Abraham worthy of receiving his reward." '[1]

Even those Tannaim and Amoraim who appraised the love of God[2] most highly, nevertheless regarded the fear of Heaven as an indispensable condition for attaining to love.[3] With reference to the verse 'And now, Israel, what doth the Lord thy God require of thee but to fear the Lord thy God' (Deuteronomy x 12) the Babylonian Talmud raises the following objection: 'Is the fear of Heaven such a small thing? Did not R. Ḥanina say in the name of R. Simeon b. Yoḥai: The Holy One, blessed be He, has naught in His treasury save a store of the fear of Heaven, as it is said: "The fear of the Lord is His store" (Isaiah xxxiii 6)?' The answer given is to the effect that in Moses' eyes the fear of God was but a small thing: 'It is like the case of a man, who is asked for a big article, and he has it, then it appears to him like a small article; (but if he is asked for) a small article, and he does not possess it, it seems to him like a big article.'[4] Apparently experience showed that there were many to whom the fear of heaven was 'a small article that they did not possess'. There were even scholars 'who occupied themselves with the Torah, but had no fear of Heaven', and in regard to them R. Jannai proclaimed 'Woe to him who has no court, but makes a gateway to his court!' (*T.B. Yoma* 72b). About two generations later, this type of scholar was compared by Rabba bar Rav Huna in Babylon 'to a treasurer, to whom the inner keys were entrusted but not the outer keys' (*T.B. Shabbat* 31b). In urging that the attribute of the fear of God should be regarded as fundamental, the Amoraim were nevertheless not led to overlook the attribute of love. Abbaye was accustomed to say: 'A man should always be subtle in the fear of Heaven, (remembering that) "A soft answer turneth away wrath"; he should be on the friendliest terms with his brethren and relatives and, indeed, with all men, even with the Gentile in the street, so that he may be beloved in Heaven and well-liked upon earth, and be acceptable to his fellow men.'[5] The dictum serves to reduce the tension between the two concepts by giving a moderate interpretation to them both. The verse 'And thou shalt love the Lord thy God' was already expounded even by the

Tannaim in the sense of 'Make Him beloved of all men', but they add 'like our father Abraham, as it is said "and the souls that they had gotten [literally 'made'] in Haran" (Genesis xii 5)... for our father Abraham used to convert them and bring them under the wings of the Divine Presence.'[6] The ways suggested by Abbaye for instilling the love of God among men do not demand proselytization; deeds that make a man acceptable to his fellow creatures are considered sufficient. Such deeds are not far removed from those characterizing 'him who is subtle in the fear of Heaven'. If Abbaye did not explicitly abolish the distinction between love and fear of God, this was done by his colleague Rava, as is clearly to be seen from the following story: 'Two disciples were once with Rava. One said to him: "In my dream they read to me 'O how great is Thy goodness which Thou hast laid up for them that fear Thee' (Psalms xxxi 20)." The other said to him: "In my dream they read to me 'But let all those that put their trust in Thee rejoice, let them even shout for joy... let them also that love Thy name exult in Thee' (*ibid.* v 12)." Said he [Rava] to them: "Ye are both wholly righteous Rabbis, one being actuated by love and one by fear." '[7] Clearly Rava's words are opposed to the teaching of R. Simeon b. Eleazar, that one who acts from love is greater than one who acts from fear, and to the concept that the reward of him who acts from love is immeasurably greater.[8] The Amora who related to Rava that they read out to him the verse wherein he was included among the lovers of God undoubtedly regarded this love as taking the form not only of devotion to the observance of the commandments, but also, without doubt, of abstention from transgression.[9] So, too, we may be sure that his colleague, who was counted among the God-fearing, observed the precepts in accord with the ruling of a disciple of Rava, namely 'He that fears Heaven will seek to satisfy both views.'[10]

CHAPTER XV

MAN'S ACCOUNTING AND THE WORLD'S ACCOUNTING

I. SIN AND DEATH

The problem of requital — reward and punishment — and the question of the existence of suffering and evil in the world arose incidentally in the course of our discussion of some of the subjects dealt with in the previous chapters.[1] Now we shall proceed to examine these questions *per se*, but in this investigation, too, we shall need to treat once again of topics whose connection with the problems under review is not always apparent, but emerges in the course of the exposition and clarification.

In the Bible itself the Sages found a variegated tapestry of the 'doctrine of requital', embroidered and interwined with threads from the skein of myth, closely linked to the feeling of belonging to the family-tribe, refined and purified in the crucible of the suffering and afflictions of prophets and poets. The daring of their protest and the heroism of their surrender in accepting and justifying the Divine judgement found expression in the words of Jeremiah and Ezekiel, in the Psalms and in the Book of Job.[2]

The Tannaim and Amoraim did not overlook the great disparities and variegation of this tapestry. They discovered contradictions between the Scriptural passages. Some were content just to note them, but others attempted to reconcile them by introducing views and concepts of which hardly a hint can be found in the verses themselves. They aimed not only at enlarging and deepening the ideas and motifs of Holy Writ, but also at raising new questions and finding new solutions to old problems. This was the outcome of their renewed examination of past events, or of their personal wrestling with the problems of their existence, or the result of the absorption of views that were current in the world in whose environment they lived and worked.

The story of Adam and his transgression against the prohibition of eating of the fruit of the 'tree of the knowledge of good and evil' establishes unequivocably the causal nexus between sin and punishment. The first sin brought into the world death,[3] birth pangs, toil, and fatigue. The story of Adam's sin does not purport in the Bible to explain men's sins and weaknesses. Furthermore, the entire episode is nowhere alluded to subsequently.[4] Ben Sira does, indeed, declare (xxv 28 [24]) 'From a woman did sin originate, and because of her we all must die.' However. these words occur in a chapter that treats of the woman in general, the first verse of the passage (*v*. 16 [13]) being 'Any wound, but not a heart-wound! Any wickedness, only not the wickedness of a woman!', and includes warnings against a wicked woman, though it ends on an optimistic note: 'A good wife (is) a good gift; she shall be given to him that feareth God, for his portion' (xxvi 3).

Ben Sira states only that iniquity began on account of woman and because of her, death came into being, but the concept of 'original sin' and predestination never entered his mind in the least. On the contrary, elsewhere (xv 14–15) he expressly states: 'God created man from the beginning, and placed him in the hand of his *yeṣer*. If thou (so) desirest, thou canst keep the commandment, and (it is) wisdom to do His good pleasure. And if thou trust in Him, of a truth thou shalt live.' Death is a natural law: 'All flesh withereth like a garment; and the eternal decree is: "Thou shalt surely die!"' (xiv 17).

The episode of Adam and Eve only marks the time when death came into being. A similar interpretation is to be given to the following sayings ascribed to R. Joshua regarding the precepts specifically devolving upon women: 'Because they brought death into the world, they are the first to go to a dead person... because she [the woman] quenched the soul of the first man, therefore she was given the precept of (kindling) the Sabbath light.'[5] Only death came with Adam's sin, but not the necessity to sin. In regard to the possibility of transgressing and the freedom of choice between the way of life and the way of death, Ben Sira made no distinction between Adam and his offspring.

As we have seen (above, p. 264), this was the opinion of R. Akiba. It is true that there were Sages who did not subscribe to his view regarding the complete separation between a man's deeds and the duration of his life in this world (above p. 265), but then did they also dispute the very concept that death was an inescapable decree? It was not possible to ignore the difficulty of attributing the actual existence of death in the world — and needless to say of other afflictions — to Adam's sin. If free will was given to men, and it is in their power to be wholly righteous, why should they be punished 'on account of the serpent'? Why does death, or the angel of death, continue to have dominion? Even the postulate that there is no righteous man who does not sin raises a grave problem. If predestination is not involved, what prevents a man from preserving his integrity? Or is man evil from birth, and this evil cannot be wholly cured? If so, who and what brought about this evil? Within the framework of monotheistic faith there is no place for a solution that puts the blame for corruption and sin on any power beyond the control of God; this fact underlies the story of Adam's transgression. The serpent, who was the cause of death, is one of God's creatures and was punished for its deed. This punishment implies a change in its original nature and qualities.[6] We have already observed (above, p. 229) that Adam was regarded, prior to his sin, as one endowed with special qualities, and there were also Sages who went to extravagant lengths in portraying his attributes. Adam's punishment consisted not only in the decree of death, but in losing his former virtues, and one might almost say that just as he brought 'death to his descendants', so he caused deterioration in their very nature and made them incline ineluctably towards sin.[7]

Was this concept known in Rabbinical circles, and, if so, what was their attitude towards it? To answer this question we shall first have recourse to an extraneous source, where this idea is formulated with great extremism, and without any qualifications. The reference is to Paul's statement (Romans v 12–21): 'Therefore as sin came into the world through one man and death through sin, and so death spread to all men because all men sinned — sin indeed was in the world before the law was given, but sin is not counted where there is no law. Yet death reigned from Adam to Moses, even over those whose sins were not like the transgression of Adam... Then as one man's trespass led to condemnation for all men, so one man's act of righteousness leads to acquittal and life for all men. For as by one man's disobedience many were made sinners, so by one man's obedience many will be made righteous.'

Paul's statements and their precise meaning gave rise to dogmatic theological discussions within Christianity,[8] and have been variously interpreted by its modern expositors.[9] But no one disputes that Paul held that the first sin affected all mankind, and that Adam bequeathed to his descendants, by his trespass, a body infected by lust and desires, and consequently they were predestined to sin. The question whether he thought this tendency already existed in the flesh to begin with and Adam's downfall was a transformation of the potential into the actual, or that it came into being with his sin, is of no importance here. The main consideration, in Paul's view, is that sin is inherent in man, and hence death, too, which comes to every human being, is a punishment for his own sin, and at the same time also the consequence of the first sin. The problem that interests us is whether this doctrine originated with Paul, who wished to serve thereby his Christological purpose, or whether he derived its basic idea from his Jewish environment and only added that, through the giving of the Torah, sin, which was already in existence, but did not yet count, became sin that does count, and from which a man can only free himself by the enthronement of grace through belief in Jesus.

The doctrine built upon the first sin and its consequences was known to the author of the *Syriac Apocalypse of Baruch* (liv 15–19), but he firmly rejected it. He states 'For though Adam first sinned and brought untimely death upon all, yet of those who were born from him each one of them has prepared for his own soul torment to come, and again each one of them has chosen for himself glories to come... Adam is therefore not the cause, save only of his own soul, but each of us has been the Adam of his own soul....' The polemical tone of his words is obvious, and the purpose is to emphasize man's personal responsibility for his deeds.

The author of *IV Ezra* comes nearer to Paul's view of the consequences of Adam's sin than to that of the author of the *Syriac Apocalypse of Baruch*; his statement is particularly significant, because he also deals with the problem of sin in relation to the giving of the Torah. In reviewing the history of mankind and that of the people of Israel, he declares: 'And to him Thou commandest only one observance of thine, but he transgressed it. Forthwith Thou appointedst death for him and for his generations, and from him were born nations and tribes... And every nation walked after their own will... And it came to pass that when Thou leddest forth his seed out of Egypt, and didst bring them to the Mount Sinai... to give Law to Jacob's seed and Commandment to the generation of Israel. And yet Thou didst not take away from them the evil heart, that Thy Law might bring forth fruit in them. For the first Adam, clothing himself with the evil heart, transgressed and was overcome; and likewise also all who were born of him. Thus the infirmity became inveterate; the Law indeed was in the heart of the people, but (in conjunction) with the evil germ; so what was good departed, and the evil remained' (iii [i] 7–23). The difference between the view of this anonymous author and that of Paul is clear.

Although the giving of the Law did not of itself uproot the evil in man, yet he was given a means of choosing the good. The author did not refrain from saying to the angel who spoke to him: 'Better had it been that the earth had not produced Adam, or else, having once produced him, (for them) to have restrained him from sinning. For how does it profit us all that in the present we must live in grief and after death look for punishment? O thou Adam, what hast thou done! For though it was thou that sinned, the fall was not thine alone, but ours also who are thy descendants!...' And the angel answered him: 'This is the condition of the contest which (every) man who is born upon earth must wage; that, if he be overcome, he shall suffer as thou hast said: but if he be victorious, he shall receive what I have said. For this is the way of which Moses, while he was alive, spoke unto the people, saying: Choose thee life, that thou mayst live!' (*ibid.* vii [v] 116–129). In the light of these words it can be seen that the primary difference between Paul and his predecessors and his circle does not lie in the evaluation of Adam's sin and its consequences, but in Paul's complete negation of the Torah. He speaks of the inability of the Torah (ἀδύνατον τοῦ νομοῦ) to give man life (Romans viii 3) and to bring about a change in his nature and character. Paul's views on sin served him as a basis on which to erect the structure of his concept of redemption.

In the dicta of R. Joshua and R. Akiba (above, p. 422) we only found that Adam's sin was blamed for the death of all the generations, but not for the sins of his offspring. Accordingly R. Akiba's disciples discussed the influence exerted by the acceptance of the Torah not on man's inclination to sin, but on the decree of death.

The word of the Lord after the giving of the Torah, 'Oh that they had such a heart as this always, to fear Me' etc. (Deuteronomy v 26), is expounded by an anonymous Tanna as follows: 'Had it been possible to remove the angel of death, I should have removed him, but the decree has already been promulgated.' R. Jose disagreed with him and said: 'On this condition the Israelites took their stand at Mount Sinai — on condition that the angel of death should not have dominion over them, as it is said "I said: Ye are godlike beings, and all of you sons of the Most High" (Psalms lxxxii 6); (but) ye corrupted your deeds, (therefore) it is written "Nevertheless ye shall die like men, and fall like one of the princes". '[10] An exposition similar to that of R. Jose was given by his colleague R. Judah, or Nehemiah, on the verse 'And the writing was the writing of God, graven [חָרוּת *ḥārût*] upon the tables' (Exodus xxxii 16): this means 'freedom חֵרוּת [*ḥērût*] from the angel of death'.[11]

In one of the sources in which this dictum is cited the homilist proceeds to interpret it by drawing a parallel between the action of Israel and that of Adam, and he concludes with the teaching of R. Jose mentioned above: 'When Israel declared "All that the Lord hath spoken will we do, and obey", the Holy One, blessed be He, said: "I gave Adam one commandment to fulfil and I compared him to the Ministering Angels, as it is said 'Behold, the man is become as one of us' (Genesis iii 22); these [the Israelites] who perform and observe 613 commandments — apart from the general rules, the detailed regulation, and the minutiae — are *a fortiori* entitled to everlasting life"... but when they said "This is thy god, O Israel", death came upon them. Said the Holy One, blessed be He, "Ye have walked in the footsteps of Adam... I said 'Ye are godlike beings', but ye followed the ways of Adam, (therefore it is written) 'Nevertheless ye shall die like men'." '[12] The view of R. Jose and his colleague

R. Nehemiah, or R. Judah, is that it was the sin of the calf that was the cause of death. The giving of the Law provided an opportunity to choose life once again and to banish death from the world. But after the Children of Israel had sinned, and the decree of death was renewed, the people of Israel re-enacted the story of Adam, who first sinned and only thereafter was death imposed upon him.

Just as there was no Tanna among R. Akiba's disciples that attributed the existence of sin to Adam's transgression, so none among them, or among their disciples, attributed the actual existence of death to human sins. However, a Baraita is cited in the Babylonian Talmud to corroborate the opinion of an Amora that 'There is no death without sin.' It reads as follows: 'R. Simeon b. Eleazar said: Even Moses and Aaron died on account of their sin, as it is said "Because ye believed not in Me" (Numbers xx 12) — (otherwise) your time to depart from this world had not yet come.'[13] The conclusion of the Baraita shows that it was not the Tanna's intention to say that if Moses and Aaron had not sinned, they would have lived for ever. He only stated that they would not have passed away before their time and it would have been granted them, as the rest of the verse implies (*ibid.*), to bring 'this assembly into the land which I have given them'. The following explanation is given in a parallel Baraita: 'R. Simeon b. Eleazar said: Moses and Aaron, too, died prematurely [literally, 'by being cut off'], as it is said "because ye sanctified Me not" (Deuteronomy xxxii 51); hence, if you had sanctified Me, your time would not yet have come to depart (this world).'[14] Another Baraita dissociates even Moses' death from his sin: 'The Ministering Angels said to the Holy One, blessed be He: "Sovereign of the universe, why did Adam die?" He replied: "Because he did not fulfil My commandment." Said they to Him: "But Moses did fulfil Thy commandments!" He answered them: "It is My decree, the same for all men, as Scripture states 'This is the law: when a man dieth' " (Numbers xix 14).'[15] The punishment for his sin was limited to the fact that he was not privileged to enter the land either in his lifetime or after his death.[16] The conception of death as a decree — whether it came into the world with Adam's sin and was never annulled, or whether it was abolished and renewed when the calf was made — puts an end to the connection between the sin of Adam and the sins of his descendants. By the same token there is no necessity to search for sins in the life of the righteous; hence sayings like that attributed to R. Eliezer Ha-Gadol 'If the Holy One, blessed be He, were to bring Abraham, Isaac, and Jacob to judgement, they could not stand before the indictment'[17] and similar dicta are not to be linked with the view that 'There is no death without sin'.[18] Exceptional is the Baraita that was considered to uphold the idea of original sin:[19] 'Four died because of the serpent, namely Benjamin the son of Jacob, Amram the father of Moses, Jesse the father of David, and Chileab the son of David.'[20] The meaning of this Baraita is unambiguous: All men die on account of their sins; and there is no death without sin.[21] There were only four exceptions to the rule, and these were not Jacob, the father of the nation, who was a man of perfect integrity, nor our teacher Moses, who delivered Israel and gave them the Torah, nor King David, the elect of the Lord, but the fathers or sons of these great men,[22] men of whose sins, it is true, nothing is known, but neither are we informed of their meritorious deeds. Only they died 'because of the serpent'. The polemical — almost paradoxical — character of this dictum, which is directed against the idea that finds expression in the Paulinian theology, is obvious, and only when thus understood does the saying become meaningful. The restriction of the effect of the first sin to the fate of four not very important persons annuls the significance of the episode, and hence takes away the basis of Paul's doctrine of redemption. A similar polemical attitude was adopted by R. Joḥanan in a passage that is cited in three places in the Babylonian Talmud, but in order to understand it, it is important to quote it as it appears in its original context. There it is related that R. Ḥiyya bar Abba and Rav Assi were sitting before R. Joḥanan, and while their teacher was dosing, R. Ḥiyya bar Abba asked his colleague physiological and physiognomical questions about animals and human beings. To the last question 'Why are the Gentiles contaminated with lust?' he replied: 'Because they eat the flesh of abominable and creeping things.' Thereupon R. Joḥanan awoke and rebuked his disciples, calling them 'infants', and in place of the naive answers, he gave them other explanations, which were deeper and more symbolical. In reply to the last question he said: 'Why are the Gentiles contaminated with lust? Because they did not stand at Mount Sinai.

For when the serpent came upon Eve he instilled contaminating lust into her; when, however, Israel stood at Mount Sinai, their lust ceased. But since the Gentiles did not stand at Mount Sinai, their contamination did not disappear.'[23] R. Joḥanan used the erotic motif of the serpent myth (see above, p. 169), and attributed to the serpent the lust of human beings, but it was taken away — contrary to Paul's teaching — precisely from those who stood at Mount Sinai and continued to infest the Gentiles. The concept of contaminating lust, dirt, and filth, became as it were — like the notion of defilement — synonymous with sin,[24] and indeed R. Joḥanan himself employs the word זיהום *zihûm* ['contamination'] in the sense of 'unfitness' and 'disqualification', in regard to the religious admissibility of a woman to be married to a priest.[25] The Amora R. Abba bar Kahana declared the contamination from the children of Jacob to have been removed even before the revelation at Sinai: 'Up to three generations — he asserts — the contaminating strain did not disappear from our ancestors: Abraham begot Ishmael, Isaac begot Esau, but Jacob begot the twelve tribes who were untainted.'[26]

The Baraita concerning the four who died on account of the serpent and the statements of R. Joḥanan and R. Abba bar Kahana regarding the contamination that was injected, likewise because of the serpent, into the human species, seem at first blush to accept the doctrine of original sin, but in actual fact they void it of all meaning in all that pertains to the question of sin and its punishment relative to the people of Israel. This very fact serves to corroborate the statement regarding the polemical character of these dicta. A polemical undercurrent, it seems to me, is also discernible in the discussion of R. Joḥanan's contemporaries, R. Ḥama b. R. Ḥanina and R. Jonathan, on the cause of the penalty of death. R. Ḥama b. R. Ḥanina said: 'Adam did not deserve to know the taste of death. Wherefore, then, was death imposed upon him? Because the Holy One, blessed be He, foresaw that Nebuchadnezzar and Hiram would declare themselves gods, therefore was death imposed upon him... Said R. Jonathan: If so, He should have decreed death on the wicked, but not on the righteous! (The reason, however, was) to prevent the wicked from presenting a hypocritical appearance of repentance — that they should not say: Do not the righteous live only because they lay up precepts and good deeds? Let us, too, lay up precepts and good deeds! Their action will thus be insincere.'[27] It was not Adam's sin that brought death to the generations that succeeded him, but, on the contrary, because of those generations that would proclaim themselves gods was the penalty of death inflicted on Adam. If there remained the slightest doubt that not just Nebuchadnezzar and Hiram alone were meant, R. Jonathan proceeds to explain not the death of the wicked generally, but that of the wicked who know how to store up precepts and good deeds insincerely. In this homily the position is completely reversed. Not through 'the obedience of one' shall the many be redeemed from sin and death, caused by the first man; on the contrary, death was decreed upon Adam for fear of the faith preached by Paul.

This polemical homily, like all the dicta and various expositions cited so far, is based on the premise that death — and certainly untimely death — is a punishment,[28] and consequently a negative phenomenon. The view of R. Me'ir is an exception. The very style of its transmission by one of the great Haggadists among the Palestinian Amoraim testifies to its unusual character. 'R. Samuel bar Naḥman said: I was riding on my grandfather's shoulder and going up from my town to Kefar Ḥanna by way of Bet Shean, when I heard R. Simeon b. R. Eleazar, as he was sitting and expounding in the name of R. Me'ir, say: ' "And, behold, it was very [מאד *mĕ'ōd*] good" — and, behold, death [מות *môt*] is good.'[29] Death is not an evil decree nor a punishment, but forms part of the order of the universe from the beginning. We do not know how R. Me'ir interpreted the story in Genesis iii, but it is not improbable that he regarded this episode as an account of the origin of death rather than an explanation of its cause. R. Me'ir's teaching influenced several Amoraim, and as we have seen (above, p. 279), they applied it to the question of Providence, developing for themselves a doctrine that removed the explanation of the existence of death from the act of the serpent and the sin of Adam. This separation in itself liberated them from the need to engage in a polemic with the adherents of the doctrine of original sin. But even an Amora like R. Joḥanan, who answered this contention in his own way (above, p. 427), independently explained the decree of death as follows: 'R. Joḥanan said: Why was death imposed upon the wicked? The reason is that as long as the wicked live, they vex the Holy One, blessed be He, as it is written "Ye have wearied the Lord with your words" (Malachi ii 17); but when they die they no longer vex the Holy One, blessed be He, as Scripture states "There the wicked cease from troubling" (Job iii 17) — there the wicked cease vexing the Holy One, blessed be He. Why was death inflicted upon the righteous? The reason is that as long as the righteous live, they wage war with their inclination; but when they die, they are at rest, as it is written "And there the weary are at rest" (*ibid.*) — (as if to say:) we have wearied ourselves enough!'[30]

Death is thus not the consequence of sin, but is linked to the doctrine of reward and punishment. R. Joḥanan, who posited free will for the individual, regarded the death of the righteous as a form of reward, since it brought to an end their exhausting struggle against their evil inclination. The death of the wicked causes them, in his view, to cease vexing God, but actually it implies punishment, since they derive satisfaction from their provocative actions. Resh Laqish, R. Joḥanan's colleague, related the subject of death to reward and punishment, only he holds that death comes to give twofold reward to the righteous and to inflict on the wicked twofold punishment: 'To give reward to the righteous, who did not deserve to know the taste of death, yet accepted it, hence (they are) promised "Therefore in their land they shall possess double" (Isaiah lxi 7); and to impose retribution on the wicked, for the righteous did not deserve to know the taste of death, yet because of them they accepted death, therefore (it is written) "and destroy them with double destruction" (Jeremiah xvii 18).'[31]

Death *per se* is not a punishment for sin. Although there was no need for the righteous to experience death, and they deserved to continue living, yet the implementation of the principle of reward and punishment — according to R. Akiba's[32] conception of the relationship between predestination and free will — necessitated imposing death on the righteous, too. The Amoraim R. Joḥanan and Resh Laqish, and likewise R. Samuel bar Naḥmani, differentiated between the death of the righteous and the death of others, following the view of R. Ḥiyya that the righteous are called living even in their death.[33]

All the sources that we cited, whether of the Tannaim or of the Amoraim, dealt with the explanation of the existence of death as a universal phenomenon either in confrontation with the story in Genesis, which they interpret and adapt, or by ignoring it. Only the Baraita concerning the 'Four who died because of the serpent', whose polemical and tendentious character we have discussed above (p. 427), postulated that each man's death is the result of his own sin. Allowing foı no exception, and motivated by a totally different purpose and ideological nexus, the Amora Rav Ammi, the disciple of R. Joḥanan and Resh Laqish, formulated the following principle: 'There is no death without sin, nor suffering without iniquity. There is no death without sin, for it is written "The soul that sinneth it shall die; the son shall not suffer for the iniquity of the father nor shall the father suffer for the iniquity of the son; the righteousness of the righteous shall be upon himself, and the wickedness of the wicked shall be upon himself" etc. (Ezekiel xviii 20). There is no suffering without iniquity, for it is stated "Then I will visit their transgression with the rod, and their iniquity with strokes" (Psalms lxxxix 33).'[34] The very linking of death and suffering to verses that are cited as proofs shows that Rav Ammi did not intend to explain the general phenomenon of death, its source and origin, but rather its place and function in the life of each individual person. It is connected with the question of the ways of expiating iniquities and the teaching of the Tannaim on this subject. An anonymous Mishna states: 'Death and the Day of Atonement effect atonement, if combined with repentance' (*M. Yoma* viii, 8). From R. Ishmael, who taught that 'There are four categories of persons with reference to atonement'[35] we learn: 'If a man committed transgressions involving premature death (*kārēt*) or execution by the court, and he repented, then repentance and the Day of Atonement suspend (the guilt), while suffering endured during the rest of the year purge it, for it is said "Then will I punish their transgression with the rod" (Psalms lxxxiv 33 [32]). If anyone desecrated the name of Heaven and repented, repentance has not the power to suspend (the iniquity), nor the Day of Atonement to atone (for it); but repentance and the Day of Atonement atone for a third (of the transgression), and sufferings atone for a third, while death, together with suffering, purges, and in relation to this it is stated "Surely this iniquity will not be forgiven you" (Isaiah xxii 14), which teaches that the day of death purges.' The Tanna R. Judah said that the day of death is like repentance, and the latter atones, like death, for (the non-fulfilment of) positive precepts.[36] R. Judah the Patriarch said: 'I might have thought that the day of death does not effect atonement. Since, however, Scripture declares "when I open your graves" (Ezekiel xxxvii 13), behold you learn that the day of death does effect atonement.'[37] The various categories of transgression for which also death atones, and the broad interpretation given to the concept of 'the desecration of the Divine Name' on the basis of a man's standing, function, and piety,[38] were able to lead Rav Ammi to the conclusion that 'There is no death without sin'. The following Midrash supports the interpretation that we have given to his statement:[39] 'R. Ḥiyya taught: Hypocrites are exposed on account of the desecration of the Divine Name, as it is said "Again, when a righteous man doth turn from righteousness and commit iniquity" (Ezekiel xviii 24). And why does the Holy One, blessed be He, set an evil path before him? In order to expose his deeds to the world, for (otherwise) if[40] anything should befall him because of his transgressions, people would complain against God's justice. Therefore the Holy One, blessed be He, exposes his deeds.' In expounding the Baraita, the Midrash based itself on the verse in Ezekiel, from which Rav Ammi learned that there is no death without sin, just as it sought support in the verse in Psalms, from which R. Ishmael deduced that suffering purges, in order to prove that 'There is no suffering without iniquity'. The connection between Rav Ammi's dictum and the view that attributed the power of atonement to death and to suffering is clear, but when did this view gain currency?

The doctrine of R. Ishmael, R. Judah, and Rabbi that death — even death without repentance — has the power to atone originated only after the Destruction, for with regard to the Temple period it is stated: 'And for all other prohibitions ordained in the Torah, be they light or grave... premature death and execution by the court, the scapegoat makes atonement' (*M. Shevu'ot* i, 6). In truth on the subject of 'the four categories of persons with reference to atonement', including the teaching 'that death purges', R. Joḥanan said: 'This is the view of R. Eleazar b. Azariah, R. Ishmael, and R. Akiba, but the Sages maintain that the scapegoat effects atonement.'[41]

We do not know who these Sages were, but since the Baraita on the categories of atonement was taught after the Destruction, for it contains no reference to the scapegoat, they must have held that even after the Destruction death does not replace the scapegoat as an atonement.

At the time when the Temple still stood, it was certainly unnecessary and inappropriate to regard death as an atonement. The scapegoat of the Day of Atonement apart, a man could bring sacrifices for his unwitting transgressions, and 'R. Eliezer said: A man may offer of his own free will a suspensive guilt-offering on any day and at any time that he pleases, and this is called "the guilt-offering of the pious". It was said of Bava b. Buṭi that he offered of his own free will a suspensive guilt-offering every day except on the day after the Day of Atonement. He said: "By the Temple! if only they permitted me I should bring one (even then), but they say to me: Wait until you can be in doubt" ' (*M. Keritot* vi, 3). Of Hillel it is told that 'Never in all his life did anyone commit trespass in connection with his burnt-offering. For he brought it unconsecrated to the Temple Court, consecrated it, laid his hand upon it, and slaughtered it.'[42] His disciple Rabban Joḥanan b. Zakkai said: 'Happy is the generation whose leader brings a sin-offering for his unwitting transgression.'[43] The offering of sacrifices was conjoined to the duty of confession;[44] and it was implied that the sacrificer was ready to repent, for the confession was the sign of penitence. With regard to the early Ḥasidim ['pious men'] R. Judah said: 'Seeing that the Holy One, blessed be He, does not allow an offence to be perpetrated by them, what did they do? They arose and made a free-will vow of naziriteship to the Omnipresent, so that they should be liable to bring a sin-offering to the Omnipresent.'[45] R. Nathan testified that R. Ishmael had written in his account book: 'Ishmael b. Elisha tilted the lamp on the Sabbath. When the Temple will be rebuilt, he will be liable to bring a sin-offering.'[46] The sacrifices only expiated iniquities between man and God, for which it was not in the power of an earthly court to impose punishment. Transgressions that were liable to punishment by a court were not atoned for by sacrifices, and only the penalty brought with it atonement for the sin. Those who were sentenced to death were told to make confession, 'For such is the way of those condemned to death to make confession, because every one that makes confession has a share in the world to come... and if he does not know to make confession, he is told: "Say, May my death be an atonement for all my iniquities" ' (*M. Sanhedrin* vi, 2). Similarly, it is stated regarding the penalty of lashes: 'Lashes are precious, for they atone for sins, as it is said: "according to [כדי *kĕdê*] the measure of his wickedness" — the lashes suffice [כדאי *kĕda'y*] to atone for his wickedness.'[47] The Sages even said 'For all who are liable to extinction, if they have received lashes, are exempted from their penalty of extinction.'[48]

When the court's right to impose the death-penalty was abrogated and the Temple was destroyed, involving the abolition of the sacrifices, a sense of despair and the feeling that Israel had been deprived of the possibility of atonement prevailed. 'It once happened that Rabban Joḥanan b. Zakkai was leaving Jerusalem and R. Joshua was walking behind him, when the latter saw the Temple in ruins. Said R. Joshua: "Woe to us that this is in ruins — the place where the sins of Israel were expiated!" Rabban Joḥanan b. Zakkai replied: "My son, be not grieved, we have a means of atonement that is commensurate with it. Which is this? It is the performance of acts of lovingkindness, as it is said 'For I desire loving kindness and not sacrifice' " (Hosea vi 6).'[49]

In the spirit of this teaching of Rabban Joḥanan b. Zakkai, the Tanna R. Eliezer b. Jacob said: 'Whoever entertains a scholar in his house and lets him enjoy his possessions it is accounted to him by Scripture as if he had offered up the daily burnt-offerings' (*T.B. Berakhot* 10b). The atonement of sins depends on the sacrifice of the daily burnt-offerings, and the Scripture 'he-lambs [כבשים *kĕvāśîm*] of the first year' (Numbers xxviii 3) was expounded by the School of Shammai thus: '*Kĕvāśîm* (are so called) because they suppress [כובשים *kôvĕshîm*] the sins of Israel.' The School of Hillel said: '*Kĕvāśîm* (are so called) because they cleanse [כובסין *kôvĕsîn*] the sins of Israel.'[50] The fasts that multiplied after the Destruction also assumed the character of a surrogate and replacement for the atonement effected by the sacrifices. This fact found concrete expression in the prayer attributed to Rav Sheshet: 'Sovereign of the universe, it is known to Thee that when the Temple was in existence, if a man sinned he would bring a sacrifice, of which only the fat and the blood were offered up, and he would be granted atonement. Now I have observed a fast and my own fat and blood have been diminished.

May it be Thy will that my diminished fat and blood be accounted as though I had offered them up before Thee on the altar, and do Thou show me favour.'[51]

In the light of the preceding dicta it is not surprising that after the abrogation of the death-penalty at the hands of the court, the power of atonement and purging was attributed also to death from natural causes. Just as execution by court decree is preceded by confession, so, R. Nathan also said, 'All who are dying require confession.'[52] But Rabbi and R. Judah were of the opinion that death, even without repentance, atones for sins that the burnt-offering expiated and for people who are endowed with knowledge of the Torah and good deeds.[53]

The Tannaim who ascribed to death and suffering the power to purge and expiate did not necessarily say that there was no death without sin. For we have seen that there were 'the early Ḥasidim', who offered up sin-offerings and brought each day a suspensive guilt-offering. In his dictum 'There is no death without sin, and no suffering without iniquity' R. Ammi took up a very extreme position, and indeed in our treatment of the subject of Divine providence and the reasons of the precepts[54] we noted that many Sages were not in agreement with his apodictic statement. Moreover, the Talmudic discussion in which his saying is cited concludes with the words: 'This proves that there is death without sin and suffering without iniquity, and Rav Ammi stands refuted.'[55] Nevertheless his saying is not an isolated view. Another, anonymous, Talmudic passage propounds the question whether '(the purpose of) burial is to save (the dead) from disgrace (so that he should not be made contemptible in the sight of those who see him dead and putrefying and disintegrating — Rashi) or to effect atonement (so that he should win atonement by the interment, for he is lowered and humbled in the recesses of the earth)', and the answer is — for atonement. To the query 'Do the righteous need atonement?' the Sages reply 'Yea! for it is written "There is not a righteous man upon earth, that doeth good, and sinneth not" (Ecclesiastes vii 20).'[56] This pessimistic view of Ecclesiastes, which was also shared by Job's friends, was approved by Rav Ammi, by the author of the interpretation of the Baraita of R. Ḥiyya (above, p. 432), and by the Talmudic passage that we have just cited. Death and suffering prove that the man who was deemed to be righteous was not really so. The aim of this approach is to demonstrate clearly and unequivocally that the world is ruled according to righteousness and justice. Obviously this view excludes any idea of inherited sin, such as might have been inferred from the story of Adam.

II. Reward and Punishment

Although it was seen that the Sages did not refrain from discussing the subject of sin and death and the teachings flowing therefrom, such opinions did not determine their views and their main dicta on the theme of sin and its punishment. The fundamental reward for the observance of the commandments and the punishment for transgressions in a man's lifetime are stated again and again in the Torah and reiterated in the Prophets and Hagiographa. If a Jew but heard the Decalogue, there would be imprinted on his memory the verses 'visiting the iniquity of the fathers upon the children of the third and fourth generation of those who hate Me, but showing steadfast love to thousands of those who love Me and keep My commandments'. If he recited the *Shĕma*ᶜ, he learned to link the blessing of the land and its produce, his own length of days and that of his children, with the keeping of the Lord's precepts, and the curse of dearth and destruction with transgressing His words. Long historical experience, with all its catastrophes and calamities, taught the Jew to evaluate the passages of rebuke in Leviticus and Deuteronomy, not as a mere threat, but as warnings that were translated into reality, and to realize that not merely the threnodies of Lamentations bore testimony thereto.

The objections and questions bound up with the problems of the relationship between the actions of the individual and collective retribution, or between the sins of the fathers and the punishment of the children, did not disappear when the belief in the judgement of the souls after death[57] and the doctrine of requital connected therewith took root, for this belief did not eradicate or nullify the view that a man is brought to judgement for the things he does in this world even in his lifetime. Thus it was taught: 'If a man says give this *sela*ᶜ to charity in order that my children may live, or in order that I may merit thereby life in the world to come, he is a wholly righteous man.'[58] This Baraita reflects a widespread belief among the people, which the Sages continued to strengthen and even to utilize in urging the observance of the commandments and in denouncing transgressors (see above, p. 349). When he stated 'And faithful is the Master of your work, who will pay you the wages of your toil; and know that the giving of the reward to the righteous is in the time to come', R. Ṭarfon made the reward in this world precede that in the world to come,[59] only the account is not concluded upon death. This thought R. Akiba expressed figuratively: 'The ledger lies open, and the hand writes, and whosoever wishes to borrow may come and borrow, but the collectors regularly make their daily rounds, and exact payment from a man whether with or without his knowledge, and they have that whereon they can rely in their demand, and the judgement is a judgement of truth, and everything is prepared for the feast.'

The collectors are the tribulations and sufferings. Sometimes a man knows why they come upon him, that is to say, he realizes that they are a punishment for his actions; but at times they befall him without his being able to justify them, and then he remembers that everything is prepared for reward in the world to come.[60] The statements were made not only in a generalized form, but even the calamities that occur to people as punishments for given transgressions were expressly specified. For instance it is taught in the Mishna: 'For three transgressions women die in childbirth: for negligence in observing the laws of menstruation, the dough-offering, and the kindling of the (Sabbath) lamp.'[61] The Tanna R. Nathan added: 'Also on account of (their) vows women die in childbirth.'[62] To this sin R. Eleazar the son of R. Simeon b. Yoḥai — followed also by R. Judah the Patriarch[63] — ascribed another tribulation, no less common than the death of women in childbirth, namely the death of young children. R. Nehemiah said: 'For the sin of causeless hatred there is great contention in a man's house and his wife miscarries, and a man's sons and daughters die when they are young.' In an anonymous Baraita causeless hatred is considered to produce disease of the bowels. 'It is taught there are four signs: the sign of transgression is dropsy; the sign of causeless hatred is jaundice; the sign of conceit is poverty; the sign of slander is cramp [or, diphtheria].'[64] Within the framework of the collective retribution mentioned in the reproofs of the Torah and the Prophets are also specified the sins that bring upon the people punishments like war, exile, plagues, and famine. The Tannaim widened the scope, classified and adapted the punishments to the sins, and taught in the Mishna 'Seven kinds of penalties come to the world for seven chief transgressions.'[65] The prevailing rule, both in personal and collective retribution in the existing world, is that of 'measure for measure'. The Mishna teaches: 'With what measure a man metes it shall be meted out to him again: she prinked herself for transgression — the Omnipresent disgraced her; she laid herself bare for transgression — the Omnipresent likewise laid her bare...; Samson went after (the desire of) his eyes — therefore the Philistines put out his eyes...; Absalom gloried [ניתנוּוה *nitnawwā*] in his hair — consequently he was hanged by his hair... So, too, in the case of good deeds: Miriam waited for Moses one hour... therefore Israel tarried for her seven days in the wilderness...; Joseph was privileged to bury his father, and none of his brothers was greater than he... Whom have we greater than Moses? Thus only the Omnipresent occupied Himself with him...'[66] This principle the Sages even introduced into their interpretation of sections of the Torah where actually both the sin and the punishment are expressly stated, such as the story of the generation of the Flood and that of the people of Sodom, and thus they expounded in a Baraita:[67] 'The men of the Flood waxed haughty only on account of the good (they enjoyed), as it is said "Their houses are safe from fear, neither is the rod of God upon them. Their bull gendereth, and faileth not... They send forth their little ones like a flock... They take the timbrel and the harp... They spend their days in prosperity, and their years in pleasures." It is this that brought it about that "They said to God: 'Depart from us... What is the Almighty that we should serve Him? And what profit should we have, if we pray unto Him?' " (Job xxi 9–15). They said "Do we need Him for aught but rain? Lo, we have rivers from which we supply our needs, and we do not require Him", as it is said "But there went up a mist from the earth, and watered the whole face of the ground" (Genesis ii 6)... Said the Holy One, blessed be He, to them: "Because of the very good that I vouchsafed you, you wax proud before Me? I shall punish you", as it is said "For in seven days I will send rain upon the earth" etc. (*ibid.* vii 4).

The men of Sodom waxed proud only on account of the good (they enjoyed). What does Scripture state of Sodom? "As for the earth, out of it cometh bread; and under it it is burned up as it were with fire. The stones of it are the place of sapphires... That path no bird of prey knoweth, and the falcon's eye hath not seen it" (Job xxviii 5–6). They argued: "Since silver and gold come forth from our lands, we do not require people to come to us, for they come only to deprive us of our possessions." Said the Omnipresent to them: "On account of the good that I lavished upon you, do you cause the foot (of the traveller) to be forgotten from among you? I shall, therefore, cause you to be forgotten from the world", as it is said "They are forgotten by travellers, they hang afar from men, they swing to and fro" (*ibid.* *v.* 4); "In the thought of one who is at ease there is contempt for misfortune; it is ready for those whose feet slip. The tents of robbers are at peace, and those who provoke God are secure..." (*ibid.* xii 5–6); it is this that brought it upon them: "in that which God brought into their [literally 'his'] hand" (*ibid.*) ....' The homilist cites the words of Job, wherein he argues and shows that the wicked are at ease and spend their days in prosperity, and it is just these verses that the expositor expounds with reference to the men of the generation of the Flood and the men of Sodom and Gomorrah, in order to refute the argument that 'the wicked man prospers'.

Numerous dicta, aphorisms, stories, and parables were added by the Sages to those already found in the Bible in order to prove that the principle of 'measure for measure' was not abolished.[68] Indeed the weighing and measuring of details, down to the minutest particulars, of actions and their consequences became an unfailing source of expository-poetic enjoyment. But just as the Halakha, which ordained that 'an eye for an eye connotes monetary damages', did not diminish the sense of justice informing the earthly court's ruling, so the Sages were not concerned with the extent to which human actions and Heaven's punishment truly correspond, but with the actual presence of 'reward and punishment' in the Divine administration of the world.

We shall later revert to the problems and difficulties aroused by the belief in reward and punishment in this world, when the Sages came to compare it with other cardinal doctrines and principles. But undoubtedly this belief was so widespread and had so many adherents that it could not be ignored even by those Sages who personally were inclined to transfer the entire subject of reward and punishment to the hereafter, or had reached the conclusion that the precept was its own reward and transgression its own punishment (see above, p. 346). How deeply rooted was the belief in reward and punishment in this world may be learnt from certain tales of a distinctly folk character, although the date of their origin is difficult to determine. But their very occurrence in ancient Midrashic collections and their numerous versions show that they were known to wide circles. We shall cite, as an example, a story taken from *Leviticus Rabba*:[69] ' "For according to the work of a man He will requite him, and according to his ways He will make it befall him" (Job xxxiv 11): There was once a man who had two sons. One of them made many contributions to charity, but the other gave no alms at all. The son who was very charitable sold his house and all that he possessed in order to give to charity. Once on the Day of הושענא *Hôshaʿnāʾ* [Seventh day of Tabernacles, now called הושענא רבא *Hôshaʿnāʾ Rabbāʾ*] his wife gave him ten fallera [small coins] and said to him "Go, buy something in the market for your children." As soon as he went to the market place, the charity collectors met him. Said they: "Behold, the philanthropist is coming." They then requested him: "Give your share in this good deed [*miṣwā*], for we wish to buy a garment for the orphan girl so-and-so." Thereupon he took the money (his wife had given him) and gave it to them. But he felt ashamed to go (back) to his wife. What did he do? He went to the Synagogue, where he saw some of the citrons carried by the children on the Day of *Hôshaʿnā*... He took some of them and filled his sack and sailed away on the Great Sea [the Mediterranean], until he reached a distant land [literally 'a country overseas']. When he arrived there, it was found that the king was suffering from a bowel complaint. His physicians said to him: "If you had one of the citrons that the Jews carry on the Day of *Hôshaʿnāʾ*, you could eat it and be cured." Messengers forthwith went and searched throughout the country and in all the ships, but found none. They went, however, and found the (charitable) man lying on his sack. Thereupon they said to him: "Have you aught to sell?" He replied: "I am a poor man, and possess nothing." They then opened his sack and found it full of citrons. They asked him: "Whence are these?" He answered: "They are citrons that Jews use during Divine service on the Day of *Hôsha'nā'*." So they brought him before the king... who ate of the citrons and was cured. He [the king] then ordered: "Empty his sack and fill it with denars"... Then the king said to him: "Make any request, and I shall fulfil it." He replied: "I request that my possessions be restored to me and that all the people come forth to meet me." His request was fulfilled. When he reached the harbour, the herald went before him and all the people went forth to meet him, and his brother and his sons also went out to meet him. When they crossed the river, the current swept them away and carried them off. It thus came about that when he entered his home, he took possession of his own property and inherited that of his brother, in fulfilment of the Scripture "For according to the work of a man He will requite him" etc.' Stories of this kind and many parables about the relationship between a master and his workmen and hired labourers[70] were of help to preachers and teachers in encouraging and inspiring their listeners to observe the commandments and eschew sin and transgression. However, as against such stories the homilists easily found, without doubt, examples and episodes testifying to the success of the wicked and transgressors and to the sufferings and afflictions of those who kept the precepts and feared the Lord. Nor did the Sages confine their questioning to the two commandments whose reward is expressly mentioned in the Torah; thus it is argued in the Talmud 'Now if his father said to him "Go up to the loft and fetch me some pigeons", and he ascended to the loft and let the dam go and took the young, and on his return he fell and died, where is his happy life and where his length of days?'[71] Although they conjoined with the reward in this world the reward of the world that is wholly good, and with the punishments of this world also the punishments of the hereafter, yet they did not intend to minimize the former on account of the latter. At any rate this was not the intention of those scholars who taught in the Mishna: 'These are the things whose fruits [מפירותיהן *mi-pêrôtêhen*] a man enjoys in this world, while the capital is laid up [מתקיימת *mitqayyemet*] for him in the world to come',[72] and it was certainly not in the mind of those who urged the observance of the precepts on the basis of the promised reward. Especially difficult was their explanation of the afflictions and sufferings that befell righteous men for no particular reason. The argument that these righteous people were due to receive compensation after death was treated with derision in various quarters, as may be seen from the remarks put into the mouth of the Sadducees, who said: 'The Pharisees have a tradition that they afflict themselves in this world, and have nought in the world to come.'[73]

The conventional 'doctrine of reward and punishment' underwent a grave crisis in the period of Hadrian's religious persecution, which led to a change in Rabbinic thinking on theodicy. It was not the tribulation that came upon the righteous from a higher power that called for an explanation, nor the bitter outcry against the troubles that were equally the lot of the wicked and the righteous that demanded an answer, but the fact that the resolve to observe the commandments was itself the cause of death and suffering!

However, there is not wanting the stereotyped explanation that views the tortures and sufferings of the (ten) martyrs as punishment for miniscule transgressions: 'When R. Ishmael and R. Simeon went forth to execution, R. Simeon said to R. Ishmael: "Master, my heart is ill at ease, because I know not the cause of my execution." Said R. Ishmael to R. Simeon "Did it never happen that a man came to you for judgement, or to ask you a law, and you kept him waiting until you finished sipping your drink, or you tied your sandal, or put on your cloak? But the Torah declared 'If thou delay [usually rendered 'afflict'] in any wise', and the principle applies irrespective of whether the delay is long or short." Thereupon he replied "Master, you have comforted me." '[74] Clearly this source was influenced by the Mishna cited earlier (p. 438) 'The sword comes to the world on account of the delay of justice.' In a later source[75] the Rabbis did not wish to attribute so grave a sin to Rabban Simeon b. Gamaliel, and reacting to this explanation, R. Simeon said: 'The attendant was instructed that whether I was sleeping or dining, no one should be prevented from entering.' R. Ishmael then raised another possibility: ' "Perhaps when you were sitting and expounding on the Temple Mount and all the multitudes of Israel were sitting before you, you grew arrogant?" He replied: "Ishmael, my brother, a man must be prepared to accept his affliction." '

It seems, however, that these explanations do not emanate from the generation that suffered the persecution; at all events they did not satisfy R. Akiba.[76] He and his colleagues were not required to commit transgressions that made them liable to the death penalty, and concerning which it was ordained that 'a man should let himself be killed rather than transgress'. With regard to persecutive decrees of this nature it could be said that the people on whom they were imposed 'were liable to death at the hands of heaven',[77] and thus they attained their punishment and atonement and share in the world to come. But R. Akiba and those of his colleagues — but not all of them[78] — who adopted his attitude observed the commandments[79] demonstratively and in defiance of the ruling power. 'Once when R. Akiba was being tried before the wicked Tineius Rufus, the time arrived for reading the *Shĕma'* and he began to recite it joyfully. Said he [T. Rufus]: "Old man, old man, either you are a magician or you bear pain with contumacy." R. Akiba answered him: "Woe to that man! I am neither a magician nor do I bear pain with contumacy; but all my life I have read this verse: 'And thou shalt love the Lord thy God with all thy heart and with all thy soul [i.e. life] and with all thy might [i.e. wealth].' (Truly) I loved Him with all my heart, and I loved Him with all my wealth, but I was never called upon to face the ordeal of 'with all my soul'. Now that I experience (the test of) 'with all my soul', and the time for reading the *Shĕma'* has arrived, and I have not thrust it aside, therefore I am reciting the *Shĕma'* with joy." '[80] This acceptance of suffering is voided of its reason and significance, if it is explained as a punishment for any sin. Indeed it is told that 'When R. Akiba was killed at Caesarea, the news reached R. Judah b. Bava and R. Ḥananiah b. Teradion. They arose and girded their loins with sackloth and rent their garments and cried: "Oh, our brethren, hearken unto us! R. Akiba was not slain for robbery, or for not toiling in the Torah with all his strength. R. Akiba was slain only as a sign, as it is said 'Thus shall Ezekiel be to you for a sign; according to all that... then ye will know that I am the Lord God' (Ezekiel xxiv 24)".'[81] This doctrine of R. Akiba, which regards the acceptance of suffering with love as the highest goal of him that serves the Lord, performing the commandments in the spirit of 'with all thy soul — even though He takes thy soul', has no parallel[82] except in the conduct and words of Socrates before his death[83]; but the difference in the manner of their execution should be noted. R. Akiba, and his disciples who followed in his footsteps,[84] not only saved, by their acts, Israel's Torah and the observance of its precepts, but also radically transformed the evaluation of the relationship between the troubles and tribulations that befall the individual or the community, and sin and iniquity.

III. The Reason for Suffering

The change that occurred in R. Akiba's own outlook is reflected in a twofold tradition concerning R. Akiba's visit to the house of his teacher R. Eliezer, who was on his death bed. In one tradition it is stated: 'When R. Eliezer fell ill, his disciples came to visit him. Said he to them: "There is fierce wrath in the world." They burst into tears, but R. Akiba began to laugh. Said they to him: "Why do you laugh?" He countered: "And why do you weep?" They answered: "Shall we not weep when a 'scroll of the law' lies in distress?" R. Akiba rejoined: "For this very reason I am laughing. So long as I saw that my master's wine did not go sour, nor was his flax smitten, nor did his oil become rancid, nor did his honey ferment, I thought: Perchance my master has received his reward in this world. But now that I see my master in distress, I rejoice." Thereupon R. Eliezer asked him: "Akiba, have I omitted aught of the whole Torah?" He answered: "You have taught us, O our master, 'For there is not a righteous man upon earth that doeth good and sinneth not.' " '[85] Here R. Akiba still cleaves to the view accepted by himself and his teachers that we must not rebel against suffering, for no man is without sin. In the parallel account[86] R. Akiba's colleagues say 'whereas my master is for this world and the world to come'. But R. Akiba observed 'Suffering is precious'. The author of the story describes the surprise of R. Eliezer, who said: 'Support me that I may hear the words of my disciple R. Akiba, who has declared "Suffering is precious". He then asked him "Akiba, how do you know this...?" '[87] Although the period of evil decrees and religious persecution came to a close, yet the example set by R. Akiba, demonstrating that we are enjoined to die for the sanctification of the Name, remained in the Halakha for generations, and his watchword 'Suffering is precious' was examined again and again by his disciples,

R. Eliezer b. Jacob, R. Me'ir, R. Nehemiah, and R. Simeon b. Yoḥai, in order to find therein a justification and explanation for the normal sufferings that come to a person even in times free of evil decrees and religious persecution. 'R. Eliezer b. Jacob said: Scripture declares: "My son, do not despise the Lord's discipline" etc. Why? "For the Lord reproveth him whom He loveth" (Proverbs iii 11–12). You say so? Come and see, what was it that enabled the son to obtain his father's forgiveness? You must say, suffering... R. Simeon b. Yoḥai said: "Suffering is precious, for three good gifts were given to Israel... and they were granted only through suffering, to wit, the Torah, the Land of Israel, and the world to come... Which then is the way that leads a man to life in the world to come? You must say "It is suffering." '[88] Also in the School of Ishmael it was taught: 'Anyone who for forty days has known no suffering has received his reward in this world.'[89] Just as R. Akiba's martyrdom exerted a historic influence, and his disciple R. Eliezer b. Jacob was the first of the Sages to mention that Abraham was thrown into the fiery furnace,[90] so, too, an anonymous Tanna adorned the first believer with the merit of suffering as a sign of love: 'Before the advent of our father Abraham (so to speak), the Omnipresent judged the world ruthlessly: When the men of the generation of the Flood sinned, He drowned them with storm winds upon the face of the waters; when the men of the Tower (of Babel) sinned, He scattered them from one end of the world to the other; when the men of Sodom sinned, He swept them away with fire and brimstone. But when Abraham our father came into the world, he was vouchsafed suffering, which gradually began to manifest itself, as it is said: "Now there was a famine in the land, and Abram went down to Egypt" (Genesis xii 10). Should you ask: Why does suffering come? On account of (God's) love for Israel, (as it is said): "He fixed the bounds of the peoples according to the number of the sons of Israel (Deuteronomy xxxii 8)." '[91]

Even the view that corporate suffering was a sign of the love of God for His people and its righteous men, which found expression in the teaching of R. Eliezer b. R. Zadok — 'The Holy One, blessed be He, inflicts suffering upon the righteous in this world in order that they may have an inheritance in the world to come'[92] — did not reduce the tension and self-scrutiny and search for sins. At a time when the means of livelihood were scarce and the Sages earned a living with difficulty, R. Simeon b. Eleazar said:[93] 'Have you ever seen a wild beast or a bird practising a craft? Yet they sustain themselves without distress. Now they were created only to serve me, and I was created to serve my Maker; how much more ought not I to sustain myself without worry? But I have done wrong and have (thus) forfeited my sustenance.'[94] However, this searching and delving is a matter for the individual who suffers and is being chastised, not for anyone else. Another person transgresses the prohibition 'Ye shall not wrong one another; but thou shalt fear thy God', if, seeing that his fellow is subjected to disease and pain and buries his children, he says to him 'As Job's companions said to him: "Is not thy fear of God thy confidence, and thy hope the integrity of the ways? Remember, I pray thee, who ever perished, being innocent? Or where were the upright cut off?" (Job iv 6–7).'[95]

From the close of the Tannaitic period we find stories about Sages who invited suffering to come upon them for fear lest they were guilty of any transgression. But there were some who were accustomed to do this, even when they had no such fear,[96] like the pious men of old who wished to offer a guilt-offering even when it was obvious to them that they had committed no transgression (above, p. 433). The earliest Amoraim distinguished between two kinds of suffering: suffering that is not due to iniquity is suffering of love, but visitations due to sin are not chastenings of love. Signs indicative of the suffering of love were transmitted in the name of R. Joḥanan, namely afflictions that do not involve interruption of Torah study or of prayer.[97] On the other hand the same Amora said: 'If anyone is able to occupy himself with the (study of the) Torah and fails to do so, the Holy One, blessed be He, inflicts ugly sufferings upon him.' Similar sayings were transmitted in the name of the Babylonian Amoraim Rav Huna,[98] Rav Ḥisda, and Rava. In the name of the last two it is reported: 'If a man becomes subject to suffering, let him search his deeds, as it is said "Let us search and try our ways, and return to the Lord!" (Lamentations iii 40). If he searched and found no fault, let him attribute it to neglect of the study of the Torah, as it is said "Blessed is the man whom Thou dost chasten, O Lord, and whom thou dost teach out of Thy law" (Psalms xciv 12). If he did so and (still) found no fault, it is assuredly suffering of love, as it is said "For the Lord reproveth him whom He loveth" (Proverbs iii 12).' Those who accept suffering lovingly and consciously bring salvation to the world.[99] There were also Sages who did not wait for the coming of suffering, but performed acts of self-affliction and mortification. In conformity with the teaching of R. Akiba that 'vows are a fence for abstinence'[1] they made vows to restrain themselves and withdraw from the pleasures of the world, and to spur themselves to observe the precepts. Thus R. Joḥanan said: 'I vow to fast until I finish my chapter, (or) until I complete my Scriptural section.'[2] But most fasts were linked to the fear of sin. R. Ḥiyya bar Ashi, the disciple of Rav, who practised extreme abstinence and fought against his inclination, was given to fasting all his life until he died thereof.[3] Even the fasts attributed in Amoraic sources to Tannaim on account of slight transgressions, which are alluded to in Tannaitic texts, point to the tendency that prevailed in the time of the Amoraim. Once R. Joshua said: 'I am ashamed of your words, O School of Shammai'; but when their reason was explained to him by one of the Shammaite disciples, 'R. Joshua retracted and taught according to the explanation of the disciple. He said: "I crave your forgiveness, O bones of the School of Shammai." ' But the Babylonian Amoraim were not content with this; they were not satisfied until they had asserted that R. Joshua prostrated himself[4] upon the graves of the School of Shammai, adding that 'all his days his teeth were blackened on account of his fasts'. The same thing was told of R. Simeon, because it was considered that when he said 'And until the day of his death R. Akiba used to declare it unclean, but whether he retracted after his death, I do not know' he was disrespectful to his teacher.[5] Similarly the Amora R. Hananiah said of R. Eleazar b. Azariah 'His teeth became black on account of the fasts', which he observed because he had acted in a certain matter contrary to the will of the Sages.[6]

Alongside this tradition concerning the last of the Tannaim and the Amoraim, who invited suffering and fasted much, there existed a parallel tradition voicing opposition to the practice of mortification and self-affliction, irrespective of its motives.[7] The reasons for this opposition were many and varied[8]; we shall mention only those that give expression to the antithesis between the Halakha and asceticism.

In the name of Resh Laqish it is stated: 'A scholar may not practise fasting, because he diminishes the work of heaven'[9], and Rav Dimi said in the name of R. Isaac with reference, in general, to those who make vows: 'You are not content with what the Torah has forbidden you, but you seek to augment the things prohibited to you.'[10] The opponents of asceticism also adopted a different attitude to suffering. In a Baraita it is taught[11] that if a man's body is racked with pain, his life is no life. So that it should not be said that they had received their reward in this world, these scholars were prepared to fulfil the duty of suffering at a minimum. According to Rava 'Even if a man put his hand in his pocket to take out three (coins) and he took out only two' (this is accounted suffering).'[12] As a means, too, of purging sins Rava saw no need for suffering; instead he prayed: 'And the sins that I have committed wipe out in Thine abundant mercies, but not through suffering and evil diseases.'[13] By appealing to the Lord's mercies to purge his sins, Rava actually implied that strictly he deserved to be subjected to suffering and evil diseases, and his view is thus not different from that of other Amoraim who said 'Is then the Holy One, blessed be He, suspect of dispensing justice unjustly?'[14]

IV. The Attribute of Justice and the Attribute of Mercy

Whence and when did the idea originate that it was possible to request, as did Rava, for iniquities to be purged by the Lord's mercies? Moses, it is true, proclaimed 'The Lord, the Lord, a God merciful and gracious, slow to anger... forgiving iniquity and transgression and sin', but he continued 'but who will by no means clear the guilty, visiting the iniquity of the fathers upon the children and the children's children, to the third and the fourth generation' (Exodus xxxiv 5–6). The psalmist (ciii 7–13) explained Moses' words as follows: 'He made known His ways to Moses... The Lord is merciful and gracious... He does not deal with us according to our sins... For as the heavens are high above the earth, so great is His steadfast love toward those who fear Him... As a father pities his children, so the Lord pities those who fear Him.' Not the complete purging of iniquities without any punishment is promised here, but the diminution of the sin, so that the retribution should not be according to the full measure of the sin; furthermore, both the steadfast love and the mercies are promised only to those who fear Him but have stumbled. Even he who prays 'But He, being full of compassion, forgiveth iniquity'... concludes by saying 'and doth not stir up all His wrath' (Psalms lxxviii 38). The Lord's compassion only diminishes the severity of the sentence, but does not annul it or replace it.

It seems that in the Book of Jonah, too, the outlook is not different. The people of Nineveh repented after Jonah's proclamation, nevertheless they expressed themselves with doubt; they said in their prayer 'Who knoweth, God may yet repent and turn from His fierce anger, so that we perish not.' Indeed it is then stated 'When God saw... how they turned from their evil way, God repented of the evil.' Regarding this episode Jonah declares 'For I knew that Thou art a gracious God, and compassionate, long-suffering, and abundant in mercy, and repentest Thee of the evil' (Jonah iii 9; iv 2), that is to say, he cites the words of Moses in the sense that the nullification of the punishment on account of the penitence of the sinner is an act of grace and compassion on the part of God. Also in the seventh benediction in the order of service for fast days — 'May He that answered David and his son Solomon in Jerusalem answer you and hearken to the voice of your crying this day. Blessed art Thou, O Lord, that hast compassion on the land'[15] — compassion follows only after repentance and acts of atonement, as is shown by the reference to David's act after the famine that visited the land (II Samuel xxi) and to Solomon's prayer (I Kings viii 36–39). The fulfilment of God's promise is also considered to reveal His mercy, and when R. Eliezer was asked when prayers should be offered up for the rains to cease, he replied: 'When a man should stand on the top of Ophel and dabble his feet in the brook of Kidron; but we are sure that the All-Merciful will not bring a flood upon the world. What is the reason? "For this is as the waters of Noah unto Me; for as I have sworn that the waters of Noah should no more go over the earth." '[16] The fact that God refrains, as he has sworn, from bringing another flood upon the world makes Him 'All-Merciful'. This very oath, like the readiness to take back the penitent, are examples of His mercies.

Another approach, it might seem, finds expression in the prayer of Onias the Circle-maker, who 'drew a circle and stood within it and said... "I swear by Thy great name that I will not stir hence until

Thou hast compassion on Thy children" ' (*M. Ta'anit* iii, 8). Onias asks for compassion irrespective of whether those whom he represents deserve it, according to law and justice, or not. He gives the following reason for his request: 'Thy children have turned their faces to me, for that I am like a son of the house before Thee.' Thus Onias, too, does not request compassion without any justification; his right as a 'son of the house' gives him the courage to ask for the exercise of mercy. Before, however, we elucidate the meaning of the term 'attribute of mercy', we must consider the pair of concepts, the 'attribute of retribution' and the 'attribute of good', which are current in Tannaitic literature. The actual expression 'attribute' [מידה *middā*, literally 'measure'] is linked, as we have seen (above, p. 439), to justice and law. The judge metes out the measure of punishment or the measure of good entirely in accordance with the acts of the person judged.[17] Although it is stated that the attribute of good exceeds that of retribution, yet the proof adduced for this fact shows that this surplus is also comprised within the confines of justice. 'The attribute of good exceeds that of retribution five hundred times. In the case of the attribute of retribution Scripture declares "visiting the iniquity of the fathers upon the children..."; in the case of the attribute of good it is stated "and showing mercy unto the thousandth generation". It is thus seen that the attribute of good exceeds that of retribution.'[18] But this 'mercy unto the thousandth generation' is promised in the verse only to 'them that love Me and keep my commandments'. This homily is old, for its motif was already used by R. Eleazar of Modi'im in the exposition he delivered before R. Ṭarfon and the elders.[19] Indeed there are numerous Midrashic interpretations that seek to prove that the Lord is wont to enlarge the measure of good due to a person.[20] Among these homilies there is one that confirms the construction we put on Onias' prayer.

On the verse 'If thou afflict them in any wise, and they cry out to Me, I will surely hear their cry' (Exodus xxii 22) the Sages comment 'Now if in the case of the attribute of retribution, which is scant, this is what happens when an individual cries out against the many, how much more so does it apply to the attribute of good, which is abundant, when many pray for an individual!'[21] This argument from minor to major also applies where 'an individual prays for many'.

The use of the correlatives 'attribute of retribution — attribute of good' points to the extrusion of 'compassion' [or 'mercy'] from the sphere of justice, although we found it still included therein in Scriptural passages and even in ancient translations and Rabbinic sources.[22] The attribute of justice — including the elements of beneficence and punishment inherent in it — was completely separated from that of compassion in heavenly as in human judgements.[23] Also the word *middā* changed its signification. The Sages no longer speak of 'a measure' meted out by the judge or ruler; it becomes an epithet of God, which may be used as a Divine designation in place of His name.[24] The attribute of justice and the attribute of compassion are found alongside each other, and apparently are transformed into self-subsistent powers, into hypostases, in the imagery of the homilies and dicta of the Amoraim.[25] They are careful, however, not to provide any semblance of support to those who believe in dual deities. The following homily was directed against this doctrine: ' "The Lord is a man of war" — why is this stated? Because He revealed Himself at the sea as a mighty man who wages war, as it is said "The Lord is a man of war", (and) He revealed Himself at Sinai as an old man full of compassion, as it is said "And they saw the God of Israel" (Exodus xxiv 10)... so as not to provide an excuse for the nations of the world to claim that there are two divine powers. But "The Lord is a man of war; the Lord is His name..." '[26] Whence would the nations of the world have derived this pretext? What compelled the homilist to declare that the Lord manifested himself in various forms? Apparently the homilist already bases himself on the rule that 'Where יהוה YHWH ['Lord'] occurs it refers to the attribute of compassion, as it is said "The Lord, a God compassionate and gracious"; (but) wherever אלהים *'Ĕlōhîm* ['God'] is mentioned, the reference is to the attribute of justice, as it is stated "The case of both parties shall come before God", and Scripture further enjoins "Thou shall not revile God" (*ibid.* xxii 27–28).'[27] This postulate that each Name refers to one of the attributes seeks to refute the view that the two Names allude to more than one God.[28] But even the transformation of the Names to attributes did not altogether close the door to those who were searching for indications of the belief in dualism. Now the Tanna who delivered the exposition found in the sentence 'The Lord is a man of war; the Lord is His name' an allusion to the fact that even when the Egyptians were being punished and drowned in the sea, He was still the merciful Lord, and in the expression 'the God of [אלהי *'Elōhê*] Israel', used in connection with the giving of the Torah, he discerned a reference to compassion. The use of a Name that denotes one attribute does not annul the existence of the other. Both attributes are of equal importance. The same source that seeks to refute the claim that there are two divine principles also contains the following exposition of the verse ' "This is my God [אלי *'Ĕlî*], and I will praise him, [my father's God (*'Ĕlōhê*), and I will exalt Him]": this means that He dealt with me according to the attribute of compassion, and with my fathers He dealt according to the attribute of justice. And how do we know that *'Ĕlî* signifies none other than the attribute of compassion? As it is said "My God, my God [*'Ĕlî*, *'Ĕlî*], why hast Thou forsaken me?" (Psalms xxii 2); and it is written "Heal her, O God [אל *'Ĕl*], I beseech thee" (Numbers xii 13); and Scripture further declares "The Lord is God [*'Ĕl*] and He has given us light" (Psalms cxviii 27).'[29] It is obvious that the fathers, with whom God dealt according to the attribute of justice, were not inferior in any respect to the scions, towards whom He acted in conformity with the attribute of compassion.

Many scholars have noted that Philo, too, identified the names of God with His powers, but in his view κύριος — which is the Septuagint translation of the Tetragrammaton — is the power that judges, rules and punishes, whereas θεός — the Septuagint rendering of *'Ĕlōhîm*[30] — is the power that is good and beneficent. While Zacharias Frankel was inclined to ascribe this deviation of Philo from Palestinian Midrashic exegesis to his ignorance of Hebrew[31], more recent scholars[32] have suggested that Philo's interpretation is indicative of an ancient Midrashic exposition, traces of which can be found also in Rabbinic teaching, only for polemical reasons the ancient rule was changed and reversed. However, the suggested explanation that the thesis of the sectarians — to wit, that the Jewish God, the God who judges, is jealous, and vengeful, is only the demiurgos, while the Most High God is the good and compassionate Deity — brought about a drastic change, namely the declaration that *Y.* represents the attribute of compassion and *'Ĕlōhîm* the attribute of justice, was insufficient to refute the dualistic claim, and it would, in the circumstances, have been preferable to abolish this entire distinction. Moreover, the very conjecture that *Y.* once signified 'the attribute of justice' and *'Ĕlōhîm* 'the attribute of compassion', has no foundation whatsoever in the sources,[33] nor any basis in Biblical language, whereas it is possible to find verses (Exodus xxi 6; I Samuel ii 25) in which *'Ĕlōhîm* feasibly has the connotation of judge. It is the Greek translation that caused Philo to reverse the Palestinian tradition. The rendering of *Y.* by κύριος, whether due to the reading of the Tetragrammaton as אדני *'Ădōnay*,[34] or whether it was independently chosen as a substitute for a Divine Name that was not to be pronounced, gave this word the meaning of lordship and dominion. Whilst in the original text the readers saw the Specific Name as it was spelt, and even when they did not read it according to its spelling, they knew that the spelling was of primary importance, the Hellenistic reader was confronted by the word κύριος in its accepted sense. If Philo wished to find the idea taught by Jewish tradition, namely that the God of Israel was both the God of justice and righteousness and a compassionate and gracious God — in Philo's terminology: the One who possesses 'the powers', in the dual sense of attributes and of created entities[35] — he had to adapt it to the version before him. Without doubt Philo came across verses that contradicted the principle of his differentiation — that is to say, where κύριος is used when compassion is spoken of[36] and vice versa — just as the Amoraim encountered passages that were in conflict with the rule laid down by the Tannaim. Further on we shall deal with the solutions that were suggested.

The important thing in the view of the Tannaim was to preserve both attributes. The Mishna that declares 'If a man said "To a bird's nest do Thy mercies extend"... he is silenced'[37] is not opposed to stressing God's attribute of compassion, but to giving emphasis to this attribute alone. When the Amora R. Jose bar Bun said[38] 'They do not well (to) interpret the attributes of the Holy One, blessed be He, as compassion (only)', he expressed opposition to predicating the reason for the precept of driving away the mother-bird from the nest (Deuteronomy xxii 7) on the Lord's compassion.

We have already dwelt on the anti-Gnostic character of the aforementioned Mishna, and quite possibly the dictum of R. Jose b. R.

Bun — who apparently possessed an interpretative tradition[39] — also had an anti-Christian motive directed against the exclusive doctrine of love.

The first Sage reported to have used the Divine designation 'All-Merciful' [רחמנא *Raḥmānā*] is R. Akiba: 'Rav Huna said in the name of R. Me'ir and so, too, it was taught in the name of R. Akiba: A man should ever be accustomed to say "All that the All-Merciful does is for good." '[40] This Baraita is cited in explanation of the Mishna 'A man must bless (God) for the bad even as he blesses (Him) for the good', and this anonymous Mishna conforms to the view of R. Akiba, who expounded ' "Ye shall not make with Me (gods of silver)" — (this means), that you shall not treat Me as others treat their divinities, to wit, when good comes to them, they honour their gods, as it is said "Therefore they sacrifice unto their net" (Ḥabakkuk i 16), but when tribulation befalls them, they curse their gods, as it is said "And it shall come to pass that, when they shall be hungry, they shall be enraged, and curse their king and their god" (Isaiah viii 21). But you, if I bring you good, give thanks, or if I inflict suffering upon you, give thanks... both for the bestowal of good and for that of retribution.'[41] Even he who transmitted this teaching in the name of R. Me'ir, did so in the spirit of the latter's teacher R. Akiba. Only he who held that 'suffering is precious'[42], and did not interpret it as an act of justice, for in his opinion 'compassion does not enter into judgement',[43] could bless for calamity and affliction and designate God in his benediction as 'All-Merciful', since the suffering did not come as a consequence of justice, but as a token of the Lord's love.

The saying 'All that the All-Merciful does is for good' was not interpreted according to its original meaning, but was understood as a promise of 'a happy ending'. Following upon the Baraita just cited, the version in the Babylonian Talmud contains a story intended to portray the occasion on which R. Akiba made his statement: 'R. Akiba was once going on a journey and came to a town, and he sought lodgings but was refused. Thereupon he said: "All that the All-Merciful does is for good." So he went and spent the night in the open field. Now he had with him a cock (Rashi: "to wake him from his sleep"), and an ass, and a lamp. A gust of wind came and extinguished the lamp; a cat came and devoured the cock, and a lion came and devoured the ass. He (still) said: "All that the All-Merciful does is for good." That same night a band of marauders came and captured the town. Said (R. Akiba) to them [to his disciples, or, subsequently to the townsmen]: "Did I not tell you 'All that the Holy One, blessed be He, does is entirely for good'?" The aetiological, popular character of the story is self-evident, and the late date of the attribution of the episode to R. Akiba does not require much proof. It will suffice to point to the motif, which is common to this narrative and to those concerning Nahum of Gimzo.[44]

R. Akiba's heroic conception that suffering is inherently precious, and that God in inflicting it upon a man does this for the person's benefit, and is even at that very moment the All-Merciful, is far removed from the simple, folk notion that 'every untoward happening is destined to have a happy ending'. Between these two extreme views there exist quite a number of intermediate positions. We have already referred above to the homily delivered by R. Eliezer of Modiʿim before R. Ṭarfon to the effect that the bestowal of good exceeds that of retribution, and we explained that this surplus is promised only to those worthy of it, namely, the righteous. Now the same Tanna expounded the verse 'Because ye rebelled against My commandment... in the wilderness of Sin' as follows: 'Come and see how much the righteous are beloved of the Holy One, blessed be He, for wherever He mentions their death he also mentions their transgression. What is the reason for all this? So that people may have no excuse for saying: "They must have been guilty of evil deeds in secret; hence they died." Thus (we find that Scripture) mentions the death of Aaron's sons, and wherever it refers to their death it also refers to their sin, to let you know that this was their sole offence. Now an argument from minor to major may be applied: If in the hour of wrath the Omnipresent gives such consideration to the righteous, how much more so (will He be gracious to them) at the time of favour....'[45] The syllogism at the end of this homily is reported in another source in the name of R. Ṭarfon thus: 'Now it is an argument from minor to major: seeing that when the righteous are subject to (God's) wrath they are compassionated, how much more so at the time of (God's) mercy.'[46] 'The time of mercy' corresponds to 'the time of favour', but mercy at the time of wrath is vouchsafed only to the righteous.

In accordance with this conception the verse 'In wrath remember mercy' (Habakkuk iii 2) is translated in the Targum 'And the righteous, who do Thy will, remember in mercy.'[47] The application of the attribute of mercy to the righteous is paralleled by that of the attribute of justice to the wicked. R. Simeon b. Yoḥai said: 'When is the name of the Holy One, blessed be He, magnified in His world? At the time when He executes justice upon the wicked.'[48]

A different approach was adopted by Rabban Gamaliel. He incorporated the attribute of justice into that of compassion; the Lord's compassion came as a reward for man's compassion. 'R. Judah said in the name of Rabban Gamaliel: Behold, Scripture declares "And show thee mercy, and have compassion upon thee, and multiply thee" — take hold of this principle: so long as you are compassionate, the All-Merciful will have compassion on you.'[49] Preceding this teaching of Rabban Gamaliel there is a Baraita that illustrates man's compassionate deeds and their reward: 'If a man injures his fellow, the injured must make supplication for him, even though not requested by the assailant, as it is said "And Abraham prayed unto God, and God healed (Abimelech etc.)" (Genesis xx 17). So, too, you find in the case of Job's friends, as it is said "Now, therefore, take unto you seven bullocks... and My servant Job shall pray for you" etc. And what does Scripture state (thereafter)? "And the Lord restored the fortunes of Job when he prayed for his friends...." (Job xlii 8–10)'! While Abba Saul demands that a man should imitate his Maker — 'Just as He is compassionate and gracious, so you be compassionate and gracious'[50] — Rabban Gamaliel assures the compassionate man that his Maker will have mercy on him. It is in man's power, therefore, to influence and to change the attribute of justice to that of compassion, and vice versa. This concept also made it possible to explain the deviation in the use of the Biblical Names from the rule that *Y.* signifies the attribute of compassion, and *'Ĕlōhîm* the attribute of justice. The words of Isaiah (xxvi 21) 'For, behold, the Lord cometh forth out of His place to visit upon the inhabitants of the earth their iniquity' were interpreted as meaning 'He comes forth from the attribute of justice and enters the attribute of compassion upon Israel.' The passage in Hosea 'Return, O Israel, unto [עד *'ad*] the Lord thy God' was expounded thus: 'While [*'ad*] He is still to be found in the attribute of compassion; and if not — "thy God"; ere the defence becomes indictment.'[51] This idea, that the compassion of man, and not necessarily of a righteous person, but even of a wicked man, can awaken the compassion of Heaven, was accepted to such an extent that the Amora R. Aḥa relates that the blood of Zechariah, the priest and prophet, continued to seethe after Nebuzaradan had brought eighty thousand young priests and slaughtered them: 'At that moment he (Nebuzaradan) rebuked him, saying to him: "What do you wish, that we should destroy the whole of your people because of you?" Forthwith the Holy One, blessed be He, was filled with compassion and said: "If this man, who is but flesh and blood and ruthless, was filled with compassion for my children, how much more so shall I, of whom it is written (Deuteronomy iv 31) "For the Lord thy God is a compassionate God; He will not fail thee or destroy thee or forget the covenant with thy fathers", (have mercy upon them).'[52]

The transformation of the Lord's compassion into a reward for human compassion deprived it to a certain extent of its absolute character and made this attribute subject to man's conduct. In the last story paradoxical expression was given to the idea: The Almighty requires, as it were, an *aide mémoire*, containing the verse 'For the Lord thy God is a compassionate God'. R. Aḥa, who relates this story, followed the view of R. Joḥanan, in whose name he transmitted: ' "Slow to anger [אפים *'appayim*, a dual form]" — He is long-suffering before He collects [i.e. punishes]; when He begins to collect, He does so patiently.'[53] Without doubt, it was in conformity with this doctrine that R. Ḥanina, the younger contemporary of R. Aḥa, declared 'Whoever says the All-Merciful is lax (in executing justice), may his bowels be relaxed! He is merely long-suffering, but (ultimately) He collects His debt.'[54] These Amoraim were not only opposed to making the attribute of compassion the one, absolute attribute of the Lord (see above, p. 453), but they maintained the view that the attribute of justice was of primary importance, and that the function of the attribute of compassion was to delay and slow down the collection of the debt.

In contrast to these opinions the Amora R. Samuel bar Naḥman reverts to the concept of the Tannaim that the two attributes are to begin with equal (above, p. 451), but adds that it lies within the power of the righteous and the wicked to make one of them dominant. He gave the following exposition: 'Woe unto the wicked, who transform the attribute of compassion into that of justice! Wherever *Y.* is mentioned the attribute of compassion is referred to, (thus Scripture states) "The Lord, the Lord, God compassionate and gracious" (Exodus xxxiv 6), yet it is written "And the Lord saw that the wickedness of man was great... and it repented the Lord that He had made... And the Lord said: 'I will blot out man'" (Genesis vi 5–7). Blessed are the righteous who convert the attribute of justice to that of compassion. Wherever *'Ĕlōhîm* occurs, the attribute of justice is alluded to: "Thou shalt not curse *'Ĕlōhîm*" (Exodus xxii 27), "The cause of both parties shall come before *'Ĕlōhîm*" (*ibid. v.* 8); yet it is written "And *'Ĕlōhîm* heard their groaning, and *'Ĕlōhîm* remembered His covenant" (*ibid.* ii 24), "And *'Ĕlōhîm* remembered Rachel" (Genesis xxx 22), "And *'Ĕlōhîm* remembered Noah" (*ibid.* viii 1).'[55] In the same way he also explained the verses that appear to contradict the rule concerning the Names that allude to the Divine attributes. The Amora Rava solved this problem with dialectical acuity. He did not represent the Lord as lax in the execution of justice. On the contrary, he retained for the attribute of justice its original sense of 'meting out measure for measure' and declared: 'He who forbears to retaliate — in that he does not insist on fully requiting those who hurt him, but lets his rights go unclaimed — all his iniquities are (likewise) passed over', that is to say, 'the attribute of justice is not meticulous in searching out the misdemeanours of such people, but leaves them unpunished'.[56]

One of the Amoraim of the fourth century, who transmitted many of the dicta of R. Samuel b. R. Naḥman, explained, in accordance with the latter's doctrine, the creation of man and the phrasing of the verse 'And *'Ĕlōhîm* said: "Let us make man..."' (Genesis i 26) as follows: 'R. Berechiah said:[57] When the Holy One, blessed be He, came to create the first man, He foresaw that righteous and wicked persons would descend from him. He said (to Himself): "If I create him, wicked people will descend from him; if I do not create him, how shall righteous people issue from him?" What did the Holy One, blessed be He, do? He removed the way of the wicked from before Him, made the attribute of compassion a partner in His action, and created man....' A Scriptural basis for the idea of this partnership is to be found in the wording of the verse 'In the day that *Y. 'Ĕlōhîm* made heaven and earth'. The juxtaposition of the two Names was expounded by an anonymous homilist, under the influence of R. Samuel bar Naḥmani, as follows: 'It is like the case of a king who had empty cups. The king thought: If I put hot water in them, they will crack; cold water, they will become warped. What did the king do? He mixed hot with cold water and put it in them, and they remained undamaged. Even so the Holy One, blessed be He, argued: "If I create the world with the attribute of compassion, there will be many sinners; if I do so with the attribute of justice, the world will not endure. Therefore, I shall create it with both the attribute of justice and the attribute of compassion, and may it endure! — (this is the meaning of) "*Y. 'Ĕlōhîm*".'[58] Although the creation of the world is spoken of, yet the reference is to the heart of the world — man. In keeping with this conception, the Amora R. Eleazar interpreted the verse in Psalms (lxii 13) 'Also unto Thee, O Lord, belongeth lovingkindness; for Thou renderest to every man according to his work': 'At first "Thou renderest to every man according to his work", but in the end "Unto Thee, O Lord, belongeth lovingkindness"' — that is to say, when He sees that the world cannot endure on the basis of justice alone.[59] R. Eleazar changed the order of the verse, but others expounded it as it stands, in conformity with the view of his teacher, R. Joḥanan (above, p. 457): 'Unto the Lord belongeth lovingkindness' — this implies that He delays the punishment, but thereafter He collects His debt. Whoever wished to temper the attribute of justice itself, made the deduction that God requites a man 'according to his work', but not 'his (actual) work', that is to say, He does not deal strictly with him.[60] If one held, however, that the attribute of justice was of primary importance, it was difficult for him to agree to the full partnership of the attribute of compassion in the creation of man. Indeed, following upon the homily of R. Berechiah, cited above, it is stated: 'R. Ḥanina gave a different exposition: When (the Almighty) thought of creating the first man, He consulted the Ministering Angels. He said to them: "Let us make man." They asked him in reply: "What is his nature?" He answered them: "Righteous men shall descend from him"... He revealed to them that righteous men would spring from him; for had He disclosed to them that the wicked (too) would issue from him, the Attribute of Justice would not have permitted him to be created.'

In the last homily we encounter a phenomenon to which we have already alluded, namely, that the attribute assumes the character of an independent and separate power: 'For had He disclosed to them that the wicked (too) would descend from him, the attribute of justice would not have permitted him to be created' — the Attribute of Justice becomes a prosecuting angel. Thus we find[61] the Attribute of Justice standing before the Lord and saying: 'In what way are these different from those? He answered: "These are wholly righteous, and those are wholly wicked." Justice countered: "Sovereign of the universe! It was within their power [i.e. of the righteous] to protest, but they did not do so." The Lord replied: "I know full well that if they had protested to them, they would not have accepted their protest." Said Justice before God: "Sovereign of the universe! If it was known to Thee, was it also known to them?"'

This dialogue, built up by R. Aḥa b. R. Ḥanina on the basis of Ezekiel ix 4, ended, he informs us, in an exceptional manner: for 'never was the attribute of good, once it had issued from the mouth of the Holy One, blessed be He, changed to evil — save in this one case'.

In the Haggada that we have cited, and in similar stories,[62] the Attribute of Justice strives to maintain its position unimpaired. Its aim is to prevent the scales from being unjustly inclined towards mercy, and the Lord answers its arguments. But in the course of the debate the struggle changes its aspects. From being a contest between two attributes it becomes a struggle between the Attribute of Justice and the Almighty, who becomes identified with the Attribute of Compassion. In this way R. Samuel bar Naḥmani — who, we have seen, is inclined to give precedence to the Attribute of Compassion — understood the words of Isaiah (xxx 18) 'And therefore will the Lord wait, that He may be gracious unto you, and therefore will He be exalted, that He may have compassion upon you.' Without paying attention to the continuation of the verse 'For the Lord is a God of justice' he asks: 'Seeing now that we wait and He waits, who causes the delay?' and answers 'It is the Attribute of Justice that is responsible for the delay.'[63] The Attribute of Justice assumes, as we have stated, the image of a heavenly prince or angel acting for the prosecution; it ceases to act according to its allotted function and invades a sphere that does not belong to it. This transformation also brought in its wake a qualitative change in the connotation of the Attribute of Compassion, particularly in the dicta of the Amoraim who were opposed to the preference given to the Attribute of Compassion and to the undue reliance placed upon it. The Attribute of Justice does not complain against those who say that 'the Holy One, blessed be He, is lenient', but against the readiness of God to receive back the penitent.

Resh Laqish reports in the name of R. Judah Nesi'a: 'What is the meaning of the verse "And the hands of [ידי *yĕdê*] a man under their wings" (Ezekiel i 8)? The *Kĕthîv* is *yādô* ['His hand']. This means the hand of the Holy One, blessed be He, which is stretched out beneath the wings of the living creatures to receive the penitent on account of (the opposition of) the Attribute of Justice.'[64] In similar terms R. Joḥanan said in the name of R. Simeon bar Yoḥai concerning King Manasseh: 'What is meant by the verse "And he prayed unto Him, and an opening was made [reading ויחתר *wa-yēḥātēr* instead of ויעתר *wa-yēʿātēr*, "and He was entreated of him"] for him"?... It teaches us that the Holy One, blessed be He, made a kind of opening in the sky in order to receive him in penitence on account of (the opposition of) the Attribute of Justice.'[65] In parallel sources the Attribute of Justice is not mentioned, but it is stated 'that the Ministering Angels closed up the windows so that Manasseh's prayer might not ascend to the Holy One, blessed be He'.[66]

The possibility of such an interchange in the sources — the Attribute of Justice transmuted into angels — provides proof of the growing power of the Attribute of Justice, but, paradoxically, its potential activity became at the same time contracted and a limit was set to it. When it clashes with the cardinal belief in the power of repentance, the Lord conceals His actions from it and its significance is consequently annulled.[67]

V. The Power of Repentance

The scholars who attributed primary importance to the 'attribute of compassion' did, not as we have seen, uproot justice and law, or transform the attribute of compassion into a 'law of grace', unrelated to human action and conduct (see above, p. 457). Similarly the Sages who regarded the attribute of justice as central, in that it symbolized the justice and law inherent in the ways of the Lord, proceeded to set bounds to its dominion, when it might threaten to deprive man of the ability to repent and consequently of the possibility of escaping the jurisdiction of the attribute of justice. The subjection of the attribute of justice to the power of repentance, which we observed in the last dicta quoted, raises the question of the antithesis between the principles of reward and punishment and that of repentance. We have seen how great was the interest of the Sages not only in the doctrinal existence of 'reward and punishment', but also in demonstrating their application and realization in this world (above, p. 440). Yet how could these be reconciled with the possibility of repentance at any and every moment?

Before we proceed to answer this question, let us thoroughly examine the idea of repentance as it was understood by the Tannaim and Amoraim and the transmutations that it underwent. The term תשובה *Tĕshûvā* ['repentance'] was coined by the Sages[68], but the concept it signifies is a cardinal principle of the Biblical legacy — a legacy that is intrinsically full of problems and contradictions in respect of this central theme. On the one hand repentance finds no place at all in the stories about the Flood, the Tower of Babel, and the people of Sodom. They were, it is true, all wicked and sinners, but they were not called upon to repent. Likewise in the entire account of the provocations, complaints, and rebellions of the Israelites in the wilderness there are admonitions against sin and warnings of the infliction of punishment, but no call to repentance; and even Moses in his prayers does not rely upon the regret or repentance of the people, but on the promise given by the Lord to the Patriarchs. He appeals to God 'Turn [שוב *shûv*] from Thy fierce wrath' and presents his request as a plea for the Father's honour: 'Wherefore should the Egyptians speak' etc. (Exodus xxxii 12–17). In the expiation ceremony of the Day of Atonement, as it is depicted in Leviticus xvi, reference is made to atonement, confession, and purification from defilement, but the verb *shûv* ['return', 'turn', the stem of *tĕshûvā*] does not occur in any of its various forms. On the other hand, Moses' entreaty was of no avail, and the penalty imposed upon him not to cross over to the Promised Land is not rescinded (Deuteronomy iii 23–26). Sometimes repentance removes the sin, but not the punishment, as in the case of David (II Samuel xii 7–17; xxiv 10–17), or merely suspends it, as in the case of Ahab (I Kings xxi 27–29). It also happens that God grants the prayer of a wicked person like Manasseh (II Chronicles xxxiii 10–17). God not only hardened the heart of Pharaoh, but He even said to Isaiah (vi 10), when he charged him with the mission of prophecy, 'Make the heart of this people fat, and their ears heavy, and shut their eyes; lest they see with their eyes, and hear with their ears, and understand with their hearts, and turn and be healed.' On the other hand, Jonah goes to Nineveh and proclaims 'yet forty days, and Nineveh shall be overthrown!' (iii 4), and in the end 'when God saw what they did, how they turned from their evil way, God repented of the evil which He had said He would do to them; and He did not do it' (*ibid.* v. 10). All the prophets of Israel called the people to repent, but the relationship between these appeals and the prophecies of reproof, warning, and imprecation, on the one hand, and the prophecies of consolation and salvation, on the other, is not at all equal, just as there is not a single style for calling to repentance.

Although the Sages did not consider it their function to portray the idea of repentance, its ways, and development in the Bible[69], yet they were not unaware of — nor did they overlook — the various divergent approaches. The Palestinian Amora, R. Phinehas, expounded: 'It is written "Good and upright is the Lord; therefore doth He instruct sinners in the way" (Psalms xxv 8). Why is He good? Because He is upright. The Torah was asked: "What is the sinner's punishment?" It replied: "Let him bring a sacrifice and he shall win atonement." Prophecy was asked: "What is the sinner's punishment?" It replied: "The soul that sinneth, it shall die" (Ezekiel xviii 4). David was asked: "What is the sinner's punishment?" He replied: "Let sinners cease out of the earth" etc. (Psalms civ 25). Wisdom was asked: "What is the sinner's punishment?" It replied: "Evil pursueth sinners" etc. (Proverbs xiii 21). The Holy One, blessed be He, was asked: "What is the sinner's punishment?" He answered them: "Let Him repent and I shall accept him", for it is written "Good and upright is the Lord". '[70] Obviously the homilist intended to ascribe to God the view that the power of repentance was absolute, transcending that of atonement through sacrifices and the importance of the law of retribution. Without doubt he knew that in the same chapter of Ezekiel (xviii 32) on which he based 'the view of prophecy', it is stated 'For I have no pleasure in the death of him that dieth, saith the Lord God; wherefore turn yourselves, and live'. Indeed, he did not refrain from expounding this verse as proof that God does not close the portals of penitence, even before the utterly wicked: 'Said R. Phinehas bar Ḥama, the priest: The Holy One, blessed be He, does not wish to condemn any person, as it is said "For I have no pleasure in the death of him that dieth"... And in what does He find pleasure? — in justifying His creatures... Know that this is so, for when people sin and vex him, and He is angry with them, what does the Holy One, blessed be He, do? He goes about seeking an advocate to defend them, and He opens a way before counsel for the defence....'[71] The elimination, or at least, the unqualified rejection of the law of requital, accords with what we have learnt concerning the ousting and disregard of the attribute of justice by providing an opportunity for repentance, but the view of R. Phinehas himself is only the end-result of a long development.

Primarily repentance calls for the abandonment of the way of sin and the inner resolve never to return to it, and not the outward acts that accompany it, such as fasting and prayer. On the fast day the elder spoke words of admonition: 'O brethren! it is not said of the men of Nineveh that "God saw their sackcloth and their fasting", but "And God saw their works that they turned from their evil way" (Jonah iii 10), and in the Prophets it is enjoined "Rend your heart and not your garments" (Joel ii 13).' This is the version of the admonition given in the Mishna (*Taʿanit* ii, 1). According to the Tosefta[72] the elder recited the verses Isaiah lviii 3–8, adding: 'If a man had a reptile in his hand, then even though he immersed himself in the Shiloah [Siloam] and in all the waters ever created, he can never be clean. If, however, he has cast away the reptile, immersion in forty *sĕ'ā* suffices.' Thus, too, the Bible teaches 'But whoso confesseth and forsaketh them shall obtain mercy' (Proverbs xxviii 13); and it is further stated 'Let us lift up our heart with our hands unto God in the heavens' (Lamentations iii 41). The analogy of the reptile is also old, and Ben Sira (xxxiv 25–26) uses a similar argument: 'He who washeth after (contact with) a dead body and toucheth it again, what hath he gained by his bathing? So a man fasting for his sins and again doing the same — who will listen to his prayer? And what hath he gained by his fasting?'

Despite the clear emphasis laid on the nature of repentance and the high esteem in which it is held, we have already seen (above, p. 432) that in the Tannaitic teaching on the categories of atonement repentance by itself atones only for light transgressions, whereas in respect of other iniquities it is required that repentance should be augmented by additional methods of expiation. There were also Tannaim who held that there were ways of atonement — like the Day of Atonement and the day of death — that expiated even without repentance (above, p. 435). Furthermore, specific cases are recorded where the repentance of individuals was of no avail. The Sages represent Moses as arguing: 'See what transgression I committed and how many supplications I offered up, but I was not forgiven; and see how many transgressions you committed, yet the Omnipresent said to you "Repent, and I shall receive you." '[73] The Tanna who counted Manasseh among the kings who have no share in the world to come[74] was of the opinion that his repentance, mentioned in Chronicles, was of no avail in his case. Elisha b. Avuya despaired of penitence, 'For once — he said — I passed by the Holy of Holies riding on my horse on the Day of Atonement, which fell on a Sabbath, and I heard a heavenly voice go forth from the Holy of Holies and declare: "Return ye backsliding children, except Elisha b. Avuya, who knew My power and yet rebelled against Me....'[75] His reference to the heavenly voice that he had heard reflects a view that had gained currency. Elisha b. Avuya belonged to the category of men of whom the Mishna says (*M. 'Avot* v, 18) 'Anyone who makes the many sin is not given opportunity to repent'. The Tosefta gives the following reason for this view: 'That his disciples may not descend to Sheol, whilst he inherits the world, as it is said "If a man is burdened with the blood of another, let him be a fugitive unto death; let no one help him" (Proverbs xxviii 17).'[76] However, his disciple R. Me'ir had no fears on this score, but we know nothing of the extent of Elisha's influence. At all events the negation of his repentance may also be justified on the ground that he was guilty, of 'the desecration of the Divine Name', which was implicit in his conduct, a sin that the Lord does not pardon, but exacts for it 'immediate retribution'.[77] Nevertheless, despite all the reasons that can be found to justify the heavenly voice, the abandonment of the hope of repentance, proclaimed by Elisha himself, was tainted by heresy. Indeed in the continuation of that narrative it is stated: 'After a time Elisha fell ill. People came and said to R. Me'ir: "Behold, your teacher is sick." He went to visit him and found that he was ill. Said he [R. Me'ir] to him: "Do you not repent?" He replied: "And if a man repents is he accepted?" Said [R. Me'ir] to him: "Is it not thus stated in Scripture 'Thou turnest man back to דכה *dakkā*'? — that means, he is received until life is crushed [דכדוך *dikhdukh*]." At that moment Elisha wept and passed away. And R. Me'ir rejoiced in his heart, saying: "Methinks that my teacher died in a state of penitence." '[78] The authenticity of this story is self-evident. Elisha's doubt never left him. Even after R. Me'ir had expounded (Psalms xc 3) 'he is received until life is crushed', it is not stated that Elisha repented, only that he died; and R. Me'ir only used the expression 'Methinks that my teacher died in a state of penitence'. The authenticity is also apparent in the light of the legend that follows, which tells of the fire that arose from Elisha's grave.[79] R. Me'ir did not wish to give the sectarians an opportunity to claim that man was not allowed to repent. In truth, also in other dicta transmitted in his name the importance of repentance is stressed: 'It is taught: R. Me'ir used to say, Great is repentance, for on account of one person who has repented, the whole world is forgiven, as it is said "I will heal their backsliding; I will love them freely, for Mine anger is turned away from him" (Hosea xiv 5 [4]); the verse does not say "From them", but "from him".'[80] The universal character of repentance is emphasized in the teachings of a number of Tannaim who were contemporaries of R. Me'ir: The right hand of the Lord is outstretched to all mankind[81] since time immemorial; the Lord gave a period of grace to the generation of the Flood in order that they might repent; and likewise to the men of the Tower of Babel and the people of Sodom and Gomorrah.

The dictum of R. Eliezer b. Hyrcanus 'And repent one day before your death'[82] was apparently interpreted already by himself as meaning 'that a man should say every day: Today I shall repent lest I die tomorrow'. The saying resembles the admonitions of Ben Sira:[83] '...And in the time of (committing) sins, show forth repentance... And wait not till death to be justified.' But in R. Me'ir's day, whenever doubt was expressed about the actual power of repentance, greater emphasis was laid on the possibility of repenting up to the very last moment of one's life: 'R. Judah b. Bava said: It is like the case of a man who is charged by the state: though he give ever so much money he cannot extricate himself. But thou (O Lord) sayest: "Repent and I shall accept (you)", for it is written "I have blotted out, as a thick cloud, thy transgression, and, as a cloud, thy sins" (Isaiah xliv 22).'[84] R. Simeon deduced from Ezekiel xxxiii 12–14: 'If a man was wholly wicked all his days, and repented in the end, the Omnipresent receives him, for it is stated "And as for the wickedness of the wicked, he shall not stumble thereby".'[85]

The Amoraim followed the doctrine of the Tannaim, and even enlarged the sphere and power of repentance, to the point of extravagance, yet they did not overlook the problems raised in consequence. Resh Laqish gave a cosmic character to repentance by incorporating it in the list of things that were created before the creation of the world.[86]

The Amora Ḥanana bar Isaac gave an early date to the manifestation of repentance, ascribing it to Cain. Unlike the Amoraim who interpreted the verse 'And Cain went out' (Genesis iv 16) pejoratively, he gave it an ameliorative sense: 'He went out rejoicing, as it is said "He goeth out to meet thee; and when he seeth thee, he will be glad in his heart" (Exodus iv 14). Adàm met him [Cain], (and) said to him: "What sentence was pronounced upon you?" He replied: "I repented and became reconciled." (Thereupon) Adam began to slap his (own) face (saying), "Such is the power of repentance, but I did not know it." Forthwith he arose and said "A Psalm, a Song. For the sabbath day. It is a good thing to give thanks unto the Lord" (Psalms xcii 1–2 [1]).'[87] This Amora, whose date is not certain, is apparently transmitting a homily whose source is earlier than the dispute between R. Joshua b. Levi, who holds that 'Repentance accomplishes all and prayer only half', and R. Judah b. R. Ḥiyya, who maintains that prayer accomplishes everything 'and repentance only half. From whom do you deduce this? From Cain, on whom a severe penalty was imposed, as it is written "A fugitive [נע *nāʿ*] and a wanderer [נד *nād*] shalt thou be in the earth", yet when he repented half the sentence was remitted, as it is stated "And Cain went out from the presence of the Lord, and dwelt in the land of Nod" — the text does not say here "in the land of *Nāʿ* and *Nād*", but "in the land of Nod, on the east of Eden". '[88] To this exposition R. Joshua b. Levi doubtless replied that Cain only stood and prayed, and the Lord said to him: 'Cain, had you repented, I should have released you from "*Nāʿ* and *Nād*", but now that you have left repentance and taken hold of prayer, I shall relieve you of one (only).'[89]

Even the Sage that held that Cain's repentance was not wholehearted but merely 'repentance of deception'[90] could have continued to read 'I accepted the repentance of Cain, shall I not then accept your repentance?' In the same way R. Joḥanan and Resh Laqish, who for anti-Christian polemical reasons minimized the merit of the repentance of the people of Nineveh and declared it to be 'repentance of deception', [92] could not deny the fact that it won acceptance, but were only able to argue with greater force: 'I accepted the repentance of Cain, shall I not then accept your repentance?'[91] R. Joḥanan combined prayer and repentance and explained, by their joint power, the Lord's attribute of compassion: ' "And the Lord passed by before him, and proclaimed" — R. Joḥanan said: If it were not stated by Scripture, it would not be possible to say it. The verse teaches us that the Holy One, blessed be He, drew His robe round Him like a reader and showed Moses the order of prayer. He said to him: Whenever Israel sin, let them conduct their prayers before Me according to this order and I shall pardon them. "The Lord [YHWH], the Lord" — I am He [i.e. YHWH] before a man sins and I am the same after a man sins and repents. "A God merciful and gracious".' The mercies of the Lord are assured to sinners who have repented, even as to those who have not sinned, in accordance with R. Joḥanan's own statement: 'Great is repentance, for it rescinds a man's sentence.'

Repentance finds expression in the recitation of the thirteen attributes according to the underlying intent ascribed to them by R. Joḥanan. This is the covenant made with the thirteen attributes, that they do not fail of their purpose, as Rav Judah stated.[94] R. Samuel bar Naḥman found in the verse, Psalms lxv 6, an allusion to the fact that repentance is comparable to the sea: 'Just as the sea is ever open, so are the gates of repentance ever open.'[95] R. Yuda b. R. Simon expounded: ' "Return, O Israel, unto the Lord thy God" (Hosea xiv 2) — even if you have denied the primary principle of the faith.'[96] Thereby he wished to say that there is no sin for which repentance does not atone. Continuing the teaching of the Tannaim and Amoraim concerning the help vouchsafed by Heaven to those who come to sanctify and purify themselves,[97] R. Yossa said: 'It is written "Open to Me" (Canticles v 2). The Holy One, blessed be He, said "Open unto Me an entrance no bigger than the eye of a needle, and I shall open unto you an entrance through which (entire) camps and fortifications can pass.'[98]

Although it was fully recognized that the duty of repentance devolved on man at all times, and despite the liberal view taken of the opportunity afforded man to repent, both because the demands of repentance were so small and the time allowed for it so long — until his last day — it was yet felt necessary to stress the special penitential character of certain days, namely the Ten Days of Penitence, extending from New Year to the Day of Atonement. How and when did these days acquire this specific character? The Torah appointed the tenth of the seventh month as a fast day and as the Day of Atonement — 'to make atonement for the children of Israel because of all their sins once in the year' (Leviticus xvi 1–34). The first of the seventh month is designated in the Torah only as 'a day of blowing the horn' (Numbers xxix 1), or as 'a solemn rest unto you, a memorial proclaimed with the blast of horns' (Leviticus xxiii 24). In the Book of Nehemiah it is related that Ezra the Scribe read in the Book of the Law before the congregation on the first of the seventh month, and when he had brought the people to tears, Nehemiah and Ezra said to the people 'Mourn not nor weep... Go your way, eat the fat and drink sweet wine and send portions to him for whom nothing is prepared; for this day is holy to our Lord; and do not be grieved, for the joy of the Lord is your strength' (Nehemiah viii 2–10). The verse in Psalms, 'Blow the horn at the new moon, at the full moon for our feast-day. For it is a statute for Israel, an ordinance of the God of Jacob' (Psalms lxxxi 4–5 [3–4]), comes to link, if not according to its actual meaning at least according to its Midrashic interpretation, the theme of the blowing of the horn to that of judgement. In all these sources the first of the seventh month is not designated as ראש השנה Rōsh ha-Shānā ['the beginning of the year', 'New Year'];[99] and even when we refer to the Mishnaic tractate bearing this name, we find that it ennumerates four New Years, the last being the first of Tishri, which is 'The New Year for (the reckoning of) the years (of foreign kings), of the Years of Release and Jubilee years, for the planting (of trees) and for vegetables' (*M. Rosh ha-Shana* i, 1), that is to say, the numbering of the years commences on the first of Tishri.[1] In the next Mishna it is stated: 'At four seasons in the year the world is judged: on Passover in respect of produce, on Pentecost in respect of the fruit of trees, on New Year all that come into the world pass before Him כבנומרון'[2] (νούμερον — like a troop of soldiers). 'All that come into the world' means all mankind, and without doubt this judgement may also be considered to include the things comprised in the other seasons. Furthermore, the Mishna overlooks the Day of Atonement, which is connected with the expiation of sins. But it is surely not possible that a man's sentence should be passed before his sins are forgiven! The solution of these difficulties already forms a subject of dispute among the Tannaim: 'Everything is judged on the New Year, and their sentence is sealed on the Day of Atonement — this is the view of R. Me'ir. R. Judah says: Everything is judged on the New Year, but the sentence of each is sealed in its due season: at Passover (sentence is passed) on the produce, at Pentecost on the fruit of trees, at the Festival (of Tabernacles) on water, while man's sentence is sealed on the Day of Atonement.'[3] The Mishna is formulated according to the view of R. Judah, but there was also a view that each thing is judged in its due season and that its sentence is (likewise) sealed in its due season, a view that is akin to the opinion of R. Jose, who holds that man is judged each day.[4] Yet a fourth view maintains: 'All of them are judged on New Year and the sentence of each one is (likewise) sealed on New Year.' In accordance with this opinion 'It was stated in the New Year Prayers (interspersed with the blowing of the Shofar) of Rav: This day is (the anniversary of) the beginning of Thy work [i.e. creation], a memorial to the first day, yea it is a statute unto Israel, an ordinance of the God of Jacob. Thereon it is decreed which countries are destined for the sword and which for peace, which for famine and which for plenty, and thereon the fate of every mortal is decided, whether to be recorded for life or for death.'[5] This prayer was accepted, but a way was found to reconcile it with the view that the Day of Atonement is the day on which judgement is sealed.

In the name of R. Joḥanan it is stated: 'There are three account books, one of the wholly righteous, and one of the wholly wicked, and one of intermediate persons. As regards the one of the wholly righteous — they have already received their sentence [איפופסי = ἀπόφασις] of life on New Year; as for that of the wholly wicked — they have already received their sentence on New Year; regarding the intermediate — they have already been given the Ten Days of Penitence between the New Year and the Day of Atonement: if they repent, they are inscribed with the righteous; and if not they are inscribed with the wicked.'[6] In this way specific days of repentance came into being. To those who are acquitted during these days the Lord declares 'I account it to you as though you were re-created'.[7] But, needless to say, they do not exempt a man from the duty of repentance during the rest of the year. Indeed, in the prayer of the Eighteen Benedictions recited throughout the year a special benediction was composed for repentance, which in its ancient version was composed of a Scriptural text and the closing formula of the blessing: 'Turn Thou us unto Thee, O Lord, and we shall be turned, renew our days as of old; blessed art Thou who takest pleasure in repentance.'[8]

VI. The Two Inclinations

To the question why the blessing for penitence was placed after that for knowledge the Sages replied in the words of the prophet Isaiah: 'Make the heart of this people fat, and their ears heavy, and shut their eyes... and lest they understand with their hearts, and turn.' Despite the extravagant advocacy with which they stressed how easy the way of repentance was, the Sages did not overlook the fact that it not only calls for will, but also for knowledge and understanding in man's fight against his passions.

The stereotyped phrase 'the evil inclination' [יצר הרע *yēṣer hā-rāʿ*] to express the antithesis of 'the good inclination' [יצר הטוב *yēṣer ha-ṭôv*] was coined by the Sages. This dualism in no way corresponds to the dualism of body and soul. The Sages do not maintain that the evil inclination resides in the body and the good inclination in the soul. This widespread view current in the Hellenistic world, and also in Jewish Hellenism (*IV Maccabees*), found its sharpest and most popular expression in the words of Paul (Romans vii 22–24) 'For I delight in the law of God after the inward man; but I see another law in my members... and bringing me into captivity to the law of sin which is in my members.' There is no need to emphasize that the Sages rejected this conception in the light of what we have stated above (p. 223) regarding their views on the relationship between the body and the soul. In Sirach, as in the Bible, the *yēṣer* is the natural inclination of man[9], and also in the teaching of the Tannaim and Amoraim it sometimes denotes the power of thought, or serves as a synonym for the heart as the source of human desires.[10] However, Rabbinic teaching did to some extent personify 'the Evil Inclination', to whom were ascribed attributes, aims, and forms of activity that direct man, even before he was explicitly identified, as by the Amora Resh Laqish, with Satan and the Angel of Death.[11] Just as all the angels, including Satan, are God's creatures, so, too, was the Evil Inclination created by God, only at the same time God gave man the power to rule over the Evil Inclination: 'Thus the Holy One, blessed be He, said to Israel: "My children, I have created for you the Evil Inclination, (but I have at the same time) created for you the Torah as an antidote. As long as you occupy yourselves with the Torah, he shall not have dominion over you...." '[12] In the School of R. Ishmael[13] it was taught: 'My son, if this hideous (wretch) encounters you, drag him along to the schoolhouse; if he is of stone, he will dissolve, and if of iron, he will be shattered....' Similar analogies are cited in the name of other Tannaim.[14] Despite their great faith in the power of the Torah to be of help in the struggle against the *Yēṣer*, the Sages did not think that the Torah was able, so long as it was in the possession of man, to uproot the Evil Inclination completely. The Tanna R. Nehemiah expresses, in an interesting form, the view that any distance or partition introduced between man and his God creates a domain for the activity of the Evil Inclination. He declares: 'When Israel heard (the words) "Thou shalt have no (other gods)", the Evil Inclination was eradicated from their hearts. (Then) they came to Moses (and) said to him: "Moses, our teacher, be a πρέσβεις — an emissary — between us, as it is said "Speak thou with us, and we will hear — Now therefore why should we die?" What benefit will there be if we perish? Forthwith the Evil Inclination returned to his place. (Thereupon) they went back to Moses and said to him: "Moses, our teacher, would that He revealed Himself to us a second time, would that "He would kiss me with the kisses of His mouth". He answered them: "This will not happen now, but in the time to come, as it is written: "And I will take away the stony heart out of your flesh" (Ezekiel xxxvi 26)'[15] The very fact that 'other gods' are identified with the Evil Inclination is evidence of the power attributed to him, and the consoling thought that he would be eradicated in the future was insufficient to put their minds at rest, and many, indeed, investigated his devices and methods. To R. Akiba, the teacher of R. Nehemiah, already was ascribed the simile 'At first he is like a thread of spiderweb, but in the end he becomes like a ship's hawser, as it is written "Woe unto them who draw iniquity with cords of falsehood, and sin, as it were, with cart ropes" '[16]; and continuing his thought, the Amora R. Isaac said 'At first he is like a transient lodger, then a guest, and after that the host.'[17] R. Reuben expounded ' "And the Lord will take away from thee all sickness" (Deuteronomy vii 15): this refers to the evil inclination, which is sweet at the beginning and bitter at the end.'[18] The ready response given by man to the evil inclination found expression in a widely current simile: 'And the evil inclination is (like) a king over two hundred and forty-eight parts of the body. When a person goes to perform a precept, all his bodily parts become indolent, because the evil inclination in his bowels is king over the two hundred and forty-eight parts of man's body; but the good inclination is only like one confined in prison, as it is said "For out of prison he came forth to be king" (Ecclesiastes iv 14) — this refers to the good inclination.'[19]

He who conquers the evil inclination establishes his sovereignty over his bodily members, and of him the Tanna Ben Zoma said 'Who is mighty? He who subdues his *yeṣer* ['inclination'], as it is said "He that is slow to anger is better than the mighty, and he that ruleth over his spirit than he that taketh a city" ' (Proverbs xvi 32).[20] The verse cited by Ben Zoma shows that he identifies the *yeṣer* — without the adjective רע *ra'* ['evil'] — with the tendency to anger and impatience. But in the name of the Tanna R. Joḥanan b. Nuri it is taught that they are actually the devices of the evil inclination: 'If a man pulls out his hair, rends his garments, breaks his vessels, or scatters his money in his wrath, regard him as no better than an idolater. For if his *yeṣer* had said to him "Go and worship idols", he would have done so, for such is the work of the evil inclination.' It is clear that the Tanna merely intends to say that a man who loses control of himself and does, in the moment of his anger, the things just described is liable also to go so far as to perpetrate the gravest of sins, namely idolatry.[21] Actually his dictum is no more than a commentary on R. Akiba's simile cited earlier. Other Tannaim illustrated the transition from a light transgression to other iniquities of a grave nature[22] but not necessarily idolatry. We have already referred to the widespread view that the desire for idol-worship was wholly eradicated from Israel already at the beginning of the Second Temple period.[23] But in a homily attributed to the Amora Rav or R. Joḥanan[24] it is narrated that after the prayer for the elimination of the craving for idolatry had been granted, 'the Sages said: Since this is a time of grace, let us make supplication concerning the Tempter who incites to (sexual) sin. (Accordingly) they prayed and he was delivered into their hands. Said (a prophet) to them: Beware, you will slay the whole world, if you slay him. So they imprisoned him for three days. (Then) when they sought throughout Eretz-Israel a new-laid egg for a sick person, it was not to be found... Thereupon they blinded him ['with stibium' — Rashi] and let him go; and it availed, for he no longer entices men to commit incest.' A similar exposition is quoted in the name of R. Samuel bar Naḥman:[25] ' "And, behold, it was very good" — this refers to the evil inclination. But is the evil inclination very good? Surely not! The fact is that but for the evil inclination, a man would not build a house, nor take a wife, nor beget children.' The destruction of the evil inclination also implies the annihilation of this world, for as long as a man is alive — and he lives perforce — he has a duty to perpetuate the human species. The struggle against the *yeṣer* does not therefore mean withdrawal from the world and from activity therein, but the conquest of the *yeṣer* while working in the world. The evil inclination ceases to be evil — it even becomes very good — when it is the 'inclination of life'; hence it is possible for a man to love the Lord 'with both his inclinations — with the good inclination and the bad'.[26] He who knows — as did our father Abraham — how to transform the evil into the good inclination,[27] and likewise he who fights and refuses to surrender to his evil inclination — they both love the Lord.

In the name of the Tanna R. Jose the Galilean it is reported that the righteous, the wicked, and average people are to be differentiated as follows: 'The righteous are ruled [literally 'judged'] by the good inclination... the wicked are ruled by the evil inclination... average people are ruled by both.'[28] Apparently the Tanna meant to convey a similar thought to that contained in the anonymous dictum 'The wicked are controlled by their heart... but the righteous control their heart.'[29] That is to say, the righteous man is one who makes the good inclination his ruler, and even his heart — whose inclination is evil — is under his control. Not so the wicked: the evil inclination rules them, and they are controlled by their heart. These dicta do not purport to indicate a permanent relationship between the righteous and their inclination or between the wicked and theirs. They do not seek to deny the freedom of choice granted to man,[30] who can at best expect only minimal help in his struggle, but to explain the nature both of the righteous and of the wicked, and by implication to point to the severity of the conflict.

There are differences of opinion about the methods to be employed in this struggle, and countermeasures were suggested against the wiles of the evil inclination. The School of R. Ishmael recommended the study of Torah (above, p. 472). The Tanna R. Josiah said that one's evil inclination must be adjured, for we find that all the righteous men adjured their evil inclination.[31] R. Simeon b. Laqish drew up a plan of campaign, so to speak: 'A man should always incite the Good Inclination against the Evil Impulse (Rashi: 'he should wage war against the evil inclination')... If he conquers him, well and good, if not, let him study the Torah...; if he conquers him, well and good... but if not, let him recite the *Shemaʿ*...; if he conquers him, well and good, but if not, let him bring to mind the day of death.'[32] But this same Resh Laqish also realized that there were times when no strategy availed a man without the help of the Almighty: 'R. Simeon b. Laqish said: A man's (Evil) Inclination gathers strength against him each day and seeks to slay him, as it is said "The wicked watcheth the righteous, and seeketh to slay him" (Psalms xxxvii 32), and were it not that the Holy One, blessed be He, comes to man's aid, he would not overcome him, as it is said "The Lord will not leave him in his hand, nor suffer him to be condemned when he is judged" (Psalms *ibid.*, *v.* 33).'[33] When the Babylonian Amora Rabbah heard the definition of R. Jose the Galilean as to what constitutes righteous, wicked, and average people, he commented: 'Such as we are average people.'[34] His disciple Abbaye reacted to this by saying 'The master lets no man live' (Rashi: 'If you are of the average people, there is not a truly righteous person in the world'). But in the course of time, it seems, Abbaye became convinced that his teacher was right, and from personal experience he learned that the Evil Inclination incites scholars 'more than anyone else', and because of his distress 'A certain old man came to him (and) taught him: The greater the man the greater is his (Evil) Inclination.'[35] When R. Zeʿira was meticulously careful and abstained from the slightest prohibition, he wished to avoid self-gratification and the praise of others by saying: 'Not that (Rabbi) Zeʿira is so virtuous, but we do the things to which the (Evil) Inclination assents'[36], that is to say, the deed does not pertain to the things wherein lies temptation.

Neither wisdom nor age intrinsically enable a man to withstand his Inclination. R. Joshua b. Levi said that the Evil Inclination grows with man 'from his youth until his old age, and if he finds (an opportunity) at the age of seventy, he brings about his downfall; (and even) at the age of eighty, he overthrows him.'[37] Hillel's saying 'Trust not yourself until the day of your death' (*M. 'Avot* ii, 4) served as a source for this view, and corroboration was also found for it in actual occurrences, for example: 'Once a pious man was sitting and learning: Trust not yourself until the day of your old age — like me. Thereupon a certain (female) spirit came and tempted him, and he began to bethink himself (in remorse). Said she to him: Be not distressed, I am (only) a spirit; go, be now like your colleagues.'[38] With respect to such an incident the Sages said 'If we have escaped (actual) transgression, we have not escaped sinful thoughts.'[39]

Even recalling the day of death, which appeared to Resh Laqish as the last resort in his list of expedients to be employed in the struggle against the Evil Inclination, did not, it seems, stand the test. Not all the Sages were of the opinion 'that the Evil Inclination was not to be found in the cemetery'.[40] R. Isaac expounded: ' "Wherefore doth a living man mourn [יתאונן *yit'ōnēn*], a strong man because of his sins?" (Lamentations iii 39) — even in a man's state of אנינות *'ănînût* [the period of mourning between the time of a relative's death and his burial] his (Evil) Inclination overcomes him';[41] and the Rabbis were able to tell stories that justified his words. Notwithstanding the emphasis they placed on the difficulties and severity of the struggle against the Evil Inclination and the relative value they ascribed to the resources available to man, it never entered the thoughts of the Sages to regard surrender to what they considered enticement to sin and transgression as of the least remedial worth. Certainly the Tanna R. Simeon b. R. Eleazar did not have this in mind when he said 'The *yeṣer*, a child, and a woman should be repelled by the left hand, but encouraged by the right.'[42] The phrase 'repelled by the left, but encouraged by the right' does not tell us what kind of *yeṣer* is referred to. But the juxtaposed words 'child and woman' show that it is not an evil inclination to begin with. Rashi's interpretation, therefore, seems correct: 'If a man alienated his desire completely, he would reduce the propagation of the species; and if he encouraged it completely, he would eventually do that which is forbidden, for he would not be able to restrain his passion from committing sin.' This approach was also voiced by R. Joḥanan in his saying: 'Man has a small organ — starve it and it is sated, sate it and it remains hungry.'[43] However, there were Amoraim who were indeed implacable in rejecting any compromise with the Evil Inclination, and demanded extreme resistance to his devices, yet within the area of permissibility they were prepared to concede even more than with the 'right hand'. The story transmitted in the name of Rav as a decided Halakha of the

Sages may serve as an example of the uncompromising attitude:[44] 'Once a man set his heart on a certain woman and he fell a prey to impure desires. When the doctors were consulted, they said "There is no other remedy for him but that she should submit to him." The Sages, however, said "Let him die rather than she should yield." (Said the doctors) "Then let her stand before him naked." (The Sages replied) "Let him die, but she must not stand before him nude." (The doctors then suggested that) "She should converse with him from behind a fence." (But the Sages insisted) "Let him die rather than she should converse with him from behind a fence."' Rav also demanded that a man should repent 'while he is (still) a man',[45] that is to say, while he is a young man in full vigour, but at the same time he did not call for drastic abstinence and asceticism in legitimate sexual life as a means of suppressing the evil inclination. This is attested by both his instructions to others[46] and the testimonies to his own behaviour[47] in this sphere. In order to explain these there is no need to dive into the deep waters of apologetics;[48] it will suffice to remember that Rav did not negate licit pleasure and joy,[49] and possibly he regarded them as a bulwark against the breaching of forbidden fences and barriers. His views were shared by other Amoraim in Eretz-Israel and Babylon. R. Joshua b. Levi said: 'A man should visit his wife when about to go on a journey' ('because he desires her most [at such a time]' — Rashi), and Rav Joseph glossed his ruling.[50] R. Tanḥum said in the name of R. Ḥanilai: 'A Jew who has no wife abides without joy, blessing, (or) good.'[51] And the maxim 'He that has bread in his basket is not to be compared with one who has no bread in his basket', which originally referred to food,[52] became a proverbial saying, denoting the difference between a married man and one without a wife. This approach does not imply any underestimation of the dangers threatening man, or a lessening of tension in the struggle that he must wage.

There were Sages who did not overlook the very fact that the observance of the precept of procreation involves the satisfaction of a man's desire, nor the difficulty of distinguishing between the two. The Amora R. Aḥa gave the following exposition: ' "Behold, I was brought forth in iniquity, and in sin did my mother conceive me"... in complete iniquity; even the most pious person cannot possibly be without an element [of desire]. David said before the Holy One, blessed be He "Sovereign of the universe, did my father Jesse really intend to bring me into existence? Actually he was thinking only of his own needs." You can tell that this is so from the fact that when they perform their needs, each one turns his head in a different direction and Thou dost introduce every drop that a man has. This is the meaning of David's words "For though my father and my mother have forsaken me, the Lord will take me up" (Psalms xxvii 10)'.[53] The conclusion of the homily clearly shows that R. Aḥa did not infer extreme abstinence from the drastic language that he ascribed to David, language that recalls the arguments of the Cynics.[54]

It is precisely man's weakness that serves as a reason for intensifying the demand for the suppression of human passions. A man must force himself to subjugate his inclination.[55] Hence it is taught in a Baraita that if one has the option of either unloading the burden of a friend's beast that is lying under its burden, or of helping an enemy to load, he must help his enemy, in order to subdue his impulse.'[56] R. Ḥanina and R. Jonathan acted thus even in matters that were not obligatory. When they had a choice of two roads, one leading to an idolatrous shrine and the other to the entrance of a brothel, they did not take the first path, because the craving for idolatry had already been destroyed (above, p. 22) and there was no need to overcome it, but chose the second route in order to master their inclination.[57] The dispute about the desirability of submitting to temptation in secret rather than profaning the Divine Name in public, with which we dealt already above (p. 357), is also bound up with the fear lest a man's capacity for controlling his inclination become weakened. In the name of Rav Huna, the disciple of Rav, it is reported: 'when a man commits a transgression more than once... he comes to regard it as something permitted.'[58] Wrongful acts of this kind, which people treated lightly, were enumerated by two other disciples of Rav. Rav Judah said 'Most people (are guilty) of robbery,[58a] a minority of unchastity, and all of slander.' Rav Amram regarded 'Sinful thoughts, עיון תפלה *'iyyûn tĕfillā* ['calculating on prayer'; *aliter*: '(lack of) devotion in prayer'], and slander' as sins to which a man succumbs daily.[59] In the School of Rav[60] the verse 'In that day, saith the Lord, will I assemble her that halteth... and her that I have afflicted' (Micah iv 6) was expounded as expressing God's regret at having created the Evil Inclination; and this homily R. Joshua b. Levi transmitted in the name of R. Phinehas b. Jair.[61] The same verse was used by R. Joḥanan as a basis for justifying a man who fell into sin.[62] The Lord admits, so to speak, that by creating the Evil Inclination, who incites man to sin, He was the cause of all the troubles. An anonymous preacher integrated the homilies of R. Phinehas b. Jair and R. Joḥanan and elaborated them thus: 'Israel said: "Sovereign of the universe, Thou hast caused to be written concerning us 'Behold, as the clay in the potter's hand, so are ye in My hand, O house of Israel' (Jeremiah xviii 6). Therefore, although we sin and anger Thee, do not leave us. Why? For we are the clay, and Thou art our Potter. Come and consider the potter! If he makes a jug and leaves a pebble in it, then when the vessel is taken out of the kiln and liquid is put in it, it leaks where the pebble is embedded and loses its liquid. Who caused the jug to leak and lose its contents? (Surely) the potter, who left the pebble in it!" Even so Israel argued before the Holy One, blessed be He: "Sovereign of the universe, Thou hast created within us the Evil Inclination from our youth, as it is said 'For the imagination of man's heart is evil from his youth' (Genesis viii 21). Now he is the cause of our sinning before Thee, yet Thou dost put the blame on us! We entreat Thee, therefore, remove the Evil Inclination from us, that we may do Thy will and not sin." He answered them: "Thus shall I do, as it is said 'In that day, saith the Lord, will I assemble her that halteth, and I will gather her that is driven away' ".'[63] Indeed, help is given to the righteous in this world to subdue the Evil Inclination. It is related that both R. Akiba and R. Me'ir scoffed at transgressors; so Satan once disguised himself as a woman and would not let them in peace until he heard the proclamations in heaven 'Take heed of R. Akiba and his Torah-learning', 'Take heed of R. Me'ir and his Torah-learning.'[64]

The Amoraim who told such stories about the great Tannaim did not take it for granted that they would be vouchsafed the same grace as their predecessors;[65] hence they were accustomed to add in the special prayers that they said upon waking from sleep, or in supplements to the statutory prayer, supplications for the conquest and suppression of the Evil Inclination. The School of R. Jannai said 'And I have sinned unto Thee; may it be Thy will... that Thou give me a good heart, a good portion, a good inclination....' R. Ḥiyya bar Va (= Abba) used to pray 'May it be Thy will, O Lord our God... that Thou incline our hearts to repent wholeheartedly before Thee....' R. Tanḥum (son of) Scholasticus (Σκολαστικός) composed a prayer that is wholly concerned with breaking the power of the (Evil) Inclination. It is worded 'May it be Thy will, O Lord our God... that Thou break and remove the yoke of the Evil Inclination from our heart, since Thou hast created us to do Thy will, and we are duty-bound to do Thy will. Thou dost wish it and we wish it; who then prevents it? The leaven in the dough [i.e. the incitement of the Evil Inclination]. It is well known that we have not the strength to withstand him. May it, therefore, be Thy will, O Lord my God... to remove him from us and subdue him, so that we may do Thy will as our own with a perfect heart.'[66] From this prayer we clearly learn that there is no intention to exempt man from the obligation of fighting against his inclination, nor to cast his burden on the Lord. The worshipper wishes to do the will of God with a perfect heart, and he is asking for the help promised to those who come to sanctify and purify themselves.[67] This response implies the exercise of the attribute of compassion before the commencement of judgement. It is a corollary of God's goodness. From the Almighty's answer 'I will make all My goodness pass before thee' to Moses' request 'Show me, I pray Thee, Thy glory' the Tanna R. Nehemiah concluded 'When he [Moses] approached Him wholeheartedly, the Holy One, blessed be He, responded accordingly.'[68] In this spirit the verse 'The Lord is good to all; and His tender mercies are over all His works' (Psalms cxlv 9) is expounded by the Amora R. Levi: 'The Lord is good to all and He bestows of His compassion upon His creatures.' This dictum is followed by an illuminating story: 'In the days of R. Tanḥuma, Israel needed to fast. When the people came and said to him: "O Master, proclaim a fast!" he decreed a fast — the first day, the second, and the third, but no rain fell. He then entered and preached to them, saying "My children, feel compassion towards each other, and the Holy One, blessed be He, will be filled with compassion for you".'[69]

Man's compassion derives from God's compassion, but a man must first show compassion in order that the Lord should compassionate him. In the Pentateuchal section 'on which most of the essential parts of the Torah are dependent'[70] the Lord said to Moses: 'Go say to the Children of Israel: My children, just as I am abstinent, so must you abstain (from sin); just as I am holy, so must you be holy.'[71] Holiness and abstinence are attributes of God and it is His will that His creatures should (also) cleave to them, and He even helps them, if they begin to walk in His ways. A similar exposition was given to the verse ' "May He send forth thy help from the sanctuary [*qōdesh*, literally 'holiness']" — on account of the hallowed deeds you have performed; "and support thee out of Zion" (Psalms xx 3 [2]) — on account of the distinguished acts you have done.'[72] The idea that the good God helps to bring about good, led the Sages to emphasize it and to develop it into the doctrine that the Evil Inclination was not created by the Lord.[73] He put 'the evil leaven in the dough'[74], but for the fermentation of the leaven man alone is responsible; and he may bring himself by his actions to such a stage that the help promised to one who wishes to do good will be denied him, for by sinking into uncleanness and by doing evil he may become obtuse and regard the forbidden as permitted and even deprive himself of the possibility of repenting. He may consider the Evil Inclination itself as his god, as R. Jannai put it: 'Whoever listens to his (Evil) Inclination is, as it were, an idolater. What is the reason? "There shall no strange god be in thee; neither shalt thou worship any foreign god" — make not the stranger within you your sovereign.'[75] The enthronement of the Evil Inclination is idolatry; and the prayer, customarily recited in the School of R. Jannai, 'that Thou mayest give me... a good inclination', and similarly formulated supplications (see above, p. 480), implied the acceptance of the yoke of the kingdom of heaven, and was an expression of readiness to fight against the Evil Inclination.

In the teaching of the Sages on sin and the Evil Inclination the influence of the personal experience of the man who struggles with and lives by his faith plays a prominent role. Without doubt the Tannaim and Amoraim, whose dicta and definitions we have cited above, were capable of advancing sharp-witted arguments against the views of their predecessors, against the sayings of their colleagues, and even against their own statements, just as they demonstrated these qualities in the thrust and parry of Halakhic discussion, where they spared no effort to pursue the merest shadow of a contradiction, lack of consistency or exactitude, whether the question was one of civil law or the rules governing holy things and levitical purity. Against the Stoics, whose central interest was the problem of theodicy, which they endeavoured to solve and put on a firm basis, the Academic thinkers[76] put forward a dialectic argument, such as undoubtedly could have been heard in the schoolhouses of the Sages. According to the Stoic doctrine a man is obliged to acquire good for himself; it is not given to him by the deity. This concept is a necessary corollary to the principle of free will. But if the gods are able to bestow good upon man, but do not do so, they are not good. Should you argue that they are incapable of doing this, then again they are of no benefit at all. Such a contention had no place in the world of our Sages, for their entire approach in discussing this theme was fundamentally different from that of the Stoics. They did not occupy themselves with philosophical dialectics, but with the variegated experiences of the man who believed in the good God and was tested by his ability to endure the trial of faith and trust.

VII. The Righteous and Wicked

Our exposition is further illumined by the description of the ideal of the righteous man found in Rabbinic teaching. We have learned that the struggle against and defeat of the Evil Inclination make a man righteous. The term צדיק *ṣaddîq* 'righteous' denotes in this context that a man remains pure, uncontaminated by sin. Indeed we find that the word נקי *nāqî* ['pure', 'innocent'] is translated four times in the Septuagint by δίκαιος, i.e. 'righteous';[77] so, too, Onkelos renders the verse 'and the innocent [*nāqî*] and righteous [*ṣaddîq*] slay thou not' (Exodus xxiii 7) — ודיזכי ודי נפק דכי מן דינא לא תקטול ['Him who is innocent and goes forth guiltless from judgement shalt thou not slay'].[78] Man is righteous so long as his guilt has not been proved. In this manner the Tannaim explained the verse just cited, which they exemplified as follows: 'If one witness testified that he worshipped the sun, and another that he worshipped the moon, I might have thought that their evidence should be combined and the man should be declared guilty; therefore Scripture teaches us "and the innocent and righteous slay thou not". If Reuben was pursuing his fellow to kill him, holding a sword in his hand, and (witnesses) said to him: "Take cognizance that he [the one pursued] is of our covenant and the Torah has ordained 'Whoso sheddeth man's blood, by man shall his blood be shed'" (Genesis ix 6); and he answered them: "I know, but even so." And (for a time) the witnesses lost sight of them and subsequently they found (the fugitive) in his death throes and the slayer holding a sword dripping blood, then I might have thought that he (the pursuer) should be held guilty. Therefore Scripture teaches us "and the innocent and righteous slay thou not". '[79] Alongside the use of *ṣaddîq* for a man who is declared not guilty at his trial, the term also serves as a designation for those who do God's will,[80] and for those who have accepted the Torah,[81] which fits a man to be a *ṣaddîq*.[82] The name *ṣaddîq* is also given to one who gives charity [*ṣĕdāqā*], which is simply termed 'precept',[83] and in fulfilling it a man imitates the deeds of his Creator and merits to be called by His name: ' "Whosoever shall be called [reading *Niphʿal* instead of *Qal*] by the name of the Lord shall be delivered" (Joel iii 5). But how is it possible for a man to be called by the name of the Holy One, blessed be He? The answer is that just as the Omnipresent is gracious and compassionate, so you, too, must be gracious and compassionate and donate free gifts; (just as) the Omnipresent is called *Ṣaddîq*, as it is stated "For the Lord is righteous (*ṣaddîq*), [He loveth righteousness]" (Psalms xi 7), so you, too, must be righteous....'[84] The designation of the Lord as 'the Righteous One, who lives for ever' is based on the verse 'The Lord is righteous in all His ways' (Psalms cxlv 17).[85] The Tannaim and Amoraim indulged in many hyperboles in describing the importance, weighty character, and greatness of charity [צדקה *ṣĕdāqā*, literally: 'righteousness']. It has the power to atone for iniquities, even for the sin of idolatry.[86] Thus R. Nathan taught: 'From Gareb to Shiloh is a distance of three *mil* [= 6,000 cubits], and the odour of the smoke of the (Temple) altar and the smoke of Micah's image intermingled. The Ministering Angels wished to thrust him aside. Said the Holy One, blessed be He, to them: "Let him be, because his bread is available to wayfarers."' For this reason Micah was not counted among the commoners who have no share in the world to come.[87] But acts of charity do not always atone for iniquities or deliver a man from punishment for his transgressions; sin even has the power to extinguish the merit of precepts.[88] Furthermore, if one commits transgressions with the intention of atoning for them by the performance of precepts, he remains wicked, even if he has fulfilled them. If, now, 'one who says I shall transgress and repent' does not attain to true penitence (see above, p. 464), it is obvious that if a man gives liberally to charity, but at the same time sins, he is not to be designated a *ṣaddîq*. This was the accepted view.[89] The exaggerated story set in homilies by the expiatory value of acts of charity and lovingkindness gave rise to the need for express expositions opposing the attitude of shallow levity towards the gravity of sin. With people of such mentality in mind R. Joḥanan commented on the verse 'Hand to hand, (but) he shall not go unpunished for the evil' [see Rashi *ad loc.*] as follows: 'It may be compared to the case of a man who went and committed a sin and gave the harlot her hire, but he had hardly gone out of the door of her house when a poor man met him (and) said to him "Give me alms." The man gave him and went on his way, thinking to himself: Had not the Holy One, blessed be He, wished to grant me atonement for my sins, He would not have sent that beggar so that I might give him alms and gain atonement for what I had done. Thereupon the Holy One, blessed be He, said to him: "Wicked wretch! do not suppose such a thing; but go and learn from the wisdom of Solomon, who explained, saying "Hand to hand, (but) he shall not go unpunished for the evil".'[90] Such homilies are to be found not only relative to ordinary people, and not only with regard to transgressions of the kind mentioned, but also with reference to one who 'acquired Torah like Moses our Teacher', but is filled with overweening conceit.[91]

A special term 'a book-keeping Pharisee' denotes the man who performs 'one sin and one precept, and balances one against the other.'[92] In discussing the Evil Inclination, we encountered a differentiation between those whose heart and inclination are under their control and those who are controlled by their inclination and heart.[93] The former are righteous, but if they rule their impulse and refrain from sin without doing any acts of charity, they are not deemed completely righteous. Rava reports the explanation that he heard from the Palestinian Amora, Rav Idi, of the verse 'Praise the righteous [*ṣaddîq*] when he is good, for they shall eat the fruit of their doings'

(Isaiah iii 10): 'But is there a *ṣaddîq* that is good and one that is not good? The meaning is: He that is good to Heaven and to men is a good *ṣaddîq*; he that is good to Heaven and bad to men — is a *ṣaddîq* that is not good. Similarly Scripture states "Woe unto the wicked man [רשע *rāshāʿ*] that is bad!" But is there a *rāshāʿ* that is bad and a *rāshāʿ* that is not bad? The meaning is: He that is evil to Heaven and evil to men is a bad *rāshāʿ* he that is evil to Heaven, but not to men is a *rāshāʿ* that is not bad.'[94] The homily belongs to an Amora, but the idea that it is not possible to be a *ṣaddîq* without outstanding acts of charity is old. The Sages had already decided by vote in the upper chamber of R. Ṭarfon and declared: 'Who are they that "do righteousness at all times" (Psalms cvi 3)? Should you say: They are those who teach children Bible and Mishna — but do they not eat and drink and sleep? Alternatively (should you suppose that) they are the writers of Tefillin and Mezuzot — but do they not (likewise) eat and drink and sleep? Who then are they that "do righteousness at all times"? You must conclude that this alludes to one who brings up an orphan in his home. But can you claim that he [the orphan] does not uncover himself at night? Said (the Sages): We still need the Sage of Modiʿim. R. Eleazar of Modiʿim came and taught: Scripture refers only to the piece of bread that he eats in his house.'[95]

We have already seen that even in the case of a man who is wholly righteous there is no absolute assurance that he will always remain so, 'and will not in the end rebel, and regret his former conduct'.[96] R. Joḥanan does indeed state in the name of R. Jose that the Lord acceded to Moses' request and let him know His ways, explaining to him why it may go ill with the righteous and well with the wicked. However, not only did R. Me'ir disagree with him and say that this knowledge was not vouchsafed to Moses, expounding ' "And I will be gracious to whom I will be gracious" — even though he is unworthy'; "And I will show mercy on whom I will show mercy" — even though he is unworthy; but even according to R. Jose's view the Gemara finds it difficult to discover the explanation given to Moses, and only after the rejection of one conjecture is the opinion put forward: 'A righteous man with whom it is well is wholly righteous; a righteous man with whom it is ill is not wholly righteous; a wicked man with whom it goes well is not wholly wicked.'[97] This answer does not accord with the widely current view that 'a righteous man with whom it is well' is a rare phenomenon, as Rava stated: 'The world was created only (for the following): This world for Ahab the son of Omri, and the world to come for Ḥanina b. Dosa.'[98] Although a man 'with whom it is well' may be 'a wholly righteous person'[99], yet this fact certainly does not *per se* constitute a criterion. Doubts with regard to a man's complete righteousness remain unchanged until his last day.

However, this rule, which recurs in various forms, did not prevent the creation of 'a legend of the righteous', which contains popular motifs alongside literary themes known to us from the folk-tales concerning 'men of God', saints and righteous men from outside the world of the Sages. These were integrated both with the histories of the Patriarchs, the Prophets, and other Biblical figures deemed worthy, and with the stories of men of piety and miracle workers of the time of the Second Temple and of the period of the Tannaim and Amoraim itself.

In our discussion of Providence we have already pointed out that the views of the Tannaim and Amoraim regarding the righteous and the wicked that were named before birth did not result from any compromise with a dualistic outlook. In truth it appears that primarily they emanate from the deeply rooted belief that the existence of the righteous is a condition of the survival of the world. From the verse 'But the righteous is the foundation of the world' (Proverbs x 25) the Tannaim[1] already inferred that 'One righteous man is equivalent to the entire world', and R. Eleazar b. Shammuaʿ explained the Scripture figuratively, declaring that 'the world rests on a single pillar, called "Righteous".'[2]

To a student who spoke up and said 'Master, who is greater, the world or the righteous?' the Patriarch R. Judah, the distinguished disciple of R. Eleazar b. R. Shammuaʿ replied: ' "The righteous." "Why?" (asked the scholar). (The Patriarch answered): "When Jochebed gave birth to Moses he was equivalent to the entire world." And where do we find that Moses was equal to all the people? For it is said "As the Lord commanded Moses and the children of Israel"; and it is also said "Then sang Moses and the children of Israel"; and it is further said "And there hath not arisen a prophet since in

Israel like unto Moses (Deuteronomy xxxiv 10)." '[3] Rabbi's homily referred in its source to Moses[4], but the inference drawn relative to the relationship between the righteous and the world is of general application. R. Ḥiyya bar Abba transmitted in the name of R. Joḥanan: 'No righteous man departs from this world until another righteous man like him is created, as it is said "The sun also ariseth, and the sun goeth down" — ere the sun of Eli set, the sun of Samuel the Ramathite had arisen.'[5] In this teaching the criterion of 'a righteous man like him' is laid down, but in the name of the same Amora two other dicta are reported, which indicate a progressive decline: 'R. Ḥiyya bar Abba also said in the name of R. Joḥanan: The Holy One, blessed be He, seeing that the righteous were few, proceeded to plant them in each generation, as it is said "For the pillars of the earth are the Lord's, and He hath set the world upon them" (I Samuel ii 8). And R. Ḥiyya bar Abba further said in the name of R. Joḥanan: The world exists even for the sake of one righteous person, as it is said "And the righteous is the foundation of the world." '[6]

However, R. Joḥanan reported a homily in the name of R. Simeon b. Jehozadak which states that the world exists on account of the merit of a given number of righteous men. The expositor links the words of Hosea (iii 2–3) 'So I bought her to me for fifteen pieces of silver and a homer of barley, and a half-homer of barley; and I said unto her: "Thou shalt sit solitary for me..." ' with the verse in Zechariah (xi 12) 'And I said unto them: "If ye think good, give me my hire; and if not, forbear." So they weighed for my hire thirty pieces of silver', giving the following exposition: ' "A homer of barley and a half-homer of barley" — these are the forty-five righteous men on account of whom the world exists. Still I do not know whether thirty are here and fifteen in Eretz-Israel, or thirty in Eretz-Israel and fifteen here. When, however, Scripture states "And I took the thirty pieces of silver, and cast them into the treasury, in the house of the Lord", you must infer that thirty are in Eretz-Israel and fifteen here. Abbaye said: And the majority of them are to be found in the Synagogue called "Under the Balcony".'[7] It is clear that the words 'Still I do not know' etc. belong to the redactor of the Babylonian Talmud, and 'here' means Babylon in antithesis to Eretz-Israel. It also appears that Abbaye's statement should come earlier, for it refers directly to the dictum of R. Simeon b. Jehozadak, and this is what Rashi had in mind in his annotation 'And the majority: of the righteous of Eretz-Israel'.[8]

But the homily of R. Simeon b. Jehozadak was not acceptable to R. Joḥanan. The latter did not expound the verse in Hosea at all allegorically, and on the verse in Zechariah there is reported an authentic dispute between him and Rav: ' "So they weighed for my hire thirty pieces of silver" — Rav said: These are the thirty righteous. Said R. Joḥanan to him: Has not Rav heard that the verse refers only to the Gentile nations? According to Rav "And I said unto them" means to Is[rael]; according to R. Joḥanan "And I said unto them" means to the Gentile nations. In Rav's opinion, when Israel are worthy the majority of them are in Eretz-Israel and the minority in Babylon; but when Israel are unworthy the majority of them are in Babylon and the min[ority] in Eretz-Israel.'[9] According to this tradition the verse in Zechariah, too, was not expounded by R. Joḥanan with reference to the thirty righteous men of Israel, but with regard to the Gentile nations and the thirty commandments that they will accept in the days of the Messiah.

The source of both the view of R. Joḥanan concerning one righteous man as the foundation of the world and of the opinion attributed to Rav, which the former rejects, regarding the thirty righteous men, is to be found in the dictum of R. Simeon b. Yoḥai, whose formulation is paradoxical: 'R. Hezekiah in the name of R. Jeremiah said as follows: R. Simeon b. Yoḥai declared: The world does not lack thirty righteous like Abraham. If there are thirty, my son and I are two of them; if there are twenty, my son and I are two of them; if they are ten, my son and I are two of them; if they are five, my son and I are two of them; if they are two, they are my son and I; if there is (but) one, it is I.'[10]

The conclusion of the dictum, which, like similar sayings, expresses this extraordinary Tanna's consciousness of his own worth, testifies that, although he knows the tradition of the thirty righteous by whose merit the world exists, he does not regard this number as a *sine qua non*. The world can exist even by the merit of one righteous person. However, the concept that a certain number of righteous men was needed became the accepted view of the Palestinian Amoraim in the second half of the fourth century. They found support for the theory in the Pentateuchal story about Abraham, who terminated his prayer for Sodom, when ten righteous men could not be found there (Genesis xviii 13). Furthermore, in the opening verse of the section ואברהם היו יהיה 'Seeing that Abraham shall surely become' the Sages found an allusion to the fact 'that the world does not lack thirty righteous like Abraham'[11], that is, the tradition known to R. Simeon b. Yoḥai.

The Babylonian Amora Abbaye, whom we found reacting to the tradition of R. Simeon b. Jehozadak (above, p. 488) also adopts another fixed number of righteous; however, it is not only the number, but also the definition of the function of these righteous men that is different. 'Abbaye said: The world never lacks thirty-six righteous, who greet the presence of the Shekhina in each generation, as it is said "Happy are they that wait *lô* ['for Him']" (Isaiah xxx 18) — and the numerical value of *lô* is thirty-six.'[12]

It has already been pointed out[13] that the quoted verse can hardly be interpreted to allude to Abbaye's dictum, and that apparently the choice of the number thirty-six righteous, who are vouchsafed to greet the Shekhina, was influenced by the concept prevailing in ancient Egypt[14] with reference to the dominion of the thirty-six *decani*, that is, the thirty-six gods of the sky, who appear in the course of the nights of the year in the vault of heaven. In the astrology of the late Hellenistic system a complete system was evolved that traced the influence of the thirty-six *decani* and their demons on the various organs and parts of man's body. We also know of prayers and supplications offered to the *decani* — many of them still bearing Egyptian names — as demons who protect certain organs.[15]

The Judeo-Hellenistic apocryphal work *The Testament of Solomon*[16] also enumerates thirty-six πνεύματα, which are divided according to the twelve signs of the zodiac and produce diseases in various sections of the human body. It is not to be supposed that Abbaye was the only one among the Amoraim who was acquainted with these beliefs;[17] and apparently even the numbers forty-five and thirty righteous, mentioned by the early Sages, also had the aim of establishing specifically — against the prevailing views of the influence of the thirty-six *decani*-god-demons on man — the power and influence of man. The existence of the entire world depends on a given number of righteous. Possibly the Sages purposely adopted numbers other than thirty-six, when referring to the righteous who live in the world and sustain it.

We have seen that even Abbaye left the number forty-five unchanged and only added his comment on the place where the majority of the righteous of Eretz-Israel are to be found (see above, p. 488). The number thirty-six is mentioned by Abbaye only when those who behold the presence of the Shekhina are spoken of. In relation to this dictum the Talmud cites also the teaching of R. Simeon b. Yoḥai, but there, too, the reference is not to the righteous who sustain this world, but to the group who welcome the presence of the Shekhina[18], of whom R. Simeon b. Yoḥai said: 'I have seen the men of high standing [Heaven-destined] and they are but few: if they number a thousand, my son and I are among them... if they be two, they are my son and I.' These 'Righteous who are destined to welcome the presence of the Shekhina' were compared by R. Simeon b. Yoḥai himself to the stars, and he applied to them[19] the verse 'And they that are wise shall shine as the brightness of the firmament; and they that turn the many to righteousness as the stars for ever and ever' (Daniel xii 3). While the Tanna did not fix the number of these righteous either in heaven or on earth[20] — for the essential point in this dictum, as in the parallel saying, is the emphasis given to the consciousness of his own worth — the Amora Abbaye proceeded to equate the number of the righteous who greet the presence of the Shekhina and resemble the stars with the number of *decani*.

The idea of the dependence of the existence of the world on that of the righteous led to the attempt to solve the problem of theodicy, in so far as the matter relates to the premature death of the righteous and the longevity of the wicked. 'Samuel ha-Qaṭan [the Younger] was asked: What is the meaning of the verse "There is a righteous man that perisheth in his righteousness" (Ecclesiastes vii 15)? He replied: It is fully revealed to Him who spoke and the world came into being that the righteous man would eventually degenerate. Said the Holy One, blessed be He: While he is still righteous, I shall take him away....' With regard to the wicked R. Josaiah said that the Lord shows them forbearance, 'for perchance righteous children may issue from them, for thus we find that He was forbearing with Ahaz and he sired Hezekiah; with Amon, and he begot Josiah; (with) Shimei and Mordecai was descended from him.'[21] The principle also holds good for Gentiles, since from them, too, proselytes and righteous men may come forth.[22]

The nature of the righteous man, who is the foundation of the world, is not expressly defined. The one man who is specifically given the title 'righteous' in the Bible is Noah: 'Noah was a righteous man, blameless in his generation' (Genesis vi 9); 'For I have seen that thou art righteous before me in this generation' (*ibid.* vii 1). Around his personality has been woven a widely ramified Haggada linked to the verses 'This one shall bring us relief from our work and from the toil of our hands...' (*ibid.* v 28), 'But Noah found favour in the eyes of the Lord' (*ibid.* vi 8); but its motifs — like many of those found in the legends of other righteous men of the Bible — are shared by Θεῖος ἀνήρ, the Greek man of God. He is a man beloved of the gods, mediates between them and mortals, and his life has typical features. His birth is announced beforehand and mostly takes place in unusual circumstances and conditions. The man of God matures rapidly in body, spirit, and moral understanding, and he arouses, as an infant or child, the wonder of all who see him. His knowledge comes direct from God. He has wonderful powers at his disposal: he hears and sees hidden things; he knows the secrets of the future; he is able to control both animate and inanimate nature. In his youth people persecute him, but subsequently he appears as a saviour, counsellor, and pleader, and uses his powers for the benefit of mankind, saving people from the wrath of God, warding off natural disasters, and helping the poor and suffering in everyday life. He dies an unnatural death, either as a martyr or a death accompanied by marvels, and miracles are wrought on his body. His death does not mean the cessation of existence but entering into a higher sphere.[23] In *The Book of Enoch* (cvi 1–12) we find a description of the extraordinary nature of the child Noah: 'And his body was white as snow and red as the blooming of a rose, and the hair of his head and his long locks were white as wool, and his eyes beautiful. And when he opened his eyes, he lighted up the whole house like the sun, and the whole house was very bright. And thereupon he arose in the hands of the midwife, opened his mouth, and conversed with the Lord of righteousness.' Lamech, the father of Noah, was frightened and went to his father Methuselah to ask him to find out the meaning of the matter from Enoch. A parallel to the portrayal in the *Book of Enoch* occurs in a Qumran scroll.[24] In the homiletical expositions of the Sages the child Noah is not accorded such an enthusiastic description; possibly the link with the personality of Enoch, whom the Amoraim did not regard as completely righteous,[25] sufficed to oust the legend of Noah's extraordinary birth. On the other hand the Rabbis, cleaving to the Scriptural expression 'This one shall bring us relief', emphasized the idea expounded by R. Joḥanan: 'When the Holy One, blessed be He, created man, He gave him dominion over everything: the cow obeyed the ploughman, the door obeyed the carpenter. When, however, man sinned, God caused them to rebel against him: the cow no longer obeyed the ploughman, nor the door the carpenter. But when Noah arose, they became submissive again.'[26] This motif, that upon the birth of a righteous man good comes to the world, occurs often.[27] Of Isaac we are told: 'When he was born all rejoiced — heaven and earth, sun and moon, and the planets. And why were they glad? For if Isaac had not been created, the world could not have existed!'[28] But the motifs of the apocryphal Haggada of Noah recur in the homilies of the Amoraim on the birth of Isaac and Moses. R. Ḥanina b. Levi said: 'On the day that Isaac was born the Holy One, blessed be He, made the light of the sun's orb forty-eight times as great.'[29] In the name of Rav it is reported that 'When Moses was born, the whole house was filled with light.'[30] In the Midrash that describes Moses' struggle with the angel of death, Moses testifies regarding himself: 'On the day that I was born, I was able to speak and to walk, and I spoke with my father and my mother, and I did not even suck milk. And when I was three months old, I prophesied, declaring that I would receive the Torah from the midst of flaming fire.'[31]

The signs that foretell the birth of the righteous man, his external characteristics, his beauty, his might, even his odour[32] do not yet give assurance that a righteous man is indicated. The decisive proof is to be found in his deeds, as was stated by 'R. Jeremiah in the name of R. Samuel bar R. Isaac: Each day a Heavenly Voice went forth, pealing throughout the world and proclaiming: "A righteous man will arise called Samuel." Thereupon every woman who gave birth to a son named him Samuel, but when they saw his deeds, people would say: "Is this Samuel? This cannot be that Samuel!" But when he [the true Samuel] was born, and people saw his deeds, they said: "It seems that this is he." '[33]

The righteous, by their deeds, bring blessing and prosperity to the world. R. Eleazar b. R. Simeon said: 'I approve the words of R. Jose: So long as the righteous are in the world, there is blessing in the world, but when the righteous depart from the world, blessing too departs from the world.'[34] The reference is to normal material benefits like 'plenty and ease',[35] as well as marvellous happenings and miracles:[36] 'The righteous see from one end of the world to the other.'[37] And not only the Patriarchs ruled over nature and prevailed over its laws, but the sages, righteous, and pious of every generation did so too.[38] Elsewhere we have treated of the nature of these miraculous deeds.[39] We wish to emphasize, however, that many of them are indicative of the heavy demands made on the ideal of the righteous man. The following example will suffice here: 'R. Phinehas b. Jair was once going to the schoolhouse when the river Ginnai was in flood. Said he to it: "Ginnai, why do you prevent me from going to the schoolhouse?" Thereupon it parted before him and he crossed. His disciples then said to him: "Can we cross?" He replied: "Whoever is quite sure that he never acted irresponsibly towards any Jew may cross and will not be harmed." '[40] The righteous man not only controls the laws of nature but also God's decrees, which he has the power to annul.[41] In the spiritual accountancy of the world the righteous man has a special task. With respect to every person R. Simeon b. Eleazar said: 'Because the individual is judged by the majority of his (deeds) and the world is judged by the majority of its (deeds), a man should always regard himself as half innocent and half guilty. If he performs one precept, he is blessed, for he weighed down the scales for himself and the world on the side of merit; if he commits one transgression, woe betide him! for he has weighed down the scales for himself and the world on the side of guilt.'[42]

But the righteous have an additional task: their very existence serves to influence people, for those who draw near to them, even though they do not attain to their level, yet acquire something of their fragrance, and 'it is well with the righteous (and) well with his neighbour.'[43]

However, they must not be content with this. As men of righteousness they must protest against the actions of the wicked, even though their rebuke is of no avail.[44] On the other hand the duty also rests upon them to stand before their creator as defending counsel and advocates for their fellow creatures, for they have it in their power to transform the attribute of justice into the *attribute of compassion*.[45] This power is given them only by virtue of their deeds and loyalty to the Torah and precepts. The righteous person does not become a law and precept unto himself.[46]

We find, however, that the Sages spoke in defence of the sins of the great men of the past, just as they added to the charges against certain prophets and righteous men, accusing them of misdeeds beyond what is expressly attributed to them in Scripture.[47] But we do not find, even among the most zealous defenders, anyone who is prepared to justify the transgressions of the righteous on the ground that they are not really sins, but are misjudged as such by other people who lack understanding.[48] Many attempts were made to extenuate David's crime in the affair of Bathsheba, the most extreme being the contention that 'whoever says David sinned undoubtedly errs... for he intended to do (wrong), but did not', for 'whoever went to battle in the wars of the House of David wrote a bill of divorcement for his wife... and Uriah the Hittite... was guilty of rebellion against the king's orders' (*T.B. Shabbat* 56a). But even R. Samuel bar Naḥmani and R. Jonathan and R. Judah the Patriarch, in whose name this advocacy is reported, never thought for a moment of presenting the transgression as a good deed. They merely discovered extenuating circumstances, and even this approach was rejected by Rav, who observed caustically 'Rabbi who is descended from David tries to whitewash him' (*ibid.*). Rav reduced David's sin by portraying it as a challenge to the Evil Inclination, since the king submitted himself to an ordeal and failed. But primarily he based David's vindication on the suffering and penitence that he accepted,[49] and this is also the traditional method of exoneration: 'The School of R. Ishmael taught: If you have seen a scholar commit a transgression at night, do not think ill of him by day; perhaps he repented.' This is the wording of the Baraita, but the Talmud adds anonymously ' "Perhaps"? Can there be any doubt! Unquestionably he has repented' (*T.B. Berakhot* 19a). We find here confidence that there was repentance; but there is no annulment or minimization of the sin.

However there is not lacking the feeling that there is a decline in the generations, which impairs even the power of the righteous. This feeling is accurately expressed in the following story: 'Invading troops once came to Levi bar Sisi's town. Thereupon he took a scroll of the Torah and went up to the roof-top and said: "Sovereign of the universe, if I left one word of this Book of the Torah unfulfilled let them enter; but if not, let them go!" Forthwith they were sought, but not found. His disciple acted likewise; his hand withered, but they (the invaders) went away. His disciple's disciple did the same; his hand did not wither, nor did they (the troops) leave.'[50]

Together with the stories about the diminution of the power of the revealed and well-known righteous there arose tales about 'covert men of righteousness', simple folk who by one deed won eternity for themselves and brought relief and prosperity to the world. It was disclosed to illustrious Sages in a dream that the prayer of a certain ass-driver, or of a certain theatre decorator and attendant of the dancing girls, would bring down rain. Only subsequently are the good deeds of these righteous men made known.[51]

The activity of the righteous and the influence of their merit do not cease with their death.[52] The covenant that God made with Noah and with the Patriarchs, and which He swore to remember and to fulfil, is due to the merit of the good deeds of the Patriarchs. Their descendants, it is true, are required to keep this covenant, and breaking it brings punishments in its train, as it is written: 'And if ye shall reject My statutes... but break My covenant; I also will do this unto you...' (Leviticus xxvi 15). But the punishment will not go so far as the annulment of the covenant itself on the part of God (*ibid.*, *v.* 44). To the merit of the early Patriarchs are added those of the righteous in every generation. On the respective share to be accredited to the deeds of the living generations and to the merits of former generations in preventing the abolition of the covenant, and likewise in the acts of salvation and redemption, there are differences of opinion between the Sages since the time of Shemaʿya and Avṭalyon. 'Shemaʿya said: The trust that their father Abraham reposed in Me suffices that I should divide the sea for them, as it is said "And he believed in the

Lord; and He counted it to him for righteousness" (Genesis xv 6). Avṭalyon said: sufficient is the trust that they reposed in Me that I should divide the sea for them, as it is said "And the people believed and when they heard..." (Exodus iv 31).'[53] There is a similar dispute between R. Joshua and R. Eleazar of Modiʿim, when they came to interpret the section of the manna. ' "Then said the Lord unto Moses: 'Behold, I will [הנני *hinnĕnî*] cause to rain... for you.' " R. Joshua said: The Holy One, blessed be He, said to Moses: "Behold, I shall reveal Myself forthwith and shall not delay." R. Eleazar of Modiʿim said: The text says *hinnĕnî* — only on account of the merit of Abraham, Isaac, and Jacob. "For you." R. Joshua said: It is assuredly due only to you. R. Eleazar of Modiʿim said: Scripture says "for you" — only because of the merit of Abraham, Isaac, and Jacob.'[54] There is a similar difference of opinion between the two Tannaim in connection with the section of Amalek.

Avṭalyon, R. Joshua, and the long series of Tannaim who ascribed the miracles and salvations to the merit of Israel's deeds[55], and not to that of the Patriarchs, were afraid of too much reliance on this merit and the consequent weakening of the sense of duty and of the need to fulfil the commandments. The subject is explained in the Midrashic exposition that was taught in the School of R. Ishmael: 'Should you ask: Why do the Gentiles, who ser[ve] strange gods, worship idols, and prostrate themselves to images, continue to live? (The answer is:) On account of the merit of Noah, as [it is said] "While the earth remaineth" etc. (Genesis viii 22). When will this covenant be annulled? When day and night will cease, as [it is said]: "While the earth remaineth", "And there shall be one day, it is known to the Lord" etc. (Zechariah xiv 7). Now we might argue from minor to major: If the Gentiles, who are idolaters, live because of the merit of Noah, shall not we live on account of the merit of Abraham, Isaac, and Jacob? Therefore Scr[ipture] tea[ches] us "If thou shalt keep all this commandment" — it is the reward of the commandment that gives you life, not the merit of the Patriarchs.'[56] However, no difference in principle is to be inferred here between the School of R. Ishmael and the School of R. Akiba, for we find Tannaim from both schools who stress the value of the merit of the Patriarchs,[57] and also Sages who base everything on the fulfilment of the commandment, while others conjoin the merit of the Patriarchs with that of observing the precepts.[58] In this spirit the Amora R. Avin also expounded the prayer of Moses after the episode of the golden calf: ' "Remember Abraham". Why did Moses mention here the three Patriarchs?... The Holy One, blessed be He, said to Moses: "I require of you ten, just as I did of Sodom. Point to ten righteous men among them, and I shall not destroy them." He replied: "Sovereign of the universe, I shall do so. There is myself, Aaron, Eleazar, Ithamar, Phinehas, Joshua, and Caleb." Said God to him: "These make seven; where are the (other) three?" (Moses) did not know what to do. (Then) he said to God: "Sovereign of the universe, are the dead alive?" He replied: "They are." (Thereupon) he [Moses] said: "If the dead live, remember Abraham, Isaac, and Jacob." These make ten. Hence he [Moses] mentioned the three Patriarchs.'[59] Here the merit of the Patriarchs serves only to complete the minimum number of righteous requisite for the deliverance of Israel from annihilation. In an anonymous homily God promises Abraham: 'From your seed I shall raise up shields of righteous men; furthermore, when your children will come to commit transgressions and evil deeds, I shall see one righteous man among them, who can say "Enough!" to the attribute of justice, (and) I shall take him and grant them atonement (on account of him).'[60]

Alongside the views that attribute the salvations of the past either to the deeds of those who possessed their own merits, or to the merit of the Patriarchs, or to the merit of both, we find yet another opinion, which ascribes them to the merit of the promises and the great deeds of the future. R. Ishmael himself declared: ' "Wherefore criest thou unto Me?" On account of [בזכות, *bizĕkhût*] Jerusalem I shall divide the sea for them....'[61] An anonymous preacher expounded the verse: ' "And the waters were a wall unto them on their right hand, and on their left" — Who caused Israel to be delivered? "On their right hand, and on their left"; "on their right hand", on account of the Torah, which they were destined to receive on their right, as it is said "At His right hand was a fiery law unto them"; "and on their left" — this refers to the phylactery [תפלה *tĕfillā*, sing.]. Another interpretation is: "On their right hand, and on their left" — "on their right hand" refers to the *mĕzûzā* that the Israelites would affix, "and on their left" refers to the phylacteries [תפילין *tĕfillîn*, plural].'[62] The underlying thought in these and similar dicta[63] is that historical happenings, like the redemption from Egypt or the parting of the Sea of Reeds, are not dependent on a tally of reward and punishment of the nation at the time concerned, but serve to bring near the ultimate goal that the Lord appointed for His people. The idea is repeated in the following form: 'And the Sages say: For the sake of His name did He act thus towards them, as it is said "For Mine own sake, for Mine own sake, will I do it" (Isaiah xlviii 11), and it is (also) written "That divided the water before them" (*ibid.* lxiii 12). For what reason? "To make Himself an everlasting name." '[64] From a later Midrash we learn that R. Nehemiah was the Tanna who said that the Israelites went forth from Egypt 'on account of the Torah that they were due to receive.'[65] From the concept that on account of future happenings previous generations were vouchsafed Divine grace, some Amoraim drew the conclusion that the righteous of later generations are also able to help their ancestors by their merit. They transformed the merit of the sires into that of the scions, and they said that the Israelites went forth from Egypt because of the merit of the generation of Isaiah or on account of Hananiah, Mishael, and Azariah.[66]

The dispute among the Tannaim regarding the place and importance of the merit of the fathers was not confined to the history of the nation as a whole, but also had a bearing on the nature and destiny of the individual.

In keeping with his view concerning Providence R. Akiba taught: 'The father endows the son with beauty, strength, wealth, wisdom, and (length of) years....'[67] In agreement with R. Akiba's doctrine, Rabban Gamaliel, the son of R. Judah the Patriarch, taught in the Mishnah: 'And let all who labour with the community labour with them for the sake of Heaven, for the merit of their fathers helps them and their righteousness endures for ever....'[68] In the spirit of these teachings it was related of R. Akiba himself in connection with the appointment of R. Eleazar b. Azariah as Patriarch: 'And R. Akiba sat grieving and said: Not that he is more learned in the Torah than I, but his family tree is nobler than mine. Blessed is the man who has ancestral merit; blessed is the man who has a peg to hang on.' And the narrator explains: 'What now was R. Eleazar b. Azariah's peg? He was the tenth generation in descent from Ezra.'[69] This dictum explains why it was said at the beginning of the age of the Amoraim that the Patriarchs are 'three great pegs in the world',[70] that is to say, that the world rests upon them, and this was the purport of R. Simeon b. Laqish's words, when he said that the Patriarchs are 'a throne with three pegs', and of his dictum that 'It is the Patriarchs who constitute the Chariot.'[71]

Just as we find Shemaʿya disagreeing with the opinion of Avṭalyon that the redemption from Egypt came on account of Abraham's faith, so we have ancient testimonies to a point of view that disputes R. Akiba's opinion, at least in the period close to his own time. The polemical character of the following Tannaitic homily is quite evident: ' "And there is none that can deliver out of My hand" — fathers cannot deliver their sons: Abraham cannot deliver Ishmael, and Isaac cannot deliver Esau. We have thus learned only that fathers cannot deliver sons. How do we know that brothers cannot save brothers? Scripture teaches us "No man can by any means redeem his brother" (Psalms xlix 8) — Isaac cannot deliver Ishmael, and Jacob cannot deliver Esau. And though he be given all the money in the world, he is not granted his atonement [כפרו *kofrô*, literally 'ransom'], as it is said "No man can by any means redeem his brother, nor give to God a ransom for himself [כפרו *kofrô*], for too precious is the redemption of their soul, and must be let alone for ever" (*ibid. vv.* 8–9) — too precious is the soul, for when a man sins he cannot compensate for it.'[72] We apparently encounter unmitigated opposition to the concept of ancestral merit in *IV Ezra*. To the question 'Whether in the Day of Judgement the righteous shall be able to intercede for the ungodly, or to entreat the Most High in their behalf' the angel that spoke to him answered him: '...Even as now a father may not send a son, or a son his father, or a master his slave... that in his stead he may be ill, or sleep, or be healed; so shall none then pray for another on the Day, neither shall one lay a burden on another; for then every one shall bear his own righteousness or unrighteousness.'[73]

However, the very manner in which the opposition is expressed shows how deeply the belief in the merit of the fathers was rooted. Characteristic is the story in *Liber Antiquitatum Biblicarum* ascribed to Philo. Before Deborah's death the people cry: 'Mother, you are dying and forsaking your children!... Pray for us, and after your death let your soul remember us forever.' Deborah answers the people: 'So long as a person lives, he can pray for himself and for his sons, but after his death he cannot pray for others, nor can he remember them. Put not your trust in your ancestors, they will not profit you, if you be not like them.'[74] Here a chink of compromise is opened, for it is possible to infer that if they will be like them (their ancestors) they will profit them, in the sense of 'Blessed is the man who has a peg to hang on'. However, the objections raised to reliance on the merit of the fathers did not succeed in diminishing its significance or centrality. It even found support in other principles and the difficulties they entailed. The righteous, who were not vouchsafed their reward in this world, not only stored up for themselves treasures of reward in the world to come, but, in the view of Amoraim like R. Simon and R. Phinehas, also accumulated merits for the benefit of future generations. Of a man who gives alms or performs a precept and asks for the reward thereof at once, R. Simon said that is 'like a man who says: Here is a sack, and a *sela*ᶜ, and a *se'a*, proceed to measure out! You can see that this is so, for if the fathers of the world had sought to receive the reward of the precepts that they performed in this world, how could there have existed merit for their children after them? This is the meaning of Moses' words to Israel "Then will I remember My covenant, with Jacob" etc.'[75] R. Phinehas expounded the verse ' "Hand to hand, the evil man shall not be unpunished" (Proverbs xi 21): If a man performs a precept in this world and seeks to receive his reward for it at once... he is wicked, and leaves nothing for his children.'[76] These Amoraim obligate the righteous man not to settle the account of his reward, but to see to it that those who succeed them have merit.

Without doubt these views are connected with the evaluation of acts of martyrdom since the time of the religious persecution under Hadrian, which led as we have shown elsewhere[77], to past events being interpreted retrospectively. Some of those who endowed the generations with merit were also appraised by their act of martyrdom. Not only were Hananiah, Mishael, and Azariah[78] placed on the same plane as the three Patriarchs, but the attitude to the Patriarchs themselves likewise changed.

The Tanna R. Jose the Galilean does not ascribe the parting of the Sea of Reeds to Abraham's faith in general, but to the act of the *ʿÅqēdā* ['the binding of Isaac', i.e. his attempted sacrifice], and he depicts the scene dramatically: 'When the Israelites went into the sea, Mount Moriah had already moved from its place, with Isaac's altar built upon it, and the faggots arranged on it, and Isaac as it were bound and lying on the altar, and Abraham as it were stretching out his hand and holding the knife to slaughter his son.'[79]

While in the Pentateuchal story the hero of the *ʿÅqēdā* is Abraham, and even in the benediction in the ancient order of service for fast days recorded in the Mishna (*M. Taʿanit* ii, 4) it is still stated 'May He that answers Abraham on Mount Moriah answer you...', in the tradition of the age of the Hadrianic persecutions, and especially in that of the succeeding period, Abraham is more and more ousted in favour of Isaac, the victim himself.[80] The latter is not only made a full partner in the test — ' "So they went both of them together": the one to bind and the other to be bound, the one to slaughter and the other to be slaughtered'[81] but, furthermore, the ordeal is accounted an act. Consequently Isaac became the real hero of the epic. In one of the earliest sources that testify to this change the motif is linked to a dispute that bears upon the very subject of merit: ' "And when I see the blood" — R. Ishmael said: But is not everything fully revealed to Him... wherefore, then, does Scripture say "And when I see the blood"? The meaning is that on account of the precepts that they perform He reveals Himself unto them and takes pity on them... Another explanation is: "And when I see the blood" — I see the blood of Isaac's *ʿÅqēdā*, as it is said "And Abraham called the name of that place *Adonay-yir'e* ['the Lord seeth']" etc. (Genesis xxii 14); and subsequently it is stated "The Lord beheld, and He repented Him of the evil" (I Chronicles xxi 15) — what did He see? The blood of Isaac's *ʿÅqēdā*.'[82] While R. Ishmael ascribes the deliverance of the first-born of Israel to the merit of the precepts that they fulfilled, an anonymous expositor — his contemporary or a scholar of the succeeding generation — attributes the salvation not to the merits of the fathers in general, but to the merit of Isaac and that of 'the blood of his *ʿÅqēdā*', as though it had actually been shed. Similarly another Tannaitic homily speaks of the ashes of Isaac. With respect to the verse 'Then will I remember My covenant with Jacob, and also My covenant with Isaac, and also My covenant with Abraham will I remember' (Leviticus xxvi 42) the expositor asks: 'Why is remembering mentioned relative to Abraham and Jacob, but not with regard to Isaac? The reason is that his ashes are regarded as lying heaped up on the altar.'[83] While in the Mishna proper we find no allusion to Isaac in the order of service for fast-days, there were Amoraim who introduced it into the Mishna by their interpretation: 'The ark is brought forth into the open place of the city and wood ashes are placed on the ark. R. Judan the son of R. Manasseh and R. Samuel bar Naḥman (differ with regard to the reason): one said in order to recall the merit of Abraham, and the other said in order to recall the merit of Isaac. The one who said in order to recall the merit of Abraham (permits the use of) either dust or ashes, in accordance with (the verse) "I who am but dust and ashes" (Genesis xviii 27); the one who said in order to recall the merit[84] of Isaac (allows the use of) ashes only, Isaac's ashes being regarded as heaped upon the altar.'

The verse in Chronicles (i Chronicles xxi 15), which served in Tannaitic Midrash as proof that the Lord beheld on the night of the plague of the first-born 'the blood of the *ʿĀqēdā* of Isaac', is differently interpreted by Rav and Samuel: ' "And as He was about to destroy, the Lord beheld, and He repented Him of the evil." What did He see? Rav said: He beheld our father Jacob... and Samuel said: It was the ashes of Isaac that He saw....'[85] Thus the Tannaim and early Amoraim used the expression 'the blood of the *ʿĀqēdā* of Isaac' and 'the ashes of Isaac' as synonyms for 'the merit of Isaac'.

It is true that R. Isaac Nappaḥa ['the smith'], R. Joḥanan's disciple, did not employ the phrase 'as though', and in answer to the question how did those who returned from Babylonia know the site of the altar, he answered 'They beheld the ashes of Isaac lying on that site'.[86] Nevertheless it was undoubtedly not his intention to imply that Isaac was actually burned at the time of the *ʿĀqēdā*, but that 'the ashes of the ram' took his place. R. Isaac's teaching is thus explained in a homily based on an exposition of R. Banna'a, one of the last of the Tannaim[87]: 'Since Scripture tells us that Abraham "took the ram, and offered him up for a burnt-offering" (Genesis xxii 13), is not the verse quite complete? What then is the meaning (of the words) "in the stead of his son"? Abraham said: "Sovereign of the universe, I am slaughtering the ram, look upon it as if my son were slain before Thee." When he took its blood, he said "Look upon it as if Isaac's blood were sprinkled before Thee." When he took the ram and flayed it, he said to Him: "Look upon it as if Isaac's skin had been flayed before Thee upon the altar." When he burned it, he said to Him: "Look upon it as if his ashes were heaped before Thee on the altar." '[88] Isaac's willingness to be bound and slaughtered and burned was accounted an act, and the acts performed to his substitute — the ram — were deemed as though they had been done to him; thus the Sages spoke of the blood of his *'Ăqēdā*, and the ashes of the ram were regarded as his ashes.

From being a story about Abraham's ordeal, the episode of the *'Ăqēdā* evolved, in the dicta of the Tannaim and Amoraim, into an account of Isaac's atonement. R. Banna'a's disciple, the great Amora R. Joḥanan himself, put in Abraham's mouth an explanation of the story of the *'Ăqēdā*, whose sole purpose was to provide a defence for Israel: 'R. Bevai the Great stated in the name of R. Joḥanan: Abraham said to the Holy One, blessed be He: Sovereign of the universe, it is well known to Thee that when Thou didst enjoin me to offer up my son Isaac, I could have countered and replied: But yesterday Thou didst tell me "For in Isaac shall seed be called to Thee", yet now Thou dost command me "Offer him there for a burnt offering!" Did I — Heaven forfend! — disobey Thee? No! I suppressed my inclination and did Thy will. So be it Thy will, O Lord my God, that when the descendants of Isaac, my son, find themselves in trouble, and have no one to plead their cause, do Thou defend them. "The Lord seeth": Remember unto them the *'Ăqēdā* of their father Isaac and be filled with compassion for them.'[89]

In the light of what has been stated it is not surprising that the Tannaitic pronouncements against dependence upon ancestral merit[90] did not meet with much success. As we have already indicated, the idea of the merit of the fathers became permanently entrenched in the prayers of the fast days and of the Day of Judgement, that is, New Year. R. Levi in the name of R. Ḥama Ḥanina used the following analogy: 'It is like the son of a king who had a lawsuit before his father. Said his father to him: "If you wish to win the suit before me, appoint so-and-so as your advocate (νικολόγους — successful pleader), and you will win the case before me." Even so did the Holy One, blessed be He, say to Israel: "My children, if you will cite the merit of your fathers, you will win the suit before Me." '[91] The verse Leviticus xxiii 24 is expounded allegorically: ' "One [usually rendered 'First']" — this refers to our father Abraham, "Abraham was one" (Ezekiel xxxiii 24). "A memorial proclaimed with the blast of horns" — this refers to our father Isaac, "And he looked, and behold behind him a ram caught in the thicket by his horns" (Genesis xxii 13). "A holy convocation" (Leviticus, *loc. cit.*) — this refers to our father Jacob, "Hearken unto Me, O Jacob, and Israel My called" (Isaiah xlviii 12). When shall you cite the merit of the fathers and succeed in your plea before Me? "In the seventh month" (Leviticus, *loc. cit.*).'[92]

There were indeed Amoraim who attempted to fix a date: 'How long did the merit of the fathers avail?' Some ascribed to R. Ḥiyya the view[93] that (the benefits of) ancestral merit ceased in the days of Joahaz; Samuel said that it continued till the time of Hosea. R. Joshua b. Levi said 'until the time of Elijah', and R. Judah said 'until the age of Hezekiah'. Actually the view of R. Aḥa was accepted, namely that 'The merit of the fathers endures for ever; "for the Lord thy God is a merciful God... and will not forget the covenant of thy fathers" (Deuteronomy iv 31)'[94], only the demand for Torah study and the observance of the precepts was added thereto.

Paradoxically, those who bestowed merit on the community were themselves sent, after their great deeds of martyrdom, to study Torah in the schools of their contemporaries. From the time that Hananiah, Mishael, and Azariah arose from the fiery furnace, they are no longer mentioned. To the question 'Whither did they go?' R. Joshua b. Levi replied: 'They changed their abode and went to Joshua b. Jehozadak to study Torah.' In a similar manner R. Berechiah expounded in the name of the Rabbis of Babylonia: ' "So Abraham returned unto his young men": Where now was Isaac?... (Abraham) sent him to Shem to study Torah.'[95]

The early Amoraim were not unconscious of the problem that both ways — both that which depends on ancestral merit and that which derives from the power of precepts fulfilled and good deeds performed — lack completeness and may even be dubious from the viewpoint of the integrity of faith and devotion. R. Joḥanan said in the name of R. Jose b. Zimra:[96] 'Whoever makes (his prayer) depend on his own merit, (his salvation) is attributed to the merit of others; and whoever makes (his prayer) depend on the merit of tohers, (his salvation) is attributed to his own merit. Moses made (his prayer) depend on others, as it is said "Remember Abraham, Isaac, and Israel thy servants" (Exodus xxxii 13), (hence the salvation) was attributed to his own merit, as it is said "Therefore He said that He would destroy them, had not Moses His chosen stood before Him in the breach to turn back His wrath, lest He destroy them" (Psalms cvi 23). Hezekiah made (his prayer) depend on his own merit, as it is written "Remember now, I beseech Thee, how I have walked before Thee" (II Kings xx 3), (therefore the salvation) was ascribed to the merit of others, as it is written "For I will defend this city to save it, for Mine own sake and for My servant David's sake" (*ibid.* xix 34).' Here R. Joḥanan expresses opposition to reliance on one's own merit. On the other hand Resh Laqish terms those who rely on ancestral merit as 'those who come with power', or 'those who come with a (mighty) arm'.[97]

R. Abbahu states, in connection with the interpretation of the verse, ' "Hearken unto Me, ye stout-hearted, that are far from charity": R. Joḥanan and Resh Laqish differ. One said: The whole world come [to ask Heaven for sustenance] as an act of charity, whereas these come with power [with good deeds and precepts]; the other said: All the benefits and consolations that are vouchsafed to the world are bestowed on account of their merit, but they themselves derive no benefit from them; for example, Mar Zuṭra, who, when praying for others, was answered, but for himself he was not answered.'[98] The first view is apparently that of Resh Laqish. He holds that 'the stout-hearted' is an epithet for the righteous, who come on the strength of their good deeds, and do not have to rely on the Lord's grace and charity, which are vouchsafed on account of ancestral merit. The second view is that of R. Joḥanan. 'The stout-hearted' are those who keep far from their own righteousness and do not benefit from it, but bestow the merit upon their generation. A similar opinion was also held by Rav, in whose name Rav Judah transmits the dictum: 'Every day a Heavenly Voice goes forth and declares: The whole world is sustained on account of My son Ḥanina, yet My son Ḥanina is content with a *kab* of carobs from one Sabbath eve to the other.'[99] The merit of the righteous avails others but not themselves. The righteous, by their deeds, arouse the Lord's charity, which is His attribute of compassion, or — in the phraseology of the Midrash that we have cited above — they are able to say 'to the attribute of justice — "Enough!" '.[1] This power and right were given to them by the covenant made with the Patriarchs. The merit of the fathers consists in the direction of the later generations towards their Father in heaven. The prophet (Isaiah lxiii 16) declares: 'For Thou art our Father; for Abraham knoweth us not, and Israel doth not acknowledge us; Thou, O Lord, art our Father, our Redeemer from everlasting is Thy name.' According to their simple sense, these words represent a rejection of the concept of the merit of the fathers and its power. The homily of R. Samuel bar Naḥman in the name of R. Jonathan does not divest the verse of this meaning, but in a dramatic manner, which is not devoid of humour, actually makes Isaac, the outstanding exemplar of the idea of ancestral merit, as its hero, although he is nowhere mentioned in the passage. And this is how he expounded the Scripture: (In the time to come the following dialogue will take place): 'The Holy One, blessed be He, says to Abraham: "Your children have sinned against Me." He answers Him: "Sovereign of the universe, let them be blotted out for the sanctification of Thy name."[2] God then says: I shall speak to Jacob, who knew the tribulation of parenthood; perhaps he will entreat for them. The Lord tells him: "Your children have sinned." He answered Him: "Sovereign of the universe, let them be blotted out for the sanctification of Thy name." To this God replies: "There is no reason in old men and no counsel in children." He then says to Isaac: "Your children have sinned against Me." Isaac thereupon answers God: "Sovereign of the universe, my children and not Thy children? ... If Thou wilt bear them all, well and good; but if not, let half be upon me and half upon Thee. And shouldst Thou say they are all my responsibility, behold, I have offered up my life unto Thee." (Thereupon) they (the children of Israel) begin to say "For thou art our father...." But Isaac says to them "Instead of praising me, praise the Holy One, blessed be He." Forthwith they all begin to proclaim "Thou, O Lord, art our Father; our Redeemer from everlasting is Thy name." '[3]

Taking account of the merit of the Patriarchs represents the grace and righteousness of God. But these again are vouchsafed only to those who are willing to cleave to good deeds. This thought finds expression in the dictum transmitted in the name of the Palestinian Haggadist of the fourth century, R. Berechiah: 'R. Judan bar Ḥanan in the name of R. Berechiah stated: The Holy One, blessed be He, said to Israel: "My children, if you see the merit of the Patriarchs declining and the merit of the Matriarchs tottering, go and cleave to lovingkindness. What is the reason for this? 'For the mountains may depart' (Isaiah liv 10). — this refers to the merit of the Patriarchs; 'and the hills totter' — this refers to the Matriarchs. From now on 'But My kindness shall not depart from thee, neither shall My covenant of peace decline [E.V. 'be removed'], saith the Lord that hath compassion on thee". '[4] When men on their part forsake lovingkindness, this causes the merit of the fathers to decline, whereas the renewal of devotion to lovingkindness can bring about the renewal of the merit. R. Berechiah sums up the compromise approach that we have found in the teaching of many of his predecessors (above, p. 497). On the other hand, Rava expounded the verse 'Come, now, and let us reason together' (Isaiah i 18) in a manner that stresses the disinclination of Israel to rely on the merits of the fathers. This attitude vouchsafes them the Lord's answer: 'Since you have relied upon Me, "Though your sins be as scarlet, they shall be as white as snow".'[5]

Above (p. 499) we have dwelt on the view that sought to explain the acts of redemption in the past as due to the merit of the righteous who were due to be born; in other words: the living endowed the dead with merit. This concept is not far removed from the notion that the living are able to atone for the sins of the dead. Indeed, this question also formed a subject of discussion in the schools of the Amoraim in both Eretz-Israel and Babylon in the wake of the expositions of the Tannaim. With reference to the prayer of the priests, when the heifer's neck was broken (Deuteronomy xxi 1 ff), 'Forgive, O Lord, Thy people Israel, whom Thou hast redeemed', the Sages said: '(The words) "whom Thou hast redeemed" teach us that this act of expiation atones for those who went forth from Egypt. "Forgive Thy people" — this refers to the living; "whom Thou hast redeemed" — this refers to the dead. Scripture teaches us that the dead need atonement, and we learn at the same time that he that sheds blood sins as far back as those who went forth from Egypt.'[6] The sin of shedding blood rests also on the fathers and on the fathers' fathers of the murderer, and the atonement for the living is likewise an expiation for the dead. The Tanna R. Judah declared with reference to the verse Ezra viii 35: ' "The children of the captivity, that were to come out of exile, offered burnt-offerings unto the God of Israel" — they brought them for (the sin of) idolatry.' Rav Judah explained his statement in the name of Samuel thus: 'for the idolatry that obtained in the days of Zedekiah'. In answer to the objection 'But those who sinned are dead!' Rav Papa explained: 'The tradition that a sin-offering whose owner has died must be left to die applies only to the offering of an individual but not to that of a community, because a community does not die.' The Talmud seeks to trace the source of the distinction drawn by Rav Papa and eventually suggests the homily in the passage of the *Sifre*, quoted above in regard to the calf whose neck was broken, but this conjecture is rejected, because the calf whose neck was broken comes primarily to atone for the living 'and since it atones for the living, it also atones for the dead'.[7] The conclusion of the Talmudic discussion is that the act in the days of Ezra was based on 'a temporary ruling'. However, despite the conclusion of the Gemara that there is no expiation even for a community of dead, this belief was not entirely ousted, and it emerges in various sources even with reference to individuals.

The early Amoraim already sought the reason for the fact that the Mishna did not include Ahaz among the kings who have no portion in the world to come. In the Palestinian Talmud[8] it is stated: 'R. Hoshaiah the Great said: Because his father was righteous. But was not Manasseh's father righteous? In the case of Manasseh, his father was righteous, but his son was wicked... in the case of Ahaz, both his father and his son were righteous; this is the meaning of the verse "My hand upon it! the evil man shall not be unpunished, but the seed of righteous men shall escape" — Scripture does not state here that "the seed of the righteous man shall escape", but that "the seed of righteous men shall escape", that is, seed placed between two righteous men shall escape.' This explanation, namely, that the merit of the father and the merit of the son combine to endow him that is between them with merit, is cited also in the discussion of the Babylonian Talmud[9] on this subject in the name of R. Jeremiah bar Abba, but there the text continues: 'Why did the Sages not include Amon? In deference to Josiah. Let Manasseh, then, also not be included in deference to Hezekiah? A son's merit can protect his father, but a father's merit cannot protect a son, as it is written "And there is none that can deliver out of My hand" — Abraham cannot deliver Ishmael....' Thus the Sages accept the view of the Baraita cited above (p. 500), which rejects the idea of ancestral merit, but affirm the view that sons protect their fathers with their merit after the latters' death. This concept already found expression in the laws of honouring parents, as they are taught in the following Baraita: 'The Sages taught: (the son) honours him (the father) in his lifetime and honours him in death... How does he do so in death? When he states a tradition in his name, he must not say "Thus my father said", but "Thus said my father, my teacher. May I be an atonement for his resting place!" '[10]

Atonement for the dead by the living was not restricted to sons only. Thus the Sages in the Babylonian Talmud declared that David's prayer availed to endow his son Absalom with merit and bring him to life in the world to come.[11] In a late Midrash it is stated generally: 'Should you say that having descended into Gehenna, one can no longer ascend, (this is not so). When intercession is made for him, he is cast out from Gehenna.'[12] In the spirit of this concept, there was added to the homily on the calf whose neck was broken: ' "Whom Thou hast redeemed" — this refers to those who are atoned for by the alms of the living', but already in the Middle Ages they noted that this is an interpolation[13] intended to justify the prevailing custom.

We shall conclude our exposition of the idea of the sons' endowing their fathers with merit by examining a notion that seemingly accords with the essence of our concept, but actually gives it a meaning at variance with its accepted signification. 'R. Simeon b. Yoḥai said: If one has a son that toils in the Torah, it is as though he never died....'[14] It is not said that he enables him by his merit to attain to life in the world to come, or that he delivers him from retribution,[15] but that he continues his life, so to speak. Here we return to the old conception that a man's reward is to be found in his life in this world.

This concept lies at the base of the ancient laws of inheritance, and Ben-Sira gave expression to it in the words 'When his father dieth he dieth not altogether, for he hath left one behind him like himself. In his life he saw and rejoiced, and in death he hath not been grieved. Against enemies he hath left behind an avenger, and to friends one that requiteth favour.'[16] But, while former generations regarded the surviving heir and the inheritance as constituting a name and memorial to the dead, the Tanna mentioned above found this only in the son who toiled in the Torah. This very toil of the sons, without any special acts or prayers designed to expiate the sins of the deceased or to bestow merit upon them, was a continuation of the life of the fathers. The dictum of R. Simeon b. Yoḥai, whose meaning we have just attempted to understand, may be taken as a logical sequel to this Sage's daring statement about the ability of himself and his son not only to reinstate and exempt from judgement the generations to come, but also the preceding generations.[17] Generations, like that of Simeon b. Yoḥai, who accepted the yoke of the Torah and precepts, justify the existence of the previous generations.

We have already observed (above, p. 498) that the Tannaim R. Ishmael and R. Nehemiah professed the doctrine that attributes the redemptions and salvations that were wrought for the nation in the past to the merit of the later generations. R. Simeon b. Yoḥai gave this concept an individual character; following in his footsteps certain Amoraim reversed the merit of the fathers. R. Samuel bar Naḥman[18] declared that Abraham 'was delivered from the fiery furnace only on account of the merit of our father Jacob... that is the meaning of the verse "Therefore thus saith the Lord concerning the house of Jacob, who redeemed Abraham" (Isaiah xxix 22) — Jacob redeemed Abraham.' In Babylon a similar exposition was transmitted in the name of Rav.[19]

VIII. Interpretations of Theodicy

The themes included in this chapter are the constituent elements of the spiritual stocktaking of the world and of the individual Jew. But even when the individual does this accounting from his own point of view, he is unable to overlook the fact that he is the son of the Lord's people, which was chosen from the family of nations, and that a covenant was made with him to keep the Torah. On each of the subjects treated in this chapter we found differences of opinion. Nor is there lacking parallelism between the conclusions reached by the Sages regarding one subject and those concerning another, and they certainly sought to reconcile contradictions between verses. But their explanations are not to be appraised as merely apologetic interpretations.[20] It is true that the views and conclusions arrived at by the Tannaim and Amoraim as a result of their own experiences helped them to explain Biblical passages. The actual existence of 'three successive generations of wicked men'[21] served to exemplify the truth of the verse 'visiting the iniquity of the fathers upon the children' (Exodus xx 5), but it ceased to be a binding postulate after they observed that there were also sons of the wicked who were righteous. R. Jose bar Ḥanina said: 'Four decrees did Moses, our teacher, impose upon Israel, but four prophets came and abrogated them... Moses said "visiting the iniquity of the fathers upon the children"; came Ezekiel and revoked it: "The soul that sinneth, it shall die" (Ezekiel xviii 4).'[22] But even Ezekiel's declaration, which, according to the Amora, invalidated the unfavourable decree contained in Moses' statement, was not accepted as a rule that applied at all times and in all circumstances, for, as we have seen, the martyrs who prayed for the moment when they could fulfil the precept 'and with all thy soul', testified against it. And as against the view that 'There is no death without sin', many held the doctrine that 'There is death without sin, and there is suffering without iniquity.'[23] R. Jose b. R. Ḥanina, or another Amora, could have continued in the style of the above homily and said: The prophet Ezekiel decreed that every man should die for his own sin, but R. Akiba came and repealed the decree....

The truth 'that there is no family containing a publican that may not be deemed to consist wholly of publicans, or one that contains robbers that may not be considered to consist wholly of robbers, because they protect him'[24] R. Simeon b. Yoḥai was able to learn from his personal experience, for his father Yoḥai held a position in the Roman police administration;[25] and indeed there were in his days, as in all ages, families that protected transgressors in their midst. But it is clear that even R. Simeon b. Yohai did not regard this experience as a rule, but it sufficed to interpret the verses 'And if the people of the land do at all hide their eyes from that man, when he giveth of his seed unto Molech, and put him not to death; then I will set My face against that man, and against his family, and will cut him off...' (Leviticus xx 4–5). The realities of life justify the punishment of the family, for there are families that cover up for their members; yet our sense of justice demands that the punishment meted out to the family should not be as severe as that of the transgressor. In truth the Tanna continues his exposition as follows: 'I might have thought that his family should also be liable to *kārēt* [death by Divine visitation, premature death]. Therefore Scripture states "him" — he (the offender) is to be punished by *kārēt*, but not his family, upon whom only pains are inflicted.'[26] In this part the exposition is tied to the Scriptural text, to wit, that the sinner who did not receive his due punishment at the hands of the earthly court will receive it at the hands of Heaven, either in the form of the death of *kārēt* or — according to the Sages who mitigated the punishment of the family — through suffering. But in the first part of this exposition[27] we find the concept that sin carries within itself the factor that operates the punishment. Needless to say, the deductions have but a flimsy basis in the verse: ' "And if hide they will hide" [this is the literal meaning of the words rendered above 'do at all hide']: How do we know that if they connive at one thing, they will in the end connive at many things? Therefore Scripture declares "if hide they will hide". And how do we know that if one court connived, in the end many courts will connive? Therefore Scripture states "if hide they will hide". And how do we know that if the tribal high courts [Sanhedrins][28] connived, in the end the Great Sanhedrin of Israel will connive, and they will be deprived of the right to judge capital cases? Hence it is written "And if hide they will hide".'

Weakness on the part of the court and its connivance at one offence brings in its train the collapse of the entire judiciary and the system of justice among the people. However, not only dereliction of duty by the custodians of law and justice involves penalties affecting the public as a whole, but, as we have seen, even the sin of an individual leads to the infliction of retribution upon the entire community. Numerous examples may be given, but for the present we shall only indicate that this idea is also represented in the homily dealing with the sin of Molech, from which we have quoted the preceding expositions. This concept was also read into the verse: ' "Because he hath given of his seed unto Molech, to defile My sanctuary, and to profane My holy name" — this teaches us that he defiles the Sanctuary, desecrates the Divine Name, causes the Shekhina to depart, makes Israel fall by the sword, and exiles them from their land.'[29] We have cited expositions relating to a single section, all of which are Tannaitic — if they are not ascribed to R. Simeon b. Yoḥai himself, they belong at least to his contemporaries — in order to demonstrate again the variegated spectrum of the dicta of the Sages on the doctrine of retribution comprised in just one small segment of Scriptural homilies.

It seems that there is hardly a view, which modern scholars have propounded in order to formulate the Biblical doctrine of retribution, that is not to be found in the dicta of the Sages. Only the Sages, in contrast to these savants, did not claim, even when they based their opinions on Biblical verses, that they were revealing the actual meaning of the texts. In their groping attempts to find answers to the problems of the doctrine of retribution and of cognate subjects the Rabbis did not unravel this Gordian knot, but in their tackling of it and their constant occupation with this doctrine there stand out certain beliefs that form a firm foundation common to them all. These beliefs revert again to the plain meaning of the Biblical texts, that is, to citing them without interpretation. Irrespective of the answer given to the question of 'the righteous man who fares ill and the wicked man who fares well', or of the meanings ascribed to the terms 'reward and punishment' — be it in this world or in the world to come — or of the explanation of the concept 'the reward of a precept is (another) precept', the actual existence of reward and punishment is not in doubt. It is implicit in the very idea of God, who is Judge (above, p. 28), and in the Torah that He gave to His people, in whose observance and fulfilment judgement is involved, as the anonymous homilist put it: 'It is written "O Lord, Thou hast enticed me, and I was enticed" (Jeremiah xx 7) — the Congregation of Israel said to the Holy One: "Sovereign of the universe, Thou didst entice me until Thou didst give me the Torah, and I placed upon my neck the yoke of the kingdom of the commandments, and I was punished on account of them. Had I not accepted the Torah, I should have been like one of the other nations, (receiving) neither reward nor punishment....'[30]

We have seen that the elements of which a man's sentence is composed are many, and the relative portion therein of a man's actions — the precepts fulfilled and the transgressions committed — the merit of the past and present righteous men, the attribute of the compassion of the Holy One, blessed be He, and its place within and alongside the attribute of justice — all these are moot questions and may only be evaluated conjecturally. But the demand for the justification of the Divine judgement is obligatory, and in this respect deed and theory go hand in hand: 'When they [the Romans] seized R. Ḥanina b. Teradion, it was decreed to burn his scroll upon him. They told him "It is decreed to burn your scroll upon you." He (thereupon) recited this verse: "The Rock, His work is perfect." They (then) said to his wife: "It has been decreed to burn your husband's scroll upon him and to execute you." She recited (in response) this verse: "He is a God of faithfulness and without iniquity." They (then) said to his daughter: 'It has been decreed to burn your father's scroll upon him, to execute your mother, and to put you to forced labour." She (thereupon) recited this verse: "(Thou art) great in counsel, and mighty in work — whose eyes are open... to give every one according to his ways, according to the fruit of his doings" (Jeremiah xxxii 19). Rabbi said: Great are these acts, for in the hour of their trouble they caused three verses that vindicate the Divine judgement to burgeon....'[31] The acts yielded the verses not merely because the passages occurred to righteous people in the hour of their ordeal, but because in the mouths of these martyrs they acquired significance of unmitigated and absolute justification of God's judgement. This is illustrated by the next homily: ' "The Rock, His work is perfect" — when Moses came down from Mount Sinai, all Israel came to him. They said: "Moses, our teacher, tell us, what was the nature of the attribute of justice on high." He replied: "I do not only say when the righteous are cleared and the guilty are condemned, but even when the reverse takes place, '(He is) a God of faithfulness and without iniquity'." '[32] This means to say that even if the Lord appears to convict the innocent, He remains a God of faithfulness. This absolute justification of the Divine judgement is connected with the change that occurred in the conception of the suffering that befalls man, as we have explained (above, p. 443).

When a child died in the house of R. Abbahu, R. Jonah and R. Yassa came to comfort him and they asked him to tell them a Torah teaching. On the basis of the Mishna ruling that after the burial of those who were executed by the court 'The relatives come to greet the witnesses and the judges, as though to say: Know that we bear you no grudge for you have delivered a true judgement', R. Abbahu said to them: 'If now in the case of the earthly judiciary, in which are to be found falsehood, lying, deception, partiality, and bribery, and they are here today and gone tomorrow, it is ordained: The relatives come and greet the judges and the witnesses, as though to say: We bear you no grudge, for you have delivered a true judgement, then how much more, in the case of the Heavenly Judiciary, where there is to be found neither falsehood, nor lying, nor deception, nor partiality, nor bribery, and He lives unto all eternity, are we duty-bound to accept the judgement meted out....'[33] This absolute theodicy was also adopted by the Amoraim towards drastic Biblical episodes, and it was even attributed to the heroes of the remote past, although they attempted at the same time to invest the express statements with added meaning in order to justify them. The incident recorded in II Samuel xxi concerning the delivery of seven members of the family of Saul into the hands of the Gibeonites and their hanging was regarded by the Sages as perplexing from the viewpoint of the law of retribution. Actually it is explicitly stated that the Lord said that the famine lasting three years came on account of Saul's sin, 'because he put to death the Gibeonites', and so it is to be understood, for Scripture already blames the Gibeonites for what happened, since it was they who said to David 'It is no matter of silver or gold between us and Saul, or his house... The man that consumed us, and that devised against us, so that we have been destroyed from remaining in any of the borders of Israel, let seven men of his sons be delivered unto us, and we will hang them up unto the Lord' (*ibid. vv.* 4–6); and as if the narrator was anxious from the first to whitewash the act, he added the information 'Now the Gibeonites were not of the children of Israel, but of the remnant of the Amorites; and the children of Israel had sworn unto them...' (*ibid. v.* 2). An anonymous homilist continued the defence along the lines of Scripture and even added thereto[34]; but not all the Sages were content to solve the difficulty in this way and argued: 'It is written in the Torah "The fathers shall not be put to death for the children...", whereas these died for the sin of their fathers!' Two types of solution to this problem are reported in the name of R. Hoshaʿya. One explanation follows the road of absolute theodicy: ' "And Rizpah the daughter of Aiah took sackcloth, and spread it for her upon the rock..." — what is meant by "upon the rock"? R. Hoshaʿya declared: She said "The Rock, His work is perfect".' The second explanation extends the existing story and introduces therein a new element that gives it a general application, which deviates considerably from the framework of the event in the Bible, and the injustice in it is reduced and ousted in the light of the purpose achieved by the act: 'R. Abba bar Zemina in the name of R. Hoshaʿya said: The sanctification of the Divine Name is greater than the desecration thereof. In the case of the desecration of God's name it is written "His body shall not remain all night upon the tree" (Deuteronomy xxi 23); but in the case of the sanctification of God's name it is written "From the beginning of harvest until water was poured upon them from heaven" (II Samuel, *loc. cit.*, *v.* 10).[35] This teaches us that they remained hanging from the sixteenth of Nisan to the seventeenth of Marḥeshvan, and the passers-by said: What sin did these commit that the law was changed in their case? And they were told: They stretched forth their hands against self-made proselytes. They (the Gentiles) then said: Now if these who were not converted for the sake of Heaven, the Holy One, blessed be He, avenged their blood thus, how much more so (will He avenge) him who is converted for the sake of Heaven! There is no God like your God, and there is no people like your people, and we must join you alone. At that time many became converted.'

This explanation serves to convey the Halakhic teaching that the measure of justice to be shown towards proselytes — even to those who were not converted for the sake of Heaven — may be achieved by injustice towards Jews themselves. What is the relationship between this explanation and the first? Apparently there is no contradiction between them, and in truth it is possible that both were enunciated by the same Amora, only the first was given in the original situation, without any argumentation beyond the complete justification of the judgement for which no reasons or grounds are offered, while the second explanation regards the episode from the viewpoint of passers-by and the Gentile nations, who contemplate with amazement the act of justice done for the sake of the self-made proselytes, the Gibeonites. The words 'Now the Gibeonites were not of the children of Israel' acquired a new significance. However, this explanation does not diminish the intrinsic difficulty of the problem inherent in the incident *per se*, and it still needs vindication of the Divine judgement, such as R. Hoshaʿya put into the mouth of Rizpah the daughter of Aiah, but the elucidation opened the way to instruction and moral teaching that appeared to the homilist no less important than finding a reason for justifying the retribution.

However, harsh Scriptural occurrences did not always provide an opportunity for elaboration, which, even if it did not offer a direct answer, nevertheless contained a surrogate. Nevertheless, the Amoraim did not refrain from enlarging upon them, although they thereby primarily gave added weight to the problem. In the generation after R. Hoshaʿya, Amoraim discussed the incident of Saul and Amalek: ' "And Saul came to the city of Amalek, etc." (I Samuel xv 5) — R. Ḥuna and R. Benaiah declared: He began to argue against His Creator, saying: Thus said the Holy One, blessed be He, "Go and smite Amalek" (*ibid.* v. 3). If the men sinned, what sin did the women commit, what sin did the children commit, what sin did the herd and the oxen and asses commit? (Thereupon) a Heavenly Voice went forth and said to him: "Be not righteous overmuch" (Ecclesiastes vii 16) — more than your Creator.'[36]

Another Amora expounded in similar fashion the continuation of the verse: ' "And he strove for the valley" [E.V. "And he lay in wait in the valley"] — R. Mani said: Over the affairs of the valley. When the Holy One, blessed be He, said to Saul "Go and smite Amalek", he argued: If now in respect of one soul the Torah enjoined that a heifer whose neck was to be broken should be brought, how much more so in the case of all these souls! And if man has sinned, what sin have the cattle committed? And if the adults have sinned, what sin have the minors committed? A Heavenly Voice (thereupon) went forth and said to him: "Be not righteous overmuch." '[37] These

Amoraim by their exposition enlarged and deepened the gravity of the problem. It is clear that the questions that they put in the mouth of Saul troubled the Amoraim themselves, and they had no answer except the justification of the Divine judgement both in regard to the annihilation of Amalek and in respect of the punishment imposed upon Saul. Resh Laqish, indeed, did attempt to find fault with Saul and said 'Whoever is merciful when he should be ruthless in the end is ruthless when he should be merciful. And whence do we learn that he (Saul) became ruthless when he should be merciful? For it is said "And Nob, the city of the priests, smote he with the sword" (I Samuel xxii 19).'[38] But the incident at Nob came as a result of the punishment inflicted on Saul; however, the Rabbis so formulated the dictum of Resh Laqish that it contains no explanation but only a justification of the Divine judgement: 'Whoever is merciful when he should be ruthless is in the end stricken by justice.' Rav Huna, who ascribed to Saul the argument against the injunction to destroy Amalek, also said that Saul 'never knew the taste of sin',[39] and when he compared his fate with that of David, he declared: 'How little does he whom the Lord helps need to grieve or trouble himself! Saul sinned but once and he suffered disaster, whereas David sinned twice and he did not suffer calamity!' Rav Huna employed the saying[40] in the sense that David who committed two transgressions was vouchsafed this help, whereas Saul transgressed only once and yet he was not granted this aid. The fact is recorded without any reason being sought, but possibly the reason is implied in the interpretation put by Rav Huna on Saul's sin. It was no ordinary sin but outright rebellion against the Lord's commandment and an impugnment of its justice; hence Divine help was denied him, although he subsequently confessed his sin.[41] His forfeiture of the kingdom is also given an explanation that deviates from the Biblical account. Rav Judah, the colleague of Rav Huna, stated in the name of his teacher Samuel: 'Why did the dynasty of the House of Saul not endure? Because he was free from any family stigma... for an administrator is not appointed over a community unless he has a basket of reptiles hanging over his back, so that if he becomes arrogant, he is told: Look back!' In the name of his teacher Rav he states: 'And why was Saul punished? Because he forwent the honour due to him....'

Rav and Samuel undoubtedly did not overlook the Scriptural statement 'For thou hast rejected the word of the Lord, and the Lord hath rejected thee from being king over Israel' (I Samuel xv 26 and xvi 1), only they found additional reasons for the nature of the punishment, but not for the sentence itself. They and all those Amoraim who agreed with them concerning Saul's righteousness merely justified the Divine judgement.

However, the judgement and fate of the heroes of the past have a historical explanation in the light of the subsequent development of events, and in this way there is also found a reason for justifying the Divine judgement that appeared to them preferable to that given in the Bible. The explanation offered in Chronicles (I Chronicles xxii 4–8) for the fact that the Temple was not built by David, the anointed of the Lord, but by his son Solomon, is that David shed much blood and waged great wars. But did he act on his own accord and not by the command of the Lord? This explanation did not satisfy the Tanna R. Judah b. R. Il'ai. He declares on the basis of another verse in Chronicles (*ibid.* v. 8) that the prophet Nathan said to David 'Thou shalt not build a house unto My name, because thou hast shed much blood', and the Tanna continues 'When David heard this, he was afraid and said: Lo, I have been disqualified from building the Temple... The Holy One, blessed be He, thereupon said to him "Fear not David. By your life! all the blood that you have shed (is in My sight) as that of the hart and gazelle..." Said (David) to Him "If so, why may I not build it [the Temple]?" The Holy One, blessed be He, answered him "If you should build it, it will stand enduringly and never be destroyed." He [David] countered "But surely that is a good thing!" The Holy One, blessed be He, replied "It is revealed before Me that Israel is destined to sin, and I shall assuage My wrath by venting it upon the Sanctuary and destroying it, but the Israelites will be saved." '[42] Thus it was not David's actions that prevented him from building the Temple, but the fate of his people in the distant future. The spiritual balance sheet of individuals — their reward and punishment — is not a personal one only, but part of the audit of the Congregation of Israel. Both the wicked and the righteous must pay their portion of this account, for it is not confined to their generation alone, but belongs both to the future and past generations. However, these computations are invariably made long after the actual deeds and events.

Among the Tannaim who witnessed the martyrdom of their teachers and colleagues in the days of persecution under the Emperor Hadrian, or lived close to their time, there were such as sought to fasten the blame for what occurred onto certain individual sins of the heroes. There were those who insisted on absolute justification of the Divine judgement without entering into specific calculations, or they accepted the doctrine of R. Akiba 'Precious is suffering', and regarded the hallowing of God's name by submission to martyrdom as an example to future generations. However, in the course of time, when the stories concerning the martyred Sages were combined and a kind of martyrological literature developed, in which a total of 'Ten Martyrs'[43] was reached, the theme as a whole was incorporated into the course of history and a common factor was found for all the episodes, namely the atonement of a single iniquity perpetrated in the national past, which had so far not been expiated, and this was none other than the sin of the sale of Joseph. The concept that this sin was never atoned for and that it rests on all the generations, is old, although it was rejected by the Tannaim and Amoraim. They found no stigma or disqualification in the sons of Jacob (below, p. 530). The author of *The Book of Jubilees* states that Joseph was sold on the tenth of the seventh month, and gives the event as the reason for the incidence of the Fast of Atonement on that date. This is how he expresses it: 'For this reason it is ordained for the children of Israel that they should afflict themselves on the tenth of the seventh month — on the day that the news which made him weep for Joseph came to Jacob his father — that they should make atonement for themselves thereon with a young goat on the tenth of the seventh month, once a year for their sins...' (xxxiv 18–19). When the Temple was destroyed, the sin remained without an atonement, and it appears that the burden of expiation was imposed on the righteous in each generation. And thus it is stated in the late Midrash on the Book of Proverbs in the name of the Amora R. Avin: 'In each generation ten have been punished, but the sin is still unexpiated.'[44] The influence of the literature of the *Hekhalot*, which developed the tradition of the ten martyrs, on Midrash Mishle is not in doubt,[45] and indeed before the dictum of

R. Avin we find one in the name of R. Joshua b. Levi: 'The ten martyrs were dragged to execution [נמשכו] only on account of the sin of the sale of Joseph.'[46] In the Midrash emanating from the circle of R. Moses ha-Darshan,[47] who accepted this tradition, the question is raised: 'And should you say: But the Torah ordained "neither shall the children be put to death for the fathers" (Deuteronomy xxiv 16), why then did these die for the iniquity of their fathers? This is no contradiction. (The Sages) said: This was the point of contention between the Attribute of Justice and Michael the guardian angel of Israel. The Attribute of Justice said: It is written in the Torah "For it is no vain thing for you" (Deuteronomy xxxii 47). Now the tribal eponyms sold Joseph and transgressed (the law of) "And he that stealeth a man..."; they were therefore liable to death, but neither they nor their children have yet paid the penalty for the wrong done to Joseph. Michael answered: It is, however, written in the Torah "neither shall the children be put to death for the fathers", and so the children are not liable to death on account of their fathers. Said the Attribute of Justice to the Holy One, blessed be He: Dost Thou then show respect of persons? If Thou dost give a good reward to the children because of the merit of the fathers, wilt Thou not (also) exact retribution from the children on account of the iniquity of their fathers? ... Either make the children pay the penalty or annul the oath! By this argument the Attribute of Justice defeated Michael, for there was no answer, and so he agreed that their children should pay the penalty. And their sentence was that righteous men should die rather than that the Holy One, blessed be He, should annul the oath concerning their merit.' The execution and torture of the Sages during the Hadrianic persecutions received a significance in the course of the nation's history that transcended the confines of their time and age. By atoning for the sin of Jacob's sons in selling Joseph, they saved the merit of the fathers for the benefit of future generations. From the aspect of the latter the element of the merit of the fathers outweighed in the scales of the world's moral reckoning the rule that 'neither shall the children be put to death for the fathers', which underlies the doctrine of retribution. The Attribute of Justice triumphed at the time of the religious persecutions in order that the Attribute of Mercy might prevail for the generations to come.

However, such an evaluation of the various elements composing the world's moral balance sheet is possible and permissible only in respect of the remote past. But no man may have the presumption to imagine that he may act in the present contrary to the duties and precepts imposed upon him, because he foresees the outcome. When King Hezekiah fell ill, Isaiah came to visit him and told him: 'Set thy house in order; for thou shalt die, and not live.' This visit and harsh announcement were expounded, it seems, already in the first generation of the Amoraim as follows:[48] ' "Thou shalt die" in this world, "and not live" in the world to come. Said (Hezekiah) to him: "Why all this?" He replied: "Because you did not engage in the propagation of children", (Hezekiah) answered: "The reason is that I saw by means of the Holy Spirit that unvirtuous children would issue from me." Said (Isaiah) to him: "What have you to do with the mysteries of the All-Merciful?[49] You must do what you are bidden, and that which pleases Him will come to pass." ' Hezekiah exchanged the world's reckoning for its secret. He sought to penetrate into the arcana of the future by ignoring his obligations towards his generation and his society. Actually the spiritual accounting of the individual Israelite is intimately linked to that of the Congregation of Israel. The concepts and beliefs of the Sages concerning the nature, place, and function of the latter will be treated in the next chapter.

CHAPTER XVI

THE PEOPLE OF ISRAEL AND ITS SAGES

We shall begin our portrayal of כנסת ישראל *Kěneset Yiśrā'ēl*, 'the Congregation of Israel' — this designation does not differ in signification from עם ישראל *'am Yiśra'el*, 'the people of Israel', or just ישראל *Yiśrā'ēl*, 'Israel' (see below, p. 645) — with two extraneous testimonies: the first belongs almost to the commencement of the period of which we are treating, and the second pertains wellnigh to the end of it. Hecataeus of Abdera, a writer who reached middle age in the time of Alexander the Great and was active in Egypt at the beginning of the reign of Ptolemy I (323 B.C.E.)[1], related that the work of the priests at Jerusalem was not confined to the sacrificial service and Temple duties, but also included the supervision of the observance of the Torah laws and judicial functions. The High Priest is called by him ἄγγελος τῶν τοῦ θεοῦ προσταγμάτων, 'emissary of God's precepts', that is, the supreme authority in Torah matters. Hecataeus states that at the assemblies of the people 'the High Priest brings forth the commandments of the Torah (in the sight of the people) and the people are, of their own volition, so obedient to the Torah that they forthwith fall upon their faces to the ground and prostrate themselves to the High Priest, who reads and explains (the Scriptures) to them'.[2] More than seven hundred years later the church father Augustine wrote: 'It is in truth a surprising fact that the Jewish people never gave up its laws, either under the rule of pagan kings or under the dominion of Christians. In this respect it is different from other tribes and nations; no emperor or king who found them in his land was able to prevent Jews from being differentiated, by their observance of their Law, from the rest of the family of nations.'[3] In the eyes of strangers, who lived in such widely separated periods in which the conditions of Jewish life were fundamentally different, Israel's Torah remained the decisive factor in moulding the character of this people. But just as the situation described by Hecataeus was the result of struggles against intrigue and antagonism,[4] as they are known to us from the Books of Ezra and Nehemiah, so the astonishing phenomenon referred to by Augustine was the product of the activity of generations of Sages. By their Halakhot, which embraced every sphere of life, by their religious and rational thinking, and by their struggle against trends and views of which they did not approve, they determined the image of the nation. Nevertheless, in doing this, the Sages did not cease studying the history of the Jewish people and its destiny during the vicissitudes that time had brought; they did not refrain from inquiring into the individual's position in the community, or from examining the questions relating to the nation's social and economic stratification and its political and spiritual leadership, or from investigating the significance of its survival and its place in the family of nations in the existing world with all its faults and imperfections, as well as in the world that would be wholly good at the end of days.

I. Election and Reality

The concept of Israel's election, as it is explained in the Bible, served, of course, as a basis for the homilies of the Tannaim and Amoraim on the verses of the Torah and the Prophets touching on the subject. It is not our intention to thread together a string of these homilies,[5] which elaborate the Pentateuchal and Prophetic teachings concerning the fact that the election is founded on the covenant made with the fathers at the revelation on Mount Sinai, that it is essentially dependent on the observance of the covenant by the Jewish people, and that it finds expression in the Lord's love for his people and in His acts of grace.[6] We have already discussed in another context (above, p. 138) the significance of the election in placing the people of Israel under the guidance and direct rule of God in contrast to other peoples who came under the dominion of 'Princes' and angels. Now we propose to deal primarily with specific problems with which the Sages were confronted by the belief in the election of their people, in view of the changes and vicissitudes wrought by time.

The words of the prophet Amos (iii 2) 'You only have I known of all the families of the earth; therefore I will punish you for all your iniquities' served to explain Israel's tribulation and sufferings as an educational and reformative factor, but the explanation was not identical in all ages. The author of *II Maccabees*, who described the treachery of the Hellenizers, the religious persecutions instituted by Antiochus, and the experiences of the martyrs who made the supreme sacrifice, already knew the results of the rebellion, namely the conquest of the city and the Temple. In the light of these events he explains to his readers: 'That our people were being punished by way of chastening and not for their destruction. For indeed it is a mark of great kindness when the impious are not let alone for a long time, but punished at once. In the case of other nations, the Sovereign Lord in his forbearance refrains from punishing them till they have filled up their sins to the full, but in our case he has determined otherwise, that His vengeance may not fall on us in after-days when our sins have reached their height. Wherefore He never withdraweth His mercy from us; and though He chasteneth His own people with calamity, He forsaketh them not' (vi 12–16).

The prayer that the author put in the mouth of Judah Maccabaeus and his men on the day of the purification of the Temple was: 'That they might never again incur such disasters, but that, if ever they should sin, He would chasten them with forbearance, instead of handing them over to blasphemous and barbarous pagans'. In the third century C.E., when the Jewish people had been under the rule of foreign nations for over two centuries, there were found vilifiers who made use of the verse in Amos (cited above) in order to challenge the claim of the Jews to be the Chosen People. The long duration of the exile and oppression made it impossible to give an answer like that of the author of *II Maccabees*. To the sectarians who asked 'Does a friend vent all his wrath upon those whom he loves?', R. Abbahu replied: 'The case may be compared to a man who has two debtors, one his friend and the other his enemy. From his friend he accepts payment a little (at a time); from his enemy he exacts (the whole amount) at once.'[7] The sectary who asked the meaning of the verse in Amos was undoubtedly a Christian. If the conversation took place at the end of the third century, then he himself was used to hearing the derisive remarks of the pagans against the doctrine of election held alike by the Jews and the Christians. Origen, who, like R. Abbahu, lived in Caesarea but at an earlier period, reports the argument put forward by Celsus against him: 'But, see pray, how much (God) helped them and you! Instead of being the lords of the earth, they have remained without a land and without a Temple of their own. And in regard to you, if one of you wanders secretly, he is discovered and sentenced to death.'[8] Origen's answer is not for the moment our concern, but it is evident that long before Celsus, at least from after the destruction of the Temple and even more so after the failure of the revolt in the time of Hadrian, the Jews were subjected to the derision of Gentiles who scoffed at their inferior political position and their degraded status, which were in glaring contrast to their claim to be the Chosen People and close to God.[9]

These arguments influenced the Jewish sectarians, whether they were Christians or belonged to other sects; but what certainly seemed even more dangerous to the Tannaim was the threat they posed to the faith of the members of their own community. It was to the strengthening of the latter that they devoted their attention. The replies they gave the sectaries were of a paltry nature and even the accounts of the debates themselves bear a grotesque and derisive character.[10] More weighty are the answers they gave their own people on the question of the relationship between Israel and the Gentile nations and regarding the significance of the election. Many passages that have been interpreted by scholars as polemical, as answers to pagans and sectarians, are in truth wrestlings with problems that exercised the Sages themselves and were solved by them in various ways. Some Tannaim regarded Israel's election as a cosmic act. The verse Exodus xiv 15 was expounded by the Tanna R. Eleazar of Modiʿim thus: ' "Wherefore criest thou unto Me?" — do I require an instruction where My sons are concerned? "Concerning My sons, and concerning the work of My hands, command ye Me?" (Isaiah xlv 11). Have they not already been designated to be before Me since the six days of creation? For it is said "If these ordinances depart from before Me, saith the Lord, then the seed of Israel shall also cease from being a nation before Me for ever" [Jeremiah xxxi 35].'[11]

R. Eleazar of Modiʿim merely reverts in his exposition to the concept that had been widely accepted long before the destruction of the Temple, as is also attested by extraneous sources.[12] The view that the election of Israel had been planned by God when the world was created makes the election, of course, absolute and independent of any circumstances. This was the doctrine of R. Akiba, who said 'Beloved are Israel in that they are called children of the Omnipresent. Still greater is the love in that it was made known to them that they were called children of the Omnipresent, for it is said "Ye are children of the Lord your God" (Deuteronomy xiv 1).' The great Tanna himself explained the expression and connotation of the love: 'Beloved are Israel in that He gave them the instrument with which the world was created. Still greater is the love in that it was made known to them that He gave them the instrument with which the world was created, as it is said "For I give you good doctrine; forsake ye not My Law" (Proverbs iv 2).'[13] Israel were chosen to be children of the Almighty, and to these children He gave the instrument — that is, the Torah — with which He created the world. The still greater love consists in the fact that the Lord has made known to them that they are His children and that He has given them a good doctrine. R. Me'ir, in the spirit of the teaching of his master, R. Akiba, said: 'Although they are full of blemishes, they are called children, as it is said "Is corruption His? No, His children's is the blemish" (Deuteronomy xxxii 5).'[14] On the basis of these Tannaitic expositions the Amoraim placed the Torah and Israel at the head of the things that preceded the creation of the world, and it is stated in the name of R. Samuel b. R. Isaac: 'The thought of (creating) Israel preceded everything... Had not the Holy One, blessed be He, foreseen that after twenty-six generations Israel would accept the Torah, he would surely not have written in it "Command the children of Israel"!'[15] The consciousness that their election had a cosmic and eternal character accompanied the feeling of tension that emanated from the discrepancy between this consciousness and the reality, as is attested by the words of the visionary, the author of *IV Ezra*: '...Thou hast said that for our sakes Thou hast created the world in the beginning. But as for the other nations, which are descended from Adam, Thou hast said that they are nothing, and that they are like unto spittle; and Thou hast likened the abundance of them to a drop of a bucket.

And now, O Lord, behold these nations which are reputed as nothing lord it over us and consume us. But we, Thy people whom Thou hast called Thy first-born, Thy only-begotten, Thy beloved [most dear], are given up into their hands. If the world has indeed been created for our sakes, why do we not enter into possession of our world? How long shall this endure?'[16] This feeling of tension between the reality and the spiritual consciousness found release in the belief in redemption in its various senses, which we shall discuss later (p. 649).

But not all the Tannaim and Amoraim accepted the doctrine of cosmic-eternal election. Against it can clearly be discerned other views, which may be termed a historical-relativist approach. It is related to conditions and circumstances, and in it the Chosen People plays an active role, being at times even the chooser. Thus R. Eleazar b. Azariah expounded: ' "Thou hast avouched the Lord this day... and the Lord has avouched thee this day" (Deuteronomy xxvi 17–18). The Holy One, blessed be He, said to Israel: You have made Me a unique object of your love in the world, and I shall make you a unique object of My love in the world. You have made Me a unique object of your love in the world, as it is written "Hear, O Israel, the Lord our God, the Lord is One" (*ibid.* vi 4); and I shall make you a unique object of My love in the world, as it is said "Who is like unto Thy people Israel, a nation one in the earth" (I Chronicles xvii 21).'[17] The Lord was chosen by Israel before Israel was chosen by God; R. Ishmael expressed a similar thought in his exposition: ' "And ye shall be holy men unto Me..." (Exodus xxii 30) — when you are holy you are Mine.'[18] First Israel must sanctify themselves and only thereafter do they merit to be called a holy people.

Although the view that Israel chose the Lord first is rejected in an anonymous Tannaitic Midrash, yet the process of election portrayed in it falls within the ambit of history and is not an act that preceded Creation: ' "For the portion of the Lord is his people" (Deuteronomy xxxii 9): The case is comparable to that of a king who had a field, which he leased to tenant farmers. The tenants began to steal from it; so he took it away from them and gave it to their sons. They soon proved themselves worse than the first. He thereupon took it away from their sons and gave it to their grandsons, but they showed themselves to be still worse. When, however, a son was born to him, he said to the tenants: "Go forth from my (land); you cannot remain there. Give me (back) my portion so that I may declare it to be mine." Even so when our father Abraham came into the world, there issued from him the refuse of Ishmael and all the sons of Keturah; when Isaac came into the world there issued from him the refuse of Esau and all the chiefs of Edom, and they were even worse than the first. When Jacob, however, arrived, no refuse issued from him, but all the sons born to him were worthy, as it is said "And Jacob was a perfect [תם *tām*; EVV 'quiet'] man, dwelling in tents" (Genesis xxv 27). Who is the first to be claimed by the Omnipotent as His portion? Jacob, as it is said "For the portion of the Lord is His people, Jacob the lot of His inheritance", and it is further said "For the Lord hath chosen Jacob" (Psalms cxxxv 4). But the matter still remains ambiguous and we cannot tell whether the Holy One, blessed be He, chose Jacob or whether Jacob chose the Holy One, blessed be He, therefore Scripture teaches us "Israel for His own treasure" (*ibid.*). However, the matter is still undecided, and we do not know if the Holy One, blessed be He, chose Israel for His own treasure, or if Israel chose the Holy One, blessed be He, therefore Scripture teaches "And the Lord thy God hath chosen thee to be His own treasured people" (Deuteronomy xiv 2). And how do we know that Jacob also chose the Lord?; for it is said "Not like these is the portion of Jacob" (Jeremiah x 16).'[19] The homily as we have it is composed of two homilies, and the point of their juncture is still discernible. The first emphasizes the idea of choice and clearly establishes that it was God who chose His portion, as is also to be inferred from the verse in Deuteronomy, which serves as the starting point. The second homily finds the verse Psalms cxxxv 4 ambivalent and accordingly 'we cannot tell whether the Holy One, blessed be He, chose Jacob or whether Jacob chose the Holy One, blessed be He'.[20] The expositor's solution is, as it were, a twofold concept of election. From the verse in Deuteronomy he deduces that the Lord chose Israel, and from the verse in Jeremiah, where it is stated, after the prophet had spoken about people who had elected to serve idols, 'Not like these is the portion of Jacob', he infers that Jacob chose the Lord.[21] The Lord's choice was answered by Jacob's choice, and, indeed, also the Tanna R. Judah made the latter a condition of the maintenance of the first. He disagreed with his colleague R. Me'ir and expounded ' "Ye are the children of the Lord your God"... If you act like children you are (deemed) children, but if not you are not (accounted as) children.'[22] The selective process of the election, which, continuing for generations, is enshrined in verses of the Prophets and of the Hagiographa[23], and is depicted, in a manner similar to the exposition of the Tannaim, also in the pseudepigraphical literature[24], removes the arbitrary aspect from the question of the election. The chosen people becomes the choosing people. 'A certain noblewoman put an objection to R. Jose, saying: "Your God brings near [i.e. favours] whom He wishes!" He thereupon brought before her a basket of figs from which she selected well, eating what she selected. He then said to her: "You know how to choose; (can you imagine that) the Holy One, blessed be He, does not know how to choose! When He sees one whose deeds are good, He elects him and brings him near." '[25] The Amora R. Judah b. R. Simon took the old belief that the world was created on account of the Torah and combined it with the motif of free choice, and in his hands both ideas, woven into a beautiful homily, transform the people of Israel from the Chosen to the Choosing People. ' "As a lily among thorns" (Canticles ii 2): It is like the case of a king who had an orchard. He planted in it rows upon rows of figs, a row of vines, and a row of pomegranates. After a time when the king went down to see his vineyard, he found it full of thorns and thistles. So he appointed for it mowers to mow it down. But he found in it one rose blossom; he took it and smelt it and felt refreshed. Thereupon he said: This blossom deserves that the entire orchard should be saved for its sake. Even so the whole world was created only on account of the Torah. After twenty-six generations the Holy One, blessed be He, glanced at His world and found it full of thorns and thistles, such as the generation of Enosh, and that of the Flood, and the men of Sodom. He thereupon wished to destroy it utterly, as it is said "The Lord sat enthroned at the Flood" (Psalms xxix 10). But He found there a single rose blossom — to wit, Israel — and He took it and breathed its fragrance at the time when He gave them the Ten Commandments, and His soul was refreshed when they said "We will do, and obey." '[26]

It was Israel's positive response and their acceptance of the Torah that made the election of Israel a reality, and when the Torah was accepted the world was firmly established. It was still possible, of course, to contend that the Lord had not offered His Torah to other peoples, and this very fact, even if the Israelites accepted the Law voluntarily and not under compulsion, makes the election an arbitrary act, and indeed it seems that some did argue thus. In order to answer this objection the Tannaim already completed the Pentateuchal story by declaring:

'Therefore the Gentile nations were asked to receive the Torah, in order not to afford them an opportunity to say to the Shekhina: "Had we been asked we should certainly have accepted it." Thus they were asked, but did not accept it, as it is said "And he said: 'The Lord came from Sinai' etc." (Deuteronomy xxxiii 2) — He revealed Himself to the children of the wicked Esau, and said to them: "Will you accept the Torah?" Said they to Him: "What is written therein?" He answered them: "Thou shalt not murder." They replied: "This is the heritage that our father has bequeathed to us, as it is said 'And by thy sword shalt thou live' (Genesis xxvii 40)." He next revealed Himself to the children of Ammon and Moab, saying to them: "Will you accept the Torah?" Said they to Him: "What is written therein?" He answered them "Thou shalt not commit adultery". They then said: "We are all the offspring of adultery, for it is written 'Thus were both the daughters of Lot with child by their father' " (*ibid.* xix 36). He then revealed Himself to the children of Ishmael, saying to them: "Will you accept the Torah?" Said they to Him: "What is written therein?" He answered them: "Thou shalt not steal." They replied: "This is the benison bestowed upon our father. for it is written 'And he shall be as a wild ass of a man' (*ibid.* xvi 12) and it is further written 'For, indeed, I was stolen away' (*ibid.* xl 12)." But when He came to Israel and "At His right hand was a fiery law unto them" (Deuteronomy xxxiii 2), they all cried aloud and said "All that the Lord hath spoken will we do, and obey" (Exodus xxiv 7).'[27]

By the Gentile nations [literally 'nations of the world'], to whom the expositor did not wish to give an excuse, he doubtless meant the pagans. The Emperor Julian asked the Christians: If the Deity is not only the God of the Jews but also the God of the Gentiles, why did

He send them so much grace of prophecy, and Moses, and anointing, and the prophets and the Torah... whereas we have no prophet, no anointing, no teacher, no herald, to make known to us the grace of His love, which is in store for us... Nay more, He even hid Himself from us for myriads — or, if you will, for thousands — of years, and He let all those who dwell from the rising of the sun to the setting thereof, and from the north pole to the recesses of the south, serve idols, as you call them, out of such ignorance, except for one small people that settled in a part of Palestine less than two thousand years ago....'[28]

The apostate emperor's argument was directed specifically against the doctrine of Paul and his followers, who maintained that the Gentiles who believed in Jesus had inherited Israel's place; but from the Tannaitic expositions we learn that in point of fact he repeated arguments adduced by the pagans against the Jews some two centuries earlier. The answer given by the Sages did not aim at the placation of the non-Jews, but constitutes a counterattack. It establishes a fact, as it were: The Gentiles were given an opportunity to accept the Torah, but did not do so. The precepts that prompted their refusal — 'Thou shalt not murder', 'Thou shalt not commit adultery', and 'Thou shalt not steal' — are not exclusive ordinances of the people of Israel; they are counted among the Noachide laws,[29] whose observance is incumbent upon the whole human race. Indeed in another version of the answer it is stated: 'There was not one among the nations to whom He did not come and speak and upon whose door He did not knock, (asking) whether they wished to accept the Torah... Should you think that they hearkened and accepted, Scripture teaches us "But do them not" (Ezekiel xxxiii 31), and it further says "And in anger and wrath I will execute vengeance upon the nations that did not obey" (Micah v 14). Nay, even the seven commandments that the children of Noah accepted they failed to keep, till in the end they set them aside and gave them to Israel.'[30] Undoubtedly we have here evidence of the Sages' evaluation of the ethical standard of the Gentiles with whom they came in contact[31], although it was exacerbated by the polemical trend of the source; but the effect of this homily, too, was primarily internal. It was transmitted in the course of generations and served to justify the giving of the Torah to Israel and thus to consolidate the sense of election, specifically in its active signification. On Lamentations iii 1, 'I am the man' we find the following homily:[32]

'R. Joshua b. Levi said: The Congregation of Israel said before the Holy One, blessed be He: "Sovereign of the whole universe, I am the one that is inured (to affliction); all that Thou wishest comes upon me."[33] It is like the case of a noblewoman with whom the king was wroth and she was expelled from the palace. What did she do? She hid herself, standing behind a pillar. When the king passed, he said to her "You were insolent". She answered him: "My lord, the king, so it is fitting, and so it is comely, and so it is proper for me, for no woman accepted you but me." Said the king to her: "Nay! It is I who disqualified all the women on account of you." She replied: "Nay! It is they who did not accept you." Even so the Congregation of Israel said to the Holy One, blessed be He: "Sovereign of the whole universe, thus it is proper for me (to act), for no nation received Thy law, only I." The Holy One, blessed be He, answered: "Nay! It is I who disqualified all the nations on account of you." Said she to Him: "Nay! It is they who did not accept it. Wherefore didst Thou go to Mount Seir? Was it not to give the Torah to the children of Esau, but they did not accept it? So, too, (Thou didst go) to the wilderness of Paran — was it not to give the Torah to the children of Ishmael, but they did not accept it? Wherefore didst Thou go to the Ammonites and Moabites? Was it not to give the Torah to the children of Lot, but they did not accept it?.... How many kindnesses have I not done Thee? I sanctified Thy name at the sea; I uttered song unto Thee; with joy I accepted the Torah, which the Gentile peoples did not accept. Yet after all this glorification 'I am the man that hath seen affliction'!" '[34]

The answer given in the Tannaitic homily to the charge of the Gentile nations against the arbitrary character of Israel's election is used by the Congregation of Israel in the homily of R. Joshua b. Levi as proof that the Israelites accepted the Torah of their own volition, and it opens the way again for their complaint at their cruel fate, which contradicts the fact that they are the Chosen People. This remonstrance on the part of the Congregation echoes to some extent the arguments advanced by non-Jews, which were cited above (p. 526); but it called forth varied reactions, especially from those

Sages who did not regard the election of Israel as an arbitrary cosmic act, and likewise did not wish to give up the idea that the Congregation of Israel voluntarily accepted the Torah and adopt instead the view that the Holy One, blessed be He, 'tilted the mountain over them like a cask' (above, p. 324).

It is possible to distinguish three kinds of reaction to this reproach: the first emanates from a consideration of the history of the nation and its relationship to its God since receiving the Torah; the second is based on the contemporary view of the people as a community of individuals who are responsible for one another; and the third cut the Gordian knot by opening the way to a universal conception of Israel's election.

Following close upon the acceptance of the Torah is the story of the golden calf. Some Tannaim emphasized the gravity of the sin into which the whole people fell, so that a shadow was cast upon the revelation at Mount Sinai and it lost its positive significance: 'Thus we find that our ancestors, when standing at Mount Sinai, sought to deceive the Most High, as it is said "All that the Lord hath spoken will we do, and obey" (Exodus xxiv 7) — and, so to speak, the (Heavenly) Court was deceived, as it is said "O that they had such a heart as this always" (Deuteronomy v 36). Should you suppose that not all things are revealed and known to Him, Scripture teaches us "But they beguiled Him... For their heart was not steadfast with Him". Nevertheless "He, being full of compassion, forgiveth iniquity" (Psalms lxxviii 36–38).'[35] Uttering 'We will do' before '(We will) obey,' contained an element of deception, which was manifest to the Holy One, blessed be He, only He, as it were, overlooked it, just as He was ready to grant atonement for the sin of the calf. The diminution of Israel's prestige at the revelation on Mount Sinai weakens the impression of treachery produced by the episode of the calf, and reduces the tension that finds expression in the complaint. But reference to the story of the calf sufficed even for the Sages who in no way impugned the integrity of the act of receiving the Torah to moderate the complaint. By the incident of the calf the Israelites lowered the status that they had attained at the revelation on Mount Sinai. The Tanna R. Simeon b. Yoḥai accepted the words of the prophet Amos (v 25) 'Did ye bring unto Me sacrifices and offerings in the wilderness?' etc. as a fact and interpreted it as a punishment upon Israel. 'The Israelites — he said — did not offer sacrifices. To whom then did the tribe of Levi sacrifice, for it is said "They put incense before Thee, and whole burnt-offering upon Thine altar" (Deuteronomy xxxiii 10)... The Israelites served idols, but the tribe of Levi did not worship idols, as it is said "For they have observed Thy word" (*ibid. v.* 9)'.[36] But the punishment was temporary, for the sin of the calf was neither the first nor the last transgression. Some Sages adopted the historical assessment of Ezekiel in chapter xx, which states that Israel's rebellion began when they were still in Egypt, and said that the Israelites did not hearken to Moses (Exodus vi 9) when he came to announce to them the news of the redemption, 'for it was hard for them to give up idolatry'.[37] Notwithstanding, God brought them out from Egypt and gave them the Torah and the precepts 'that they might know that I am the Lord that sanctifies them' (Ezekiel xx 12). The Amora R. Samuel bar Naḥman combined the words of Ezekiel with the verse in Proverbs (x 12) 'Hatred stirreth up strifes; but love covereth all transgressions', and gave the following exposition: 'For nearly nine hundred years Israel felt pent-up hatred for their Father in Heaven, from the time they left Egypt until Ezekiel arose and said to them "Cast ye away every man the detestable things of his eyes" etc. (Ezekiel xx 7)..." "but love covereth all transgressions" — the love with which the Holy One loved Israel, as it is said "I have loved you, saith the Lord" (Malachi, i 2).'[38] Only the 'Hatred that Israel felt for their Father in Heaven' induced the prophet Ezekiel to reveal the sin that they committed in Egypt and which in His love the Holy One, blessed be He, covered up for nine hundred years. This love finds expression in the fact that the evil deeds tend to be forgotten but not the covenant. Thus Resh Laqish said:

'The Congregation of Israel declared before the Holy One, blessed be He: "It is the way of the world that even when a human king takes an additional wife, he remembers the acts of the first; but Thou hast forsaken me and forgotten me." Said the Holy One, blessed be He, to the prophet: "Go tell the Congregation of Israel: My daughter, I have created twelve constellations in the firmament, and for each constellation I have created... and all of them have I created only for your sake, yet you say: Thou hast forsaken me and forgotten me. 'Can a woman forsake her sucking child, that she should not have compassion on the son of her womb?' (Isaiah xlix 16)...." Thereupon the Congregation of Israel spoke before Him: "Sovereign of the universe, since there is no forgetfulness before the Throne of Thy Glory, perhaps Thou wilt not forget unto me the incident of the calf." God answered her: " 'Yea, these will be forgotten (*ibid.*).' " The Congregation of Israel then rejoined: "Sovereign of the universe, since there is forgetfulness before the Throne of Thy Glory, perhaps Thou wilt forget unto me what happened at Sinai." The Lord assured her: "Yet I [the initial word of the Decalogue] will not forget thee." This, too, is what R. Eleazar said in the name of R. Oshaʿya: What is the meaning of the verse "Yea, these will be forgotten"? This refers to the episode of the calf; and "Yet I will not forget thee" — this refers to Sinai.'[39]

This conviction of Resh Laqish that Israel's response at Sinai would not be forgotten is only an expression of his trust in the eternity of the election of Israel. But it did not make him oblivious of the absence of manifestations attesting the election of Israel by the Lord and of their nearness to Him, and he explained this by the conduct of the people at crucial junctures of their history. Concerning the period of the Second Temple the Sages declared that it lacked five things possessed by the First Temple, among which they included the Holy Spirit.[40] Resh Laqish did not attribute the absence of the Shekhina from the Second Temple — as did R. Joḥanan — to the fact that the Temple was built by Cyrus, who was a descendant of Japhet, but to the exiles of his day who did not respond to his call 'Whosoever there is among you of all His people — his God be with him — let him go up [to Jerusalem]' (Ezra i 3), 'For thus said the Holy One, blessed be He, if all Israel go up the Shekhina shall rest upon them, but if not, they would have to avail themselves only of a *Bat Qol*' ('Heavenly Voice').[41]

In the generation following Resh Laqish the Sages in Eretz-Israel gave the following exposition: ' "If she be a wall" (Canticles viii 9): Had the Israelites gone up from exile like a wall [i.e. undivided, in their entirety], the Temple would not have been destroyed a second time.'[42] Thus they found the cause of the destruction of the Second

Temple to have existed already at the beginning of the era. These homilies had topical significance, for they were expounded by Amoraim in Eretz-Israel, who did not love their Babylonian colleagues.[43] More perhaps than by expressions of explicit unsympathy or dislike this is attested by the sarcastic explanation of the delay that occurred in Ezra's immigration: '...Ezra and his disciples and his colleagues did not go up at the time. Now why did Ezra not go up at that time? Because he needed to clarify his learning before Baruch the son of Neriah. Then Baruch the son of Neriah should have gone up! But (the Sages) said: Baruch the son of Neriah was a great man and old and even in a sedan-chair (*lectica*) he could not have been carried.'[44]

Even if we attribute no small part of the evaluation of the Second Temple period and its beginning, in particular, to the contemporary polemical aim of these Amoraims, we cannot overlook the element in their dicta that makes the realization of the election — its merits and its characteristics — dependent on the numerical state of the people. These views were expressed by the Amoraim in accordance with the doctrine of R. Simeon b. Yoḥai. It was actually this Tanna, who held extravagant individualistic opinions (above, p. 489), that said: 'Whence is it to be inferred that even if Israel lacked one person the Shekhina would not have appeared to them? Because it is written: "For the third day the Lord will come down in the sight of *all* the people upon Mount Sinai" (Exodus xix 11)'[45]; that is to say, the giving of the Torah, which is the quintessence of Israel's election, was conditional on the total presence of the people — not a soul was absent. With this view also R. Judah, the Patriarch, agreed.[46] But unity, and not only numerical wholeness, was required, and it was Rabbi, too, who emphasized this fact and explained its significance:

'Rabbi said: This tells us the merit of Israel. When they all stood at Mount Sinai to receive the Torah, they all resolved, with like mind, to accept the kingdom of God with joy. Nay more, they pledged themselves for one another. Nor was it for the overt acts alone that the Holy One, blessed be He, intended to reveal Himself to them in order to make a covenant with them, but also for the secret deeds. However, they said to Him: For the overt acts we shall make a covenant with Thee, but not for the secret deeds, lest one of us sin in secret and the whole community be held liable, as it is said 'The secret things belong unto the Lord our God; but the things that are revealed belong unto us and to our children" (Deuteronomy xxix 28).'[47]

The election was of one entire people and the covenant was made on condition that all 'Israel be sureties for one another (ישראל ערבין זה לזה)'.[48] R. Simeon b. Yoḥai, who stressed the importance of the wholeness of the nation at the time of their election, also explained the significance of the mutual guaranties: 'R. Simeon b. Yoḥai taught: This may be compared to people who were in a boat, and one of them took a drill and began to drill a hole beneath himself. Said his companions to him: "Why are you doing this?" He retorted: "What concern is it of yours? Am I not drilling under myself?" They replied: "Because you will flood the boat for us all!" Even so Job argued "And be it indeed that I have erred, mine error remaineth with myself" (Job xix 4). Said his companions to him: " 'When he addeth to his sin, he attacheth rebellion to us' [EVV: 'For he addeth rebellion to his sin, he clappeth his hands among us'] (*ibid.* xxxiv 37) — you attach your iniquities to us." '[49]

Only the punishment of the sinners frees the community from the responsibility resting upon it. The homily ' "And that soul shall be cut off from among his people" — then his people will be at peace' recurs in all[50] the Tannaitic Midrashim, a fact that attests its antiquity.

From the verse 'And who is like Thy people, Israel, a nation one in the earth' (II Samuel vii 23), which the Sages regarded as expressing the election of Israel (above p. 529), as 'a holy nation' in the sense of 'separated from the nations of the world and their abominations'[51], they also inferred that Israel was 'as one body, as one soul... if one of them sinned all were punished, as it is said "Did not Achan the son of Zerah commit a trespass concerning the devoted thing, and wrath fell upon all the congregation of Israel? and that man perished not alone in his iniquity" (Joshua xxii 20). If one of them is smitten they all feel pain; therefore it says "Israel is a scattered sheep" (Jeremiah l 17) — just as when a ewe is afflicted in one of its limbs, all the limbs are affected, even so is Israel, when one of them is afflicted they all suffer. But the Gentiles all rejoice at one another's downfall.'[52] Israel has become one nation by virtue of the covenant and cannot rejoice when part of it is punished or suffers as do other peoples; for even if they are members of one faith, they are divided into nationalities and fight one another. Already the Tanna R. Joḥanan b. Torta, who lived at the time of the Revolt of Bar Kochba, cited as a cause of the destruction of the Second Temple the fact that 'they hated one another without cause'[53]; and an Amora who gave a dramatic description of Abraham's intervention on behalf of his children on the night of the Ninth of Av makes the Holy One, blessed be He, give as the final reason for the Destruction '...Moreover, they rejoiced at one another's downfall.'[54] The punishment of the whole people of Israel is a consequence of their mutual responsibility and is inherent in the act of election, which made Israel one nation upon earth. The very concept of the election implies mutual responsibility and consequently also collective punishment; there is no room, therefore, for complaint, for this reciprocal suretyship makes it possible to gain atonement and to preserve the special relationship between Israel and his God. With reference to the story of Achan, in which the Sages found testimony to the fact that 'Israel are sureties for one another', R. Abba bar Zavda states in the name of Rav ' "Israel hath sinned" — this implies that although they have sinned they are still "Israel" '[55], and, as Rashi explains: 'Since Scripture does not say "the people hath sinned", their holy name still belonged to them.'

The mutual suretyship, which brings punishment upon the whole people bearing the responsibility, implies also a guarantee that Israel would return to the path of rectitude, and by the same token is an assurance of the nation's eternal existence. The verse in Jeremiah (xi 16) 'The Lord called thy name a leafy olive-tree, fair with goodly fruit' was expounded by R. Joshua b. Levi and by R. Joḥanan. The former said: 'Why are the people of Israel likened to an olive-tree? To tell you that just as an olive-tree does not shed its leaves either in summer or in winter, so Israel shall not come to an end either in this world or in the world to come.' R. Joḥanan said: 'Why are the people of Israel compared to an olive-tree? To tell you that just as the olive produces its oil only through pounding, so do Israel return to the path of righteousness only after suffering.'[56] The two homilies complement each other. The Israelites are not easily reformed, but the attribute of obduracy also assures their survival. R. Joḥanan's colleague, Resh Laqish, declared that the people of Israel were the

עזין *ʿazzîn* ['fierce, impetuous ones'][57] of the nations. The meaning of his dictum is made clear by the Baraitot cited in the same context. 'It was taught in the name of R. Me'ir: Why was the Torah given to Israel? Because they are impetuous [*ʿazzîn*]; the School of R. Ishmael taught: "At His right hand was a fiery law unto them" — the Holy One, blessed be He, said: These deserve to be given a fiery law. Some say: The laws of these are sheer fire, for had not the Torah been given to Israel, no nation or tongue could have withstood them.'[58] From the exposition of 'Some say' — that only the Torah transforms the attribute of impetuosity [עזות *ʿazzût*] into a virtue and that otherwise it might have been a source of harm to the world — we learn that the School of Ishmael regarded impetuosity as the quality that made Israel worthy of receiving the fiery law. This last dictum, which to begin with portrayed Israel's character and concluded — through its metaphor — with the thought that the giving of the Torah to Israel was also of benefit to the Gentile world, enables us to make the transition to the third group of dicta and homilies that bridges the gulf between Israel's election and its present position of subjection, as well as its history, which is replete with hard and bitter ordeals. This is achieved actually by emphasizing the universal elcment in Israel's election.

II. Election and Proselytization

In the Midrash, which was likewise taught in 'the School of Ishmael', it is stated:

' "Before the Lord God, the God of Israel" (Exodus xxxiv 23). Why is this [the last part] stated? Has it not already been said "Before the Lord God"? Why then does Scripture add, "the God of Israel"? The explanation is that He conferred His name particularly on Israel. Similarly, "Hear, O Israel, the Lord our God, the Lord is One" (Deuteronomy vi 4). Why is this [the last part] stated? Has it not already been said "the Lord our God"? What then is the significance of "the Lord is one"? The meaning is that He conferred His name particularly on us. Similarly, "Therefore, thus saith the Lord, the God of Israel" (II Kings xxi 12). Why is this stated? Has it not already been written "Behold, I am the Lord, the God of all flesh" (Jeremiah xxxii 27)? What then are we taught by the words "The God of Israel"? The fact that He conferred His name particularly on Israel. Similarly, "Hear, O My people, and I will speak; O Israel, and I will testify against thee: God, thy God, am I..." (Psalms l 7). I am the God of all people; nevertheless I have conferred My name specifically on Israel.'[59]

Apparently the practical significance attaching to this emphasis on the particular conferment upon Israel of the name of God, who is the God of all flesh, is that it is Israel's function to bring the recognition of the God of Israel to the knowledge of the world. The fact of the dissemination of Israel's faith among the Gentiles in the Jewish Diaspora and of the resultant large number of proselytes and 'fearers of the Lord' in the countries of the Roman Empire and in the area of Hellenistic civilization is well known; we shall not, therefore, discuss it in detail.[60] Our primary interest here is the reflection of these circumstances in the views expressed concerning the place of the Congregation of Israel in the family of nations and its distinctive character and mission.

Our concern will be to trace to what extent and in which way events like the destruction of the Temple, the loss of the residual political independence of Judea, the spread of Christianity, and its missionary activity influenced these views and in what measure they remained fundamental beliefs that were unaffected either by these events or by the cessation of Jewish proselytization. We shall begin particularly with dicta of the second half of the third century C.E.: 'R. Eleazar also said: The Holy One, blessed be He, exiled Israel among the nations only to the end that proselytes might join them, as it is said "And I will sow her unto Me in the land" (Hosea ii 25). Surely one sows a *se'a* in order to reap a number of *kor*[61]... R. Osha'ya said: What is the meaning of the verse "Even the righteous acts of פרזונו *pirzono* [understood as equivalent by metathesis to *pizrono*, 'His scattering'] to Israel" (Judges v 11) — an act of charity [literally: 'righteousness'] did the Holy One, blessed be He, to Israel in that He scattered them among the nations. And this is what a Min once said to R. Judah Nesi'a:[62] "We are better than you. Of you it is written 'For Jacob and all Israel remained there six months, until he had cut off every male in Edom' (I Kings xi 16), whereas you have been with us many years, yet we do you no harm." Said (R. Judah Ne'sia) to him: "If you wish, one of the disciples will take up the argument with you." R. Hoshaʿya debated with him, saying: "Because you do not know how to act. Should you think of destroying them all, they are not among you. (Should you consider destroying only) those in your midst, you would be called a barbarous kingdom."[63] Replied (the Min): "I swear by the גפא *gappā* of Rome![64] With this (thought) we rise up and with this (thought) we lie down (Rashi: 'We are constantly preoccupied with this thought')." ' The two dicta cited together reflect totally different explanations of the dispersion of the Jewish people among the nations, but it is actually the view of the younger scholar, R. Eleazar, who declared that the Lord exiled Israel among the nations only that proselytes might join them, that was the legacy of preceding generations, who gloried in the influence exerted by Israel's Torah on their non-Jewish environment[65], and was acceptable to all and remained the belief of the majority even after the decline of proselytization.[66] R. Hoshaʿya's reply was given in a specific situation and originated not as an explanation of the existence of the Dispersion, but as a polemical argument between a Min and the Sage. The Min referred to was a Gentile and a pagan,[67] only he was apparently interested in the sacred Scripture of the Jews. There were pagans who in this manner found their way either to conversion to Judaism and admission to the Congregation of Israel,[68] or to Christianity.[69] But there were also others whose antipathy and antagonism towards Judaism, ingrained in them from the first, were further strengthened by such reading. For we must not forget that even in the period when the Jewish diaspora and Israel's Torah had an appeal for the Gentile world and attracted converts, they also aroused hatred and sharp criticism,[70] which advanced arguments that laid the foundations of theoretical anti-Semitism.

The type of Gentile that they encountered and their experiences with the pagans who were drawn towards Judaism and read the Bible also determined the reactions of the Sages. Against the view of R. Eliezer that 'No Gentile has a share in the world to come', R. Joshua argued: 'But there are righteous men among the nations who have a share in the world to come' (*Tosefta Sanhedrin* xiii, 2, p. 434). Probably the dictum 'Even a Gentile who studies the Torah is like the High Priest' is only the outcome of a positive experience. In some sources it is ascribed to the Tanna R. Jeremiah, who belonged to the *entourage* of R. Judah the Patriarch and knew the relationship between 'Rabbi and Antoninus'.[71] In other sources the author of the saying is given as R. Me'ir,[72] who actually lived and worked in troubled days of religious persecution, but even in such times the Rabbis encountered exceptional individuals who stood by the Jews in their hour of adversity, and it is not surprising that they attributed the acts of these people to the merit of their study of the Torah and precepts. It was the disciple of R. Me'ir, Judah b. Shammua', who was given advice, at the time of religious oppression, by 'a certain noblewoman, who entertained all the leading Romans. She counselled them (the delegation): "Go and cry out at night." So they went and cried out at night, saying: "Oh, in heaven's name, are we not your brethren, are we not the children of one father? Why are we different from all other nations and tongues that you impose harsh decrees upon us?" The decrees were thereupon annulled.'[73] On the other hand, at times when the government was better disposed towards the Jews, many Gentiles continued to favour the policy of Hadrian. To them belonged the Min who met R. Judah Nesi'a. He made use of the knowledge he had acquired from the Book of Kings regarding the acts of Joab in Edom in order to establish his pagan charge concerning the ἀπανθρωπία of the Jews in contrast to the Graeco-Roman φιλανθρωπία.

R. Hosha'ya, to whom R. Judah Nesi'a assigned the task of replying to the Min, did not choose the apologetic approach in order to defend Joab's actions, but proceeded to counterattack. This φιλανθρωπία not only does not exist where Jews are concerned, but the Roman government has given thought to the possibility of annihilating the Jewish people from off the face of the earth — the memory of Hadrian's edicts had not yet dimmed — and if the intention was not implemented, it was because of the kindness that the Lord had done to His people in that they were only partly subject to the rule of the wicked empire, and hence it did not have the power to destroy them. The Min admits, at the end of his speech, and even swears to reinforce his words that the question of ridding the world of Jews does not cease troubling him and his associates.

This story proves that even in the period of the spread of Christianity it is not possible to speak of a rapprochement between Gentiles and Jews for the reason that 'Jews and Gentiles had to fight against the common dangerous enemy',[74] just as, on the other hand, the Jews and Christians were not allies in the common struggle against the heathen Roman Empire.[75] Although Celsus — followed by Porphyry, the emperor Julian, and others like them — was prepared to recognize and even to praise the loyalty of the Jews to the tradition of their ancestors and their laws,[76] yet at the same time they were most emphatically opposed to the claim of the Jews that their God is 'One and there is none beside Him', that they are His chosen people, and certainly to the contention that the Jews cannot give up their belief that the idols shall utterly pass away and that they are enjoined to encourage idolaters to enter the fold of Judaism. The struggle of the Christians against idolatry did not make them partners of the Jews, since this struggle was waged by the Christians while cleaving to the postulate that the election of Israel had been completely annulled and with it the age of the Torah and precepts had likewise passed away, and that the Church, 'which had been gathered from among the Gentile peoples'[77] had replaced the Congregation of Israel. In their endeavour to condition the minds of the pagans to accept their Gospel, the Christians were at the same time fanning the flames of hatred towards 'Israel in the flesh', and preparing the background for the anti-Jewish legislation and persecutions of the Jews in the fourth century,[78] after 'the entire kingdom [i.e. Roman Empire] had gone over to the Christian heresy'.[79] From that time on the Sages regarded it as 'The wicked kingdom, which seduces the world and leads it astray with its falsehoods'.[80]

For about a hundred and fifty years, from after the Revolt of Bar Kokhba until Christianity became dominant in the Roman Empire, the Sages of Israel stood embattled on two fronts — one facing them and the other at the rear. They joined issue with the pagans, who proceeded to negate Israel's election with politico-territorial arguments: a subjugated people, which had neither independence nor temple, could not be regarded by them as a chosen but as an inferior people; and they polemized against the Christians, who boasted that they had inherited the election-birthright of the Jewish people and its covenant with its God, as well as the accompanying spiritual attributes, precisely because they were 'not a people' but 'a church of the peoples'.[81] Although the polemic — as we noted even in the case of the pagans — was conducted on the basis of Scriptural verses, their interpretation and exposition, yet it was also nourished by actual relations and deeds which determined, in no small measure, its form and its intensity. The reply given by R. Hoshaʿya to the pagan Min, at the injunction of the Patriarch, was not delivered in a vacuum but as a result of definite knowledge of the heathen's thoughts and his attitude towards the Jews. This attitude was not peculiar to this Min alone, but it is likewise clear that he and his congeners did not represent the whole of pagan society.[82] Just as his point of view justified the answer that the dispersion of Israel was a means of protecting them from annihilation, so does the existence of pagans who come to be converted form the background of R. Eleazar's explanation that the dispersion of the nation was due to the desire of Providence to augment the number of proselytes. Undoubtedly this fact was also known to Rav Hoshaʿya, but it would have been out of place to emphasize it in the debate with his interlocutor. On the other hand Origen tells of a disputation that he had, with one who was accounted a scholar among the Jews, on the passage in Isaiah lii 13–liii 8. When Origen gave it a Christological interpretation, the Jew said to him: 'That these prophecies refer to the whole people as though they were a single individual, for they are scattered in exile and are afflicted, so that as a result of the Jews' being dispersed among other peoples, many of the latter may be converted'. In this way the Jew interpreted the verses: 'So marred was his visage unlike that of a man', 'For that which had not been told them shall they see'.[83] R. Eleazar's dictum is given here verbatim, only while the Amora based his teaching on Hosea ii 25, Origen states that the Jewish Sage with whom he debated expounded the verses in Isaiah lii–liii. But it seems that the Church father abridged his opponent's argument, for to begin with he reported in his name 'that the Jews are in exile and afflicted', but in the continuation he explains only the fact of the dispersion. Needless to say, Origen is concerned in his work not with the Jew but with his antagonist Celsus, and it is him that he wishes to convince of the correctness of the Christian claim that the verses in Isaiah, mentioned above, referred to Jesus, and thus prevent him from using the Jewish interpretation that it is the people of Israel which is spoken of. But what is important to us is the fact that, even in disputations with churchmen of the type of Origen, a Jewish Sage would make use of the proselytizing mission as a justification of the exile. It is inconceivable that a Jew would have advanced this argument, if it could have been easily refuted by an actual situation at variance with it. The importance of the continuing fact of proselytization in Judaism's struggle with Christianity is attested by Origen himself in another passage: 'Although Celsus, or the Jew whom he represents, may deride what I have to say, let it nevertheless be stated that many have turned to Christianity as though by compulsion: some spirit — through a vision by day or by night — suddenly changed their mind from hatred of the Gospel to readiness to die for it.'[84] Against such successes and their dialectical exposition it was possible to retaliate only by counteraction. This background enables us to understand the homily — apparently of the Amora R. Phinehas of the end of the fourth century — ' "If he do not declare it, then he shall bear his iniquity" (Leviticus v 1): the Holy One, blessed be He, said to Israel: If you will not declare my Godhood among the nations of the world, I shall exact retribution from you....'[85] At the same time the Sages did not deny the actual fact of degradation inherent in subjection and the imposition of an alien yoke, nor did they hide it from would-be proselytes. The procedure governing the reception of converts as taught in the Baraita undoubtedly reflects the condition prevailing after the promulgation of Hadrian's edicts: 'When an intending proselyte comes to be converted[86] at the present time, we say to him: "What reason have you for seeking conversion? Do you not know that Israel today are in travail, persecuted, swept (from place to place), harassed, and full of suffering?" If he answers: "I know and I am unworthy", he is immediately accepted....' This version appears to be a more general formulation of the text that was composed actually at the time of the persecution, namely: 'But do you not see that this people are the most debased and afflicted of all the peoples and are full of suffering... and they are slain for circumcision, ritual immersion, and all the other precepts, and cannot conduct themselves in public like all other people....'[87] These very statements are reported as the argument of Hadrian. When his relative Aquila came to inform him of his wish to be converted to Judaism, he said to him: 'You wish (to join) this people? How much have I degraded them, how much have I massacred them! You wish to attach yourself to the most despised of the nations...?'[88] In the second recension of the procedure of conversion it is prescribed that after the proselyte has come up from his ritual immersion, 'We speak (to him) kindly and comfortingly: "Happy are you! To whom do you cleave? To Him who spoke and the world came into being, blessed be He; for the world was created only for Israel's sake, and only Israel have been called children unto the Omnipresent, and we said all those things only for the purpose of increasing your reward." '[89] In another version of the story of Aquila's conversion he bases himself on the advice given by Hadrian in matters of business: 'Whatever merchandise you see debased and fallen to the ground trade in it, for eventually it will rise (in value) and you will make a profit.' He [Aquila] argued thus: 'I went the rounds of all the nations, and I did not find a nation so lowly and prostrate as Israel, but in the end it will rise, for so said Isaiah (xlix 7): "Thus saith the Lord, the Redeemer of Israel, his Holy One, to him who is despised of men, to him who is abhorred of nations, to a servant of rulers: kings shall see and rise, princes and they shall prostrate themselves, because of the Lord that is faithful, even the Holy One of Israel, who hath chosen thee." '[90] Presumably Aquila heard these words of comfort at the time of his conversion. Words of consolation were said to the proselytes, but the actual existence of candidates for conversion was a source of solace to the converters, for it served to bridge the gulf between the reality of the situation in which they found themselves and the consciousness of election, which we discussed above (p. 526). We may reasonably conjecture that such were not the sentiments expressed at the induction of proselytes before the promulgation of Hadrian's edicts, and even less so when the Temple existed; however, we are not dependent in this matter on mere supposition, but have express testimony as it has survived in the Tannaitic homily[91] on Deuteronomy xxxiii 19: ' "They shall call peoples unto the mountain": From this you may infer that the nations and kings foregathering to do business in Eretz-Israel would say: "Since we have gone to the trouble of coming here, let us go up and see what Jerusalem is like." Thus they go up to Jerusalem and see the Israelites serving one God and eating one kind of food — for in the case of the Gentiles the god of the one is not that of the other, nor is the food of one person like that of another — and they declare: "This is the best people to join." How do you know that they do not stir from there until they become converted and go and offer up sacrifices and burnt offerings? Therefore Scripture declares "There shall they offer sacrifices of righteousness" (Deuteronomy, *ibid.*). The people of Israel is not compared here to poor merchandise, but even when it appears in this guise, it does not cease being a chosen people and the nexus between election and proselytization remains. The homiletical discourses of the Sages in the synagogues and the colleges, at the time of assemblies, on occasions of rejoicing, or of mourning, attracted non-Jewish listeners, and in the name of Rabbi it was stated: 'There is a kind of pigeon that is fed and its companions smell her and come to her cote. So, too, when the elder sits and delivers his exposition, many proselytes are converted.'[92]

It is not feasible to attempt to classify the Sages according to their dicta relative to proselytes and to distinguish between those who had a liberal-universalistic outlook and spoke in favour of converts and conversion, and those who, holding a particularistic-exclusive view, were opposed to proselytization and spoke disparagingly of proselytes.[93] Such a division is an oversimplification, as is evidenced by the Tanna R. Simeon b. Yoḥai. He was the strongest opponent of the Roman Empire, and completely refused to give it credit for its philanthropic and civilizing acts. In his opinion 'All the improvements that they have made are for their own benefit. They established market-places in order to instal harlots there; baths for their own pleasure; bridges with a view to levying tolls.'[94] Despite this attitude and his bitter, disillusioning experience with proselytes and 'fearers of the Lord',[95] which induced him to say 'The best of the heathens slay', it was just this Tanna who taught: 'Behold Scripture says "But they that love Him shall be as the sun when he goeth forth in his might" (Judges v 31). Now who is greater, he who loves the king or he whom the king loves? You must say: He whom the king loves. And it is written "And loveth the stronger" (Deuteronomy x 18).'[96] This exposition and the homiletical hymn 'Beloved are proselytes, for they are everywhere given the same designations as Israel' were intended to encourage both the converts and the converters, 'so as not to close the door before future proselytes'.[97] His hope for proselytization led Simeon to rule that even outside Eretz-Israel, if one sees an idol, one must say the benediction for its eradication, 'because (the idolaters) are destined to be converted, as it is said "Then will I turn to the peoples a pure language, that they may all call upon the name of the Lord, to serve Him with one consent" (Zephaniah iii 9).'[98]

R. Simeon b. Yoḥai's attitude tends to show that the harsh expressions employed by other Sages, too, regarding Gentiles and proselytes do not necessarily attest opposition in principle to conversion or even to action in this respect, just as contrariwise kindly remarks about non-Jews do not of necessity imply enthusiasm for drawing them near to Judaism. R. Joḥanan[98a] is the author of the following dicta: 'Whoever says a wise thing among the nations of the world is called a sage' (*T.B. Megilla* 16a); 'Gentiles outside Eretz-Israel are not idolaters; they are merely keeping to their ancestral customs' (*T.B. Ḥullin* 13b). But at the same time he held, in opposition to the view of Tannaim (above, p. 543): 'A Gentile who studies the Torah is deserving of death, as it is said "Moses commanded us Torah (for) an inheritance" (Deuteronomy xxxiii 4) — it is an inheritance for us, but not for them' (*T.B. Sanhedrin* 59a). The exposition of the verse supports the assumption that the claim of the Christians, who sought to make the Torah their heritage, led to this sharp repudiation; but experiences of the kind that befell R. Judah Nesi'a (above, p. 542) suffice to explain such reactions. However, in actual practice it seems that R. Joḥanan held that even with regard to Minim 'one should thrust them aside with the left hand and bring them near with the right', and he even encouraged 'the bringing of people beneath the wings of the Shekhina.'[99]

R. Ḥelbo's saying, which has received wide publicity[1] as testimony against proselytization, that 'Proselytes are as difficult for Israel (to endure) as a scab [ספחת *sappaḥat*], as it is said "And they shall cleave [ונספחו *wĕ-nispĕḥû*] to the house of Jacob" (Isaiah xiv 1)' is not clear and unambiguous evidence, for other things are described as difficult[2]; nevertheless a man is not obliged, nor is he even able, to refrain from them. Incidentally, it is R. Ḥelbo who maintained the view that the Lord adjured Israel not to rebel against the non-Jewish governments.[3]

Nor does there appear to be any development from a more lenient to a stricter attitude, or evidence that later Amoraim are more inclined to close the door before proselytes. Actually the most unequivocal dictum against those who accept proselytes was uttered by a Sage who lived in the generation before R. Ḥelbo, namely R. Isaac Nappaḥa, who said 'Evil after evil shall come upon those who accept proselytes'.[4] He was not content to state that converts were hard to endure, but curses those who receive them. Possibly this clear opposition originated in unpleasant experiences with גרים גרורים *gērîm gĕrûrîm* ['dragged-in' proselytes, who converted out of fear][5], and in the desire to prevent blurring of the distinction between proselytes who joined the Jewish people and those of the Gentiles who turned to the new church. Against their usurpative claims R. Isaac fought a hard and bitter fight,[6] and many of his dicta against the Gentile peoples can be clearly understood only if we regard them as directed against the church from among the peoples.[7] His saying was therefore an ephemeral expression of opinion emanating from his policy towards the new trouble that had befallen the Congregation of Israel. But it was actually a Sage that lived about two generations after R. Isaac, namely R. Berechiah, who did not agree with this approach, and did not even interpret the verse, Isaiah xiv 1, according to R. Ḥelbo, although as a rule he transmitted his expositions.[8] R. Berechiah's teaching is linked to an anonymous homily, which was also, it seems, enunciated close to his own time. We shall cite the exposition fully: '...Job said "The stranger will not lodge in the street", for the Holy One, blessed be He, disqualifies no one, but accepts everyone; the gates are open at all times and all who wish to enter may do so. Therefore the text says "The stranger will not lodge in the street"... the reference is to the Holy One, blessed be He, who bears with His creatures. R. Berechiah said: With respect to whom is it said "The stranger will not lodge in the street"? The meaning is that proselytes [the same as that rendered 'stranger'] will in time to come be priests ministering in the Temple, as it is said "And the stranger shall join himself with them, and they shall cleave to the house of Jacob" (Isaiah xiv 1), and "cleaving" means none other than priesthood, as it is said "Put me, I pray thee, into one of the priests' offices" (I Samuel ii 36).'[9] It may well be that R. Berechiah was reacting to the homily of R. Ḥelbo. Although proselytes are difficult to endure, nevertheless people generally are also difficult, yet the Lord bears with them. The anonymous homilist disagreed with R. Isaac's view, and maintained that proselytes should be accepted, for the Almighty does not disqualify any creature, but accepts everyone.

The hope for conversion did not cease so long as the belief in Israel's election and in the power of the Torah was a living and dynamic faith that deemed its purpose to be the perfection and renewal of the world. This faith was shared by both the first and the last of the Amoraim, both in Babylonia and in Eretz-Israel. R. Joḥanan said 'Just as a thorn-bush is used to make a hedge for a garden, even so is Israel a hedge for the world.'[10] In keeping with this thought 'R. Joḥanan declared: I am to whom I am (cf. Exodus iii 14) applies to individuals, but where the multitude is concerned, I shall reign over them perforce, against their will, though their teeth be shattered, as it is said "As I live, saith the Lord God, surely with a mighty hand, and with an outstretched arm, and with fury poured out, will I be king over you" (Ezekiel xx 33).'[11] The eternity of Israel for the sake of the world is linked in another dictum — which in a number of versions is transmitted in the name of R. Joshua b. Levi — with the nation's dispersion: 'For I have spread you abroad as the four winds of heaven, said the Lord...' 'This is the meaning: Just as the world cannot be without winds, so the world cannot be without Israel.'[12] Their great contemporary in Babylonia, Rav, found satisfaction in the fact that there were many Gentiles who, though they had not become converted, yet esteemed Israel and his God. He is the author of the dictum: 'From Tyre to קרטיגיני (Carduene) Israel and their Heavenly Father are recognized, but from Tyre westwards and from קרטיגיני (Carduene) eastwards neither Israel nor their Father in Heaven are recognized.'[13] In the name of R. Joḥanan's disciple, R. Abbahu, it is reported by R. Berechiah that the very election of Israel posits the continued election of proselytes: '...But had it been stated "And I set the nations of the world apart from you" the nations of the world would not have survived. But (it says) "And I have set you apart from the peoples, that ye should be Mine" (Leviticus xx 26), (signifying) that He chooses the good from the bad, choosing again and again; but when He selects the bad from the good, he does so once but not again.'[14] However, the attraction of proselytes was dependent on Israel's conduct. R. Berechiah describes an analogy, the moral of which is: 'So long as they [Israel] do the will of the Holy One, blessed be He, then whenever He sees a righteous person among the nations of the world — like Jethro, Rahab, and Ruth, and like Antonius — He makes him come and join Israel....'[15] Rav Ashi, the greatest of the last Amoraim in Babylonia, said that the guiding star (מזל *mazzal*) of the proselytes was present at the Revelation on Mount Sinai and that the contaminating lust injected by the Serpent into man left them just as it left the Israelites.[16] He was dissatisfied with the paucity of proselytes in his day and he declared that the inhabitants of his city were stubborn 'for they see the glory of the Torah twice a year and not one of them is converted'.[17]

The intensity of the consciousness of election found its true expression in the orders of the prayers and benedictions among the Jews. On the Day of Atonement the High Priest pronounced, during the service, eight benedictions, including 'who choosest the Sanctuary', 'Who choosest Israel', 'Who choosest the priests'.[18] R. Eleazar b. R. Zadok reports that his father, who still lived in the Temple period, used to pray on Sabbath evening as follows: 'And out of Thy love, O Lord our God, that Thou didst love Israel, Thy people, and out of Thy pity, O our King, that Thou didst feel for the children of Thy covenant, Thou didst give us, O Lord our God, this great and holy seventh day in love.'[19] The blessing for the Torah, which was originally a separate blessing formulated like 'Who choosest the Torah', 'Who hast given the Torah unto Israel',[20] was also prefaced by thanksgiving for the election of Israel. The Babylonian Amora, Rav Hamnuna, gives us the wording of the blessing that he regards as 'the best of the benedictions': 'Who hast chosen us from all the peoples and hast given us Thy Torah, blessed art Thou, O Lord, who hast given the Torah.'[21] In the Palestinian version of the liturgy we find: 'Blessed art Thou, O Lord, King of the universe, who hast chosen the flocks of Thy sheep and hast made known to them the ways of Thy will.'[22]

The closing benedictory formulas for Israel's election occur in the recensions of the second benediction preceding the *Shema*ʿ (which is also a kind of blessing for the Torah), namely in אהבה רבה *'ahăvā* *rabbā* ['With abounding love'], the version recommended by Samuel and R. Eleazar, and in the formulation of the 'Rabbanan' [Rabbis], אהבת עולם *'ahăvat ʿōlām* ['With everlasting love'].[23] It would be superfluous to add examples from the liturgical formulas of the festivals, in which the idea of election is central; but we would point out that with reference to the נעילה *Nĕʿîlā* ['Closing of the Gates'] prayer of the Day of Atonement — at one time it used to be recited also on fast-days and at the מעמדות *Maʿămādôt*[24] — which was essentially a confession, it is likewise related that ' ʿUlla bar Rav (once) descended (to the reader's desk) — in the presence[25] of Rava (and) commenced "Thou hast chosen us" and concluded "What are we, what is our life?" and he praised him.' The combination of the confession according to Samuel's formulation — which expresses, not in the singular but in the plural, the insignificance of man standing before his Maker, a fact that won the approval of the great Amora Rava — with the prayer 'Thou hast chosen us from all the peoples' sheds light on the meaning of Israel's election.

The active conception of the election, which postulates that Israel chose his God (above, p. 529), at least in the sense of proclaiming the uniqueness of His name and power in the world, was censured as a source of self-gratification: a homily, whose date it is difficult to fix[26], declares: ' "I said unto the Lord, Thou art my Lord; My gratefulness is not with thee" (Psalms xvi 2): The Congregation of Israel said before the Holy One, blessed be He: "Sovereign of the universe, be grateful to me that I made Thee known in the world." He answered "My gratefulness is not with thee" — I am grateful only to Abraham, Isaac, and Jacob, who were the first to make Me known in the world, as it is said "With the holy that are in the earth; they are the mighty ones in whom is all My delight" (*ibid.* v. 3).'[27]

III. Indictment and Defence of the Congregation of Israel

The consciousness of election did not blind the Sages from seeing the weaknesses of the Congregation of Israel, and they had no need of the accusations of extraneous traducers — idolaters and all kinds of sectarians. It was just these charges that led to counter-attacks, but at times also to a manner of defence that could only be described as 'brushing aside with a reed'. But neither type of rejoinder was able to put a good complexion on negative facts; it will suffice to underline what occurred in the episode of the golden calf. Needless to say this incident was seen by the Tannaim in all its gravity and characteristically they gave added emphasis to the matter. They not only justified the twofold punishment that the people suffered at the hands of Moses and of God,[28] and even augmented it,[29] but they allowed the shadow of the sin of the calf to fall upon the revelation at Mount Sinai and even impugned the sincerity of the people's response at the time;[30] similarly they called in question the liberality of their offerings for the erection of the Tabernacle. R. Simeon b. Yoḥai said: 'To what may the matter be compared? To a man who welcomed Sages and disciples and everyone praised him. Then Gentiles came and he welcomed them (too) and people said: "It is his nature to welcome everybody." Even so Moses said: "And 'Di-zahab' (Deuteronomy i 1) [interpreted as 'much gold'] — (they gave) to the Tabernacle and 'Di-zahab' (they gave) to the calf." '[31] The lesson drawn from the parable is not analogous to the parable, for the episode of the calf preceded the work of the Tabernacle; this is a clear indication that the parable was of primary importance to the Tanna. He wished to rebuke men of wealth who befriended Sages and disciples and at the same time also sought the intimacy of Gentiles from among government circles. Whether he referred to the period before the Revolt and to people like his father, who were state officials, or whether he had in mind burghers in Galilee after the Revolt, his words were directed to his own people, and the story of the calf merely served as a peg for his criticism, but was not his primary concern. But when the Gentiles began to vex Israel 'and said to them: "you made the calf" ', and consequently even God had, as it were, exchanged them for others, the Amoraim adopted polemical and apologetic measures. The Haggadist R. Samuel bar Naḥmani took an extreme line of defence, saying 'The Israelites are exonerated from that episode, for had the Israelites made the calf they would have said "These are our gods, O Israel". It was the proselytes who went up with Israel from Egypt and also the mixed multitude that went up with them (Exodus xii 38) who made the calf and vexed them, saying to them "These are thy gods, O Israel" (*ibid.* xxxii 4).'[32] In conformity with the rule enunciated by R. Samuel b. Naḥmani that when the Lord sees the nations of the world gleeful at the thought that He is about to chastise Israel, He transmutes the chastisement into benefit,[33] R. Levi came and found confirmation of the view that God Himself 'investigated the charges and found no substance in them', and therefore He enjoined that the ox should head all the sacrifices.[34] It was actually R. Isaac, opposed though he was to accepting proselytes (above, p. 551), who did not blame them for the sin of the calf. To the Gentile nations who say 'This people has changed its Glory', Israel answered, he states, as follows: 'If now in one moment I have become so guilty, how much more so are you (blameworthy)! Furthermore, the Israelites say to the nations of the world: We shall tell you what we are like: we are comparable to a prince who went forth to the pasture-land adjoining the city and the sun beat down on his head and his face was tanned. But on entering the city (again), with the help of a little water and a little bathing in one of the bath-houses, his body became white again and his beauty was restored as at first. Even so is it with us, if the sun of idolatry scorched us. But you are scorched from your mother's womb. While you were still in your mother's womb you worshipped idols. How? When a woman is pregnant, she enters her pagan temple and kneels and prostrates herself to the idol — both she and her son.'[35] The conclusion accords with R. Isaac's opposition to the acceptance of converts and for a good reason: people who have already served idols in their mother's womb are not likely to be weaned from it. But this fact in no way diminishes the sin of the calf. When they were not engaged in controversy, other Amoraim also regarded this incident as a reminder of iniquity. Thus R. Abbahu gave the following exposition: ' "And with twain he covered his feet" (Isaiah vi 2) — so that they should not behold the presence of the Shekhina, as it is written "and the sole of their feet was like the sole of a calf's foot" (Ezekiel i 7), and it is further written "They have made them a molten calf" (Exodus xxxii 8), for Scripture declares "And it shall be no more the confidence of the house of Israel, bringing iniquity to remembrance" (Ezekiel xxix 16).' In this way, too, R. Abbahu explained the reason underlying the Halakha taught in the Mishna of *Rosh-ha-Shana*: 'All *shofars* are valid save that of a cow' (*M. Rosh ha-Shana* iii, 2), 'because it is the horn of a calf, and it is written "They have made them a molten calf", for Scripture declares "And it shall be no more the confidence of the house of Israel, bringing iniquity to remembrance." '[36]

Like R. Simeon b. Yoḥai (above, p. 555), one of the early Amoraim, R. Ba bar Aḥa[37], proceeded to compare Israel's conduct when the calf was made and when the Tabernacle was erected, and he came to the general conclusion: 'One cannot understand the nature of this people: if appealed to for the calf they give, and if appealed to for the Tabernacle they give.'[38] This dictum expresses the fickleness and polarity that marked Israel's behaviour and hence it is difficult for this Amora 'to understand the nature of this people'. This evaluation recalls the homily of the Tanna R. Judah on the destiny of the nation, which also fluctuates from one extreme to the other: 'R. Judah b. R. Ileʿai expounded ...this people are likened to the dust and to the stars; when they decline, they go down to the dust, and when they rise, they ascend to the stars.'[39] The Amora R. Judah bar Pazzi reached a far more pessimistic conclusion than that of R. Ba b. R. Aḥa.[40] He also compared the story of the calf with that of the Tabernacle, but he added comparisons with the account of the giving of the Torah, of the exodus from Egypt, and of the spies, and he sums up as follows: 'Shall we read and not feel abashed? For a good cause (we find) "as many as were willing-hearted" (Exodus xxxv 22), but for evil "And all the people broke off the golden rings which were in their ears" (*ibid.* xxxii 3); for good "And Moses brought forth the people" (Exodus xix 17), for evil "And ye came near unto me every one of you" (Deuteronomy i 22); for good "Then sang Moses and the children of Israel" (Exodus xv 1), for evil "And all the congregation lifted up their voice, and cried" (Number xiv 1).' The homilist stresses that the tendency of the Israelites towards evil, during their stay in the wilderness, was stronger than their inclination to do good, and in this respect he associated himself with similar appraisals found in the Prophets (above, p. 216); but as in their case the focal interest in this evaluation and similar pronouncements lay in their bearing on the present and on the attitude of the Sages to the Jewish people in their own times. However, it is precisely in this sphere that the fundamental difference between the Sages and the Prophets is clearly to be seen. The Rabbis contemplated the prophetic work and reproof as well as their outcome, and they studied and eval-ated the reciprocal relationship between the Prophets and Israel.

R. Akiba said that only for Israel's sake did the Lord speak with Moses, 'for during the entire period of thirty-eight years that He was wroth with Israel He did not speak with him.' His disciple, R. Simeon b. Azzai, added to his teaching, saying that 'God spoke with all the Prophets only for Israel's sake.'[41] The Prophets were called upon to offer their lives for Israel; they were God's messengers and transmitted His word, but they were also the representatives of the people. Although it was likewise the Prophet's task to demand that the honour of the Father be respected, yet it was forbidden him to ignore the honour due to the son. Jeremiah was a prophet who sought to assure both the Father's and the son's honour. Elijah, on the other hand, claimed only the honour due to the Father, and therefore the Lord said to him ' "And Elisha the son of Shaphat... shalt thou anoint to be prophet in thy room" (I Kings xix 16) — now there was no need to say "prophet in thy room"; the purport is: I do not desire your prophecy.' Jonah insisted on the honour of the son but not on that of the Father; therefore it is said ' "And the word of the Lord came unto Jonah the second time, saying" (Jonah iii 1) — He spoke to him a second but not a third time.'[42] The reference in this homily is to Jonah's flight and refusal to go and prophesy to Nineveh. However, the use made already by the Gospels of the story of Jonah brought in its train another interpretation of Jonah's flight. The authors of the Gospels argued: 'The men of Nineveh will arise at the judgement with this generation and condemn it; for they repented at the preaching of Jonah, and behold something greater than Jonah is here.'[43] The words of the Midrash read as a reply to this, namely that Jonah's flight was not due to the fact that he did not wish to rebuke the men of Nineveh, but 'Jonah said to himself as follows: "I shall go outside the borders of Israel, where the Shekhina does not reveal Itself, for the Gentiles soon repent, and I shall thus avoid condemning Israel." '[44] But the Lord rejected Jonah's argument; Israel had no reason to fear the repentance of the people of Nineveh. Only the exacerbation of the Judeo-Christian conflict led to the negation of the value of this penitence.[45]

Just as the Sages regarded the prophet's function as that of one who demanded both the honour due to the son and to the Father, so they considered themselves to hold a brief for both the honour of the prophets and of the people. In the wake of the testimonies of the Bible regarding the bad relationship between Israel and its prophets, legendary tales were current in various circles that supplemented what was missing in Scripture. Verses like 'Shall the priest and the prophet be slain in the sanctuary of the Lord' (Lamentations ii 20), or 'Nevertheless they were disobedient, and rebelled against Thee, and cast Thy law behind their back, and slew Thy prophets that did forewarn them to turn them back unto Thee...' (Nehemiah ix 26), opened the way for visionaries to embroider the story of the prophets' lives and to relate their end and death and even to indicate their burial place. Such tales were preserved in their entirety in apocryphal works, which the Fathers of the Christian church adopted and even made interpolations in them: but their Jewish and Hebrew origin is not to be doubted.[46] Fragments of them have been preserved in the Talmuds and Midrashim. Simeon b. ʿAzzai said that he had found 'a scroll of genealogical records in which was written... Manasseh killed Isaiah'[47], and Amoraim in Eretz-Israel and in Babylonia even transmitted details of the story of how Isaiah was sawn asunder at the command of King Manasseh[48], a legend that is also known to us from the pseudepigraphical work *The Ascension of Isaiah*.[49] Around the verse in Lamentations concerning the priest and prophet who were slain in the Temple, a cluster of tales has been woven about the murder of the prophet Zechariah.[50] It is not surprising that the authors of the Synoptic Gospels seized upon this legendary tradition, in which they found support for their charges against 'Jerusalem, which killest the prophets and stonest them that are sent unto thee.'[51] The Fathers of the Church discovered in these stories parallels to the be haviour of the Jews towards Jesus and his apostles and already in the middle of the second century Justin argues against Trypho: 'Had your teachers and sages known and understood (the passages in the Bible alluding to Jesus), they would assuredly have taken care to expunge them, just as they suppressed the story about the death of Isaiah.'[52]

However, the truth is, as we have seen, that they did not suppress the story of Isaiah's martyrdom, either in the time of the Tannaim or in that of the Amoraim. Even more, in a Tannaitic Midrash it is stated generally 'In the end you will do violence to the prophets',[53] and in the name of R. Me'ir it is transmitted that 'The men of Jerusalem were smitten because they contemned the Prophets.'[54] The Amora R. Judah b. R. Simeon described Isaiah's appointment as a prophet dramatically, making his readiness to accept suffering the central feature of his account: 'Isaiah said: I was walking about in my schoolhouse, when I heard the voice of the Holy One, blessed be He: "Whom shall I send, and who will go for us?" (Isaiah vi 8); I sent Micah and they smote him on the cheek, as it is written "They smite the judge of Israel with a rod upon the cheek" (Micah iv 14); I sent Amos and they called him ψελλός... that inarticulate fellow... whom then shall I send and who will go for us? Forthwith I said "Here am I: send me" (Isaiah *loc. cit.*). Said God to him: Isaiah, My children are sinners and troublesome, if you will agree to be abused and beaten by My children, you can go on My mission; but if not, do not go. Isaiah replied: Even so, "I gave my back to the smiters, and my cheeks to them that plucked off the hair" (*ibid.* l 6).'[55] From the same verse it is deduced, in another homily, that the righteous have a duty to restrain their people, 'to suffer abuse for the sanctification of the Name, and to accept and suffer blows from Israelites as the prophets suffered at the hands of Israel, for Jeremiah endured much trouble from Israel, and so did Isaiah....'[56] This willingness to suffer is indicative of the Prophets' readiness to assert the honour due to the Father, but we have already seen that Tannaim criticized Elijah for not fulfilling his mission properly, in that he did not insist on the honour due to the son. Just as the travail and sufferings of the Prophets were generalized and Jonah did not remain the only one to 'demand the honour of the Father', so, too, the Amoraim transferred the character of Elijah to other Prophets. Let us begin with the homily of R. Simon, the father of R. Judah, to which were juxtaposed the dicta of Amoraim who preceded him and served him as a source:[57] ' "Look not upon me that I am swarthy" (Canticles i 6) — R. Simon began his exposition thus: "Slander not a servant unto his master" (Proverbs xxx 10), the Israelites are called servants, as it is said "For unto Me the children of Israel are servants" (Leviticus xxv 55) and the Prophets are called servants, as it is said "For the Lord God will do nothing,[58] [but He revealeth His counsel unto

His servants the prophets]" (Amos iii 7). Thus we learn that a servant should not slander a (fellow) servant. The Congregation of Israel says to the Prophets: you have denigrated me before Him who spoke and the world came into being. None loved me more than Moses, yet because he said "Hear now, ye rebels" (Numbers xx 10) it was decreed that he should not enter Eretz-Israel. Nor was there anyone that loved me more than Isaiah, but because he sa[id] "Woe is me! for I am defiled [נטמאתי]..."[59] (Isaiah vi 5), the Holy One said: You may proceed, of yourself you are perm[i]tted (to speak thus). "And I dwell in the midst of a people of unclean lips" — why? You see what is written there "Then flew unto me one of the seraphim, with a רצפה *riṣpa* ['glowing stone'] in his hand" (*ibid.* *v.* 6). What does it mean? [R.] Samuel bar Naḥman said *riṣpa* (connotes that) the mouth of him who speaks evil of Israel is to be crushed [רוצצים *rôṣĕṣîm*]. It is likewise written of Elijah (I Kings xix 10) "I have been very jealous for the Lord, the God of hosts; for the children of Israel have forsaken Thy covenant..." Said God: It is My covenant; is it then yours? "And thrown down Thine altars" — Said God to him: It is My altars; are they then your altars? — "And slain Thy prophets with the sword"—Said God (to him:) They are My prophets; what concern are they of yours? Said (Elijah) to God[60] "And I, even I only, am left" — what is written there? "And he looked, and, behold, there was at his head a cake baked on the hot stones [*rĕṣāfîm*]" (*ibid.* *v.* 6); R. Samuel bar Naḥman said: The mouth of him who speaks ill of Israel is to be crushed.' R. Simon transmitted R. Samuel bar Naḥman's exposition, and made it the basis of his own homily in answer to the accusations levelled by the Prophets against Israel, and it seems that also R. Joḥanan's dictum on this theme was reported by R. Simon as follows: 'R. Joḥanan heard it [the homily] in connection with the following verse: "The burden of Damascus. Behold Damascus... The cities of Aroer are forsaken" (Isaiah xvii 1–2) — he stands in Damascus and makes a proclamation concerning Aroer, but Aroer is surely within the borders of Moab! The meaning, however, is that there were six hundred and sixty-five idol shrines in Damascus and they used to worship each one on a particular day, but there was one day when they worshipped all of them on that day.[61] Said the Holy One to him: Elijah, instead of denouncing these, go and denounce these; "Go, return on thy way to the wilderness of Damascus...." ' Although a polemical note is to be discerned in R. Joḥanan's words, which is attested by the expression 'instead of denouncing these, go and denounce these', yet they were not said for polemical reasons only. The verse from Proverbs cited above R. Joḥanan interpreted in the name of R. Simeon b. Yoḥai as follows: 'Even a generation that curse their father and do not bless their mother, slander not a servant unto his master', and he learnt this from Hosea: 'R. Joḥanan said ...The Holy One, blessed be He, said to Hosea "Thy children have sinned"; he should have answered "They are Thy children, the children of Thy favoured ones, the children of Abraham, Isaac, and Jacob; be compassionate to them." Not enough that he did not speak thus, but he said before Him: "Sovereign of the universe, the whole world is Thine — exchange them for another people." Said the Holy One, blessed be He: "What shall I do with this old man? I shall tell him: Go and take a harlot and beget children of harlotry, and thereafter I shall say to him: Send her away. If he will be able to send her away, then I, too, will send Israel away." '[62] Doubt about the actual effectiveness of a general indictment is expressed in another dictum of R. Joḥanan: 'Pharaoh's removal of his ring to validate the oppression of Israel in Egypt was more beneficent than the forty years of prophesying against them by Moses, for the former resulted in redemption but the latter did not bring redemption.'[63] R. Abba bar Kahana, who mostly transmits dicta in the name of R. Joḥanan, formulated the idea in more general terms: 'Of greater avail was the removal of the ring (by Ahasuerus) than the forty-eight prophets and seven prophetesses that prophesied to Israel, for none of them restored the Israelites to the path of rectitude, whereas the removal of the ring did bring them back to the way of righteousness.'[64] His homily is formulated this time after the pattern of Resh Laqish's dictum: 'The removal of Ahasuerus' ring had a greater effect upon Israel than sixty myriads of prophets in the day of Elijah....'[65] The criticism of these Amoraim was directed against the all-embracing denunciation and the arraignment of the Congregation of Israel, which they regarded as an act of denigration on the part of the prophets in view of its ineffectiveness. However, it is clear that their purpose was not to criticize the prophets, but to point the moral for their own conduct. The following story is linked with the name of Resh Laqish: 'R. Abbahu and Resh Laqish were entering Caesarea, when R. Abbahu said to Resh Laqish: Why are we going into the city of blasphemers and revilers! Thereupon Resh Laqish alighted from his ass and took sand and put it into his mouth. Said (R. Abbahu) to him: What is the meaning of this? Resh Laqish replied: Does the Holy One then take pleasure in one who speaks ill of Israel?'[66]

Whilst in the homilies treating of the prophets the Amoraim criticize them for not fulfilling their function in demanding the honour due to the son — that is to say, they did not crave to justify the children of the Holy One, blessed be He, nor were they averse to condemning them[67] — in the story just cited opposition is expressed to the use of derogatory expressions regarding the Congregation of Israel, or concerning an entire city in Israel, even if no 'tale-bearing' is involved. Undoubtedly, Resh Laqish does not intend to deny the Sages the right and the duty to rebuke. This duty is ordained in the Torah, and the Sages regarded it as incumbent upon every individual Jew and even determined its proper measure: 'Whence do we know that when one observes something reprehensible in his fellow that he must rebuke him? For Scripture declares הוכח תוכיח *hôkhēaḥ tôkhîaḥ* "Thou shalt surely rebuke" (Leviticus xix 17). If he rebuked him, but he did not accept it, whence do we know that he must rebuke him again? Because the verse states תוכיח *tôhîaḥ*, "Thou shalt rebuke" [i.e. the expression of rebuking is repeated: *hôkhēaḥ tôkhîaḥ*, literally, 'Rebuke thou shalt rebuke'], in any circumstances. One might have assumed (that this is to be done) even if his face changed colour; hence the Torah teaches "Thou shalt incur no guilt because of him." '[68] With regard to the extent of the rebuke, even Amoraim differed: Rav said: To the point of smiting — that is, until the offender smites the rebuker; and Samuel said: until he curses; and R. Joḥanan said: until he loses his temper. The same dispute is transmitted in the name of the Tannaim R. Eliezer, R. Joshua, and Ben Azzai.[69] But other Tannaim, who were contemporaries of theirs, wondered if it was at all possible to rebuke: 'R. Ṭarfon said: Upon my faith! There is no one in this generation capable of reproving; R. Eleazar b. Azariah said: Upon my faith! There is no one in this generation able to receive reproof. R. Akiba said: Upon my faith! There is no one in this generation who knows how to reprove.'[70]

IV. The Status of the Sages in the Days of the Hasmoneans

The phrase 'There is no one in this generation' shows that, although the statements were made in connection with the precept to rebuke, which devolves on each individual, they actually refer to the leaders of the generation, who regard themselves as responsible for shaping its image. The responsibility is necessarily linked to a feeling of authority. This section will be devoted to the elucidation of the nature of this authority, its sources, and its manifestations in the position of the Sages within the Jewish community. Some of the facts may be gleaned from the sources we have cited with reference to the evaluation of the work of the prophets in relation to the people of Israel, but we have to enlarge the canvas in two directions. On the one hand, we shall consider the general appraisement of the phenomenon of prophecy by the Sages and, by implication, their self-evaluation through confrontation with it. On the other hand, we shall carefully observe the social situation at the different periods and places in which the Sages have expressed their views about themselves and their people.

The prevailing feeling in the Books of the Maccabees, as in all the Rabbinic sources, is that prophecy was absent in the era of the Second Temple, either throughout the period or, at least, from the beginning of Greek rule in the days of Alexander.[71] Prophecy is a highly complex phenomenon and when its disappearance is spoken of the question arises: Which of its elements are being referred to? The prophets appear in the Bible as ecstatics, as folk miracle-workers, who were unusual in their attire and customs and left the impression of 'madmen', as apostles who uttered words of rebuke and brought tidings of consolation.[72] Which of all these aspects ceased to exist? What remained of all these qualities, and how was the prophetic image conceived? It is clear that the Baraita which states 'When the last prophets, Haggai, Zechariah, and Malachi died, the Holy Spirit departed from Israel'[73] refers to the ending of prophecy as a part of the Holy Scriptures. Josephus, who tells us much about prophets in his time and in the preceding generations as miraculous men, who foretold future events and reprimanded, declares at the same time that 'From Artaxerxes to our own time the complete history has been written, but has not been deemed worthy of equal credit with the earlier records, because of the failure of the exact succession of the prophets... For, although such long ages have now passed, no one has ventured to add, or to remove, or to alter a syllable.'[74] However, the cessation of prophecy was not understood merely as the exclusion of the words of the prophets that had appeared, or were destined to appear, from the canon of the Biblical Prophets. From this aspect, there were not only a hundred and twenty myriads of prophets, or sixty myriads of prophets, mentioned by the Amoraim Rav Samuel bar Isaac and R. Joḥanan[75], but also 'one prophet in the morning and another at twilight', to whom Rabbi refers, and twice the number transmitted in the name of R. Nathan,[76] and even the prophets that are expressly cited in the Bible and are enumerated in the Baraita among the 'forty-eight prophets and seven prophetesses who prophesied to Israel,'[77] yet none of these had their utterances published. The explanation given of this phenomenon is: 'Every prophecy that was required at the time and was (also) needed for future generations was published, but the prophecy that was required at the time, but was not needed for future generations was not published.'[78]

From the postulate concerning prophecies that were needed at the time is to be inferred that their authors had the authority to demand that their generation should listen to them. The non-incorporation of prophetic utterances from the Holy Scripture is not yet sufficient, therefore, to negate their authority or that of their authors. This, however, is precisely the implication of the Baraita that links the cessation of prophecy with the beginning of Greek rule: 'This is Alexander the Macedonian [i.e. Alexander the Great], who reigned 12 years. Till now the prophets prophesied through the medium of the Holy Spirit; from now on incline your ear and hearken to the words of the Sages.'[79] Here the most characteristic feature of prophecy is negated, namely the express and manifest mission of the prophet, who claimed for himself direct authority in the name of the Lord, who speaks with him.

There may be visionaries and seers, men who foretell future events and work miracles and wonders — and, in truth, we have seen that there were many such in the days of the Second Temple and also in the period of the Tannaim and Amoraim, even in their very own circles — but they do not appear as prophets and messengers of God.[80]

Elsewhere we have noted the process that led to the divestment of prophecy of all authority in relation to the Torah and precepts and to the liberation of the latter from all dependence on supernatural forces. We have seen that, indeed, not all easily forwent supernal revelations even in these spheres; but the development that took place in the Oral Law and the struggles of its banner-bearers against sects and doctrines that launched attacks against it and its sources weighed down the scales in favour of the authority of the Sages, their expositions, and decisions. The enactments, practices, and innovations introduced by the prophets, of which information has come down to us, derived not from the power of their prophecy, but was the product of their explanations and argumentation, or the traditionary lore that they had received — in other words, the prophets were also Sages.[81] It would be superfluous to prolong this discussion in order to disprove the theory that connects the termination of prophecy with the dominance accorded the Torah in the days of Ezra. This hypothesis — whether it interprets the causal nexus unfavourably by supposing that prophecy could not survive in a framework of a fixed and crystallized Law of worship and precepts[82], or whether it interprets the link favourably by suggesting that the Torah, which grew to be the practical rule of life in the time of the Second Temple, made the reproofs of the prophets unnecessary[83] — overlooks two factors in the reality that emerges from the sources of the Oral Law, namely the attitude of the Torah exponents, the Sages, to prophecy and the prophets, on the one hand, and the function of these Sages as mentors, on the other.

The Baraita that makes the age of Alexander the Great the close of the era of 'those who prophesied by the Holy Spirit', and transfers their preaching and reproof to the Sages, was undoubtedly formulated at the conclusion of the process, and it merely retrojects the end-results to the initial stage. However, the various stages leading to the creation of the unique class of the Sages in actual history, and to its emergence as an elite of leadership unfold, *pari passu* with the crystallization of a given concept of prophecy and the prophets.

The prophets, whose teachings were conjoined with those of the Torah and who were portrayed as a link in the chain of tradition preceding the Men of the Great Synagogue, were not connected through their work with any particular social class, and were not affiliated to any state or cultic institution. Nor did they constitute a class of their own after the manner of their predecessors in the days of Samuel and in the days of Elijah and Elisha.

The Divine word that they uttered, their prophetic visions, their symbolic and ecstatic acts, their personal experiences — these were all directed to the improvement of the social order in all its aspects — in the spheres of worship, ethics, and justice — and to educating people to see the connection between their way of life and their attitude to the precepts of the Lord, on the one hand, and their destiny in the past, present, and future, on the other. However, their appearance as prophets and the consciousness of the direct mission that inspired them all, despite the individual differences between them, gave the prophetic teachers the image of a special and separate class.

We know neither the nature nor the date of 'the Great Synagogue', to whose members the prophets handed down the Torah (*M. 'Avot* i, 1).[84] But it is clear that these men — at least the majority of them — were not prophets, and we shall not err if we call them 'Sages'.[85] At any rate the earliest dictum attributed to them 'Be deliberate in judgement, raise up many disciples, and make a fence around the Law' shows that they were interested in the dispensation of justice and its methods, in making enactments and decrees, and in increasing the number of disciples[86] from whom Sages would arise. It seems that this was the highest legislative institution, which met whenever necessary.[87]

The statement that Simeon the Just was one of the last of the Great Synagogue implies that it was dissolved near his time. It is possible that the Greek conquest, which led to the establishment of Macedonian colonies, brought about administrative changes[88] that rendered the 'Great Synagogue', as an institution representative of all the people of the land, an impossibility or a fiction, and it was replaced by the 'Gerousia', the council that functioned in conjunction with the High Priest and represented Jerusalem and the adjacent region. At any rate it is only after the liberation of Judea in the days of Simon the Hasmonean that 'the Great Synagogue' reappears (below, p. 570).

Ben-Sira, who wrote in the years 190–170 B.C.E., shortly after Eretz-Israel passed from the rule of the Ptolemies to that of the Seleucids, describes the situation in his time as one marked by a great gulf between those engaged in work and those who wielded power and dominion. It is true that without the farmer, the smith, the refiner, and the potter 'a city cannot be inhabited, and wherever they dwell they hunger not. But they shall not be inquired of for public counsel, and in the assembly they enjoy no precedence. On the seat of the judge they do not sit, and law and justice they understand not' (xxxviii 32–33). On the other hand, the sage has no occupation; he sits upon the judge's seat 'and sets his mind upon the Law of the Most High; who searcheth out the wisdom of all the ancients, and is occupied with the prophets of old... who serveth among great men, and appeareth before princes' (*ibid.* xxxix 1–4). The Sages, as Ben-Sira portrays them, were wealthy and saw in their function election and mission. They were members of the Court of Justice and members of the Supreme Council, which is the γερουσία mentioned in the letter of Antiochus III, of the year 190 B.C.E., together with the 'priests and the scribes of the Temple'.[89] These members of the Gerousia, like the men of 'the Great Synagogue' who preceded them, or the members of the Sanhedrin who came after them, took no pay whatsoever for their public and judicial work. The scribes of the Temple were, it appears, custodians of the Holy Scriptures, called 'the books'. At first their work consisted only of writing and of copying the Holy Scriptures, and of taking meticulous care in transmitting them correctly. The explanation of their name given in a later period, namely 'Therefore the early Sages were called *Soferim* [understood here as 'Counters'; usually rendered 'Scribes'], because they counted all the letters of the Torah' (*T.B. Qiddushin* 30a) is not to be regarded as an etymology but is correct in substance. The revisers of the Temple scrolls, who were considered to have special authority, received their salary from the Temple fund,[90] and in all probability were priest-scribes. At any rate they did not belong to the highest hierarchy, and neither they nor the scroll-writers outside the Temple were rich. Ben-Sira also regarded the wisdom of the scribe as a form of art, which did, in truth, increase wisdom, but did not advance one to a position of power.

There was a difference between the scribes and the Sages similar to that which subsisted, as we know from the history of the earliest period of Roman jurisprudence, between the jurists, who decided and fixed the law, and the ancient interpreters of the legal prescriptions.[91] However, the Sages, too, were not merely legalists, but, as Ben-Sira states (xxxix 1–4), they set their minds upon the Law of the Most High, meditated upon prophecies, searched out the wisdom of all the ancients, the discourses of men of renown, the deep things and hidden meanings and parables. To meditation and knowledge they added also piety, which found expression in prayer, in thanksgiving, and in deducing wise instruction. Undoubtedly the Sage of Sirach, like that of the Book of Proverbs, was required to be constant in his fear of the Lord and the performance of the precepts (i 23; xix 20; xxv 14–15), to keep far from violent and presumptuous men and to associate with saintly men. But the wise man is not found as a sociable type. Although the public spoke in praise of him, and many lauded his understanding, yet he was not close to them, nor do we hear of his activity in their midst and on their behalf. The saying of Jose b. Jo'ezer, who lived in the generation preceding the Maccabean Revolt, 'Let your house be a meeting-place for the Sages, and sit amid the dust of their feet, and drink in their words with thirst' (*M. 'Avot* i, 4), fits the exclusive character of the class of the Sages in the Hellenistic period prior to the Maccabean Revolt. However, next to this dictum there is a demand of an entirely different kind expressed by his contemporary Jose b. Joḥanan of Jerusalem, who declares 'Let your house be opened wide and let the needy be members of your household' (*ibid.* i, 5). But although this saying emphasizes charitable and welfare work, and not wisdom, it does not diminish the aristocratic and philanthropic character of the request addressed by both of them to the householder. The restrictive edicts of King Antiochus Epiphanes directed against the Jewish religion in 167, the acts of martyrdom that followed in their wake, the raising of the standard of rebellion, at the head of which stood the priestly family of the Hasmoneans of Modi'im, who were joined by 'those who were seeking righteousness and justice' and 'a company of Hasideans... every one who offered himself willingly for the Law', the military victories of the Maccabees and the growing strength of Judea — all these factors led to the establishment of a new leadership. The solemn decision in 140 B.C.E., 'in a great congregation (ἐπὶ συναγωγῆς μεγάλης) of priests, and people, and chiefs of the nation, and elders of the country',[92] to appoint Simon as High Priest and Ethnarch opened the era of the Hasmonean monarchy with all the hopes and disillusionments, as well as the political and spiritual struggles, it involved. The changes that occurred in the institutional and governmental sphere are less apparent. Indubitably the rise to power of the House of the Hasmoneans resulted in the deposition of families of noble lineage who belonged to the extreme Hellenizers, while elevating, together with the new rulers, the families of the loyal fighters to governatorial and administrative positions. The replacement of the family of High Priests descended from Zadok by the priestly families of the Hasmoneans had political significance, but did not express the primary transformation. Typologically, Simons son John (Johanan) Hyrcanus approximates the figure of the 'Judge', the leader-deliverer. He was High Priest and also *'Av Bet Din* [Head of the Court of Justice]; he introduced reforms in the order of the Temple service[93] and made politico-religious enactments in regard to the collection and distribution of the tithes.[94]

Josephus, moreover, not content with this, attributed to him the power of prophecy: 'He was the only man to unite in his person three of the highest privileges: the supreme command of the nation, the high priesthood, and the gift of prophecy. For so closely was he in touch with the Deity, that he was never ignorant of the future; thus he foresaw and predicted that his two elder sons would not remain at the head of affairs.'[95] Although the Sages do not mention prophecy, for in their view the Holy Spirit ceased in Israel 'when the last prophets, Haggai, Zechariah, and Malachi died', yet they, too, related in a Baraita: 'Johanan the High Priest heard (a voice) from the Holy of Holies (saying) "The youths that went to do battle at Antioch were victorious" '; and the teacher of the Baraita added: 'And they determined the exact moment and found that it was precisely at that time that they triumphed.'[96] John Hyrcanus, however, was a unique phenomenon. It is certain that in his days men who belonged to the 'company of Hasideans' and those who offered themselves for the Law came to fulfil functions in the Temple and in institutions of the judiciary and Halakhic decisions, and it was the period of the activity of the 'Bet Din [Court, Sanhedrin] of the Hasmoneans'.[97] Although the priests continued to be scribes and judges in civil cases, yet the Sages penetrated all these classes, and from now on there were Sages who were priests, Sages who were judges, and Sages who were Ḥasidim ['Pietists'].

The earliest Sages about whom we have any tradition of real significance appear to us like the early prophets — Nathan, Gad, Ahijah, and Elijah — as reprovers of kings and despots. Only their reproof did not emanate from prophecy and their influence was not due to charisma, but to their wisdom; and this wisdom implies knowledge of the Torah and Halakha and absolute faithfulness to their injunctions and principles.

Let us piece together the tradition in our possession concerning the first Sage, who belongs to the Hasmonean period, namely Simeon b. Sheṭaḥ. We meet him sitting in the Bet Din to judge the slave of King Jannaeus, who had killed a person. In accordance with the Halakha that the owner of the slave must appear before the Bet Din, Simeon b. Sheṭaḥ summoned Jannaeus, 'And when he came, he said to him: "King Jannaeus, stand up and let them [the witnesses] testify against you..." Said he [the king] to him: "It is not as you say, but as your colleagues will say." When (Simeon) turned to the right, they [his colleagues] looked down at the ground, and when he turned to the left, they looked down at the ground. Whereupon Simeon b. Sheṭaḥ said to them: "Are you full of thoughts (of expediency)? Let the Master of thoughts [i.e. God] come and call you to account...." '[98] Simeon's colleagues may have shared in his function (as judges), but they did not share his views.

Simeon's activities were directed to the improvement of judicial procedures. This is attested by his rulings in regard to the examination of witnesses, so as to prevent punishment on the basis of estimated testimony, that is, on the basis of circumstantial evidence; so, too, with respect to the punishment of זוממים *zômĕmîm* witnesses [i.e. false witnesses against whom other witnesses testify that the former were with them elsewhere at the time of the crime].[99] His general instruction to judges was: 'Examine the witnesses diligently and be cautious in your words lest from them they learn to tell falsehood' (*M. 'Avot* i, 9). His enactment that the husband should write in his wife's *ketubba* ['marriage contract'] that all his property is pledged to her, was intended to make hasty divorce difficult and to secure the economic position of the woman on being divorced.[1] According to one source Simeon b. Sheṭaḥ enacted 'that children should go to school'.[2] The exact nature of the enactment and how it fits into other traditions concerning the establishment of a school system are not clear, but for our purpose this very statement regarding his activity in the field of popular education is of importance. We find Simeon b. Sheṭaḥ rendering assistance to poor nazirites and helping them to free themselves from their nazirite vows and to bring the sacrifices incumbent upon them.[3] As in the case of Elijah, so it was also related of Simeon b. Sheṭaḥ that he performed an act of zealotry, ordering, as an emergency measure, that eighty women be hanged in Ashkelon for engaging in witchcraft and illicit love.[4] The narrative tradition also portrays Simeon b. Sheṭaḥ as on friendly terms with King Jannaeus.[5] He dines with him at a banquet in honour of the emissaries of the King of Persia, who recall his words of wisdom on previous visits. But even in these narratives the extent of the Sage's individualism and independence is stressed. In his conversation a reproachful tone blends with friendliness. Undoubtedly this period of concord was the time to which many of his acts and enactments, mentioned above, belonged. However, he attributed his honour and status entirely to his Torah-knowledge. For his livelihood he engaged in flax work, and his principle in commercial transactions was so to conduct himself as to inspire people to glorify the name of his God, to declare 'Blessed be the God of the Jews'.[6]

In these fragmentary notices concerning this ancient Sage are enshrined a number of fundamental attributes that were to characterize the Sages throughout their generations, and served as ideals that they were brought up to honour and which, in turn, they inculcated in others. The work of the Sage and the administration of his community were not necessarily dependent on the fulfilment of any official function. Whether he held office or not, he was duty-bound to guide and to lead the community. The power of his leadership he drew first and foremost from his knowledge of the Torah. His attitude to the government and to wealth was determined only by the conduct of the officers of the government and the owners of the wealth. He did not seek their intimacy, but he did not shun them either. He preserved his independence and freedom and earned his livelihood by working. The dictum of Shemaʿya, the disciple of Simeon, 'Love labour and hate mastery and seek not acquaintance with the ruling power' (*M. 'Avot* i, 9), is a kind of briefing, emanating from the life-story of his master, that defines the ideal to be followed by the Sage in his relationship to work, the exercise of power, and the government. The activity of the Sage aimed to ameliorate the life of the community in the sphere of justice and righteousness, and in that of family relations and the education of the people in Torah and piety. Even the attributes and virtues that are absent from Simeon b. Sheṭaḥ's limited spectrum of activity are instructive. It contains no contemplative-mystical, or miraculous-supernatural, element. One may certainly not infer from this that Simeon b. Sheṭaḥ adopted a negative attitude to these aspects; but they are not to be regarded as dominant characteristics. Miracle-workers lived in close proximity to Simeon. Onias, the Circle-maker — like Elijah before him — delivered his people by his prayer from severe drought. Onias's importunate pleading before the Lord, expressed in the terms 'I swear by Thy great name that I shall not stir from here until Thou shalt take pity on Thy children', and the prominence he gave to himself by saying 'Thy children have turned their faces to me' were not pleasing to Simeon b. Sheṭaḥ. Although Onias's prayer was answered, yet Simeon did not refrain from sending him a message in which rebuke and recognition were, so to speak, intermingled: 'Were it not that you are Onias, I would decree a ban against you. But what can I do with you? For you importune the Omnipresent and he fulfils your will, like a son who importunes his father.'[7] Although this pronouncement does, to some extent, find fault with Onias's method of working, yet it contains, at the same time, an acknowledgement of his standing with his Creator, and also, apparently, of the esteem in which he was held by wide sections of the people.

If we find that Simeon b. Sheṭaḥ assumed one facet of the early prophets' activity, namely to intervene in political life, to reprove rulers and men of power openly, and to wage war against corrupt conduct, Onias, on the other hand, the first of the line of pietists and miracle-workers who are known to us by name, inherited the ability to perform miracles and wonders. In the case of the early prophets the two aspects were integrated; and although they are separated here, they existed in juxtaposition. Undoubtedly the simple folk looked upon Onias as a type of Elijah and the bringing down of rain even enhanced his popularity. Simeon, however, was content to put his own interpretation on the episode. God fulfilled Onias's wish as a father fulfils that of his son. Simeon b. Sheṭaḥ's attitude to Onias is characteristic of that of the Sages towards concepts and beliefs, trends and tendencies, that were not wholly to their liking. Their approach was to set their seal upon them by penetrating the affected circles and adopting them as their own. On account of this attitude they did not hasten to ban or eliminate phenomena or groups of which they did not approve, even when they had the power to do so. This is attested by the history of the relations between the Sages and the Sadducees. Whereas the latter, when they held office and were in power, sought to turn their opponents into a group of secessionists — and hence they also designated them 'Pharisees' [פרושים *Pĕrûshîm*, literally 'Separated', i.e. seceders][8] — yet when the Sages prevailed and their influence was decisive, they did not oust the Sadducees. At any rate the tone of the discussions between them and the testimonies concerning them[9] do not bear out such an aim. Although the attitude towards sectarians became greatly exacerbated, yet this exacerbation came as a reaction to the secession of individuals or sects, like the Christians in the second century[10], who on the one hand argued that the Congregation of Israel should cease to exist as a separate entity, and on the other wished to be regarded as its inheritors.

The Sages' desire and intent to live amidst the broad strata of the people, to lead them and guide them, was prompted to no small extent by the fact that they themselves came from all classes and strata. There were among them priests of noble lineage, men of wealth, sons of big landowners, poor artisans, metayers and farmers, hired labourers, and sons of proselytes. This entire variegated community, without exception, the Sages wished to mould and to guide. Undoubtedly Hillel's teachers, Shemaʿyah and Avṭalion, also acted in accordance with his maxim 'Keep not aloof from the community' (*M. 'Avot* ii, 4). But this principle did not exhaust the communal policy of these Sages. They refused to swear an oath of allegiance to Herod, but Shemaʿyah's dictum 'Seek not acquaintance with the ruling power' was complemented by the teaching of his colleague Avṭalion 'Oh Sages, give heed to your words, lest you incur the penalty of exile' (*M. 'Avot* i, 11). A tyrannical ruler like Herod might sentence those who spoke incautiously to be banished from the country, or to work in the mines. He must not easily be provided with a pretext for ridding himself by this method of the leaders, who knew his nature, and so deprive the broad masses of their leadership.

The popularity of these Sages and their relationship to the contemporary High Priest — the reference may be to Aristobulus the Hasmonean, or to a High Priest appointed by Herod — is indicated by the following story: 'It once happened that a certain High Priest went forth from the Temple and all the people escorted him; but when they saw Shemaʿyah and Avṭalion they left the High Priest and followed them. Finally Shemaʿyah and Avṭalion came to take their leave of the High Priest and said to him: "May the son of Aaron go in peace!" He replied: "May the descendants of the Gentiles come in peace!" They riposted: "May the descendants of the Gentiles, who act like Aaron, come in peace, but may not the son of Aaron, who does not act like Aaron, come in peace!" '[11] The two Sages paid due honour to the High Priest. But when he, incensed by the preference shown by the people for the Sages, expressed himself contemptuously by alluding to their non-Jewish origin, they replied that what mattered was not genealogy — belonging to the sons of Aaron — but acting like Aaron. In the spirit of this answer their disciple Hillel enjoined: 'Be of the disciples of Aaron, loving peace and pursuing peace, loving mankind and bringing them nigh to the Torah' (*M. 'Avot* i, 12). All who possess these attributes are deemed disciples of Aaron, and they are to be preferred to the sons of Aaron who do not walk in his ways.

The families of the High Priests, who occupied the important posts of treasurers and trustees (*Amarkalim*), made the Temple the pivot of their activities. Dynasties were created in which appointments were concentrated for generations, and they also had knowledge of certain cultic services, whose secrets they guarded from generation to generation. One Sage, Abba Saul b. Botnit, who owned a store in Jerusalem shortly before the destruction of the Temple, criticised the priestly dynasties and the concentration of functions in their hands as well as the violence of the office-bearers. He declared: 'Woe is me because of the House of Elisha, woe is me because of their fist, woe is me because of the House of Ishmael b. Phiabi, who are High Priests and their sons are treasurers and their sons-in-law are trustees, and their servants come and beat us with sticks!'[12] Indeed we also hear in another source of 'the leading priests', who came and took by force the skins of the holy offerings in the Temple and prevented their just division among the priestly watches.[13] The houses of the experts, who refused to teach their craft to others, the Sages mentioned unfavourably and said that they intended to enhance their own glory and to diminish that of Heaven.[14] Nor did the Sages refrain from protesting against the exaggerated scrupulousness of the priests in regard to the laws of purity and impurity, 'so that the uncleanness of the knife was considered by them a graver matter than the shedding of blood'.[15] But the Sages were not content merely to voice their criticism; they also endeavoured to permeate the sphere of the Temple and its service with their influence and views, and to weigh down the scales in favour of the traditions and the customs, or the interpretations of the details of the service arrangements that they approved.

V. Hillel's Character and Work

Hillel, who immigrated from Babylonia, influenced the Sons of Bathyra — also apparently a Babylonian family — who had been appointed to one of the important Temple offices, after Herod had deposed the Hasmoneans from the High Priesthood. In his debate with the Sons of Bathyra he made use of the seven exegetical rules by which the Torah is expounded in order to prove that the offering of the Passover sacrifice overrides the Sabbath, if the fourteenth of Nisan falls on the Sabbath, and this accorded with the tradition he had received from his teachers Shemaʿyah and Avṭalion. This Halakha was forgotten and differences of opinion arose on the subject, not necessarily because it but rarely happens that Passover eve falls on the Sabbath. Not only was his teachers' tradition on Hillel's side, but it seems that the masses of the people who went on pilgrimage were of the same opinion. When the Sons of Bathyra said to him 'If so, what will be the position with regard to the people who have not brought their knives and their Passover offerings to the Temple?' he replied: 'Leave it to them; the holy spirit rests on them. If they are not prophets, they are sons of prophets.'[16] Indeed the people found a way of bringing their Passover lambs and knives to the Sanctuary, and they undoubtedly acted as did their fathers.

The way in which Hillel expressed himself — 'The holy spirit rests on them. If they are not prophets, they are sons of prophets' — is of great significance. While, on the one hand, he himself went to the trouble of applying the principle of 'the standard rule' and the argument *a fortiori* in his exposition and even made use of the tradition he had received from his teachers, Shemaʿyah and Avṭalion, in order to prove that the Passover sacrifice overrides the Sabbath, on the other hand, he evaluated the popular usage as a reflection of prophecy, as a kind of Heavenly Voice. The holy spirit had departed from individuals, but it rested on the community as a whole. The aphorism uttered by Hillel at the Water-Drawing Celebration 'If you will come to My home, I shall come to your home; but if you will not come to My home, I shall not come to yours'[17] contains an allusion to the etymological exposition of R. Joshua b. Levi: 'Why is it called בית השואבה *Bêt ha-Shô'ēvā* [literally 'House of Drawing'; rendered above 'Water-Drawing']? Because the holy spirit is drawn from there.'[18] The holy spirit as a permanent factor ceased to exist in the days of the Second Temple, but certain situations of exaltation and joy deriving from the performance of a Divine precept bring about its reappearance; more than this, however, the generation does not merit. This explanation is confirmed by another story concerning Hillel: 'It once happened that when the Sages entered the house of Guryo in Jericho, they heard a Heavenly Voice say "There is a man here who is worthy of the holy spirit, but his generation is not worthy of it and they all looked at Hillel...."[19]

The very expressions 'a generation worthy', 'a man worthy', in relation to the holy spirit and prophecy point to a fundamental change that had occurred in the conception of this phenomenon. In the Bible we find no description whatsoever of the prophetic attributes considered essential qualifications for the gift of prophecy. The prophet is called and responds or is sent and runs away; a mighty hand takes hold of him, and the prophecy is like a fire shut up in his bones; while according to the Sages a man is vouchsafed the holy spirit by virtue of his fitness and the qualities of character and virtues that he has acquired[20], and even these are insufficient and he requires certain external, objective conditions.[21] Prophecy evolved into a mystic experience.[22] It is told of Hillel 'that he had eighty disciples, thirty of whom were worthy that the Divine Presence should rest upon them... the most junior of them all was Rabban Joḥanan b. Zakkai'[23] and with his name, in truth, are linked the earliest traditions and accounts of the experiences of those among the Sages who occupied themselves with the 'Work of the Chariot'. But this mystic encounter remained an esoteric doctrine, the tradition relating to it being restrained and reserved.[24] Even if it raised the status of its heroes in the estimation of their friends, it was not the factor that gave them authority and standing, just as these were not acquired by the performance of miracles, although they may have brought those who wrought them fame in the eyes of the masses.[25] The 'Work of the Chariot' became a theme of Torah study, a part of the wisdom of those Sages who continued to learn and expound it. It was the Amora R. Avdimi of Haifa, who himself belonged to this type of Sage[26], that stated: 'Since the destruction of the Temple prophecy was taken away from the prophets and given to the Sages'[27]; and, apparently, by 'prophecy' he meant a mystic experience, which could be acquired only by one who was also a Sage. The Sage could also be a prophet, but one who professes to be only a prophet, is not even a prophet. This is what Amemar had in mind when he said 'a Sage transcends a prophet.' One aspect of prophecy — namely foretelling future events — also continued to be found among the Sages. In this sense Amoraim said that certain Tannaim 'foresaw' or 'divined' by the holy spirit, and actually the stories show that this 'holy spirit' was their understanding and wisdom or a miraculous act.[28] R. Joḥanan referred to foretelling and divining the future in his dictum 'Since the day that the Temple was destroyed, prophecy was taken away from the prophets and was given to idiots and children.'[29] He not only interpreted the verse 'And thine ears shall hear a word behind thee' (Isaiah xxx 21) to mean that 'one may make use of a Heavenly Voice [literally 'the Daughter of a Voice']'[30], in the sense of divining the future and drawing inferences from a voice heard by chance, but he acted in accordance with this rule. The voice of a lad, who read in his school the verse 'And Samuel died', led him and Resh Laqish to the conclusion that the Amora Samuel in Babylonia had died, and caused them to put off their intended journey to Babylonia in order to visit him.[31] The voice may be of a child or of a woman, but it is used for instruction. A different connotation attaches to the expression 'a Heavenly Voice went forth', which refers not only to that which went forth from the Holy of Holies, or was heard at the time when the voice of prophecy had not yet become silent; the phrase 'a Heavenly Voice went forth and said' serves at times as a substitute for 'the holy spirit said'.[32] Tannaim and Amoraim also heard 'a Heavenly Voice' of this kind.[33]

It is, nevertheless, clear that neither the manifestations of prophecy in its later aspects, nor the working of miracles, nor the demonstration of superhuman power in bestowing good upon the meritorious and in punishing the wicked, nor ardent words of revelation (which, however, were delivered as interpretations of verses) are characteristic of the Sages in the context of their status among the people and their leadership of the Congregation of Israel. The stories about R. Simeon b. Yoḥai and R. Joḥanan, who cast their eyes on people and turned them into 'a heap of bones',[34] are not different from many other stories regarding righteous and saintly men. The homilies of Sages and others that contain hyperbolical descriptions of the world to come recall the visions of the apocalyptists.[35] What stamps them as Sages is the fact that, like their colleagues who were not known as miracle-workers, they lived in the midst of their people, and that all their actions, expositions, and Halakhot served to guide and perfect the Congregation of Israel. This aim unites the Sages from first to last, despite the differences of type and many divergences of view.

Let us revert to Hillel. The fact that he was found worthy of the inspiration of the holy spirit highlights his personal attributes and virtues as they are revealed in his deeds and activities, which endowed him with influence and status. Even if his appointment as Nasi [Patriarch, Chief] by the Sons of Bathyra had only limited significance — that is to say, he was accepted as Nasi over them[36], as a teacher of Halakhot in the sphere of the Sanctuary — his influence is nevertheless also proved by his enactments. One concerned the Temple treasury, which likewise served as a depository in the charge of trustees and treasurers. In order to circumvent the law of the Torah, which gives the seller of a house in a walled city the right to redeem it during the entire period of twelve months, the buyers used to hide themselves on the last day of the year, so that the seller should not find them and the house should become theirs permanently. 'Hillel, however, ordained that he [the seller] should deposit his money in the (Temple) Chamber.'[37] This enactment obliged the trustees and the treasurers in charge of the Temple treasury to carry out certain banking operations — to register the name of the depositor and the name of the buyer to whose credit the money was deposited. The one who sold his house was certainly a person in distress, and Hillel's enactment was prompted by concern lest he be deprived of his right to return to his house, just as the enactment of *Prosbol*, which Hillel introduced, sought to secure the interests of artisans, shopkeepers, and small businessmen who were in need of credit — 'so as not to close the door to borrowers'.[38] This enactment, which in practice annulled the law of the cancellation of debts in the Sabbatical year, preserved its purpose and its spirit.

As we have seen, the Sages were not always pleased with the ways of the kings and princes, with the members of the Sanhedrin, with the actions of priests and with the practices obtaining in the Temple. But their criticism did not lead them to negate these institutions or to secede from them. On the contrary, they held to the principle: to protest against wrongdoing by members of the administration and government, whilst maintaining an attitude of esteem and respect for the hallowed institutions of the people, namely the Temple, the Sanhedrin, and the priesthood. Furthermore, neither the earthly kingdom of the Hasmoneans[39], nor even that of the House of Herod, was completely and absolutely invalidated.

The merit of Herod himself, 'a slave of the House of the Hasmoneans'[40], was not impaired as a builder of the Temple; and a saintly Sage, Bava b. Buṭa, one of the elders of the House of Shammai[41], was his counsellor in this undertaking.

King Agrippa, the validity of whose lineage was in doubt, won the praise of the Sages when he publicly demonstrated his faithfulness to the Torah.[42] The verse 'The sceptre shall not depart from Judah' was rendered by Onkelos 'Rulership shall not depart from the House of Judah',[43] and in this version it appeared at the end of the High Priest's prayer in the Temple[44], when kings who were not of the House of Judah reigned.

As for the age of Hillel, to it also is applicable the statement in the Mishna that the elders of the Beth Din used to adjure the High Priest not to change anything of all that they had instructed him regarding the order of the service.[45] It appears that due to Hillel's endeavours there were to be found High Priests who were themselves Sages, or at least disciples of the Sages.[46] If we come to evaluate the influence of the Sages in Temple matters and in the ordering of the service, we must not forget that the cultic arrangements, the offering of the sacrifices and cereal oblations, the laws of sacred dedications and vows of evaluation, the Sanctuary structures, its chambers and Temple equipment, were in practice for centuries in the hands of the priests. Needless to say, the priestly families, the officers, and the trustees were well versed in these laws, and they also determined what was to be preserved and what had to be changed.[47] Not a few of the cultic forms and temple ceremonies of the Gentile peoples of antiquity were taken over by the Temple of Jerusalem, which, at the same time, came under their architectural influence,[48] and imported gates as well as craftsmen from Alexandria.[49] On the other hand, specific details of many laws were directed against practices that had wide currency among non-Jews. In certain matters differences of opinion arose between the families of the High Priesthood, and when they were in power, they imposed their own procedures.[50] The Sages ceased to regard the Temple and the sacrificial laws as a priestly code and made them an order of their Mishna. The Sages decided between the various traditions; such a decision was made by Hillel in regard to the offering of the Passover sacrifice on the Sabbath. In this matter — of a sacrifice that every individual Jew was obliged to bring — he also took into account the usage prevailing among the people (above, p. 577). The Sages gave particular attention to the glorification of ceremonies and the observance of precepts in the Temple in which all the people participated. Apart from the laws connected with the Passover offering they strove to consolidate customs and precepts about the details of which there were divergent opinions — for instance, the offering of 'the sheaf' — or such as were entirely disputed, like the libation of water and the ceremonial use of willows on the seventh day of the Festival of Tabernacles. In rituals of this type, in processions and festivities, in offering the First Fruits, in the Water-Drawing Ceremony, or on the occasion of the Assembly [הקהל *Haqhēl*, Deuteronomy xxxi 10–13] at the termination of the Year of Release, the participation of the masses of the people was ever of primary importance.[51] Reference has already been made to the meticulous care with which the priests observed the laws of levitical purity and impurity (above, p. 576), and there are copious testimonies, both internal and extraneous, regarding this scrupulousness in all that concerns the Temple and its environment,[52] and about the multiplicity of preventive measures to safeguard the hallowed things and the priests from being defiled.[53] The restrictive decrees and enactments of the early Sages, like Jose b. Jo'ezer, Jose b. Joḥanan, and Simeon b. Sheṭaḥ, dealt with matters of levitical purity and impurity. Ancient regulations in this sphere that had been forgotten were renewed in later courts,[54] and the Tanna R. Simeon b. Eleazar said of the earlier generations: 'Come and see, how far the observance of the laws of purity had spread among Israel!'[55]

However, the desire to make it easier for the pilgrims who went up to Jerusalem for the festivals and enable the multitudes to participate to a greater extent in the experiences of staying in the Temple, and to show them its glory and greatness, led to the introduction of many alleviating practices and rules, and it appears that these not only had the consent of the Sages, but were even due to their initiative. The roads by which the Babylonian pilgrims were accustomed to go up to Eretz-Israel were pronounced clean, although they formed part of the land of the Gentiles which had been declared unclean.[56] It was the duty of every Jew to purify himself for the festival,[57] and no one entered the Temple Court — even if he was clean — until he had undergone ritual immersion.[58] Hence even the ignorant people [עמי הארץ *'ammē hā-'areṣ*, 'peoples of the land', who were not scrupulous in the observance of the laws of purity and in separating the tithes] were trusted in Jerusalem at festival times even in respect of the heave-offering.[59] They [the Temple officials] used to bring forth and show the table to the pilgrim, 'and they entered the chamber of vessels and brought forth from there ninety-three utensils of silver and gold'.[60] After the festival they 'entered upon the cleansing of the Temple Court' and immersed the vessels in the Temple;[61] once it happened that 'they immersed the candelabrum on a festival and the Sadducees said: "Come and see, the Pharisees are immersing the light of the moon".'[62] The reason for these lenient rulings was explained by R. Joshua b. Levi in the following homily: ' "Jerusalem that art builded as a city that is compact [*ḥubbĕrā*] together" (Psalms cxxii 3) — a city that makes all Israel חברים *ḥăvērîm* ['Associates'; scholars who observe the laws of levitical purity].'[63] Similarly it is taught in a Baraita that the reason for accepting sacrifices from 'people who are like cattle (Rashi: 'wicked')' and from 'Israelite transgressors' is 'that they might repent'.[64]

The ideal of the Sages was to make all Israel 'associates', and not merely at the time when the people went up to Jerusalem. Hence we must consider the social consequences of the insistence on the meticulous observance of the laws of purity and impurity in everyday life. The prevailing view in the Halakha is apparently that all the laws of purity and impurity — followed also by the Rabbinical rules of impurity — really affected only priests and Nazirites, and they concerned the Israelites as a whole only when they came into contact with Temple matters and hallowed objects. Even the verse 'Of their flesh ye shall not eat, and their carcasses ye shall not touch; they are unclean unto you' (Leviticus xi 8), which applies to all Israel, is explained as referring only to the time of the festivals.[65] However, not only individuals — priests, Levites, Israelites, and proselytes — were accustomed to eat unconsecrated food in various degrees of purity[66], but from early sources, Mishnayot and Baraitot, there emerges what appears to be an Order of *Ḥăvērîm* (חברים), who share the ideal of observing 'the principles of associateship' in matters of purity and impurity, the separation of heave-offerings and tithes, and the avoidance of certain forms of contact with those who do not belong to their associateship, namely those called *ʿam ha-ʾareṣ*. Separate societies organized for the observance of the laws of purity and holiness, sects who remained apart from the other members of their community, city, or people, are known in the framework of other religions.[67] To the enrolment procedure of the *Ḥăvûrā* of Pharisees there are parallels in the order of initiation into the group of Essenes, as described by Josephus, and especially in the system of initiation of the sect of 'the Men of the *Yaḥad*' [the Qumran Covenanters] not only in respect of its regulations and their ceremonial details, but also in regard to the phrasing and expressions of the ritual.[68]

However, despite all the similarities in details and major aspects, there is a fundamental difference between the Pharisaic groups and the Essenes and the Qumran Sect. The object of the Pharisaic groups was to facilitate the observance of the laws of purity in all their stringency. Joining a group meant separation from those who were not Associates — from the *ʿam hāʾāreṣ* — and this not only gave rise to problems in everyday life, but was a problem in itself, and could create class and sectarian polarity. Although we are unable to determine the exact time when the groups first appeared, it seems that initially they limited the separation to necessary spheres and maintained unity in the matters that they shared with non-Associates. After all it appears that the Pharisee Associates were closer to the *ʿammê hā-ʾāreṣ* than sects of the type of the Essenes or the Men of the *Yaḥad*. In the view of the latter the laws of membership held no problem or difficulty, but on the contrary, served to fortify a society that was separated from 'the habitation of men of wickedness'; it was essentially an order of brethren, living in community and sharing their property, an order that created for itself substitutes for all the institutions that were sacred to the nation as a whole. The Men of the *Yaḥad*, who called themselves 'holy men', 'men of truth', 'men of the destiny of God', regarded those who did not belong to them 'as men of violence', 'men of wickedness', 'men of corruption', and 'men of the destiny of Belial',[69] but not as *ʿam hā-ʾāreṣ*. On the other hand, in the world of the Sages the connotation of the term *ʿam ha-ʾāreṣ* underwent a change. It does not only mean one who does not eat unconsecrated food in purity, or is suspected of not setting aside the tithes,[70] but also one who is not learned in the Torah and does not study it. In this sense apparently Hillel already used the term *ʿam hā-ʾāreṣ*; and from the context it seems possible that he even employed it vis-à-vis people of the type of the Men of the *Yaḥad*. His dictum 'A brutish [בור *bûr*] man dreads not sin, and an *ʿam hā-ʾāreṣ* cannot be saintly' consists of two parallel members.[71] *ʿAm hā-ʾāreṣ* corresponds to *bûr* in the sense of brutish and empty of Torah.[72] The antithesis between *bûr* and 'Sage' in the following Baraita is particularly instructive for our subject: 'He who begins (a benediction) with YH [יה, part of the Tetragrammaton] and concludes with YH is wise [a Sage]; (begins) with YH and concludes with *ʾAlef Lamed* [אל, 'God'] is brutish [*bûr*]; (begins) with *ʾAlef Lamed* and concludes with YH is intermediate; (begins) with *ʾAlef Lamed* and concludes with *ʾAlef Lamed* — this is another [i.e. heretical] way.'[73] In another version of this Baraita 'brutish' is applied to one who begins with ʾEl and ends with ʾEl, and 'another way' is referred to one who is only careful to end with ʾEl.[74] Indifference in regard to the benedictory formulas was characteristic of the members of the Qumran sect, who used the name ʾEl in the conclusions of benedictions.[75] This method was termed 'another way' or the act of a brutish man, although those who followed this practice intended to demonstrate 'fear of sin', for a 'brutish' person is not sin-fearing. And as 'a brutish man' is the antithesis of 'a Sage', so does *ʿam hā-ʾāreṣ*, which is a parallel term, denote one devoid of Torah knowledge, who, even if he observes abstinence and purity, cannot be deemed saintly. It is not accidental that the Mishna which speaks of the attitude to property designates the one who says 'Mine is yours and yours is mine' — that is the one who believes in community of wealth and property — an *ʿam hā-ʾāreṣ*.[76] It is obvious that ordinary *ʿammē hā-ʾāreṣ* were not wont to speak thus; apparently the reference is to an *ʿam hā-ʾāreṣ* who is to be identified with the members of a sect similar to that of the Qumran Order.[77] It is possible that the Men of the *Yaḥad* adopted for their purpose earlier procedures of 'Associateship' (חברות *ḥăvērût*), just as these methods of adaptation are evident in the Halakhot of the Sages. Thus it is stated: 'Even a disciple has to accept (Associateship), but a Sage who sits in the academy need not accept (Associateship) for he already accepted it when he took his seat (in the academy). Abba Saul said: Even a disciple need not accept (Associateship). Furthermore, even others may accept (Associateship) before him.'[78] The compiler of this Baraita had in mind the Mishna of Abba Saul in which he taught that a disciple — and not only a Sage — need not accept (Associateship).[79] Abba Saul was a contemporary of R. Ṭarfon, and like the latter testified to matters that occurred in the Temple,[80] as well as to the rules applicable to 'Associates' and *ʿammê hā-'āreṣ* in regard to partaking of sacrifices of the lower grade and second tithe in certain parts of the city of Jerusalem.[81] The Mishna that he taught represents, therefore, the state of affairs shortly before the destruction of the Temple. It also appears that in the version of the Baraita cited above there are discernible two stricter views, which represent two earlier stages, namely the opinion that even a Sage must accept (Associateship), and the view that an appointed Sage (= one who sits in the academy) does not need to so, but a disciple must. Of the stringent ruling R. Joḥanan said: 'This Mishna was taught in the days of the son of R. Ḥanina b. Antigonus.'[82] He, too, was a Tanna who lived in Temple times. The aim reflected in these rulings is to assure preferential standing for a Sage and a disciple even in the framework of the *Ḥăvûrā* of the Pharisees. The Associations of the Pharisees were not all of the same character, and certainly did not observe the same stringencies at all times and in all matters. The divergences are still reflected in the statements of the later Tannaim in which the Halakhot of the earlier generations are embedded. It seems that in the ancient period, when the associates were not numerous, their laws were stricter, but when the ways of the *Ḥăvûrā* became popular practice, the tendency towards leniency developed. Sometimes this difference is expressly stated: '*At first* they used to say: An associate who became a tax-collector is expelled from his society. *Subsequently they declared*: So long as he is a tax-collector he is not deemed trustworthy; but once he gives up his work as tax-collector he is (again) trusted.'[83] Apparently even laws that have not been formulated in this way, but as a dispute between Tannaim, are, in truth, Halakhic traditions belonging to different periods; for example: 'And none of them, if they retracted, are ever accepted again — this is the view of R. Me'ir. R. Judah said: If they retracted openly (παρρησία) they may be accepted (again); if they did so covertly, they may not (again) be accepted [i.e. if they reverted to their former evil practices secretly, but outwardly acted like associates, they may not be accepted on account of their hypocrisy]. R. Simeon and R. Joshua b. Qorḥa [said]: In either case they are accepted.'[84]

It is difficult to regard R. Me'ir's statement as his personal opinion, because it is a complete contradiction of his teaching concerning the power of repentance (above, p. 466); hence it is to be viewed only as a relic of stringent regulations of a society, which has a parallel in the *Scroll of the Rule of the Yaḥad* [Manual of Discipline] vii, 1: 'If a man utter a curse... then he is to be excluded and never allowed to return to the Council of the Community.' Although the extant laws of associates were taught in the period of Usha, yet it is clear that this fact does not indicate the date when the laws[85] came into being, but merely that at that time, or approximately so, they were resuscitated with a view to making regulations that had once pertained to small societies the Halakhot of corporate Israel. This is implied by R. Me'ir's dictum 'Whoever lives permanently in Eretz-Israel and eats unconsecrated food in purity and speaks the holy tongue and reads the *Shĕma*ʿ morning and evening is assured of life in the world to come.'[86] R. Me'ir wished to introduce greater stringency, whereas the Tannaim who disagreed with him preferred to proceed along the path of leniency. The renewal of these laws after the Revolt of Bar Kokhba is also to be explained, perhaps, by the general ascetic trend prevailing at the time.[87] However, it appears that in practice these stringencies were chiefly confined to the Sages and their disciples. Possibly this tendency is reflected in the dispute between Rabban Simeon b. Gamaliel and Rabbi, which was epitomized in the Talmudic dictum: 'Rabbi holds that an Associate prefers to transgress a minor prohibition so that an *ʿam hā-'āreṣ* should not transgress a major prohibition; and Rabban Simeon b. Gamaliel maintains that an Associate prefers an *ʿam hā-'āreṣ* to transgress a major prohibition rather than that he himself should transgress even a minor prohibition.'[88] It is probable that Rabbi had in mind an Associate who was primarily a Sage, just as in enunciating the rule 'An Associate does not require admonition, because admonition serves only to distinguish between one who commits a transgression unwittingly and one who does so wittingly.'[89] Rabbi's colleague, R. Jose b. R. Judah, was thinking primarily of a Sage and not necessarily of a *Ḥāvēr* in the earlier connotation of the term. In the Amoraic period the designation *Ḥāvēr* became a synonym for a scholar [literally, 'disciple of the Sages'], so that it was possible to say '*Ḥăvērîm* are none other than scholars'.[90]

Now we must examine how the development that we have described in the meaning of the terms *Ḥāvēr* and *'am hā-'āreṣ* affected the mutual relationship of the two types. Was not the combination of wisdom and Torah-knowledge with the observance of the laws of purity and impurity and scrupulous care in regard to the laws of tithes liable to exacerbate further the rift between the Sages-Associates and the *'am hā-'āreṣ*? Ostensibly we have already answered this question in the negative; but actually we have considered only the measures taken to prevent sectarian secession and preserve unity within the framework of the sacred institutions common to all. But this does not provide a complete answer. At any rate an additional examination of the question of the relationship between the Sages and the broad masses is necessary. Let us revert to the image of Hillel. At his funeral eulogy no mention was made of the fact that he was worthy that the Shekhina should rest upon him, but it was said 'Alas, the humble man, alas the saint, the disciple of Ezra!' The reference to Ezra is to be explained by the dictum of Resh Laqish: 'When the Torah was forgotten in Israel, Ezra came up from Babylon and re-established it; when it was again forgotten, Hillel the Babylonian came up and re-established it.'[91]

Hillel founded the Torah anew by virtue of the fact that he was both saintly and humble. His saintliness found expression in the testimonies to his acts, which were all for the sake of Heaven (above, p. 340), and to his absolute faith in God, which left no room for misgivings or fears.[92]

The attributes of humility, patience, love of one's fellows, and the pursuit of peace, which Hillel displayed, did not diminish the stringency of his ethical and religious demands, or prevent him from placing full responsibility on man, whom he required to act for his own perfection and for the public weal. Man is obliged to make endeavours, for 'If I am not for myself, who will be for me?' But he cannot achieve much through seclusion and separation, and he must remember 'And being for my own self, what am I?' Nor may he forget that his time is limited and he dare not procrastinate — 'And if not now, when?' (*M. 'Avot* i, 14). Man's relations with his fellow man were defined by Hillel not only in the rule attributed to him as a reply to a proselyte who asked to be taught the whole Torah while standing on one foot — 'What is hateful to you do not do to your fellow'[93] — the like of which the would-be proselyte might also have heard from others, but in the demand that one must not pass hasty judgement on the actions of another person, just as one is forbidden to be confident of one's own righteousness. The principle is: 'Be not sure of yourself until the day of your death, and judge not your fellow until you come into his place' (*M. 'Avot* ii, 4). However, a man's humility and self-criticism are no excuse for keeping aloof from the community. Hillel even instructs the Sage who has acquired the qualities of saintliness and humility: 'Sever not yourself from the community... and where there are no men strive to be a man' (*ibid.* ii, 5).

In the cycle of stories about Hillel's humility and patience the strictness of Shammai is also portrayed.[94] One may ask if the tales about Shammai do not act merely as a background and literary device that serve to highlight the attributes of the real hero, whose virtues are presented as an example for future generations. This question is undoubtedly justified in regard to details of the stories even in the light of Shammai's dictum 'and receive all men with a cheerful countenance' (*ibid.* i, 15). But the actual tradition regarding Shammai's severity is not to be denied. This is evidenced not necessarily by lack of politeness and impatience, but by his insistence on the scrupulous observance of commandments without considering the consequences, to the point of endangering the life of a child; and this is true not solely of the individual and personal sphere, but also of the laws and precepts that appertain to the entire community.[95] Only four disputes between Hillel and Shammai,[96] it is true, have come down to us, and one of these was a subject of controversy in earlier generations, namely that of סמיכה *sĕmîkhā* (see below). But it is clear, on the one hand, that there were other matters on which they differed, but they still adhered to the old Halakhic traditional method of citing only 'a decided Halakha without controversy'.[97] On the other hand, it appears that even the three controversial matters referred to were transmitted in this form only because no decision had been arrived at, and afterwards the issues were decided in accordance with neither view.

Hillel's attributes and his conduct were responsible for the fact that not only his enactments but also his views were accepted, even when others differed from him. Thus 'When the Alexandrians married, one would go and snatch the bride from the street, and a case of this kind came before the Sages. They wished to declare their children bastards; but Hillel the Elder said to the Alexandrians: "Bring me your mothers' *kĕtubbā* [marriage contract]." They brought them and it was found written therein: "When thou shalt enter my house, thou shalt be my wife according to the Law of Moses and Israel." '[98] We do not know who were the Sages who wished to declare the Alexandrians bastards, but it is clear — as in the case of the Passover sacrifice — that Hillel considered the public custom authoritative. As Naḥmanides explains:[99] 'And although it was an ignorant custom, he ruled in accordance with it, as if they had acted on the instruction of the Sages. And although they had become used to writing thus without Rabbinic mandate, he made this practice a (court) condition... since it was a simple custom and every one acted in this way...' R. Solomon b. Abraham Aderet (Rashba) went further[1] in explaining the broad-minded understanding of Hillel: 'In the matter brought up before Hillel, it was not the *kĕtubbôt* of the mothers of those who were being stigmatized as bastards that were produced, but the meaning is that he was shown the *kĕtubbôt* of other people of that place. From these he learned that the local people were accustomed to write thus, and on the basis of these documents he also validated all the others that were not drawn up in precisely the same manner, but in general terms....' This decision, like his enactments, gave Hillel such standing and authority among the people, that they deemed the time opportune to come to a decision also in respect of the one disputed issue that had not been decided in the course of the generations, namely the question of *sĕmîkhā* [putting hands on the head of a sacrifice]. Despite the many strange conjectures advanced concerning this controversy, the reason for its continuance for generations and its background has not been elucidated; only one thing is clear, that the point involved was whether or not *sĕmîkhā* could be performed on a festival.[2] Hillel not only stated theoretically that one was allowed 'to put on hands', but he acted accordingly in practice, and thus brought about a decision with the help of the people who supported him: 'It once happened that Hillel the Elder performed *sĕmîkhā* on a burnt-offering in the Temple court, and the disciples of Shammai gathered about him in protest against his action... (however,) he put them off with words and they went away.'[3]

The abolition of the laying on of hands on a festival resulted in the diminution of those who brought offerings. This is how it is explained in a story of later origin: 'After a time the School of Shammai prevailed and they wished to decide the Halakha according to their ruling; now Bava b. Buṭa, one of the disciples of the School of Shammai, was present and he knew that the Halakha was in accord with the view of the School of Hillel. Once, on entering the Temple court, he found it deserted. Thereupon he said: May the homes of those who have made the House of our God desolate become desolate! What did he do? He ordered three thousand lamb[15] of the sheep of Kedar to be brought and he examined them for blemishes and placed them on the Temple Mount and proclaimed: "Hearken unto me, O my brethren of the House of Israel! whoever so wishes let him bring burnt offerings, (let him bring) and lay on hands; let him bring peace offerings and lay on hands." At that moment the Halakha was determined according to the School of Hillel, and no one said a word to the contrary.'[4] This episode, which occurred at the time when the Shammaites prevailed — we shall still revert to this incident — teaches us that Hillel, in acting as he did, decided in favour of *sĕmîkhā*[5] for a similar reason — that is to say, that the Temple court should not be desolate on a festival — but he gained the decision by virtue of the persuasive power of his arguments. As in the case of the decision taken in regard to the offering up of the Passover sacrifice on the fourteenth of Nisan that fell on a Sabbath, when account was also taken of the current trend and attitude of the people, Hillel's own dictum was exemplified in himself: 'My humiliation is my elevation, and my elevation is my humiliation.'[6] His personality became an educational exemplar, and when later generations highly eulogized a departed Sage they said: 'Ah, humble man, ah saint, disciple of Hillel!'[7]

In the dispute between the School of Hillel and the School of Shammai regarding the interpretation of the dictum of the Men of the Great Assembly 'And raise up many disciples', the view expressed by the Hillelites reflects the outcome of Hillel's activity. His maxim 'Be of the disciples of Aaron, loving peace and pursuing peace, loving your fellow creatures and drawing them near to the Torah' (*M. 'Avot* i, 12) means 'the disciples of Aaron', but not necessarily 'the descendants of Aaron'. 'Fellow creatures' in general — even if they are not Sages and meek, of good family and worthy — should be drawn near. Accordingly the School of Hillel said: 'One should teach everyone'; and they based their teaching on the result of this approach, 'for there were many transgressors in Israel, but when they began to study Torah, there came forth from among them righteous men, saints, and worthy men.'[8] Hillel was responsible for the fact that the Sanhedrin, which consisted of 'priests, Levites, and Israelites who could give their daughters in marriage to priests',[9] became a Sanhedrin of 'all Israel', as it is designated in Mishnayot and Baraitot that refer to the period after Hillel, as for instance in the Mishna 'The Chamber of Hewn Stone — there the Great Sanhedrin of Israel used to sit and judge the priesthood.'[10] Confirmation of the general character of the Sanhedrin is contained in the following statement of R. Joshua, who, like the redactor of the Mishna cited above, lived when the Temple was still in existence: 'Did proselytes then enter the *Hêkhal* [the Holy]? Lo, no Israelite entered the *Hêkhal*! The meaning is that they sat in the Sanhedrin and taught the words of the Torah.'[11]

Hillel and his disciples pursued the path of gradual penetration into the institutions of the Temple and the Sanhedrin and endeavoured to influence their methods and actions, but at the same time they did not regard themselves as an élite that aspired to power and leadership, but as an élite that served as an example.

Love of one's fellow creatures, which was Hillel's guiding principle, his open policy, and his readiness to receive into the circle and association of the Sages all who came to learn, served to reduce the tension and to limit the gulf between the sections of the people, dangers that were inherent in the laws of fellowship governing levitically clean foodstuffs, heave-offerings, and tithes, and in the emergence of an intellectual stratum that had also gained influence in the institutions of government and authority. But we may state that at least until the destruction of the Temple, and even till the period of Jabneh, the principal task of the Sage still remained in the field of teaching and Halachic ruling, in works of charity and acts of lovingkindness. He lived among the multitude of the people. He sought to influence the sacred institutions of the people — the Temple, the Sanhedrin, and the priesthood — and to decide Halachic matters. But the power of his influence was derived solely from his wisdom, and the source of his authority lay in his deeds and qualities of character. This is the testimony of Josephus at the end of his work *Antiquities of the Jews*, concerning a period close to that of Hillel: 'For our people do not favour those persons who have mastered the speech of many nations, or who adorn their style with smoothness of diction... But they give credit for wisdom to those alone who have an exact knowledge of the law and who are capable of interpreting the meaning of the Holy Scriptures.' Concerning these Sages he observes elsewhere 'that even when they speak against a king or high priest, they immediately gain credence'.[12]

VI. The Regime of the Sages after the Destruction of the Temple

In the world of the Sages in the days of the Second Temple until the time of Hillel we find no bureaucratic organization, no system whatsoever of appointments, no promotion, no remuneration, and in truth no training arrangements or definition of functions. But it was just the success and achievements of Hillel's acts that led to a far-reaching change in the status of the Sages. It is a fact that for the first time we encounter *Bêt Hillēl* (the 'House of Hillel') as denoting a dynasty, although the son and grandson of Hillel — Rabban Gamaliel and his son Rabban Simeon — were not נשיאים *Nĕśî'îm* ('Princes') in the sense that Simeon the Hasmonean was a נשיא *Nāśî'*, nor in the connotation given to the function of the *Nĕśî'îm* of the House of Hillel in the period following the Destruction.[13] But undoubtedly they had a special status in the Sanhedrin, and enactments made in certain spheres bore their name. Rabban Simeon b. Gamaliel decided the Halakha in a matter concerning the Temple in a manner resembling that of his grandfather Hillel: 'It once happened that a pair of doves in Jerusalem cost a golden denar. Said Rabban Simeon b. Gamaliel: "By this Temple! before the night is over they will cost but a (silver) denar." He entered the *Bet Din* ('court') and taught: If a woman suffered five miscarriages that were not in doubt... she need bring (only) one sacrifice and she may then partake of the animal offerings, and she is not under obligation to bring the other offerings. That same day the price of a pair of doves went down to a quarter of a denar each.'[14] On the other hand it must be pointed out that the intervention of the Sages in the affairs of the Temple and their influence over the priests did not prevent antagonism between them and 'the Bet Din of the priests',[15] whose views differed from those of the Sages, and the latter did not always have the power to oppose the priests and to effect a decision contrary to their opinion.

Until the beginning of the Revolt the differences of opinion, which grew with the increase of the number of disciples, did not lead to sharp schisms between the two schools — the School of Shammai and the School of Hillel. On the contrary, 'Joezer of the Bira [Temple structure] was one of the disciples of the School of Shammai and he said: 'I asked Rabban Gamaliel the Elder, when he was standing in the Eastern Gate'.[16] Joḥanan the Ḥoronite, although a disciple of Shammai, always acted in accordance with the views of the School of Hillel.[17] On the other hand we find that 'the more scrupulous of the Hillelites used to act according to the School of Shammai',[18] 'And once the elders of the School of Shammai and the elders of the School of Hillel went into the upper chamber of Jonathan b. Bathyra and ruled that there was no prescribed length for fringes [see Numbers xv 37 ff]; so, too, they decided that there is no prescribed length for the palm-branch [used on the Festival of Tabernacles].'[19] The position changed with the start of the Great Revolt; whereas previously the Sages were able to adopt a positive attitude in principle to the actual institutions of the state and government, without refraining from protesting against acts of injustice and without seeking unduly close relations with the ruling power, once the Revolt broke out, which seemed to many an obligatory war, and to others a hopeless struggle that endangered the existence of the people, the relationship between the two Schools became severely strained, and it may well be that the dividing line did not correspond precisely to the academic division. It is clearer to us today than ever before that the Zealots — the freedom-fighters in the years of the Great Revolt — not only were not a sect motivated by a given philosophy, but were more divided and diversified in respect of their views and their ideological affiliation than in regard to their politico-strategical and social outlook.[20] The discovery of a scroll at Massada[21], the like of which is to be found only among the Qumran writings, proves, beyond any shadow of doubt, that there were also members of this sect among the Zealots and fighters, and that the case of John, the Essene, who is mentioned in Josephus[22] as one of the commanders, was not exceptional. Undoubtedly there were, on the other hand, Essenes and Qumran covenanters who were opposed to the zealotry of their colleagues. Political zealotry both united and divided. Rabban Simeon b. Gamaliel supported the preparations for the Revolt and cooperated with John of Gischala.[23] Zechariah b. Eucolus is regarded in the Talmudic stories about the destruction of the Temple as responsible for stopping the offering of sacrifices for the welfare of the state.[24] Josephus, who puts the blame for this incident on Eleazar b. Ananias, the High Priest, an official of the Temple, mentions Zechariah b. Eucolus as one of the extremist Zealots, who, jointly with Eleazar b. Simeon, invited the Idumeans to Jerusalem.[25] In the Talmudic sources we are told that the disciples of the School of Shammai stood with swords and spears 'and slew disciples of the School of Hillel'[26], forcing them to accept their restrictive decrees, that is 'the decrees of the eighteen measures'. These decrees were not promulgated in the Temple, nor on the ascent of the Temple Mount, but in the upper chamber of Eleazar b. Ḥananiah b. Hezekiah b. Garon, one of the Shammaite disciples, who had previously filled the office of general of the army in Idumea.[27] In a late Midrash[28] there is preserved an ancient source portraying fragmentary incidents that took place in the war against the Romans, and it is stated there: 'And Eleazar went up accompanied by disciples, and they smote Elhanan and cut him up into pieces.' The reference, apparently, is to the murder of Ḥanan b. Ḥanan [Ananus], the High Priest, by the Idumeans;[29] and it is not surprising that the Idumeans are called 'disciples', for the Sages declared, with reference to the time when the School of Shammai prevailed, that 'there were Idumean disciples in the School of Shammai'[30], and we have already seen (above, p. 591) that an attempt was even made to change a Halakha, once decided by Hillel, regarding *sĕmîkhā* on a festival. The appraisement of the younger generation, who, if they did not themselves witness the episode that occurred that day, could have heard about it from those who did, is reflected in the words of R. Eliezer and R. Joshua: 'That day they overfilled the measure', or 'struck the measure'; and some said that that day 'was as grievous for Israel as the day on which they made the calf.'[31] The politico-military struggle was exploited for the purpose of securing decisions by force.

It is almost certain that this event had political consequences, for it led the disciples of the School of Hillel to adopt a negative attitude towards the groups of freedom-fighters. The internal dissensions, which became aggravated, caused R. Ḥanina, the prefect of the priests, to say in those hard times: 'Pray for the welfare of the state, for were it not for the fear of it, we should have swallowed [בלענו *bālaʿnû*] each other up alive.'[32]

It appears that Rabban Joḥanan b. Zakkai's attitude to the Revolt was from the outset more reserved than that of Rabban Simeon b. Gamaliel, who cooperated with him in Halakhic decisions.[33] Although it is not known that Rabban Joḥanan held any official position when he was in Jerusalem,[34] he acted like his master Hillel and strove to infiltrate the views of the Sages into the Temple service and into the sacrificial regulations[35], and without doubt he had access to both the circles of the High Priesthood and the leaders of the group of rebels. His moderate attitude at the time of the victories at the beginning of the Revolt after the defeat of Cestius Gallus found expression in his admonition: 'Be not in haste to pull down the high places of the Gentiles, lest you have to rebuild (them) with your own hand; lest you pull down those made of bricks and they order you: "Rebuild them of stone!", or those made of stone and they enjoin you: "Rebuild them of wood!" '[36] It is not to be inferred from these words 'that R. Joḥanan b. Zakkai advised the acceptance anew of the Roman yoke'.[37] It seems, however, that when internal schisms became intensified, that is to say, 'when the murderers multiplied',[38] he saw danger threatening the very existence of the people and resolved to work for peace. Possibly the following homily of his contains an apologia for his attitude: 'It is stated "Thou shalt build... of unhewn [שלמות *shĕlēmôt*] stones' (Deuteronomy xxvii 6) — stones that bring peace [שלום *shālôm*]." It is an argument from minor to major: If now the stones of the altar, which neither see nor speak, yet, because they make peace between Israel and their Father in heaven, the Holy One, blessed be He, said "Thou shalt lift up no iron tool upon them"; how much more so shall one who makes peace between man and man, between a man and his wife, between city and city, between nation and nation, between government and government, or between family and family, not suffer tribulation.'[39]

According to one version of the story about the attempts of Rabban Joḥanan b. Zakkai to come in touch with the emperor Vespasian, who had laid siege to Jerusalem, the Sage was aided by his sister's son, Abba Siqra, chief of the outlaws.[40] At any rate Rabban Joḥanan b. Zakkai left Jerusalem, after he was convinced that the fate of the City and the Temple was sealed, and he received permission to go to Jabneh, the seat of a Bet Din, which was apparently administered by the Sons of Bathyra, who were also *personae gratae* with the Roman authorities.[41] The destruction of the Temple he regarded as a punishment and he reacted to it as did Eli when Shiloh was destroyed[42], but primarily his thoughts and deeds were devoted to his reconstructive activity, and in this respect he was able to rely only upon the power of his influence. Whether he served from the beginning as head of the Bet Din, or whether he left this office to the Sons of Bathyra, it is clear that their Bet Din was based on the authority of the members collectively. This trend is also reflected in the designation 'the place of assembly' and in Rabban Joḥanan b. Zakkai's enactment 'that wheresoever the head of the Bet Din might be, the witnesses should go only to the place of assembly'.[43] It is possible that on account of this Rabban Joḥanan b. Zakkai preferred to dwell in Beror Ḥayil, in order to remove from himself any suspicion that he was seeking his own honour. His main aim was to restore unity to the association of the Sages and to heal the breaches. Testimony to this activity of Rabban Joḥanan b. Zakkai in the House of the Assembly at Jabneh is to be found, to my mind, in the old and original portion of the

Mishna and Tosefta of *ʿEduyot*: 'When the Sages entered the Vineyard of Jabneh, they said: A time will come when a man will seek a Torah teaching and not find it, a ruling of the Scribes and not find it... so that one precept of the Torah would not be like another. (Hence) they declared: Let us begin with Hillel and Shammai.'[44] The Sages who assembled came to rectify the position that one precept of the Torah was not like another. The purpose of the convention was not therefore literary — it was not to systematize the Halakhot — but to arrive at decisions regarding disputed Halakhot. They began to discuss differences of view between Shammai and Hillel themselves, and 'decided neither according to the one or the other'; they collected Halakhot in respect of which 'the School of Hillel retracted and ruled in accordance with the view of the School of Shammai', and the Halakhot on which the two Schools agreed. In these decisions they were aided by the testimonies of the elder Sages of the generation, like R. Hananiah, the prefect of the priests; R. Dosa b. Harkinas, whose younger brother Jonathan was a disciple of Shammai but he himself decided according to the School of Hillel;[45] R. Joḥanan b. Gudgada; R. Zadok; and apparently also ʿAqaviah b. Mahalalel, who, however, held firmly to his views and did not give way to the opinion of the majority. It appears to me that the story related about this last Sage is significant for determining the status of Rabban Joḥanan b. Zakkai; we shall therefore cite it verbatim and explain it: ʿAqaviah b. Mahalalel testified to four matters... a woman proselyte and a freed bondwoman are not made to drink of the waters of bitterness... They said to him: It happened in the case of Karkemit, a freed bondwoman who was in Jerusalem, and Shemaʿyah and Avṭalion gave her to drink. He replied: It only appeared that they made her drink.'[46] The reliance on an incident that took place in Jerusalem, expressed in this wording, shows that the testimony of 'ʿAqaviah was not given in Jerusalem but in Jabneh.[47] The Sages disagreed with him in three other matters and said to him: 'ʿAqaviah, retract the four opinions that you expressed and we shall make you Av (Father of the) Bet Din of Israel. He replied: It is better that I be called a fool all my days than become for a while a wicked man before God; lest people say that he retracted for the sake of attaining to high office.' At what particular time was this suggestion made to

ʿAqaviah b. Mahalalel? I am inclined to conjecture that the incident occurred near the time of Rabban Joḥanan b. Zakkai's death, and just as Rabban Joḥanan b. Zakkai himself was not appointed and did not succeed anyone, so, too, he did not transfer his status and did not appoint a successor. The position was offered to a Sage of whom it was said 'that the Temple court was not closed to any man in Israel so wise and sin-fearing as ʿAqaviah b. Mahalalel'; but the condition was that he should yield to the majority opinion.

The problem of appointments and the exercise of authority in the world of the Sages is discernible here in its initial stages. It is a fact that shortly after Rabban Joḥanan b. Zakkai we find in Jabneh not an Av Bet Din, but a Nasi [Prince, Patriarch] who was descended from Hillel, namely Rabban Gamaliel, and his position was authorized by the governor in Syria.[48] This circumstance is indicative of the status of his rule externally, and internally, too, he appears as a leader of the nation, whose authority is derived not only from his being Av Bet Din and a Sage, but also from the prestige of his lineage.

Indeed the dynasty of the Patriarchs of the House of Hillel — which at a later period discovered a geneological table showing that 'Hillel was descended from David'[49] — stood at the head of the nation for over three hundred years, until the last Rabban Gamaliel died — the fifth or sixth — without an heir — in the reign of Theodosius II, *circa* 425 C.E.[50] The very fact that the office remained in one family for so long a period, marked by numerous changes, fluctuations, and vicissitudes, bears testimony to the high standing and esteem that it had achieved.

Clearly much depended on the personality, scholarship, and the administrative capacity of the Patriarch, and to no small extent also on the relations between him and extraneous factors, namely the Roman authorities. But it is precisely the fact that not all the Patriarchs were alike in stature and ability, and that the government's attitude towards the Jews of Eretz-Israel and their institutions was not the same at all times, which also serves to demonstrate the stability of the Patriarchal institution. Although this durability is primarily noticeable when measured in terms of centuries, yet when we scrutinize it closely, in so far as we have evidence, the crises in the institutions' history are many. Just as its strength derived from a general desire to regard it as a remnant of national freedom and independence — a kind of shadow monarchy — so, too, the crises and difficulties arose chiefly from its character as such. Since the existing leadership emanated from the body of Sages, there was the danger that the people would look upon all the Sages as the ruling class, and would also blame them for all the faults and perversions connected with government. This danger was largely averted owing to the fact that in all periods there were to be found among the Sages outstanding men who undertook to continue the struggle of former generations against governmental authorities, High Priests, kings and despots, only this struggle was presently directed against a ruling power and authority that stemmed from their own midst and now sought to dominate them. Political circumstances imposed upon the Patriarchs duties that had formerly belonged to other institutions. The supervision of Halakhic decisions in civil and religious law found expression in the centralization of appointments and in the strict selection of disciples. Rabban Gamaliel II of Jabneh considered it a function of the Patriarchate to organize a judicial system in the towns and settlements and to establish a link between them and the central authority, as well as to maintain relations with the Diaspora communities, which involved not only journeys to Rome, where the Patriarch himself had travelled accompanied by elders, but the sending of emissaries to distant parts — to Arabia, Cilicia, Africa, Galatia, Cappadocia, and Gazaka in Media.[51] All these activities necessitated the appointment of office-bearers and the installation of public administrators.[52] The supervision of the Halakhic decisions, introduced by Rabban Gamaliel, led him not only to denounce severely the Sages who continued to stand for freedom in Halakhic rulings, but even to punish them,[53] and this resulted in a revolt against Rabban Gamaliel and in his deposition from the Patriarchate. Although the revolt ended in a compromise that created a kind of oligarchic administration,[54] yet there were several Sages who would not submit even to this control and insisted on complete freedom in Halakhic decisions. R. Eliezer b. Hyrcanus (the great Tanna that was placed under the ban), who dwelt in Lydda,[55] eulogized the understanding vouchsafed to Nethanel, the Nasi of Issachar,[56] the tribe that had maintained law courts in Egypt, saying 'that he brought his offering immediately after the king, because he was learned in the Torah, and it was he who had advised the tribes to bring wagons.'[57] Possibly these homilies were intended to emphasize the difference between a Nasi that is learned in the Torah and advises the tribes and one who is a king. R. Eliezer did not agree to submit even to the majority view and adhered to his tradition and opinion against the view of the Sages, and it was this attitude that led to his being banned.[58] However, Eliezer was exceptional. In this first crisis, as in crises that were to take place subsequently, the majority were not inclined to undermine the actual existence of the patriarchal institution linked to the House of Hillel, and were content to protest with extreme vehemence against this or that Patriarch, or to condemn his actions and practices.

A most serious phenomenon that changed the economic and social position of many Sages, and even endangered their moral image, was connected with the maintenance of the Sages who fulfilled public functions. The acceptance of remuneration from the public was forbidden. If they were not wealthy with means of their own, the leader of the generation, the Patriarch, was charged with their maintenance. However, the support of the Patriarch, as the common benefactor who provided many Sages with their livelihood, served as a decisive factor in underscoring the class and social distinctiveness of the Sages. A confrontation was created between scholars who made the Torah their profession and those who followed other vocations. The conception of 'Torah' as a vocation also opened the way to its being passed on from fathers to sons like other skills. Dicta that emphasize the thought that the Torah cannot be transferred as a legacy are directed against the trend to bequeath Torah-knowledge and its ranks, including the privileges attached thereto, to the Sages' own families. The very formation of a spiritual and national leadership, which combined with instruction in the Torah and elucidation of the Halakha also the administration of the community by means of institutions and modes of government, establishing a hieraschical system and ceremonial honours — all this constituted a change. It created the image of a Sage that is not only a teacher and guide, and as such draws people nearer to the Torah and engages in beneficent works, but is, at the same time, an administrator, appointed over the community, who transmits his office to his sons. These developments were factors contributing, at the close of the Tannaitic age and during the Amoraic period, to the distinctive character of the Sages, who became a class of men that were differentiated 'by their manner of walking, of speaking, and by the cloak they wore in the street.'[59]

Strangely it is the time of R. Judah ha-Nasi (Rabbi), who not only knew how to conduct his patriarchate on a high level and to consolidate anew the position of the nation and to heal its disaster, but also won recognition as a Sage, so that none challenged his religious-Halakhic eminence — it is just the period of this Patriarch to which critical testimonies are found. The criticism was levelled not only against his 'honouring the rich' and against the style of living, the exercise of authority, and the royal pomp that obtained in Rabbi's court, but against the very institution of the Patriarchate in Eretz-Israel and the office of Exilarch in Babylonia.[60] Rabbi himself was not oblivious of the problem of conflicting aims in the attempt to combine the custodianship of the ideals of the world of the Sages, whose base was the Torah and precepts and its apex the Kingdom of Heaven and the world to come, with the ways of hegemony, whose outward expression was wealth and lordship. Indeed in his will the great Patriarch enjoined the separation of the two domains: the Patriarchate by itself and the headship of the Bet Din by itself.[61] This severance of the Patriarchate, as the supreme politico-national administrative institution of the people, from the headship of the colleges prevailed in practice, even when the Patriarch himself was a great scholar, throughout the existence of the Patriarchate after Rabbi. The dichotomy characterizes the Jewish leadership in Babylonia from its inception as, on the one hand, the institution of 'the Exilarch'[62] — which appears definitely for the first time at the end of the reign of R. Judah ha-Nasi — and, on the other, as the headship of the academies.

With the increase of the evidence about the Babylonian centre our information about the tension and clashes between the Exilarchs and the heads of the academies likewise grows. The disputes were concerned both with the problems of the relative authority of the institutions and with questions regarding the proper mode of life and the methods of government. The duality of authority did not prevent schisms in the circle of the Sages itself, for there were not a few among them who maintained close family ties with the House of the Nasi in Eretz-

Israel or with the House of the Exilarch in Babylonia, and many of them carried out functions on behalf, and in the vicinity, of the central administrative institutions. It was natural that such Sages should tend to restrict their criticism and to give greater recognition to the authority and status of the administration. In this way they, too, came into conflict with scholars who adopted an extreme attitude in their criticism and refused to compromise with aspects that appeared negative to them, to the point of forgoing all contact with the authorities. Tannaim like R. Phinehas b. Jair and R. Jonathan b. Amram avoided even the semblance of benefiting from honour shown to their Torah erudition, and the Amora R. Eleazar not only refused to receive gifts from the House of the Patriarch, but did not even accept the Patriarch's invitations, whereas R. Zera permitted himself such benefits, declaring 'They are honoured by my presence' ('They are honoured by the fact that I dine with them; hence it is not a gift' — Rashi).[63] The very rivalry between the authorities, and likewise the mutual criticism, prevented the relaxation of the moral tension among the Sages and preserved the distinctive character of their leadership, whose strength lay not in the exercise of power and in institutions, but in their personalities and devotion to their main function, which was to study the Torah, to teach disciples, and to direct the life of the nation throughout its strata and classes.

VII. The Struggle Between Learning and Practice in the Creation of the Image of the Sage

Our last remarks here, expressed in general and summary terms, require methodical elucidation, which may also provide a substantive explanation. The nature of our sources — to which we have repeatedly referred in various contexts — makes it particularly difficult to appraise personalities and their relationship to their colleagues and to members of other classes. In one respect the character of a given Sage may be emphasized with particular and extreme sharpness, but in another respect there may be found contradictory testimonies, which are sometimes given no less prominence. There are certainly stories and legends whose aim is harmonistic, that is to say, they seek to make the attributes congruent and this congruence is in the form that appeals to the narrators and transmitters. We must not, however, overlook the possibility that diverse and conflicting testimonies do not necessarily cancel one another, but may be explained on the basis of different experiences, separated from one another by long intervals of time, occurring in the life of the same Sage. Caustic expressions and harsh words of denunciation are not infrequently clear indications of temporary reactions and not of fundamental attitudes. Undoubtedly there are many sources whose principal aim is to speak in praise of certain Sages and their virtues, but on the other hand there are by no means lacking narratives and testimonies that are very far from the literary category of 'eulogies'; intentionally or unintentionally they underline occurrences, qualities of character, and deeds that are negative. A correct assessment of the sources is particularly important and difficult in regard to the subject that we shall soon be summing up, namely: the Sages of Israel and the Congregation of Israel. Therefore, before we commence this summation, we shall consolidate our general remarks on other aspects of social relations. We shall augment our previous remarks about the attitude of the Sages to the exercise of authority and rulership, and we shall devote some attention to the question of the relations between the Sages in the sphere of the academy. I believe that observation of the relationships in internal areas will make it easier to give a more balanced evaluation of the attitudes towards other classes.

We have seen (above, p. 600) how R. Akiba fought for freedom of Halakhic decision, but at the same time supported Rabban Gamaliel in organizing the centre at Jabneh. We do not know the date of Rabban Gamaliel's death, but it is certain that his son did not succeed him. Scholars are divided on the question of who stood at the head of the Sages in the period prior to the Bar Kokhba Revolt. But it is certain that there was no Patriarch at their head.[64] The dynastic principle was annulled and the way was prepared for the recognition of Bar Kokhba as Patriarch, which administratively meant the separation of the national-political rule of the Patriarch from the spiritual-religious leadership of the Sages and their contemporaries. It is not surprising, therefore, that R. Akiba enjoined his son R. Joshua: 'Do not dwell in a city whose heads are scholars!'[65] The renewal of the centre in Usha was connected with the restoration of the crown of leadership to the Hillelite dynasty of Patriarchs, but the leadership remained in the Patriarch's hands only in so far as he recognized the authority of the Sages and cited decided Halakhot agreed to by his Bet Din.[66] R. Judah b. R. Ile'ai, who is designated 'the first of the speakers on every occasion'[67], was 'the teacher of the House of the Nasi'.[68] On the other hand, R. Me'ir was not reconciled with the Patriarchate of R. Simeon b. Gamaliel, and even after the surrender of R. Nathan, his comrade in rebellion, he did not yield and refused to appease the Patriarch.[69] Also R. Simeon b. Yoḥai remained faithful to the charge of his teacher R. Akiba, and prided himself on not being a judge.[70] Clashes of this type recurred repeatedly in subsequent generations in varying degrees of bitterness. From personal experience Rabban Simeon b. Gamaliel came to the conclusion that 'There is not a single scholars' session without complaints being heard as to why so-and-so participated and so-and-so did not';[71] and indeed his words were fulfilled in the case of his descendants.[72] However, the centuries that the Patriarchate existed created a hierarchy and protocol not only in respect of the Patriarch. The following Baraita belongs to the time of R. Simeon b. Gamaliel: 'When the Patriarch entered, all the people stood up and did not sit down until he told them: "Be seated!" When the Av Bet Din entered, two rows were formed, one on each side, until he came in and was seated in his place; when a Sage entered, one stood up and one sat down, until he came in and sat in his place; the sons of Sages and the disciples of Sages, when needed by the public, may even leap over the heads of the people....'[73] About five generations later, the Galileans asked who was to be called to the Torah after the Kohen and the Levite, and R. Isaac Nappaḥa replied: 'After them are called up scholars who have been appointed public administrators, and after them the sons of scholars whose fathers have been appointed public administrators, and after them the heads of synagogues and the general public.'[74] The special status granted to scholars who were appointed public administrators, and even to their sons, testifies to a trend that regards this synthesis of Torah with communal work as a blessing.[75] Indeed R. Joḥanan, the teacher of R. Isaac Nappaḥa, considered it a duty and a privilege for scholars to shoulder the burden of administration. This, in his estimation, was the way to obviate the appointment of unworthy persons. Indeed he also said 'If you see a hypocritical and wicked man leading the generation, it were better for the generation to fly in the air, and not to make use of him.'[76] However, he was not content with protest, but demanded that the scholars should be 'builders', that is, 'should occupy themselves with the building of the world',[77] and he even defined 'Who is a scholar that may be appointed a public administrator?' 'Who is a scholar whose lost property may be returned to him on the basis of his general impression [without his specifying any particular identifying marks]?' and 'Who is a scholar whose fellow townsmen are enjoined to do his work?' and insisted that the scholar's outward appearance should be immaculate. In his view it is not only 'a disgrace for a scholar to go out to the market place with patched shoes', but 'any scholar on whose garment a grease spot is to be found is deserving of death.'[78] Undoubtedly there were Sages who conformed to R. Joḥanan's definition that a scholar is 'One who is able to answer a Halakhic question on any subject', nevertheless they avoided accepting the yoke of public administration,[79] because they regarded all occupation, with the exception of Torah-study, as worthless. They thus expounded the verse ' "Surely oppression [העשק *hā-ʿōsheq*] makes the wise man foolish" (Ecclesiastes vii 7): whoever occupies himself [המתעסק *ha-mitʿassēq*] with communal affairs forgets his learning.'[80]

R. Simeon b. Yoḥai's extremism does not necessarily find expression in his demand that scholars should devote themselves entirely to the study of the Torah, without giving a thought to questions of livelihood. His colleagues, too, shared this approach, with differences of emphasis, not only in their dicta,[81] but also in their way of life.[82] Of greater significance, however, for our subject is the following story: 'It once happened that R. Simeon b. Yoḥai was visiting the sick, when he came across a man who was languishing and lying prostrate with a bowel ailment and was reviling the Holy One, blessed be He. Said he to him: "Wretch, you should be making supplication for yourself; instead you are reviling!" The other replied: "May the Holy One, blessed be He, remove the sickness from me and give it to you." He (R. Simeon b. Yoḥai) said: "The Holy One, blessed be He, acted rightly towards you, for I left the study of the Torah and occupied myself with worthless matters." '[83] Possibly R. Simeon b. Yoḥai's reaction was due to the sick man's curse, but the actual formulation of the statement testifies that R. Simeon b. Yoḥai understood the words 'The study of the Torah is equal to them all'[84] literally. Undoubtedly he went far beyond the view of his teacher Akiba. Although it was R. Akiba who gained the decision in the house of Nitza in Lydda on the question 'Which is greater? Is study greater or is practice greater?' when he said 'Study is greater', yet those who answered after him 'Study is greater, for study leads to practice' understood his reason, a fact that is demonstrated by the following episode: 'It once happened that one of his pupils became ill, and the Sages did not come to visit him. But R. Akiba did visit him, and because he [R. Akiba] swept and sprinkled (the floor) before him, he [the sick man] said to him: "Master, you have given me new life!" (Thereupon) R. Akiba went forth and taught: "If one fails to visit the sick, it is as though he shed blood." '[85] We do not know which incident occurred first, and whether R. Akiba wished perhaps to teach the disciples who made light of the precept of visiting the sick a lesson. Without doubt it is possible to argue that R. Simeon's conduct accords with the characteristics of his personality as we know it (above, p. 491), namely that of an absolute individualist, who esteems the person who acquires perfection by the hard way of suffering and tribulation. Unlike his teacher R. Akiba, who knew how to use his laughter as a means of dissipating pain and despair (*T.B. Makkot* 4b), R. Simeon b. Yoḥai held that it was forbidden 'for a man to fill his mouth with laughter';[86] no wonder, therefore, that he was disinclined to reconcile himself to human weaknesses. However, in the case under discussion it is possible to argue *per contra* that opposition to those in authority and to despots does not necessarily go hand in hand with the attitude of forgiveness and indulgence towards the frailty of ordinary folk. R. Simeon b. Yoḥai was different from both his colleagues — from R. Judah, 'the teacher of the Patriarch' and from R. Me'ir, the opponent of the Patriarch. When a man said to his wife 'קונם *Qônām* [a form of vow] that you shall not benefit from me until you make R. Judah and R. Simeon taste of your cooking, R. Judah tasted, saying: It stands to reason: If now in order to make peace between a man and his wife the Torah enjoined: Let My name, written in sanctity, be blotted out by "the waters that curse" in a matter of doubt; how much more so I! R. Simeon did not taste, saying: Let all the widow's children die rather than Simeon should move from his position.'[87] Like R. Judah acted also his Halakhic opponent, R. Me'ir, the bitter adversary of the Patriarch Rabban Simeon b. Gamaliel. In order to enable a woman — who had been forbidden by her husband to come home, unless she first spat in R. Me'ir's face — to fulfil her husband's vow, he pretended to suffer pain in his eyes and had it proclaimed that any woman who knew how to cure a (sore) eye by charm should come and perform the charm on his eye. The woman who had been expelled from her home by her husband's vow came and spat seven times in R. Me'ir's eye.[88] When his disciples said to him 'Is the Torah to be thus abused?', he replied to them: 'Should Me'ir's honour exceed that of his Maker?' And he continued: 'If now with regard to the Holy Name, which was written in sanctity, Scripture enjoined that 'it should be blotted out by the water in order to make peace between a man and his wife, how much more so in the case of R. Me'ir's honour!'[89] R. Akiba's disciple, R. Judah b. R. Ileʿai, acted in his master's spirit. It was told of him 'that he used to interrupt his study of the Torah to attend a funeral or a wedding ceremony... and he used to take a twig of myrtle and dance before the bride....'[90] Undoubtedly the author of the following Baraita was right, when he summed up the situation of the Bar Kokhba Revolt thus: 'And the world was desolate until R. Akiba came to our masters in the south and taught it [the Torah] to them, namely R. Me'ir, R. Judah, R. Jose, R. Simeon, and R. Eleazar b. Shammuaʿ, and it was they who revived Torah learning at that time.'[91] R. Judah's portion was not less than that of R. Simeon. The generation of which it was said that six disciples covered themselves with a single garment and studied the Torah was called 'the generation of R. Judah b. Ileʿai.'[92]

Just as the problem of the livelihood of the Sages in the framework of the question of studying Torah and practising a craft did not cease troubling, complicating, and confusing the circles of the Sages,[93] so, too, no unambiguous solution was found to the question of the relationship between learning Torah, on the one hand, and performing good works and occupying oneself with communal needs, 'both religious and mundane', on the other. With reference to the Baraita, 'The pious men of old used to wait an hour, and pray for an hour, and again wait an hour', the question was raised 'Since they spend nine hours a day in prayer, how is their Torah-knowledge preserved and how is their work done?' The answer given was: 'Because they are men of piety, their Torah-learning is preserved and their work is blessed.'[94] At least in all that appertained to the study of the Torah even Pietist-Sages were not inclined to rely on this explanation. The extravagant praise bestowed upon students of the Torah was undoubtedly on occasion prompted by prevailing circumstances at periods and places that witnessed a falling-off in Torah-study,[95] but chiefly it attests the complete identification of Torah-students with their Torah-study, and it served to weaken their allegiance to other values and at times even to exchange and substitute them. The establishment of a scale of relationships and the discovery of a ratio between Torah-study and occupation with worldly affairs, work and marital connection, and between studying Torah and observing the precepts, were themselves difficult topics in the teaching of the Sages, who wrestled and struggled with them throughout the generations. On the one hand, we find the injunction of the Men of the Great Synagogue 'Raise up many disciples' (*M. 'Avot* i, 1); in the same spirit Hillel declared 'And he that does not study is deserving of death'[96], and the School of Shammai enjoined 'Fix a period for the study of the Torah' (*ibid.* xvi), and R. Neḥemiah b. Ha-Qana stated 'Whoever accepts the yoke of the Torah, from him the yoke of the kingdom and the yoke of worldly care are removed' (*ibid.* iii, 5), and R. Me'ir urged 'Lessen your occupation with business and busy yourself with the Torah' (*ibid.* iv, 8); and this, too, is the burden of all those extreme statements of the Amoraim that we shall cite subsequently. But on the other hand, there is the dictum of Shemaʿyah 'Love work and hate lordship' (*ibid.* i, 9); that of R. Zadok 'Make not of the words of the Torah a crown wherewith to aggrandize yourself, nor a spàde wherewith to dig... whoever makes profit out of the words of the Torah destroys his own life' (*ibid.* iv, 5); and that of Rabban Gamaliel, the son of R. Judah the Patriarch, 'An excellent thing is study of the Torah together with worldly occupation, for the toil in them both puts sin out of mind; but all study of the Torah without work comes to naught in the end and brings sin in its train [גוררת עוון].[97] Let all who labour with the community do so for the sake of Heaven....' (*ibid.* ii, 2).

This dictum of the Patriarch can easily be credited to his experience, and that of his family, in dealing with the problem of the livelihood of the Sages and with the difficulties encountered in appointing Sages to public posts. But this explanation, as in similar instances, does not exhaust the nature of the problem nor the facts. Rav Huna, who worked his own fields and picked his fruit himself, and, when people came before him for judgement, asked that someone be appointed to irrigate his field,[98] taught that 'Whoever occupies himself with Torah only is like one who has no God.' In the spirit of this homily it is related in a Baraita in the Babylonian Talmud that R. Ḥanina b. Teradion said to R. Eleazar b. Peraṭa: 'Happy are you that you have been seized on five charges, but will be saved. Woe unto me who have been seized on one charge and will not be delivered! For you have occupied yourself with Torah-study and deeds of benevolence, whereas I engaged in Torah-study only.'[99] R. Abbahu was a wealthy man and close to the government and was called 'leader of his people'.[1] He himself knew Greek and wished to teach this language to his daughter[2], and without doubt he also occupied himself, in addition to his Torah-study, with 'both secular and religious matters'. Nevertheless, when he learned that his son R. Ḥanina, whom he had sent to Tiberias to study Torah, occupied himself with charitable works, he sent him this message: 'Is it because there are no graves in Caesarea that I sent you to Tiberias?'[3] But we shall certainly be wrong if we attempt to explain the dicta that speak in praise of Torah-study and give it precedence over everything else as though they were directed solely to students. R. Samuel bar Naḥmani said in the name of R. Jonathan: 'Scholars who engage in the study of the Torah anywhere in the world are regarded by Me as though they burned and offered oblations unto My name.' Two sayings are reported in the name of R. Joḥanan: one — 'Scholars who occupy themselves with the study of the Torah at night are accounted by Scripture as though they were engaged in the Temple service'[3a]; the other — 'When scholars occupy themselves with the laws of the Temple service, it is accounted to them by Scripture as though the Temple were built in their days.' While Resh Laqish expounded the verse ' "This is the law for the burnt-offering, for the meal-offering, for the sin-offering and for the guilt-offering" (to mean that) whoever occupies himself with the study of the Torah is deemed as though he had offered up a burnt-offering, a meal-offering, a sin-offering, and a guilt-offering', and R. Isaac taught 'Whoever occupies himself with the law of the sin-offering is regarded as if he offered up a sin-offering, and whoever occupies himself with the law of the guilt-offering is regarded as though he offered up a guilt-offering.' Rava came and said 'Whoever occupies himself with the study of the Torah needs no burnt-offering nor sin-offering, no meal-offering nor guilt-offering.'[4] The wording of Rava's dictum 'needs no' etc. is more extreme than the dicta of his predecessors and their like, such as 'A Sage who sits and expounds (Torah) in public is accounted by Scripture as though he offered up fat and blood upon the altar',[5] for all these sayings contain the expression 'as though (if)'. Even in the anonymous homily that states 'When the Temple is not in existence, how shall you find atonement? Occupy yourselves with the words of the Torah, which are comparable to the sacrifices and they shall make atonement for you...',[6] the study of the Torah serves only as a surrogate and replacement for atonement by the sacrifices. Even this concept is already the result of a late development, for when the Temple was destroyed, Rabban Joḥanan b. Zakkai declared that acts of charity and benevolence were Israel's atonement,[7] while others again looked upon fasts as substituting for and replacing sacrifices.[8] The supersession of fasting and the practice of benevolence as a means of expiation by the study of Torah accords with the views of various Sages who chose the way of R. Simeon b. Yoḥai, rather than that of R. Judah b. Ile῾ai.

Rav Joseph cited a Baraita[9] to the effect that when Mordecai became viceroy, he found favour only with the majority of his brethren, not with all of them; some of the Sanhedrin left him, 'because he ceased to study Torah and entered upon rulership'. The Sage drew the moral 'Greater is the study of the Torah than the saving of lives.' Indeed Rav Joseph also said that the Torah protects and saves both when one is studying it and when one is not studying it, whereas the precept saves only when one is performing it. This, too, is an inference, which he derived from the teaching of R. Menaḥem b. R. Jose: 'Scripture equates the commandment with a lamp... just as a lamp protects only temporarily, so the commandment also protects only temporarily; but the Torah is equated with light to tell you that just as light protects permanently, so the Torah protects for ever... another explanation is: Sin quenches the commandment, but it does not extinguish the Torah.'[10] The dictum of the Babylonian Amora 'Study of the Torah transcends the building of the Temple, for as long as Baruch the son of Neriah was alive, Ezra did not leave him to go up (to Eretz-Israel)' may possibly be regarded as an apologia for the continued residence of the Sages in Babylonia;[11] but this certainly does not apply to the saying of the same Amora 'Study of the Torah transcends honouring father and mother.' Rava followed the view of Rav Joseph, and his statement that he who occupies himself with study of the Torah has no need of burnt-offering or sin-offering emanates from the absolute conviction of these Rabbis that the expiatory power of Torah-study is greater than that of sacrifices. This is further indicated by the following dispute between Rava and Abbaye, which is linked to the homily of R. Samuel bar Naḥmani in the name of R. Jonathan: 'Whence do we know that a Divine decree accompanied by an oath is not abrogated? For it is said "Therefore I have sworn unto the house of Eli that the iniquity of Eli's house shall not be expiated with sacrifice nor offering" (I Samuel iii 14).' On this Rava commented 'It is not expiated with sacrifice or offering, but it is atoned for with study of the Torah'; as against this Abbaye said 'It is not expiated with sacrifice or offering, but it is atoned for by Torah-study and the practice of benevolence.' The anonymous view of the Talmud expresses agreement with the opinion of Abbaye by stating: 'Abbaye and Rava were descended from the House of Eli. Rava who engaged in Torah-study only lived forty years; Abbaye[12] who occupied himself with the study of the Torah and with the works of benevolence lived sixty years.' Rava prepared in anticipation, as it were, an answer to this proof by his dictum 'The length of one's life, children, and sustenance are not dependent on merit but on fate.'[13]

Rava's appraisement of Torah-study as the supreme value also found expression in his attitude to prayer. With reference to the Baraita wherein it is taught 'Associates who are engaged in the study of the Torah interrupt their study for the reading of the *Shĕma'*, but not for the Prayer [Eighteen Benedictions]', the view of R. Joḥanan was cited in Babylonia: 'This was taught only with respect to scholars like R. Simeon b. Yoḥai and his colleagues, in whose case Torah-study was their sole occupation, but such as we must interrupt our study for the reading of the *Shĕma*ʿ and for the Prayer.'[14] It is hard to imagine that Rava, who engaged in wine trade, possessed fields and ships, métayers and slaves[15], acted as a judge and even imposed floggings, and had contacts with royalty and with princes[16], considered himself — unlike R. Joḥanan — as one 'whose Torah-study was his sole occupation'. Nevertheless, when he saw Rav Hamnuna prolonging his prayers, he said 'They forsake eternal life and occupy themselves with ephemeral existence.'[17] Also in relation to prayer the study of the Torah is exalted to an absolute value, irrespective of the amount of time that a man devotes to such study, and without any demand, as a result of this conception, for one's complete withdrawal from all other interests of the world. However, despite the absolute character of Rava's appraisement, it is certain that we may not attribute to him any lack of reverence for all those matters of which he held Torah-study took precedence. It will suffice to note the number of times that Rava's name appears in discussions relative to the Halakhot of prayer and the Halakhot of the Temple and its sacrifices. These subjects, just like the laws of Shabbat and the festivals, of damages and levitical purity, constitute that very Torah that he praises and extols; and undoubtedly he did not forget the fact that 'the Torah begins with an act of benevolence and ends with an act of benevolence'.[18] We find, moreover, express dicta of his that serve to balance the element of hyperbole that characterize his sayings in praise of the Torah. Needless to say, he did not regard the study of the Torah as an offset to transgressions. Against such an opinion Rava declared: 'Whoever has intercourse with a married woman, even if he has studied Torah — of which it is written "It is more precious than rubies [מפנינים *mi-pĕnînîm*]", that is, than the High Priest who enters the innermost part [לפני ולפנים *lifĕnay we-lifĕnîm*] of the Temple — will be hunted down by her to the judgement of Gehenna.'[19] It is actually of Rava that it is related that he was accustomed to say 'The goal of wisdom is penitence and good deeds; a man should not study Bible and Mishna and rebel against his father and his mother and his teacher, or one who is superior to him in wisdom, as it is said "The reverence of the Lord is the beginning of wisdom, a good understanding have all they that do thereafter" (Psalms cxi 10) — Scripture does not say "to all those who study them [לומדיהם]" but "to all those who do thereafter [עושיהם]" ....'[20] It is he, also, who added each day after his prayer 'My God, before I was formed I was unworthy, and now that I have been formed I am as though I had not been formed; I am dust in my lifetime, how much more so in my death. I am before Thee as a vessel full of shame and confusion. May it be Thy will, O Lord my God, that I sin no more, and the sins that I have committed before Thee purge away by Thy great compassion, but not by suffering and evil diseases.'[21] A man who sees suffering coming upon him he advised first to examine his deeds, and only 'If he finds no reason, should he attribute it to neglect of the study of the Torah.'[22] Right practice is harder to achieve and less commonly found than the fulfilment of the duty of Torah-study, and Rava himself declared 'Is there any virtue in propounding problems... the Holy One, blessed be He, requires the heart, for it is written "But the Lord looketh on the heart" (I Samuel xvi 7).'[23] In the spirit of his teacher, Rav Pappa explained the obscure Baraita of R. Jose, 'Whoever says he has no (interest in the study of) the Torah, has no (reward for the study of the) Torah' in the sense of 'Whoever says that he is only concerned with the study of the Torah, receives no (reward) even for (the study of) the Torah... "that ye may learn them and observe to do them" — whosoever observes is also regarded as studying, but he who does not observe is not regarded as studying.'[24]

Rav Pappa adopted the view of Rav Huna and almost repeated his words verbatim despite the changes that had occurred in the intervening years and despite the differences in the circumstances of the lives and character of the two Sages. It is important to note that the views and dicta that we have cited on the themes under discussion not only reflect divergent opinions between different Sages and diverse trends, but also contradictions in the teachings of a single Sage, which are the outcome of inner questing and struggles. We have encountered them in the sayings of the Amora Rava,[25] and we shall come across them again, if we revert to that personage of ostensibly unequivocal approach and character, namely R. Simeon b. Yoḥai.

We have seen him as one who rejects any synthesis of Torah-study with another occupation and as one who prefers occupation with the Torah to any deed of benevolence, leadership, or position of authority. However, not only does an Haggadic tradition represent him as effecting an improvement for the benefit of Tiberias[26], and as going on a mission of intercession in order to get an edict rescinded in Rome[27], but a homily is cited in his name praising the existence of juridical institutions: 'R. Simeon b. Yoḥai: Why do the civil laws precede all other precepts of the Torah? Because when there is a lawsuit between a man and his fellow, there is strife between them. But once the case has been decided, peace reigns between them.'[28] However, it was actually as judges that Sages came to know difficult litigants and realized that peace did not always follow the verdict. Nevertheless they agreed in principle with the dictum of Rabban Simeon b. Gamaliel that the world 'rests on judgement, truth, and peace' (*M. 'Avot*, i, 18). But, taking the view that 'Where there is judgement there is no peace, and where there is peace there is no judgement', R. Joshua b. Qorḥa came to the conclusion that arbitration should be preferred to law, and that it was 'meritorious to arbitrate', But R. Eliezer the son of R. Jose the Galilean said: 'It is forbidden to arbitrate, and he who arbitrates commits a sin, and whoever blesses an arbitrator actually contemns ... but let the law pierce through the mountain.'[29] This dispute was not decided, and one could say in this matter that 'not all men, or places, or times are alike'. However, even those Sages who undertook to establish the land by justice and to make litigants obey the court by imposing the fear of 'the judges' instruments'[30], which they had at their disposal, observed the counsel of R. Jonathan: 'A judge should always imagine himself as having a sword hanging over his head [literally 'lying between his thighs'], and Gehenna gaping beneath him.'[31] The verse 'The king by justice establisheth the land; but the man of *terumot* [literally 'heave-offerings'; the usual rendering is 'he that exacteth gifts'] overthroweth it' (Proverbs xxix 4) is interpreted as referring to a man 'who makes himself like a heave-offering, which is cast in a corner of the house and declares: Why should I bother with the affairs of the community, why should I concern myself with their lawsuits, why should I have to hear their noise? Peace be upon you, O my soul! — such a person destroys the world.'[32] But from the same verse the

Sages also learned at that time: 'If a judge is like a king, who is in need of naught, he establishes the land; but if he is like a priest, who makes the rounds of the threshing floors, he overthrows it.'[33] R. Simlai, who was a member of the household of the Patriarch, found in the verses 'And I charged your judges at that time' (Deuteronomy i, 16), 'And I commanded you at that time' (*ibid. v.* 18), 'an admonition to the community that they should show the judge due deference, and an admonition to the judge to be forbearing towards the community.'[34] Those Sages who, on account of the awe with which the act of judging filled them, refrained from accepting the burden of judgeship were also not free from pangs of conscience, as the following story testifies: 'When R. Assi was about to depart from the world, his sister's son came to visit him, and found him weeping. Said he to him (to R. Assi): "Master, why are you weeping? Is there a part of the Torah that you did not learn or teach? Behold, your disciples sit before you. Is there an act of benevolence that you did not perform? Yet despite all your attributes you eschewed giving judgement, and never allowed yourself to be appointed as administrator of communal affairs." He answered him: "My son, it is for this very reason that I weep, lest I am held culpable for having been able to dispense justice to Israel (but not having done so)." '[35] The disciple considered the avoidance of exercising authority a virtue, but when R. Assi 'drew near to the shadow of death'[36] he began to doubt the rightness of his attitude.

The retreat from giving decisions and sitting in judgement is also to be explained against the background of the ramification of Torah-study, of the proliferation of expositions and interpretations, and of the harmonization of conflicting Mishnayot, Baraitot, and traditions. R. Akiba's maxim 'Why should we concern ourselves with the practice? I am not concerned with the act but with the express Scriptural statement'[37] opened wide the way to freedom of Halakhic decision that was no longer subjected to institutions and testimonies regarding acts of the Bet Din. Nor was he disturbed by the question 'Shall we impose on this woman (the severer penalty of) death by burning because you expound the *Waw* of the word ובת *û-bat* ['and the daughter']?'[38], but interpreted the text and harmonized it with the traditional law.[39] In truth the expositions conquered the Halakha,[40] but the signification of the term 'Halakha' underwent a change. At the beginning of the Amoraic period it no longer connotes 'A practice that continues from earlier times to the end, or the path in which Israel walks',[41] or a firmly fixed decision, but denotes the result of argument and study, not a practical ruling, so that it became necessary to coin a special term 'a practical Halakha' in order to restore its original sense. Samuel said 'The whole of the Halakha at the beginning of the last chapter of Nidda obtains in theory but not in practice.'[42] Of R. Joḥanan it is related that he expounded the law to the men of Tiberias 'according to the view of R. Simeon b. Eleazar; he taught it to them theoretically, but they thought it was to be observed thus in practice....'[43] According to another tradition: 'R. Assi said to R. Joḥanan "When the master tells us that the Halakha is so and so, may we act accordingly?" He replied: "Do not act accordingly, unless I declare it to be the law for practical purposes." '[44] R. Joḥanan even went so far as to say that an expressly stated Mishna was taught only with a view to sharpening the minds of the disciples.[45] R. Bun and the Rabbis put several questions to R. Ze'ira concerning the laws of the 'booth', to which he replied; commenting on his answers R. Abbahu said: 'All these statements serve the purpose of argumentation, but it is forbidden to rule thus.'[46] Possibly this caution was actually the result of R. Joḥanan's aim 'to make the teaching agree with the Halakha' and to lay down rules for deciding in matters that were disputed by Tannaim; but this procedure did not put an end to the disputes. Indeed we find that his disciples disagree as to whether a 'Halakha' derived by rules of this kind is a real Halakha, or merely a case where we 'incline towards', or 'favour' the view in question. The Amora Rav Mesharshia said, again in the form of a rule, 'The Halakha is not according to these rules.'[47] It was the realization that underlying these rules was the desire to obtain a substantive decision in a given matter in conformity with a given view[48] that engendered the attitude of scepticism towards them, even if — or, perhaps, just because — they were formulated by Sages who were well known for their power to decide. Rav Naḥman said of a series of Baraitot containing conflicting views of Tannaim on matters of civil law, in which he was considered a leading expert: 'The Halakha is according to R. Judah, and according to R. Jose b. Judah, and according to Rabban Simeon b. Gamaliel.' When, however, Rav Kahana reported his statement to Rav Zevid, he said: 'It was not the Halakha that was stated but the principle (which all three follow).'[49] When Rav Naḥman said in the name of Rav 'The Halakha in the entire chapter (is in accordance with the Mishna) except where there is a difference of opinion, Rav Sheshet remarked: I should say that Rav was half asleep and going to bed when he stated this tradition.'[50] The Sages not only pointed out the errors in the decisions of other scholars, but Rav Naḥman himself, and subsequently Rava — several times — announced in public 'I erred in the statement I made to you.'[51] An additional difficulty in fixing the Halakha was to be found in what appeared to be a contradiction between the prevailing practice and local customs[52], between the conclusions derived from the discussion in the schoolhouse and the sources or traditions in the possession of the Sages.[53] On the one hand there was the desire to reach as far as possible a unified decision, and on the other, unity could only be attained by concessions to local customs and by leaving questions open to various possible decisions. The Tannaitic homily ' "לא תתגדדו *Lō' titgōdĕdû* [usually rendered 'ye shall not cut yourselves']" — you shall not form factions [אגודות *'aggûdôt*], but you shall all be a single band [אגודה *'aggûdā*]'[54] was already considered in the period of the Tannaim a desideratum to be prayed for and corresponded to the reality only in a very general way.

The sharply worded statement in the Baraita 'When the disciples of Shammai and Hillel who had not waited upon their teachers sufficiently grew in number, the disputes in Israel increased and two Torahs were formed'[55] may perhaps be linked to the schisms that took place before the Destruction. But actually the Baraita describing the state of reconciliation provides even stronger evidence: 'Although the School of Shammai differed from the School of Hillel in regard to associate wives, sisters, a woman whose marriage is in doubt, an old bill of divorce, one who marries a woman with something worth a *peruṭa*, and a man who divorces his wife, but she spends the night with him at the (same) inn, nevertheless the Shammaites did not refrain from marrying women from Hillelite families, nor the Hillelites women from Shammaite families, but truth and peace prevailed between them as it is said "Therefore love ye truth and peace" (Zechariah viii 19). Although these prohibited and the others permitted, they did not refrain from preparing levitically pure food with one another [i.e. using one another's utensils], fulfilling the Scripture "Every way of a man is right in his own eyes; but the Lord weigheth the hearts" (Proverbs xxi 2). R. Simeon said: They did not refrain from doubtful matters, but did refrain from that which was certain.'[56] Not only the statement of this R. Simeon as well as the restrained wording in the Mishna,[57] but even the idyllic phrasing of the Baraita does not indicate a diminution of the disunity. This is attested by the Baraita which already knows that 'the Halakha is always according to the School of Hillel'; nevertheless it finds fault only with one who acts according to the stringent rulings of both or according to the lenient decisions of both, but not with one who acts in agreement with the opinion of the School of Shammai, 'in accordance with both their lenient and stringent rulings'[58]; moreover, the Sages continued to mention 'the view of an individual among the majority'.[59]

The Amoraim Abbaye and Rava drew the requisite inference from the existing situation. Abbaye said: 'We apply the rule of *lō' titgōdĕdû* only where there are two courts in one town, and the one decides according to the School of Shammai and the other according to the School of Hillel; but there is no objection to two courts in two towns (ruling differently).'

Rava went further and said: 'We apply the principle of *lō' titgōdĕdû* only in the case of a court in one town half of which decide according to the School of Shammai and half according to the School of Hillel; but there is no objection to two courts in one town (ruling differently).'[60] For 'the battle of the Torah is Torah'; and this included also what was defined as 'Messianic laws' (see above, p. 313, n. 96), and as 'what happened happened' (above, p. 305, n. 62). With regard to them R. Eliezer the son of R. Jose the Galilean already expounded the verse in Proverbs (xxiii 27): ' "Prepare thy work without" — this refers to Scripture, Mishna, and Talmud; "and make it ready for thee in the field" — this refers to good deeds; "and afterwards build thine house" — this means: Research and receive reward.'[61] Between 'Scripture, Mishna, and Talmud' and 'Research and receive reward' the Tanna inserts the demand for 'good deeds'. Likewise Rava said 'The goal of wisdom is penitence and good deeds' (above, p. 613);

by 'wisdom' he referred to the wisdom of the Torah. An anonymous homilist broadened the canvas and expounded the words of the prophet (Jeremiah ix 22) as follows: ' "Thus saith the Lord: Let not the wise man glory in his wisdom": If he does not know who created him, how can he be wise? Even among the wicked there are those who are wise in their own eyes, men who recognize the sun and the moon and the planets... and determine the months according to the solar cycle... they are wise to know the work of God in the sky, but they are unable to recognize Him who created them, even the whole world. They are also wise to build up provinces and districts and houses, to make weapons... they are wise to put things right for others, but lack the sagacity to set their own soul in order. They are wise in all respects, but in one matter they are foolish; thus through one thing they lose their wisdom, in that they have failed to recognize God....'[62] By undertaking not only to learn Torah but to teach it[63] and to engage in the thrust and parry of its 'warfare'[64], the Sages created in the world of the Torah — despite all the antitheses and dichotomies to be found in it — an educative and reformative instrument for themselves and their people.

VIII. The Internal Relations in the Academies of the Sages

The concomitant phenomena that are familiar in every academic society that values intellectual achievements of erudition, acuity of reasoning, and dialectical ability[65], did not pass by the academies of the Tannaim and Amoraim. Debates on principles and objective disputes were not free from personal overtones and the desire to annoy one's opponent: 'After R. Me'ir's death R. Judah said to his disciples: Let not R. Me'ir's disciples enter here, because they are disputatious and would come not to learn but to overwhelm me with Halakhot...'[66] There exist dicta of the Palestinian Sages, R. Oshaʿya and R. Isaac, that speak in praise of their compatriots, who are gracious and pleasant to one another in Halakhic discussion, and in dispraise of the Babylonian Sages, who are hurtful and bitter towards one another in Halakhic debate.[67] However, it is quite clear that in reality this distinction did not depend on territorial boundaries.[68] In the course of the sharp debates it also happened at times that a colleague was offended, and that harsh expressions and abusive words were exchanged in the moment of anger, and not necessarily by Sages who did not value good manners. Collegiates did not always view with favour the addition of disciples to their ranks. Rabbi himself complained: 'When I went to study Torah under Rabbi Eleazar b. Shammua', his disciples converged upon me like the cocks of Bet Buqya ('experienced and fierce, and they did not allow a strange cock among them' — Rashi), and did not permit me to learn more than this one thing in our Mishna.'[69] 'When R. Eleazar b. R. Simeon entered the college — it is related — Rabbi's face fell.'[70] Rabbi is the author of the dictum 'I learned much from my teachers, and even more from my colleagues, but most from my disciples.'[71] But he himself said of his disciple Levi 'It appears to me that he has no brains in his skull';[72] and he enjoined his son Rabban Gamaliel: 'Conduct your Patriarchate with men of high standing, and throw bile among the disciples [i.e. insist on strict discipline].'[73]

Resh Laqish, who expressed strong opposition to anyone speaking ill of Israel (above, p. 563), is also the author of the dictum 'When two scholars are gracious to each other in Halakhic discussion, the Holy One, blessed be He, hearkens to them.'[74] However, when R. Ḥiyya bar Joseph cited, upon immigrating to Eretz-Israel, a ruling by Rav, Resh Laqish did not refrain from observing contemptuously: 'Who is this Rav, who is this Rav? I don't know him....' Even when R. Joḥanan reminded him, he still asked 'What was his forte?' In this instance he yielded;[75] but he called two Sages, who were considered worthy of intercalating the year, 'cowherds' and they regarded him as 'a troublesome fellow'.[76] Indeed he was very strict with his colleague R. Eleazar.[77] The same R. Eleazar, when asked R. Me'ir's reason for a certain ruling, replied crossly: 'You ask me in the schoolhouse about a matter for which the earlier scholars gave no reason in order to put me to shame!'[78] Rav replied to Rav Huna's question 'It seems that this Rabbi thinks that people cannot explain a tradition'; in similar style Rav Assi reacted to R. Ze'ira's question, and 'Ulla to R. Abba's question.[79]

The practice of recounting the praise of disciples is already ascribed to Rabban Joḥanan b. Zakkai (*M. 'Avot* ii, 8). At times the discussion would begin with censure and end with praise. When R. Akiba taught that the priests who blew the trumpets had to be perfect, without blemish, R. Ṭarfon strongly opposed him, saying: 'How long will Akiba keep piling upon us (groundless teachings): I cannot tolerate it any longer'; but when he was convinced of the correctness of his disciple's teaching, he said to him: 'By the Temple Service! you did not invent this. Be happy, O Abraham our father, that Akiba went forth from your loins. Ṭarfon saw and forgot; Akiba gives his own exposition and is in agreement with the Halakha. Lo, whoever departs from you is as one who departs from his life!'[80] Some looked upon this eulogizing as redress for the harsh language employed. Isi b. Judah said: 'Why do scholars die prematurely? Not because they commit adultery, nor because they commit robbery, but because they abuse one another.'[81] Indeed, he recounted the praise of Sages and gave them epithets. So long as the observations were confined to an assessment of the qualities and the method of study of former Sages, even if they contained no particular tribute, they aroused no response, but not so if they referred to Sages who were still alive. Isi b. Judah himself learnt that even encomiums could lead to an unexpected reaction.[82] He said of R. Simeon 'He learns much and forgets little.' However, when R. Simeon met him, he said to him: 'Why do you babble about me to the scholars?' Isi answered R. Simeon's complaint with surprise, but at the same time amended his previous remarks, saying: 'What then did I say about you, except that you learn much and forget little; and what you forget is merely the bran of your study?'[83] R. Simeon had no need of the esteem of others, and he himself said to his disciples: 'My sons, learn my rules, for my rules are *crème de la crème* of those of R. Akiba.'[84] And if he took objection to praise that did not appeal to him, it is certain that Sages of lesser standing and self-assurance were not pleased with praise that in the end turned out to be censure, and needless to say they took umbrage at express dispraise, for it was a common phenomenon that those Sages who were accustomed to be lavish of their praises were also not sparing of censorious and disparaging remarks. The Sage that praised had to give heed not only to the reaction of the person praised, but also to that of his colleagues. Rabbi, who was skilled at appraising Sages and their character, once eulogized R. Ḥiyya extravagantly, when he entered the schoolhouse, saying: 'Let R. Ḥiyya the Great enter further in front than I. Said R. Ishmael b. R. Jose: Even in front of me?' Then Rabbi replied: 'Heaven forfend! I mean: Let R. Ḥiyya the Great enter into the interior [i.e. front benches] and R. Ishmael bar Jose into the innermost part [i.e. the very first bench].'[85] We should also bear in mind that in appraisements figurative phrases were transmitted as stereotyped formulas and *façons de parler*, to which no particular weight should be attached. When Rabban Simeon b. Gamaliel wished to give expression to the importance of R. Simeon b. Yoḥai, he said to his son that, compared with R. Eleazar the son of R. Simeon, he was like 'a lion the son of a fox *vis-à-vis* a lion the son of a lion'.[86] A similar figure of speech was used many generations later by Rav Naḥman bar Isaac. When Rav Naḥman bar Rav Ḥisda invited Rav Naḥman bar Isaac to come to him, he said to him 'We have learned in a Baraita: R. Jose said: It is not a man's place that honours him, but he that honours his place....' But when Rav Naḥman bar Ḥisda expressed his readiness to come to him, he said to him: 'Rather let a "mina" the son of "half a mina" [i.e. an eminent person the son of a less eminent person] come to a "mina" the son of a "mina" than that a "mina" the son of a "mina" should come to the son of "half a mina".'[87] This story also shows how swift was the transition from standing on one's dignity to submission. Rav Naḥman bar Isaac himself had an eloquent tongue, and he was full of witty sallies, in both praise and dispraise.[88] This attribute also characterized his great colleague Rava. On the one hand we find him saying of Rav Judah and Rabba bar Abbuha: 'Why did I interfere with the interpretation of the elders!'[89] ('Why did I have to dispute the ruling of these elders' — Rashi), and he calls his colleagues 'the lion of the company', 'a great man', 'an eminent person'.[90] Of Rav Sheshet he said: 'The question was raised by a hard man, who is as hard as iron.'[91] On the other hand, he rebuked his disciples and said to them: 'Have I not told you not to ascribe "empty bottles" [i.e. valueless opinions] to Rav Naḥman....'[92]; and he called his colleagues 'black pot' ('earthen vessel' — Rashi), 'untrained [literally 'arbitration'] judges'.[93] Of the stubborn and disputatious R. Jeremiah, who called Rav Sheshet, Abbaye, and even Rava 'foolish Babylonians',[94] Rava said: 'When one of us goes up there [to Eretz-Israel], he is worth two of them. For R. Jeremiah, who did not know what the Rabbis were talking about, when he went up there called us foolish Babylonians.'[95] But even with regard to Rav Sheshet, when Rami bar Ḥama praised his question in the words 'Here is a man and here is a question!' Rava replied 'I see the man, but I do not see [the point of] the question.'[96] Friction was also caused by competition for distinguished disciples, who wandered from the school of one Rabbi to that of another.[96a] The attempts of disciples to evaluate their teachers, even if they were careful not to offend them but only to praise that which seemed to them worthy of praise, aroused objection and tension. Rav Ḥisda said to the Sages: 'I should like to tell you something, but I am afraid that you will leave me and go away: Whoever studies Torah under one master, never makes real progress. So they left him and went to study with Rava. He explained to them, however, that this is true of logical deduction ('to acquire sharpness and subtlety of mind' — Rashi), but oral tradition it is preferable to learn from one master.'[97] The rule stated by Rav Ḥisda was brought from Eretz-Israel — from the school of R. Jannai — to Babylonia, but in Eretz-Israel Tannaim already held this view before R. Jannai.[98] It was accepted by scholars without their giving due attention to Rav Ḥisda's qualification. Thus it is related that Rav Isaac bar Rav Judah, who was accustomed to attend the discourses of Rami bar Ḥama, left him one day and went to Rav Sheshet. When Rami bar Ḥama met him and charged him with pride and presumptuousness, he replied that he acted as he did because he preferred the erudition of Rav Sheshet to the argumentations of Rami bar Ḥama.[99] Rav Ada bar Abba used to say to the disciples: Instead of going to gnaw bones (i.e. to acquire paltry knowledge) with Abbaye, come and eat fat meat with Rava.[1]

The debates at the colleges of the Tannaim and Amoraim were conducted in a free spirit. There were scholars who made their teachers wise[2], and the decision did not depend on age or status, but on reasons and arguments.[3] Many dicta are to be found against undue strictness on the part of the teacher[4], just as, on the other hand, the disciple's conduct and duties toward his teacher are defined with the greatest particularity.[5] There were scholars who said: 'Never should a man speak in praise of his fellow, because through praising him he will come to speak ill of him.'[6] But the reality was different. Sometimes praise served only as a preamble to dispraise.[7] In the light of all that we have stated above, there is no need to cite many additional examples in order to show that in practice many could not resist the great temptation of belittling their fellows. In everyday relations even the gentlest of the Sages were not always — as R. Joḥanan demanded[8] — like an angel of the Lord; nevertheless students also sought Torah from the Sages who were exacting and abusive.[9] Disciples who did not give due heed to their teachers' honour in all respects[10] disputed their views, and were not concerned if they put them to shame publicly;[11] while the relationship between colleagues — both Sages and disciples — sometimes led to *nidduy* [lighter ban] and *ḥerem* [severer ban].[12] Despite all the eulogies showered on earlier scholars and expressions of self-abasement before them, R. Oshaʿya did not refrain from saying: 'Rabban Gamaliel gave that general a fallacious answer'; and Resh Laqish reported in his name 'R. Akiba gave a fallacious answer to that disciple';[13] and Rava said: 'May the Lord forgive R. Ṭarfon!'[14] The story that 'R. Neḥunya b. Haqana was asked by his disciples "What is the cause of your longevity?" and he replied "I have never sought honour through the degradation of my colleague" ' and the parallel account about R. Zera, who replied to this question 'I have never rejoiced at my colleague's downfall' prove that the narrators of these stories did not regard these qualities as very common.[15]

We have described the internal relationship at the academies of the Sages in their various aspects, but it is clear that all the antitheses, clashes, and sharp words in no way detract from the integrated character of the class of the Sages. Verses like 'As arrows in the hand of a mighty man, so are the children of one's youth. Happy is the man that hath his quiver full of them; they shall not be put to shame, when they speak with their enemies in the gate' (Psalms cxxvii 4–5) were applied to students of the Torah, but undoubtedly the true position is also portrayed by the statement of R. Ḥiyya bar Abba: 'Even a father and son, a master and disciple, who study Torah at the same gate [the same academy, or subject], become hostile to each other, but they do not depart thence until they become friends again.'[16]

The bitterness of debate and the acerbity of the verbal exchanges at the academies did not prevent the creation of class consciousness, which found expression, as we saw, in many of the sources that we cited, either expressly or implicitly, and we shall augment them with dicta that speak in favour of the feeling of solidarity and fellowship, and emphasize and justify the right of scholars to preference and privileges. We shall now cite principally dicta of the greatest of the last of the Babylonian Amoraim. Although they designate the Sages צורבא מרבנן *ṣôrĕvā mē-rabbānān* ['a student of Rabbinical lore'] — a term found only in the Babylonian Talmud[17] — the sayings do not reflect, in their content, merely the personal opinions of those who utter them, but epitomize the views of many generations in a clear and trenchant formulation. In truth parallels can be cited for most of them from early sources.[17a] Rava permitted a *ṣôrĕvā mē-rabbānān* to make known, in a place where he was unknown, that he was a Rabbinical scholar, so that he might benefit from the privileges due to him such as the right to have his case decided before that of others, to take precedence in all things like a priest, and to receive exemption from paying the poll-tax.[18] In Eretz-Israel the dictum 'a scholar must make himself known' was transmitted in the name of Abbaye, but it was interpreted there thus: 'When a man knows one tractate and goes to a (new) place, and they honour him as though he knew two, he must declare: "I know (only) one tractate." '[19] This interpretation restricts the scholar's right to make himself known by imposing the duty of exactitude. In the style of 'Remember unto me, O my God, for good' Rava said: 'May I be rewarded for this, that if a scholar came before me for judgement, I did not lay my head on the pillow until I had sought out (arguments) in his favour.'[20] The consideration shown to litigants who were scholars[21] in the sense that their case was dealt with before that of others, and that they were exempted from the duty of standing when adducing their arguments — for their sake their opponents also enjoyed this privilege[22] — is attributed to Rabba bar Rav Ḥuna, to Rav Naḥman, to Rav Joseph[23], and to Rav Papa (in this instance 'the court messenger' made the *ʿam hā-'āreṣ* stand, and Rav Papa did not object). When Rav Yemar came to testify on behalf of Mar Zuṭra, Amemar made even the witnesses sit, and when Rav Ashi observed to him: 'All agree that witnesses must stand — since it is written "then both the men... shall stand"

(Deuteronomy xix 17)' — he answered him: 'The one is a positive commandment and the other is a positive commandment; the positive commandment of honouring the Torah takes precedence.'[24] However, even Sages who acted according to this rule had doubts as to whether they were not neglecting the principle of justice and inviting disaster. When Rav Ashi said that legally the plaintiff may demand an oath from the defendant 'but if he is *ṣôrĕvā mē-rabbānān,* we do not impose an oath upon him', Rav Yemar said to him: 'May a *ṣôrĕvā mē-rabbānān* strip people of their cloaks? But we do not attend to his case' (he is not compelled to swear, so that he should not appear to be under suspicion, but neither do we collect for him, if his opponent demands: 'Swear to me!').[25] Mar bar Rav Ashi recused himself from trying the case of a scholar and gave his reason: 'He is as dear to me as myself, and a man does not find arguments to his own detriment.'[26] Many of the concessions granted to the Sages appear to be due to the difficulty experienced in solving the problem of providing the Sages with a livelihood.[27] But frequently none of the remissions helped, and the Sages were unsuccessful in their business: 'Simon bar Wa (Abba) was an expert in pearls and in all things, but he had no bread to eat, and R. Joḥanan applied to him the verse "neither yet bread to the wise" (Ecclesiastes iv 11).' It appears that this Sage, too — who was for a time in Damascus, and in the meantime his juniors received appointments, but he was not appointed to any office[28] — had no alternative but to ask R. Judah Nesi'a for a testimonial letter, which contained a recommendation, in order that he might find a livelihood.[29] But even the appointments to offices did not solve the problem, since Sages who received appointments, but were not wealthy or the owners of prosperous businesses[30], were dependent for their maintenance on the support of the local people.

Numerous dicta accord high praise and promise great reward to those who support and maintain Sages and their disciples.[31] To the support given to Torah-scholars by 'precept-performers' (i.e. generous donors to charity) the Rabbis devoted a whole series of homilies that symbolized the recipients and donors under the figure of the two tribes Issachar and Zebulun: 'Issachar occupies himself with the study of the Torah, while Zebulun sails the seas and, on his return, supports him [Issachar], and thus is the Torah promoted in Israel.'[32] The evidence of the homilies and hortatory dicta is transcended by the stories that tell of the honour that great Sages showed to householders who helped to maintain Sages.[33]

It is clear that even those Sages who exhorted the people to support scholars were not unaware of the danger that threatened the status of the Sages in the estimation of those householders who had means and from whose possessions the scholars benefited. On the one hand R. Eleazar said: 'Whoever does not benefit a scholar with his possessions, never sees a sign of blessing'[34], and 'whoever marries his daughter to a scholar, and does business on behalf of scholars, and benefits scholars with his possessions, is regarded by Scripture as though he cleaved to the Shekhina [Divine Presence]'; and it was only on account of such deeds that he found it possible to assure the ignorant [*ʿammē ha-ʾărāṣôt*] of resurrection.[35] On the other hand he could not overlook the fact that the honour of the Sages was lowered in the eyes of their supporters, and he declared: 'What is a scholar like in the eyes of an ignorant person? At the outset he appears to him like a golden ladle... once he has benefited from him he seems to him like an earthen ladle ...'[36] At the same time it must be stressed that the mutual attachment between scholars and ignorant folk, or between *ṣôrĕvā dĕ-rabbānān* and 'the ordinary person', left its mark even when no family relationship was formed. The hosts who gave of their bounty to their guests received bounty in return. In Eretz-Israel they said of scholars who entered the homes of the ignorant: 'That they feed them with words of the Torah... that they teach Israel to distinguish between the clean and the unclean, and instruct them to do the will of their Father in heaven.'[37] Rava also had this in mind, when he said: 'He who loves the Rabbis will have sons that are Rabbis; he who honours the Rabbis will have sons-in-law who are Rabbis; he who is in awe of the Rabbis will himself become *ṣôrĕvā mē-rabbānān*; and if he has not the capacity for this, his words will be heeded as those of a *ṣôrĕvā mē-rabbānān*.'[38]

Rava's dictum, which begins by praising those who honour and love the Rabbis, ends by stating the purpose for which this homily is preached, namely that the words of the Sages should be accepted by their congregation. This dictum holds a warning for the researcher who proceeds to collect Rabbinic sayings that treat of such questions as the maintenance of Sages, their social standing, their relationship to other classes, and the like. The stringing together of these dicta so that they ostensibly form combinedly an account of a complete subject gives no assurance of the reliability of the account, even if one succeeds in fitting it into moulds that are eminently suited to sociological terminology. The criterion adopted is easily capable of causing 'visual distortion' and one-sidedness, not merely because great store is set by sayings and homilies whose forceful wording is intended to persuade and exhort, but because in dealing with them one is inclined to overlook homilies and dicta that are formulated at times with no less extremism by the same Sages in other fields. The sources serve less as testimony to the existing social structure than to the painful struggles between loyalty to ideals and the hard reality, as well as to inner conflicts regarding the determination of priorities in the scale of various values. When we deal with the subject of the maintenance of the Sages in its various aspects, we must not forget the homilies and Halakhot and acts of the Sages, from the first to the last, in matters of charity and benevolence, which affected every poor and needy person in Israel.[39]

The test of the Sage was whether, and in what measure, his deeds and conduct conduced to the sanctification or the desecration of the Divine Name. The principle, attributed already to Simeon b. Sheṭaḥ (above, p. 572), remained valid and was given a superabundance of detailed annotation. A kind of epitome may be found in a Baraita transmitted by Abbaye: ' "And thou shalt love the Lord thy God" (Deuteronomy vi 5): This means that the Name of Heaven may become beloved through you — that a man should study the Scriptures and the Mishna and attend upon scholars, and his dealings with people should be courteous. What will people say of him? Happy is the father who taught him Torah, happy is his teacher who taught him Torah, woe to the people who have not learned Torah! This man who has learned Torah — see how gracious are his ways, how faultless his deeds! Of him Scripture declares "And He said unto me: Thou art My servant, Israel, in whom I will be glorified." If, however, one studies the Scriptures and attends upon scholars, but his business is not done honestly and his conversation with people is not courteous, what do people say of him? Woe to this man who studied Torah — see how corrupt are his deeds and how ugly his words...!'[40]

All questions of honour and status fell away, perforce, wherever there was any danger of desecrating the Divine Name. The rule 'Wherever desecration of the Divine Name is involved no deference is shown to a Rabbi' is reported in the name of Rav and Samuel, and in the name of Rav Ashi, and as an anonymous statement of the Gemara.[41] The strict insistence on the upright conduct of the individual Sage served to prevent any decline of the honour in which the class of the Sages and their institutions, and in the final analysis of the Torah in general, was held: 'If an Associate is caught committing a transgression, he is disgraced, because he mingles pure with impure things. He contemns the very Torah that was so precious to him.'[42]

However, the Sage was not permitted to be satisfied with his personal perfection. Since he was required to lead, instruct, and guide his community, he was guarantor to the whole Congregation of Israel. Although this feeling of being surety was required of every Jew (above, p. 539), yet it had a special significance where the Sage was concerned. The Tanna R. Nehemiah interpreted the verse 'My son, if thou art become surety for thy neighbour, if thou hast struck thy hands for a stranger' (Proverbs vi 1) thus: 'It speaks of *Ḥăvērîm*. So long as a man is an Associate, he need not be concerned with the community and he is not punished on account of it. But once a man has been placed at the head and has donned the *Ṭallît* [cloak of office], he may not say: I have to look after my welfare, I am not concerned with the community; but the whole burden of communal affairs rests on him. If he sees a man doing violence (βία, violence, wrong) to his fellow, or committing a transgression, and does not seek to prevent him, he is punished on account of him, and the Holy Spirit cries out: "My son, if thou art become surety for thy neighbour" — thou art responsible for him. "If thou hast struck thy hands for a stranger [*zār*]" — you have entered the arena [*zîrā*]; he who enters the arena is either conquered or conquers....'[43]

IX. The Sages Among Their People

When they entered the arena as reprovers, guides, and teachers of the people the Sages found themselves most of the time in a dilemma regarding their relations with their community and congregation. On the one hand they wanted to maintain intimacy with the public and enjoy its support; they longed to show it good will and to be accepted by it. But on the other hand they were enjoined to refrain from realizing this aspiration at the cost of principles. The Babylonian Amora Abbaye gave extreme expression to this danger. He said that when a scholar is beloved of his fellow townsmen, it is not a sign of his exceeding virtue, but of the fact that he fails to rebuke them properly.[44] However, it was not reproof alone that caused tension between the Sages and different sections of the community. Indeed a distinct trend is discernible to emphasize equality and to demolish social barriers not only in respect of everything that bears on Halakhic questions, but also in matters of usage and etiquette. In the name of R. Ishmael and R. Akiba it was taught 'All Israel are worthy of that robe'[45], and R. Simeon declared: 'All Israel are princes.'[46] At the same time R. Akiba demanded an attitude of reverence towards scholars, and he gave a most daring expression to his demand in his exposition: ' "Thou shalt fear (את *'et*) the Lord thy God" — this comes to include scholars.'[47] Yet he also admonishes his colleagues, with similar forcefulness, against the vice of haughtiness and pride. From his personal experience before he became a Sage he knew that arrogance caused the *ʿammê ha-'āreṣ* to hate the Sages.[48] Hence he said: 'Whoever exalts himself on account of his knowledge of the Torah, to what is he to be compared? To a carcass lying in the road; everyone that passes by puts his hand to his nose and proceeds to get far away from it.'[49]

The attempt to find a middle way between preserving the attitude of deference towards the Sage, which was regarded as also implying respect for the Torah, and the avoidance of hauteur — concerning which R. Akiba[50] declared 'What caused you to become a base fellow through Torah-learning? The fact that you exalted yourself thereby' — followed a chequered course. The possibility of reconciling, on the one hand, the demand for faithfulness to principles, and even for a measure of stubbornness and self-sacrifice where they were concerned, with the requirement, on the other hand, to complement this, at the same time, with love of one's fellow-man was epitomized, as it were, by sayings of the last of the Babylonian Amoraim. Rav Ashi said: 'A scholar who is not as hard as iron is not a true scholar, for it is said "And like a hammer that breaketh the rock in pieces" (Jeremiah xxiii 29)... Ravina said: Even so, a man must train himself to be gentle, for it is said "Therefore remove vexation from thy heart, and put away evil from thy flesh" (Ecclesiastes xi 10).'[51]

Our conclusions regarding the evaluation of the specific and factual significance of Rabbinic dicta, homilies, and stories concerning the internal relationship between the Sages themselves, and between them and their disciples, hold good also for understanding those sources that give clear expression to the complex of relations between the Sages and the *ʿam ha-ʾāreṣ*. As we have seen (above, p. 588) there can be no doubt about the actual fact of the separation and schism between *Ḥăvērîm* and Sages, on the one hand, and the *ʿammĕ ha-ʾāreṣ* and uncultured, on the other. This situation, which continued for centuries, is reflected in sharp verbal exchanges between the two sides. The vehemence of expression does not necessarily testify to a great gulf dividing the classes. It is likely that even at times when a rapprochement took place between the ignorant folk and the Sages and their disciples, the scholars continued to employ the same stereotyped phrases that were commonly applied to the *ʿammê ha-ʾāreṣ* in earlier generations and even added some of their own, when they denounced those that had little knowledge of the Torah, behaved coarsely, and lacked culture and refinement. The Sages of Usha, who sought to re-establish the study of the Torah, are cited as the authors of many of these dicta, which reveal their own orientation and also that of the Tannaim and Amoraim who came after them and expressed similar ideas. The struggle to attract the masses to the study of the Torah and the observance of the precepts was accompanied by denunciation of the contemptuous attitude shown towards the performance of the commandments and the negative manifestations and practices that were current among various strata of the people, and not necessarily among the poor classes. In Galilee there were to be found powerful burghers who lent money on interest, removed the yoke of imposts from their own necks and placed 'the yoke of taxation on the poor and needy and unfortunate', offered sums of charity in public but failed to pay them,[52] hated scholars,[53] and prevented the local children from receiving a Torah education.[54] The extent to which the designation *ʿam hā-ʾāreṣ* came to be used loosely and had deviated from its original signification is shown by the following discussion in the Babylonian Talmud. In the Mishna (*M. Berakhot* vii, 1) we learn 'and a Cuthean may be included in the three required for common grace', and an objection is raised to this in the Talmud:[55] 'Why should he not be regarded simply as an *'am hā-āreṣ*? For the master has taught: An *'am hā-'āreṣ* is not included in the company for the purpose of saying common grace. Abbaye said: The reference is to a Cuthean who is a *Ḥāvēr*. Rava said: You may even refer the ruling to a Cuthean who is an *'am hā-'āreṣ*, but here the term *'am hā-'āreṣ* is used according to the definition of the Rabbis. For it is taught (in a Baraita): Who is an *'am ha-'āreṣ*? Whoever does not eat non-sacred food in levitical purity — this is the view of R. Me'ir. But the Sages say: Whoever does not tithe his produce properly. Now the Cutheans are meticulous in observing what is enjoined in the Torah. The Rabbis taught: Who is an *'am hā-'āreṣ*? Whoever does not recite the *Shĕma'* morning and evening — this is the view of R. Eliezer.[56] R. Joshua says: Whoever does not put on *Tĕfillīn*. Ben 'Azzai declares: Whoever has no *mĕzûzā* on his door or fringes on his garment. R. Jonathan bar Joseph[57] is of the opinion: Whoever has sons and does not bring them up to study the Torah. Others hold: Even if one studied the Scriptures and the Mishna, but did not attend on scholars, he is deemed an *'am hā-'āreṣ*.' In the continuation it is narrated that Rami bar Ḥama did not wish to include Rav Menashia bar Taḥlifa in the quorum for common grace because he had not attended on scholars.

From the possibility of a 'Samaritan *Ḥāvēr*' to Rav Menashia bar Taḥlifa, whom Rami bar Ḥama judged to fall within the category of *'am hā-'āreṣ*, is a very far cry, and the various definitions given by the Tannaim of the nature of the *'am hā-'āreṣ* show that the term had gradually ceased to be a defined designation and had become a pejorative epithet for those who were neglectful of the observance of the precepts, and it is now manifest that he who observes these commandments does not deserve this epithet, and even if he is not an Associate in the ancient connotation, he can be an 'Associate' in the sense of a 'Sage'. Resh Laqish warned the wives of 'the scholars of the School of Jannai' that 'I am an *'am hā-'āreṣ* in respect of levitical purity'.[58] All the laws that were connected with 'acceptance as an Associate', so as to remove one from the category of *'am hā-'āreṣ*, have no relevance to the definitions of an *'am hā-'āreṣ* given by R. Eliezer and R.

Joshua, Ben ʿAzzai and R. Jonathan bar Joseph, which are cited in the second Baraita. Furthermore, a *Ḥāvēr* and a trustworthy man [נאמן *ne'ĕmān*, epithet for one who is scrupulous in giving tithes and heave-offerings] and even a pietist [חסיד *ḥāsîd*] could be included in the definition of *ʿam hā-'āreṣ*, of whom R. Simeon b. Yoḥai said: 'An *ʿam hā-'āreṣ*, even if he is upright, even if he is a holy and trustworthy man, is cursed unto the God of Israel.'[59] The expression 'trustworthy man' is derived from the laws governing Associates.[60] A complete Talmudic discussion[61] has been preserved in which there is a collection of Tannaitic and Amoraic dicta that speak in similar vein about the *ʿammê hā-'āreṣ* and which also mention harsh expressions of animosity uttered by the ignorant against scholars. 'R. Eleazar said: An *ʿam ha-'āreṣ* may may be stabbed (even) on the Day of Atonement that falls on a Sabbath. Said his disciples to him: Say "to slaughter him [i.e. ritually]". He replied to them: The one requires a benediction, whereas the other [i.e. stabbing] does not require a benediction. R. Eleazar further said: It is forbidden to join company with an *ʿam hā-'āreṣ* on the road. R. Samuel bar Naḥman said in the name of R. Jonathan: An *ʿam hā-'āreṣ* may be torn asunder like a fish. Said R. Samuel bar Isaac: Even along the back.[62] It is taught [in a Baraita], R. Akiba said: "When I was an *ʿām hā-'āreṣ*, I used to say: Would that I had a scholar (in my power) and I would bite him like an ass." Said his disciples to him: "Master, say like 'a dog'."[63] He replied to them: "The one [the ass] bites and breaks a bone, while the other bites without breaking a bone." It is taught: R. Me'ir used to say: If a man gives his daughter in marriage to an *ʿam hā-'āreṣ*, it is as though he bound her and put her in front of a lion. Just as a lion rends and eats (his prey), and feels no shame, even so an *ʿam hā-'āreṣ* beats (his wife) and has sexual intercourse, and has no sense of shame. It is taught: R. Eliezer said: Were it not that we are necessary to them for trade, they would kill us. It is taught: R. Ḥiyya said: If one studies Torah before an *ʿam hā-'āreṣ*, it is as though he raped his betrothed before him... The animosity felt by *ʿammê hā-'āreṣ* towards the scholar exceeds the hatred felt by the Gentiles towards Israel, and their wives are even more hostile. It is taught: One who studied the Torah and then abandoned it (nurses) the greatest (enmity) of them all. The Rabbis taught: Six things have been said with regard to the *'ammê hā-'āreṣ*: We do not commit testimony to them, nor do we accept any from them; we reveal no secret to them; we do not appoint them guardians of orphans; we do not appoint them administrators of the charity fund; and we do not join company with them on the road. And some say: We also do not proclaim their lost property.' In the Talmud the question is raised: 'And the first Tanna?' — that is to say: Why did he not also include the proclamation of lost property? The answer given is: 'Sometimes they have worthy descendants.' This very conclusion shows that even the redactors of the Talmud did not understand R. Ḥiyya's statement about one who studies the Torah before an *'am hā-'āreṣ* in an absolute sense. R. Ḥiyya's great efforts to spread knowledge of the Torah in the towns where there were no 'primary teachers'[64] also show that he did not mean to oppose the teaching of Torah to *'ammê hā-'āreṣ* generally, but only to one kind of them, namely those who hated the scholars, and apparently the reference is to *'ammê hā-'āreṣ* who were close to the *Mînîm* [Sectarians]! This is indicated by the additional passage introduced by the word תנא *tĕnā'* ['It is taught'], which includes in the term *'am hā-'āreṣ* 'One who studied the Torah and then abandoned it', and possibly there is an allusion to the matter — though it constitutes no actual proof — in the figure 'it is as though he raped his betrothed'[65] and in the phrase 'exceeds the hatred felt by the Gentiles towards Israel'.[66] The Geonim have already pointed out that in this Talmudic discussion the reference is not to one type of *'am hā-'āreṣ*, for 'the *'am hā-'āreṣ* has many aspects.'[67] 'When R. Eliezer says that an *'am hā-'āreṣ* may be stabbed even on the Day of Atonement that falls on a Sabbath, would anyone with any sense suppose that this may be done to any *'am hā-'āreṣ*? For even the execution of those who are put to death by the Bet Din for idolatry, and cursing God, and the penalty imposed on (the inhabitants of) a condemned city [see Deuteronomy xiii 13–18] does not override the Sabbath....'[68] Although Rav Sherira sought to refer this dictum to 'an *'am hā-'āreṣ* who pursues his fellow with the intent to slay him on the Day of Atonement that fell on a Sabbath',[69] he did not refrain from remarking that the earlier Baraitot are 'like the laws of right conduct, or like stories in condemnation of *'ammê hā-'āreṣ*, or like rhetorical hyperbole'. Indeed the undertone of mockery is palpable in the dialogue between R. Eliezer and his disciples, and even the Baraita concerning 'the six things (that) have been said with regard to the *ʿam hā-'āreṣ*', which 'are all Halakhot', does not allude to a single type. Only one who has no knowledge of Scripture, or Mishna, or right conduct, that is, 'one who is uncivilized'[70] did R. Joḥanan disqualify as a witness;[71] while Rav Papa said that nowadays we accept the testimony of an ordinary *ʿam hā-'āreṣ*, and he relied for this ruling on the statment of R. Jose in the Baraita: 'Why are all trusted throughout the year in regard to the levitical purity of the wine and oil (that they bring for use in the Temple)? Lest each one go and build a high place for himself and burn a red heifer for himself.'[72] Obviously an *ʿam hā-'āreṣ* to whom a secret is not revealed because he is suspected of being an informer[73] does not belong to the type of person of whom it is necessary to state that they may not be appointed administrators of charity funds. Indeed, this distinction between ordinary ignorant people and sectarians and informers is explained in the interpretation of R. Joshua's teaching: 'The evil eye, the evil inclination, and hatred of his fellow-creatures put a man out of the world. How is this to be understood? It teaches us that a man should not have it in his mind to say: Love the Sages and hate the disciples, love the disciples and hate the *ʿammê hā-'āreṣ*; but (he should say:) Love all of them and (only) hate the sectarians, the apostates, and the informers. So, too, David said: "Do not I hate them, O Lord, that hate Thee? And do not I strive with those that rise up against Thee? I hate them with utmost hatred; I count them mine enemies" (Psalms cxxxix 21–22).'[74] Also the persons to whom the words were addressed largely determined their tone, and at times even their content. R. Me'ir's severe words concerning 'one who gives his daughter in marriage to an *ʿam hā-'āreṣ*' (see above, p. 634) were not necessarily directed to scholars; likewise the *ʿam hā-'āreṣ* spoken of was of a special type, and there is even evidence for this. In a Baraita that does not deal with an *ʿam hā-'āreṣ* that did not study Bible or Mishna, but treats of the laws of Associateship, we learn: 'We may buy male and female slaves from an *ʿam hā-'āreṣ*... and we may take their daughters who are minors in marriage, but not those who are of age; so R. Me'ir. But the Sages say: (Even) a daughter who is of age, provided she undertakes (to observe the laws of Associateship). We do not, however, give them in marriage either daughters who are of age or minors; so R. Me'ir. But the Sages say: A daughter who is of age may be given to an *ʿam hā-ʾāreṣ* in marriage, provided it is stipulated that she should not prepare levitically pure food in his home.'[75] As in another passage, so also here R. Me'ir taught ancient and stringent laws of Associateship (above, p. 588), but they contain no revilement or aspersions. On the other hand the reason underlying the dictum 'One who gives his daughter in marriage to an *ʿam hā-ʾāreṣ*' is ethical; it does not refer only to an *ʿam hā-ʾāreṣ* who is not observant of the laws of levitical cleanness and uncleanness. While R. Me'ir denounced one who married his daughter to an *ʿam hā-ʾāreṣ*, the same Talmudic section[76] contains several Baraitot that require every Jew to marry a scholar's daughter: 'The Rabbis taught: A man should always sell all that he has and marry a scholar's daughter. If he does not find a scholar's daughter, let him marry the daughter of (one of) the great men of the generation. If he did not find the daughter of (one of) the great men of the generation, let him marry the daughter of (one of) the Synagogue-heads. If he did not find the daughter of (one of) the Synagogue-heads, let him marry the daughter of (one of) the charity treasurers. If he did not find the daughter of a charity treasurer, let him marry the daughter of a primary schoolteacher. But he should not marry the daughter of *ʿammê hā-ʾāreṣ*, because they are detestable and their wives are reptiles, and of their daughters it is said "Cursed be he that lieth with any manner of beast".'[77]

This Baraita is addressed to 'a man' in general, encouraging him to marry the daughter of a scholar and admonishing him, in forceful language, not to marry the daughter of an *ʿam hā-ʾāreṣ*. Clearly 'a man in general' in this and similar Baraitot, which exhort one to marry the daughter of a scholar and to give his daughter in marriage to a scholar, and which promise that by virtue of this meritorious action he would have sons that are scholars, are not addressed to scholars only, but it is equally certain that they are not directed to *ʿammē hā-ʾāreṣ*, 'who are detestable and their wives are reptiles' etc. — that is to say, to clear transgressors, and it need hardly be said that such were to be found at all times and at all places.[78] As we have seen (above, p. 628) R. Eleazar found a remedy for the *ʿam hā-ʾāreṣ* who is ignorant even of Torah law, namely that he should marry his daughter to a scholar, for he hoped, like the authors of the Baraitot cited above, that out of this union there would issue sons dedicated to the Torah. The same R. Samuel bar Naḥmani, who said in the name of R. Jonathan that an *ʿam hā-ʾāreṣ* may be torn asunder like a fish, also reported in the latter's name 'Whoever teaches the son of an *ʿam hā-ʾāreṣ* Torah, even if the Holy One, blessed be He, pronounces a decree, He annuls it for his sake.'[79] R. Zera's dictum, which he cited in the name of Rav Judah, 'Take heed of the sons of *ʿammê hā-ʾāreṣ* for knowledge of the Torah shall issue from them'[80] was prompted by the realization that many of the Tannaim and Amoraim — if they were not originally like R. Akiba, who was himself an *ʿam hā-ʾāreṣ* — were the sons of *ʿammê hā-ʾāreṣ*, or of fathers who were not scholars. It is indeed reported in the name of R. Joḥanan 'If one is a scholar, and his son is a scholar, and his grandson is a scholar, knowledge of the Torah will never cease from his descendants'[81]; and basing himself on the same verse in Isaiah lix, R. Jeremiah said 'Henceforth Torah learning is hereditary in the family [literally: 'goes round to its lodging place'].' But not only did the Tanna, R. Jose the priest, say 'Fit yourself to study the Torah, for it is not an inheritance of yours' (*M. 'Avot* ii, 12), as an admonition to scholars not to rely on their lineage, but it was taught in Tannaitic Midrashim: 'Lest you say: There are the sons of the elders, the sons of the great... Scripture teaches us that all are alike in regard to the study of the Torah'; ' "A heritage" but not "an inheritance", so that the son of an *ʿam hā-ʾāreṣ* should not say, "Since I am not a scholar, what benefit shall I gain by studying the Torah?" — but "Water shall flow from his buckets [דליו *dolyaw*]" (Numbers xxiv 7), from the lowly ones [דלים *dullim*] among them.'[82] The Amoraim, from Rav Joseph to Rav Ashi and Ravina — that is for a century and more — occupied themselves with seeking an answer to the question 'Why do we find that the sons of scholars are not scholars?' While the answer of Rav Joseph — 'That it should not be said that the Torah is your inheritance' — and that of Rav Shisha son of Rav Idi — 'In order that they should not dominate the community' — explain the phenomenon and even discover a positive aspect to it, Rav Ashi, on the other hand, regarded it as a punishment and said 'Because they call people asses'.[83] He referred not just to the contemptuous attitude adopted towards the simple folk, but also to the abusive epithets that the scholars were accustomed to use in the academies.[84]

At all events the pedigree of a Sage was not a determining factor. When R. Perida was told: 'Rabbi Ezra, the grandson of R. Avṭilos, who is the tenth generation from R. Eleazar b. Azariah, who (in turn) is the tenth generation from Ezra, is standing at the gate, he replied: Why all this? If he is a scholar, it is very fine; if he is a scholar and of noble ancestry, fine; but if he is of noble ancestry but not a scholar, may fire consume him!'[85] The very fact that the academy was open to all and the free competition therein prevented the rise of a genealogical aristocracy in the sphere of the Torah and assured a stream of fresh, creative forces. The contact of the Sages, in all generations, with broad strata of the people of all classes not only led to the discovery of manifestations of estrangement from Judaism, of disrespect for the Torah and precepts, of abuse of the Sages and the like, but also to the revelation of good qualities, of simple faith, of piety and outstanding acts of charity and benevolence on the part of the common people. With the same honesty and candour with which the sources preserved the negative views of the Sages about the *ʿammê hā-ʾāreṣ* and the evidence of the mutual tension between them, they also reported the positive phenomena among the fringe classes of Jewish society, and even cultivated a tradition of stories in which the *ʿammê hā-ʾāreṣ* appear as the teachers of the Sages in virtues, and the reproved become reprovers. These narratives[85a] are better evidence of the self-criticism of the Sages in respect of their relationship to other classes than direct statements that speak in praise of the *ʿammê hā-ʾāreṣ*, of their merits, and the duties towards them. Let us begin with a story about the Tanna R. Simeon b. Eleazar of the generation of Usha: 'The Rabbis taught: Once R. Simeon b. Eleazar[86] was coming from the house of his teacher at Migdal-Geder and he was riding on an ass in leisurely fashion along the lake-shore, feeling greatly elated at having learned much Torah. On the way he chanced to meet a man who was exceedingly ugly. Said he to him: "Wretch, are all the people of your city as ugly as you?" The man replied: "Go and tell the Craftsman who made me 'How ugly is this vessel that Thou hast made!'" Realizing that he had done wrong, he [the Sage] dismounted from the ass and, prostrating himself before the man, said to him: "I crave your pardon, forgive me!" But he answered: "I shall not forgive you until you go to the Craftsman who made me and say to Him: 'How ugly is this vessel that you have made!' " He followed him until he reached his city. When he came to his city, the men of his city came to meet him [the Sage], saying: "Peace be unto you, O master!" Said (the man) to them: "Whom do you address as 'Master' (Rabbi)?" They replied: "Him that is following you." Said (the man) to them: "If he is a Rabbi, may his type not increase in Israel." Said they to him: "Heaven forfend! What did he do to you?" He told them: Such and such a thing he did to me. They (then) said to him: "Even so, forgive him, for he is a great Torah scholar." He replied: "I forgive him, only let him not make a habit of behaving thus." (Thereupon) R. Simeon b. Eleazar entered the schoolhouse and expounded: Let a man ever be pliant as a reed, and not hard as a cedar.' This maxim, the like of which is found among non-Jewish proverbs[87], was possibly cited in praise of the ugly man, and it served as a reason for quoting the story as a sequel of the theme, which dealt with the reed and the cedar. But clearly it is not the focal point of the story, which comes to show what even a great Sage may do when he becomes overweening through the joy of having learned much Torah.

About two generations after R. Simeon b. R. Eleazar it is related: 'Once R. Jannai[88] was walking along the way, when he met a man who was handsomely attired. Said he [R. Jannai] to him: "Would the master mind being my guest?" He replied: "As you please." He then took him home and questioned him on Bible, but he knew nothing; on Mishna, but he knew nothing; on Talmud, but he knew nothing; on Haggada, but he knew nothing. (Finally) he asked him to say grace. He replied, however, "Let Jannai say grace in his house." He then asked him: "Can you repeat what I tell you?" He answered "Yes." He then exclaimed: "Say 'A dog has eaten Jannai's bread.' " (Thereupon the guest) rose and seized him, demanding of him: "What of my inheritance with you, that you are cheating me?" Said (R. Jannai) to him: "What inheritance of yours have I?" He replied: "The children recite 'Moses commanded us the Torah, an inheritance of the congregation of Jacob' (Deuteronomy xxxiii 5). It is not written here 'congregation of Jannai' but 'congregation of Jacob'." When they became reconciled, (R. Jannai) asked him: "Because of what merit was it granted to you to eat at my table?" He replied: "Never have I heard slander about anyone and repeated it to him; nor did I ever see two people quarrelling without making peace between them." He (R. Jannai) then said: "You conduct yourself so well, yet I called you 'dog'!" Thereupon he applied to him the verse "And to him that שם [pointed שָׂם *śām*, with a *Sîn*, and usually rendered 'ordereth aright'] his way will I show the salvation of God" (Psalms l 23): it is written with a *Shîn*, signifying "He that appraises his way is to be highly appraised".' R. Jannai brought home a rich man whose external appearance deceived him, so that he thought him to be, if not a scholar, at least one who moved among the Sages; but when he realized his mistake, he reviled him. He discovered, however, that this man knew how to direct and appraise his ways in matters in which even Sages failed to make the grade. At times the Sages came to realize — no doubt with pleasure — that even simple folk, who were unknown to them, not only possessed noble qualities of character and fine manners, but also had knowledge of Torah and could debate successfully.

It is related of R. Jonathan[89], the younger colleague of R. Jannai: 'R. Jonathan was going up to pray at Jerusalem, when he passed by a certain terebinth (πλάτανος) and a Samaritan saw him. Said the Samaritan to him: "Whither are you going?" He replied: "To pray at Jerusalem." The Samaritan retorted: "Is it not better for you to pray on this blessed mountain than on that dunghill?" The Sage then asked him: "Why (do you think that) it is blessed?" The Samaritan answered: "Because it was not inundated by the waters of the Flood." R. Jonathan could not for a moment think of a rejoinder. (Thereupon) his ass-driver said to him: "Master, permit me to answer him." R. Jonathan answered 'yes'. Said the ass-driver to the Samaritan: "If it is one of the high mountains, then it is written 'And all the high mountains... were covered' (Genesis vii 19); and if it is one of the lower hills, the Bible ignored it." Forthwith R. Jonathan dismounted from the ass and made the ass-driver ride on it three miles, and he applied to him the following three verses: "There shall not be male or female barren among you, or among your cattle" (Deuteronomy vii 14) — even among your cattle-drivers; "Thy temples (*raqqātēkh*) are like a pomegranate split open" (Canticles vi 7) — even the ignorant (*rêqānîn*) among you are as full of counterarguments as a pomegranate (is full of seeds). This is the meaning of the verse "No weapon that is formed against thee shall prosper" (Isaiah liv 17).'[90]

Although there were *ʿammê hā-'āreṣ* of the type of this ass-driver, yet it is obvious that there were also others of a different sort.[91] Hence there is undoubtedly an element of exaggeration in the eulogy no less than in the disparaging remarks that we have cited above, but after allowances have been made for hyperbole in each case, there remains a grain of truth in both groups of sources. It is not possible to fix boundaries of development and to differentiate between the beginning of the Usha era and the subsequent age, ascribing to the former all the harsh statements against the *ʿammê hā-'āreṣ*, and to the latter the kindly and pleasant dicta and friendly acts. Such a theory is refuted by all the sources that we have cited above, belonging as they do to periods before and after Usha,[92] and other passages to this effect can also be quoted. We shall content ourselves, however, with citing only the words of R. Judah the Patriarch 'Tribulation comes upon the world only on account of the *ʿammê hā-'āreṣ*'[93], and the saying of Resh Laqish, the Sage who was careful not to speak ill of Israel (above, p. 563), 'Though a scholar be vengeful and unforgiving like a serpent, yet gird him upon your loins; but even if an *ʿam hā-'āreṣ* is pious, do not dwell in his vicinity.'[94] A scholar who does not behave like a pious man is preferable to an *ʿām hā-'āreṣ*, who is liable to act like a foolish pietist, whom R. Joshua numbered among 'the destroyers of the world'.[95] In the Palestinian Talmud the explanation is given: 'Who is a foolish pietist? One, for example, who saw a child struggling in the river and said: "When I have taken off my phylacteries I shall rescue him." While he takes off his phylacteries, the child breathes his last!' In the Babylonian Talmud a different example is cited: 'If a woman, for example, was drowning in a river, and he said: It is improper for me to gaze upon her and (this precludes my) saving her.'[96] It is manifest, however, that the Amoraim were not always pleased even with the scholarly pietists who preceded them.[97]

The last observation is not intended to minimize the demand to keep away from the *ʿam hā-ʾāreṣ* expressed in Resh Laqish's dictum. Although R. Akiba enjoined his son not to live in a city whose leaders were scholars (above, p. 604), yet Resh Laqish is only repeating, in point of fact, the admonishment of the Tannaim in different words, for example, the dictum of R. Dosa b. Harkinas (*M. ʾAvot* iii, 10), who counted 'sitting in the meeting-houses of the *ʿammê hā-ʾāreṣ*' among the things that put a man out of the world; or the Baraita that counted sitting down to a meal 'in the company of *ʿammê hā-ʾāreṣ*'[98] among the things unfitting for a scholar. The meeting-houses of the *ʿammê hā-ʾāreṣ* and their companies were considered places without holiness or Torah. This, too, is how R. Simeon b. Eleazar's saying 'On account of two sins do the *ʿammê hā-ʾāreṣ* die: because they call the holy ark 'chest' and because they call a בית כנסת *Bêt Kĕneset* [synagogue, meeting-house] בית העם *Bêt hā-ʿĀm* [the people's house]'[99] is to be understood, for it is as though they took away the sanctity and uniqueness of the synagogue. Statements of this kind concerning the *ʿammê hā-ʾāreṣ* and their institutions — the scathing criticism and acrimonious expressions — are to be regarded in the same light as the parallel phenomena that we have encountered in the internal problems of the world of the Sages. They reflect an authentic reality — not infrequently expressed in a particularly extreme and vehement form — from a circumscribed viewpoint. But it is clear that the authors of these dicta did not intend to reconcile themselves to the situation that they defined or denounced, since the Sages never made concessions at the expense of the integrity of the Congregation of Israel in all its sections and factions. Undoubtedly the Sages were far from overlooking faults, but the acceptance of the yoke of the Torah, in the sense of the duty of elucidating and inculcating it to the masses, strengthened their faith in the power of repentance, whose gates were never closed to the individual Jew and *a fortiori* not to Jewish groups and associations. R. Judah b. R. Ileʿai, in whose name there are also recorded disparaging remarks about the *ʿammê hā-ʾāreṣ* — although not to the same extent as those ascribed to his colleague R. Me'ir — gave the following exposition: '"Hear the word of the Lord, ye that tremble at His word" (Isaiah lxvi 5) — this refers to scholars; "your brethren have said" (*ibid.*) — this refers to Bible students; "that hate you" (*ibid.*) — this refers to Mishna students;

"'that cast you out" — this refers to the *'ammê hā-'āreṣ*. Should you think that their hope is completely cut off, Scripture teaches — "That we may gaze upon your joy; but it is they who shall be put to shame" — and not "Israel shall be put to shame." '[1] This Tanna was lenient in his demands where the *'ammê hā-'āreṣ* were concerned, and stringent in regard to scholars. He expounded: ' "And declare unto My people their transgression and to the house of Jacob their sins" (Isaiah lviii 1): "Declare unto My people their transgression" — this refers to scholars, whose unwitting mistakes are likewise accounted intentional sins; "and to the house of Jacob their sins" — this refers to the *'ammê hā-'āreṣ*, in whose case even the intentional sins are deemed unwitting errors.' R. Me'ir went even further: he not only did not give up the hope of reclaiming deviationists and sinners, even if they belonged to the category of 'one who studied (Torah) and abandoned (it)', like Elisha b. Abuya,[2] but he regarded Israel's election as absolute, and, in opposition to R. Judah, he declared that, whether they acted as sons or not, the Jewish people were children of the Omnipresent.[3] This sentiment arose from the conviction that it was within the capacity of his colleagues to strive, if not for the complete removal of sin, and hence of sinners, from the world,[4] at least for the ideal of drawing their fellow men nearer to the Torah by their willingness not merely to reprove others, but to prefer in their own case reproof above all eulogy. Thus he stated: 'If you have companions, some of whom rebuke you while others praise you, love him that rebukes you and dislike him that praises you; because he that reproves you brings you to life in the world to come, whereas he that lauds you puts you out of the world.'[5] There is hardly any need to add that in the light of their experience, R. Me'ir and the other Sages, both those who came before him and after him, realized that the formulation of a dictum of this kind was easier than its practical observance. However, the Sages, who knew the weakness of human beings generally as well as their own but engaged all their life in an unceasing struggle against the evil impulse and its temptations, motivated by a desire to attain to love of their fellow men, felt in their very being a compulsion to preserve the existence of the Congregation of Israel and to transform it from a chosen to a choosing people.

The Sages endeavoured to fulfil, towards the Congregation of Israel as a whole, R. Me'ir's teaching concerning the attitude a person should adopt towards his reprovers and his praisers. R. Simeon b. Laqish said: 'This people is like a vine: its branches are the burghers, its clusters are the scholars, its leaves are the *ʿammê hā-'āreṣ*, its twigs are the worthless in Israel.' Anonymously the Babylonian Talmud adds: 'This is the meaning of the message sent from there [Eretz-Israel]: "Let the clusters pray for the leaves, for were it not for the leaves the clusters would not exist." '[6] Needless to say the dictum refers not only to intercession, but also to action leading to the sinners' repentance through the scholars' willingness to 'be sureties for their fellows' (above, p. 539). Like Resh Laqish others, too, thought that only the preservation of unity could bridge the differences between the various sections of the nation in respect of their religious-ethical level and at the same time assure the improvement of those who were backward and those who were weak. An anonymous preacher stressed the thought in the form of an allegorical interpretation of the Torah precepts relative to the 'four species' (Leviticus xxiii 40): ' "The fruit of goodly trees" refers to Israel; just as the *'etrôg* (citron) has flavour and fragrance, so does Israel contain people that possess knowledge of the Torah and good deeds. "Branches of palm-trees" refer to Israel; just as the date has flavour but no fragrance, so are the Israelites; they contain people that have Torah-learning but no good deeds. "And boughs of thick trees" refer to Israel; just as the myrtle has fragrance but no flavour, so do the Israelites contain people that possess good deeds but no Torah-learning. "And willows of the brook" refer to Israel; just as the willow has neither flavour nor fragrance, so are the Israelites — they comprise people that possess neither knowledge of the Torah nor good deeds. What now does the Holy One, blessed be He, do with them? To destroy them is not possible. Hence the Holy One, blessed be He, declares that they should all be bound together as a single bunch, so that they may atone for one another.'[7] These and similar homilies are very significant, particularly in the light of their portrayal of the many problems with which the Sages contended in daily life. These included both the internal attitudes of their alma mater — the evaluation of the scholars' functions and the determination of the correct relationship between the study of the Torah and the responsibilities of leadership and administration, between withdrawal and the acceptance of life's realities, on the one hand, and activity and struggle, on the other — and all that concerned the complex of relations with other classes and the Sages' place as leaders and teachers of the people. In their actions and ways the Sages were guided by the consciousness that they were teachers and educators and that it was their duty to teach and train the entire people of Israel, in accordance with the Midrashic exposition: ' "And Moses and the priests the Levites spoke" (Deuteronomy xxvii 9): What words were spoken there? The verse teaches you that the Israelites came and said to Moses: "You have taken the Torah and given it to the priests", as it is said "And Moses wrote this law, and delivered it unto the priests" (*ibid.* xxxi 9). Said Moses to them: "Is it your wish that they should make a covenant with you that whoever desires to study Torah should not be prevented?" They replied "Yes". So they stood up and swore that no one should be prevented from reading the Torah, as it is written "unto all Israel saying"[8] (*ibid.* xxvii 9). Moses then declared to them "This day thou art become a people" (*ibid.*).' Our account has raised the question of the conflicting aims inherent in the combination of the principle of preserving high ideals with that of carrying out administrative and tutorial duties. The Sages realized that in the existing order of the world there was no possibility of achieving the fulfilment of social and hegemonic ideals in their purity. Nevertheless they undertook to work within the Congregation of Israel as it was with all its defects, knowing full well their own weaknesses and the difficulties involved in their labours.

This 'Congregation of Israel', despite its dispersion and despite the absence of all those hallowed institutions that characterized its existence in the past, did not cease to be, in the estimation of the Sages, identical with the people of Israel — separate, sanctified and elect. There is no ground whatsoever for the conjectures that the term 'Congregation of Israel' [*Kĕneset Yisrā'ēl*] was accepted in the early centuries of Christianity owing to the fact that the Christian community was designated ἐκκλησία[9], or because the 'Congregation of Israel' meant the 'Jewish Church' in the sense of Catholic Judaism, but, in contrast to Catholic Christianity, it was inclusive and not exclusive, and also incorporated within itself seceders and deviationists.[10] These explanations not only do not fit the content of the statements made about the 'Congregation of Israel', but they also disregard the nature of the sources in which the expression occurs. It does not appear at all in Tannaitic literature,[11] even when the relationship of the Holy One, blessed be He, to His people is compared to that between a bride and bridegroom,[12] nor does it occur in the MSS. of the ancient Haggadic Midrashim.[13] It is chiefly found in homilies on verses of the Prophets that liken Israel to a woman, a mother, or a daughter,[14] or on passages of Canticles that were interpreted allegorically as referring to Israel,[15] but even in homilies of this type 'Congregation of Israel' and 'Israel' are used indiscriminately.[16] The phrase 'Congregation of Israel' did not enter into the formulations of the prayers and benedictions either. These speak only of 'His people Israel', 'Thy people Israel', or of 'Israel'.[17]

In the Amora R. Berechia's exposition of verses in Canticles the Congregation of Israel declares 'Before the Holy One, blessed be He... My Beloved is unto me...';[18] but the same Amora, who delivered ardent homilies in favour of proselytization (see above, p. 553) interpreted 'Behold (הן *hēn*), ye are nothing (מאין *mē-'ayin*), and your work is a thing of naught' (Isaiah xli 24) as follows: '*Hen* is a Greek word (ἕν — one)... The Holy One, blessed be He, said: You are one nation unto Me from among the nations of the world; *mē-'ayin*, from among those of whom it is written "All the nations are as nothing (אין *'ayin*) before him".'[19]

In Christianity the annulment of nationalism became an actual problem, since it espoused the idea that the Messianic era had already begun and the dominion of the princes of the nations had come to an end. The cosmopolitan conception of Alexander the Great's kingdom — the abolition of antagonism between peoples — and likewise the Hellenistic doctrine that regarded the national gods as satraps of the Most High God, who formed a kind of administrative hierarchy,[20] could be integrated into the new religion. There were, however, Christian teachers who did not ignore the difficulties and perceived that although the σφραγίς [seal] gives the same colour to all the sealed objects, yet after a time their appearance changes again and acquires different tints. But Eusebius found the solution in the Roman Empire[21], which overcame, in his opinion, the problem of peoples and nationality. Since the angel had brought the tidings of peace at Jesus' birth, peace came in the days of Augustus. The national states disappeared from the world, and with the triumph of the new religion the national religions followed suit. He saw the earthly kingdom — the Empire — as corresponding to the Heavenly Kingdom.[22] In the estimation of the Sages the antithesis 'Israel — nations of the world [Gentiles]' remained unchanged, whether the reference was to pagan or Christian nations. Paul had expounded ' "But in Isaac shall thy seed be called" (Genesis xxi 12). That is, They which are the children of the flesh, these are not the children of God; but the children of the promise are counted for the seed' (Romans ix 7–18), as though it was his intention to oppose the teaching of the Mishna (*Nedarim* iii, 11) '[If he said, "*Qônām*!] if I have any benefit from the seed of Abraham!" he is forbidden to have benefit from Israelites, but not from other nations.' In order to counter Paul's homily and the claims of those who followed in his footsteps, the Amoraim added to the Mishnaic statement their exposition of the aforementioned verse: 'And Ishmael is not included among the seed of Abraham; "But in Isaac shall thy seed be called", and Esau is not included among the seed of Isaac.'[23] In order to avoid any possibility of mistaking who is meant — whether Esau or Jacob — the Sages cited the exposition of R. Gershom in the name of R. Aḥa: ' "A star hath stepped forth from Jacob" (Numbers xxiv 17): From whom did a star step forth and is destined to rise in the future? From Jacob';[24] and they added the homily of R. Aḥa in the name of R. Huna: 'The wicked Esau will wrap himself in a Ṭallit and take his seat among the righteous in the Garden of Eden in the time to come, but the Holy One, blessed be He, will drag him out from there.' Esau, who wraps himself in a Ṭallit, is the kingdom that has gone over to 'sectarianism'.

The Sages regarded the kingdom that conquered their country, destroyed their Temple, and exiled their people as a wicked kingdom, and the alliance made between the religion that issued from its bosom and this empire increased their opposition to both. The words of Zephaniah (iii 9) 'that they may all call upon the name of the Lord, to serve Him with one consent' remained linked to the act of future redemption and 'to the abolition of Israel's subjection to the world.'[25]

The Sages' views of the nature and significance of this redemption we shall discuss in the coming chapter.

CHAPTER XVII

ON REDEMPTION

The teaching of the Sages concerning the Redemption are closely linked to verses in the Pentateuch, to the promises of the Prophets, and to the visions recorded in the Book of Daniel. However, their interpretations and homilies were not aimed at elucidating the original meaning of the Scriptural passages; possibly in this sphere, more than in regard to any other theme, there is evident the independent approach of the Sages, which finds expression in a variety of views and conceptions. At times this diversity exceeds the standards of normal differences of opinion and reaches down to fundaments. It is not confined to divergences within the framework of the generally accepted system of concepts, but reaches antitheses that imply the complete negation of one doctrine by the other. Needless to say there are also not wanting intermediate and harmonizing attitudes.

The polarity and variegation are the result of numerous factors: the great divergences marking the use of the verb גאל *gā'al* ['to redeem'] and the noun גאולה *gĕ'ûlā* ['redemption'] in all their different forms, even in the Bible itself;[1] the integration of the concept into a terminology that is only in part derived from the Scriptures, and in part from a later source. The terms referred to are: 'end of days', 'End', 'days of the Messiah', 'resurrection of the dead', 'the world to come', 'the future to come', 'the new world'. Ostensibly all these concepts appear to be close to the idea of redemption, but they are not necessarily identical with it. The growth and consolidation of some of them are connected with entirely different questions and phenomena. The notions of 'the world to come' and 'the resurrection of the dead' are bound up with the problem of reward and punishment, and the doctrine of the soul and retribution. The portrayals of the 'End' and 'the days of the Messiah' are drawn from the vision of 'the end of days' conceived by the prophets of Israel.[2] This vision already has two aspects: The one regards the future as the time when the existing world would be perfected, when it would be freed from its faults, from wickedness and injustice, from wars and catastrophe, and the world would be full of knowledge, and the spirit of the Lord would be poured upon all flesh (Isaiah iv 2–6; xi 6–9; Joel iii 1–4). The other aspect conceives 'the day of the Lord' as a day of ruin and destruction of the present world. That day will be 'a day of darkness and gloom' (Zephaniah i 15). The earth will again be without form and void, and the Carmel a wilderness (Jeremiah iv 23).

The transition to redemption is conditioned by revolutionary upheaval, by catastrophe.[3] In prophetic teaching the idea of the world's 'end of days', in both its aspects, is linked to the new revelation of God as the universal God and to the realization of the kingdom of the Almighty, to the redemption of the people of Israel and to its liberation from the servitude to the (Gentile) kingdoms. The integrity of the world is dependent on the integrity of Israel.

To the array of terms connected with the idea of redemption and the various ways of understanding them, to which we have alluded, is also linked the evaluation of the redeemer's image, and here, too, there are many possibilities. One is that God Himself will redeem the people, and the redeemed people will be His servant, in the sense of 'I, even I, am the Lord; and beside Me there is no saviour... therefore ye are My witnesses, saith the Lord, and I am God' (Isaiah xliii 11–12); or he might be a human king who would appear — like the judges and kings of old — as a saviour who conquers foes, in fulfilment of Balaam's prophecy 'There shall step forth a star out of Jacob, and a sceptre shall rise out of Israel, and shall smite through the corners of Moab, and break down all the sons of Seth' (Numbers xxiv 17). Although he will be a shoot out of the stock of Jesse, yet he will not strike with the sword, but 'He shall smite the land with the rod of his mouth, and with the breath of his lips shall he slay the wicked. And righteousness shall be the girdle of his loins, and faithfulness the girdle of his reins... unto him shall the nations seek; and his resting-place shall be glorious' (Isaiah xi 1–10). In addition there is the description of the servant of the Lord who 'shall prosper, he shall be exalted and lifted up, and shall be very high', but before this 'He had no form nor comeliness... But he was wounded because of our transgressions, he was crushed because of our iniquities... and the Lord hath made to light on him the iniquity of us all' (Isaiah lii 13; liii 2–6). Each one of the prophetic concepts could be restricted or expounded.

In the days of the Second Temple, in the period preceding the Hasmoneans, there were circles that assumed, primarily, one of the functions of the prophets, namely to foretell coming events. The vision of the future became central in apocalyptic literature. One of these works, the vision of Daniel, found a place in the Bible — not, it is true, among the Prophets but in the Hagiographa — and hence became an authoritative source to which interpretations and homilies were attached.[4] However, it is clear that the Sages were familiar with apocalyptic writings, both of those that have come down to us and of similar compositions that have been lost. In this type of literature, too, called apocryphal or pseudepigraphical, no uniform picture emerges of the theme of redemption, but the features that these books have in common far exceed the differences, a fact that finds expression not only in their indubitable eschatological trend, but also in their style and formulation. Some of the Sages not only knew compositions of this kind, but were actually close, in their spiritual leanings and turbulent imagination, to the circles from which they emanated, and were very susceptible to their ideas and visions. When we seek to explain the doctrines of the Sages concerning redemption and to distinguish between the different elements of which they were composed, we are compelled to have recourse to the apocryphal-apocalyptic literature, to the writings of the early Christians, and now also to the Qumran Scrolls. They are all important both for determining the dates of very many ideas in the Rabbinic doctrine of redemption, and for differentiating between concepts that are a heritage from ancient generations and views that represent reactions to certain events and actions, or are due to opposition to notions that appeared alien and even dangerous to them.[5] They are also of value for ascertaining clearly the meaning of eschatological terms that are often used in different senses[6], like 'world to come', which 'is neither the Messianic era nor that of the resurrection of the dead, but refers to the celestial world in which the souls of the righteous abide.'[7] The existence, on the one hand, of separate terms, and their fusion, on the other hand, into a single term through semantic blurring, show that the different trends did not come into being interrelated and linked together.[8]

While the idea of reward and punishment after death already appears about a century before the destruction of the Temple[9], we do not find any explicit statements in Rabbinic sources about redemption and the days of the Messiah before the generation of the disciples of Rabban Joḥanan b. Zakkai. However, the absence of express dicta about redemption dating from the days of the Second Temple is no proof that there was no concern with the subject in the long, tempestuous period from the time of the dominion of the High Priests, under the auspices of the Persian kingdom, to the destruction of the Temple. It may well be that belief in redemption actually found expression and a permanent formulation, which remained unchanged, while the Temple was still standing. That this was indeed the position can be definitely proved in the case of 'resurrection'.[10] There can be no doubt that in various passages of the Bible — in almost all its parts — there are to be found figures of speech and similitudes that recognize the possibility of the resurrection of the dead and the power of God — and even of the prophets — to revive the dead. But we are referring to the belief in the *general* resurrection of the dead at the end of days. The subject is mentioned in the Mishna: 'And these are they that have no share in the world to come: he who says that there is no resurrection of the dead, and (he who says that) the Torah is not from Heaven, and an Epicurean.'[11]

The very fact that R. Akiba adds to this Mishna the words 'Also he who reads apocryphal books and he who utters an incantation over a wound' shows that the first part of the Mishna preceded his time, but the belief in the resurrection of the dead is regarded as traditional already in *II Maccabees*. The author of the book makes the martyrs, at the time of Antiochus' religious persecution, say: ' 'Tis meet for those who perish at men's hands to cherish hope divine that they shall be raised up by God again; but thou — thou shalt have no resurrection to life' (vii 14). The Mishna commentators already found it difficult to explain the threat that one who denies the resurrection will have no share in the world to come. But it is clear that the entire Mishna — including R. Akiba's supplement — is directed against sectarians who held certain views.[12]

Here there is a difference between the world to come and resurrection. The latter refers to the return of the soul to the body, which becomes resuscitated, and the belief is based on the notion of the unity of body and soul, and is in no way connected with the Hellenistic concepts regarding the immortality of the soul. Underlying the latter ideas is actually the absolute antithesis between the soul and the body, which is only a prison from which the soul longs to be freed. This concept is the basis of the Platonic myth of the transmigration of souls. Josephus attributed the belief in the resurrection of the dead to the Pharisaic sect, while the belief in the survival of the soul, which, escaping to freedom after a long servitude, is uplifted 'with joy on high', he ascribed to the Essenes and related to the Greek view.[13] The Essenes held that the world to come, as the sequel to this world, is the sphere of the redeemed souls. The Mishna, however, denies those who do not believe in resurrection even a share in the world to come. The verses in Daniel — 'And many of them that sleep in the dust of the earth shall awake, some to everlasting life, and some to reproaches and everlasting abhorrence' (xii 2), 'But go thou thy way till the end be; and thou shalt rest, and shalt stand up to thy lot, at the end of the days' (*ibid.* v. 13) — place the resurrection before reward and punishment in the world to come in the form of the three groups referred to in the dicta of the School of Shammai and the School of Hillel.[14] The very resurrection to everlasting life is the reward, and the author of *II Maccabees* has in mind the pious martyrs who offered up their lives for the sanctification of His name, and was not content with 'the good name', which constituted human survival according to Ben-Sira. The mention of 'the resurrection of the dead' in the Mishna in *Tractate Sanhedrin* does not attest the commencement of this belief, but the struggle for its acceptance against its opponents.

Let us now see whether we can determine the nature of the beliefs in the redemption of the nation and country in the period preceding the Destruction. In the order of service for fast days given in the

Mishna twenty-four benedictions are mentioned, 'the daily eighteen, to which six are added'. The additional blessings begin with the benediction for redemption, and in the Tosefta and in the Baraitot we find the version used in the Temple, namely 'Blessed be the Lord, the God of Israel, from everlasting to everlasting; blessed be the Redeemer of Israel.'[15] Clearly the benediction and prayers that were added on public fasts were introduced, like the fasts themselves, for current troubles, like drought. But what of the actual benediction for redemption in the Eighteen Benedictions? Is it a Messianic prayer for the political redemption of the Jewish people, for its liberation from subjection? The formulation of the prayer, in its Palestinian form, 'Behold our affliction and champion our cause and redeem us speedily for Thy name's sake; blessed art Thou, O Lord, the Redeemer of Israel'[16], and likewise other recensions, remain undecisive. The Amoraim tried hard to show that, as R. Aḥa had stated in the name of R. Joshua b. Levi, 'Also he that composed this Prayer [Eighteen Benedictions] did so according to a fixed order', and to the question 'and what was their reason for juxtaposing... the benediction for forgiveness to that for redemption' R. Jeremiah replied by referring to the passage in Psalms ciii 3–4 'Who forgiveth all thine iniquity; who healeth all thy diseases; who redeemeth thy life from the pit.'[17]

This explanation is based on the conception that the prayer for redemption speaks not of national redemption, but of the redemption of individuals from their affliction, trouble, and distress, just as the term 'redeem' is used in many verses[18] for the deliverance of an individual. Actually this conception is already expressed in *Midrash Tannaim.* With reference to Moses' blessing the Tannaitic homilist declares: 'Scripture teaches us that when Moses began (to bless Israel), he did not commence with Israel's needs, but with the praise of the Omnipresent... and likewise the Eighteen Benedictions, which the early Sages had ordained that Israel should recite as prayer, do not begin with Israel's wants, but with the praise of the Omnipresent — in the words of the Prayer: 'the great, mighty, and revered God... holy art Thou and revered is Thy name', and then 'loosest the bound', followed by 'healest the sick', and thereafter 'We give thanks unto Thee'.[19]

Undoubtedly by 'loosest the bound' the expositor had in mind the Benediction of Redemption, and mentioned its theme but not its closing formula, just as he did in 'We give thanks unto Thee'. Alongside the reason we have cited for the position of the Benediction of Redemption in the Eighteen Benedictions another reason is given by the Amora R. Aḥa: 'Why was "who redeemest Israel" made the seventh benediction? To teach you that Israel will be redeemed only in the seventh year (of the Messiah's advent).'[20] This explanation is given in the Babylonian Talmud in the name of Rava.[21]

In the Talmud a difficulty is pointed out by reference to a distinctly eschatological Baraita[22], which describes the events of the septennium preceding the advent of the son of David, and in which it is stated 'in the *sixth* year (Heavenly) sounds; in the seventh, wars; and at the termination of the septennium the son of David will come', and the Gemara answers 'War is also the beginning of redemption.' It is obvious that these Amoraim regarded the benediction of redemption as referring to the redemption of the Jewish people by their Messiah. Rashi who realized the difference between Rava's dictum and what preceded — where the statements are cited in the form of a Baraita — found it necessary to note 'And although this redemption does not refer to redemption from exile, but is a request that (God) should redeem us from the troubles that constantly come upon us, for as regards the prayers for the gathering of the exiles and the rebuilding of Jerusalem and the branch of David, each one constitutes a separate benediction apart from this prayer for redemption, yet since it bears the name redemption, it has been inserted in the seventh benediction.'[23]

Rashi's remarks certainly hold good for the period of the Second Temple. So long as the Temple stood and self-rule in one form or another obtained in Judea, the national-Messianic hopes were not expressed in general terms of redemption, but in particular forms with concrete meanings. Indeed a Mishna dating from Temple times sheds light on them. In the order of the service of the Day of Atonement we are told that the High Priest read from the Torah, and thereafter it is stated: 'And he pronounced thereon eight benedictions: for the Torah, for the Temple-Service, for the Thanksgiving, for the Forgiveness of Sin, for the Temple, for Israel, for the Priests, and for the rest a (general) prayer.'[24] In the Palestinian Talmud the portion of the Mishna pertaining to our subject is explained thus: 'For the Temple, "who choosest the Temple" — but Rav 'Idi said: "who dwellest in Zion";[25] for Israel, "who choosest Israel"; for the Priests "who choosest the priests". 'Clearly the reference here is to the closing formulas of the prayers, of which the general theme only was known. Maimonides writes as follows:[26] 'And he said a separate benediction for the Temple, whose theme was that the Temple should (continue to) stand and the Divine Presence (dwell) therein, concluding it "Blessed art Thou, O Lord, who dwellest in Zion". And he pronounced a separate benediction upon Israel, which was a petition that the Lord should deliver Israel and that a sovereign should not depart from them, and concluded it "Blessed art Thou, O Lord, who choosest Israel". And he uttered a separate benediction for the priests, requesting the Omnipresent to accept their acts and service with favour and bless them, and concluded it "Blessed art Thou, O Lord, who sanctifiest the priests".' Other commentators cited different versions, for example: 'May it be Thy will, O Lord our God and God of our fathers, that Thou shouldst let Thy Temple stand before Thee for ever, and that Thou shouldst be pleased with it and cause Thy Divine Presence to dwell therein constantly. Blessed art Thou, O Lord, who choosest the Temple.'[27] Undoubtedly even at the outset the formulations of the High Priest's prayers were not uniform, and it was common practice to make innovations in them and to variegate them according to circumstances; similarly the Tosefta explains the phrase 'and for the rest a (general) prayer' not by citing a text, but by defining the content thus: 'And for the rest a prayer, petition, and supplication that Thy people Israel need to be delivered before Thee, concluding "who hearest prayer".' We possess an ancient prayer of this kind for the salvation of Israel in the *Book of Sirach*.[28] The worshipper appeals to God to show the Gentiles anew his mighty deeds, entreating 'Subdue the foe and expel the enemy'. In clear allusion to Habakkuk ii 3 he adds 'Hasten the end and ordain the appointed time.' Without doubt the reference is to actual events that were connected with the Ptolemaic and Seleucid kingdoms. The phrases in which he expressed the hopes and expectations inherent in salvation are: 'Gather all the tribes of Jacob, that they may receive their inheritance as in the days of old' — an expression that corresponds to 'who gatherest the banished ones of Thy people Israel'; 'Compassionate the people that is called by Thy name' corresponds to 'who choosest Israel'; 'Compassionate Thy holy city' parallels 'who choosest the Temple'. The nexus with the Eighteen Benedictions and the prayers of the High Priest is clear. The verse 'Fill Zion with Thy majesty, and Thy Temple with Thy glory' may indicate the content of the High Priest's benediction, whose closing formula 'Who dwellest in Zion' is cited by Rav 'Idi, and the theme of the prayer for Jerusalem that was recited in place of our text.

We gain further clarification of the Messianic hopes and expectations in the pre-Hasmonean period in chapter li of *Sirach*[29], which is patterned after the Great Hallel of Psalms cxxxvi, and from the viewpoint of its content and language has much in common with the prayer of the *ʿĂmîdā* [Eighteen Benedictions]. We shall quote the lines that appertain to our subject: 'Give thanks unto the Keeper of Israel... Give thanks unto the Redeemer of Israel... Give thanks unto Him that gathereth the banished ones of Israel... Give thanks unto Him that buildeth His city and His Sanctuary... Give thanks unto Him that maketh a horn to sprout for the house of David... Give thanks unto Him that chooseth the sons of Zadok to be priests... Give thanks unto Him that hath chosen Zion.' This psalm has been omitted in the Greek translation, and apparently it has not been wholly preserved in its original recension. But its general authenticity cannot be doubted.

In the light of what we have shown above, both by reference to chapter xxxv of the *Book of Sirach* and with regard to the prayer of the High Priest and the prayer of the *ʿĂmîdā*, the psalm is a synthesis of thanksgiving for hopes and expectations that had been realized and supplication for assurances and promises that were still being hoped for. 'The Redeemer of Israel', like 'the Keeper of Israel', is the Lord, who rises up to help His people and redeems them from troubles and misfortunes; the Sanctuary is built, the elect sons of Zadok the (High) Priest minister in it, but the gathering of the banished ones of Israel has not been completed, and 'the sprouting of a horn unto the house of David' is still hidden in the womb of time; all the hopes bear a realistic and sober character, and contain no catastrophic-eschatological elements. Of all the eschatological images found in the utterances of the Prophets Ben-Sira mentions only the words of Malachi concerning the mission of Elijah 'before the coming of the great and terrible day'; but while the words of the last prophet 'And he shall turn the heart of the fathers to the children, and the heart of the children to their fathers' (Malachi iii 23–24) may be interpreted as the hope of the realization of a social ideal that would put an end to family strife and to tension between the generations,[30] Ben-Sira retains the first half of the verse, 'To turn the heart of the fathers to the children', but continues 'and to restore the tribes of Israel',[31] that is to say, Elijah will play a role in the restoration of the diaspora — in his own words, cited above, 'that they may receive their inheritance as in the days of old'. It would seem that also the ancient version of the fourth blessing of the grace after meals contained at first a prayer for the deliverance of Israel and the restoration of the kingdom of the House of David and the ingathering of the dispersed sons of Israel. In the name of R. Eliezer it was taught 'Whoever has not mentioned... the kingdom of the House of David in the benediction "who buildest Jerusalem" has not fulfilled his obligation', but R. Jose b. R. Judah said that the conclusion of the benediction should be 'Who savest Israel'.[32] In the Genizah fragments of the Palestinian version the blessing includes the verse 'The Lord doth build up Jerusalem, He gathereth together the dispersed of Israel', and there is ancient, extraneous testimony for this recension.[33]

The conception of redemption in *Sirach* and also in sources close to it in time is realistic, and is primarily concerned with the supplementation of the deficiencies of Israel's sovereignty, well-being, and prosperity. The belief in the resurrection of the dead is not found there, and the notion of reward and punishment in the world to come is also wanting. Indirectly this confirms our thesis that the belief in resurrection dates from the beginning of the Hasmonean era.

This period intensified the sense of revival and redemption, and this is attested by the coins of the epoch, which carried the inscription 'To the redemption of Zion'.[34] The reference, however, is not to the redemption of 'the time of the end', but to redemption from national trouble, for which it was ordained that Hallel be recited; in the words of the Sages: 'The prophets among them instituted that the Israelites should say it [the Hallel] at every turning point and every trouble — Heaven forfend! — and when they are redeemed they should recite it (as a thanksgiving) for their redemption' (*T.B. Pesaḥim* 117a).

Nevertheless, for the present there stood at the head of the people a family of priests that was not of the House of Zadok, and a shoot of the House of David had not appeared. The pietist rebels and the Hasmoneans themselves were not influenced by the idea of 'the end of days'. The author of *I Maccabees* put into the mouth of Mattathias before his death the sentence 'David, for being merciful, inherited the throne of a kingdom for ever and ever' (*I Maccabees* ii 56). After Judah the Maccabean had entered Jerusalem and the desecrated altar had been pulled down, its stones were hidden in a special place 'until a prophet should come and decide concerning them' (*ibid.* iv 46; see *M. Middot* i, 46). The decisive step in the appointment of Simon is described thus: 'And the Jews and the priests were well pleased that Simon should be their leader and high-priest for ever, until a faithful prophet should arise' (*I Maccabees* xiv 41). The belief in the appearance of Elijah continued, nor did the belief in the kingdom of the House of David cease, but it is not characterized by a sense of urgency and actuality. This feeling found expression in a Baraita: 'When the First Temple was destroyed the (Levitical) cities with pasture land [cf. Numbers xxxv 2] were abolished, the Urim and Thummim ceased, and there was no longer a king from the House of David, and should anyone insinuate a doubt, quoting "And the governor said unto them that they should not eat of the most holy things till there stood up a priest with Urim and Thummim" (Ezra ii 63), (say to him: The verse speaks of the remote future), as one who says to his fellow "Until the resurrection of the dead and the advent of the Messiah son of David." '[35] The true prophet Elijah will come to announce the Messiah's advent and will resolve matters in doubt, but the expansion of the borders of the land and the settlement of the Jews in their inheritance were carried out by the Hasmoneans. Furthermore, after they had proclaimed themselves kings, the Sages recognized them as kings of Israel. The Mishna ruling 'The king neither judges nor is judged' was interpreted as applying to Israelite kings, but not to kings of the House of David, and tradition regards this Halakha, which implies that the monarch is deprived of the right to give judgement and is not subject to the authority of the Sanhedrin, as a compromise reached after the clash between Simeon b. Sheṭah and King Jannai.[36]

In principle the Sages recognized the kingship of the House of the Hasmoneans. The enactments of John Hyrcanus were accepted,[37] and we find Simeon b. Sheṭaḥ also on good terms with King Jannai.[38] The clashes and expressions of opposition do not go beyond what we know of the attitude of the prophets to the kings of the House of David and even to David himself. It was the open rebuke of strong-willed and dominating men. In the collision between the Pharisees and Jannai, Judah b. Gedidiah did not argue against Jannai's right to be king. On the contrary, he said 'Be content with the crown of sovereignty; leave the crown of priesthood to the seed of Aaron',[39] and even here the reason was not one of opposition in principle to the unification of two domains, but the fact 'that it was said: His mother was taken captive at Modiʿim.' Shemaʿyah and Avṭalion went to greet the High Priest and paid him due honour, and it was only when the latter insulted them publicly by alluding to their low origin or to their being proselytes that they reacted sharply. Despite all the criticism that they levelled against the conduct and leadership of the last of the Hasmoneans and of the kings of the House of Herod,[40] the Sages never went so far as to negate the existing institutions of the monarchy, the priesthood, and the Temple. Nor did they withhold appreciative recognition from Herod for his work of rebuilding the Temple, or words of praise and comfort from Agrippa.[41] There were some Sages who held office in administrative and governmental institutions. They infused their spirit and ideals into the affairs of government and administration[42], but they considered their primary function to be the teaching of Torah, the clarification of Halakha, the interpretation of the Holy Scriptures, and the devoted instruction of the people in the principles of faith in Divine Providence, in reward and punishment, and in the resurrection of the dead. But very little is said on 'esoteric subjects'[43] or about attempts to penetrate the arcana of the future. Apart from the dispute between the School of Shammai and the School of Hillel in regard to the three companies[44] we find only one tradition, and again it relates to Elijah:

'R. Joshua said: I have received a tradition from Rabban Joḥanan

b. Zakkai, who heard it from his teacher, and his teacher from his teacher, as a Halakha given to Moses at Sinai, that Elijah will not come to declare clean or unclean, to put away or to bring nigh, but to put away those that were brought nigh by violence and to bring nigh those that were put away by violence. The family of Bet Ṣerefa was in Transjordan and Ben Zion put it away by force. And yet another (family) was there, and Ben Zion brought it nigh by force. The like of these Elijah will come to declare clean or unclean, to put away or to bring nigh.'[45]

For the elucidation of the matters *per se* — such as family purity and trustworthiness — Elijah was not required. These things fall within the jurisdiction of the Sages, but the authorized institutions were too weak to right wrongs that were perpetrated by force, and therefore they left them to Elijah.

Another function was thus assigned to Elijah. But the fundamental aspects that characterized the conception of redemption in the preceding era remained unchanged, and apparently were also shared by Jewry in the Diaspora, at any rate to the extent that they found expression in Philo's writings.[46] There were other circles, however, whose interest was centred essentially on these themes and all that they involved. The authors of works like the *Book of Enoch*, the *Testaments of the Twelve Patriarchs*, the *Sibylline Oracles*, the *Apocalypse of Baruch*, *II Esdras* [Apocalypse of Ezra], *et al.* took over a single aspect of the ancient prophecy — the vision of the future. They made use of motifs derived from prophetic utterances and visions, but since their works were pseudepigraphical,[47] ascribed to great men of the past, they were completely unrestrained in their depiction of the scenes in the upper worlds. Despite feelings of awe and trepidation they continue to walk about in them and to stand in close contact with Guardian Princes and angels, drawing nigh to the Chariot and to Him who sits upon the Throne of Glory, and they are easily able to acquire information and receive revelations concerning the changes and upheavals that are about to take place in the history of the Gentile nations and kingdoms, and regarding the role that the people of Israel and their Messiah are destined to play in this drama (see Daniel vii 13–19). They are able to describe the Day of the Lord as a day of world judgement in all its detailed terrors; the fulfilment of the Messianic promises, determining their dates and portents; and likewise the figure of the Messiah (Book III of the *Sibylline Oracles* and *Enoch*); the dominion of death until the end of the corrupt world; the resurrection of the dead, their judgement, and the rise of a new world in which human beings will resemble angels (*Apocalypse of Baruch*). It is not to be denied that the belief of apocalyptic circles was nourished by their disillusionment with the existing reality, both with the Maccabean War, and with the Temple, in which priests who were not of the sons of Zadok ministered, and with the dominion of wickedness holding sway in Israel and in the world. They saw no possibility of improving the present world, and hence the urgent need for salvation and redemption. Since the exact date of some of these works is not known, it is difficult to determine certain events, depicted as though forming the background of the vision. The attempts made in this direction have led at times to various extraordinary conjectures, but the principle underlying them remains valid. In the work known as the *Testaments of the Twelve Patriarchs* two Messiahs are referred to — a Messiah who is a priest and one who is an Israelite. In the 'Testament of Reuben' it is stated 'For to Levi God gave the sovereignty... because he shall know the law of the Lord, and shall give ordinances for judgement and shall sacrifice for all Israel until the consummation of the times, as the *anointed* [Messiah] High Priest....' In the continuation, again, concerning Judah we find: 'because him hath the Lord chosen to be king over all the nation. And bow down before his seed... and will be among you an eternal king' (vi 7–12). Similar statements, with different nuances and additional motifs, are to be found also in other testaments. Scholars were amazed by the idea of the two Messiahs, and various theories were advanced in order to resolve the difficulty, but from the Qumran scrolls it is clear that this belief in two Messiahs was accepted by the *Yaḥad* [Qumran] sect.[48]

Because of the opposition of these sectarians to the transfer of the High Priesthood to the Hasmoneans, who pursued the path of warriors and conquerors and adopted a Hellenistic style of life, they departed to the wilderness under the leadership of a Priestly Teacher of Righteousness.

Influenced by the prophecies of Zechariah, who refers to 'the two anointed ones' (iv 1–2, 14), they developed this eschatological conception of the Messiah descended from Aaron and out of faithfulness to the promises given to the House of David in the Scriptures — including Zechariah (xi 4) — they juxtaposed to him the Israelite Messiah. The Messianic idea in *The Rule of the Community* [*Yaḥad*] bears a distinctly restitutive character, and in *The Rule of the Congregation* [*Hā-ʿEdā*] the Messiah does not even appear as the one who brings the redemption.[49]

It appears that consequent upon the internecine strife within the House of the Hasmoneans, the wars between the brothers Aristobulus and Hyrcanus, and the capture of Jerusalem by Pompey, which came in their wake in 63 B.C.E., the Messianic consciousness acquired greater strength and actuality. Wc possess the work called *The Psalms of Solomon*[50], which has been preserved in Greek translation only, but was originally written in Hebrew at Jerusalem; it treats of the events in the years 70–45 B.C.E. The author is vehemently opposed to the monarchy of the Housc of the Hasmoneans and to the ruling circles in Jerusalem; he attributes to them every kind of criminal and abominable act; and he describes the capture of Jerusalem by Pompey, at the invitation of Aristobulus, in anguished language mixed with irony:

> The princes of the land went to meet him with joy: they said unto him:
> Blessd be thy way! Come ye, enter ye in with peace. They made the rough ways even, before his entering in;
> They opened the gates to Jerusalem, they crowned its walls.
> As a father (entereth) the house of his sons, (so) he entered (Jerusalem) in peace;
> He established his feet (there) in great safety.
> He captured her fortress and the wall of Jerusalem;
> For God Himself led him in safety, while they wandered.
> He destroyed their princes and every one wise in counsel;
> He poured out the blood of the inhabitants of Jerusalem, like the waters of uncleanness.
>
> (viii 18 [16]–23 [20]).

In truth the struggle against the Roman conquerors did not cease, and for two decades (57–37) the revolts of Aristobulus and his sons continued, but the author placed no real hope either in what was done or in the doers, although he was granted to hear of Pompey's death in the year 48 and to portray his bitter end as Divine retribution on the wicked (ii 26–37). The anonymous poet sees hope of salvation only in the coming of the Messiah of the House of David and in the perfection of the world in the kingdom of the Almighty. Psalm xvii — the Messianic psalm, which commences with the words 'O Lord, Thou art our King for ever and ever, for in Thee, O God, doth our soul glory' — rejects, in unambiguous terms, the monarchy of the Hasmoneans:

Thou, O Lord, didst choose David (to be) king over Israel,
And sworest to him touching his seed that never should his kingdom fail before Thee.
But, for our sins, sinners rose up against us...
They set a (worldly) monarchy in place of (that which was) their excellency...
But Thou, O God, didst cast them down, and remove their seed from the earth,
In that there rose up against them a man that was alien to our race...

The Hasmoneans are usurpers who introduced an alien form of government into the country. The poet does not distinguish between Aristobulus and Hyrcanus; he has but one prayer:

Behold, O Lord, and raise up unto them their king, the son of David,
At the time in which Thou seest, O God, that he may reign over Israel Thy servant.
And gird him with strength, that he may shatter unrighteous rulers...
At his rebuke nations shall flee before him...
And he shall gather together a holy people...
And he shall divide them according to their tribes upon the land.
And neither sojourner nor alien shall sojourn with them any more...
And he shall purge Jerusalem, making it holy as of old;
So that nations shall come from the ends of the earth to see his glory...
And he (shall be) a righteous king, taught of God, over them,
And there shall be no unrighteousness in his days in their midst.
For all shall be holy and their king the anointed of the Lord.

For he shall not put his trust in horse and rider and bow,
Nor shall he multiply for himself gold and silver for war,
Nor shall he gather confidence from(?) a multitude for the day of battle.
The Lord Himself is his king, the hope of him that is mighty through (his) hope in God.
All nations (shall be) in fear before him,
For he will smite the earth with the word of his mouth for ever...
And he himself (will be) pure from sin, so that he may rule a great people.
He will rebuke rulers, and remove sinners by the might of his word...
His words (shall be) like the words of the holy ones in the midst of sanctified peoples.[51]
Blessed be they that shall be in those days...
May the Lord hasten His mercy on Israel! ...
The Lord Himself is our king for ever and ever
(xvii 23 (21)–51 (46)).

I have quoted many verses from this Messianic document, and although its elements appear to be no more than an amalgam of prophetic promises and the utterances of visionaries like Daniel, yet its distinctiveness lies not in the combination of the themes, but in the centrality of the figure of the Messiah son of David, who although manifestly a redeemer of the land and nation, is at the same time a cosmic redeemer, who promises the kingdom of the Lord upon earth. This document is also unique in respect of what it omits. It does not mention either reward or punishment in the world to come, or the resurrection of the dead, nor does it describe catastrophic scenes. Although the document contains no indications of a sectarian orientation, yet at the same time it clearly represents only a faction within Pharisaic Judaism about a century before the Destruction, for despite all the frictions the majority of the Sages continued, as we have already emphasized, to adopt a positive attitude even to the last representatives of independent rule in Judea. Both those who subsequently supported the revolt against the Romans and those who endeavoured to come to terms with the foreign rule, so long as the Temple stood in its place and some measure of independence was allowed them in internal affairs, did not consider the Messianic expectation a matter of immediate and practical significance. Both sections understood the concept of redemption realistically, as implying the enlargement of Jewish independence, whether by force of rebellion and war, or by virtue of patience and reconciliation. The belief that the Messiah, who was due to come, must necessarily be of the House of David, was primarily used to reject the claimants to the crown of the Messiah.[52]

With the destruction of the Temple and all that it involved the question of redemption and its entire conception underwent a great change. From the aspect of the sources in our possession, the apocalyptic literature is now augmented by such books as the *Apocalypse of Baruch* and *IV Ezra*. But alongside of them there exists an abundance of Rabbinic dicta and homilies dealing with the problems of redemption, in which are to be found the variegation and polaric contrasts that we discussed at the outset. Comparison with the apocryphal works enables us to distinguish between such views as form the ancient heritage of the Sages and concepts that were absorbed through the closer mutual understanding between the Sages and certain apocalyptic circles, and also to discern, in no small measure, the realities behind the words.

Rabban Joḥanan b. Zakkai, who sensed the approaching Destruction, began to prepare the people to live without Temple and sacrifices. In a Haggadic Baraita, which might be called 'an apocalypse in reverse', it is related:

Forty years before the destruction of the Temple the lot did not come up in the right hand, nor did the crimson strap become white, nor did the westernmost light burn; and the doors of the היכל *Hêkhāl* [the *Holy* of the Temple] opened of their own accord (Rashi: 'A sign to the enemies to enter'), until Rabban Joḥanan b. Zakkai rebuked them. He said to it [the Temple]: '*O Hekhal*, *Hekhal*, why do you alarm yourself? I know full well that you are destined to be destroyed, for Zechariah the son of Ido has already prophesied concerning you "Open thy doors, O Lebanon, that the fire may devour the cedars" (Zechariah xi 1).'[53]

We know from Josephus[54] that years before the Destruction there walked about Jerusalem prophets and presagers who spoke about the Temple in ruins, and visionaries and sectarians who, in their enthusiasm, already saw a glorious new Temple descending from

Heaven. The destruction of the Temple was a shattering blow to the Jews of that generation. For the Temple service was one of the three things on which the world rested, and the effect of the disaster on Rabban Joḥanan himself is depicted thus: 'Rabban Joḥanan was sitting and looking towards the wall of Jerusalem to see what would happen to it, as it is narrated of Eli "Lo, Eli sat upon his seat by the wayside watching" (I Samuel iv 13). When Rabban Joḥanan b. Zakkai saw that the Temple was destroyed, and the *Hekhal* was burnt, he rose and rent his garments, and took off his phylacteries, and sat and wept and his disciples with him.'[55] But already then he started the work of reconstructing the life of Torah and precept, and although he did this in the hope that the Sanctuary would be rebuilt and the people redeemed, he realized that these things could not happen in the near future. 'Once Rabban Joḥanan b. Zakkai was going forth from Jerusalem, followed by R. Joshua, when he saw the Sanctuary in ruins. Said R. Joshua: "Woe unto us that this place, where the iniquities of Israel were expiated, lies in ruins!" Said (Rabban Joḥanan) to him: "My son, be not grieved! We have a means of atonement that is its equal, namely the practice of benevolence, as it is said: 'For I desire lovingkindness, and not sacrifice' (Hosea vi 6)."'[56] It may be that this answer was also intended to contradict R. Joshua's view: 'I have heard that sacrifices may be offered although there is no Temple; and that the most holy sacrifices may be eaten although there are no curtains; and the lesser holy sacrifices and the second tithe although there is no wall; because the first sanctification availed for its own time and for the time to come.'[57] The immediate urge to attempt to rebuild the Sanctuary and to proclaim that the Messiah would come soon did not cease. It is against them, apparently that the dicta of Rabban Joḥanan b. Zakkai are directed; possibly they were not uttered at one time, although they are aimed against similar trends: 'If the young people say to you "Let us go and build the Temple", do not listen to them. But if the old people say to you "Come, let us pull down the Temple", listen to them, because the construction of youths is destruction, and the destruction of the aged is construction. Proof of this is Rehoboam the son of Solomon.' Another dictum is: 'If there was a plant in your hand, and you are told: "Behold, the Messiah is here", go and plant the plant, and then go forth to welcome him.'[58] All his life Rabban Joḥanan b. Zakkai occupied himself with making enactments, with laying foundations for the national institutions, and with inculcating Torah and precepts and ideals that would improve the life of the individual and the community, and also with the acceptance of the yoke of the kingdom of Heaven. Thus he expounded: 'Why was it seen fit to bore the ear...? Because it heard on Sinai "For unto Me the children of Israel are servants, they are My servants", yet he removed the yoke of Heaven and caused the yoke of flesh and blood to reign over him....'[59] Undoubtedly Rabban Joḥanan b. Zakkai held to the actual belief in the advent of a redeeming Messiah, but since the early accounts of the study of mystic doctrines and the Work of the Chariot, which are linked with the name of Rabban Joḥanan b. Zakkai and the circle of his disciples, are distinguished by their unpretentious and restrained character,[60] he saw no reason for detailed discussions about the Messiah and his times and acts.

Only near to his death, he revealed a little of his Messianic ideal, corroborating what we have stated thus far: 'R. Jacob bar Idi said in the name of R. Joshua b. Levi: Rabban Joḥanan b. Zakkai sensing the approach of death, said: "Clear the house on account of defilement, and set a throne for Hezekiah king of Judah." '[61]

King Hezekiah, to whom a number of Isaiah's Messianic prophecies are applied,[62] is the monarch concerning whom Scripture testifies: 'And he wrought that which was good and right and faithful before the Lord his God. And in every work that he began in the service of the house of God, and in the law, and in the commandments, to seek his God, he did it with all his heart, and prospered' (II Chronicles xxxi 20–21). Him R. Joḥanan b. Zakkai sees at the time of his death as coming to greet him, and it is only fitting to prepare a throne for such a Messianic king and to welcome him.

Dicta have been transmitted in the names of R. Joḥanan b. Zakkai's disciples relating to the study and discussion of the principles and details of the future redemption. The Tannaim R. Eliezer b. Hyrcanus and R. Joshua differ on the relationship between penitence and redemption. The dispute has come down to us in two versions. According to one of them: 'R. Eliezer said: If Israel repent they will be redeemed, but if not, they will not be redeemed. Said R. Joshua to him: If they do not repent, they will not be redeemed? Nay, the Holy One, blessed be He, will raise up for them a king whose decrees will be as brutal as those of Haman, and (in consequence) Israel will repent, and he will thus bring them back to the right path.'[63] In this short text the type of redemption is not defined, but we may assume that both Tannaim had in mind religious-national redemption, which would restore the former position, that is to say, liberation from servitude, renewal of national freedom, rebuilding of the Temple as a condition requisite to perfecting the world under the sovereignty of the Almighty and to the fulfilment of the prophetic promises concerning the end of days and all that this entails. R. Eliezer makes redemption dependent on repentance: 'If they do not repent, they will not be redeemed.' Repentance comes first. Redemption is not, therefore, an eschatological act, having an independent existence, and it has no fixed time. R. Joshua, too, does not sever the nexus between repentance and redemption, only he incorporates this in the eschatological act, for it is inconceivable that Israel will not be redeemed, even if they do not repent. Hence the Lord will raise up a king, whose decrees are as brutal as those of Haman, and Israel will ineluctably repent. Upon examination it becomes clear that the dispute, which is ostensibly centred on the question of redemption, is actually concerned with the predetermined End. According to R. Eliezer there is no 'time of the end' or absolute 'end of the wonders', and consequently there is no point in all the attempts to discover this End and the signs connected with its coming. R. Joshua's view makes room for 'the calculators of the End', for those who envision catastrophic events and 'the throes of the Messiah', which precede the redemption; but there is one condition, namely that the act of repentance must be fitted into all these.

That the basis of this dispute is related to the apocalyptic visions is clearer still in the parallel tradition in which each one of the Tannaim brings Scriptural proof for his viewpoint. Against R. Eliezer's verse 'Return, ye backsliding children, I will heal your backslidings' (Jeremiah iii 22), R. Joshua adduces the verse 'Ye have sold yourselves for naught; and ye shall be redeemed without money' (Isaiah lii 3), and so they continue to counter one prophetic passage with another, until R. Joshua says: 'But it has already been stated "And I heard the man clothed in linen, who was upon the waters of the river, when he lifted up his right hand and his left hand unto heaven, and swore by Him that liveth for ever that it shall be for a time, times, and a half; and when they have made an end of breaking in pieces the power of the holy people, all these things shall be finished" (Daniel xii 7).' The transmitters of this tradition conclude the debate with the words 'Rabbi Eliezer went away', or 'And R. Eliezer was silent.' When R. Joshua sought support in the words of an apocalyptic vision of the type of Daniel, R. Eliezer saw no further possibility for continuing the argument, for it was precisely this view that he opposed in his dictum 'If they do not repent, they will not be redeemed.' However, R. Joshua also did not accept the vision of the End without a certain compromise. He placed repentance before redemption by relying on the power of a wicked king like Haman to force Israel back to the right path. It should be noted that in the battle of verses R. Eliezer did not seek support in Isaiah lix 20 'And a redeemer will come to Zion, and unto them that turn [ולשבי *û-lĕ-shāvê*] from transgression in Jacob'. Possibly both R. Eliezer and R. Joshua already knew an interpretation of this verse which they rejected. Whereas the Masoretic version supports the view of R. Eliezer, and Aquila, Symmachus and Theodotian rendered it accordingly, the Septuagint translates: καὶ ἀποστρέψει ἀσεβείας ἀπὸ Ἰακούβ ('and He shall turn away [ישיב *yāshîv*] ungodliness from Jacob'.[64] Paul, too, cites the verse in this version (Romans xi 26). According to the interpretation inherent in this translation repentance does not actually precede redemption, but it is the redeemer who puts transgression away. This translation accords with the antinomian doctrine of Paul, which taught that 'Therefore by the deeds of the law there shall no flesh be justified in his sight: for by the law is the knowledge of sin' (*ibid.* iii 20). Hence there is no possibility of repentance, in his view, before the advent of the Messiah, 'For Christ is the end of the law, that every one who has faith may be justified.' Paul himself indicates the apocalyptic character of his words by declaring (*ibid.* xi 25) that he came to reveal by his words μυστήριον, which is the tidings of the redemption unto the Gentiles, who are 'all Israel' (*ibid. v.* 26), and He made a covenant with them after He had removed their sins. According to this view Paul also changed the first part of the verse from the Septuagint, and instead of ἕνεκεν Σιὼν he read ἐκ Σιὼν, that is to say, the redeemer will not come to Zion, but from Zion to the Gentiles.[65] Obviously this was not R. Joshua's conception. At any rate it is reported in the name of R. Jose the Galilean 'Great is repentance, for it brings redemption near, as it is said "And a redeemer will come to Zion", because of "them that turn from transgression in Jacob".'[66] This homily accords with the view of R. Joshua and contradicts the translation cited above. Hence, despite the absolute value R. Jose attributed to redemption, he could not but make repentance precede it. R. Eliezer did not wish to rely even on catastrophic events as reliable incentives to repentance. Repentance was an absolute value in itself. However, he, too, was acquainted with apocalyptic portrayals and visions — and undoubtedly not only with those in the Book of Daniel — but he endeavoured to limit their absolute value. The following homily is transmitted in his name: 'If you will succeed in keeping the Sabbath you will be delivered from three visitations: from the Day of Gog and Magog, from the throes of the Messiah's advent and from the Day of the Great Judgement.'[67] When his disciples asked him 'What shall a man do to save himself from the throes of the Messiah's coming?', he replied 'Let him occupy himself with the study of the Torah and with the practice of benevolence.'[68] If repentance alone makes redemption possible and brings it near, then there is no need for the Messianic sufferings.

Another dispute between R. Eliezer and R. Joshua is concerned with the month in which the Israelites are destined to be redeemed. According to R. Eliezer 'In Nisan they were redeemed (from Egypt), and in Tishri they will be redeemed in time to come', and according to R. Joshua 'They were redeemed in Nisan, and in Nisan they will be redeemed in time to come.'[69] Undoubtedly they based themselves on expositions of verses[70]; yet it appears that this dispute is related to the first dispute, and is likewise grounded in a principle. R. Joshua likens the last redemption to the first even from the aspect of time, and just as the redemption from Egypt was given a fixed date at the 'Covenant between the Pieces' — and according to one view the Israelites were devoid of all religious observance, and were even idolaters, and it was only to endow them with some merit that they were given just before the hour of redemption two commandments, the blood of circumcision and the blood of the passover offering[71], in order that they might be worthy of redemption — so also would it be in the coming redemption. On the other hand, in the opinion of R. Eliezer the future redemption would occur only in the month of Tishri, the first day of which was the anniversary of Creation, the Day of Judgement, and the Day of Repentance. R. Joshua's compromise in considering redemption to have a predetermined time combined with repentance makes it easier for him to accept literally the catastrophic events before the advent of the Messiah. One must not overlook the fact that the element of compromise is not wholly wanting in the apocalyptic literature itself. The author of *IV Ezra*, who was a contemporary of R. Eliezer and R. Joshua, and whose visions are full of portents of the End, declares that he heard from the archangel that the world to be would not come into existence until the number of the righteous is complete, 'For he has weighed the age in the balance, and with measure has measured the times... neither will he move nor stir things, till the measure appointed be fulfilled' (iv 36–37).

In the tradition relating to the dispute between R. Eliezer and R. Joshua 'Redemption' is spoken of generally, but there is no reference to the days of the Messiah, or the coming of Messiah the son of David, and certainly the concept of redemption is not defined as including the End, 'the resurrection', 'the time to come', 'the new world' — all those terms, in fact, that are closely linked to the idea of redemption. We shall now seek to discern to what extent and in what way the various views have affected the relationship between repentance and redemption, the conception of the nature of redemption itself and its component elements, and the conception of the redeemer's image.

The attitude to practical movements of redemption was determined to no inconsiderable extent by the two views cited above. When indications of redemption appeared — troubles and cruel suffering, or a lenient attitude on the part of the (Roman) government, or a political constellation that appeared to signalize its fall could all be reckoned as signs of redemption — it was possible to entertain hopes that indeed 'the voice of the turtle was heard in our land and the time had arrived for Israel to be redeemed' (*Canticles Rabba* ii, 13). R. Joshua b. Hananiah himself knew such an experience. In his days 'the (Roman) government decreed that the Temple should be rebuilt'. The story attributes the failure of the project to the calumniations of the Samaritans (Cutheans). Thereupon the Jews wished to revolt, but R. Joshua b. Hananiah dissuaded them from doing this by citing the fable of the Egyptian heron that put its beak into the lion's throat and left unhurt. Even so, said R. Joshua, 'Let it suffice us that we came among this nation in peace and left in peace'.[72] R. Joshua strove to convince his people that the time had not yet arrived to rebel against the government.

The criterion of repentance that R. Joshua conjoined to the belief in the End always made it possible, after the failure of attempts at redemption and of the Messiah to appear, to put the blame on the fact that the generation was not yet worthy. It may be assumed that R. Akiba adopted his teacher's doctrine. He did not abandon the idea of the End, but he saw the possibility of hastening it in a generation that merited it.[73]

In the light of the information now available to us about the period of Bar Kokhba from the letters and finds in the caves of the Judean desert[74], that generation may be largely considered as one of penitent and observant Jews. Nay more, R. Akiba held, like the author of *IV Ezra*, that a generation could even be saved by the virtue of its righteous men alone, and of the redemption from Egypt he declared that by 'the merit of the pious women in that generation were they [the Israelites] redeemed.'[75]

This approach made it easier for R. Akiba to adopt a positive attitude to Bar Kokhba; he saw the question of the redemption of the nation and the land as an internal, practical process in the world of history. From Bar Kokhba and his triumph he expected only the realization of Haggai ii 7, and, according to another source, the fulfilment of Zechariah's prophecy (viii 4) 'There shall yet old men and old women sit in the broad places of Jerusalem, every man with his staff in his hand for very age.'[76] He did not connect the restoration of the Ten Tribes and their resettlement in the land with this redemption,[77] nor did he find therein a role for Elijah, or the realization of the visions concerning 'the day of the Lord' or 'that day', and he certainly did not await new revelations or hope to penetrate into the Work of Creation, or the upper worlds, or the mystery of the Godhead.

R. Akiba did, however, occupy himself with the Work of Creation and the Work of the Chariot, and he was the only one of whom it is stated that 'he went up in peace and came down in peace', and apparently the reference is to 'seeing the Chariot'.[78]

The catastrophic events he transferred to 'the time to come', and in his Mishna he taught 'The judgement of Gog and Magog (Ezekiel xxxviii–xxxix) in the time to come will endure twelve months, the judgement of the wicked in Gehenna will endure twelve months'.[79] The Sages, who disapproved of R. Akiba's attitude to Bar Kokhba, also disagreed with his principles. When R. Akiba applied to Bar Kokhba[80] the verse 'There shall step forth a star out of Jacob, and a sceptre shall rise out of Israel' — a verse that had already been translated and expounded in an early period with reference to Messiah the son of David[81] — R. Joḥanan b. Torta reacted sharply and said 'Akiba, grass will grow out of your jaws, and the Son of David shall not yet have come.' This Tanna's opposition emanated apparently from his view that the Messiah must necessarily be descended from the House of David.[82] In addition to proof of his descent, evidence was also required of the fulfilment of the signs postulated by the prophet Isaiah with regard to the shoot of the stock of Jesse. In an anonymous Haggada it is narrated in the Babylonian Talmud: 'Bar Koziba reigned two and a half years. He then said to the Rabbis: "I am the Messiah." They answered him: "Of the Messiah it is written that he can judge by the scent. Let us see: If he can judge by the scent, well and good; if, however, he cannot, let us kill him." When they saw that he could not judge by the scent, they slew him.'[83] The Tanna R. Eleazar of Modiʿim, who according to one account was killed by Bar Kokhba,[84] taught that in reward for the observance of the Sabbath 'The Holy One, blessed be He, will give you six good portions: the Land of Israel, the world to come, the new world, the sovereignty of the House of David, the priesthood and the Levites' offices.'[85] The observance of the Sabbath does indeed assure redemption, but the Sage visualized it in the form of the monarchy of the House of David, and connected it with the world to come and the new world.

It is against the background of such opinions that the sharp rejoinder of R. Joḥanan b. Torta is to be understood, and it may be assumed that the attitude to Bar Kokhba caused a schism not only in Rabbinic circles. The same R. Joḥanan b. Torta said: 'But in the time of the Latter Temple we observe that they toiled in the study of the Torah and were meticulous in giving the tithes. Why then were they exiled? Because they loved money and hated one another. This teaches you that hatred between people is grievous in the sight of the Omnipresent.[86]

The failure of Bar Kokhba's revolt and the religious persecutions that followed brought in their wake various reactions to the hopes of the early advent of the Messiah. The Sages of the time devoted their attention to the survival and consolidation of the Jewish settlement in Eretz-Israel. Thus we learn in a Baraita: 'Let a man dwell in the Land of Israel, even in a town inhabited mainly by Gentiles, rather than outside the Land, even in a town that is entirely inhabited by Israelites. This teaches us that dwelling in the Land of Israel is as meritorious as the observance of all the precepts of the Torah....'[87] R. Simeon was strict in forbidding departure from Eretz-Israel, applying the prohibition even in periods of dearth and distress, and he apparently was also the one who said '... So long as they [the Israelites] are on it, it is as though the Land were not conquered; if they are not on it, it is as though the Land were conquered... whoever leaves the Land in peacetime and goes abroad, he is accounted an idolater ...', and R. Simeon b. Eleazar said 'Israelites living outside the Land of Israel are idolaters....'[88] The Tanna R. Nathan expounded ' "Of them that love Me and keep My commandments" — this refers to the Israelites who dwell in the Land of Israel and give their lives for the commandments. "Why are you going forth to be decapitated?" "Because I circumcised my son." "Why are you going forth to be burnt?" "Because I read the Torah." "Why are you going forth to be crucified?" "Because I ate the unleavened bread." "Why are you being lashed?" "Because I performed the ceremony of the Lulav [palm-branch and the other three species]." And it says: "Those with which I was wounded in the house of my friends" (Zechariah xiii 6): these wounds caused me to be beloved of my Father in heaven.'[89] The same R. Nathan declared with reference to the Scripture (Habakkuk ii 3) 'For the vision is yet for an appointed time, but at the end it shall speak, and not lie: though he tarry, wait for him; because it will surely come, it will not tarry' — 'This verse penetrates down to the very deep.'[90] The meaning of his words is as Rashi explains: 'Just as the deep has no end or limit, even so man cannot understand the ultimate significance of this verse, for there is no final date for the Messiah, but "though he tarry, wait for him", for he is under no limitation of time.' He who cited this Baraita of R. Nathan added: 'Nor according to R. Akiba, who expounded ' "Yet once, it is a little while, and I will shake the heavens, and the earth", but... and the kingdom of Ben Koziba (shall last) two and a half years.' It is obvious that R. Akiba also applied the continuation of the passage — Ḥaggai ii 7 — 'And I will shake all nations, and the choicest things of all nations shall come, and I will fill this house with glory, saith the Lord of hosts' to Bar Kokhba. Whoever interpolated in the Gemara the words 'but' etc. took the passage from *Seder 'Olam Rabba*, or from its source, that is, from the Baraita of R. Jose b. Ḥalafta, according to which the reign of Bar Kokhba lasted two and a half years.[91]

The failure of the redemption of the country on the stage of history and its separation from the Utopian-apocalyptic events also led to a totally different reaction from that of R. Nathan, namely complete abandonment of the realistic elements surrounding the redemption and its absolute integration into supernatural processes built on the ruins of existing history and actualities. The passage in *T.B. Sanhedrin*, chapter *Ḥēleq* ['Portion'] (XI), from which we cited the statement of R. Nathan, consists chiefly of Baraitot and homilies that read like actual parallels to the apocalyptic literature. It will suffice to compare the Baraita about the septennium at the end of which the son of David will come — in part we have already encountered it as a dictum of Rava — with the Syriac *Apocalypse of Baruch:*

Baraita

> The Rabbis taught: The septennium at the end of which the son of David will come — in the first year the following verse will be fulfilled 'And I will cause it to rain upon one city and cause it not to rain upon another city'; in the second, the arrows of famine will be sent forth; in the third, there will be a great famine and men, women, and children, men of piety, and miracle

workers will die, and the Torah will be forgotten by its students; in the fourth, there will be partial plenty; in the fifth, there will be great plenty, and people will eat and drink and rejoice, and the Torah will be restored to its students; in the sixth, there will be (heavenly) voices; in the seventh, wars; at the end of the septennium the son of David will come.[92]

Apocalypse of Baruch

And I answered and said: 'Will that tribulation which is to be continue a long time, and will that necessity embrace many years?'

And He answered and said unto me: 'Into twelve parts is that time divided, and each one of them is reserved for that which is appointed for it. In the first part there shall be the beginning of commotions. And in the second part (there shall be) slayings of the great ones. And in the third part the fall of many by death. And in the fourth part the sending of the sword. And in the fifth part famine and the withholding of rain. And in the sixth part earthquakes and terrors... For these parts of that time are reserved, and shall be mingled one with the other... so that those may not understand who are upon the earth in those days that this is the consummation of the times.

Nevertheless, whosoever understandeth shall then be wise... And it shall come to pass when all is accomplished that was to come to pass in those parts, that the Messiah shall then begin to be revealed....[93]

There is a difference of style. The visionary sees the heavens open, and a voice from on high makes the proclamation to him. In the Baraita, which begins with a verse, the words are transmitted as though they were a tradition. But there are also revelations of Elijah. To this category belongs the famous Baraita: 'A Tanna of the School of Elijah taught: The world will exist six thousand years: for two thousand years there was desolation; for two thousand, Torah; and for two thousand years there will be the Days of the Messiah.'[94] Clearly this Baraita was taught before the end of the fourth millenium, that is to say, in the middle or the end of the second century C.E.

Since it is known only in the Babylonian Talmud, but not in the Palestinian Talmud or the ancient Midrashim of Eretz-Israel,[95] it probably reflects the influence of the Iranian apocalyptic chronology.[96] The expectation that the Messiah would come suddenly found expression in the Baraita that enunciates the Halakhic rule that one who vows ' "I shall be a Nazirite on the day when the son of David comes may drink wine on Sabbaths and festival days (Rashi: 'For the Messiah will certainly not come then'), but is forbidden to drink wine on any weekday' (Rashi: 'in case he comes').[97] It is possible that those who vowed this type of Naziriteship intended to bring nearer the day of the coming of the son of David. At the close of the Tannaitic era we find evidence again, for a short period, of a practical conception linking the hopes of redemption to an actual historical event. It is associated with the particular personality of R. Judah the Patriarch. R. Ḥiyya the Great and R. Simeon b. Ḥalafta said 'This is the way of Israel's redemption: to begin with it comes little by little, but as it progresses it grows greater and greater.'[98] To Rabbi was applied the verse 'The breath of our nostrils, the anointed of the Lord.'[99] The watchword 'David, king of Israel continues to live' was chosen as a signal for the sanctification of the new moon.[1] Rabbi wished to abolish the fast of the Ninth of Av[2], and to him is attributed a question put to R. Ḥiyya 'Has one like me to bring a he-goat?' [see Leviticus iv 23][3] — that is to say, was his law like that of a king? Possibly there is a connection between the discovery of the genealogical scroll in which it is stated 'Hillel is descended from David',[3a] the Sages' going up to Jerusalem and the renewal of 'the holy congregation in Jerusalem'[4], on the one hand, and the realistic Messianic hopes on the other. But if there were such hopes, they were quickly dissipated, and already in the period of the first Amoraim a Utopian trend prevailed in the vision of redemption. This was undoubtedly due to the decline of the Roman empire, the wars it waged against the Persians[5], the degeneration in the economic position, and also the criticism levelled against the administrative institutions, the Patriarchate, and the courts. There actually exists a kind of competition in depicting anarchy and upheaval as indications of the advent of the son of David. The two sons of R. Ḥiyya — Judah and Hezekiah — declared, when they were dining with Rabbi and had become intoxicated: 'The son of David will not come until the two dynasties in Israel come to an end, namely the Exilarchate in Babylonia and the Patriarchate in Israel.'[6] It may be presumed that they did not think up this criticism on the spur of the moment, but repeated a saying that was bandied about just as R. Simlai stated in the name of R. Eleazar b. R. Simeon 'The son of David will not come until all the judges and officers come to an end in Israel'.[7] R. Joḥanan, the leading Amora of Israel, said 'If you see a generation continually declining, wait for him [the Messiah]'; he was also the author of the dictum 'The son of David will come only in a generation that is wholly wicked.'[8] The magnitude of the degeneration, anarchy, and sufferings heralding the Messiah will be matched by the brilliance and glory of the Days of the Messiah; and indeed the sons of R. Ḥiyya, mentioned above, and R. Joḥanan pictured Jerusalem in the time to come in a manner recalling the accounts that the apocalyptists transmitted in the names of angels, only the Amoraim based their descriptions on verses.[9] R. Ḥiyya bar Abba reports in the name of R. Joḥanan 'All the prophets prophesied (in speaking of redemption) only of the Messianic era, but as for the world to come, "the eye hath not seen, O Lord, beside Thee" '[10], an interpretation that completely contradicts the view of R. Akiba and those who followed his opinion. Hence the Gemara adds, with reference to R. Joḥanan, 'Now he disagrees with Samuel, for Samuel said: the present world differs from the Messianic era only in respect of the servitude of the kingdoms.' R. Jose b. R. Ḥanina, the disciple and colleague of R. Joḥanan, drew a practical inference from the Utopian conception of redemption, and basing it on the verse 'I adjure you, O daughters of Jerusalem' (Canticles ii 7), he expounded: 'There are two oaths here, one for Israel and one for the nations of the world. He adjured Israel that they should not rebel against the kingdoms, and He adjured the kingdoms that they should not make Israel's yoke oppressive, for if they were to make Israel's yoke oppressive, they would cause the End to come prematurely.' 'The End at its due time' is something different from liberation from the servitude of the kingdoms, and cannot be attained by rebellions.[11]

R. Joḥanan also conceived the figure of the Messiah as transcending all previous conceptions of him. While Rav said 'The world was created only for David', and Samuel said 'for Moses', R. Johanan said 'for the Messiah'.[12] R. Joḥanan also did not refrain from depicting the work of redemption in anthropomorphic language that has erotic overtones. Balaam's words 'Alas, who shall live after God hath appointed him?' R. Joḥanan expounded as follows: 'Alas for the nation that will be found (obstructing), when the Holy One, blessed be He, is engaged in the redemption of His children. Who would (dare) cast his garment between a lion and a lioness at the moment of copulation?'[13] The actual image has its roots in the allegorical interpretations of Canticles, but it appears to be directed against the 'nation' that intervenes and desires to separate the Congregation of Israel from its God, in order to inherit its place. Corroboration of this interpretation can be found in Rash Laqish's exposition of this verse: 'Alas for him who restores himself to life by the name of God' [*mi-śûmô 'ēl* is interpreted as *mi-shĕmô 'ēl*].

Even among the Amoraim there were not wanting 'calculators of the End', who were vouchsafed revelations of Elijah and added meanwhile the years that had passed since the previous revelations. Thus it is related: 'Elijah said to Rav Judah, the brother of Rav Salla the Pious: The world shall endure not less than eighty-five jubilees, and the son of David shall come in the last jubilee. Said Rav Judah to him: "At the beginning (of the jubilee) or at the end?" He replied: "I know not." "Shall it be completed or not?" He answered: "I know not".'[14] Actually less importance is to be assigned to the fact that the calculation is in jubilees than to the end of the story regarding its uncertainty. The explanation is to be found in another story concerning the revelation of Elijah to the same Sage. Elijah said to Rav Judah, the brother of Rav Salla the Pious: 'You say: Why does not the Messiah come? Now today is the Day of Atonement, yet were many virgins violated in Nehardea.'[15] Against the calculators of the End R. Samuel b. R. Naḥmani declared in the name of R. Jonathan: 'Blasted be the bones of those who calculate the End, for they used to say: "Since the (time of the) End has arrived, but he has not come, he will never come.'[16] The disillusionment after the passing of the dates fixed for the End was profound, and it was precisely those who waited and hoped that feared the disappointment of the weak in faith. The extreme view against any figure of a human Messiah was represented by the Amora R. Hillel, who said 'Israel will have no Messiah, for he has already been vouchsafed to them in the days of Hezekiah.'[17] The Babylonian Amora Rav Joseph reacted sharply to this: 'May his Master forgive R. Hillel! When did Hezekiah live? In the period of the First Temple. Yet Zechariah, prophesying during the era of the Second Temple, said: "Rejoice greatly, O Daughter of Zion; shout, O daughter of Jerusalem; behold, thy king cometh unto thee! he is just, and having salvation; lowly and riding upon an ass, and upon a colt the foal of an ass".'[18] When Rabba exclaimed, on hearing an account of the throes of the Messianic era, 'Let him come, but may I not see him!', Rav Joseph retorted 'Let him come, and may I be privileged to sit in the shadow of the dung of his ass!'[19] The Messianic fervour of this Amora was tremendous, and apparently he also took the trouble to obtain apocalyptic writings, without investigating their origin and source. Thus it is narrated: 'Rav Hanan bar Taḥlifa sent (word) to Rav Joseph: "I met a certain man, who had in his possession a scroll written in Assyrian [i.e. square] characters and in the holy tongue. So I asked him: 'Where did you get this?' He replied: 'I hired myself as a mercenary to the Persian forces, and I found it among the Persian archives. It is stated therein: After four thousand two hundred and ninety-one years after the creation of the world, the world will be orphaned. (Of the subsequent years) some will be marked by wars of the sea monsters, some by the wars of Gog and Magog, and the remainder will constitute the Days of the Messiah, and the Holy One, blessed be He, will renew His world only after seven thousand years.' " '[20] This scroll, which a soldier found in the archives of Persia, is on the face of it suspect, lest it was written by an Iranian eschatologist. The name of R. Hanan bar Taḥlifa, who is not known from any other passage of the Talmud, could add another element of strangeness to this story. But the truth is that the word *Pāras* ['Persia'] was introduced here by Marcus Marinus Brixianus, the censor of the Basel printing press (1578–1581), who erased the name *Rômî* [Rome] wherever it occurs and sometimes changed it to 'Babylonia' or 'Aramaea'. In this particular case, it seems, he chose 'Persia' in order to confuse scholars, and indeed he succeeded in no small measure.[21] At all events, in all the MSS. and the early editions the text reads 'I hired myself to the Roman forces, and I found it in the Roman archives.'

In some of these recensions the name of the Sage who sent the information to Rav Joseph is given as Rav ʿAnan bar Taḥlifa, one of the disciples of Samuel.[22] From the aspect of structure and motifs this scroll adds nothing to what we know from other apocalyptic writings.[23] The date 291 is a corruption of 231[24], and this date appears also in another apocalyptic Baraita: 'It is taught in a Baraita: After four thousand two hundred and thirty-one years *anno mundi*, if one should say to you "Buy a field worth a thousand denars for one denar", do not buy.'[25] The date was determined on the basis of an exposition, being equivalent to four hundred years after the destruction of the Second Temple, and just as the first redemption came after four hundred years of servitude in Egypt, so shall it also be in the case of the last redemption. About a century after Rav ʿAnan had sent the information about the contents of this scroll to Rav Joseph, Jerome wrote[26] that the Jews of his time used to say that just as Pharaoh, king of Egypt, and all his host were drowned in the Red Sea after holding the people of Israel in captivity for four hundred and thirty years,[27] so, too, the Romans would be destroyed by the vengeance of the Lord when they would have ruled over the Jews that number of years. The discovery of the scroll in the archives of Rome in the days of Rav Joseph served to give this exposition the aspect of an ancient vision; in the words of R. Me'ir ha-Levi Abulafia in his book *Yad Rama* on Sanhedrin: 'And the reason for informing us that it [the scroll] was written in square characters and in the holy tongue was to show that the Romans had not written it, but that it was brought from the exiles of Jerusalem.'[28]

Needless to say, it was just the apocalyptic stories and dicta of the Sages that were not always handed down in their original form; sometimes the narrators presented them in a sharp dialectical form that appeared to nullify their original intention. It is related, for instance, that R. Joshua b. Levi met Elijah at the entrance of R. Simeon b. Yoḥai's burial-cave and asked him: "When will the Messiah come?" He answered him: "Go and ask him himself." "Where does he abide?" — "At the entrance of Rome" — "How is he to be recognized?" — "He sits among the sick; now all of them untie and tie up (all their bandages) at one and the same time, while he unties and reties (his bandages) one at a time, saying (to himself): In case

I am needed, I shall not be delayed." So he [R. Joshua b. Levi] went to him (and) said to him "Peace be upon you, O my master and teacher!" He replied: "Peace be upon you, O son of Levi!" He then said to him: "When will the master come?" His reply was "Today". He [R. Joshua b. Levi] then returned to Elijah, who asked him "What did he tell you?" He answered him "Peace be upon thee, O son of Levi!" Said (Elijah) to him "He assured you and your father of (a share in) the world to come." (R. Joshua b. Levi) rejoined "But he lied to me; for he told me 'I shall come today', yet he did not come." Said (Elijah) to him "This is what he meant: 'Today, if ye will hearken to His voice'." '[29] In this story, which does not lack overtones of humour and irony,[30] R. Joshua b. Levi is told, after he had troubled Elijah and the Messiah himself, that which his contemporary, Rav, had said in more prosaic form: 'All the (calculated) dates of redemption have passed, and the matter now depends upon repentance and good deeds.' Now he himself disagreed with Rav and said 'It suffices the mourner to keep his mourning'[31], implying that even without repentance Israel will be redeemed. The narrator undoubtedly held similar views to those of the hero of his narrative, that is to say, he belonged to the circles of the Sages that cultivated the Messianic vision in the apocalyptic spirit. These were the Sages who, projecting the present into the past, said of the Israelites in Egypt: 'This teaches us that they possessed scrolls, in which they took delight on Sabbaths, and these held out the promise that the Holy One, blessed be He, would redeem them.'[32] The Haggadist's witness is, therefore, reliable, namely that precisely in these circles, despite all their attachment to the fantastic conception of redemption, they again accepted the doctrine of R. Eliezer that 'If they do not repent, they will not be redeemed.'

Confirmation of our view is to be found in another dictum, transmitted in the name of R. Joshua b. Levi, in which he explicitly makes the figure of the Messiah — whether his place is among the clouds of heaven, or whether he is a poor man riding on an ass — depend on the merits, that is, the deeds of Israel.[33]

The synthesis of repentance with the apocalyptic Messianic system enabled the Sages who cultivated it to adopt ideas that ostensibly should have been rejected on polemical and apologetic grounds. In truth the fact that certain modern scholars ignored the role played by the integration of the idea of repentance led them to account for matters that appeared surprising to them by discovering signs of polemics in expressions that were perfectly innocent in themselves.

We shall discuss two motifs to both of which references were already found in the sources that we have cited. One concerns the 'pre-existence' of the Messiah. In several sources[34], which enumerate six or four things that preceded the creation of the world, 'the name of the Messiah' occurs. Louis Ginzberg[35] regards the reference to 'the name of the Messiah' instead of the 'Messiah' as an intentional change for anti-Christian polemical reasons, just as he discovered a distinction between real pre-existence and ideal pre-existence in the source that includes the Messiah's name among the things that were planned to be created and not among the things that were actually created. However, among the latter are counted only the Throne of Glory and the Torah, which may be said to have actually preceded Creation, whereas 'the name of the Messiah' is mentioned together with the Patriarchs and with Israel, which preceded it in thought. As for 'the name of the Messiah, it is clearly linked to the verse on which its pre-existence is based, namely 'His name burgeoned before ever the sun was' (Psalms lxxii 17, which is rendered in JPS 'May his name be continued as long as the sun'). In one source, which I published from a MS.,[36] the author of the list of pre-existent things is given as R. Simeon b. Laqish. This same Resh Laqish gave an allegorical, apocalyptic interpretation to the second verse in Genesis: 'R. Simeon b. Laqish interpreted the verse with reference to the kingdoms: "Now the earth was waste and void" — this is Babylonia (as it is written): "I beheld the earth, and, lo, it was waste and void" (Jeremiah iv 23); "and void" — this means Media... "and darkness" — this refers to Greece... "over the face of the deep" — this alludes to the present wicked kingdom, just as the deep is unfathomable, so the wicked kingdom is unfathomable; "and the spirit of God hovered" — this connotes the spirit of the Messiah, as it is said "And the spirit of the Lord shall rest upon him" (Isaiah xi 2). By what merit does its ministration begin? — "hovered over the face of the waters", through the merit of repentance, which is likened to water, (as it is said:) "Pour out thy heart like water" (Lamentations ii 19).'[37] Here 'the spirit of the Messiah' is mentioned; there are no grounds, therefore, for the distinction between the 'pre-existence' of his name and the 'pre-existence' of his personality.[38] It is the pre-existence of repentance that also prepared the way for the 'pre-existence' of the Messiah. It is noteworthy, however, that in seven sources out of nine[39] the 'Torah and repentance' invariably head the list and 'the name of the Messiah' concludes it, in conformity with the homily of Resh Laqish.

Circles that, like R. Joshua b. Levi, lived the Messianic hope very intensely and deemed it important to know where the Messiah, who dwelt in secret, was to be found, endeavoured also to discover his name, especially since the Christians called the Messiah by a personal name. The conjectured names, their sources, and explanations are highly variegated. Most of them — such as David, Ṣemaḥ, and Menaḥem — are based on Messianic verses.[40] Some of the passages mention not only the supporting verse but also the names of the homilists themselves,[41] their attributes, or their views about the nature of the redemption and the image of the redeemer.[42] Among the names suggested on the basis of various verses is also found the name חוליא *Ḥûlyā* ['the ailing one'],[43] based on the verse 'Surely he has borne our sicknesses and carried our pains; yet we esteemed him stricken, smitten by God and afflicted' (Isaiah liii 4). We have already met, in the story about R. Joshua b. Levi, the poor and afflicted Messiah, who sits in the gateway of Rome.

His disciple, R. Alexandri, did not refrain from expounding the verse 'And הריחו *hărîḥô* [usually rendered 'his delight shall be'] in the fear of the Lord...' thus: 'This teaches us that He loaded him with precepts and suffering as with a millstone [ריחים *rêḥayîm*].'[44] The verse Ruth ii 14 is expounded by R. Joḥanan allegorically of the King Messiah, and the expositor accordingly declares: '"And eat of the bread" — this means the bread of sovereignty; "and dip thy morsel in the vinegar" — this refers to the suffering, as it is said "But he was wounded because of our transgressions". "And she sat beside the reapers" — this connotes that his kingdom would temporarily be taken away from him...; "and they reached her parched corn" — this signifies that it is destined to return to him... R. Berechiah in the name of R. Levi said: The last redeemer would be like the first: just as the first redeemer was revealed and then hidden again from them (Israel) ... and how long would he be hidden from them?... forty-five days....'[45]

The second part of the homily is derived from Daniel xii 11–12 and is found in parallel passages[46] without any connection with the verse in Ruth. But the interpretation of the dipping into vinegar as referring to the sufferings of the Messiah is reminiscent of John xix 28–29: 'That the scripture might be fulfilled, saith, I thirst. Now there was set a vessel full of vinegar; and they filled a sponge with vinegar and put it upon hyssop, and put it to his mouth'; the intent was to fulfil the verse in Psalms (lxix 22) 'and in my thirst they gave me vinegar to drink'.[47] The manifestation of the Messiah and his disappearance for forty-five days are alluded to in Daniel, but they become days in which the faith of the people is tested, for the Messiah leads them into the wilderness, where they eat salt-plants and brooms. One receives the undoubted impression that in these Messianic Midrashim there exists a trend similar to that in the Gospels, namely to find the fulfilment of all the Scriptures and visions containing Messianic descriptions. Only while in the Christian sources these are referred to the lifetime of a Messiah who had already lived and died, in the homilies of the Sages the allusions are to the Messiah who has still to come. When the Christians themselves began in the second century[48] to speak of the delay in δευτέρα παρουσία, the signs and portents that were interpreted with respect to the Messiah's first appearance inevitably lost their significance. The Rabbis felt no misgivings, therefore, in applying to the Messiah even a verse like Zechariah xii 10 'And they shall look unto Me because they have thrust him through; and they shall mourn for him, as one mourneth for his only son.'[49] Thus it is stated in a Babylonian Baraita:[50] 'The Holy One, blessed be He, will say to Messiah the son of David — may he be destined to reveal himself speedily in our days! — "Ask Me for anything and I will give it to you", for it is said "I will tell of the decree... this day have I begotten thee, ask of Me and I will give the nations for thy inheritance." But when he will see that Messiah the son of Joseph has been slain, he will say to Him "Sovereign of the universe, only life do I ask of Thee." Then He will say to him: "Life? Before ever you spoke, your father David already prophesied concerning you, as it is said "He asked life of Thee; Thou gavest it him" ' (Psalms xxi 5). This source, which is termed a 'Baraita', is apparently connected with the preceding debate in the Babylonian Talmud regarding the interpretation of the verse in Zechariah: 'R. Dosa and the Rabbis differed on the point: one held that it [the mourning] was on account of Messiah, son of Joseph, who had been slain; while the other maintained that it was on account of the Evil Inclination, which had been slain.' This dispute is identical with that of the 'two Amoraim' in the Palestinian Talmud:[51] 'One said: This refers to the mourning for the Messiah; and the other said: This refers to the mourning for the Evil Inclination.' Thus according to the Amora who interpreted the verse in Zechariah as alluding to the Messiah, there is no difficulty in assuming a nexus between this motif and the Haggada that declares that the Messiah 'would be revealed and then hidden again'. Apparently apocalyptic circles no longer had misgivings about interpreting the verse with regard to a suffering and afflicted Messiah. Such views were put by Justin Martyr in the mouth of Tryphon. He accepts the view that the Messiah will suffer after his first advent, but he rejects Justin's belief that this Messiah was Jesus.[52] Be the source that gave rise to the figure of Messiah the son of Joseph[53] what it may, it was not the motif of the suffering and afflicted Messiah that produced it. The truth is that cautious and hesitant homilists used this motif in order to liberate the image of the Messiah the son of David from suffering, afflictions, and death.

In the speculations about the figure of the suffering Messiah there is naught left apparently of the idea of repentance as a factor in the process of redemption, but deeper examination of the problem leads us to a different conclusion.

The afflicted and suffering Messiah, who 'is wounded because of our transgressions', who is slain or is compelled to disappear, actually contains a paradox, since it diminishes his power as a redeemer, and in fact deprives his function, as the one that fulfils the redemption, of its absolute character. It is not the redemptive act *per se* that liberates the world from sin and transgression, but there is need of the purging sufferings and afflictions of the Messiah, which are preconditions of the work of redemption. Actually it is nowhere stated in the ancient Amoraic sources that the afflictions and suffering of the Messiah constitute in themselves an atonement and redemption, as Paul had stressed (Romans iii 23). Even in *IV Ezra* the apocalyptist negates the possibility of 'vicarious' repentance. His opinion is unambiguous: 'For then every one shall bear his own righteousness or unrighteousness' (vii 105). R. Simlai expounded the verse in Isaiah liii 12 with reference to the first redeemer, Moses, as follows: ' "Because he poured out his soul unto death" — for he delivered himself unto death...; "Yet he bore the sin of many" — because he made atonement for the making of the golden calf; "And made intercession for the transgressors" — for he entreated that the transgressors of Israel might repent' (*T.B. Soṭa* 14a). Even the late apocalyptic homilist, living at the end of the period of Byzantine rule in Palestine, who reunited the figures of Messiah the son of Joseph and Messiah the son of David into one Messiah, 'Ephraim our righteous Messiah', and made the subject of his afflictions and suffering a central theme in his 'Messianic Tractate', which is incorporated in *Pesiqta Rabbati*[54], concluded his exposition of the verse, Isaiah lxi 10, as follows: ' "As a bridegroom decketh himself with a garland" — this teaches us that the Holy One, blessed be He, will clothe Ephraim, our righteous Messiah, with a garment whose splendour will span the world from end to end...; "And as a bride adorneth herself with her jewels"... just as a bride is not accepted without her adornments, even so the Congregation of Israel does not put her adversaries to shame except by merit...'[55] It is this merit that gives assurance that the Congregation of Israel will never return to her servitude. Just as the Amora's interpretation of the mourning in Zechariah xii as lamentation for the Messiah — an exposition that marks a climax in straining the apocalyptic aspect of redemption — still requires its measure of repentance, so, too, the homily of the Amora who takes a different view and explains the words of the prophet as a lament for the slain 'Evil Inclination', reveals its apocalyptic-eschatological ingredients, which combined with the idea of repentance as a decisive factor in the process of redemption. Ostensibly it is repentance that must bring about the destruction of the Evil Impulse, but rightly the Talmud raises an objection to this interpretation: 'Should there be mourning for such an event? (On the contrary) there should be rejoicing! Why then should they weep?' The answer is: 'As R. Judah b. R. Ile'ai expounded: In the time to come the Holy One, blessed be He, will bring the Evil

Inclination and slaughter him in the presence of the righteous and the wicked. To the righteous he will appear as a towering mountain, while to the wicked he will seem like a (mere) strand of hair. Both groups will weep. The righteous will weep and say: How were we able to conquer this towering mountain! And the wicked will weep, saying: How was it possible for us not to vanquish this strand of hair!'[56]

Notwithstanding all their hyperbolical estimates of the power of repentance (see above, p. 462), even those Tannaim and Amoraim who expounded its merit and ability to hasten the coming of redemption, Sages of the type that taught that 'If Israel were to repent but a single day, the son of David would come forthwith'[57] — even they learnt from their long historical experience how hard was the road of repentence for individuals, and still more so for an entire nation. Nor were all of them sure of the power of afflictions and misfortunes to hasten the process. Regarding the people of Sodom R. Jeremiah b. Eleazar said: 'Twenty-five years the Holy One, blessed be He, brought upon them volcanic eruptions and earthquakes, so that they might turn to repentance, but they did not.'[58]

The conduct of Pharaoh, concerning whom Scripture testifies 'for I have hardened his heart', drew the attention of two scholars whose interest in the subject of redemption and repentance we have already pointed out.

R. Joḥanan did not hesitate to say 'This provides an opportunity for the sectarians to say: It was not in his power to repent.' In the light of what we have stated earlier, it will not be difficult to identify the sectarians who could cite this verse to confirm the negation of the power of repentance. Although R. Simeon b. Laqish said 'May the mouth of the sectarians be closed!' yet he continued: 'For the Holy One, blessed be He, warns a man once, twice, and thrice, and if he does not retract, then He closes his heart to repentance in order to punish him for his sins. So was it with the wicked Pharaoh... The Holy One, blessed be He, said to him: "You have made yourself stiff-necked and hard of heart; therefore I shall add defilement to your defilement" ' (*Exodus Rabba* xiii, 2). It is true that repentance, according to Resh Laqish, preceded the creation of the world, but he, too, recognized that there are situations in which the way of penitence is hidden from mortals. To prevent the Evil Impulse from returning in the time to come, and to enable man to be redeemed from the tendency to sin, it seemed to Rav Judah — an Amora who had no special interest in redemption in the national sense — that the surest course was for God Himself to come and slaughter the Evil Impulse in the presence of the righteous.

A parallel manifestation of the removal of the work of redemption from human control is also to be found in the other aspect — in the conception of redemption in the national-political connotation. The fear that there might be renewed servitude after the coming redemption continued to cling to the Tannaim and Amoraim, and they gave expression to it in various ways.[59] The Amora R. Aḥa, who possibly witnessed the Emperor Julian's attempt to rebuild the Temple, expounded, out of a sense of disillusionment, ' "The cords of Death compassed me"... I turned hither and thither, but I have no redeemer but Thee.'[60] In an anonymous homily the expositor attributed the following argument to the people of Israel: 'Israel said to the Holy One, blessed be He: "Hast Thou not already redeemed us by the hands of Moses and of Joshua and of judges and kings? And now we are again enslaved and put to shame, as though we had never been redeemed!" Said the Holy One, blessed be He, to them: "Because your redemption was by human agency, and your leaders were mortals who are here one day and in the grave the next, therefore your redemption was of a temporary nature. But in the future I, who live for ever, shall redeem you Myself; I shall redeem you with an everlasting redemption." '[61]

The homilist in effect negates the figure of the personal Messiah. The Holy One, blessed be He, will Himself be the ultimate Redeemer, and only His redemption will be everlasting. This homilist expresses in his own way the view of Hillel 'Israel has no Messiah.'[62]

The abolition of the figure of the personal Messiah is thus to be found in both conceptions of redemption — in that which regards it as the time of the End, and also in that which integrates it with preliminary repentance. Furthermore, dicta of Tannaim who held different conceptions of the actual nature of redemption lend support to this view. If we have regarded R. Akiba, who separated the national redemption from all other events of the end of days, as the outstanding representative of restitutory pattern, it must be borne in mind that it was nevertheless he who remarked with reference to the verse 'Before Thy people, whom Thou didst redeem Thee out of Egypt, the nations and their gods' (II Samuel vii 23): 'Were not the verse written, it would be impossible to say it. So to speak, Israel said to the Holy One, blessed be He, "Thou hast redeemed Thyself"...'[63] The God who redeems Himself together with His people from exile does not need even a deliverer like Moses; He can also make use of Bar Kokhba, or choose any other way. Redemption was, of course, subject to the condition that the people would wish to be redeemed; but the Sages were not always sure of this desire. The Amora R. Berechiah gave expression to the scant enthusiasm for redemption in his exposition of the verse 'Egypt was glad when they departed' (Psalms cv 38) with the help of the following analogy: 'It is like a stout man riding on an ass; the ass waits for the moment when the man will get down from him, and he waits for the moment when he will get down from the ass. When he does so, the man is glad and the ass is glad. But I do not yet know who rejoices more; you must conclude that the ass rejoices more. Even so was it with Israel in Egypt: The plagues were coming upon the Egyptians and they were awaiting the moment when the Israelites would depart, and the Israelites were waiting for the moment when the Holy One, blessed be He, would redeem them. When the Exodus took place and they were redeemed, both sides were glad. But we do not know who rejoiced more, until David came and said "Egypt was glad when they departed"; thus we know that the Egyptians rejoiced more.'[64]

However, also in the name of the Sage who opposed R. Akiba's attitude to Bar Kokhba, namely R. Eleazar of Modiʿim — he held a different doctrine, which identified the national redemption with the transformation of the nature of the world — a homily is transmitted that abolishes the role of the personal Messiah in the eschatological task and bases everything upon the absolute belief in redemption:

'As R. Eleazar of Modiʿim said: The Guardian Angels of the heathen nations are destined in the time to come to denounce Israel before the Holy One, blessed be He, saying: "Sovereign of the universe, these [i.e. the Gentiles] were idolaters and these [the Israelites] were idolaters, these committed incest and these committed incest, these were guilty of bloodshed and these were guilty of bloodshed. Why then do these [the heathens] go down to Gehenna, but not the others?"[65] The Holy One, blessed be He, will answer them, saying: "If so, let all the peoples descend with their gods to Gehenna." This is the meaning of the verse "For let all the peoples walk each one in the name of its god" (Micah iv 5). R. Reuben said: If Scripture had not written it, it would be impossible to say it. So to speak, "For by fire will the Lord be judged [the literal meaning of נשפט *nishpāṭ*]" (Isaiah lxvi 16). It is not written here "The Lord will judge" [שופט *shôfēṭ*], but "will be judged" [*nishpāṭ*]. This is implied in what David said through the holy spirit: "Yea, though I walk through the valley of the shadow of death, I will fear no evil for Thou art with me" (Psalms xxiii 4).'[66]

PUBLICATIONS OF THE PERRY FOUNDATION FOR BIBLICAL RESEARCH OF THE HEBREW UNIVERSITY OF JERUSALEM

U. Cassuto / Biblical and Oriental Studies.

U. Cassuto / From Adam to Noah.

U. Cassuto / From Noah to Abraham.

U. Cassuto / Exodus.

U. Cassuto / The Documentary Hypothesis.

U. Cassuto / The Goddess Anath.

E. E. Urbach / The Sages (two vols.)

ב' אופנהיימר / הנבואה הקדומה.

א"א אורבך / חז"ל — פרקי אמונות ודעות.

י' היינמן / התפילה בתקופת התנאים והאמוראים — טיבה ודפוסיה

מ' הרן / בין ראשונות לחדשות.

ש"א ליונשטם / מסורת יציאת מצרים בהשתלשלותה.

י' ליוור / פרקים בתולדות הכהונה והלוייה.

י' ליכט / הניסיון — במקרא וביהדות של תקופת הבית השני.

ע"צ מלמד / פרשני המקרא.

מ"ד קאסוטו / תורת התעודות.

מ"ד קאסוטו / פירוש על ספר בראשית.

מ"ד קאסוטו / פירוש על ספר שמות.

מ"ד קאסוטו / ספרות מקראית וספרות כנענית.